Modern Social Thought
An Introduction

Anthony Thomson

OXFORD
UNIVERSITY PRESS

OXFORD
UNIVERSITY PRESS

Oxford University Press is a department of the University of Oxford.
It furthers the University's objective of excellence in research, scholarship,
and education by publishing worldwide. Oxford is a registered trade mark of
Oxford University Press in the UK and in certain other countries.

Published in Canada by
Oxford University Press
8 Sampson Mews, Suite 204,
Don Mills, Ontario M3C 0H5 Canada

www.oupcanada.com

Copyright © Oxford University Press Canada 2016

Library and Archives Canada Cataloguing in Publication

Thomson, Anthony, 1949-, author
Modern social thought : an introduction / Anthony Thomson.

Includes bibliographical references and index.
ISBN 978-0-19-900240-5 (paperback)

1. Social sciences--Philosophy. 2. Social sciences--History.
3. Sociology--Philosophy. I. Title.

H61.T56 2015   300.1   C2015-904233-X

Oxford University Press is committed to our environment.
This book is printed on Forest Stewardship Council® certified paper
and comes from responsible sources.

Printed and bound in Canada

1 2 3 4 — 19 18 17 16

Contents

Part III ◆ From Radicalism to Juggernaut 203

CHAPTER 9 The New Left and Feminism 205

CHAPTER 10 Structuralism, Microsociology, and Foucault 234

Preface

•◆•

Social theory is conventionally divided between classical and contemporary. This book surveys selected parts of critical Western social thought from the early years of the twentieth century to the contemporary period, a span of time that may be referred to as post-classical or modern. The book begins with a brief sketch of classical sociological theory and *fin-de-siècle* social thought. It concludes with an overview of some significant contemporary approaches to social theory defined as post-structuralist and late-modern. *Modern Social Thought: An Introduction* is intended as a post-classical companion to the study of classical social theory presented in *The Making of Social Theory: Order, Reason, and Desire*.[1] The main features of this introductory book are the historical and critical framework within which social thought is contextualized; the multi-disciplinary nature of social thought; and the multiplicity of social perspectives that reflect social theory relating to gender and racialized constructions.

A primary purpose of reading theory is to understand ideas in the context of time and space, relative to the social characteristics of the author and in relation to preceding and subsequent social thought. As a result, the structure of this text is organized within two interlocking frameworks: chronology and theme. The chapter set-up is broadly historical: Part I focuses on the first half of the twentieth century; Part II covers the early post-1945 decades; and Part III introduces significant developments in contemporary theory.

Strict chronology, however, may confuse as much as it helps frame social thought. Within each part, and particularly in Part III, where ideas and theorists most clearly overlap and interpenetrate, chapters incorporate thematic organization so that related ideas are discussed together. Saussure's theory of linguistics, for example, was published in 1916, but it is discussed in Chapter 10 because it is foundational for structuralism. In contemporary thought, the ideas of postmodernists, post-structuralists, third-wave feminists, and the theorists of late modernity overlapped in time. Their ideas, which are presented systematically in the last three chapters, developed both in relation to and in opposition to one other. The inclusion of a timeline at the beginning of each part is designed to help keep chronology in mind.

Modern Social Thought: An Introduction is intended to provide a framework for finding meaning in the progression of ideas. My perspective derives from an interest in social change and the history of ideas in relation to critical theories and the emergence of social movements rooted in unequal gender and class relations, and racialization—hence, the historical framework and the integration of alternative perspectives, which reflect marginalized populations. This perspective is the underlying bias shaping the selection and the interpretation of material, which is contextualized by descriptions of the historical context and biographical descriptions.

This book grew out of my efforts to teach social theory to second- and third-year undergraduates. Students frequently approach the study of intellectual history and theory, in my experience, without a systematic framework of time and space within which to link ideas or to connect what they are learning with wider cultural experiences. While this observation is reflected in the teaching of classical social thought, I have also found that undergraduate students could use a better understanding of the social history of the last century. My approach to social thought is to connect ideas with their historical and intellectual context. Connecting information is an important component of understanding; otherwise, information is discrete, incomprehensible, and easily forgotten.

This text is meant to provide a contextualized introduction to the development of social thought over the last century. It may usefully be supplemented with excerpts from primary sources to provide students with challenging opportunities for analysis and interpretation. Understanding primary works requires contextualizing them in time and social context, and in relation to previous, contemporary, and emerging social thought, which is the organizing principle of this text. Texts on contemporary theory are often not comprehensive in their coverage of post-classical social thought. Texts on intellectual history, on the other hand, while comprehensive and interesting, provide too much summary detail and do not focus enough on certain key, critical thinkers.

In addition to conceptualizing theories in time and social context, it is also important to reflect the language and terminology employed by academics who do not write specifically for undergraduate students. I strive to strike a balance between the need to understand and employ the concepts with which ideas are developed and presented and the need to help make these thoughts intelligible for a wider audience. The challenge of making theories comprehensible increases as social thought becomes more contemporary. First, academics have proliferated and each is required, by virtue of the occupation, to add novelty to the literature. Second, time is required to identify views that have a lasting impression and that, to some extent, transcend their time of production. Third, instructors who have gone through the process of theorizing themselves and who instruct social thought develop their own interpretations and judgments about what is significant and worthy to be taught.

My interests are in social thought broadly defined to include some consideration of the emergence, evolution, and consequence of ideas expressed by recognized social and political theorists, but also reflected in the work of poets, novelists, and visual artists. Ideas are multi-disciplinary. This book evolved with the idea of integrating these perspectives. It attempts to provide an overview of the development and context of primarily critical, post-classical theory, while offering more in-depth examination of selected theorists.

The introductory chapter summarizes important developments in nineteenth century thought, which the last century inherited, including positivism, decadence, feminism, socialism, and psychoanalysis. This brief summary of important highlights of late classical social thought reviews ideas that are usually covered in detail in classical social theory. The chapter grounds the subsequent coverage of post-classical, modern social thought that follows.

Acknowledgments

Life seems to be a series of contingencies punctuated by a few minor miracles. One miracle was the opportunity my wife, Heather Frenette, and I had to live and study in England. The sabbatical year we spent in China with two small children in tow was another. The birthing of children is always miraculous. And publishing a book requires an air of good fortune and favourable winds.

This book had a particularly long germination. The idea of writing a multidisciplinary mash-up of social thought came to me as an undergraduate while I was rehearsing for the role of Jacques Roux in the play *Marat/Sade*. My reading of literature, social history, politics, and biology revealed a great deal of overlapping ground. The idea of the book was nourished through classes in the histories of modern art and cinema, which I had initially thought of as "bird courses." The cross-disciplinary approach to social thought first sprouted in a Bachelor of Education project on curriculum development. The actual writing began many years later when I was teaching intellectual history to graduate students in Beijing and found that I had to produce my own readings. *The Making of Social Theory: Order, Reason and Desire*, an earlier Oxford University Press book on classical social theory, was the first result. This introduction to modern social thought is the second artifact of this long developmental process.

Writing is as much a collective as an individual effort. I owe a deep debt of gratitude to my students, colleagues, and teachers. Working in a small university provided numerous opportunities for the cross-fertilization of ideas with supportive scholars from a variety of disciplines. On campus, the library is one of my favourite places. Librarians are the most helpful people in academia, and Acadia's librarians always came through for me. The noon-hour basketball crowd gave me as much mental relaxation as exercise.

At Oxford University Press, I am grateful for Mark Thompson's work steering my proposal through the acquisitions stage and for the anonymous reviewers who found some merit in the idea. Tanuja Weerasooriya helped develop the project, providing encouragement and critical suggestions. Eric Sinkins diligently chased down difficult permissions beyond the initial refusal. I am particularly grateful for Colleen Ste. Marie's dedicated work on the manuscript. This stage of the editing process is humbling and sometimes mortifying. Colleen called attention to the most egregious errors with amazing tact and always made positive suggestions and revisions. I certainly take responsibility for the errors that remain despite the best efforts of the editors at Oxford.

I want to take this opportunity to remember George and Eva Thomson, who sometimes referred to themselves as "George & Dragon." What a trying family my mother raised, including two bohemian daughters, Eva and Lyn, who still make me look especially square. My father was an autodidact who could teach himself anything, from repairing wind-up watches to facing granite with stone chisels. I am blessed with six people who most closely share my life: Julia and Ryan, and Devon and Lindsay have become young adults I am proud to admire. Little Miss Kira Barnes always warms my heart. And, above all, I want to thank my wife, Heather, for sharing with me our long and enduring emotional and intellectual life journey.

Introduction

Lankes: Title: BARBARIC, MYSTICAL, BORED.
Bebra: You have given our century its name.[1]

—Günter Grass, *The Tin Drum*, 1959

In his post-World War II novel about the first half of the twentieth century, German author Günter Grass characterized the era in pessimistic terms. He did not call it the century of progress, democracy, rationality, science, or civilization. Grass was coming to terms with totalitarianism, the Holocaust, economic collapse, and the threat of nuclear annihilation. As a result, he implied that the term *barbaric*—an ethnocentric term that referred to the supposed inferiority of an uncivilized, cruel East distinct from a civilized, enlightened West—best characterized the history of the West in the twentieth century. The promise of rationality had collapsed in the face of the sinister manipulation of the irrational, mystical, and emotional. Rather than being engaged in the serious problems of the times, people were inclined to be disengaged, bored, and indifferent.

Implicit in Grass's act of giving the twentieth century its name is a dualistic interpretation of human nature that, to a degree, shapes social theories that are both traditional and modern. One of the aims of contemporary postmodern and "late-modern" social thought is to efface this binary classification as well as other two-fold distinctions that have been foundational in social theory.

In the long-standing tradition of binary concepts in social thought, humans are simultaneously thinking and emotional creatures. These two elementary components of human nature are interwoven in innumerable ways in the great variety of social theories that have been devised to make sense of history. Theories rooted in the rational tend to focus on logic and on the physical reality that makes the material world. Theories of the emotional and the unreasonableness of human action, on the other hand, focus on irrational desires and passions, which may be reflexive in the body or buried deeply in the subconscious mind. Somewhere in the middle are theories of implicit, unthinking customs and traditions that shape actions, and the world of imagination, with its feet in the world of the possible and its head in the clouds of pure speculation and spiritualism.

People create theories out of the almost infinite variety of combinations of these elementary principles. For most of human history, theories about the world were dominated by non-rational beliefs, by traditions and customs. They were rooted in imaginative speculations about spirituality, generally expressed in some form of socially constructed religion. In traditional societies, rational theories were subordinated to spiritual ones.

In Europe during the early modern era (approximately from the sixteenth to the eighteenth centuries), a social revolution took place that transformed the whole range of social, political, and economic institutions inherited from the traditional past. Simultaneously, a revolution in social thought took place. Previously dominant theories, founded on non-rational and spiritualist principles, lost pride of place to theories based on human reason and materialism. In this new Age of Reason or Enlightenment, human reason was to be applied to all technological and social problems. Over time, it was believed, rational humanity would construct a reasonable, fair, and just social order. This doctrine, which may be termed **Enlightenment rationalism**, became the ideology of science, business, and government—in short, the new dominant ideology of the modern era.

The older, spiritual ideology survived in many forms, although religion had to compete with growing secularization. Yet the new social order of the Age of Reason and industrial capitalism did not deliver the promised just and fair society. The dominant social classes embraced the narrowest type of rationality as their goal and purpose in life (individual monetary profit; science in the service of economic growth; government as domination; media as manipulation). In response, new varieties of anti-rationalist thought emerged. The Romantic rebellion of the nineteenth century, which began as a movement in the arts and literature, jettisoned human reason in favour of emotion, extreme experience, spirituality, and passion. The Romantics sought to locate what they believed to be a deeper kind of meaning and understanding, more profound than science or rationality. They focused on the world inside themselves, their subjectivity, rather than on the material world of objects existing outside the self. This type of thought may be termed **Romantic subjectivism**.

Concretely, most social theories attempt to account for this duality of nature and humanity. If a tree falls in the forest, its rapid motion creates waves in the air molecules. But that is not sound. Sound requires, at the other end, a brain capable of receiving these waves and converting them into something we call "the noise of a falling tree." Without receptors and brains, the world would be an entirely silent one, even if a whole mountain came crashing to the ground. Without the mountain and the air there would be nothing for the receptors to receive. There is no sound in space, as the film, *Gravity* pointed out, despite the increasing number of ears and brains now floating in zero gravity.

The many counter-tendencies of Romanticism coexisted in the underground world of alienated intellectuals. As social thought developed in the nineteenth and into the twentieth century, rationalism dominated socio-economic life. The theorist Auguste Comte attempted to employ the methods of science, which had worked so well to explain the physical world, to understand the social world. He created the discipline of sociology as the result of this scientific method. On the basis of his social science, sociology emerged in nineteenth century Europe principally from the work of Émile Durkheim in France and Max Weber in Germany, among others. Both Durkheim and Weber responded to and critiqued the theories of Karl Marx, who had developed his own social scientific theory of modern society. The ideas of these three social theorists, as well as other social thinkers of the period, are still central to the debates and controversies of most contemporary sociologists, as Part III of this book illustrates. In the twentieth century, the ideas of Durkheim, Weber, and Marx were classified as "classical" sociological theories to represent their foundational status for modern sociology.

Classical Sociological Theory

Beginning in the eighteenth century, the Enlightenment represented a crucial reorientation of European thought. Sociological theorists of the time developed the notion that they were living in a new, modern society that stood in absolute contrast to the traditional order that was being overcome. Traditional thought consisted primarily of theological speculation. Culture was rooted in tradition and custom, within a fixed hierarchy of status positions. Humans were regarded as "fallen," humble creatures with a flawed capacity for independent thought. Truth was given by authorities and was not the province of the individual human mind. The economy was agrarian and static. The political was dominated by traditional authority.

However, in the centuries leading to the modern era, Europe underwent an ideological and social transformation. Change was brought through a diverse set of cultural, economic, and political movements with at least two elements in common. The first of these was individualism—the elevation of the individual above society. In Protestantism, the individual was alone before the deity, without benefit of the hierarchy of clergy as intermediaries. In culture, individuals were the creators of art and literature, and the discoverers of scientific knowledge. Individual entrepreneurs were regarded as the source of economic wealth through their individualistic pursuit of economic advantage. In political liberalism, the individual was the creator of the government, the state, and social order through the concept of a social contract.

The second element these diverse movements had in common was the importance of the human capacity for rational thought based on evidence produced by the senses and understood by the mind. The Renaissance celebration of human "potential" meant above all that humans were superior because of their capacity for rational thought and action. All natural and social problems could be solved by the scientific method, the application of human reason, and the experimental method.

Classical sociological thought, which developed roughly in the century between the fall of Napoleon (1818) and World War I (1914–18), took as its central theme the distinction between the traditional world in Europe and the emerging modern world. The central question was how the transition from traditional to modern could best be explained. Marx, Durkheim, and Weber focused attention on different primary factors that distinguished the traditional from the modern.

For Karl Marx (1818–83), *economic individualism*—specifically, the rise of capitalism—was the essential feature that had undermined the traditional world and created the modern one. The capitalist is a rational economic actor who makes economic decisions based on rational calculations of self-interest. As capitalism developed, merchants who bought and sold goods or loaned money accumulated wealth in vast amounts. The bigger capitalists drove the smaller ones out of business and grew larger. Land was converted into private property and the people who traditionally worked the land were forced out. With no way to earn a living independently, these people migrated into the newly emerging cities where capitalists were investing their wealth in the factory system. The migrants found wage-work in the factories, producing the profits that the capitalists further accumulated and reinvested. Industrial capitalism took off as a world-wide system of production and exploitation. Conflict naturally grew between the workers and the capitalists. Marx anticipated that, just as capitalists had risen to power and overthrown traditional authority, as capitalism became increasingly concentrated into fewer hands, the working class would lead their own revolution. They would create a new, socialist system of political and economic equality.

Émile Durkheim (1858–1917) lived within this world of class conflict, which he saw as a social disease that needed to be cured within the framework of the existing system. The key difference between traditional and modern societies, as Durkheim saw it, was not specifically capitalism, but the *industrial system*. The modern occupational structure was becoming increasingly specialized as the modern division of labour expanded. Individuals were increasingly separate from each other, and the old customs and beliefs that they had shared, and which held society together, had disappeared. It was increasingly difficult for society to have the solidarity it needed to be peaceful and orderly. Moving to socialism would not solve these problems, which were inevitably part of industrialism. But Durkheim believed that capitalism could be reformed. Education could inculcate feelings of solidarity. Although it was necessary to have unequal pay for different jobs in order to motivate individuals to perform the more difficult and responsible occupations, the gap between rich and poor could be substantially reduced. And once income inequalities became more rational and fair, according to Durkheim, conflict would diminish.

Max Weber (1864–1920) believed that the fundamental difference between traditional and modern societies was the rise of *rationality*. Rationality shaped all modern institutions, from religion to economics and politics. Weber believed that the form that modern rationality took, however, caused social problems. Not just capitalism, but government, science, even culture to some extent were government by "instrumental" rationality that was concerned only with success—finding the most efficient way to achieve the institution's goal (profit-making, acquiring power, dominating people through ideas, and so on). As institutions grew more rational and became more controlling, they threatened to put individuals into an "iron cage" of rationality from which there was no escape. Moving to socialism, which centralized power even more than did capitalism, would only strengthen the "iron cage," according to Weber. It was important to recognize that individuals were reasoning and feeling beings. Sociology must take into account these features and not assume that external factors simply determine human actions.

None of the three dominant "classical" sociologists theorized at length about issues of racialization or gender. The nineteenth century also bequeathed to the next a history of black emancipation and a vigorous and strong women's movement. Not until the early twentieth century would a movement for civil equality revitalize African-American struggle. A widespread movement for women's emancipation straddled the turn of the century. Most first-wave feminists had narrowed the aim of their movement to political equality, essentially, gaining the vote. Women fought for this modest goal relentlessly, sometimes violently, and ultimately successfully in the face of determined opposition. Some feminists demanded a wider set of social and economic goals, such as economic independence and the right to control their whole person, including sexuality. These demands would resurface decades later in a new mass movement of women that has continued into the present.

Romantic Subjectivism

Time is not real, Govinda. I have realized this repeatedly. And if time is not real, then the dividing line that seems to lie between this world and eternity, between suffering and bliss, between good and evil, is also an illusion.[2]

—Hermann Hesse, *Siddhartha*, 1951

The view that existence was first of all objective was central to Enlightenment rationalism and, as argued above, to classical sociologists. There was, however, an alternative type of social thought based on subjectivity, which assumed that reality was essentially in the mind. The rational, linear, progressive sense of time, as it was represented in the West, was not real; it did not represent time as it was actually experienced by people. Subjectively, time was fast or slow; it flowed backward or forward. Ultimately, nothing could be known to exist except your own mind (I know that I am thinking; therefore, I exist—or at least I know my mind exists).

Romantic subjectivism did not become the dominant mode of Western thought, however. The dominant Western ideology continued to be rationalism, science, technology, and bureaucracy. But an alternative view arose that was composed of many different strands, without a single centre principally expressed in the arts and literature. The alternative perspective was largely an intellectual expression of opposition to the dominant view. It had few practical consequences for the power structure of society and existed primarily among some intellectuals at the margins of economic and political power.

Romanticism reached back to English liberalism, particularly to the emphasis on individualism and freedom, while denying the central importance of human rationality. Individuals were not rational but were motivated by emotions and feelings; they understood things intuitively. What was really important—beauty, music, self-expression, and, above all, freedom—could never be understood by rational science. Late nineteenth-century painting, for example, abandoned the realism that was connected to "bourgeois" thought—rationalism and science—in favour of expressionism. Rather than depicting nature or real social conditions, Romantic works expressed emotion, irrationality, and subjectivity. Writers, furthermore, tried to express that which could not be expressed in words, giving rise to twentieth century stream of consciousness literature, nonsense poetry, and surrealist paintings.

For the Romantics, the rational part of the brain was secondary to the intuitive, emotional essence, which included the most basic and primitive impulses, particularly sexuality. Human rationality, in their view, became little more than rationalisms, explanations that merely excuse or justify our actions, which, in reality, spring from deep, unconscious processes. The Enlightenment belief in rational thought, then, was wholly mistaken, according to the Romantics. Rather, people were motivated to act by non-rational factors. This belief explained the hold that religion had on so many people.

It was precisely irrationality that Sigmund Freud (1856–1939) sought to subject to scientific understanding. Freud saw himself as a scientist who developed the theory of the unconscious mind to explain people's irrational and sometimes psychotic behaviour. Human beings were born with powerful instincts that were the essential foundations of their behaviour and actions.

Among the most powerful of the instincts, according to Freud, were those of life and death. Life instincts were primarily expressed through sexuality. Ultimately, much of an individual's life could be understood by examining the way a person's psychic life had unfolded, comparing this actual development with a "normal" sexual development that produced heterosexuality and the normative masculine/feminine binary. The second essential instinctual force was a death instinct, which was at the root of violence and aggression. Civilization could be explained by the application of life instincts to progress; the equal history of violence and terror resulted from the uninhibited operation of the death instinct. Freudianism is still an important theory that contemporary social theorists employ more or less critically.[3]

Decadence

Cecil Vyse (Daniel Day-Lewis): I have no profession. My attitude, quite an indefensible one, is that so long as I'm no trouble to anyone, I have the right to do as I like. It is, I dare say, an example of my decadence.[4]

—A Room with a View, 1986

In European social thought, the end of the nineteenth century has become synonymous with cultural decadence, a variant of Romanticism, which the twentieth century inherited in major doses. Decadents refused to follow the rules of humanity or deity; they were guided only by their individual desires and feelings. The moral relativism of the decadents drew from Charles Darwin's theory of evolution the lesson that the only sensible response to a meaningless world was hedonism and self-expression. A movement that was primarily expressed in literature and the arts, Romanticism presented itself as the instinctive enemy of bourgeois society and, potentially, of any society whatsoever. Although the Romantics generally shared with the socialists many of the criticisms of modern society, they believed their antipathy was more profound since it rested on a cult of the individual. Romantics rejected the materialism and morality of bourgeois society, but in periods of pessimism they tended to abandon any hope of social revolution or reform.

The avant-garde artists of the turn of the century, anticipating Freud, explored their own subjectivity, the intricacies and paradoxes of their own psyche, their desires and self-destructiveness. Literature and art took a symbolic turn, using words to evoke indirect suggestions rather than using direct description to express emotions and ideas. Poetry used words as sounds, bringing it closer to music. In painting, artists examined the form of art itself rather than its symbolic content, focusing on colour, texture, and design, abstracting from reality.

Decadence was influenced by the reissue in the 1880s of the works of the dissolute and Romantic aristocrat, the Marquis de Sade, and by the pessimistic philosophy of Arthur Schopenhauer. In *The World as Will and Idea* (1819), Nicholls argues, Schopenhauer emphasized the central role in life of human "will," a blind and irrational force that was expressed above all in appetites and desires. In a universe that lacked sense and logic, in which humans were thought of as full of egoism, hatred, and malice, art became self-consciously anti-social, leading ultimately to the pessimistic embracing of death.[5]

The centrality of the human "will" became the axis around which Friedrich Nietzsche (1844–1900) wrote his nihilistic, late-nineteenth century philosophy. "Doubt" was the weapon that Enlightenment rationality had turned against traditional thought. Nietzsche turned the same weapon against scientific rationality. In his view, scientific knowledge could not claim any more certainty than any other form of knowledge. Behind each claim about knowledge and truth was a group that sought to have its version of truth accepted and, through this means, to acquire power.

Knowledge was what those in dominant positions had the power to *make* true. As the 1960s anarchist Abbie Hoffman said in *Revolution for the Hell of It*, "I don't want to get philosophical but there is really no such animal [as Truth]."[6] In Nietzsche's view, people have a "will to power" that is fundamental. A natural elite group exists always and everywhere in society. Socialism is impossible because human beings are and want to be unequal. Christians and socialists both exercise their "will to power" by trying to make the powerful modest, meek, and egalitarian, bringing them down to the level of mediocrity. Nietzsche's critical, anti-rationalist stance was influential at various points in the twentieth century, as the following chapters demonstrate, through the rise of postmodernism in the 1980s.[7]

The Organization of This Book

The book is divided into three parts. Part I, "From Disillusionment to the Abyss," introduces important historical currents that occurred in the immediate post-classical period, from World War I to the close of World War II. These include the Russian Revolution, the Great Depression, the emergence of Keynesianism, and the rise of fascism in the 1930s. This section traces social thought in a variety of intellectual contexts, including in literature and the arts, with a focus on the Chicago School, Fordism, Western Marxism, and the Frankfurt School.

Part II, "From Repression to Rebellion," discusses the development of critical social thought in the early post-World War II decades. Critical thought emerged in the context of large and radical social movements of African Americans and women, in the fear and opposition inspired by Cold War and the threat of nuclear war, and in the opposition to colonial wars in Africa and Asia. This section discusses structural functionalism, postwar cultural rebellion, post-colonialism, feminist revival, existentialism, and critical social thought.

In Part III, "From Radicalism to Juggernaut," the narrative traces the development of social thought from the social movements of the 1960s, principally those involving a "counter-culture," women, and African Americans, to the contemporary period. This section introduces structuralism, interactionism, postmodernism, third-wave feminism, and a number of sociological versions of "late" modernity. It includes an overview of major figures, such as Lévi-Strauss, Goffman, Garfinkel, Becker, Foucault, Baudrillard, Smith, Hill Collins, Butler, hooks, Habermas, Giddens, and Bourdieu. And finally, the conclusion briefly considers the current state of globalization, social change, and ecological crisis, and the need for an equally comprehensive, historical, and comparative, global sociology.

We turn now to Chapter 1, "Modernism and Discontent," which considers early twentieth century social thought as it responded to the initial call to arms and the resulting devastation of World War I.

Timeline

1903   Henry Ford opens the Ford Motor Company. Produces Model "T" in 1908.

1903   W.E.B. Du Bois publishes *The Souls of Black Folks*.

1905   Albert Einstein presents his theory of relativity.

1909   The *Futurist Manifesto* is published in Italy, written by Filippo Marinetti.

1914   World War I begins.

1916   Marcus Garvey moves from Jamaica to the United States.

1917   February Revolution and October (Bolshevik) Revolution take place in Russia.

1918   Armistice ends World War I. Treaty of Versailles signed in 1919.

1919   Civil War in Russia. Winnipeg Strike begins (May); repressed by police (June).

1921   Civil War in Russia ends; Bolsheviks implement the New Economic Policy.

1921   Yevgeny Zamyatin publishes *We*, his dystopian, anti-Soviet novel.

1922   Benito Mussolini seizes power in Italy, marking the first fascist government in Europe.

1923   Georg Lukács publishes *History and Class Consciousness*.

1924   V.I. Lenin dies in January; the struggle over the direction of the revolution begins.

1924   André Breton publishes the first *Surrealist Manifesto*.

1925   Sergei Esenin, disillusioned poet and Isadora Duncan's ex, hangs himself.

1925   Robert Park, Ernest Burgess, and Roderick McKenzie publish *The City*.

1925   Harlem Renaissance poet Langston Hughes publishes *The Weary Blues*.

1929   British Cabinet rules that women in Canada are legally defined as "persons."

1929   With Joseph Stalin in power, collectivization of agriculture begins in the USSR.

1929   The stock market crash spirals the US and much of the world into the Great Depression.

1933   National Socialist German Workers' (Nazi) Party, under Adolf Hitler, takes power in Germany.

1935   The populist Social Credit Party wins the provincial election in Alberta.

1936   Trotsky publishes *The Revolution Betrayed*.

1936   John Maynard Keynes publishes his *General Theory*, foundational for the welfare state.

1939   Hitler and Stalin sign non-aggression pact and invade Poland, starting World War II in Europe.

1940   Helen MacGill publishes her dissertation, *News and the Human Interest Story*.

1943   Everett Hughes publishes *French Canada in Transition*.

1944   The socialist Co-operative Commonwealth Federation wins election in Saskatchewan.

1945   World War II ends in Europe (April) and Japan (August).

I From Disillusionment to the Abyss

Charlie Chaplin (1889–1977) is probably the most recognizable actor and filmmaker of the silent era of American cinema. *Modern Times* (1936) is a biting satire of the inhumanity of modern technology and its Fordist production practices. Working at a conveyor belt endlessly tightening bolts, Chaplin is a small cog in the big industrial machine, into which he inadvertently gets swallowed, ending up entangled in its inner gears. In another scene, Chaplin is a guinea pig for the ingenious Billows Feeding Machine, which automatically pushes food in the mouths of assembly line workers so they don't have to stop working to have lunch. The factory scenes in *Modern Times* critique the dehumanizing effects of modern technology, the oppression of capitalists, and the inhumanity that stands in the way of social justice for the honest and hard-working poor. Chaplin's sympathies were broadly socialist. Later, during the Cold War hysteria of the 1950s, Chaplin was hounded by anti-communist watchdogs of the US government and was threatened with deportation (Chaplin had been born in Britain). He left the United States and settled in Switzerland, where he died.[1]

Image: Charlie Chaplin, in *Modern Times*, is sucked into the gears of the assembly line. He becomes nothing more than a dehumanized machine—a cog in the wheel of capitalist production. © AF archive / Alamy

The year 1914 marked the beginning of World War I—the "war to end all wars," or so it was said at the time. Instead, the war began a century in which the productive potential of an increasingly globalized capitalism was matched (or overshadowed) by the expansion of its capacity for physical, social, and environmental destruction. If the celebrations that marked the war's beginning reflected the Romantic age of honourable conflict, the daily horrors of total war quickly replaced such romanticism with an unprecedented social pessimism and despair. The classical sociologists were caught between their sense of nationalism and their wider commitment to a world of justice and peace. African Americans responded to continuing racism with a cultural revolution that tried to define the response of the black community to white oppression and develop a distinctive, black culture in the Harlem Renaissance.

In 1917, a communist-led revolution in Russia created the first state socialist government, which embarked on a drive for quick industrialization under conditions of severe austerity, state repression, and continuing conflict. Western Marxism, meanwhile, focused on the analysis of culture. The Frankfurt School, for example, argued that mass culture had become a tool of domination. In Chicago, sociologists embarked on an ambitious analysis of culture and communities in the supposed melting pot of American immigration.

As the world was plunged into the Depression following the stock market crash of 1929, social democratic governments increased the economic and social role of governments. In Europe, authoritarian governments took advantage of the economic chaos to capture political power and lead much of the world into the abyss of another war.

CHAPTER 1

Modernism and Discontent

Learning Objectives

- To understand and illustrate the consequences of World War I on social thought
- To examine the role of nationalism in Max Weber's and Émile Durkheim's theories
- To examine modernism in European culture as a response to social anxiety and disillusionment
- To understand the feminist views of Virginia Woolf in the context of the early women's movement

[I]n or about December, 1910, human character changed.[1]

—Virginia Woolf, "Mr. Bennett and Mrs. Brown," 1924

Woolf was not alone in believing that human character, at least in Europe, had changed fundamentally in the new century. Nineteenth-century Victorianism had been dethroned in the era of decadence and the **New Woman**, and old standards of taste, morality, and truth had been undermined. By suggesting that human character had changed on a fairly precise date, however, Woolf ridiculed positivism and scientific certainty. And while relations between husbands and wives had also shifted, she knew that *male* character had not changed nearly enough.

Whatever "human character" might have been in 1910, it was about to be severely tested. The late nineteenth century was a period of tremendous technological change and cultural innovation. The intellectuals of the modern era were,

however, uncomfortable with the prevailing social order. In 1918, the German historian Oswald Spengler published *The Decline of the West*, a title that reflected his belief that, as had happened to ancient Greece and Rome, European civilization was beginning to spiral downward to its doom. Writing while the nations of Europe were literally destroying one another in the Great War, Spengler's work gave voice to widespread social pessimism, which had replaced Victorian notions of optimism and progress.

The sentiment expressed by the title of Spengler's book reflected a belief that the new century marked a widening gulf between the past and the present. The twentieth century had arrived and, almost by fiat, what was in the past no longer counted. In modern society, new generations tend to believe that theirs is the "in" or *au courant* generation. The generation coming into maturity now, in the early twenty-first century, for example, has a sense that the world reshaped by the microchip is fundamentally different from that of the late twentieth century. Indeed, our world has shrunk in both distance and time. Events that occur on other continents can impact us both rapidly and profoundly. As a result, even more than previous generations we are aware of the dark side of modernity, the persistence in the twenty-first century of oppression, injustice, and alienation.

Similarly, when philosopher Bertrand Russell said that "something very fundamental was needed to put the world right,"[2] he could have been speaking to a contemporary audience. World War I helped shape the diverse and contradictory set of ideas and movements that stood opposed, in different ways, to the dominant, modern world.

The "Great War": From Romanticism to Disillusionment

Oh God! What a lovely war.[3]

—Guillaume Apollinaire, "The Cavalier's Farewell," 1913–16

Apollinaire's phrase quickly became ironic; it is hard to imagine that he meant it quite literally, that, in the beginning, World War I seemed romantic. But some nations, such as the United States and France, were born of war and revolution, and romantic myths of combat are part of the national psyche. Even today, when Western countries are being drawn once again into the "war on terrorism," with an apparently implacable and demonized enemy, the mythology of previous wars helps to shape public acquiescence, if not enthusiasm. And so it was that when Britain declared war in 1914, and Australia and Canada were automatically at war as part of the British Empire, volunteers flocked to recruiting stations out of Imperial patriotism—but also out of a sense of adventure and a manufactured belief in the evil of the enemy.

While the most terrible features of Western civilization were about to materialize in the chaos and slaughter of war, the majority of intellectuals, even progressive ones, welcomed the coming conflict. As novelist H.G. Wells had said in 1897, "the war-fever that occasionally runs through a civilized community" had gotten into everyone's blood.[4] Walking among the crowds near Trafalgar Square in London, Bertrand Russell was amazed that ordinary people welcomed the war so gleefully: "the anticipation of carnage was delightful to something like ninety per cent of the population."[5] He had "fondly imagined" that "wars were forced upon a reluctant population by despotic and Machiavellian governments."[6]

English poet Rupert Brooke thanked God that war had come in time to awaken his sleeping generation. He rushed head-long into the conflict, like a swimmer "into cleanness leaping," away from "a world grown old and cold and weary" with its ". . . sick hearts that honour could not move, / And half-men, and their dirty songs and dreary."[7] Macho, "whole-men" clamoured to enlist in the army, Brooke declared, leaving the "half-men" at home with the women and children. The term "whole-men" proved to be ironic, however. Hundreds of thousands (if not millions) of soldiers returned from the front lines missing arms or legs, with seared lungs and shattered minds.

For German novelist Thomas Mann, war promised "a purification, a liberation, an enormous hope." Germany might be out-manned, but the German soul would be victorious over mere materials and numbers. A triumphant victory would establish the power of the superior German civilization over all Europe, fulfilling the historic mission of the German nation.[8] The historic mission of the French, on the other hand, was revenge: they wanted to reverse the humiliation they had suffered in 1871, when the Prussian Army had marched triumphantly down the Champs-Élysées in Paris. France may have been an industrial underdog compared with Germany but, inspired by the belief in their irresistible will, the French postured aggressively. French intellectuals and generals alike were convinced that the mystical French spirit, or *élan vital*, could change the odds decisively in their favour, which otherwise were stacked heavily against them.[9]

War appeared to promise excitement, adventure, and romance. Many young men in England, for example, yearned to escape from the black-coated army of office clerks who worked for "Thirty Bob a Week," the title of John Davidson's 1894 poem. The poor English clerk in this poem drags himself each day to the London underground, which conveys him from the suburbs to the city and back, "like a mole . . . in the dark." But if the millstone of the clerk's daily grind showed he was already "lost and damn'd" in hell, the real hell on earth was yet to come.[10]

For many, war enthusiasm persisted even in the face of the carnage on the Western front. In 1915, Canadian physician John McCrae wrote the oft-quoted poem *In Flanders Fields*, in which he imagined the voices of dead soldiers calling on the living to pick up the torch and join the honourable fight. From the trenches in the middle of the bloodbath, French poet Apollinaire romanticized the war. The earth, he wrote, had been "yawning with boredom."[11] Now it had come to life. Bomb shells were "fireworks in steel" exploding like "Diamonds blossoming at night."[12] Flares were "Like two breasts unbound / raising their nipples insolently."[13] In his poem "War," Apollinaire said we shouldn't weep for the horrors of war because a better future would arise from the destruction. When the war is over, he wrote, we will be masters, not only of the earth's surface, but its subterranean depths and "aerial space," and farther still beyond the Earth.[14] Destruction was the birth companion of progress.

In 1917, Wilfred Owen, an English poet who had enlisted two years previously, received orders to join a regiment on the Somme. He described his feelings at the time:

This is a Regular Regiment, so I have come off mighty well. . . . It is a huge satisfaction to be going among well-trained troops and genuine "real-old" officers. . . . This morning I was hit! We were bombing, and a fragment from somewhere hit my thumb knuckle. I coaxed out one drop of blood. Alas! No more!! There is a fine heroic feeling about being in France, and I am in perfect spirits. A tinge of excitement is about me. . . .[15]

These lines were written two years in to the war that would kill "half the seed of Europe, one by one."[16] At the time, Owen still found the prospect of fighting exciting and heroic, although his first impressions about life at the Front were of being perpetually wet and eating out of old tins among harassed-looking officers and men who were little more than "expressionless lumps." As he wrote in "Insensibility,"[17] some troops simply cease feeling because only by becoming as dull as possible could they stand "The tease and doubt of shelling, / And chance's strange arithmetic"—the randomness with which one soldier survives an attack while another dies. Of course, death was not always random. The officer class ordered the lethal assaults but stayed behind to measure the yards temporarily gained, to count the bodies, and to collect medals. The Australian film *Gallipoli* shows arrogant British officers ordering an attack on an impregnable hamburger hill, resulting in the wholesale slaughter of raw Australian recruits, who count even less in the ledger of the British army because they're merely "colonials."

The romantic conception of the glories of individual combat died an early and painful death in the no man's land strung along the French and Belgian borders. By 1916, British writer D.H. Lawrence said that the "excitement had gone out of the war" because there was too much death and horror.[18] In his stark, realistic prose, Ernest Hemingway described picking up from the battlefield detached bits of human anatomy, blown to pieces by high explosives, with bodies ripped apart "along no anatomical lines."[19] Furthermore, Newfoundland poet E.J. Pratt referred to war enthusiasm as "a virus in the air."[20] The concreteness of total war and the useless suffering and whole-scale massacre of the youth of Europe overshadowed and silenced naive, idealistic optimism for many.

Similarly, Wilfred Owen's graphic letters soon recorded his growing disillusionment with the slaughterhouse of the Western Front, where men "die as cattle."[21] From his hospital bed, he imprinted on paper the fundamental lesson that "one of Christ's essential commands was: passivity at any price! Suffer dishonour and disgrace, but never resort to arms. Be bullied, be outraged, be killed; but do not kill."[22] Despite his new pacifist sensibility, in the summer of 1918 Owen disembarked once more in France, where he shed not merely more than one but his last drop of blood. On the fourth of November, a week before the armistice, Owen became another victim of chance's strange arithmetic. He was killed by German machine gunners trying to cross the Sambre Canal.[23]

By the end of the war, young German boys were being draped with ill-fitting uniforms and shoved toward the trenches. Those were the days, novelist Günter Grass wrote, "when every male who could stand halfway correct was being shipped to Verdun," where the air of France was "famed for its iron and lead content." These sorry soldiers soon underwent "a radical change of posture from the vertical to the eternal horizontal."[24] In one of his most bitter drawings, German artist George Grosz depicted a doctor examining a mangled corpse and asserting it was "Fit for active duty."[25]

What had gone wrong? Many blamed people's feelings of patriotism and nationalism. Sigmund Freud, however, blamed people's inherent nature. For Freud, the deadly nature of modern warfare was proof that our species possessed an inherent instinct for aggression and destruction. Humans were wolves to their own species, according to Freud. Socialists linked the slaughter of mostly working men to the capitalist system and to imperialism. The German soldiers in Remarque's novel *All Quiet on the Western Front* speculate that the rulers caused the war: the kings, the generals, and those who profited from it (see Box 1.1).[26]

The romantic writers and artists who had flocked to the banner of their respective nations soon felt the heavy weight of disillusionment. As more and more of the young seeds of Europe did not return from France, the scale of this great slaughter led to a thorough intellectual pessimism about humanity, society, and the universe as a whole. Philosopher George Santayana feared that "the catastrophe won't be great enough . . . and that some false arrangement will be patched up. . . . [because] People are not intelligent."[27]

Some "false arrangement" was indeed patched together at the end of the war. Germany surrendered before the allied armies had set foot on German soil. Patriotic Germans quickly cultivated the myth that the German army had not lost the war; rather, the nation had been sold out by its own politicians and intellectuals, who were guilty of a great national betrayal. They had stabbed the German army in the back. Adolf Hitler, who was a corporal at the end of the war, believed this carefully cultivated myth and vowed to restore the German nation to greatness and domination.

Nationalism had trumped internationalism in 1914, and national identity continued to be a potent political force after the war. The map of Europe was drawn anew. New nation-states were created as old empires crumbled. The long-standing lines of linguistic and cultural identity, however, did not follow the new national boundaries. Some of the new states were multi-ethnic, such as Yugoslavia and Czechoslovakia, planting shallow seeds of future discord. Other state borders divided a single ethnic group among several nations, creating other dangerous fault lines in central Europe. Both the wish to reconstruct a **Greater Germany** and

⚜ BOX 1.1 · THEORY IN CONTEXT ⚜

All Quiet on the Western Front

At the beginning of the war, Germans also expressed enthusiasm for hostilities, which is skilfully depicted in the great, anti-war novel *All Quiet on the Western Front* (1929) by Erich Maria Remarque. The novel describes the conflict from the German point of view. The novel's protagonist, Paul Bäumer, was one of a group of ordinary German soldiers recruited from school and thrust into the thick of trench warfare. Caught up in the thrill of the moment, "beside themselves with joy," the raw recruits believed that duty to their country was their most noble aim. No one, Paul Bäumer said, "had the vaguest idea what we were in for."[28] The inhumanity of mutual slaughter was revealed, briefly, on Christmas Eve, 1914, when soldiers from both sides spontaneously put down their arms and embraced each other in no man's land. Remarque recounts this episode in his novel. As a German soldier in *All Quiet on the Western Front* realized, "Any non-commissioned officer is more of an enemy to a recruit, and schoolmaster to a pupil, than they [the French] are to us."[29] Some unknown person signs a document declaring war, and instantly murder, for which society had imposed its severest penalty, becomes "our highest aim."

At a pivotal point in Remarque's novel, Paul Bäumer fatally stabs a French soldier in the shell hole in which both soldiers had sheltered from the bombardment. Up to that moment, death had seemed distant and abstract; suddenly, war became face-to-face, graphic, and intimate. Locked in the fatal embrace of combat, Bäumer sees the "poor devil's" face and feels their human fellowship.[30] Stabbed with remorse, Paul resolves that after the armistice he will fight against war. To provide a final exclamation point on the tragic waste of warfare, Paul is killed, just like Wilfred Owen, when all is almost quiet and the ceasefire practically at hand.

---

to recapture German territories overseas fuelled the Nazi movement, rooted ideologically in the romanticism of "race" and the denunciation of liberalism and Marxism alike (see Chapter 4).

Newer nations, such as Australia and Canada, emerged from the war with a newly constructed nationalism that had not previously existed, based on the blood and sacrifice that the war had demanded. Alden Nowlan's retrospective poem *Ypres: 1915* romanticizes Canadian valour and grit, imagining a young soldier standing up to the advancing enemy: "you want this god damn trench / you're going to have to take it away / from Billy McNally of the South End of Saint John, New Brunswick."[31] Nowlan recognized that the sentiment was ridiculous "and nothing on which to found a country," except that, as a cultivated myth, it had. By the 1920s, the Dominions of the British Empire—Australia, Canada, and New Zealand—were beginning to act independently of Britain. They opened negotiations with Britain to make each country equal in its nationhood, a status finally granted by the British Parliament in 1931. For Canada, however, the dominating presence of the United States often overshadowed cultural and economic nationalism.

Classical sociologists Émile Durkheim and Max Weber addressed the question of nationalism, which remained one of the most potent mythical forces of the twentieth century. Both contributed to the war effort on behalf of their combatant countries.

Durkheim and Weber: Nationalism and Gender

Émile Durkheim (1858–1917)

For French sociologist Émile Durkheim, World War I was catastrophic. Initially, he and Jean Jaurès, his socialist friend, were opposed to war. Jaurès was later assassinated for his anti-war politics, a loss Durkheim felt deeply. Giddens says that Durkheim's generation viewed the outbreak of the war as a tragic shock. For Durkheim, patriotism was an expression of collective conscience that would be superseded by "world patriotism." German nationalism, however, was markedly different: it reflected a pathological, collective anomie. As a system of power that recognized no moral limits, the single-minded German state was like an amoral individual within a world community,[32] a view derived from Hobbes. Durkheim believed, moreover, that behind Germany's drive for war was a national character of unbounded "will-mania" that sought power and world domination and that was entrenched in a widely shared system of ideas that were made for war. He feared a repeat of the military debacle of 1870, when Prussian troops occupied his hometown, and he was greatly relieved in September 1914 when the German army was halted before it could take Paris.[33]

Once France was at war, Durkheim performed his national duty, though not in uniform. His work consisted of writing and organizing. He

said that he hadn't worked so hard in two decades. The work and the anxiety took its toll, however. His son, André, who had enlisted in the army, was declared missing on the Bulgarian front early in 1916. Not until April was it confirmed that André had been killed. Durkheim never recovered from the psychological trauma of loss. Lukes says that he withdrew into a "ferocious silence" that was "as glacial as death itself," and he forbade anyone from mentioning his son's name.[34]

When his worry over André's fate was at its deepest, Durkheim was attacked publicly on two occasions as being a pro-German Jew with a German name. Along with other French citizens of foreign descent, he was called a traitor to France. Feverish and ill, he sought relief in more work. Late in 1916 Durkheim suffered a stroke. He died in November 1917 at the age of 58, while the slaughter continued on the Western Front.[35] His hopes for society had been eclipsed by personal and world events.

Durkheim sought to understand "the *raison d'être* of national sentiments and patriotic faith" beyond the doctrinaire claims that they are merely leftovers of barbarian prejudice. Lukes says that Durkheim was strongly, although not militantly, patriotic and was motivated in his work to contribute to the moral regeneration of the French nation. For Durkheim, nationalism, like any concept, was a mental and a social phenomenon, a **social fact** that was "subject to laws that the human will cannot upset simply by willing." Nationalism was rooted in the reality and usefulness of mutual sympathy and human sociability. Such sentiments are expressed only within closed and confined social groups, and nations are one such group.[36] At his most optimistic, Durkheim thought that World War I might inspire a period of collective effervescence in France, a time when the French spirit would move beyond destruction to reconstruction, not only materially but spiritually.

According to Lukes, Durkheim was a patriot but not a nationalist; for Durkheim, nationalism assumed that one's national culture was "above all others," but one must not think of patriotism as "putting France above all."[37] Patriotic loyalty to the nation was real and valuable. People have an obligation and duty to their country, which they "do not have the right to cast off." But Durkheim was no single-minded patriot. The moral ideals to which he subscribed were international and not exclusively French, although he believed they were perhaps more clearly reflected in French history than in any other nation.[38] He opposed revolutionary **syndicalism** and socialism, which declared the working class to be the enemies of the nation and of patriotism. Durkheim argued that these revolutionary sentiments reflected a blind, emotional force that must be muzzled by intelligence and reason. For Durkheim, workers and capitalists had many interests in common; they "lived in the same social environment," were members of the same society, and were "impregnated with the same ideas."[39]

On Gender and Marriage

For Durkheim, France was undergoing an appalling moral and ethical crisis, in common with other industrializing nations. The task of sociology, he said in 1888, was to expand the spirit of collectivity among people. The individual is "the organ of an organism" and must learn that "what is valuable is conscientiously performing one's role as an organ."[40] In part, playing your social role meant learning to control your impulses and bodily urges, among the most potentially disruptive of which was sexuality. Human sexuality, for Durkheim, was necessarily subject to society's morals and social character. He did not support sex education in schools because sex was an exceptional act that was "obscure, mysterious, forbidding." Treating sexual relations openly reduced it to a biological function, in Durkheim's view, on the same level as digestion. Reflecting the Victorian age in which his own values were formed, Durkheim believed that we respond to

sexuality in a contradictory fashion: it shocks and repels us, but also attracts us.[41] The attraction may be rooted in biology, but on top of this primitive desire, society has erected a complex scaffolding of morality and **regulation** that is expressed in the sentiments of shock and repulsion, and keeps sexuality private and mysterious.

Above all social institutions, the rules of marriage provide the regulating framework for sexual expression. Durkheim believed that marriage was an important social institution providing men, in particular, with a strong moral bond that helps them resist their passions and "curb" their enthusiastic desires. Durkheim did not support an absolute prohibition on divorce—it was acceptable where continuing the marriage was literally impossible—but he disagreed with divorce by mutual consent. Marriage was the basis of the family, and preserving the family intact was essential for providing a moral influence over the whole of life. The social obligations of family stability, he wrote in 1906, significantly outweighed the right to flee from these duties. In most unhappy marriages where children were involved, Durkheim argued, both parents were sufficiently aware of their obligations to "fulfil their roles," and they made accommodations within the framework of their marriage.

According to Durkheim, the law must reinforce the strict preservation of marriage because it provides "the moral force necessary to support courageously" an unhappy relationship. His belief was similar to a line from the silent film *The Crowd* (1928): "Marriage isn't a word, it's a sentence."[42] Marriage is to be endured for the sake of society. Furthermore, Durkheim argued, divorce by mutual consent would not decrease suffering or increase happiness, contrary to what one might expect. Marriage gives men a definite object for their desires and, in the process, moderates and appeases them. In the absence of the moral bonds of marriage, desires would become aggravated, leading men to "the pursuit of ends that are always new and always changing" but, says Durkheim, "become boring once they are attained, leaving nothing behind but weariness and disenchantment." Marriage, he claims, "prevents the search after pleasures that are unattainable or disappointing."[43]

Durkheim's views on marriage and divorce were quite conventional for his time, but, contrary to the era, his nationalism was neither aggressive nor imperialistic. Nationalism emerged from the organic reality of social life and imposed a duty on individuals to act for the common good. But when it was harnessed to the aims of conquest and domination, nationalism no longer reflected the conscience of the people.

Max Weber (1864–1920)

Sociologist Max Weber (1864–1920), Durkheim's counterpart in Germany, was also variously and ambivalently attracted to liberal and nationalist ideas. Weber's domineering father was traditionalist and patriotic; his mother, spiritual and humanitarian. Initially, Weber's politics were largely conservative. As a university student, Weber adopted aristocratic habits and joined a duelling society, soon sporting the obligatory facial scarring; being able to "show your scars" was a sign of manliness in Germany's aristocratic, military culture.[44] He dutifully enlisted in the army to serve his period of compulsory training and formed life-long habits of self-discipline and ascetic living.[45] It might be said of Weber what novelist Heinrich Mann had said of Diederich Hessling, his fictional German patriot in *Man of Straw* (1918): He "was proud and glad of his excellent training. The students' corps, his military service and the atmosphere of Imperialism had educated him . . . to become a pioneer of the spirit of the times."[46]

Weber was always ambivalent, however, of the spirit of his times. He was not initially in favour of

war, but in 1914 he fell in with the war enthusiasm of the moment, referring to the actual engagement of warfare as "great and wonderful." As a reserve officer in the German army, he worked during the first year of the war to establish and run military hospitals. As the war became prolonged and stalemated, Käsler says, Weber's attitude changed. His views were expressed through regular contributions to German newspapers. As a public intellectual, Weber came up against the strictures of military censorship. He opposed expanding the German Empire in Europe through territorial annexations, a policy that was demanded by the ultra-nationalists and, he said, was supported by "munitions manufacturers and agrarian capitalists." He concluded that Germany needed a new political order, including a democratic parliament, a constitutional monarchy, and a new federal constitution, for which he wrote a draft.[47]

Early in 1918, he and his wife, Marianne Weber, campaigned together for political office. Marianne was a leader of the German women's movement and was elected as a provincial deputy. Her husband was unsuccessful in being elected or being appointed to political office, although he became an advisor to the Ministry of the Interior. As conditions deteriorated and some German provinces wanted to secede from the nation, Weber argued for maintaining the unity of Germany. He opposed the Marxist revolutionary movement that took power for a brief period in Munich, which he called a "bloody carnival."[48]

Weber's career was dogged by mental-health troubles. From his long period of psychopathology, Weber derived a deep interest in the irrational forms of cognition. According to Sica, Weber was impressed by Nietzsche's "seductive work" and by Freudianism, which was becoming popularized in Germany by 1904. Weber sought to traverse the divide between "intuition" and "intellect" without reducing one to the other.[49]

Giddens says that Weber's work constitutes an attempt to integrate Marx's historical materialism with Nietzsche's anti-rationalism.[50] Weber wished to support realistic, rational involvement in the world, and he opposed over-optimistic attempts to remake the world anew, such as leaping into impractical and unachievable revolutionism. At the same time, he rejected equally all pessimistic renunciations and rejections of the world, such as escaping into religious mysticism. Above all, Weber sought to clarify the need for making political and social decisions by distinguishing between rational means to attain a desired end and the ethical considerations or value judgments that went into choosing an end or goal.

On Rationalism, Religion, and Eroticism

In "Religious Rejections of the World," Weber discusses the tension that develops in the modern world between the spiritual and secular, between anti-rational religious ethics and this-worldly life forces, and he extends this analysis to "the spheres of **aesthetic** and erotic life."[51] According to Weber, the modern world had become largely disenchanted through the effects of science and rationality, although some people still withdrew into religious mysticism. More importantly, new, secular forms of escape were largely taking the place of the spiritual, including art and sexuality.

In Weber's view, in the modern era, people desired to escape from the increasingly impersonal, amoral, and utilitarian world that was overwhelming them, but increasingly the religious option was not available. Secularism undermined the traditional, spiritual and "other-worldly" paths of escape people had taken in troubled times. On the one hand, art and aesthetics in general became secularized. Art was understood increasingly as an independent value existing in its own right, as art for art's sake. On the other hand, in response to the growth of secular rationalization,

art provided people with the alternative of a this-worldly escape: "It provides a *salvation* from the routines of everyday life, and especially from the increasing pressures of theoretical and practical rationalism." Weber says that art in the modern world became valued as "a realm of irresponsible indulgence."[52]

The second form of secular "salvation" or escape in the modern world was sexuality. Weber believed that sexual love is the "greatest irrational force of life"; hence, religion is in profound tension with it. Societies have placed widely varied value emphasis on eroticism. Originally, Weber says, there was a close connection between sexuality and religion, linked in "magic orgiasticism within which every ecstasy was considered 'holy.'" Weber suggested that the early, "naive naturalism of sex" had been transformed as sexuality evolved away from naturalism and as culture became rationalized and intellectualized. In the process, society constructed normative and legal conventions to regulate eroticism "by veiling the natural and organic basis of sexuality."

As culture became increasingly rationalized and divorced from nature, the special position of eroticism was enhanced, in Weber's view. Sexuality was sublimated into a consciously cultivated eroticism, "raised into the sphere of conscious enjoyment." As everyday life became routine, specialized, and increasingly ascetic through the mechanisms of rationalization, eroticism came to represent "a gate into the most irrational and therefore real kernel of life."[53] With tension increasing between routine, everyday life and the possibility of temporary escape into the sensual and erotic, "extramarital sexual life . . . could appear as the only tie which still linked [a] man with the natural foundation of all life." Similar to aesthetics, then, Weber speaks of eroticism as "an inner-worldly salvation from rationalization." The erotic is a "joyous triumph over rationality." It takes the place of the equally radical rejection of other-worldly religious salvation, which finds its "climax" in "the triumph of the spirit over the body." The high value of the erotic sensation "re-interprets and glorifies all the pure animality of the sensation," in sharp contrast to a religion of salvation.[54]

There is, then, Weber believed, a tension between religions of salvation, such as Christianity, and sexuality. Religions that tend to the more rational and ascetic reject and critique sexuality as irrational and animalistic. Sexuality is "an unmediated slipping from the mystic realm of God into the realm of the All-Too-Human." For religions of salvation, according to Weber, eroticism is nothing but the "purely fortuitous flaming up of passion"; it is an idiosyncratic, pathological obsession. Passion is a loss of dignified self-control and wisdom. Consequently, only rational marriage is acceptable. Marriage is a divine ordination "given to man as a creature who is hopelessly wretched by virtue of his" lust.[55] Similar to Durkheim's argument, Weber believed that the institution of marriage in the modern world attempted to fulfill the same functions of rational control of sexuality that religion had fulfilled in the past.

For Weber, rationalization demystified religion, but it did not become an adequate replacement. As rationalization increases and religious mysticism declines, people turn to self-cultivation, including "the conscious cultivation of esthetic and erotic enjoyment." The value of art and eroticism increases "as life-enchanting antidotes to the deadening dominance of" rationality. Art and eroticism then emerge as conscious and autonomous value spheres expressing what is claimed to be "real" life.[56] For Weber, however, Brubaker argues, this attempt to escape rationalization is doomed to failure because modern romantic irrationalism is itself an intellectual rationalization. That is, once raised to consciousness, art and eroticism are subject to the scientific lens of rationalization, and the goal of escaping in either of these realms is therefore self-defeating.[57]

For Weber, eroticism had replaced mystical religion as an escape from an overly rational, bureaucratic, and nationalistic world. Nationalism, however, could be infused with irrational feelings and beliefs, and become a kind of substitute for religion. Weber did not live to see German nationalism yoked in this fashion to Nazism. But he was certainly aware of the central place of irrationalism and the erotic in what became known as modern art.

Modernism and Doubt

I want anything that breaks the monotony, subverts the perceived respectable order of things.[58]

—Margaret Atwood, *The Handmaid's Tale*, 1986

For the early generation of sociologists, modernity was a dynamic force that had to be understood and, if possible, controlled. After the Great War and contrary to the claim expressed by novelist Margaret Atwood, re-establishing the "respectable order of things" had not always appeared the sensible thing to do. Indeed, for the radicalized generation of artists and writers who gathered, mostly in Paris, to decode the entrails of traditional Europe, the old social order had been the root of the greatest evil. Atwood's quote, above, expresses that group's transgressive tendencies. As intellectuals, they believed they had a social responsibility to challenge and undermine this assumed respectability.

Disillusioned by modern society, some intellectuals, such as poets T.S. Eliot and Ezra Pound, were drawn to the fringes of the emerging fascist movement. Eliot was one of a handful of poets who were creating modern poetry and, in the process, defining the culture of the modern age. *The Lovesong of J. Alfred Prufrock* (1915), his early poem, depicted the frustrated anguish of the modern man, afraid to act in the world and, hence, doomed to failure and despair.

The Wasteland (1922) later defined the post-war era and the orientation of the generation of lost intellectuals. The poem's central image is that modern humanity is living in a wasteland or desert, which is not simply a place that may be found in "remote southern tropics." The modern wasteland is a spiritual desert.[59] The poem is a statement of pessimism and anguish, reflecting an age when, at least in respectable middle-class society, even lovemaking is instrumental and meaningless.[60] Later in his life, Eliot resolved the dilemma of living in a wasteland, at least for his personal peace, by converting to Anglicanism and thereby adopting a conventional religious solution to his angst.

If someone abandons the hope of positive social change, the usual alternatives present themselves: a turn inward to subjectivity and self-indulgence, suicide, or hedonism. Art attempts to externalize that inner anguish or vision. Thus, a return to romantic subjectivism dominated painting, literature, music, and dance of the time. It was just such a vision that had driven the avant-garde at the end of the nineteenth century to recreate the arts. The Great War was absolute proof, if it was needed, that the struggle of the individual artist-as-genius was against society as it had been constructed.

Following a long line stretching back to the Romantics and Nietzsche, the worm in modern society was variously identified as logic, rationality, or science. Cubist painter Georges Braque believed that science simply and falsely reassures whereas art is "meant to disturb," to break social rules and question certainties. In one sense, Braque spoke too soon in his claim that science offers certainties. The inherited laws of the physical universe were overturned in the early years of the twentieth century, although Nietzsche had already eroded faith in Enlightenment rationality. Since Newton, modern science had followed the dominant paradigm of the gradual accumulation of knowledge that was expected to reveal the hidden truths about the laws of nature. By following

the empirical and rational rules of science, scientists claimed to discover ever-closer approximations to truth and reality. Scientific theory and its application to technology had become the twin engines of human progress. But the new technologies that promised to benefit humanity were two-faced. Explosives, for example, could level mountains and expose the riches of the earth, but their power could also unleash weapons of mass destruction. Cartoonists pictured the apparatus of colonialism, moreover, as a gigantic sausage machine, squeezing the life out of Africans and Asians, turning their blood into profit.

What modernism transformed first was not society, but the supposed certainty of the laws of science, most dramatically by Albert Einstein's theory of relativity (1905) and by quantum physics. After Einstein, time, mass, and energy were no longer physical constants, as assumed in the Newtonian paradigm. It was unclear whether light was essentially a particle or a wave phenomenon, or some unstable combination of both. At the same time, it was impossible to predict the position, direction, and speed of subatomic particles, such as electrons. Any physical attempt to measure one characteristic of an electron has an impact on its motion, necessarily changing its conditions of existence in apparently unpredictable ways.

Just as positivism had been modelled after the supposedly fixed laws of Newtonian physics, the theory of relativity and subatomic unpredictability shaped modern conceptions of culture and society. Science has always been a contested domain in which claims to truth compete directly with each other. When **paradigms** are eroded, however, the weaknesses in foundational knowledge are exposed. The revolution within early twentieth-century science lent credence to the philosophical attacks on Enlightenment rationality, logic, and judgment, which had been inherited from nineteenth century intellectuals, such as Dostoyevsky, Nietzsche, and Bergson. The apparent erosion of the scientific process itself undermined the principle of certain truth and the notion that knowledge was a more or less close approximation to a precise, existing reality.

Perhaps ironically, the present age of supposed scientific uncertainty has led to an unprecedented and exponential growth of sophisticated technology that has fuelled contemporary mass consumption. The material applications of Einstein's hypothesis are even more earth-shattering. On the basis of his theory, expressed as $E = mc^2$ (minute quantities of mass could be converted into enormous amounts of energy), the Atomic Bomb was conceptualized, built, and devastatingly detonated. The tendency for modern science to break through supposed limits, moreover, was punctuated in 2011 when subatomic particles were measured travelling faster than the speed of light, which Einstein had said was impossible. Of more social importance, however, was the observation that science still operates in a world of human ethics and choices. The destructive consequences of some scientific knowledge and the risks posed by new discoveries (genetic engineering, for example) fuels an anti-rational rejection of reason as the arbiter of human affairs.

Varieties of Modernism

If new, radical doubt rippled through the twentieth-century community of physical science, the arts were inundated by irrationalism. Modern cultural explorations emphasized novelty, deconstruction, and innovation. Attacks on rationality fuelled by *fin-de-siècle* decadence buttressed anti-rational cultures and philosophies. The revolt of the artist against conventional society and the unsophisticated "masses" produced new styles in all the arts that became known collectively as "modernism."[61] *Modern* conveys the idea of newness, of being up-to-date, replacing the obsolete with something better. In many respects, however, *modern* is an extremely

unsatisfactory word. In a rapidly changing capitalist society, what is "modern" today will be outdated tomorrow. If you call one style of art "modern," what can you call a new style that condemns the modern as outdated and claims the title "most modern" for itself?

The centre of the artistic avant-garde was Paris, particularly the bohemian sections on the left bank of the Seine and in Montmartre. There, contemporary artists migrated, painted, or performed, drank, ate, and argued, living obscurely, sleeping in garrets, creating in their lifestyles the image and reality of the alienated, if misunderstood and unappreciated, genius. Similar districts existed in other cities—Soho in London, Schwabing in Munich, Greenwich Village in Manhattan— where artists and intellectuals created "modern" sensibilities.

This avant-garde splintered into an unprecedented number of movements, styles, tendencies, and innovations. The principal value these artists espoused was novelty, the drive to go beyond what had been done. Impressionism, then, gave way to post-impressionism, symbolism, cubism, expressionism, Fauvism, futurism, Dada, **surrealism**—a seemingly never-ending litany of "isms" embraced by the increasingly imprecise term *modern*. Poetry, novels, and painting expressed the era through images of mutilated bodies, multiple perspectives, lost limbs, corpses, anxiety, and despair. In the eyes of the avant-garde, violating the rules of syntax and spelling, as well as the traditions of realism and naturalism, reflected their rejection of the mores and practices of bourgeois society—"vulgar rationalism and chop logic," in André Breton's phrase.[62]

Not all of the artists who gathered in such areas as the Left Bank of the Seine in the decade following World War I lived their lives in genteel obscurity, however. Surrounding the dominating figure of Gertrude Stein, who experimented with words as the jazz musicians experimented with notes, was an alienated coterie of expatriate Americans called the Lost Generation. Bohemian

Paris was the inspirational centre of European culture, where the conventions of strict Victorian morality could be flouted with impunity. For the new generation of decadents, excess was, ironically, the only reasonable response to the blight of the modern age. Siddhartha, the character seeking the meaning of life in Hermann Hesse's novel of the same name, thought he had found it in the heightened anxiety and risk of gambling: Siddhartha won and lost thousands, but his aim was not simply material gain: "He loved that . . . terrible and oppressive anxiety which he experienced . . . during the suspense of high stakes. [F]or in this feeling alone did he experience some kind of happiness, some kind of excitement, some heightened living in the midst of his satiated, tepid, insipid existence."[63]

Interest in the supposedly "primitive" was widespread and influenced other artistic movements. Civilization, it was argued, had put a veneer over the most basic of human instincts, which nevertheless were the deep and unconscious wellsprings of creativity and life. Through such techniques as exaggeration or distortion, symbolists sacrificed the accurate depiction of appearance to gain an appreciation of the inner turmoil and anguish of the alienated twentieth-century individual. As Freud was interpreting humanity in terms of libido and sexuality, the Norwegian painter Edvard Munch was utilizing symbolism in, for example, *Puberty* (1894) and linking sexuality with death in *The Dance of Life* (1899–1900). Munch anticipated the movement known as expressionism with his most recognizable painting, *The Scream* (1893).

Not all forms of modern art, however, were intentionally anti-rational. In the movement known as cubism, the representation of the natural gave way to an analytical study of forms, geometric shapes, and intersecting planes. In his painting *Les Demoiselles d'Avignon* (1907), Pablo Picasso began to take apart the artistic representation of the body by exploring different perspectives, depicting his models from several points of view simultaneously.[64] Picasso's perspectivism was influenced by so-called primitive art styles represented, for example, by African masks.

Particularly in painting and music, the attention to the *content* of the image or sound gave way to a focus on its *form*. Abstract art presented the pure expressiveness of colour or the analytical geometry of design, but both were removed from any attempt to represent the "real." Once you raise the question, "What is art??" perhaps the answer is, "Everything and nothing." The movement known by the nonsense term *Dada* was consciously in rebellion against all conventions of literature and art. Poems could be generated by stitching together random words cut from a newspaper; a sculpture was anything that an artist defined as a sculpture and that a gallery curator agreed to display—as with Marcel Duchamp's *Fountain*, a mass-produced, porcelain urinal exhibited in New York. As an artistic expression of nihilism, Dada was short-lived—if anything can be defined as art, nothing can be distinguished as "art" from anything that is "not art." Nevertheless, the impulse for nihilistic artistic creation persists and re-emerges at various times and places. Surrealism, Dada's more socially conscious cousin, has been longer-lasting (see Box 1.2).

Early Feminism

Surrealism, at least in the beginning, as with avantgarde culture generally, was largely masculine. The nineteenth-century New Woman had pried open and entered the majority of occupations that had been previously monopolized by men, although not without great sacrifice and not beyond a quite visible and low ceiling. Women writers reacted ambivalently to the Great War. A body of patriotic writing by women mourned the dead but stood proudly by the patriotic sacrifice of their sons and lovers. On the other hand, women found new opportunities for independence in their private and

⚘ BOX 1.2 • THEORY IN CONTEXT ⚘

Realism and Surrealism

Realism in the arts attempted to depict things as they actually were, to represent (on canvas, in novels, in drama) the "real." In this sense, a still-life painting generally recognizable as a fruit bowl is realistic. In radical hands in the nineteenth century, however, "social realism" had become a tool of critique. When the subject or content of the art is intended to represent the real consequences of social problems, such as the injuries of a battered wife, the misery of an abandoned orphan, or the fatigue of a factory worker who has shuffled home after a 12-hour shift, realism becomes a tool of social criticism and a call to action. Nineteenth century realism was often subversive of established authority.

The term "sur"-realism implies moving beneath the surface appearance to uncover a deeper or more problematic "reality." The aim of surrealism was also subversive but its approach was different. Merely representing the evils of the social world does not transform them. Surrealism claims to undermine certainties and to suggest that there are alternative realities, such as the reality of the unconscious, that should be merged with the world of the perceivable. Surrealists imagined absurd objects, such as limp watches that could not indicate time, or they juxtaposed representations of realistic-looking objects that could not exist together, or painted optical illusions that could only exist on a two-dimensional plane, or represented images dredged from the unconscious mind.

The surrealist imagination is portrayed humorously in the 2011 film *Midnight in Paris*, written and directed by Woody Allen. Gil Pender, a Romantically inclined American

working lives when the men went overseas. Prince Edward Island author Lucy Maud Montgomery's *Rilla of Ingleside* has a subversive side in its depiction of strong, female characters and a Christian pacifist, and she subtly questions the senseless slaughter of the war.[65]

The suffragette movement had inserted women minimally into normative politics, conceding the vote but opening only the occasional, token political office to women. The liberation of women's desire, however, was another matter entirely. Even most of the radical nineteenth-century feminists, such as George Sand, stopped short of demanding women's equality in sexual enjoyment. The right to love and be loved did not cross the threshold of the **patriarchal** bedroom. Free love had been largely a masculine ideal when only primitive means of preventing pregnancy existed. The anarchist, Emma Goldman, had demanded equality in sexuality, but she was on the political fringe (see Box 1.3).

For the surrealists and Picasso, and modernism generally, women were essentially objects, defined in relation to men. And women in the 1920s did not always help their own cause. After the militancy of the suffrage movement, Firestone asserts, women endured the "fifty-year ridicule," a period when their political consciousness was anaesthetized. That assertion is a great exaggeration, however, plausible only in light of a shroud

screenwriter visiting Paris with his fiancée, is in a perplexing situation. Every night he is picked up by a mysterious Peugeot and transported back in time to Paris in the 1920s, the era that sparks his deepest longing. Once back in time, he meets the disillusioned American artists and writers of the Lost Generation and the Parisian avant-garde. He is soon attracted to Picasso's girlfriend. Pender keeps his time travel secret until he confesses to the surrealists—photographer Man Ray, filmmaker Luis Buñuel, and painter Salvador Dali—that he is actually from the future. All three react as if he had announced he was visiting from next door; they are completely unfazed by the idea of time travel. Man Ray says there is nothing strange about living in two worlds; this is "Exactly correct." Everyone lives in more than one world. Pender's particular insurmountable problem, however, is that he is in love with a woman from a different era in time. That dilemma kindles the surrealist imagination: Man Ray sees a photograph; Buñuel imagines a film; and Dali says, absurdly, "I see a rhinoceros."

Behind the symbols and the apparent absurdity of much of the surrealist movement, its purpose was to question the status quo, which would putatively reveal that what appeared to be "real" was merely one possible (taken-for-granted and undesirable) "reality." Its other purpose was to stimulate action to bring about an alternative reality.[66] Surrealist artists could critique, ridicule, and question taken-for-granted realities, but their art tended toward negation rather than construction. For a while, many surrealists were attracted to revolutionary Marxism, but it was a relationship of convenience, based more on shared antagonisms than on fundamental principles. The revolt of the Surrealists was as much against society in general as against, strictly speaking, *capitalist* society.

draped over 1930s radicalism and in contrast to the revival of feminism in the 1960s. Firestone highlights what she calls the false liberation of 1920s eroticism, the time of the flappers—young women in short, shapely dresses with low backs, open fronts, and sheer fabrics. Paris may have been the centre of "high style and lascivious behaviour . . . where there were no rules beyond the demands of style and entertainment," but the new fashions in apparel and demeanour radiated across Europe to New York and the sunny beaches of California. Life during wartime, Antonio Gramsci argued, had caused a sharp repression of "even the most normal" of sexual instincts among large numbers of young adults. Heightened by the death of so many young men from all social strata and the resulting sexual imbalance, a crisis of morality occurred after the war, shaking the inherited sexual institutions and resulting in new forms of enlightened sexuality.[67]

Artist Tamara de Lempicka epitomized the bisexual fringe of the Left Bank subculture. Born in and married to privilege in pre-revolutionary Russia, after the Bolsheviks took power de Lempicka became a political *émigré* in Paris, where she made her reputation as a painter. She employed a synthetic style, critic Fiona McCarthy says, "to startlingly voluptuous effect in images of women reclining, women bathing, women embracing, laconically stroking one another's thighs." Her flamboyant

---

✎ BOX 1.3 • BIOGRAPHY ✎

Emma Goldman (1869–1940)

Emma Goldman was born in Kovno, Lithuania, in 1869 and immigrated to the United States in 1885.[68] Goldman became an American citizen through marriage but was divorced within a year. Her developing left-wing politics were honed by the state repression that followed the Haymarket bombing in Chicago. After a bomb killed a policeman during a demonstration demanding the eight-hour day, four anarchists were executed. There was no evidence to link them to the bomb other than their anarchist association. In New York, Goldman became politically and romantically attached to the anarchist Alexander Berkman. In 1892, Berkman attempted to assassinate industrialist Henry Clay Frick, the managing director of a Pennsylvania steel company involved in the bloody repression of a strike. Goldman was suspected of being a party to the conspiracy but did not face prosecution.

In the early decades of the twentieth century, Goldman became a controversial spokeswoman for a variety of causes, speaking on feminist issues including sexuality and free love, education, and freedom of speech. Goldman was active in support of the 1909–10 general strike by women garment workers in New York. In 1910, she published *Anarchism and Other Essays*. She was arrested and jailed for short periods in 1915 for lecturing about birth control. In 1917, Goldman and Berkman were sentenced to two years in prison for actively resisting compulsory military service for men during World War I. Upon her release, under the Alien Act Goldman's American citizenship was revoked and she was deported from the United States, along with several hundred other socialists and anarchists as a result of the "red scare" that followed the Bolshevik Revolution in Russia.

In exile in Russia in 1920–21, Goldman was critical of the Bolsheviks' suppression of free speech and repression of Russian anarchists, publishing her attack in *My Disillusionment in Russia* (1923). During the next decade, Goldman lived in Canada and Europe, lecturing on her critique of Soviet Russia and warning about the rise of fascism in Italy and Germany. She published an autobiography in 1931 (*Living My Life*). During the mid-1930s she sought to raise money to support the Loyalists in the **Spanish Civil War**. Goldman died in Toronto in 1940, and is buried in Chicago near the grave of the anarchists executed for the Haymarket bombing.

---

self-portrait in an open sports car, *Tamara in the Green Bugatti*, was defined at the time as symbolic of women's liberation.[69]

The 1920s was also the era of F. Scott Fitzgerald's *The Great Gatsby*, of the fast, "young and rich and wild" crowd who serve "champagne . . . in glasses bigger than finger-bowls." Lucille, one of Fitzgerald's characters in the novel, confesses, "I never care what I do, so I always have a good time."[70] For Firestone, women of the period were chasing a superficial and shallow sensuality that left them neurotic rather than satisfied. Their search for fulfillment was reduced to personal style and the tyranny of fashion and glamour as pictured in the pages of *Vogue* or *Cosmopolitan*.[71] The highest aspiration for a woman was to be beautiful, frivolous, and alluring, the future that Daisy, another character in *The Great Gatsby*, despairingly wished for her daughter. When the nurse told Daisy she had given birth to a girl, Daisy said "I turned my head away and wept. 'All right,' I said, 'I'm glad it's a girl. And I hope she'll be a fool—that's the best thing a girl can be in this world, a beautiful little fool.'"[72]

In the arts, while women remained principally objects rather than creators, dance—one of the most evocative and sensual of the arts—was an important exception. Dance became subjective, spontaneous, and passionate, and the artistic individualism of the male poets and painters was matched in dance by the pioneers of modern movement, such as Isadora Duncan (1878-1927), an innovator who helped move artistic dance away from traditional choreography to improvisation. Duncan danced in bare feet and legs, and flimsy Greek tunics, rejecting conventional mechanical ballet for modern, expressive movements.[73] Duncan's scandalous, naturalistic dancing was matched only by her bohemianism. Like most artistic rebels of the period, her flamboyance was no less apparent in her lifestyle as in her art. She had children while remaining unmarried. Although the term *jet set* had not yet been invented, she was part of the fast, automobile set in the 1920s.

Duncan went to revolutionary Russia in 1921 to open a dance school. She married a Russian poet, Sergei Esenin, and returned with him to tour in the United States. The pair was hounded by moralists, immigration authorities, and the police. In defiance, during one performance, Duncan "divested herself of her sole garment, a red sash, and waving it above her head, shouted 'I am a Red!'"[74] Esenin and Duncan had a brief, celebrity marriage before he returned to Russia and committed suicide spectacularly, writing a final poem in his own blood. Duncan died two years later, in 1927, tragically strangled by her scarf, which had become tangled around the axel of her Bugatti sports car.

Women's liberation in the 1920s may appear to have been shunted onto an individual and personal track, a route for individual power and creativity rather than a collective and political one. While most women who found work in the new art, motion pictures, found more manufactured glitz than independent substance, a few matinee idols achieved creative power and success. But the overall screen image defined female power in all the traditional ways of the second sex. There was more to 1920s feminism, however, then the beginnings of the liberation of desire. It included the struggle for pacifism and the gradual movement out of the household and into new careers. The **Settlement Movement**, for example, spread from Britain to the United States and to Toronto, Canada (1899), bringing women's potential for activism into cultural and political reform movements that did not so much transcend gender as provide avenues for feminist activism, including campaigns for peace and justice.

Winning the vote undercut the mass participation of women in a social movement for their civil rights, but suffrage was the beginning, not the culmination, of the battle for political equality. In Canada, a clause in the Act of the British Parliament that had established Canada as a separate country in 1867 specified that only "persons" were eligible to be elected to political office. "Person" had been interpreted narrowly to refer only to men. This exclusive definition had been used to keep women from a variety of roles, including certain professions. In 1927, five women from Alberta, including Nellie McClung, petitioned the Supreme Court to rule on whether women could be appointed to the Senate, Canada's upper House of Parliament (similar to the British House of Lords).[75] The Canadian Court responded by reaffirming the rule that only men were "persons."

Finally, the five women appealed to the British Cabinet (Privy Council), which ruled in 1929 that women were included in the definition of persons in Canada. The legal victory cleared away an anachronistic legal impediment to women's participation in national politics. In between the suffragette movement and 1960s women's liberation, the ideal of women's equality did not slumber. Among the early feminists was British novelist Virginia Woolf, although she rejected the term *feminist*.

Virginia Woolf and Feminism

Sometimes I live in the country, / Sometimes I live in town, / Sometimes I get a great notion, / To jump into the river and drown.

—Huddie Ledbetter (Lead Belly), "Goodnight Irene," 1936

Lead Belly's "Goodnight Irene" was a blues hit several years before Virginia Woolf (1882-1941) took her own life, driven by the public fear of rising fascism and the private demon of recurring depression. As a novelist, Woolf experimented with a highly subjective voice and helped revolutionize the modern novel. She was also connected to the early women's movement in Britain. Her relationship to feminism, however, was complex; toward the end of her life, Woolf put aside the particular claims of women in favour of confronting the threat of tyranny.

Schooled at home, Woolf's intellectual heritage was rich and diverse.[76] Her father, Leslie Stephen, was a skeptical, liberal critic. Emotionally, however, Woolf's adolescence was traumatic. Both her parents died before she turned 20, and her mother's death precipitated a mental collapse. By her early twenties, Woolf had also lost a brother and half-sister. She later revealed that she had experienced sexual abuse as a child at the hands of her step-brother.[77] In 1904, the orphaned Woolf and her sister, Vanessa, moved to Bloomsbury, an address that would become a central fixture in the intellectual life of Britain between the wars. As early as 1904, Woolf was at the centre of an intellectual salon that debated political and aesthetic issues. The Bloomsbury Group included historian Lytton Strachey, novelist E.M. Forster, economist John Maynard Keynes, and Clive Bell, a critic who had married Virginia's sister, Vanessa. In 1912, Virginia married Leonard Woolf (1880-1969), a publisher and writer, providing some stability in a periodically difficult life. The **androgynous** protagonist in *Orlando* (1928), Woolf's fantasy novel, was modelled after Vita Sackville-West, a writer with whom Woolf had a relationship during the period of her most intense writing.

Woolf turned her hand very early to writing. While she wrote hundreds of reviews and essays, her literary reputation is founded on a handful of novels she published in the 1920s. Besides finding a voice for the perspective of women in her fiction, in *A Room of Her Own* (1929) Woolf explored the limitations imposed on women writers. Woolf wrote, "A woman must have money and a room of her own if she is to write fiction."[78] She was galled by the entrenched inequality that sent ill-suited boys to university while frustrating the ambitions of their talented sisters. Marriage was the only institution open to women, where they served as little more than mirrors to enlarge the egos of their husbands.

In her fiction, Woolf quickly rejected the conventional, realistic style, feeling that it was necessary to get beneath the surface appearance of reality to understand its subjective creation. In an essay on modern fiction, Woolf complained that even modern science-fiction writers, such as H.G. Wells, were mere materialists, concerned with the body rather than the spirit. They "write of unimportant things," she argued, spending immense skill and "industry making the trivial and the transitory appear the true and the enduring."[79]

In his initially notorious novel *Ulysses*, Irish author James Joyce presented a highly subjective style of writing that was called the stream of consciousness. This new style not only revealed the inner workings of a character's mind, but was also subjective in its structure, written as the mind apparently works: now in the here-and-now, suddenly reminiscing with a flashback from the past, then soaring in imagination. Stream of consciousness was a clear rejection of the dominant tradition of writing novels in a straightforward, realistic, and linear style. Virginia Woolf brought a feminine and feminist sensibility to the stream of consciousness. In *Mrs. Dalloway* (1925), Woolf explores the thoughts of an interconnected set of people on a single day, through subjective time, however, as the novel moves fluidly through the past and future. And in *To the Lighthouse* (1927), Woolf applied the modernist concerns with states of consciousness and interior monologue to women's subjectivity, presenting a feminine alternative to a materialistic view of reality as unproblematic.[80]

Three Guineas (1938), Woolf's treatise, debated the role that women should play in the fight against fascism, arguing that fascism was a particularly brutal form of patriarchy and that the struggles against both forms of oppression were linked. In the 1930s, she shared a deep fear with her husband, who was Jewish, that Nazi Germany would conquer England. They contemplated committing joint suicide in such an eventuality. Just past her fifty-ninth birthday, in the early, foreboding days of World War II, and in the early stages of another serious mental breakdown, Virginia Woolf acted alone. She filled her pockets with stones and waded into the River Ouse near her Sussex home.[81]

Woolf's Construction of Women's Reality

She felt herself transfixed by the intensity of her perception. . . . [H]er own voice [was] saying without prompting undeniably, everlasting, contradictory things.[82]

—Virginia Woolf, *To the Lighthouse*, 1927

Naomi Black argues that Woolf was inclined to a feminism of difference rather than a feminism of equality. The latter form calls for equal access to the spheres dominated by men. A feminism of difference, on the other hand, is rooted in the belief that men and women are essentially different but women's superior abilities are subordinated by men in patriarchal societies. Values that are specific to women should be honoured, respected, and given pride of place.[83]

Woolf explores the gender-specific ways of viewing the world in *To the Lighthouse*. Mr Ramsay, the philosopher, exhibits a typically logical, linear mind. Like Dickens' utilitarian schoolmaster, Gradgrind, Mr Ramsay "never tampered with a fact." He is working his way through knowledge alphabetically, beginning with *A*. He has reached *Q* but has bogged down in this systematic quest, being unable to move on to *R*—the letter of his surname, reflecting his incapacity for self-knowledge. His male ego is all surface, without depth. Ramsay pursues truth in a straightforward, masculine manner, with an "astonishing lack of consideration for other people's feelings."

In contrast to masculine logic, Mrs Ramsay feels truths emotionally and intuitively. Unlike her husband, she tampers with facts, altering "a disagreeable word to suit the pleasure or convenience" of someone. While Mr Ramsay is "incapable of untruth"—the narrow truth of "facts uncompromising"—Mrs Ramsay holds a more social conception of tact and nuance. She fits her words to circumstance, occasion, and need rather than to a static universe of absolute truths. For Woolf, women are particularly adept at understanding the psychology and motivations of people; indeed, psychological insight is their "only qualification."[84]

In an essay entitled *Three Guineas*, Woolf agrees that men and women possess many natural similarities: "many instincts are held more or less in common by both sexes." The gulf between them, however, is constructed from their differences. The most defining psychological difference is that, among men, there is an apparent instinct that compels fighting to develop certain "manly qualities." This male propensity for killing has been exaggerated by laws, social institutions, and practices.[85] Fighting is as foreign to women "as centuries of tradition and education can make it." Consequently, women are indifferent to the claims of patriotism. Their unconcern with nationalism, however, is based on reason as well as instinct. According to Woolf, the facts of gender inequality demonstrate that women have little for which to thank their society. Throughout most of history, any educated woman would have said that her country "has treated me as a slave." Women remain outsiders and must proclaim, with Woolf, "As a woman I want no country."[86] No one can know what woman *is* fundamentally "until she has experienced herself in all the arts and professions open to human skill" and had success or failure in them all.[87]

Woolf believed that the would-be independent woman is faced with unjust laws and the "unpaid-for-education" of marriage, "the one great profession open to our class since the dawn of time."[88] She is dogged by the image of the pure, virtuous, and self-sacrificing housewife, a phantom Victorian woman she calls "The Angel in the House," much like the members of the Abnegation faction in *Divergent*, the 2011 novel and film. Women must tell lies to succeed, Woolf says, and never reveal they have minds of their own.[89]

In *To the Lighthouse*, Woolf foregrounds the gendered split between the private and public spheres. Mrs Ramsay is ostensibly "only" a housewife. Her responsibilities, however, are enormous. At home, she constantly massages the fragile ego of her philosopher husband; she mediates family conflicts rooted in deep psychological complexities; ultimately, she is responsible for the continual social construction of the family's private sphere. With maternal pride, she oversees the masculine development of her son, James, who identifies with his father, yet also deeply resents him. Mrs Ramsay will live in the public sphere only as a mother, through the accomplishments of the men she raises as sons. She imagines James "all red and ermine on the Bench or directing a stern and momentous enterprise in some crisis of public affairs."[90]

In the novel, Woolf exposes patriarchy as fundamentally hollow. Mr Ramsay is introduced as the classic Freudian patriarch, "lean as a knife, narrow as the blade of one," who has pleasure in "disillusioning his son and casting ridicule upon his wife." Mr Ramsay's youngest daughter, Cam, has equally ambivalent feelings. She is attracted to no one more than her father, but his tyranny is intolerable. Mrs Ramsay's daughters defer to parental authority, but, in silence, they have minds of their own—as young Virginia doubtless had in her own family. In the minds of these girls there is "a mute questioning of deference and chivalry, of the Bank of England and the Indian Empire, of ringed fingers and lace."[91]

On the whole, the men in *To the Lighthouse* are a sorry lot—Mr Ramsay above all. They are sarcastic, narrow-minded, and self-centred, glibly prattling an endless stream of "ugly academic jargon." For all his patriarchal bluster, Mr Ramsay is nevertheless dependent on others' praise, particularly that of his wife, and Mrs Ramsay must continually soothe and sustain his fragile ego. In the private sphere, however, where women occupy a predominant place of influence, Mrs Ramsay dominates. At 50, she is "formidable to behold." She has astonishing power, and even her shadow is full of authority. She has managed "her husband, his money, and his books." Moreover, she has been fertile, bearing eight children. She feels protective of the men in her life for reasons she cannot explain but that include "an attitude towards herself which no woman could fail to feel or to find agreeable, something trustful, childlike, reverential."[92]

What Mrs Ramsay has done with her life, daily, hourly, minute by minute, is recreate the conditions of everyday existence. The realization of this fundamental maternal role comes to her unexpectedly, while ladling out soup at the dinner table. She feels suddenly outside an eddy in the flow of life. Things stand still; everything exists separately. She realizes the "whole of the effort of merging and flowing and creating rested on her." Without hostility, merely as fact, she feels "the sterility of men" because, if she does not bring the parts together and begin again the business of socially constructing the everyday world, no one else will.[93]

Feminism and Patriarchy

Virginia Woolf had a complex relationship with modern feminism. As a young woman she had worked for the suffragist cause, as much out of duty as enthusiasm.[94] Feminist concerns, however, suffuse both her fiction and non-fiction. In class-divided Britain, Woolf intentionally addressed middle-class women who, like her, were the economically self-sufficient daughters of educated men. Despite their common class origin, middle-class men and women existed on opposite sides of a fundamental barrier that restricted communication across the gender line.

While educational opportunities had been opened marginally to British women in the 1870s, many of the most important professions had remained monopolized by men. As a result of their different experiences, while men and women viewed the same world, according to Woolf, they "see it through different eyes." Women saw the world of professional, public life from the perspective of the private household. Few women were permitted entry to the public world and, once admitted, they were confined to lowly paid occupations. In the other, private world, women were not paid for their work. It was as if "the work of a mother, of a wife, of a daughter, [is] worth nothing to the nation in solid cash." As Woolf saw it, any time a woman tried to take her place in the

masculine, public sphere, the same resentments and opposition surfaced. Encamped inside and guarding the "sacred gates" of privilege, men reiterated the old arguments that God, nature, law, and property were on their side.[95]

Woolf wonders, however, whether money is, in itself, a desirable possession. Gaining an equal share in the professions and in the management of wealth also required participation in the capitalist system. From being the victims of patriarchy, full economic involvement would make women "the champions of the capitalist system." Woolf was skeptical whether the presence of women in the professions would make a difference, however. If women entered the same professions, they would learn the same ways that men had learned. After a century passed, she asks, "shall we not be just as possessive, just as jealous, just as pugnacious, just as possessive" as men are presently?[96]

In addition, Woolf believed that women must eschew "prostitution of the brain," which is the worst offence. In her case, this would refer to writing something solely for money, not because she felt a desire to write it. In Woolf's view, it is better, psychologically, to suffer derision and ridicule than to receive fame or praise. Finally, Woolf exhorted women to free themselves from nationality, "religious pride, college pride, school pride, family pride, sex pride and those unreal loyalties that spring from them." Instead, Woolf urged women to find new words and create new methods.[97]

In the 1930s, Woolf declared that the word *feminist* no longer had a useful meaning; it had become a dead, distorted, and obsolete word. The true struggle of the nineteenth century was not merely for women's rights, but for "the great principles of Justice and Equality and Liberty" for all, men and women alike.[98] Feminists fought only for the rights of women. But in the face of the universal threat posed by Nazism, Woolf believed that women must fight to protect the rights of all. And while she was unequivocal in her rejection of the term *feminist*, she was not in her rejection of patriarchy: women must fight independently of men in their own organizations, a conclusion that reflected her "feminism of difference." Woolf imagined a type of organization that would later be similarly imagined in the **New Left** of the 1960s: an Outsiders Society that would have no funds, "no office, no committee, no secretary; it would call no meetings; it would hold no conferences," possess no oaths or ceremonies and be "anonymous and elastic before everything." It would have no leaders or hierarchy, and include self-consciously middle-class women who worked as housewives and mothers.[99]

Woolf's politics generally leaned left—she and Leonard were members of the **Labour Party**—but her socialist sentiments were tinged with guilt, due to, as she stated, "'the psychological hindrance of owning capital.'"[100] Unlike some of her contemporaries in the 1930s, she was not attracted to communism nor to the social experiment being constructed in Soviet Russia. And, while she expressed many feminist ideas, in the context of the 1930s, she was more concerned with the unity of men and women in the face of state tyranny.

Conclusion

In the aftermath of World War I, the suffragette movement succeeded in opening up formal politics to women. Woolf understood how limited these legal victories were in the face of entrenched patriarchy. The war also brought the classical sociological era to an end. Four of the principal sociological theorists died between 1917 and 1923: Durkheim, Simmel, Weber, and Pareto. Marx and Spencer had died earlier, in 1883 and 1903, respectively. Marx's legacy would be powerfully shaped by the outcome of the Bolshevik Revolution in Russia (1917), as Marxism weaved a complex set of paths that moved in and out of sociology. Chapter 2 explores the theory and practice of state socialism in Russia and the Marxist response in the West. In the context of Bolshevism and other political forces in the 1920s and 1930s, Marxist theory in Europe took a subjectivist turn, focusing on the role of consciousness, culture, and the unconscious.

Questions for Reflection

1. Thinking of now and 1914, do wars always lead to disillusionment and pessimism? How do governments seek to win people's "hearts and minds" in favour of the "war on terrorism"?

2. Is Weber right in considering indulging in artistic freedom or eroticism an escape from a too rational and routine world? What forms of escape from the all-too-real do people turn to today?

3. Is the purpose of art to represent the way things are or to critique society? What would be a contemporary online equivalent of surrealism that makes people question the way things are today?

4. Are women and men essentially different in their ways of conceiving, understanding, and acting in the world?

5. What arguments does Woolf make about women and feminism that are still relevant today?

CHAPTER 2

The Bolshevik Revolution and Western Marxism

Learning Objectives

- To distinguish the theoretical and practical differences between reformist and revolutionary Marxism in the context of the Russian revolution
- To understand the origins and characteristics of early twentieth century fascism
- To review the development of a critical, Western Marxism that sought to understand the failure of revolution in the West
- To apply Fordism to economic developments in twentieth century capitalism

After the death of Karl Marx in 1883, his theory and the movement for socialism he inspired became so fractured that there appeared to be as many versions of Marxism as there were varieties of mushrooms. By World War I, the most significant line of division was between revolutionaries, who believed only a violent insurrection could end the capitalist era, and reformists, who thought that capitalism could evolve peacefully into socialism. Nowhere was this division more momentous than in Russia in 1917. In the face of widespread revolt of workers, peasants, and soldiers, Russia was in full revolutionary mode. The basic uncertainties were which political group would lead this revolt and with what results.

The first part of this chapter explores the theoretical and practical differences between the reformist and revolutionary parties that had their origins in Marxism. After the October Revolution in 1917, political power in Russia (which later became the Union of Soviet Socialist Republics—USSR) was in the hands of the Bolshevik or Communist Party. Perhaps strangest of all, according to the usual Marxist interpretation of history, Russia in 1917 had been a poor candidate for a socialist revolution. This chapter explores the theoretical and practical nature of the social system established in the USSR.

In Western Europe, Marx's theory was further divided by being taken out of the practical context of the workers' movement and being adopted by academics. In their hands, twentieth-century Marxism was divorced from practical change and became a useful theoretical tool to understand society. Western Marxists in the 1920s and 1930s explored the philosophical foundation of social theory and investigated the importance of culture. The context for this change in focus from economics and politics was the failure of revolution to occur in Western Europe despite the presence of the necessary objective conditions, including large, Marxist-led workers' movements. To understand the failure of revolution, Karl Korsch and Georg Lukács theorized the subjective factors of revolution: the need for a revolutionary consciousness that had not spread beyond a minority of workers. The conditions of advanced capitalism threw a veil of mystification over workers' understandings of their society, preventing them from seeing the system clearly and critically.

In Russia, culture—music, drama, novels, poetry—was a political weapon that could inspire commitment to the Bolshevik system or undermine the regime's legitimacy. In the early 1920s, Russian artists and writers, many of whom were hostile to the new, socialist society, experienced a period of freedom to produce and publish critical works. This literature offers insights into some of the contradictions of the new Soviet society.

The Anti-Soviet Internal Émigrés

Russia was a featherweight industrially but a heavyweight in world literature. A few of the artists and writers who lived through the years of revolution supported the Bolshevik cause, although never without reservations or criticisms. For some, their initial enthusiasm turned into disillusionment. Among them was Sergei Esenin (1895–1925), a popular poet who initially supported the Revolution, although not as a Marxist. When no peasant paradise emerged in Russia after the Bolshevik Revolution—"The stern October"—Esenin became despondent. His final, symbolic rejection of the Revolution was spectacular and dramatic. On Christmas Day, 1925, Esenin cut his wrists, dipped a pen in his blood to write a final poem, and then hanged himself.[1]

Most Russian artists and writers of the time, however, were hostile to the Bolsheviks and supported the anti-Bolshevik Whites in the civil war fought between 1918 and 1921. (Whites in the Russian Civil War were a coalition of anti-Bolshevik forces, including monarchists, liberal democrats, and reform socialists; they were assisted by Western army units.) When the Whites lost, many of them, including a number of artists and writers, became émigrés by going into exile abroad. Many others, however, remained in Russia even though they opposed the regime. During the relative freedom of the early 1920s, they were able to publish works that were critical of the new, Marxist world. They became known as *internal émigrés*.

One of the most strident internal émigrés was Yevgeny Zamyatin (1884–1937). As a student, Zamyatin had joined the Bolsheviks, and was arrested and exiled. By 1917, however, he was no longer a Bolshevik and, during the early 1920s, worked with other intellectuals advocating artistic freedom.[2] He published a historical play that was set during the Spanish Inquisition but that was actually a satire on the Cheka, the first Soviet secret police.[3]

We (1921) was Zamyatin's most politically significant novel. *We* describes a society 1000 years in the future that is dominated by an all-powerful, "perfect, modern, standardized State" ruled over by the Benefactor. Citizens are nameless and are known only by numbers and letters. All wear blue-grey uniforms and live in glass houses, open to public view. The Single State is subject to mathematically precise rules, enforced by the power of Guardians.[4] The State claims to achieve maximum happiness by imposing maximum equality, which Zamyatin defines as absolute sameness and the absence of freedom. The principles of strict rationality and surveillance were applied to 23 hours of the day, enforcing the group conformity of the "we." Freedom and equality are incompatible, Zamyatin says. Equality can only come at the price of uniformity, state control, and ultimately the loss of human individuality. *We* is a negative utopia (or dystopia), which inspired Huxley's *Brave New World* and Orwell's *1984*.

In 1931, Zamyatin was permitted to become a genuine émigré and moved to Paris, where he lived in poverty and died in 1937.

Mikhail Bulgakov (1891–1940) also opposed the Bolsheviks from the start. He worked as a physician until 1920 when, as a professional writer, he too became an internal émigré. During the early years after the end of the Civil War, it was still possible to maintain a critical distance from the Soviet government—Russia officially became the Union of Soviet Socialist Republics (USSR) in 1922. Bulgakov's satires offered biting critiques of Soviet life from the point of view of the disappointed urban upper-middle class. By 1930, however, he was forbidden to publish his writings. Bulgakov died in 1940, although not as a victim of one of the many purges of the time.

In "The Fatal Eggs" (1925), Bulgakov imagines an epidemic that destroys the poultry industry in the Soviet Union. At the same time, a scientist fortuitously discovers a remarkable red-spectrum ray gun with extraordinary life-giving powers. Rokk, a member of the Communist Party, plans to use the special ray to accelerate the breeding of hens. By a bureaucratic error, however, he receives crocodile and anaconda eggs instead of chicken eggs. Once they are treated with the ray gun, the reptile eggs hatch, grow enormously, and bring destruction wherever they go.[5] Scientific experiments can have unexpectedly disastrous consequences, Bulgakov says, and the Russian Revolution was a social science experiment that did not merely go wrong; it was doomed from the start.

Bulgakov's satirical novel, Heart of a Dog, published in 1925, satirized the Marxist hope for a better humanity. For Karl Marx, human nature was not fixed in time and space but was subject to change. Humans were only as good as their circumstances; and class societies, such as feudalism and capitalism, heightened the worst aspects of human nature. Marx expected that once new generations had been brought up in socially just and egalitarian circumstances, the ordinary nature of

humanity would improve. Socialism would not only build a new society but would people it with "new" men and women. The protagonist in Heart of a Dog, Philip Philippovich, is a surgeon who works out of a seven-room apartment—quite luxurious by Soviet standards.[6] On the side, he is a private entrepreneur who conducts a sordid medical practice for rich clients, transplanting organs from other species into humans for the purpose of rejuvenation. Into a middle-aged woman with a new, young lover, for example, he transplanted monkey ovaries.

One day, Philippovich has in mind a reverse experiment: transplanting human organs in an animal. He lures a stray mongrel, named Sharik, to his apartment. Soon, Sharik is on an operating table next to a petty criminal who had died violently. Philippovich removes the testes and the hypophysis from the criminal and transplants the organs into his stray dog. Sharik quickly begins to grow, stand on his hind legs, lose his tail, and speak obscenities. Philippovich realizes that, rather than rejuvenation, he has produced humanization. Sharik (newly named Sharikov) proceeds rapidly through the "chain of evolution" and is transformed into a new man, although he is short and poorly built. His low forehead, fleas, and vulgar manners reflect his hybrid nature.[7] The vile Sharikov has the worst characteristics of both "dogness" and humanity.

Sharikov is a parody of the "new socialist person." Bulgakov believed in a fixed human nature that no circumstances, however advanced, could change. The Marxist "new person" was a chimera. You could artificially raise the ordinary person and put him or her in charge, but the result would be disastrous. Every year, Bulgakov wrote, nature produces a small number of superior individuals, "stubbornly selecting them out of the mass of scum."[8] All that is necessary, Bulgakov says, is to allow the natural elite to rule and they will take charge of the "scum."

During the early years of the Revolution, it was still possible to write a literary critique of Bolshevik socialism, which could pass as a criticism of middle-class ideology, expose the inequalities that persisted in the USSR, or warn against the danger posed by the class of entrepreneurs and peasants who were growing rich. Bulgakov's main argument, however, is that the *promise of equality* itself is a sham; social levelling must inevitably fail and bring social ruin.

Theories of Reform and Revolution

For most Marxists in 1917, building socialism in an unindustrialized country such as Russia was contrary to the laws of historical materialism. The expectation that a socialist revolution could occur only in an advanced, capitalist country was shared by almost everyone in the international socialist movement. For Marx, capitalist industrialization and the experience of liberal rights and democratic practices were necessary to prepare the proletariat for acquiring and maintaining power. He expected that taking power would still require a violent insurrection.

Marx was mystified by the failure of the British working class—the most developed proletariat in the world—to embrace revolutionary socialism. They seemed mired in struggles to better their share of the capitalist pie rather than bake a new one. Marx's collaborator, Friedrich Engels, thought that workers had been "bought off" from the super profits Britain extracted from its worldwide empire. By the 1890s, the question being debated in the Marxist movement was whether social and economic conditions had changed so much since Marx had died that a new theory of socialism was necessary. The **reformists** argued that, following the Marxist laws of capitalist development, small enterprises were being eliminated by big ones, to the point that soon there would be a monopoly in each branch of industry. The next logical step in evolution was for the state to take over the enterprises in the interests of society as a whole; and state ownership meant socialism. Capitalists were unnecessary; managers would run the state-owned enterprises in the interest of the people, not private profit. Even the class structure of modern capitalism was changing. Workers were getting richer rather than poorer; small businesses were surviving; and a new middle class of administrators, professionals, and technicians was growing in between the bourgeoisie and the proletariat. Socialism was not just inevitable, it could come peacefully through a democratic election.

In *The Secret Agent* (1907), novelist Joseph Conrad paints an exaggerated portrait of the evolutionary socialist, for whom all of history is as predetermined as the certainty of one's own death. The watchwords of the reformists, Conrad declares, are *patience, inactivity,* and *fatalism.* Following this logic, "it's no use doing anything—no use whatever."[9] Socialists, apparently, had merely to await the inevitable future utopia with their hands in their pockets and let capitalism gradually change into socialism.

Revolutionaries disputed the logic of reformism. If a socialist party was elected into power and actually tried to implement radical, socialist policies, capitalists would use their money to overthrow the government by force. Violence would come, one way or the other. For Lenin, what the proletariat needed was a small, well-organized, centralized, and tightly disciplined party of dedicated professional revolutionaries whose life work was to prepare and lead the socialist revolution. From 1903, Lenin began developing this new revolutionary force—the **Bolshevik** Party. Lenin's bold assertion about party organization and membership was condemned by most Marxists, including many revolutionaries. In Germany, Rosa Luxemburg accused Lenin of planning a coup instead of a revolution, "a desperate attempt of a minority to fashion the world after its own ideal."[10]

A small, revolutionary cabal might succeed, for a time, in winning power but could never hold onto it. Without deep roots among the people, which could be developed only through a mass, democratic workers' movement, the Bolsheviks would find themselves isolated. Their fragile hold on power would soon be smashed by the old regime. Luxemburg argued that there was no quick and easy route to socialist revolution.

Among the most important of the non-Bolshevik Marxists in Russia was Leon Trotsky, who was born Lev Bronstein in 1879. His parents were ethnic Jews and well-off farmers. Trotsky's first politics were anarchist. In 1898, he was arrested for his political activities and exiled to Siberia. Trotsky read Marxism and positioned himself as an independent Marxist with no permanent connection to either the Lenin-led Bolsheviks or to their opponents.[11]

Trotsky was especially critical of Lenin's conceptualization of the centralized, tightly disciplined revolutionary party. For Trotsky, the group of "'professional revolutionaries' was not marching *at the head* of the conscious proletariat, it was acting . . . *in the place* of the proletariat." By "*politically substituting*" itself for the working class, a committee of intellectuals did the thinking for the proletariat rather than following the democratic practice of educating and mobilizing them.[12] The proletariat, Trotsky believed, was far more ready and willing to act on their own than either the Bolsheviks or the reformists gave them credit for. In 1917, the debate about reform and revolution in Russia seemed to have been resolved in favour of the latter. Coming out of the disastrous world war against Germany, Russia experienced not one but two revolutions.

The Bolshevik Revolution: Socialism and Its Discontents

[The Franco-Prussian war of 1870] is leading . . . inevitably to a war between Germany and Russia. . . . And such a war No. 2 will act as

the midwife of the inevitable social revolution in Russia.[13]

— Karl Marx to Friedrich Sorge, 1870

In his letter to Sorge (see epigraph above), Marx meant a **bourgeois revolution**, not a socialist one; that is, a revolution that would overthrow a feudal system and bring in democratic reforms and a capitalist economy. By 1917, Russia had suffered three years of bloody and futile war resisting the invasion by the German army. People were starving in the cities, peasants were seizing land in the countryside, and under-equipped, incompetently led soldiers were deserting from the Eastern Front. Then, in February 1917 Russia plunged head-long into popular revolution—a Russian Spring. In the cities, workers took over their factories and established workers' councils (soviets) to run them. The old regime was swept aside and, in its place, the triumphant rebels erected a provisional government consisting of liberals, moderate reformists, and peasant-led parties. The Achilles heel of the new government was its intention to continue the war against Germany in the name of national honour and defence. When Lenin returned to Russia from exile early in 1917, the Bolsheviks opposed the provisional government and worked to consolidate control in the workers' soviets that were being formed in the industrial cities.

When the February Revolution broke out, Trotsky was in New York. His return to Russia was delayed when he was arrested en route by the British in Halifax and was interned for several weeks in a camp near Amherst. He spent his time politicizing imprisoned German submariners. After he returned to St Petersburg, Trotsky quickly became an energetic and important leader. He was elected chairman of the Petrograd Soviet in October and, abandoning his earlier reservations about Lenin's "substitutionism," he joined the Bolsheviks.[14]

Since the proletariat was a small minority of the population, the Bolsheviks intended to create a worker–peasant alliance and offered peasants the right to own their own land. Soldiers deserted the front lines to join the revolutionaries, helping the Bolsheviks gain ground. As revolutions go, the October Revolution, by which the Bolsheviks captured political power—*Ten Days that Shook the World*—was relatively swift. The real revolutionary war, however, was still to come.

Lenin's short-term plan was to hold on to power in Russia and await the imminent European socialist revolution that must surely come from Germany's defeat in the war. Some German soldiers did mutiny, and workers' councils were formed in many factories. But even the firebrand Rosa Luxemburg had trepidations about the movement. The German proletariat in 1918 was fragmented; an insurrection, she thought, would be premature.[15]

But instead of revolution, disaster struck. The new Republican government in Germany, which included prominent members of the reformist Social Democratic Party, fought the revolutionaries in the streets with a combination of regular troops and *Freikorps*, a mercenary army comprised of the unemployed and ex-soldiers. The government unleashed a "white terror" against Marxists, militant workers, and revolutionary leaders, among them Rosa Luxemburg, who was captured and summarily executed in January 1919 by army officers.[16] Although insurrections continued into the early 1920s in Germany and elsewhere in Europe, the back of the movement had been broken. No similar revolutionary movement occurred in North America after World War I, but labour unrest intensified in the immediate post-war years and strikes were interpreted by company and government officials as, potentially, revolutionary. A widespread "red scare" was whipped up in the United States and Canada. Labour militancy in Canada was condemned as communist and insurrectionary, and state repression was unleashed (see Box 2.1).

Following the defeat of the revolutionary movement in Europe, the counter-revolution was then carried directly into Russia. Anti-Bolshevik forces began to coalesce in the Russian countryside and they were joined by troops from Western countries who wanted to snuff out the revolution as quickly as possible. Civil war was underway in earnest in 1919. The futurist poet Vladimir Mayakovsky (1893–1930) crowed that neither the "crowned British lion" nor the "hirelings" of foreign powers could crush the Russian commune. Rather than look behind, Russia was moving full-speed into a leftist future, determined to "break history's old horse":[17]

On the world's throttle
tighten
the proletariat's fingers!
Chests out with pride!
Stick flags on heaven!
Who marches by the right?
By the left!
Left!
Left![18]

Mayakovsky was the dominant figure in Russian **futurism**, a largely negative movement that attacked all previous art and all bourgeois social conventions in favour of a new, future-oriented art.[19] The Futurist Manifesto of 1912 was titled *A Slap in the Face of Public Taste*. Not all futurists saw the Bolsheviks as the wave of the future, but during the civil war, Mayakovsky enlisted his impassioned pen in the revolutionary cause.[20] His longer works, such as "Vladimir Ilyich Lenin" (1924) and "It's Good" (1927), were enthusiastic political pieces of propaganda.[21]

The civil war brought tremendous hardship to the Russian people. In the bitter winter of 1920, food was scarce and famine swept the country, fanned by a severe drought. With no fuel, people in St Petersburg burned furniture, books, and doors in an effort not to freeze.[22] Mayakovsky

✢ BOX 2.1 • THEORY IN CONTEXT ✢

Winnipeg, 1919

When soldiers were demobilized after the war, they returned to an economy of high unemployment and sharp increases in the cost of living. Labour relations in 1919 were particularly explosive in Winnipeg. Workers were drawn to the socialist movement and the One Big Union idea. When workers in the Winnipeg metal and building trades demanded higher wages and a shorter working day, their employers refused to recognize the council that the workers had elected to represent their interests. As a result, workers went on strike for the basic rights of union recognition and collective bargaining, demands that were hardly radical or socialist.[23]

As radicals were elected into union leadership, the situation was inflamed by the "red scare." Members of Parliament raised the spectre of workers' **soviets** appearing in Canada.

The Winnipeg Trades and Labour Council (WTLC) supported the strike and held a vote among its members for a general strike in the city. By about a 20 to 1 margin, workers voted to strike, including most firefighters and police officers.[24] The WTLC created a General Strike Committee to organize the strike. On 15 May, about 24,000 workers walked off the job; sympathy strikes followed in dozens of towns and cities. In response, Winnipeg's employers organized a Citizens' Committee of prominent businessmen, professionals, and officials, which recruited about 4000 men into an irregular militia. The Committee claimed that a Soviet-type regime had been installed and that Winnipeg was "'under red rule.'"

The federal government declared the strike an attempt at revolution and prepared to repress it. The Winnipeg police were loyal to the strikers, however, so members of the federal Royal Canadian Mounted Police were sent to Winnipeg. The government also sent a battalion of troops, armed with two Lewis machine guns. Government workers on strike were ordered to return to work or be fired. Many strikers were immigrants, so the Immigration Act was amended to allow the deportation of British-born immigrants. Strike leaders were arrested in the early hours of 17 June and locked up in Stony Mountain Penitentiary. They faced newly widened charges of sedition.

On Saturday, 21 June, thousands of strikers demonstrated to protest the arrest of their leaders. Mounted police and deputized specials went through the crowd, first with batons and baseball bats, and then with revolvers drawn. Two protesters were killed in the fusillade.[25] As demonstrators fled into adjacent streets, they were met by the Citizens' Committee "special police," armed with baseball bats. The city was under military rule. Armed soldiers arrested more than 100 people and patrolled the streets with machine guns mounted on their vehicles. The Winnipeg General Strike was crushed and workers returned to work with their demands unsatisfied. Subsequently, the "red scare" tactic and the force of state power were used elsewhere in Canada in the 1920s against militant workers[26]—even though their demands could have been met within the terms of regular collective bargaining and social reform. During World War II, the basic union rights of recognition and bargaining were normalized in Canada.

understood the people's sufferings. In the villages along the Volga, he wrote, the chimneys were "like death candles," and even the crows had disappeared. In the city, "the clay / has all been eaten / and every thorn."[27] Mayakovsky blamed the "fat-bellied lords [and] crowned heads" of Europe for the starvation, and he prophesied that the purifying "world-wide blaze" was coming.[28] Over time, however, Mayakovsky became increasingly disillusioned with revolution. He was found dead in 1930, shot through the heart. Officially, his death was declared a suicide, caused by a romantic breakup with yet another young actress. Questions about how and why he died, however, provide continuing fodder for serious historians and conspiracy theorists.[29]

By 1922, the foreign armies had withdrawn and the counter-revolution was defeated. The Bolsheviks cast off into the unchartered future without the leader who had first set the course: Lenin died in 1924 following a succession of strokes that had left him increasingly incapacitated. The result was a struggle among the leading Bolsheviks over the kind of socialism that would be built in Russia and, inevitably, for dominance in the Bolshevik (Communist) Party.

The Nature of the Revolution

The Bolsheviks inherited a vast, loosely connected territory of diverse nationalities and ethnic groups that had been devastated by war. Russia was isolated from the world and surrounded by enemies. Moreover, it was a theoretical anomaly: a backward, largely agrarian country with a Marxist party in power. The Bolsheviks were left to devise a new path to build socialism in a country without much industry, without a history of political or legal rights, and without a majority of people being working class. The theory the Bolsheviks inherited from Marx had no provisions for such a contingency.

During his exile in Switzerland, Lenin had undertaken an analysis of the current stage of capitalism and the revolutionary possibilities the new stage portended. In *Imperialism: The Highest Stage of Capitalism*, Lenin argued that Russia was not only on the precipice of a bourgeois revolution; it had a small but highly militant, centralized, and class-conscious working class. Furthermore, Lenin argued, since capitalism in Russia was dominated by foreign capitalists, the country did not have a strong, national capitalist class that could lead a Russian bourgeois revolution. If the capitalists were too weak to defend Russia from the exploitation of **imperialism**, by default only the proletariat could assume such a role.

Marxists abroad wondered at Lenin's audacity. What would a Marxist party do as the government of an unindustrialized, technologically backward, and largely peasant country? The immediate and pressing need was to help the economy recover from the devastation of years of war and revolution. In 1921, the Bolsheviks implemented a temporary economic program called the **New Economic Policy (NEP)**. Peasants who owned their own land were given the right to sell their produce in the open market; small businesses were allowed to flourish; professionals and administrators from the old regime were put back into positions of authority; and cultural expression was liberalized.[30]

Lenin was aware that the New Economic Policy was a retreat to capitalism and would lead to the creation of a new capitalist class. But the economic retreat was necessary under the circumstances to increase productivity. Under the NEP, the rural economy revived and consumer industries began to recover their pre-war position under the injunction to make a profit. Heavy industry, the core of the socialist strategy, lagged far behind and survived on state subsidies.[31] The NEP led to the development of a characteristically capitalist economy complete with fiscal restraint, a stock market, the opening of trade relations with Western powers, foreign investment, unemployment, and labour unrest. In place of workers' councils to manage industrial enterprises, the Bolsheviks imposed a system of one-man management.[32]

A workers' group in the Bolshevik party denounced the NEP as a compromise with capitalism—NEP, the group said, stood for the "new exploitation of the proletariat."[33] By the time a crisis in the Bolshevik party erupted in 1923–4, occasioned by the worsening illness and then death of Lenin, the party was seriously divided.

Stalin and Soviet State Socialism

He can read. He can write. He has ideas. . . . Ergo, he is an intellectual. Of course, he'll have to be shot later when ideas become a hindrance.[34]

— Doris Lessing, *The Golden Notebook*, 1962

When Lenin died in January 1924, the main differences in the Bolshevik Party coalesced around Leon Trotsky and two long-time Bolsheviks: Nikolai Bukharin and Joseph Stalin. Over the next three years there were intense struggles within the party over the policies the Communist Party of the Soviet Union (CPSU) would follow in developing socialism in the USSR and who would emerge as the dominant leader. Stalin was triumphant. As Doris Lessing's observation suggests, even Bolshevik intellectuals would not fare well under Stalin.

The first to go was Trotsky. Bukharin, with Stalin's support, was committed to the further expansion of capitalism in Russia—as long as the Bolsheviks controlled the government, private profits and riches were positive. A workers' group in the Bolshevik Party, with which Trotsky sympathized, thought the party should roll back the growth of capitalism and implement a socialist model based on centralized economic planning and heavy industry. A workers' dictatorship should advantage the working class, according to Trotsky, not the capitalistically inclined peasants.

But by 1927, the Bukharin program based on supporting the peasantry appeared to have won out. Trotsky was purged from the Communist Party and then exiled, first to Siberia and then permanently from the USSR. Once abroad, Trotsky became the most famous revolutionary critic of the state-socialist system that was constructed in the USSR under Stalin. In 1940, Trotsky was assassinated in Mexico City by an agent of the Soviet government.[35]

After Trotsky was removed from the seat of Russian power, debate in the Communist Party resumed over the fate of the NEP. In the face of serious food shortages and the apparent strength of world capitalism in the 1920s, Stalin pushed for creating a fully socialist, industrial society in the USSR. He turned against Bukharin and initiated a drive to industrialize the USSR as rapidly as possible. As a result, the urban private sector was nationalized; state economic investment was concentrated in heavy industry (steel, power, railways, hydroelectricity) at the expense of rural and consumer industries; and five-year economic plans were introduced. In 1929, with Stalin firmly in control, the farms that had been owned individually by peasants were expropriated and concentrated into large collectives or state-owned farms. In just a few years, then, economic policy in the USSR was reversed more than once.

Collectivization meant depriving peasants of their independent ownership of land. Many resisted, burying crops or killing animals rather than turning them over to the collective farms. Famine and starvation returned to the Soviet Union; millions died. Political repression deepened. Defiant peasants and political opponents were interred in forced labour camps or executed. In addition, the Communist party exercised tight control over such institutions as the media and education. The process of collectivization was conducted like a military operation against the better-off peasants. The punitive methods were justified by the claim that they established the foundation for what, in the future, would be a better, more equal industrial society. Critics said that the USSR was undergoing **primitive accumulation**, to use the Marxist economic term, and that the peasantry was being exploited in favour of industrial growth. Stalin attempted to justify the oppression by arguing that the Soviet Union was engaging in class struggle with the capitalists. In fact, in 1936 he declared that the USSR had reached the stage of socialism and that there were supposedly no longer any antagonistic classes in the country.

With private property replaced by state or collective ownership, and a planned economy substituted for the capitalist market, the Party had created a socialist economic shell. Under a series of five-year plans, the USSR was marched in lock-step by top-down industrialization into modern industry. Single-enterprise, "one-man management" was strengthened. One by one, the regime reversed the revolutionary measures put into place after 1917:

- Inequalities in pay and benefits widened.
- Traditional ranks in the military were restored.
- Traditional methods of teaching were reinstated in the schools, including "examinations, certificates, gold medals, and uniforms."
- Traditional gender roles were reinforced.[36]

The party was filled with bureaucrats and state officials whose personal careers were tied directly to the enterprises they controlled and to their positions in the party hierarchy. Since there were no longer any antagonistic classes in the USSR, Stalin claimed that opponents of forced collectivization and heavy industrial development must be agents of foreign capitalists. In response, the Communist Party purged itself of all open opposition. The last of the Bolsheviks were summarily executed after spectacular trials. Other than state ownership and centralized economic planning, the socialist policies of the Soviet Union were scooped out like a pumpkin, leaving an empty shell.

If we were looking at the USSR from abroad, through uncritical lenses, it would be easy to be impressed by the economic advances, even while wages for most people were kept depressingly low, housing was scarce, and consumer industries lagged seriously behind the production of heavy industry. The extensive labour camps were far from the eyes of visitors to the USSR. Soviet Russia demonstrated that it was possible to industrialize a society—albeit unevenly and at an enormous human cost—without a traditional class of capitalists. While the state press trumpeted economic achievements, for whom was the socialist experiment being constructed? The exiled Trotsky had an answer that was not flattering to the new men of power in the USSR.

Trotsky explained his theory in *The Revolution Betrayed* (1936). A new elite consisting of administrators, managers, and technocrats had consolidated its hold on the Party and the nation. This was not technically a "ruling class." Factory managers did not legally own the enterprises they controlled, and their children could not directly inherit their parent's wealth or position. Trotsky pointed out that the governing bureaucracy was increasingly privileged in terms of salaries and other benefits, such as housing. The new, dominant elite in the USSR may not yet have been a class, but it was "something more than a bureaucracy." The "soviet caste" was "the sole privileged and commanding stratum" and was living at the expense of the deprived majority in Soviet society. The working class had been expropriated from political power.[37]

Ultimately, Trotsky said, if the bureaucracy continued to hold on to power, over time it would inevitably transform itself into "a new possessing class." But, for Trotsky, the question of the ultimate class character of the Soviet Union, which he called a degenerated workers' state, had not yet been decided by history.[38] In 1989, the USSR collapsed and state property was privatized. The denouement was the last act of a long, drawn-out erosion that Trotsky had documented decades before.

Bolshevism and the "Woman Question"

A similar degeneration occurred in the status of women in the USSR. A powerful international women's movement formed during the first decades of the twentieth century aimed principally at securing legal rights for women, especially the right to vote. While socialists certainly agreed that women must fight for their political emancipation, the fundamental question was the relationship between women's emancipation and socialism. For Marx and Engels, only the revolutionary overthrow of capitalism and the development of socialism could genuinely liberate women.

In the view of German socialist and feminist Clara Zetkin (1857-1933), working women should fight for their political and legal rights, but a *socialist* women's movement should have a longer-term vision. Political rights alone would not end the exploitation or oppression of women under capitalism. Zetkin believed that the conflict between classes was more powerful "than the social antagonism between the sexes."[39] The class struggle of working-class women and men against the dominant class (women and men) was the revolutionary aim of the socialist movement. Women's fate, therefore, was bound up with the emancipation of the working class.

Women's full integration into paid employment was necessary if they were to develop a proletarian class consciousness and take their place in the socialist revolution. Employment gave women financial independence and also drew them out of the narrow, private circle of patriarchal isolation and household dependence, bringing them into contact with other women and other workers. Once integrated into employment, women would become part of the class struggle.[40]

This was not the view of all socialists, however. Reformists in Germany, for example, spoke on behalf of many male industrial workers when they blamed the breakdown of the working-class family on women's employment. When women entered the workforce and competed for jobs, such reformists believed, they lowered men's wages. As a result, women should stay out of paid labour and let men financially maintain their wives and children.[41] This traditional gender-based policy monopolized employment for men, reinforced the private, patriarchal household with women as domestic slaves, and meant that men controlled the finances of the working class family.[42]

Feminist socialists argued that the condition for women's participation in the struggle for socialism was that women's demands for fairness, equality, and an end to oppression should become part of the immediate struggle, and not be put off until sometime in the future. They wanted a separate socialist women's organization to struggle specifically for women's issues. When women in the Bolshevik Party did indeed establish an independent women's organization in 1919, many Bolsheviks opposed it as too feminist. But as Russian women gained experience organizing and discussing among other women, they carried their new practice into their trade union and Party work.[43]

If genuine women's emancipation required socialism, the second axiom of Marxist feminists in what was termed the **woman question** was that there could be no socialism without the liberation of women. Unless the new socialist society took steps to create equal conditions for women, it could not claim to be genuinely socialist. Patriarchal attitudes would persist after the revolution and would have to be confronted individually and organizationally. One important measure of the success of a revolution, Lenin said, is "how much the women take part in it."[44]

In the Soviet Union, however, deeply rooted traditions worked against women's emancipation.[45] Most husbands, Lenin said, had a backward mentality regarding women. They considered housework to be women's work and beneath men's privileges and dignity. Lenin argued, "The ancient rights of her husband, her lord and master, survive unnoticed. . . . We must root out the old slave-owner's point of view, both in the Party and among the masses."[46] Political work among women was the task equally of men and women in the Party, he said; it was "as much as half of all the Party work." Despite the new laws emancipating women, "she continues to be a *domestic slave*, because *petty housework* crushes, strangles, stultifies and degrades her, chains her to the kitchen and the nursery, and she wastes her labour on barbarously unproductive, petty, nerve-wracking, stultifying and crushing drudgery." The solution will come when petty housekeeping is socialized and made unnecessary through such means as public cafeterias, nurseries, and kindergartens, which are shoots of communism, Lenin suggests.[47] Furthermore, women had to take an active part in the administration of socialized enterprises and the state. Lenin called for the election of more women to positions of political power:[48] "This transition is a difficult one, because it involves the remoulding of the most deep-rooted, inveterate, hidebound and rigid 'order.'"[49]

Initially, the Bolshevik Revolution established many of the necessary conditions for the liberation of women, legalizing divorce, opening daycare centres at work sites, operating some workers' cafeterias, and granting access to medical abortions, among other legal and social measures. But many of these policies were reversed in the 1920s and 1930s.[50] Under Stalin, patriarchal authority was upheld in the family. In the effort to populate "Mother Russia," women had to be put back into the kitchen, the bedroom, and the nursery.

In addition to full economic participation and equality of legal and political rights, modern feminists are at least as likely to ask questions about the character of the personal and sexual relationships that socialist men form with the women in their lives. Lenin discussed questions of sexuality and free love with German Marxist Clara Zetkin. The widespread discussion of sexuality, Lenin declared, was a fad derived from Freud. Bourgeois women are absorbed in the problems of sexuality "the way an Indian saint is absorbed in the contemplation of his navel."[51] Among the absurd criticisms of the Soviet Union was the claim that women were becoming the common property of all men. Coming from a patriarchal world in which men "owned" women, socialism could presumably mean only that women were now collectively rather than privately owned. Lenin discussed with Zetkin the problems he believed were created by sexual emancipation (see Box 2.2).

The Development of European Marxism

For many Marxists in the 1920s, Marx's theory was in need of an overhaul. Central to the early discussion were the philosophical and cultural theories of Karl Korsch, Georg Lukács, and Antonio Gramsci. Korsch and Lukács developed close ties, and, in the early 1920s, both became members of their national Communist parties. Both argued that scientific Marxism ignored the importance of philosophy as well as class consciousness and ideology in the workers' movement. In 1924, Korsch briefly attended an International Congress in Moscow where he and Lukács were denounced as mere "professors" or anti-Marxist intellectuals.[52] Korsch left the Communist Party in 1926 while Lukács continued his membership, but both considered themselves independent Marxists.

Karl Korsch (1886–1961)

Karl Korsch was born to a middle-class family near Hamburg in north Germany. At the University of Jena, he became a member of the Free Student Movement, a group that rejected the traditional

⚜ BOX 2.2 · THEORY IN CONTEXT ⚜

Lenin and the "Glass of Water" Theory of Sexuality

[The following conversation with Lenin on sexual emancipation and Bolshevik politics was reported by Clara Zetkin in 1926.]

Lenin: "I was told that sex problems are a favourite subject in your [German] youth organizations. . . . In our country, too, considerable numbers of young people are busy 'revising bourgeois conceptions and morals' in the sex question. . . . Of course, women and young people are taking a deep interest in the tangle of problems which have arisen as a result of . . . the present messy state of sex relations. Young people rebel against them with the vehemence of their years. This is only natural. . . . However, it is hardly a good thing that sex, already strongly felt in the physical sense, should at such a time assume so much prominence in the psychology of young people. The consequences are nothing short of fatal. . . .[53]

"I am an old man, and I do not like [the prominence given to sex]. . . . [Q]uite often this so called 'new sex life' of young people—and frequently of the adults too—seems to me . . . simply an extension of the good old bourgeois brothel. . . . No doubt you have heard about the famous theory that in communist society satisfying sexual desire and the craving for love is as simple and trivial as 'drinking a glass of water.' A section of our youth has gone mad, absolutely mad, over this glass-of-water theory. . . .

"I consider the famous 'glass-of-water theory' . . . anti-social. . . . To be sure, thirst has to be quenched. But would a normal person normally lie down in the gutter and drink from a puddle? Or even from a glass whose edge has been greased by many lips? . . .

"As a communist I have no liking at all for the 'glass-of-water' theory, despite its attractive label: 'emancipation of love.' . . . In bourgeois practice it materialised into emancipation of the flesh. . . . [T]oday, in my opinion, the obtaining plethora of sex life yields neither joy nor strength. On the contrary, it impairs them. . . .

". . . You know the young comrade X [unnamed]. . . . I am afraid that he will never amount to anything. He has one love affair after another. This is not good for the political struggle and for the revolution. I will not vouch for the reliability of . . . the men who run after every petticoat and let themselves in with every young female."

[end dialogue]

Lenin sprang to his feet, slapped the table with his hand and paced up and down the room. . . . "Promiscuity in sexual matters is bourgeois. It is a sign of degeneration. The proletariat is a rising class. It doesn't need an intoxicant to stupefy or stimulate it, neither the intoxicant of sexual laxity or of alcohol. . . . Self-control and self-discipline are not slavery; not in matters of love either."[54]

German student emphasis on military training, rituals, anti-Semitism, and excessive drinking. Korsch also became a socialist while studying in Jena. He travelled all over Germany as a member of the Free Students, during which time he met Hedda Korsch, who became his wife and companion.

Between 1912 and 1914, in his mid-twenties, Korsch worked in England, where he was impressed by arguments favouring workers' control of factories.[55] In 1914 he was recalled to Germany to join his military regiment. According to Hedda Korsch, there was no jubilation when the German troops left to go to war. A band played music and women threw bouquets of flowers, but both had been arranged by the government. The men, however, "were moody, sullen or weeping." As a political protest, Korsch led his troops into battle without carrying arms himself. He was decorated several times for bravery. As the war deteriorated into stalemate, his company became increasingly radicalized. By 1917 they were mutinous and known as the Red Company. When rebellious troops established soldiers' councils (modelled after the workers' soviets in Russia) at the end of the war, Korsch's company was in the forefront of the revolt.[56]

Between 1920 and 1923, Korsch taught law in Jena, in the German state of Thuringia. Revolutionary sentiment was strong in the state, and a coalition government was formed between communists and left-wing social democrats. Korsch became a deputy in the state parliament and Minister of Justice. When the federal German government sent troops to Thuringia to prevent a working-class uprising, the revolutionaries were forced underground.[57]

After the Nazi Party took power in Germany in 1933, it passed a law that no government employee could be politically "unreliable"—that is, a socialist or a Jew. Korsch lost his university post, and the Nazi government confiscated his savings account. He remained in Berlin trying to organize anti-Nazi resistance. Korsch evaded capture,

until he finally escaped into exile. In England, the local communists denounced him to the British government as a Nazi agent, Hedda Korsch says, "because since he was not a Jew, he had no reason to behave strangely and leave Germany in the way he had."[58] In 1936, Korsch went to the United States, where he worked for a time with the Institute for Social Research. His health deteriorated after 1957. Well before then, he had become pessimistic about the possibilities of revolution and especially about the nature of the regime in the Soviet Union.[59]

Korsch's initial contribution to Marxist theory was "Marxism and Philosophy" (1923). In his view,[60] the era of revolution that Europe was experiencing had polarized Marxism between vulgar Marxists who revised historical materialism into a reformist and evolutionary movement, and ideological purists who claimed to be restoring Marxist original theory. It was necessary, Korsch said, to use Marx's dialectical method to understand the history of Marxism itself, including its recent degeneration into dogma and useless abstract theory.

The failure of revolution did not appear to result from economics—the capitalist fleece seemed ever more ready to be shorn. The crisis of Marxism had to be understood in terms of ideology and culture. Marxism originally was not a theory of economics alone but a theory of historical and social development understood as a unified whole. Conscious social action, ideology, and practice were important interconnected components of the theory. Orthodox Marxist theorists had made the mistake of focusing on separate elements of society in isolation from the whole, particularly on economics. As Marxism became little more than an analysis of capitalism and economic policy, theory was separated from revolutionary practice and Marx's theory of social revolution was lost. Marxism in the West had withered into sociological analysis and simple reform of the separate institutions of bourgeois society.

The theoretical purists who rejected reformism, however, were equally wrong. They attributed the collapse of Marxism into reformism as a consequence of the dishonesty, opportunism, or stupidity of its leaders. Workers were said to have a "false consciousness" because they were being systematically misled. For Korsch, it was no longer possible to consider workers' consciousness and ideology to be merely "false" or unimportant. On the contrary, if people's consciousness was backward, there had to be real, material reasons for the backwardness. Workers' consciousness could only be changed by understanding the material foundation of their thought and then changing people's action or practice. Throughout their writing, Korsch argued, Marx and Engels had had a dialectical appreciation of the relationship between consciousness (ideology) and reality, and had argued that change came about not through thought alone, but through practice—theoretically guided action: "[A]ll forms of social consciousness . . . are not mere chimeras, but 'highly objective and highly practical' social realities and consequently [they] 'must be abolished in a practical and objective manner.'"[61] Despite their daily exploitation, workers did not automatically gravitate toward Marxism. The reasons for their non-Marxist consciousness were complex and deeply embedded in the framework of capitalism. With his theory of reification, Georg Lukács sought to unravel the puzzle of workers' consciousness.

Georg Lukács (1885–1971)

In his 1923 essay "Reification and the Consciousness of the Proletariat," Lukács examines the implications that the modern form of industrial capitalism had for workers' thinking. He identifies the primary problem of modern capitalism to be "reification." In Marxist thought, **reification** is the process through which people come to regard something that is actually a human creation as being more powerful than humanity, a force that controls people from outside rather than being actually produced by people in the first place. For example, people invented the idea of God, but then they "reified" the concept by coming to believe that God was an independent being, more powerful than people and controlling their lives. What is humanly created is experienced by people as being "natural" and beyond their control. What is natural and normal is beyond the possibility of change.

Marx applied the idea of reification to the capitalist production system. In capitalism, the existence of propertyless workers and rich capitalists and the relationship between them, as dependent factory workers and owners, are assumed to be natural rather than an arrangement of people and resources created by human beings. Rather than being a particular arrangement of society, developed historically by humans, Marx saw capitalism as an independent and objective power that controls peoples' lives. The illusion is that workers are fed by the industrial leaders, whereas the reverse is true.[62] Workers have no sense that they actually produce the very capital that is used to dominate them. As workers are treated merely as "things," as instruments of production determined by an impersonal "system," people are conditioned to see themselves as things, and to treat other people and the natural environment as objects that are to be manipulated and dominated.

Above all, reification means assuming that existing social arrangements are natural; but it is not just a matter of indoctrination. Horkheimer and Adorno argue that ideology does "render the oppressed stupid and deflect them from the truth," but it is more fundamentally "the concrete conditions of work in society which enforce conformism." The powerlessness of the workers is not merely a trick of the rulers "but the logical consequence of industrial society."[63]

The structure of people's working and private lives, and the whole culture that surrounds them, continually reproduce the conditions that make reification the world view of even the most oppressed people. Reification is more than just an idea; it is embedded in how people live their daily lives. Hence, for Lukács, reification was a profound barrier to class consciousness. Overcoming reification was a necessary part of any successful theory of proletarian revolution. For Lukács, theory could explain reification but overcoming it required changed practices. Workers' control of factories, for example, gave workers the practical experience of making decisions and seeing the results of their actions. Combined with the theory that guided these actions and made sense of the results, workers would be able to develop a deeper consciousness of capitalism, their place within it, and their potential to construct new relations of production.

Fordism and Twentieth Century Capitalism

By the late nineteenth century in Western Europe and North America, the early competitive phase of capitalism was being transformed into large-scale, corporate capitalism. A handful of dominant companies or "trusts" came to dominate the major branches of industry in a nation, including oil, steel, rubber, and chemical. Changes in industrial organization affected similar changes in agriculture. As depicted in John Steinbeck's novel *The Grapes of Wrath*, destitute farmers were being displaced from their land by the mechanization of farming. They had not "known the power and danger of machines in private hands" until the machines had suddenly pushed them out and they found themselves on the road, looking for temporary work on the ranches and plantations of the west.[64]

When farming industrialized, farms became larger, but there were fewer of them. The owners were usually absentee, Steinbeck said, and workers resembled slaves, crawling like bugs between the rows of cauliflower and lettuce. The land was ploughed by hired hands in diesel tractors who didn't know the touch of the ground and weren't "one with the soil." The land was mechanically raped, "methodically . . . without passion."[65] The great owners vertically integrated their businesses: they owned the big California fruit farms and they also owned the canneries, so they could buy the fruit from their farm operation at next to nothing and gain all their profit from selling canned fruit at an inflated price. Meanwhile, with the cost of growing the fruit so low, "the little farmers who owned no canneries lost their farms, and they were taken by the great owners, the banks, and the companies."[66]

The changes in the capitalist economy had ramifications throughout society. The Italian revolutionary Antonio Gramsci analyzed these changes, which he called **Fordism**, as well as their effects on the working class and on anti-capitalist social movements.

Antonio Gramsci (1891–1937)

Antonio Gramsci was born in Sardinia, Italy. He was radicalized in university and, following the Bolshevik Revolution, joined the Communist Party.[67] Early in his career, Gramsci supported the emergence of workers' councils, or **soviets**, through which working people took over the management of the enterprises they worked. Through their direct experience in running their own enterprises, Gramsci believed, workers would develop the confidence and ability to expand their control from the factory to local and, ultimately, national government. Class consciousness could be transformed only through experience and empowerment. Gramsci was a leader of the revolutionary movement in Italy but, as in Germany, that movement was suppressed. In 1922, the first fascist government in Europe seized power in Italy. Gramsci was arrested and died in prison.[68]

The failure of the Red years in Italy and the rise of fascism led Gramsci to reconsider the conditions under which revolutionary consciousness was produced. In *Selection from the Prison Notebooks*, which he wrote in prison, Gramsci theorized that workers were subject to a dominant ideology, propagated by the Church, the media, schooling, and the state, that made the present economic and social system seem natural and legitimate. Through the exercise of this ideological hegemony, revolution was not just forestalled, but the opportunity for critical thought was truncated. Social change required, first, a successful campaign of counter-hegemony to denaturalize workers' views of capitalism and the state. In his prison notebooks, Gramsci discussed the development of Fordism and its introduction into Italy.

By the 1920s, the railway boom that had knit national economies and nations together was giving way to the automobile age, a new mode of transportation that would fundamentally re-make the economy, alter the use of living space, and bring a truncated form of the American dream within the reach of millions of middle-income consumers. Capitalism has always been driven by technological innovations, which make production more efficient and profitable. In the nineteenth century, manufacturing was carried out by skilled craft workers. This older, artisanal form of work demanded "a certain active participation of intelligence, fantasy and initiative on the part of the worker." The personality of the craft workers was reflected, Gramsci said, in the objects they created, and "the link between art and labour was still very strong."[69] Productive knowledge was vested in the workers, and they protected their relative privileges through highly organized, exclusive, and often militant craft unions. Through their unions, workers resisted the imposition of technological innovations that would strip them of the knowledge of the entire production process, centralize this knowledge in the hands of management, and impose technical and supervisory control over the daily work regime.

Craft workers, in most cases, were fighting a losing battle. The assembly line was the novel form of rationalized production in the early twentieth century. With control over the work process, management could devise the most rational division of labour for turning raw materials into finished products in the shortest amount of time. Scientific managers analyzed and dissected the work process, and workers became small cogs in an immense complex of machinery. Workers were trained to complete one small fragment of a complex manufacturing process, endlessly repeating the most efficient motions while the conveyor belt moved the piece along toward the next station. The film comedian Charlie Chaplin satirized the dehumanizing effects of mass production in *Modern Times* (1936). Frederick Taylor popularized the modern style of scientific management and became the guru of the industrialists. Under his robotic regime, productive work became automatic, rationalized, and reduced "exclusively to the mechanical, physical aspect." Human labour, Taylor boasted, could be reduced to the level of a trained gorilla.[70]

The new principles of rationalized production were introduced into automobile manufacturing by Henry Ford (see Box 2.3). Antonio Gramsci used the term *Fordism* (or "Americanism" when it was introduced into Europe) to refer to the "ultramodern form of production and of working methods" pioneered by Ford. Economic rationalization included the vertical integration of an industry, as corporations expanded beyond production into the direct rational management of transportation, distribution, and retailing. The lower production costs associated with Fordist production were reflected in lower selling prices, which expanded the domestic market for widespread consumption. Ford anticipated selling affordable cars to the general public, thereby beginning the present era of mass consumption.[71]

⤷ BOX 2.3 · BIOGRAPHY ↶

Henry Ford (1863–1947)

Henry Ford's name is synonymous with the automobile and the factory assembly line, although he invented neither. His father was an Irish immigrant who settled on a farm in Dearborn, Michigan. At the age of 16, Ford left the farm for factory work in Detroit. He spent most of the next decade around small steam engines and studying self-propelled machine locomotion. In 1891, he returned to Detroit, newly married to Clara Bryant. The couple's only child, Edsel, was born two years later.[72]

The four-wheel horseless carriage, powered by a gasoline internal-combustion engine, was developed first in France and Germany. Ford's first self-propelled experimental vehicle hit the Detroit streets in 1896. In 1903, when small automobile companies were quickly going bankrupt, the 40-year-old Ford and his backers opened the Ford Motor Company. Ford's vision, realized through Model "A" to the famous Model "T" (1908), was to build a purely functional car that could be sold to the multitudes of average income earners. The Ford Motor Company proved to be an enormously profitable venture.[73] For years, demand outstripped supply. Ford's second innovation was the adaptation in 1913 of a system of moving conveyer belts—the assembly line—to his new Highland Park assembly plant. Mass production was underway. The next year, Ford announced the $5 day. By 1921, two-thirds of all cars sold were Fords, although General Motors soon replaced Ford as the number one seller.[74]

The most notable feature of Fordism was the relatively higher wage paid to the semi-skilled plant workers. Higher wages were designed to correct the central difficulty of the automobile industry, which was the high turnover of labour. Many workers preferred to return to lower-wage industries—neither wage differentials nor the threat of unemployment were sufficient inducements. Rationalized work, Gramsci concluded, is "more wearing and exhausting;" as a result, "in the given conditions of society as it is," higher wages are not sufficient recompense.[75]

The high-wage economy associated with Fordism was also necessarily transitory. The introduction of rationalized methods of production occurred in the post-war period, which was marked by endemic unemployment. In situations of more or less "normal" employment, high wages alone would not be sufficient to induce workers to work on what was at the time a new and especially alienating assembly line: "[c]oercion has therefore to be ingeniously combined with persuasion and consent." Once initiated, the high-wage policy and rationalized production methods would be generalized and diffused industry-wide. The result would be a return to unemployment and, consequently, a decline in overall wages. Higher wages in America were basically a consequence of the new methods of production: "Monopoly wages correspond to monopoly profits." But as

Henry Ford became an American folk hero, the embodiment of the American dream and native ingenuity. Many prominent people wanted him to run for president. Yet, Ford was incurably anti-Semitic. According to him, Jewish bankers in Germany had started the Great War, and Jews were responsible for the immoral suggestiveness of jazz and the short skirts and revealing blouses of the twenties' flappers. Moreover, he suggested, American movies were trivial and demoralizing because they were "entirely Jew-controlled." In 1919, Ford bought a newspaper, the *Dearborn Independent*, which became the mouthpiece for his racism. Adolph Hitler had a framed picture of Ford in his office. Imitating the American autocrat, Hitler commissioned the production in Germany of an affordable people's car, the Volkswagen.

As a manufacturer in Detroit, Ford was a member of an employer's association that was vehemently anti-union. Ford ran a union-free shop, **blacklisted** union leaders, and condoned high-handed supervision of the workers. In 1928, Ford was called an "industrial fascist—the Mussolini of Detroit" by the *New York Times*. Although Ford vowed to keep unions out of his plants, he was soon confronted by the powerful United Auto Workers (UAW). As a union campaign began in front of his main plant, Ford employed Gestapo-like tactics. Photographers caught thugs, ex–prize fighters, and gangsters beating up union leaders, and kicking and slapping men and women distributing leaflets. The National Labor Relations Board found evidence of "'organized gangsterism'" in every Ford factory. Finally, in 1941, under a federal order, workers in Ford's main Detroit plant were allowed to vote for their union choice. Fewer than 3 per cent voted "no union"; almost 70 per cent voted for the UAW. With an aged Henry Ford clearly on the way out, the union and Ford management finally signed an agreement that became a model for the industry.[76]

the new methods become common in the United States and abroad, Gramsci concluded, both high wages and high profits would disappear.[77]

Fordism (rationalized capitalism), Gramsci believed, was fashioning "a new type of man suited to the new type of work and productive process." "[T]he new methods of work are inseparable from a specific mode of living and of thinking and feeling life." Obsessional work, Gramsci says, "provokes alcoholic and sexual depravation." Consequently, industrialists attempted through a body of inspectors to intervene in workers' lives. Economic rationalization required a parallel discipline of the sexual instincts, a new form of the regulation and stability of sexual relations, and

the strengthening of the family. The emphasis on familial morality was contradicted, however, by the sexual liberties of the post-war 1920s. Workers sometimes spent their higher wages on alcohol and other vices, which were thought to undermine their work efficiency. Industrialists wanted workers to spend their money rationally, to maintain and renew their physical energy appropriate for the rigours of the assembly line.[78]

Industrialists such as Henry Ford investigated the private lives of their workers and attempted to control private morality through the imposition of inspection services. In this collective effort to generate "a new type of worker" suited to rational production, Ford and his ilk were not motivated by concern for the workers' humanity or spirituality, according to Gramsci. Work could become humane again only when production was rooted in creativity. The problem with the rationalization of labour, Gramsci argues, is that the worker is exhausted by the new methods of production. The Fordist attempt to manipulate the worker's private life outside work was a purely external and mechanical intervention to prevent workers from physically collapsing and an attempt to maintain a stable, well-adjusted, and permanent labour force.[79]

In Gramsci's view, America was rent by an increasing moral gap between the lifestyle and morality of the working classes and "the ever more numerous elements of the ruling classes." Workers' sexual lives, in Gramsci's view, came to resemble the daily life of the pre-industrial peasant, whose hard physical labour was satisfied by the uncomplicated love of his "sure and unfailing" wife, who was free of any affectation. Industrialism, Gramsci believed, demanded monogamy and relative marital stability. Workers were creating "a new form of sexual union shorn of the bright and dazzling colour of the romantic tinsel typical of the petit bourgeois and Romantic layabout." Divorce in the United States, for example, was more frequent among the upper classes than among the working classes. Social passivity in the US was growing, according to Gramsci, especially among upper class women who were turning into "'luxury mammals'" obsessed with beauty and fashion, with nothing to do but travel and engage in barely disguised forms of semi-prostitution. In the longer run, Gramsci believed, social strata in America would solidify into castes similar to those in Europe.[80]

For an activist who supported workers' councils during the revolutionary post-war years in Italy, it may be surprising that Gramsci did not condemn the introduction of Fordist production techniques in Europe: Fordism was not a "malignant phenomenon," he said. Gramsci considered Fordism a progressive development that was transforming the old economic individualism in the direction of a planned economy. Enlightened workers would support rationalized production as long as it was part of a conscious, society-wide transformation of living and working conditions led by a progressive state. Rather than subordinating the workers' mind as it reduced physical labour to repetitive mechanical motions, "the brain of the worker, far from being mummified, reaches a state of complete freedom." The rhythm of the routine gesture becomes muscle and nervous-system memory "and leaves the brain free and unencumbered for other occupations." A worker will work mechanically and be free to contemplate as easily as anyone who goes for a walk.[81]

Fordism was resisted by the working class through militant craft unions. In Gramsci's view, crafts unions protected the corporate privileges of the labour aristocracy, and he concluded that "the industrialists' attempt to curb them had a certain 'progressive' aspect."[82] In the American context, however, **industrial unionism**, which combined factory-wide industrial trades into a single, large union, was the more progressive development. A wide, militant, and effective organizing drive in the 1930s, through which large industries such as automobile production were unionized, swept the United States and Canada. Industrial unionism was the labour counterpart to Fordism. The high-wage economy, which continued into the 1970s, was the product of union strength rather than employer manipulation. Fordism and industrial unionism had risen and would decline together.

Conclusion

The Russian Revolution and the establishment of the Soviet Union were defining moments of the twentieth century. For the next 70 years, world politics had to take into account the existence of a socio-political system that was an alternative to capitalism. In many parts of what became known as the Third World, the Soviet model of state-dominated national development appeared to be a way out of perpetual poverty and Western domination. In Western social theory, the emergence of a more or less official version of Marxism ("soviet Marxism") further divided critical intellectuals. The fate of Marxism in the West has gone through bullish periods, even times of academic respectability, as well as deep troughs when Marxism was deemed obsolete. Social thought and social movements were polarized between left and right in the 1930s, which was also an era of capitalist reform in the West. Radical and communist parties in the West grew stronger in the Depression years, as the next chapter demonstrates.

Questions for Reflection

1. Distinguish between criticisms of the Soviet Union that are rooted in a theory of human nature and those that are rooted in problems of social organization.

2. How do we view the USSR now? Do the theoretical ideas that the revolution was premature or the idea that a new ruling class was emerging help explain the social and political problems in the Soviet Union?

3. Is the hook-up culture that is common on campuses today similar to the glass of water view of sexuality?

4. In what ways can it be argued that we are now in a post-Fordism economy?

CHAPTER 3

The Polarized 1930s

Learning Objectives

- To provide an overview of the emergence of urban sociology in the Chicago School
- To connect social realism to the critique of the economic and social order of the Depression era
- To contrast the differing responses of Booker Washington, W.E.B. Du Bois, and Marcus Garvey to the colour line in the US
- To understand the emergence of an explicit African-American culture of racial pride and national identity

The apparent collapse of capitalism during the Great Depression of the 1930s polarized public opinion and social thought. Varieties of fascism came to power in many countries and attracted significant support in others. Simultaneously, economic crisis combined with the apparent economic prosperity of the USSR pushed and pulled many working people and intellectuals to the left. Many conservatives acquiesced to some measures of fiscal planning; liberals became New Dealers or reform socialists; and Communist Parties grew in size and influence.

It was easier to criticize the existing institutions than to develop new, more satisfying, and humane practices. That was one of the lessons social theorists had derived from the Enlightenment and the French Revolution. On the left, the determination to create just, equitable, and democratic social institutions continued to challenge social reformists. Capitalism could not, and did not, go on as it was. Stability and a return to prosperity required government intervention and regulation, guided by the new economics of Keynes and the American New Deal.

As part of the cultural shift leftward, artists and intellectuals made the 1930s an era of social protest and critique. The social problems that beset American cities in the early twentieth century became fodder for urban sociology as it developed in the Chicago School. In the African-American community, a new sense of racial pride set the cultural foundation for later social movements. Writers emerged from the despair and ennui that had reflected the great pessimism of the early twentieth century. *The Grapes of Wrath*, the great American novel by John Steinbeck, reflects the 1930s turn to social realism.

Sociology in the United States developed, for a time, independently from the classical, European theorists. A distinctly American social science emerged rooted in the philosophy of pragmatism—the view that philosophical questions can best be answered by examining the actual results that come about when an idea is put into practice. Sociological inquiry had a practical goal that linked sociologists with a long-standing concern in the United States with social reform. Following World War I, in Chicago, sociologists applied the tools of anthropology to the study of the characteristics and social problems of the rapidly expanding urban metropolis in America.

The Chicago School and the Development of Urban Sociology

In 1892, John D. Rockefeller, the industrial baron of Standard Oil, founded the new University of Chicago. The school attracted a wide range of young scholars, including John Dewey (philosophy), Thorstein Veblen (economics), and George Herbert Mead (psychology). The Chicago School was rooted in the philosophy of pragmatism, which held that an idea, social policy, or program could be judged solely on the basis of its practical consequences. In this eclectic atmosphere, departmental walls were porous and Chicago fostered multi-disciplinary research. Nowhere in the US were the problems of society more exposed and raw than in Chicago, a rapidly growing metropolis that had become the second-largest American city. Chicago was the new home of a mosaic of recent arrivals from various European countries and from the American Midwest who carried with them expectations of a better life. Immersed in the many worlds of urban Chicago, sociologists developed two main sociological orientations. One was social psychology, an approach developed by G.H. Mead, which led to symbolic interactionism, which is discussed in Chapter 10. In addition, Chicago sociologists pioneered urban ethnography, the empirical study of communities that entailed a variety of research methods.[1] William

Thomas and Robert Park helped shape the development of urban sociology in the United States.

W.I. Thomas (1863–1947)

William Isaac Thomas was born to a poor farming family in the US south but managed to attend university, where he developed an interest in **ethnography**. Research in this anthropological tradition involved immersing oneself in a culture and studying it from the inside. In 1894, Thomas became a graduate student at the University of Chicago, where he studied the consequences of mass migration from rural to urban, and from Europe to America. The Polish community in Chicago was Thomas's particular corner of the urban laboratory, and the results of his studies appeared in *The Polish Peasant in Europe and America* (1918, co-authored by Florian Znaniecki). In 1918, along with his lover, a 24-year-old married woman whose husband was serving with the American forces in France, Thomas was arrested by the FBI for registering under a false name in a Washington hotel.[2] As a result, Thomas was fired from the University of Chicago for infringing the sexual mores of the university.[3] His liberal attitudes about sexual relations and his lifestyle scandalized the conservative university establishment. Thomas's most important contribution to contemporary sociology is the "**definition of the situation**." To understand the effect brought about by a social phenomenon, it isn't enough to study it objectively. We must understand the meaning that it has for the people involved, their subjective standpoint. Social causes, then, must include both objective and subjective elements, both values and attitudes.[4]

While individuals express their attitudes through their actions, Thomas said that sociology is the theory of social organization. It entails the study of more general attitudes and values that are made explicit through formal rules of behaviour, such as mores, laws, and the ideals of the group. Rules of behaviour and the actions that correspond to them constitute a number of connected systems known as social institutions, such as the family, the tribe, and the community, the sum of which constitute the social organization of a group. Sociology focuses on the "active relations between individual members of the group and between each member and the group as a whole."[5]

Groups at the lower stages of social evolution tend to control most of their members' activities. The strict customs or mores of early tribal or kinship groups, for example, provided a rigorous and particular "set of definition." Tribal group members react identically because they have been socially trained to accept and act according to the traditional rules of behaviour, which impose certain ways of defining and solving the situations of daily life. Modern society is marked by widespread disorganization, according to Thomas, because it values most highly the liberty of the individual to make her or his own definitions. Civilized societies, Thomas and Znaniecki say, are characterized by a much greater variation of responses to social rules and by the search for personal definitions.[6]

In society, people have to act within practical, existing situations that have been formed independently of them. A given situation includes the totality of values and the pre-existing attitudes of all the members of the group. Given any set of conditions and attitudes, Thomas says, any number of actions is hypothetically possible, but only one action ultimately takes place. This action occurs only when these conditions and attitudes "are selected, interpreted, and combined." This conscious process of reflection constitutes "[t]he definition of the situation"; that is, the conscious understanding and interpretation of these existing conditions and attitudes. Either an existing social definition is applied, as in the case of a traditional custom, or the group or individual has to work out a new definition of the situation and act accordingly.[7]

When a husband finds his wife has been unfaithful, Thomas and Znaniecki say, he must define the situation by taking into account all the *values* prevailing within the concrete conditions, which include the institution of marriage; his neighbours, who give him "half-ironical pity"; his economic circumstances; and the fact of the infidelity. The husband has certain *attitudes* to these various values, some of which he has recently adopted and some of which are traditional. In the midst of these often conflicting values and attitudes, he must "define the situation for himself, focusing on some of the conditions, ignoring others, and interpreting them in light of the values he cherishes the most." Finally, among the myriad conditions, values, and reflective schemes that are possible, one attitude prevails and is realized in action, becoming a solution to the situation. The husband may decide to leave his wife, or reconcile with her, or ignore the infidelity, or take some other action. Crucial to understanding the action that is actually taken is the subjective appreciation of the individual's definition of the situation.[8]

For each individual case, the social scientist will have to know all the important conditions, values, and attitudes, and the definition of the situation that each individual develops. The problem of understanding is infinitely compounded when you take into consideration not one but many individuals facing similar situations. For social science, the reasonable approach is to identify the *types* of situations that are typically found in a particular social activity and the typical "schemes and plans of action" (definitions) that arise in these situations. Social science can develop only generalizations, which can then be applied carefully to the specific case.[9] Above all, social reformers who wish to implement change must be aware of the important role played by people's values and their definitions of the situation before social reformers try to implement their reforms. Failing to take subjective conditions into account will result in **unanticipated consequences** and the proposed reform's likely failure.

Robert E. Park (1864–1944)

Robert Park became a colleague of Thomas at Chicago. Park's father was a businessman in Minnesota, but Park chose to attend university rather than follow his father's occupation. In the atmosphere of turn-of-the-century progressivism and under the influence of John Dewey at the University of Minnesota, Park became a social reformer. He studied at Harvard and then in Germany, where Georg Simmel was an important influence. Park received a Ph.D. at the age of 40, although he didn't immediately continue an academic career. Instead, he went to the US south to observe race relations and work as an aide to Booker T. Washington. Race relations gave Park's flair for journalistic muck-raking an endless amount of material. In his most outspoken piece, Park exposed the extreme brutality of the Belgian colonial regime in the Congo.[10]

Park joined the sociology department in Chicago in 1914, at the age of 50.[11] As a sociologist, Park inspired the ethnographic study of Chicago as a great, urban laboratory of social change. Along with Thomas, he was more interested in objective and scientific study of society than social reform.[12] His understanding of the dynamics of race relations prevented Park from seeing society simply as a static structure. He analyzed social relations among groups in terms of conflict and competition, as well as accommodation and **assimilation**. In part, different ethnic and racial groups adjust to each other spatially, carving out territories or ecological niches in different zones of a city.[13] With the publication of *The City* in 1925, a collection of single-authored essays, Park and his two colleagues Edgar W. Burgess from Ontario and Manitoba-born R.D. McKenzie helped to initiate urban sociology in the United States.

A community is a collection of people and institutions "occupying a more or less clearly defined area." Communities can be classified by the number and variety of their economic, political, and cultural institutions.[14] Within a community, the population and institutions "will tend to group themselves in some characteristic pattern," which McKenzie calls the ecological organization of the community. The theory of human ecology, as described by Burgess, claims that the population and institutions of a city typically develop from an urban core according to a consistent pattern of concentric circles.[15] The development of the city follows the rational decisions of different groups of people in a variety of circumstances, creating a general pattern that can be discerned and understood and that reflects the size, distribution, and concentration of the population. The city's social organization is shaped by physical and emotional distances, and by class, ethnic, and racial divisions. Some neighbourhoods create segregated immigrant or racial colonies, within which intimacy and solidarity are preserved.[16]

The city, for Park, Burgess, and McKenzie, was more than merely a physical construction; it was "a state of mind." The organization of urban space, they believed, is matched by an organized set of attitudes and sentiments that shape the population's cultural and moral customs and traditions. Social control in the immigrant ghetto is first rooted in the customs of the home country. In the second generation, however, these rules break down and the conditions of social control are changed. Over time, neighbourhoods in a city become diverse and lack both permanency and intimacy. The "habits, sentiments, and character of the urban population" change. Primary, face-to-face relationships are transformed into indirect, secondary associations of individuals. As local attachments decline, as population grows, and as mobility increases, "the restraints and inhibitions of the primary group" are weakened. Vice and crime grow. Park did not attribute the increase in urban crime in the US at the time to the failure of immigrant groups to be assimilated into American culture.[17] In his view, recent immigrants contribute least to the social problems of the city. Immigrant groups that are able to maintain "their simple village religions and mutual aid organizations" are better able to "withstand the shock of the new environment." The Chinese and Japanese, for example, organized what Park calls "control organizations" in their neighbourhoods to deal with internal disputes among themselves and to negotiate disputes with outside communities. Mexicans, however, who lacked such organizations, "have the highest crime rate of any immigrant group in the United States."[18]

Park applied an old German adage to the modern city: "city air makes men free." Freedom in this context means, first, freedom of the market and the money economy. According to Park, the city produces an ever-expanding proliferation of occupations with particular points of view, and it accentuates what he terms the "mobilization of the individual man." Relationships in the city are more numerous, but also more transitory and unstable, "fortuitous and casual." An individual's status is now determined "by fashion and 'front'— and the art of life is largely reduced to . . . style and manners." Because the city is actually "a mosaic of little worlds," individuals can pass "quickly and easily from one moral milieu to another" and from one world to another. The city introduces "an element of chance and adventure," adding to the stimulus and attractiveness of city life.[19]

For Park, Burgess, and McKenzie, it is understandable that the city attracts so many young men and women, who abandon their rural security. While small communities may merely tolerate their eccentric individuals, cities reward eccentricity. Individuals are free to develop their dispositions for good or ill. In each city emerges what Park calls "moral regions," in which a deviant moral code prevails, a "detached milieu in which vagrant and suppressed

impulses, passions, and ideals emancipate themselves from the dominant moral order." These regions can become "vice districts," which, along with the "eccentric and exceptional people who inhabit them," must be accepted as part of the natural life of a city.[20]

Under modern conditions of life, leisure becomes a restless pursuit of excitement, a "romantic quest [that] finds its most extreme expression in the dance halls and jazz parlors." Wishing to escape reality, urban people hunt "the bluebird of romance . . . with automobiles and flying machines." Park argues that the modern "thirst for adventure" is largely "barren and illusory, because it is uncreative. We are seeking to escape from a dull world instead of turning back upon it to transform it." Rather than art, politics, and religion, leisure is spent improvidently, and in this pursuit, "the greatest wastes in American life occur."[21]

For Park, the hobo is "the most elementary expression of the romantic temperament." But the hobo wanders without a destination: "he has gained his freedom, but he has lost his direction." The restless desire to escape from the dull routines of everyday life becomes merely change for the sake of change. Like drugs, this search for escape becomes a habit that creates a vicious circle. The hobo is too much an individualist, has too much of the temperament of the artist. For society to have permanence and to progress, according to Park, the individuals who compose it must be located consistently in a specific space to maintain mutual communication, "for it is only through communication that the moving equilibrium which we call society can be maintained."[22]

The ethnographic and ecological approach to social research pioneered in Chicago by Park, Burgess, and McKenzie was exported to Canada. A department of sociology was established at McGill University in Montreal in the 1920s. Three of Robert Park's students—Carl Dawson, Everett Hughes, and Helen MacGill—studied immigration and Quebec society in the newly established department.

Helen MacGill (1903–1992) and Everett Hughes (1897–1983)

Helen MacGill was born in Vancouver, British Columbia. Her university-educated mother, who earned four degrees, was a suffragette who corresponded with Jane Addams, a prominent Chicago activist in the women's movement. MacGill studied at the University of British Columbia and at Toronto, where she read political economy and took classes from Harold Innis, whom she recalls reading his lectures in a monotone without glancing at his audience. After attending a lecture given by Robert Park in 1925, MacGill decided to enter the Ph.D. program at the University of Chicago, earning a Masters and later a doctorate degree.

In 1940, Helen MacGill published her dissertation on the American news industry, *News and the Human Interest Story*. MacGill was interested in the widening of topics that were becoming defined as newsworthy for the urban masses. By the latter nineteenth century, the *New York Sun* was covering everyday crime stories drawn from the magistrate's courthouse, helping to sell papers and, unintentionally, making trials "public circuses and criminals, public characters." At the other end of the social scale, newspapers provided society news, detailing the lives of the rich and famous for the entertainment of the poor. Local news, particularly sensational and "human-interest" stories, sold papers.[23] Revealing the "human side" of political stories made them more accessible. Today, for example, organizations solicit donations on television to provide health care and education in poor, Third World countries, and use the personal stories of impoverished children to gain sympathy and charity. MacGill pointed out that once human interest stories had attracted a mass audience to the daily newspapers, these

newspapers were given the opportunity to focus on other purposes, such as advertising as well as propaganda. Business news items were presented in the form of success stories.[24] Ordinary people could enter imaginatively into the world of the powerful and the curiously deviant. Politicians, such as President Roosevelt, were personalized and made "folksy" as part of their political appeal. The newspaper magnate Randolph Hearst used stories of personal suffering as well as sensationalist and ultra-patriotic jingoism—a style known as yellow journalism—to sway public opinion in 1898 in favour of an American war against Spain.[25]

While a student in Chicago, MacGill married Everett Hughes, a fellow graduate student. Everett Hughes was born in Ohio, the son of a free-thinking Methodist minister. He began graduate studies at the University of Chicago in his mid-thirties, joining the Department of Anthropology and Sociology then dominated by Robert Park, who became Hughes's supervisor. Hughes's approach to sociology reflects the ethnographic and interactionist approaches to field work developed in the Chicago School, "telling it how it is, 'fully, freely, and bitterly.'"[26]

Newly out of graduate school, Everett Hughes joined the sociology department at McGill University in Montreal, accompanied by his wife. With Canadian sociologist Carl Dawson, Everett Hughes embarked on the French Canada project, which investigated English–French relations in Quebec. Everett and Helen Hughes conducted field work together in a small industrial city in Quebec, the results of which were published in *French Canada in Transition*. Conventionally, the work was printed under Everett Hughes's name. He noted in the Foreword to the book that "My wife, Helen MacGill Hughes, and I jointly did the field work for the study."[27] The two ethnographers were particularly interested in the tension and conflict between the traditional, agrarian French and the industrializing, modern English.[28]

After a decade in Montreal, Everett Hughes returned to the United States in 1938 as a faculty member at the University of Chicago. Helen Hughes was excluded from employment at the patriarchal University of Chicago, which forbade the employment of spouses—meaning wives. The 1930s was a difficult time for women academics. In 1938, Helen MacGill Hughes was employed part-time ("the only kind [of work] I have ever had") as an editor of the *American Journal of Sociology*.[29] Once back in the United States, she established a publishing career in media studies, working in the margins of the academic world. Everett Hughes developed the sociology of work and occupations and helped define the sociology of health and health care. His study of physicians drew attention to the license with which the medical profession defines for everyone the nature of health and illness.[30] Hughes's work on social and economic transition in Quebec provides a picture of the region on the verge of socio-cultural change.

Quebec in Transition

Immediately upon my arrival, last fall,
I started to explore Montreal. . . . What did
I discover except perfect imitations of the
most authentic American emporia?[31]

—Lionel Groulx, *The Iron Wedge*, 1922

When Everett Hughes and Helen MacGill moved to Montreal in the 1930s, the nationalist cause was still vibrant. They found urban Montreal to be a cosmopolitan city and said that, outside the city, Quebec was the "most stable and archaic rural society" in North America. The ties of ethnic, language, and religious homogeneity ran deeply in the villages and small towns. Indeed, social regulation was closely managed by the Roman Catholic Church.

Quebec faced the formidable challenge of rapid cultural change. Much of the new urbanized culture coming into Quebec was American,

including films, confession-type magazines, and advertisements for brands that soon became familiar fare. In Montreal, the lower-middle classes were more risqué in their entertainment. They went out to night clubs, sang Parisian café songs, would "dance in close formation," and make ribald jokes. The clergy and conservatives condemned this behaviour as vulgar and obscene. Priests used their moral influence to prevent dance halls and drinking establishments in small-town, rural Quebec.[32] As novelist Claude-Henri Grigon put it, the mission of Quebec's clergy was "to prevent the torch of Christ from being extinguished by the wind of materialism."[33] No wall separated religious from secular authority. Like the small American town portrayed in *Footloose* (1984), public dancing was closely regulated.

A nationalist movement had developed in Quebec in the early twentieth century, punctuated by the conscription crisis in World War I. The principal issue was whether French Canadians should be compelled to fight in a war that implied loyalty to Britain. Lionel Groulx was one of the most articulate leaders of this national movement, which he championed in politics, journalism, and literature. The patriotic, "vigorous atavistic instincts" of French Canadians, he complained, had been lulled to sleep by the false promises of Canadian Confederation.[34] His novel *The Iron Wedge* (1916), more literally translated as "The Call of the Race," explores the pitfalls of inter-marriage between English and French.

The protagonist of *The Iron Wedge*, Jules de Lantagnac, had studied and practised law in Montreal, becoming thoroughly English in his sentiments. He marries a young English woman, Maud Hill, and together they raise four children. By his early 40s, however, Lantagnac seeks a higher calling. He immerses himself in his native language and the history of Quebec, and these studies drive an iron wedge between the two warring cultures within him. Liberated from Anglo-Saxon ideology, he resolves to return to his roots and bring his children up in the traditional Catholicism and culture of the French race, taking them away from their English upbringing and their mother. Their mixed marriage had been his original mistake. They had constructed "a homestead of ill-matched, fragile materials." Lantagnac resocializes his children into the "Grace . . . true culture, poise [and] spiritual refinement" of his Franco-Latin heritage.[35]

As the wedge between English and French drives the family apart, the race instinct also reawakens in Maud. Driven by her race, blood, and "imperialist sentiments," Maud leaves Lantagnac when he unequivocally accepts the leadership of the French nationalist cause in Canada. She takes two of the four children with her. A third, Victoria, chooses Catholicism and plans to enter a convent. The eldest son converts to the French nationalist cause "wholly and enthusiastically." He renounces his Anglo-Saxon first name and his English fiancée.[36]

In *Quebec in Transition*, Hughes explores the social and economic factors shaping this cultural divide. The farms in Quebec were relatively prosperous and family-owned—rural Quebec was not a poor backwater, economically or culturally.[37] Landownership was kept intact by limiting inheritance to a single son. Hughes likens rural Quebec to a strong dam with a spillway through which the excess population runs off to the industrializing towns and cities. Social stability in Quebec was challenged by capitalist modernization, however, which had begun to transform the region, drawing people from rural parishes into expanding urban areas, such as Montreal. Hughes's ethnographic research highlighted the social problems brought about by the spread of a new way of life dominated by English-speaking people.[38]

The new, large industries in Quebec's towns and cities were owned by outside corporations. They brought into rural Quebec an influx of English-speaking migrants, "an alien minority," who occupied dominant economic positions. They worked as managers, engineers, and skilled technicians. French-Canadians found labouring jobs in the new industries, eventually becoming differentiated occupationally.[39] National sentiments were inflamed in Quebec in the 1930s by the rise of the Union Nationale party, which won the 1936 provincial election on the strength of a coalition between nationalist and conservative politics. The Union was supported by conservative businessmen in Quebec and by alienated, young French-Canadian men who claimed that the provincial government had sold out Quebec to English corporations. Women in Quebec did not win the right to vote in provincial elections until 1940.[40]

Hughes argues that "French Canadians are being swept into the very life which their intellectual and spiritual leaders decry." Quebec had been drawn by "culturally alien agents" relatively late into twentieth-century capitalist industrialization. The great divide was between the persistence of a spiritual and cultural heritage, and the world of bread-and-butter employment, which was dominated by the English minority. Quebec experienced a clash between two cultural worlds,[41] the *Two Solitudes* that author Hugh MacLennan wrote about in his 1945 novel of that name.[42]

What Everett Hughes and Helen MacGill captured in their ethnography was a subjugated nation on the verge of a cultural revolution. As in MacLennan's novel, the solitudes examined in the ethnography are more than French/English; they are also traditional/industrial, Catholic/Protestant, male/female, and urban/rural. These divisions persisted throughout the twentieth century and into the new millennium. Quebec nationalism spawned a short-lived extremist group in the 1960s and a more deeply rooted political movement that came within a hair's breadth in 1995 of consummating the dream of a sovereign Quebec.

Literature and Art: Social Realism

*There was a big high wall there that tried
to stop me.
The sign was painted, said "Private Property."
But on the backside, it didn't say nothing.
This land was made for you and me.*

—Woody Guthrie, "This Land Is Your Land," 1940

Much of the literature of the 1920s had emphasized disillusionment or withdrawal into subjectivity. This was as true for T.S. Eliot (*The Wasteland*) as it was for the experimental novelists such as D.H. Lawrence, Virginia Woolf, and James Joyce, who undertook a circuitous journey into themselves. In the economic crisis of the 1930s, romantic subjectivism acquired the odour of flagrant indulgence while its second cousin surrealism proved to be more adept at exposing illusions than it did at supplanting them. The times, it seemed, demanded a more socially conscious and realistic literature and art. In the face of what had once seemed inconceivable—the apparent breakdown of capitalism and the rise of fascism—many artists conceived their role to be the conscience of the nation, undermining the bland assumptions about democracy, prosperity, and "the land of the free" with a heavy dose of realism. Woody Guthrie wrote "This Land Is Your Land" in 1940 as a radical antidote to Irving Berlin's patriotic song "God Bless America," released in 1938. When Guthrie's song was released as a single in 1951, the producer deleted the radical lyrics condemning "private property." The remaining lyrics still emphasize the democratic notion that America belongs equally to all Americans.[43]

In the 1930s, writers and artists turned to social realism to critique the failing capitalist system. Novelist Doris Lessing suggests that a similar turn to **social realism** occurred in the 1950s when the idea resurfaced in literature "that little novels or plays about the emotions don't reflect reality. The reality . . . is economics, or machine guns mowing people down who object to the new order." The novel, Lessing writes, had a journalistic function: "we read novels for information . . . to find out what is going on."[44]

African-American poet Alice Dunbar-Nelson in *The Proletariat Speaks* (*The Crisis*, November 1929), contrasts the aspirations of ordinary people for a life of harmony and beauty with the harsh realities of their daily lives: "I love beautiful things," she writes, "Great trees . . . exotic blooms . . . spacious rooms . . . and sweet cool spray." But the reality of everyday life is nothing like these dreams:

And so I work
In a dusty office, whose grimed windows
Look out on an alley of unbelievable
    squalor. . . .
And so I eat
In the food-laden air of a greasy kitchen
At an oil-clothed table:
Plate piled high with food that turns my
    head away. . . .
Or in a smoky cafeteria, balancing a
    slippery tray
To a table crowded with elbows
Which lately the busboy wiped with a
    grimy rag. . . .
And so I sleep
In a hot hall-room whose half-opened
    window,
. . . . Admits no air, only insects, and hot
    choking gasps
That make me writhe.[45]

In many ways, the art of photography was best equipped to reveal the human faces and tragedies behind the headlines exposing joblessness and homelessness. Images of loss and despair flooded the popular magazines: of robust men with placards yoked around their necks begging for work; of the exposed foundations of prairie houses blown free of soil; of the anguished faces of mothers with nothing to feed their children. Probably the most recognizable image is Dorothea Lange's haunting 1936 photograph of a 32-year-old migrant worker and mother of seven, which became known as "Migrant Mother." The subject was Florence Thompson, a woman from the Cherokee First Nation, originally from Oklahoma.[46] While artists working in more traditional mediums also painted images of hunger, alienation, and defiance, photography appeared to reveal the stark truth.

Socially Conscious Art and Politics

The dominant American image of the "hungry thirties" was the displaced farmer, driven off the land by a combination of a devastating drought that turned fertile farmland to a "dust bowl" and by rapacious bankers eager to foreclose mortgaged land and evict desperate families. By word of mouth, would-be migrants heard "how great it would be when they got to California," where "you could live pickin' fruit off'a the trees while you was walking down the street," as novelist Walter Mosley depicted the myth.[47] The plight of the migrant families who attempted to realize this myth is movingly told by John Steinbeck in *The Grapes of Wrath* (1939), a novel that was made into a powerful motion picture in 1940. For the dispossessed, California seemed to be the Promised Land.

The Grapes of Wrath is a searing indictment of the collapse of the small farm and the plight of migrant labourers. The Joads are impoverished, Depression-era farmers forced off their dust bowl farm in Oklahoma and making the trek along Route 66 to find work and prosperity in California. The fruit ripens in California all at once, Steinbeck writes, and 3000 people find work—for two weeks. But 3000 other migrant labourers are still begging on the road and they'll work for less pay. So wages are low and work is scarce, and when the last peach is picked, the Sheriff's deputies break up the migrants' camps and force them out of town. If the workers organize or resist, they are put in jail or added to the list of agitators and "reds" who are blacklisted. The frightened

and angry owners were ready "ta kill ever'body in the worl'" to hang on to what they had.[48]

The poor have nowhere to turn other than to each other. Camped together at night, the migrants spontaneously create an informal world of rules and ethics, constructed by their hearts and brains.[49] Joad draws together the lessons he has learned. When you're dead, there is no ice cream on golden plates. Right now, one man owns a million acres while a hundred thousand farmers starve. He commits himself to a life of social activism: "Whenever there's a fight so hungry people can eat, I'll be there. Where ever there's a cop beatin' up a guy, I'll be there. . . . An' when our folks eat the stuff they raise an' live in the houses they build—why, I'll be there."[50]

Many socially committed artists and writers in the 1930s became more explicitly socialist in their ideologies. For these more radical intellectuals, art was created to speak to the working class about the evils of capitalism and the possibilities of change. Change did not, however, necessarily imply revolution. Popular movements of protest can take many forms, including conservative and socialist versions of populism (see Box 3.1). As the world seemed to be polarized in the 1930s between the Soviet model of state socialism and fascist dictatorships of the right, in Canada, social democratic reform represented an alternative social theory.

Canada was a political creation undertaken in 1867 by elite, eastern interests. Under the National Policy, the Canadian government raised taxes on imports (tariffs) to keep out manufactured goods from the United States and Britain, creating a national market for industries in Ontario and Quebec. The Prairie Provinces were opened to settlement by European immigrants, creating an agricultural hinterland that supplied wheat and beef to the metropolitan, eastern cities, and serving as a market for high-priced Canadian industrial goods. Monetary and transportation policies favoured eastern industries, and western farmers found themselves in debt to large, eastern banks. The western provinces

⚘ BOX 3.1 · THEORY IN CONTEXT ⚘

Left and Right Agrarian Populism

In the 1930s, two distinct movements arose in western Canada: right-wing populism in Alberta and socialist-populism in neighbouring Saskatchewan. Middle-class groups, such as farmers, merchants, and professionals, could support either left-leaning or right-wing parties. According to Brym, the varied political responses can be explained by differences in social conditions and class-based coalition politics in the two provinces.[51]

In the years before the Depression, the United Farmers of Alberta (UFA), a left-of-centre party, dominated provincial politics. The UFA excluded merchants and other middle-class townspeople from membership. After 1929, however, the effects of the Depression were felt equally by both urban and rural classes. A new populist and Christian coalition developed that united farmers with urban merchants, professionals, and Protestant preachers.[52] They adopted the social credit ideas that had been formulated by C.H. Douglas, a British engineer.

Douglas calculated that the total value of goods produced in the British economy was less than the total paid out in wages, salaries, and dividends; in short, there was not enough money in circulation to buy all the goods being produced. He proposed that the government distribute a fund of money—social credit—to consumers to supplement their wages. Ordinarily, the influx of additional money into consumers' pockets causes a sharp price rise, eliminating any benefit to consumers. Douglas said that the distribution of social credit would have to be matched by a government policy of fixing prices to prevent inflation. These core economic principles were adopted by the Social Credit Party of Alberta, founded in 1935 by William Aberhart, a Baptist minister. Aberhart used his popular radio program to preach to Albertans about social credit principles and conservative, Christian values. Aberhart's Social Credit Party won the election of 1935, at the height of the Depression, and remained in power until 1971. The party, however, was unable to deliver its promised economic reforms.

became an internal colony in Canada, creating feelings of alienation among westerners, which persists in contemporary Canada. Dissatisfaction also increased the potential for populist protest movements (see Box 3.1).[53]

Depression and Keynesianism

Just how fundamentally different was modern, corporate capitalism from the model of competitive capitalism analyzed by Adam Smith and critiqued by Marx? One argument advanced by economist James Burnham in *The Managerial Revolution* (1941) was that modern forms were different in principle. In competitive capitalism, owners actively managed their enterprises and asserted their will over the industrial process. In corporate capitalism, on the other hand, ownership had become diffused among multiple shareholders. Firms and economic decisions were made by hired managers

Farmers in the adjacent province of Saskatchewan had a history of collective action through marketing and consumer co-operatives. The province was hit hard by the Great Depression, but instead of forming an alliance with merchants and business owners, farmers in Saskatchewan joined with working people and labour unions in the towns. A political coalition of farmers, workers, and urban socialists led to the founding in 1932 of a political movement known as the Co-operative Commonwealth Federation (CCF). The leader of the party, J.S. Woodsworth, was a Methodist minister.[54] The following year, the party worked out a political platform called the Regina Manifesto. The Manifesto declared the following:

WE AIM TO REPLACE the present capitalist system, with its inherent injustice and inhumanity, by a social order from which the domination and exploitation of one class by another will be eliminated. . . . The present order is marked by glaring inequalities. . . . [I]n an age of plenty it condemns the great mass of the people to poverty and insecurity. Power has become more and more concentrated into the hands of a small irresponsible minority of financiers. . . . We believe that these evils can be removed only in a planned and socialized economy in which our natural resources and principal means of production and distribution are owned, controlled and operated by the people.[55]

In terms of practical politics, the manifesto called for a national economic planning commission, government control of the financial industry, and the public ownership of utilities. The CCF laid down the principles of the welfare state, including pension rights, a minimum wage, and health and unemployment insurance. The manifesto promised a socialized, publicly organized medical and health service extended to all people. In 1944, the CCF won the provincial election in Saskatchewan under the leadership of Tommy Douglas, a Baptist minister. Under Douglas, the CCF implemented a provincial Medicare scheme in Saskatchewan, the first step toward a state-operated Canadian health-care system. National health care was legislated in the 1960s by the federal Liberal government. The CCF dropped its socialist rhetoric in the 1950s and morphed into the New Democratic Party in 1961.[56]

who made rational economic decisions that were, in principle, different from those made by individuals who identified their own fortunes with the enterprise. The fictional character von Gerlach in Jean-Paul Sartre's play *The Condemned of Altona* (1959) wanted to pass along his wealth and position to his son, but he realized that the old-style, single, dictatorial master was a historical relic: "I wanted you to run the firm after me," von Gerlach told his son. "But it does the running. It chooses its own men. . . . I own it, but I no longer run it. . . . It trains and recruits its own managers."[57]

Over the long term, as technology replaced workers and as more goods were produced with lower levels of productive employment, the potential market of buyers tended to shrink. In short, capitalism tended toward the overproduction of goods—the economy was capable of producing goods to a value that was greater than the economy's capacity to consume. If the wages and salaries in the economy were insufficient to purchase the goods the economy produced, there was a built-in tendency toward crisis. Once an industry produced a quantity of goods that was excessive, to the point where large, unsold inventories accumulated in warehouses, it was necessary to close down production, lay off workers, and concentrate on reducing the inventory.

After the apparent economic boom of the 1920s, the United States' economy teetered on the brink of collapse. Heavy speculation on the stock market pushed share values beyond the economy's capacity to sustain, and banks were over-extended in poorly secured loans. Millionaires held paper fortunes that had no real foundation. In 1929, the stock market collapsed catastrophically; many investors were wiped out overnight. Caught up in the plummeting market, banks recalled their loans. Small businesses, homeowners, and over-extended farmers began to spiral into bankruptcy, consumer spending contracted, unemployment grew, and the American economy plunged into the Great Depression. Moreover, the centrality of the American economy spread the effects of the Depression worldwide. To maintain somewhat profitable agricultural prices in the United States, hogs were slaughtered and buried and some grain crops were ploughed under rather than being harvested, while the unemployed and homeless were hungry and malnourished. One of the characters in Joseph Heller's absurdist novel *Catch-22* was a farmer who got rich in the 1930s from government subsidies, which he was paid for *not* growing alfalfa to prevent an oversupply.[58] As novelist John Steinbeck noted, there was something essentially wrong with a system in which excessive wealth existed alongside abject poverty, disease, and despair.

The failure of capitalism in its unregulated, competitive phase was suddenly apparent. Depressions are painful mechanisms of adjustment in capitalism. Smaller, less competitive firms are the first to go under as the economy is further centralized in fewer, larger corporate hands. The depth of

the Great Depression and the radicalization it precipitated called for drastic counter-measures. The system required state-led regulation of the economy in the interests of returning private capital to productivity. The solution to periodic depressions was suggested in the work of John Maynard Keynes (1883–1946), an economist who had participated in the Bloomsbury group with such British intellectuals as novelist Virginia Woolf.

Over time, through careful manipulation of such key economic indices as interest rates, money supply, and government spending, Keynes argued that capitalism could manage its growth. Interest rates could be lowered in bad times, allowing businesses and consumers to borrow and not be faced with devastating repayments. Government could effectively borrow money and expand the money supply, stimulating the economy through construction projects and other forms of subsidies. Giving unemployed workers social assistance and putting poor families on social welfare would put purchasing power in the hands of families that otherwise would be destitute. These initiatives and many more were part of the New Deal implemented by President Franklin Roosevelt in the United States. Arguably, **Keynesianism** was insufficient to bring the United States out of depression; the new foundation of American prosperity was military spending. World War II ended the Depression and started the United States on a quarter century of unprecedented economic expansion.

Keynesianism was behind the rise of the welfare state in the post-World War II decades, which managed the economy and simultaneously undermined any movements for radical change. One consequence of large-scale government economic intervention was a deepening public debt, but economists argued that, once the economy was returned to normal growth, ordinary taxation would grow, allowing the state to pay back its temporary borrowings. In a few decades, the problem of government debt, which was fuelled by massive military expenditures, would begin to collapse Keynes's liberal solution to capitalist crises.

Well before the crisis of the welfare state of the 1970s, social movements arising from social groups excluded from the economic and political mainstream began to challenge the status quo. Civil rights rallied African Americans to action in the 1950s, but the movement was built on cultural changes in the black communities that had developed decades before.

African-American Social Thought

The new Negro has no fear.

—Universal Negro Improvement Association (UNIA) slogan

Progressive ideas about race had to contend with a tradition of racist theorizing in American anthropology. In the nineteenth century, biologists had debated the question of human races. Were all humans one species, or did each race actually evolve separately in different regions of the world? Observers of racial differences among humanity debated whether the different races they recognized derived from one single human ancestor (monogenism) or whether each race evolved from distinct ancestors (**polygenism**). If polygenism was accepted, different races were actually different subspecies, a view that supported the belief that some "races" were genetically inferior to others. By the latter half of the nineteenth century, many biologists and anthropologists had adopted the theory of polygenism. This idea was behind the 1882 US Chinese Exclusions Act, which tried to limit the influx of assumed inferior races into the United States, and behind other restrictive immigration laws as well.[59] Despite this racist background, however, Franz Boas (1858–1942), a dominant early figure in American anthropology, fundamentally rejected the argument that there were any significant natural differences among

the human groups labelled "races" (see Box 3.2). Whatever differences there were, were cultural not biological. Nevertheless, oppressed people typically also feel culturally inferior. Developing race pride was a driving force in the African-American community in the 1920s and 1930s.

Although Boas and his students had undermined any scientific claim that appeared to buttress racism and the policy of eugenics, the "colour bar" continued to be one of the defining characteristics of society in the United States. Africans, unlike other migrants to the Americas, had been brought to the New World in chains, as enslaved labour. In the United States, African Americans experienced a caste status superimposed on the complex class structure of a new, multi-ethnic immigrant nation. The absolute oppression of Africans in America's past is the root of all subsequent race relations.

The emancipation of African Americans did little at first to change their economic position or social status. By the end of the nineteenth century, the colour line separated the world of legal segregation and caste in the South from more subtle forms of racism and exclusion in the North. Black educator Booker T. Washington's philosophy was that African Americans should learn the virtues of hard work and thrift, gain the advantages of education, and strive for economic independence. Agitation for social and political rights immediately was counter-productive, Washington said, because it causes whites to resist and holds back the movement toward equality. He was not about to challenge the **colour line**. For novelist Sinclair Lewis, the "Booker Washington school of Negroes" counselled "patience in the new subjection of the Negroes to slavery." Young black rebels should "seek improvement within their own souls."[60]

Washington's call for a withdrawal from politics appealed to many blacks and to even more whites. White businessmen responded to Washington's leadership by donating money to his Institute and by bending the colour bar on his personal

⚜ BOX 3.2 · THEORY IN CONTEXT ⚜

Franz Boas and Racism

Boas was a German scientist who, on a mapping trip to the Arctic, found the indigenous people more interesting than the landscape. He conducted field research among Aboriginals, including a group of Inuit in northwest North America, learning their language and keeping careful notes about their culture. He expanded his research by studying other Aboriginal peoples, emphasizing the importance of detailed ethnographic observation. Boas immigrated to New York, where his Jewish background was generally more accepted than it had been in Germany, and, in 1899, became professor at Columbia University. He introduced the concept **cultural relativism** to anthropology, which meant studying a culture in its own terms instead of ethnocentrically—interpreting it in terms of one's own cultural biases. Boas also rejected the idea that societies evolved from lower to higher stages, arguing that the assumption that less technologically developed cultures were inferior to modern Western ones reflected an ethnocentric cultural bias.[61]

Boas argued in favour of the determining effects that culture and environment have on society and the views of individuals within it. Distinct cultural traditions play a significant role in shaping the great diversity of cultures that exist, emphasizing cultural distinctions rather than common patterns.[62] Each culture perceives the world through its own distinct lens. By emphasizing the role of culture, Boas rejected the "biology is destiny" argument, which was especially important in refuting racist claims that inequalities among groups reflected innate superiority and inferiority. His studies of two generations of immigrants to the United States demonstrated empirically that not just a person's character or actions but even his or her physical characteristics are influenced by environmental and cultural factors. In 1908, Boas concluded that the anthropological evidence refuted the belief that Africans were racially inferior to whites and unfit to undertake any significant role in modern societies. Logically, Boas criticized the US Immigrant Exclusion Act on the grounds that it was unscientific; in his view, it was ethnocentric, "Nordic nonsense."[63] He campaigned vigorously against the US policy of eugenics, the sterilization or elimination of groups assumed to be inferior. In 1940, Boas's student Ruth Benedict called these unscientific policies and prejudices "racism."[64]

behalf. He travelled in private railway cars and stayed in expensive hotels, advised the president on African-American issues, and wielded power in the black community. He became a model for the aspiring black middle class.[65]

However, not all prominent African Americans agreed that political and social aims should be subordinated to patient and long-term economic development. In the view of William Du Bois (1868–1963), Washington had struck a self-serving compromise with the Establishment, which was rewarding him for counselling African Americans to tone down their demands for civil rights. Over time, Du Bois became increasingly radical in his writing and in his political activities. His book *The Souls of Black Folk* (1903) was his analysis of the American colour line and of the failures of Washington's strategy of legal reform.

Du Bois's focus was not exclusively on race and racial pride, but on both sides of the hyphen of being an African-American person. The soul of black folks, he said, was split, causing a "two-ness" in their consciousness. African Americans experienced a dual identity: they were African, but they were also a people who identified with the values and goals of the United States. As novelist Richard Wright argues, African Americans were pulled in different directions. They were close to and part of the civilization that was seeking to exclude them; and their consciousness was shaped by the culture that oppressed them. They were Americans who wanted to share the goals, incentives, and rewards that America offered others.[66] In Du Bois's view, under the existing conditions in the US, assimilation could bring only sameness, the loss of the unique elements that black Americans brought to the national culture.[67] America is woven from a variety of strands, Du Bois said. The two "world races" must not just co-exist; if each race could contribute its best talents and abilities, America would be transformed and become stronger and better.

Marcus Garvey (1887–1940)

The world moves in a circle like a roulette wheel. In the beginning, black is on top, in the middle epochs, white holds the odds, but soon Ethiopia shall stretch forth her noble wings! Then place your money on the black!

— Ralph Ellison, *Invisible Man*, 1952

A new appreciation for black culture in Africa and America was an important element of the rise of black consciousness in the United States after World War I. In literature, the **Harlem Renaissance** extolled the energy and creativeness of American black culture, and Marcus Garvey fostered black pride and the importance of African identity.

Born in Jamaica and descended from the rebellious Maroons,[68] Marcus Garvey founded the Universal Negro Improvement Association (UNIA) in 1914. In Garvey's words, the UNIA "represents the hopes and aspirations of the awakened Negro. Our desire is for a place in the world, not to disturb the tranquillity of other men, but to lay down our burden . . . by the banks of the Niger and sing our songs and chant our hymns to the God of Ethiopia." Garvey told Jamaican blacks to look to Ethiopia, where a black king would be crowned and would become their redeemer.

In 1916, Garvey moved to the United States, settling in Harlem, New York, where he opened a chapter of the Universal Negro Improvement Association and began publishing the *Negro World*, a weekly newspaper. He quickly turned the UNIA into a mass organization, complete with religious revival-style meetings; ornate uniforms; and a distinctive red, black, and green flag. In the midst of the revival of racist violence in the United States after World War I, achieving integration and equality appeared less and less possible. Garvey argued, instead, in favour of black pride, black enterprise, a new Negro Nation, and a return to Africa. Garvey's racial purity message—essentially that black is beautiful—stimulated a new consciousness among African Americans. His message about black nationalism was his answer to the dilemma of black consciousness posed by Du Bois's portrayal of the "two-ness" of the black "soul." Garvey was seen as a messiah by many black Americans, who, like Richard Wright's character Bigger Thomas in *Native Son*, "felt that someday there would be a black man who would whip the black people into a tight band and together they would act and end fear and shame."[69]

For Garvey, racial pride among blacks was linked to their common heritage in Africa, and he repudiated the European-centred view of Africa as the "Dark Continent." The theme of returning to their African roots recalled the ancient longing of American slaves, which had been expressed in their Christianity. During their enslavement in the United States, blacks had equated their plight with the Israelites, who had been enslaved in Egypt before the prophet Moses led them to Israel and freedom. For Garvey and many blacks, the ancient kingdom of Ethiopia symbolized the black homeland in Africa. Ethiopia was the only part of Africa that, up to that time, had not been colonized by Europeans. Decades earlier, in 1895, Ethiopia had decisively defeated an Italian invasion, after which Italy had been forced to concede that Ethiopia was an independent kingdom. This resistance solidified the identification of many American blacks with Ethiopia, a link that was strengthened in 1931 when Ras Tafari Makonnen was crowned Emperor of Ethiopia, adopting the name Haile Selassie. For some African Americans, the black emperor in the ancestral homeland became the "redeemer" Garvey had prophesized.

For Garvey, the image of God as "white" reflected the racism of the dominant society. Blacks, he believed, should imagine god in their own image: "since the white people have seen their God through white spectacles, we have only now started out to see our God through our own spectacles."[70] The UNIA would worship "through the spectacles of Ethiopia." The "black is beautiful" message had an unfortunate consequence, however, in that it implied that darker skinned blacks were more racially pure than lighter-skinned African Americans. This led to charges that Garvey's UNIA was racist. Black racism would linger as a shadow behind black nationalism in the United States, dogging later nationalists such as Malcolm X.

The UNIA policy on racial purity was also directly linked with the organization's gender politics. Women were valued, not as equals, but predominantly as mothers, as the producers of new generations of black children. Men dominated the UNIA, and women's organizations in the association were secondary and under male control. As a result, in the 1930s substantial numbers of women abandoned the UNIA in favour of a new religious movement founded by George Baker, who called himself Father Divine. While the Diviners' creed was inter-racial (integrating whites and blacks), they segregated the sexes in model communes and demanded celibacy. These principles contradicted Garvey's beliefs in black nationalism and amounted to racial suicide.

For Africans in the New World, Marcus Garvey became the prophet of Africa. Like his Maroon ancestors, many of whom had gone back to Africa in the early 1800s, Garvey preached repatriation to Africa, despite the fact that virtually all African Americans had a lengthy ancestry in the New World. In addition, Garvey believed in the importance of black economic independence. He organized many African-American-owned companies, most significantly the Black Star Line, a steamship company having as one of its aims to assist the return of blacks to Africa. Garvey's business ventures, however, typically failed through lack of capital.

Politically, Garvey was much more successful. His Universal Negro Improvement Association had four million members at its highest point in the 1920s. He was a vigorous, charismatic orator. Even though the explicit aim of returning to Africa had little appeal for most blacks in the United States, Garvey's message of black pride, consciousness of race, and black nationalism was a threat to the status quo. Ironically, the UNIA scheme of repatriation was endorsed by white racists who wished to expel African Americans rather than simply induce their emigration. The views of white racists are depicted in the 1962 movie *Pressure Point*, in which a black psychiatrist, played by Sidney Poitier, tries to understand the racist ideology of a Neo-Nazi patient, played by Bobby Darin:

PATIENT: "This isn't the place for you. Why, you people are trying to be white and respectable. You want to be doctors, psychiatrists. Why don't you wise up?"

PSYCHIATRIST: "How would I do that?"

PATIENT: "Go back to Africa."[71]

More threatening than a return to the African homeland was the image of African Americans as a self-conscious nation within white-dominated America. Shorn of the chimera of overseas migration, the theory of black pride and economic independence would inspire a new generation of black nationalists who would seek to carve a black homeland on United States soil. Rebellion within the American union was the real threat behind the UNIA, and it made Garvey a politically dangerous leader. He was a Jamaican and, therefore, in the eyes of the US government, an undesirable alien. He was eventually convicted of mail fraud and deported back to Jamaica.[72]

The Harlem Renaissance

Tis a noble gift to be brown, all brown.[73]

—Effie Lee Newsome, "The Bronze Legacy (To a Brown Boy)," 1922

When Marcus Garvey brought his UNIA to the United States, he settled in Harlem, not only the largest black urban community in the country, but the centre of a vibrant celebration of African-American culture. Music was at the centre of this culture—not only the blues, a musical form that had originated in the cotton fields in the south, but particularly jazz, which liberated the musician from the constraints of the written score, emphasized spontaneity, and inspired uninhibited and explicit dances. African-American music reflected the bipolar nature of the black experience:

despair and resignation in the blues; exuberance and celebration in jazz. Every Sunday in church, the cultural keystone of much African-American experience, both of these traditions were united in the evangelical message and the gospel choir.

The revolution in popular music brought about by the invention of jazz had widespread cultural significance. The early jazz musicians created an innovative and improvised musical style. The specific history of jazz is complicated and multi-layered; emerging at the turn of the century, jazz had its roots in African rhythms. Although initially the centre of jazz was New Orleans, the style spread to the north, to Memphis and Chicago, and to Harlem in the east. While the blues remained essentially African-American until the 1960s, jazz was adopted by the white middle class and nouveaux riches, as the "Jazz Age" contributed to the cultural roar of the twenties. In 1917, jazz musicians performed in Europe, creating a sensation. In the 1920s, Louis Armstrong became the most famous and emulated jazz musician, the virtuoso of the long solo.

Harlem emerged after World War I as the largest concentration of African Americans in the northern states. In this vibrant centre, black artists created a new cultural movement and cultivated a new image, the **New Negro**. Like the "New Woman" of the 1890s, African Americans demanded full participation in American life and expressed a new pride in their heritage.

The heart of the Harlem Renaissance was a new, black literature. In 1913, W.E.B. Du Bois had written, "The time has not yet come for the great development of American Negro literature." Literature required leisure and poise, neither of which was permitted by African Americans faced with economic stress and bitter racial persecution.[74] But by the mid-1920s, Du Bois sensed new stirrings within the black community, "the beginning of a new appreciation of joy, of a new desire to create, of a new will to be" that "dimly mourns the past and dreams a splendid future." The new generation of black youth, led by writers such as Countee Cullen and Langston Hughes, "bears this mighty prophecy on its breast, with a new realization of itself, with new determination for all mankind."[75]

Writing in *The Messenger* in 1920, Randolph and Owen claimed that the "New Negro" was one manifestation, in the United States, of the postwar, worldwide liberal and radical revolt.[76] In "The New Negro—What Is He?" (1920) Randolph and Owen argued that in all respects the New Negro was unlike the old. In politics, rather than seeking spoils and patronage, the New Negro demanded equality and universal suffrage. In economics, "he demands the full product of his toil." Socially, "he stands for absolute and unequivocal '*social equality*'" including the right of intermarriage. The most important distinction between old and new, according to Randolph and Owen, was in their methods. The New Negro was a worker who gave support to a political party of the working class. The New Negro created consumer co-operatives, joined the trade union movement, and organized black unions in place of reactionary, white unions. In addition to the obvious importance of education, the New Negro claimed the right to "physical action in self-defense." While the African Americans of old taught the doctrine of non-resistance, the New Negro believed that fighting back was the only justifiable response in the face of violent racism. Old leadership should be abandoned, Randolph and Owen argued, and new leaders should emerge.[77]

Five years later, Alain Locke challenged the sociologists who, he said, had failed to understand the psychology and spirit of the New Negro. African Americans had seen their own race through the distorted mirror of stereotype as a social problem—"more of a formula than a human being." Sociologists of the great racial divide had replaced black humiliation and submission with what Locke termed "hurtful counter-prejudice." They were blind to a new

African-American culture, centred in Harlem, that connected American blacks with the international awakening of their race. Garveyism was its most spectacular manifestation.[78]

The heart of the New Negro movement, Locke said, could be found in the artistic and cultural contributions of African Americans. The New Negro became a "conscious contributor . . . and . . . collaborator and participant in American civilization." Rather than being restricted to the "arid fields" of racial debate and conflict, the New Negro turned to "the productive fields of creative expression." The result, Locke declared, was a spiritual, new coming of age, foreshadowing, if not yet indicting, the full initiation of African Americans into American society and democracy.[79]

Much of the poetry of the Harlem Renaissance spoke directly of the "bread of bitterness" of the racial divide. Fenton Johnson wrote that he was "tired of work; I am tired of building up somebody else's civilization." He imagines himself going to the Last Chance Saloon to shoot dice, drink a gallon of gin, and sleep it off. It is easy to overlook the Swiftian irony in Johnson's bitter conclusion: "Throw the children into the river; civilization has given us too many. It is better to die / than to grow up and find that you are colored."[80] Similarly, Richard Wright, one of the talented black authors of the period, walked the cultural tightrope between white stereotypes and the real African-American experience. Wright was in his early twenties when the Depression struck. He describes his coming of age in *Black Boy* (1945; see Box 3.3).

Ruth Whitehead Whaley, following Fenton Johnson's turn of phrase, said that there was something more oppressive than just being coloured. In the Negro world "there is one figure who is the victim of a two-fold segregation and discrimination— the new Negro Woman . . . . [H]er closed doors are of the thickness of two—she is first a woman, then a Negro."[81] In the introduction to *Double-Take: A Revisionist Harlem Renaissance Anthology*, Venetria Patton and Maureen Honey set out to correct

✍ BOX 3.3 · BIOGRAPHY ✍

Richard Wright (1908–1960)

Dick, look, you're black, black, *black*, see? Can't you understand that?
— Richard Wright, *Black Boy: A Record of Childhood and Youth*, 1945, p. 160

The central importance of the colour line, of being black, is the crucial theme of Richard Wright's autobiographical narrative of his childhood. Wright was born in Mississippi in 1908. The dominant figure in his early life was his mother, who worked as a schoolteacher and later as a cook in white folks' households. She looked after Richard and his brother after their father deserted his family. Most of Wright's youth was spent on the streets of the many southern towns to which his family took him. His living arrangements were unstable—often with his mother, sometimes with an uncle, for a time in an orphan home when his mother could not afford to look after him, and then with his evangelical grandmother after his mother's paralytic illness. By the time Wright was nine, he "had not had a single unbroken year of schooling."[82] His education and consciousness, as a result, were formed by a sense of rejection. He responded negatively to the religious fundamentalism of his grandmother and, through this rejection, alienated himself from the centre of the black community. The fraternity he established with other youths was always tentative, although his assumptions about race "sprang spontaneously out of the talk of black boys who met at the crossroads."[83]

By the age of 12, Wright had developed street-smart survival skills along with a cynical shell and what he later described as "a conviction that the meaning of living came only when one was struggling to wring a meaning out of meaningless suffering." Through his social alienation, Wright developed an ability to distance himself from the world and see it objectively. His attitude to life, Wright explains, "directed my loyalties to the side of men in rebellion."[84] In 1927, Wright migrated north to Chicago, finding work in the post office until falling victim to Depression-era unemployment. He eventually found work under the Federal Writer's Project, meeting radicals through the John Reed Club.[85] Through their influence, Wright joined the Communist Party. Wright focused on the imposed degradation of African Americans and the vast gulf that separated them from even the few whites who believed they had the interests of blacks at heart.

Wright deliberately used the word *black* rather than *Negro*, arguing that the word *Negro* was a white man's word that recalled the limitations of segregation and caste.[86] In 1947, his experiences of racism in America and the political persecution arising from his former communist sympathies drove Wright and his family into voluntary exile in France, where he was celebrated by the existentialist writers of the period. He continued to write in a variety of mediums until his death in 1960. Gastor says that Wright's books had been

continued

censored in the US, and the more explicit passages, about race, politics, and sex, had been excised. It wasn't until 1991 that unexpurgated versions of his works were published.[87]

Wright's nightmare world of black migrants recently arrived in the urban North is full of oppression, anger, hatred, and violence. Critic James Baldwin called Wright's naturalistic novel *Native Son* (1940) "the most powerful and celebrated statement we have yet had of what it means to be a Negro in America."[88] The novel was a milestone in American fiction, became a best-selling book-of-the-month-club selection, and opened publishing space in white-controlled companies for African-American writers who followed.

historical gender-blindness. Until **second-wave feminism** spread beyond its middle-class, white origins into the communities of colour, the Harlem Renaissance was remembered as a masculine enterprise. Black feminist scholarship of the last decades of the twentieth century, however, has revealed that women artists were among the most notable figures in the movement. Their early work "signaled the creative independence and assault on demeaning stereotypes with which the Harlem Renaissance first identified itself."[89]

Women had fewer institutional outlets for their creativity, Patton and Honey note. Male, white patrons supported black, male writers. Coming from middle-class backgrounds generally, black women authors tended to avoid the vernacular and "primitiveness" in their writing—because of its association with the stereotypes of sexuality surrounding black women—using instead more traditional poetic forms and writing about middle-class, educated subjects. While voicing their double oppression, Patton and Honey assert, "they grappled uneasily with the sometimes conflicting imperatives of racial solidarity and feminist revolt."[90]

Gender studies have further uncovered questions about the role of homosexuality and bisexuality in the movement. Both Greenwich Village and Harlem were centres of gay life in New York in the 1920s.[91] Alice Dunbar-Nelson (1875–1935) was an important women Harlem Renaissance writers. A teacher, activist, and poet, Dunbar-Nelson was married several times to men and also had passionate affairs with women. In 1921 she wrote the unpublished *You! Inez!* about a black woman whose "dusk eyes" and red mouth stirred "the depths of passionate desire."[92]

Langston Hughes (1902–1967)

Langston Hughes is one of the most celebrated writers of the Harlem Renaissance. Sociologist W.E.B. Du Bois criticized Hughes for feeding white stereotypes. Despite the poet's obvious concern for the colour line, Du Bois could not accept Hughes's use of the everyday black idiom in his poetry, or his celebration of the underside of African-American culture, the excitement and hedonism of the after-midnight life, buoyed by booze, gangsters, and prostitutes. Yet there were similarities between the two writers. Both were conscious of the need to foster race pride among African Americans, although their approaches differed. Both recognized that the lines of race and class intersected, leading them to accept versions of socialism and internationalism, though Du Bois's radicalism deepened over time while Hughes equivocated in the face of post-World War II repression.

Hughes had performed his own version of the black migration, being born in Missouri and eventually coming to Harlem, where he published his first book of poetry, *The Weary Blues*, in 1926. In contrast to many black writers of the time, who sought inclusion in white markets by denying their racial origins (the literary equivalent of socially "passing" for white), Langston Hughes knew that the desire to be recognized as a "poet" rather than as a "Negro poet" was a denial of the essential self. Hughes wrote in his 1926 essay "The Negro Artist and the Racial Mountain" that "it doesn't matter" whether white people were pleased or not with his writings. In his poem "Dinner Guest: Me," Hughes demonstrated his sensitivity to the dilemma of the black artist seeking to be an authentic voice of African-American experience, in its beauty as well as its warts, in an environment dominated by white liberals whose patronage of black art was saturated with guilt.

The black Renaissance in 1920s Harlem was precisely defined by the expression of a distinctive black consciousness and experience—an incipient form of black nationalism. Much of Hughes's poetry, for example, celebrates the exuberance of black life to the rhythm of jazz, the "eternal tom-tom beating in the Negro soul."[93] For Hughes, the central dilemma of his early period (the 1920s) was the jarring incongruity between the ideals that America proclaimed—the "dream"—and the realities of deeply rooted racism. For blacks, Hughes wrote, the American dream had been deferred, its realization postponed. In his poem "Harlem," Hughes poses the question, "What happens to a dream deferred?" Does it dry up? Fester? Sag? Or, Hughes asks, "Does it explode?" In the 1960s, Hughes would live to see the social explosion he had anticipated decades earlier. In the mid-1920s, however, acutely conscious of the so-called Negro problem, Hughes was uncertain of the way out. In "Dinner Guest: Me" he imagines dining with the upper class, who dish up a large serving of "white guilt," but "solutions to the Problem, / Of course, wait."[94]

Hughes's focus on black nationalism was tempered early in his writing career when he realized that numerous sores festered in America besides racial ones. In *Union* (1931), for example, Hughes recognized the need for unity between the poor and oppressed of the world, both black and white. By that time, Hughes had been attracted to communism. In 1932, in the midst of the repression of a mass protest against the government's treatment of World War I veterans during the worst days of the Great Depression, Hughes published the poem "Good Morning Revolution." In it, he describes the situation of the boss, who "eats swell," owns many houses, breaks strikes and bribes the police, and contrasts this life of plenty with his people who have been living from hand to mouth too long. "Ain't you?" he concludes, turning the poem around to challenge the reader and incite action.[95]

It was not only Langston Hughes who was drawn to radical politics. Some blacks in the 1930s were attracted to the Communist Party for several reasons. African Americans had been hit hard by the Depression. They were the last hired and first fired, the most likely to be tossed out of their tenements by rapacious landlords, the most likely to feel the door to the American dream closed firmly in their faces. The radical, anti-capitalist ideology of the Communist Party coupled with the image of an industrializing Soviet Union attracted many new members, not merely blacks, from the industrial working class as well as intellectuals. In the new industrial unions, black workers often achieved their first sense of collective, material success. And for a time, the Communist Party supported black nationalism and the continuing struggle for political and social equality. Anna, a character in Doris Lessing's novel *The Golden Notebook*, "became a 'communist' because the left people were the only people in the town with any kind of moral energy, the only people who took it for granted that the colour bar was monstrous."[96] In the Party, blacks could feel equal to whites and feel that they were struggling not just for racial justice but also for class justice. Indeed, the Communist Party supported the Scottsboro Boys, nine black youths falsely charged with rape who were railroaded by Southern injustice despite the brilliant defence of Sam Leibowitz, the New York lawyer. Leibowitz's Yankee origins and Jewish ethnicity alienated the Southern establishment, who fought as though the old Northern liberal alliance with Southern blacks was being revived.

Langston Hughes was a revolutionary in style as well as political commitment. He spoke on behalf of the oppressed in general, but voiced particularly the plight of African Americans, speaking to them in their own dialect. He expressed the rich cultural life of blacks in America that contrasted so sharply with their meagre, material existence. In Hughes's words, he expressed their "soul," not just their bleak experience.

Conclusion

Several things conspired to make the 1930s in the West what Stromberg called the "Pink Decade."[97] First, capitalism was undergoing its most severe depression. Economically, the capitalist system appeared to have collapsed as many Marxists had expected, producing catastrophic consequences for ordinary people. Many intellectuals were not loyal to the capitalist system in any event; they had good reason in the 1930s to reject it even more thoroughly.

In addition, many Western intellectuals held a generally positive view of the Soviet experience. Unlike the entire West, engulfed in a deep depression, the economy in the USSR appeared to be expanding rapidly. The Soviet experience seemed to be a model of rapid economic growth that could be followed by other, poor counties in the colonized world. Internationally, the USSR had considerable prestige. It was not clear to everyone at the time how much the Bolshevik revolutionary legacy had been sacrificed on the altar of rapid, forced, top-down industrialization. The Soviet Union was also, it appeared in the mid-1930s, steadfastly anti-fascist. In a world where capitalism had failed and been transformed into the barbaric dictatorship of fascism, and revolutionary socialism appeared to be a realistic alternative, it was essential for capitalism to be reformed. Keynesianism initiated a period of state supervision of capitalism that brought with it the beginning of the welfare state and the consolidation of liberal democracy in the West.

The Great Depression was an essential ingredient for the rise of fascism in Europe. In the face of capitalist collapse and the threat of socialism, elites in countries such as Spain, Germany, and Italy turned to fascism, to barbarism, and to war. The anti-fascist cause united a large number of forces in the West, from liberal democrats to anarchists. In Spain in the 1930s, for example, while Western governments turned their backs on an elected government and thereby passively supported the Spanish fascists (known as the Falange), liberals and leftists from Europe and America joined the International Brigades, fighting against the fascist counter-revolution in Spain. Chapter 4 discusses the Nazi movement and the rise of critical theory, developed by German Marxists in the Frankfurt School.

Questions for Reflection

1. Is social realism an effective form of social critique or does it desensitize people and normalize the problems?

2. Keynesianism could work when governments had power over their nation's economy. In the new global world, they have less power. Is a global Keynesianism possible today?

3. Are there cultural and political similarities between the French community in Quebec and African Americans in America?

4. Does the contradiction in the black cultural renaissance between reinforcing negative stereotypes of African Americans and stimulating black pride continue in contemporary African-American music?

CHAPTER 4

Fascism and Critical Theory

———— ◆ ————

Learning Objectives

- To recognize futurism as a cultural forerunner of fascism
- To review the foundations and consequences of Nazism in Germany
- To connect the fascism of the past with contemporary neo-fascism and "friendly fascism"
- To understand the development of cultural Marxism undertaken by theorists in the Frankfurt School
- To assess the Frankfurt School's analysis of the "culture industry"

Writing on the eve of the German Revolution of 1919, the German revolutionary Rosa Luxemburg declared that the choice then facing the working class was "revolution or barbarism"—in other words, socialism or fascism. It was a prescient observation. With the exception of Russia, socialist revolutions were crushed in the years following World War I. From these insurrections grew fascism, a modern movement of counter-revolution and authoritarian capitalism.

A fascist movement established an iron grip on Italy by 1923. By the 1930s, similar authoritarian governments were in power in Germany, Italy, Hungary, Spain, and Portugal, while other Western liberal democracies faced pressure from homegrown fascist movements. While having elements in common, distinctive characteristics shaped fascist-type movements in different countries. Today, *fascism* is an imprecise word that is used to describe a wide range of right-wing, conservative, and authoritarian regimes, movements, and ideas.

Fascism brought the worst of governments and the worst of times. How can such an appalling movement be explained? Brutal military regimes were commonplace in Latin America, but their eruption in Europe, the heartland of liberalism and democracy, of Renaissance and Enlightenment, seemed shocking and unprecedented. But fascism did not drop from the sky; it grew in fertile soil prepared by an elitist, anti-democratic ideology and scientific racism, and it was nourished by elements of both anti-rationalist and rationalist strands of modernism. In Italy, fascism was foreshadowed by futurism, an artistic movement that had also sprouted in Russia prior to the Bolshevik Revolution.

Futurism and Fascism in Italy

I wanted to be really great, epic, colossal,
I wanted to accomplish something gigantic,
unheard of, that would change the heart of
men and the face of the earth. Either that,
or nothing.[1]

—Giovanni Papini

Giovanni Papini (1881-1956) was a controversial Italian novelist and critic, and an early member of the futurist movement. His ambitions were grandiose and so were the aims of the movement he joined. Futurism began as a literary revolt founded on the subjective philosophies of Henri Bergson and Friedrich Nietzsche and had its clearest expression in Italian painting and sculpture. Italian intellectuals at the beginning of the twentieth century were acutely aware of the sharp incongruence between Italy's cultural past—from the expansive Roman Empire through to the Renaissance—and its "bourgeois" present. Rather than trying to revive the glories of past greatness and celebrate rural nostalgia, the futurists wanted to create a new Italy, free from the mothballs of the old. For them,

the storied city of Venice was the epitome of the decaying state of contemporary Italy. In 1910, futurists dropped 800,000 leaflets entitled "Against Past-Loving Venice" from the clock tower in the storied city. The leaflet denounced the old, feeble Venice of "universal imbecility" and stated the intention of curing "this putrefying city." A once dominant sea power, Venice had degenerated into a tourist brothel full of "little one-eyed businesses" where merchants peddled their contemptible wares for philistine foreigners. To make way for a new, industrial, and military Venice, the gondolas were to be burned and the stinking canals were to be filled in with the debris from its disintegrating palaces.[2] The old world was to be demolished to give birth to the vibrant, exhilarating new one. In

❧ BOX 4.1 • BIOGRAPHY ☙

Filippo Marinetti (1876–1944)

Filippo Marinetti was the first distinctive voice of Italian futurism. Born into a rich, northern Italian family, Marinetti became a performance or conceptual artist. Wyndham Lewis described him as a "flamboyant personage adorned with diamond rings, gold chains and hundreds of flashing white teeth." On the platform to perform his poetry, Lewis said, Marinetti was "a frenzied Jack-in-the-Box. He sprang about, a torrent of words pouring incessantly from his mouth. . . . All of them added up to one thing—to force, to speed, to power."[3] In 1930, Marinetti began a campaign against the most essentially Italian of foods: spaghetti. He declared spaghetti "obsolete . . . heavy, brutalizing and gross" and claimed that it induced "scepticism, sloth, and pessimism."[4] The futurist definition of beauty was the dynamism and speed of modern technology, as represented by the racing car with its explosive exhaust. In the *Futurist Manifesto*, Marinetti proclaims that "a roaring car that seems to ride on grapeshot is more beautiful than the *Victory of Samothrace*," a Greek sculpture of the goddess of victory.[5] The futurists, Jeffery Meyers claimed, "insisted on the importance of the present, praised the joys of speed and advocated violent action which would destroy the bankrupt artistic culture that still clung to decorative arts and outworn values."[6]

More than 50 futurist manifestos were written between 1909 and 1915. In 1910, five futurists (not including Marinetti) proclaimed another Manifesto to an audience of 3000

his dream of utter destruction, the "perfect anarchist" in Joseph Conrad's *The Secret Agent: A Simple Tale* expressed the same idea: "what's wanted is a clean sweep and a clear start for a new conception of life."[7]

Italy was the heartland of this new, futurist ideology, a nation whose northern cities, such as Milan and Turin, were undergoing a late transition to industrial capitalism. Italian visual artists illustrated the theory of futurism by attempting to render on canvas and two-dimensional space violent movement, speed, and force—all of which these artists associated with superior masculinity and the dynamism of modern industry. The futurists sought to merge elite and mass culture. They identified with the world of material consumption, the urban crowd, industrial growth, and mass culture.[8]

The *Futurist Manifesto*, written in 1909 by Filippo Marinetti (see Box 4.1), challenged the artists of his generation to break free from the shell of reason and to throw themselves "like pride-ripened fruit into the wide, contorted mouth of the wind!" Futurists, according to Marinetti, should give themselves utterly to the unknown and the absurd. The *Futurist Manifesto* expressed indignation about the state of Italian culture and demanded the destruction of libraries, museums, and art academies, all of which had become dull, insignificant mausoleums. In place of sleepy immobility, futurists were dauntless. They extolled the love of danger and admiration for courageous, "audacity and

artists, students, and young factory workers. On the triumphalist basis of modern science, the new "free moderns" declared that an abyss separated them from the "docile slaves of past tradition." Italy was now a country being reborn politically and culturally in which "millions of machines are already roaring."[9] Futurist poetry was meant to grasp ideas and sensations "brutally and hurl them in the reader's face."[10] Antonio Gramsci argued that in the field of culture the futurists were revolutionaries. They aimed to destroy "spiritual hierarchies, prejudices, idols and ossified traditions" and were unafraid of innovations, audacities, and monsters. The futurists "have had confidence in themselves, in the impetuosity of their youthful energies." They have realized that the new age needs "new forms of art, philosophy, behaviour and language . . . [a] sharply revolutionary and Marxist idea."[11]

Marinetti's activism was directly political and the futurists explicitly politicized art. Indeed, futurism began as a politics of revolt, a harbinger of a new, exciting age. In the end, however, the Italian futurists became mired in **fascism** and, inevitably, in imperialism and war. Futurists cheered the aggression of Italian imperialism against Libya in 1911, and during World War I they became a propaganda mouthpiece for Italian nationalism. War exemplified in real life, much better than could be captured in art, the experience of power, dynamism, and modern technology. In war, the futurists believed, the old world would, indeed, be destroyed, and the way made clear for a new future.

Marinetti stood for election as a Fascist candidate in the 1919 election, which was won by the Socialists.[12] He helped write the 1919 Fascist Manifesto, which, at the time, was peppered with socialist and liberal ideas, such as a minimum wage, the eight-hour day, and a progressive tax on capital.[13] In 1935, Marinetti volunteered as part of the Italian invasion of Ethiopia. He remained loyal to the movement until his death in 1944.[14]

revolt . . . aggressive action, a feverish insomnia, the racer's stride, the moral leap, the punch and the slap."[15] The *Manifesto* also glorified violence and destruction: "We will glorify war—the world's only hygiene—militarism, patriotism, the destructive gesture of freedom-bringers, beautiful ideas worth dying for, and scorn of women."[16]

British novelist Wyndham Lewis said that futurism expressed the fascist doctrine of force in its purest expression: "There is no better guide to fascism, its meaning and its methods, than this great verbal diarrhoea, its original inspiration."[17] From the fantasies of futurism, fascist ideology developed its doctrine of force, authority, and brutality, and brought it into everyday politics in Italy. Italy emerged from World War I with crushingly high unemployment and an economic crisis that quickly became political. Industrial workers engaged in a wave of strikes and factory occupations during the Red Years of 1919 and 1920, creating factory councils to manage enterprises under workers' control (similar to Russian workers' soviets in 1917). Peasant rebellions broke out in the Italian countryside as peasant tenants and hired workers tried to wrest land from their landlords.

In the context of dangerous rebellion from below as well as the revolutions in Russia and Germany, the dominant classes allied with the traditionalist Catholic Church to defend private property and protect their privileges and power. As the class struggle intensified, however, the elite turned away from liberal, democratic politics to the new, fascist movement led by Benito Mussolini (1883-1945). Playing on the fear of social revolution, the Fascists became the only effective paramilitary force that was capable of defending the rights of the propertied. As Mussolini's Black Shirts took control of several Italian cities, Italy's government became increasingly isolated. With the backing of the conservative nationalists and the business classes, Mussolini was declared premier in 1922.

Over the next several years, Mussolini took steps to consolidate the one-party Fascist state with him as the sole leader. By 1925, all other political parties were outlawed, the press was placed under Fascist control, judicial matters were handled by Fascist tribunals that imprisoned political opponents, and independent unions (those not under control of the Fascist government) were banned. Mussolini set up large government bureaucracies to stimulate and control the economy. Despite his efforts, however, the Italian economy was mired in depression throughout the 1930s. To maintain his upper hand, Mussolini embarked on military adventures, invading Ethiopia in 1935, sending troops to support the fascist movement in Spain in 1936, and concluding a military alliance with Nazi Germany. This last move finally brought Italy into World War II on the side of Germany and, thereafter, to humiliating defeat. Mussolini was assassinated by Italian anti-Fascists in 1945. They hung his body by the feet in a public square in Milan.

Nazism in Germany

Wherever books will be burned, men also, in the end, are burned.

—Heinrich Heine, *Almansor: A Tragedy*, 1823

However brutal and authoritarian, fascism in Italy was frequently incompetent and corrupt. In Germany, fascism took on a more wolfish, virulent, and evil form. Many social theorists were struck by the way evil under Nazism took on a routine, even banal character. Nazism had deep roots in German elitism, authoritarianism, and militarism. In the words of Prussian historian Heinrich von Treitschke, the virile and brave German race was in perpetual conflict with the weak and cowardly, with the sentimental and feminine.[18] The chief defining characteristic of German Nazism was its deeply rooted racism and anti-Semitism.

By the middle of the nineteenth century in Europe, Joseph de Gobineau's pseudo-scientific doctrine of white racial superiority had taken hold. According to this doctrine, the noblest among the white race was the Aryan, and Germans were the most racially pure of the Aryans. The doctrine of racial and cultural purity was given a specific formulation in Oswald Spengler's *The Decline of the West* (1918). The "coloured people" of the world, Spengler said, threatened European civilization externally through the **Yellow Peril** and from within by the inter-breeding of races (miscegenation), which debased and lowered the supposedly superior, white race. Preserving the assumed purity of the race was imperative for German strength and success. Taken to its end point, the doctrine of racial purity led to genocide. Novelist Joseph Conrad gave an early echo of what became Nazi ideology in *The Secret Agent* (1907). The character known as the Professor referred to the weak as the "source of all evil" and dreamed of their extermination.[19]

Friedrich Nietzsche's cultural elitism was also enlisted in support of the Nazi cause. There was no right or wrong, Nietzsche had said; there was only power, and power defined what was right. It was necessary to abandon the illusions of equality, democracy, and liberalism and embrace the dynamic principles of struggle, power, and domination. A new breed of creative geniuses, a new cultural elite, would arise and become *Übermenschen*—super men—re-establishing a great civilization. German National Socialists claimed to be members of the new, dynamic elite, and they identified Hitler as *the* superman. Alfred Rosenberg, a theorist of Nazism, predicted that 80 per cent of the new elite would possess the "superior blood" of the Nordic type.[20]

Anti-Semitism is one of the specific defining characteristics of Nazism. The Nazi Party inherited a history of anti-Semitism that was as long as the First and Second Reich combined. As black novelist Walter Mosley said, "In Europe the Jew had been a Negro for more than a thousand years."[21] In his influential *Foundation of the Nineteenth Century* (1899), Houston Stewart Chamberlain warned that

German blood was threatened by one "alien element" in particular: the Jews. Jews, Chamberlain said, were engaged in a life-and-death struggle with pure Germans.[22] Making race an issue implied the policy of **eugenics**: selective breeding, the need for a race to remain pure in its "blood," and the sterilization or murder of the inferior and unfit.

Hitler claimed that in the beginning he was not anti-Semitic. The Jews in Linz, his hometown, had a history of assimilation, and "their external appearance had become European and human," he wrote. Jews were persecuted only because of their "strange religion." In Vienna, however, Hitler's anti-Semitism grew. Walking in the inner city, he came across an orthodox Jew, dressed in the traditional caftan and with long sidelocks. As he stared at the strange face and scrutinized the man's features, he became hostile and averred that Jews were "other" than German.[23]

Hitler claimed that his anti-Semitism resulted from reason and logic rather than prejudice. He came to believe that Jews were behind every corrupt practice in Vienna. What was worse, they were also the leaders of Marxian **social democracy**, a doctrine he had long hated. For Hitler, Marxism was a Jewish doctrine that rejected the natural principles of aristocracy, force, and strength, and substituted mere numbers. Finally, Hitler said, he "turned into a fanatical anti-Semite."[24] In the struggle of racial groups, the world had been turned unnaturally on its head. The superior, German race was being dominated, humiliated, and adulterated by inferior races, according to Hitler, above all, by the Jewish "race." Historian Allan Bullock points out that Hitler was convinced that behind the social troubles of pre-war Germany was hidden a worldwide Jewish conspiracy to subdue the Aryan race.[25] Hitler poured his invective into the pages of an autobiographical and political polemic that he called *Mein Kampf* ("*My Struggle*"). After he seized power in 1933, owning this book became a symbol of German loyalty and orthodoxy.

Elitism is one side of Nazi ideology. The other side is the belief in the perpetual incompetence of the masses. While Hitler believed ordinary people to be intellectually weak, he recognized the importance of mass support and cultivated the styles and symbols of charismatic leadership to harness them for his cause. In his autobiography, he demonstrated contempt for ordinary people. The masses, he writes, prefer strong rulers who teach an absolute doctrine rather than being faced with the challenge of liberal freedom. The masses are like women who willingly "submit to the strong." They do not recognize when they are being terrorized spiritually and submit only to force and brutality. In Hitler's words, he came to realize the "importance of physical terror against the individual and the masses."[26]

Ordinary people, Hitler writes, are driven by feelings, and they believe anything that is presented ruthlessly, fanatically, and one-sidedly. Their attitudes are deeply held because they are rooted in sentiments and emotions, not reason and knowledge. The masses are animated by fanaticism and hysteria, and they can be won over through willpower and strength. Propaganda, therefore, must present people with dogmatic certainty through stereotypical formulas and constant repetition. Their "primitive simplicity causes ordinary people to fall victim to a great lie more readily than to a small one."[27]

According to Nazi theory, people are united in blood and connected through history. They have a destiny, and a will that is unconscious until it is realized through the agency of the leader, or führer. In the will of the leader, the will of the people is realized. He transforms their feelings and instincts into a conscious movement that expresses their objective destiny.[28] The Führer principle requires from the people complete deference to authority and demands unswerving allegiance to the movement.[29] As the character Loki (Tom Hiddleston) explains in *The Avengers* (2012), "It is the unspoken truth of humanity that you crave subjugation."[30]

The masses were already infused with patriotism and a belief in German destiny. They saw the world in terms of nation and race, and they blamed their economic troubles on the owners of the banks and the big businesses: men, Hitler said, who were predominantly Jewish. At the same time, being poor, displaced, and alienated from their own society, the masses were susceptible to being drawn into radical movements, including some version of socialism. Many of the socialist leaders in Germany and Russia, including Marx himself, Hitler noted, were Jews. Behind the ruthlessness of big business and the international Marxist movement, Hitler imagined a worldwide **Jewish conspiracy**. And like any conspiracy theory, playing into peoples' prejudices was more effective than providing evidence. Nazism appealed to youthful idealism, a sense of being on the side of history and of belonging to a cult-like movement that was exciting and visionary. Hitler promised to deliver Germany from the inglorious past and to restore German power, pride, and prosperity. Even after defeat in World War II and the exposure of the full horrors of the Nazi regime, including the Holocaust, many ordinary Germans believed that Hitler had done a lot of good for Germany. Indeed, many middle-class German men continued to sport a small, brush-style Hitler moustache into the 1950s.

When the Nazi movement had first crawled toward power, it had its clearest support among the disinherited middle classes: small business owners, shopkeepers, and artisans; petty officials and municipal government workers—those groups in the population threatened by economic and social crisis.[31] The 1920 Nazi Party platform was nationalist and racist, but it was also anti-big business. All excessive profits, including the windfalls that had been made during the Great War, would be confiscated by the state. The fascist state would nationalize the big industrial trusts, and the profits of other large industries would be shared with the state. Land rents were to be abolished; and speculation in land, halted. The death penalty was to be imposed for "usurers and profiteers."[32] The Nazi Party platform was designed to appeal to the broad range of classes in Germany. As time passed, however, Hitler found these demands increasingly embarrassing. They were useful as rhetoric to stir up the population during elections, but they were especially damaging when the Nazis sought financial support from big industrialists and large landowners.[33]

Support from the business class was instrumental in Hitler's rise to power. The Nazi Party fought expensive elections against the socialists and communists. Campaign contributions from big business kept the party afloat, including paying the armed thugs who made each election violent and bloody. Once he was in power, Hitler had promised the industrialists, he would put an end to elections.[34] "[W]e have formed the inexorable decision to destroy Marxism in Germany down to its very root," Hitler declared.[35] Economic prosperity requires a strong state and, just as a business is run as an autocracy and not a democracy, so, too, must the state be run by a single leader, according to Hitler. The Nazi Party applied the *führerprinzip* (the concept of a single, autocratic leader) to industry: each industrialist would be führer in his own domain. German industrialists became "wildly" enthusiastic and contributed large sums to the Nazi Party.[36] As playwright Lillian Hellman put it, the Nazis "came in on the shoulders of the most powerful men in the world."[37]

Once financed, the fascist movement attracted a wide following, bringing in unorganized workers, independent farmers, members of the armed forces, the unemployed, and young people from all social classes who had lost any opportunity for economic security.[38] With lots of money to pay thugs to terrorize opponents and conduct a propaganda war—making today's attack ads look like flattery— the Nazi Party won the largest number of seats in the 1933 election: 288 out of 647. With 43.9 per cent of the vote, however, once again the Nazis fell short of a majority.[39] Arguably, the German people did not vote Hitler directly into power.

Armed with a legal mantle that he quickly shed, Hitler assumed absolute political control. The Third Reich had begun. Fascism used state power to institute its political counter-revolution. Trade unions and working class parties were smashed; and their leaders killed or imprisoned. The routine practices of liberal democracy—freedom of the press, parliamentary elections, individual rights—were eliminated. The state moved wholesale into rearmament and preparation for a new war of imperialist expansion.[40] Given the particular racial element inherent in Nazism, Jewish businesses were confiscated. All Jewish professionals were deprived of their jobs, status, and income. Under new, anti-Semitic laws introduced at the 1935 Nuremberg Nazi Party rally, Jews were stripped of their German citizenship. Jews, socialists, homosexuals, minority races such as the Roma, disabled people, the mentally ill, and other groups were systematically deported to labour camps and, ultimately, became victims of the Holocaust. Playwright Peter Weiss describes the horror of the Nazi death camps:[41]

the oppressor
could expand his authority
to a degree never known before
And the oppressed
was forced to yield up
the fertilizing dust
of his bones

Many Jews attempted to emigrate. The most well-educated or reputable were welcomed in rival imperialist countries. Socially progressive émigrés, such as Einstein, went to the United States; the more conservative, such as Freud, went to Britain. In the face of anti-foreigner pressure and widespread anti-Semitism, however, there was nowhere to go for most of the threatened population. Ordinary Jewish migrants trying to escape from Nazi Germany were summarily denied entry into the United States and Canada; the culture of anti-Semitism was widespread.

The Holocaust marched on in Germany and Eastern Europe, under Nazi rule. After the war, the rest of the world wondered who to blame and punish for these crime against humanity: Hitler alone? The leaders of the Nazi Party? Anyone who contributed directly to the Holocaust? Or anyone who acquiesced knowingly but silently while genocide was carried out (see Box 4.2)?

Nazism and Women

Give me the silent, German wives, / That go to bed demure and still.[42]

—Heinrich Heine, *Anno*, 1839

Nazism endorsed, officially, a restrained Puritan-like sexuality, confined to legitimate marriage for the purpose of reproducing the race. So-called sexual perversions were signs of degeneracy and

---

⁂ BOX 4.2 • THEORY IN CONTEXT ⁂

Who's to Blame?

"You're to blame. And you are, too. You're most to blame, You! you! you!"[43]
—Günter Grass, *The Tin Drum*, 1959

Who was to blame for Nazi war crimes? Were only the top leaders responsible or were millions of otherwise ordinary German people guilty, as suggested by Günter Grass? French philosopher Jean-Paul Sartre debated the question of collective and individual guilt in his 1960 play *The Condemned of Altona*. One character, Von Gerlach, is an industrialist who enriched himself using slave labour during the Nazi regime. In his view, it was a dirty trick to condemn 80 million Germans such as him. At most, he says, there were three dozen criminals—the top Nazi leaders. They alone should be hanged; the rest should be rehabilitated.[44]

Few Germans were tried for war crimes. The earliest important trial of Nazi leaders took place in Nuremberg. Between 1945 and 1946, a military court tried 24 Nazi leaders for war crimes and crimes against humanity. Hitler was not among them. He had committed suicide and his body burned as the victorious Russian Army converged on his Berlin bunker. No corpse of Hitler remained to be hung upside down on public display, the fate that had befallen Italy's Mussolini.

The Nuremburg show trial did not satisfy most Holocaust survivors, for whom it was merely tokenism, giving only the appearance of justice because the real villains were in the millions.[45] In the last mass trial, in 1963, 22 ordinary members of the Nazi Party were put on trial in Frankfurt. The defendants included middle- or lower-level SS members, doctors who selected inmates for work or extermination, and *kapos* (camp inmates who exercised power under the Nazis). They represented the many Germans who bore some part of the **collective guilt**.[46] The character, "V" in *V for Vendetta* might have been speaking to Germans of the 1930s about their authoritarian leaders rather than to Britons of the fictional future when he claimed that it was "*you* who gave them the power to make your

impurity. While homosexuality was tolerated among some prominent Nazis, in general homosexuality was condemned. Those convicted of being homosexual were sent to concentration camps, identified by a pink triangle, and destined for extermination.

The emergence of the "New Woman" was more challenging to Nazi ideology. In Germany, the New Woman—the "self-assertive, sexually and financially independent female . . . unmarried and employed by choice"—was a post-1914 phenomenon.[47] With her "short bobbed hair," fashionably slim figure, and an "athletic body without fat and [traditional] erotic womanliness," the New Woman was stylistically American.[48] As historian Ritta Horsley points out, German patriarchal authority responded to the challenge of the emancipated woman by reiterating traditional ideas, including the assumed-to-be natural role of women in the bourgeois family[49]—the silent German wives

decisions for you. . . . You have accepted without question their senseless orders. . . . You could have stopped them. All you had to say was 'No.'"[47]

Playwright Peter Weiss used transcripts from the Frankfurt trial to construct the dialogue of his play *The Investigation*. The refrain of the accused at the war crimes tribunals was that they were only following orders from their superiors that they were duty-bound to follow: "There wasn't anything I could do about it. . . . I would have been put up against the wall." Accused # 22 (SS Corporal Stark) in Peter Weiss's play places the blame on the pervasive indoctrination carried out by the Nazi Party. From Grammar School, he says, "It was hammered into us" that the Jews "were to blame for everything. . . . In leadership school / we were taught above all / to accept everything without question. . . . We weren't supposed to think for ourselves."[48]

In 1960, the escaped commander of **Auschwitz**, Adolf Eichmann, was captured by Israeli secret service agents and put on public trial in Israel. German author Hannah Arendt, who had gone into exile to escape Nazi persecution, watched Eichmann in his bulletproof glass cage and listened to him defend himself as merely a soldier following orders. For Arendt, coming face-to-face with evil was a harrowing experience—not because evil was revealed to be blatantly monstrous but for the opposite reason: because it appeared to be so ordinary, so "banal."[49] An image of the routine and bureaucratic nature of the Holocaust appears in Steven Spielberg's film *Schindler's List*. As thousands of displaced Jews disembark from cattle cars, dozens of average civil servants arrive to set up makeshift desks to process the new arrivals. As the nondescript clerks shuffle papers, stamp forms, and move the lines along, the visual image reflects Arendt's notion of the banality of evil. The whole regime is bureaucratic, impersonalized, and mechanical, as novelist Franz Kafka describes what he believes to be the outcome of any revolution from below:

They are masters of the street and think that they are masters of the world. And yet they are wrong. Behind them come secretaries, bureaucrats, professional politicians—all of the modern sultans whose accession to power they are facilitating. The revolution subsides, leaving only the slime of a new bureaucracy. The chains of tortured humanity are forged from administrative papers.[50]

favoured by poet Heinrich Heine. Playing the part of a new career woman as a typist or office clerk was permissible for a while, but with maturity would come conventional marriage and child-rearing.

The Nazi ideologue Alfred Rosenberg claimed that "Emancipation of women from the women's emancipation movement is the first demand of a generation of women," which would save the *Volk* ("the people") from its decline.[54] After Hitler's capture of power in 1933, women could work in paid employment and contribute to the cause of National Socialism, especially while they were single, but they were not to be independently careerist. Given its obsession with blood and breeding, fascism typically endorsed traditional attitudes toward women. That is, according to fascism, the function of women was to breed sons who would be soldiers, willing to fight and die under the authority of the leader for the good of the nation, the state, and the race. Nevertheless, women had also to be drawn out of the family and the home to fulfill the political purpose of the regime. To complete their ideological training in patriarchal power, young German women were enrolled into the League of German Girls, the counterpart of the masculine Hitler Youth. Economic prosperity in Germany extended into the domestic economy. Under Hitler, novelist Günter Grass said, housewives were able to abandon the outdoor rack, on which they beat the dirt out of carpets, and buy power vacuum cleaners.[55]

While women might work outside the home in the acceptable times and places, Nazism demonstrates that economic independence is only part of the foundation of women's emancipation. Sexuality was officially confined to a narrow, Victorian cage. Consequently, the flapper image of young women was condemned. The flappers took their liberation into the after-hour clubs, the theatres, and the bedrooms. They were deemed decadent, unnatural, and unwholesome. Liberalized sexuality tended to be associated with demands for birth control and abortion rights, which the Nazi Party refused in the case of Aryans. These eugenics policies (and worse) were reserved for those they deemed undesirable "others."[56]

Feminist criticism has linked Nazism with patriarchal violence. Part of the appeal was spectacle: the parades at night, the mass rallies, and the aggressive speeches, which were watched live or carried by radio waves into homes and workplaces. In Elaine Martin's view, under the cover of night, in the midst of a crowd of excited, like-minded people, and under the influence of too much beer, people felt that normative moral boundaries had evaporated. Certain, previously condemned behaviours became socially acceptable and the boundary between right and wrong appeared permeable. Rage could be expressed openly and violently against the despised and vulnerable, even sometimes against the socially superior. As Crista Wolf says, what emerges in times of social chaos, whether temporarily in rioting or more permanently during war, is "naked, hideous male gratification" expressed in murder and rape.[57] The connection between war and rape is ancient and by no means particular to fascism. With its glorification of authority and violence, militarism and racism, however, fascism is a particularly dangerous form of sexual domination and aggression. In some feminist theories, the male lust for violence is linked to men's fear of the feminine, of being dominated and engulfed by women.[58] In war, men can act out their fantasies of being completely in control by objectifying women as instruments of their desire and denying their status as fully human. "Enemy" women become the common property of victorious men.

The *führerprinzip*—the principle that one man shall be master in every domain—sanctioned patriarchal power and violence in the home. While Nazism unleashed male sexual violence, under its tightly controlled hierarchy of power, Martin argues, female sexuality was confined and controlled. The idea of women's independent sexuality was intolerable to Nazi men whose conception of manhood was connected to their sense of superiority.[59]

Fascism and Neo-Fascism in the West

It must be, I thought, one of the [human] race's most persistent and comforting hallucinations to trust that "it can't happen here"....And now it was happening here.[60]

—John Wyndham, *The Day of the Triffids*, 1951

Fascist movements also appeared in other Western nations. The American Liberty League, for example, was organized by prominent businessmen and Republicans to topple Roosevelt from power. Father Charles Coughlin, a Roman Catholic priest, used radio evangelism to send anti-Semitic and pro-fascist messages to millions of Americans. In Quebec, Adrien Arcand founded the National Social Christian Party to spread his message about the need for a strong, authoritarian political leader. And during World War II in both the US and Canada, fascist supporters were interned along with otherwise patriotic citizens of German and Italian descent, a political decision that smacked, ironically, of homegrown fascism.

The word *fascist* has been applied widely to a variety of authoritarian and right-wing movements and governments. The more generalized the term, the less precise it is and the more it appears potentially meaningless. Rather than narrowing the definition to the classical cases in Italy and Germany, however, it is useful to think of these regimes as ideal types to which modern movements may be more or less compared. In this light, contemporary fascism comes in numerous forms and, for many current groups, the connection to the fascism of the past is indirect. Among the most virulent contemporary forms is the ultra-nationalist movement in Europe, which targets immigrants, especially Muslims, as well as racial minorities and homosexuals.

Contemporary fascism dons a variety of guises, and groups go to some trouble to disguise their origins. As Sinclair Lewis first noted in the 1930s, neo-fascism downplays its unpopular connection with the Nazi regime and seeks to align its policies with hot-button issues, such as immigration, that agitate many people. What emerges is "friendly fascism," a right-wing agenda under the guise of conservatism that works through the mainstream political process. As Europe continues its recovery from the economic crisis that began in 2008, the worst collapse since the 1930s, the new far right is increasing its mass appeal. In the 2012 vote for the French presidency, the leader of the right-wing National Front ran a bitter and racist anti-immigration campaign and finished third, with 18 per cent of the vote. Far-right adherents play on fears and anxieties, such as the breakdown of law and order and of the traditional family, but they also reach out to the distressed middle classes by criticizing as socialist any attempt to ameliorate the worst conditions of the poor, to regulate the economy, to protect the environment, and to muzzle workers' organizations.

Naomi Klein, a popular left-wing journalist and critic of globalization and consumerism, warned of creeping fascism in the United States; so, too, did Noam Chomsky, the celebrity left-wing theorist. Naomi Wolf, another contemporary feminist, argues that American democracy is being slowly eroded through an evolution that brings it closer to the ideal fascist scenario. It can happen here, she cautions, pointing to a number of warning signs, including the following:

- Identifying a terrifying enemy that is external to the homeland but also exists underground at home (Islamic terrorism)
- Undermining important civil liberties in the name of national security
- Creating an extra-legal process of detention (rendition), imprisonment (Guantanamo Bay), and torture (water-boarding), which is run by a privately contracted, "thug caste"
- Establishing a widespread national system of surveillance
- Making it difficult for citizens' groups to protest peacefully

- Harassing outspoken and high-profile public critics of the regime
- Attempting to control the press, for example, through the use of the "big lie" (Bush's weapons of mass destruction in Iraq; Putin's claim of no Russian troops in Ukraine)[61]

She could have added other warnings, such as branding even liberal opinion as subversive; targeting and **scapegoating** minorities (the war on drugs, immigration); expanding police powers and the gulag of public and private prisons; and supporting overseas war in the interests of big business. None of this litany of growing conservatism amounts to classic fascism, but Klein argues it amounts to the erosion of democratic practices, to which a fearful public simply acquiesces. All of these signs are characteristics of classical fascism, which continues to be relevant in the contemporary world.

Understanding fascism in 1930s Europe and its contemporary appeal is a complex undertaking. In the short run, fascism in power appeared to meet the interests of both the middle class and the elite. Germany, for example, with its war economy in full swing, quickly pulled out of the Depression. Employment was strong, economic reconstruction and militarization were underway, and businesses were profitable. Few Germans in the 1930s worried about their country's possible defeat in the next war. Even after the devastation caused by World War II, many average Germans still said that at least with Hitler Germans had had prosperity.

In the long run, however, with its control of the state and military, fascist governments led both Germany and Italy into brutal war and utter defeat. The political control of a fascist state is an unpredictable tool for the maintenance of elite rule and for preserving the interests of the dominant class. In 1942, Franz Neumann said the Nazi state was a behemoth, a beast of enormous, uncontrolled destructive power. Neumann was associated with a group of German critical theorists, including Theodor Adorno, who were members of the Institute of Social Research at the University of Frankfurt, known collectively as the Frankfurt School. Adorno theorized that violence was part of the so-called authoritarian personality, which he believed was at the psychological root of fascism. From its inception, the Institute's program was explicitly Marxist, but it was not connected to any political party or movement.[62] Frankfurt School theorists attempted to bring into Marxist analysis psychological and cultural insights that would provide a corrective to Marx's theory, which they saw as one-sidedly economic.

The Frankfurt School and Critical Theory

Reason is a poor ally of reaction.[63]

—Max Horkheimer, "The Social Function of Philosophy," 1939

In the desperate European context of failed revolution and fascist success, the theorists of the Frankfurt Institute of Social Research sought to rescue Marx's original dialectical theory from the errors of Marx's twentieth-century followers.[64] Above all, they emphasized the importance of reason for understanding society and its potential for change. As Max Horkheimer believed in 1939, reason was the ally of truth and freedom, and the enemy of tyranny and reaction. Thought, according to Horkheimer and Adorno, "is the servant which the master cannot control at will."[65]

But reason, in its full, critical sense, had been squeezed out of twentieth-century social theory, including Marxism. Enlightenment rationality had become a tool of domination rather than of human liberation.[66] Most of the members of the Frankfurt Institute considered themselves adrift in a doctrine in crisis, which was deepened by the rise of fascism. Following the rise of Nazism in Germany, the Institute relocated to Columbia University in New York. Under Max Horkheimer, the director of the Institute between 1930 and

1958, the members sought to adapt Marxism to suit the new social world.

Max Horkheimer (1895–1973), the son of a prominent Jewish manufacturer, was born in Stuttgart, Germany. Like many sons of rich capitalists, it was assumed he would follow his father into business. Horkheimer's parents had more trouble accepting his wife than his radicalism. They were aghast when Horkheimer married his father's gentile (non-Jewish) secretary, who was eight years his senior. The family rift was sharp but brief. Reconciliation was all the easier because his radicalism did not entail a bohemian or faux working-class lifestyle.[67] For Horkheimer, the happiness of theoretical contemplation was possible only with a substantial material foundation—a solid middle-class career. In his words, wisdom could not "go hand in hand with misery" and reason could not grow among "people who literally led a dog's life."[68]

Along with Horkheimer, Theodor Adorno (1903–1969) was the most influential member of the Frankfurt School in the United States. Adorno did not join the Institute until 1938, several years after his immigration to America. Adorno's father was a successful Jewish wine merchant in Germany, and his mother was a professional singer. Throughout Adorno's life, Jay says, he was a cultural elitist who was most comfortable around artistic or intellectual cliques, such as he found in the Institute. Adorno's writing style was also high-brow. His prose was intricate, Jay says, and difficult for the average reader, who was challenged by the philosophical language.[69]

Horkheimer and Adoro had initially accepted socialism and the important role of the working class, which in 1944 they still referred to as "the true universal."[70] After moving to the United States, however, where the labour movement had become largely apolitical, they gradually abandoned the idea of proletarian revolution. In pre-Hitler Germany as well as in the United States, the working class appeared to have made its compliant accommodation to authoritarianism and capitalism.

The Frankfurt School integrated elements of Marxism with ideas derived from philosophers and theorists whose views had been defined in the Marxists movement as varieties of "false consciousness." They called the approach they created **critical theory**. Horkheimer argued that a dialectical approach should extract relative truths from any philosophy and integrate them into a more comprehensive theory. His approach was to theorize the mediating influence of economic developments in society; the psychology of individuals and groups; and cultural forms, including art, fashion, and sport. The Institute's stated goal was to analyze **praxis**, or practice.[71] Praxis in this context, however, did not mean engaging in conscious action to implement change.

For Horkheimer and Adorno, understanding, or reason, is the foundation of any progressive social theory. In the widest sense, the goal of enlightenment is to liberate people from fear and make them the architects of their own lives. Eighteenth-century **Enlightenment** doctrines of universal freedom and self-determination had been the ideological instrument with which the bourgeoisie had taken power.[72] But enlightenment has a second element that contradicts its rebellious side; it also contains a principle of domination related to the growth of technological rationality and expanding production. In the modern world, the opposite side of human reason had been turned into a means of dominating and controlling people and nature. Enlightenment had become **totalitarian**: "Enlightenment stands in the same relationship to things as the dictator to human beings. He knows them to the extent that he can manipulate them."[73]

Horkheimer and Adorno distinguished between a lower level of "understanding" and higher "reason." The lower type of understanding was characteristic of modern science and of **positivism** in social theory. Positivism focused narrowly on fragmented and isolated phenomena in society, as if something could be understood without appreciating the way it was connected to much larger and more complex social wholes. By restricting thought to the immediately perceivable and logical, positivism was blind to anything that didn't exist or that couldn't be expressed in words. Positivism remained at the level of apparent facts (superficial understanding) and reified the existing social structure.[74] Reason had been shorn of its critical potential and whittled down by science and technology to mere "instrumental rationality," a tool the dominant class used to control the masses.

Higher reason, in contrast, revealed existing phenomena in terms of their full social, historical, and human meanings, including their possibilities for change.[75] Reason, according to Horkheimer and Adorno, is inherently critical and is the basis on which the world can be judged, not just accepted as it is; hence, the idea of critical theory is to judge the world in terms of the higher standard of reason.[76] It was precisely critical thought that Horkheimer and Adorno found missing in the United States. Indeed, they found American culture to be highly anti-intellectual and dismissive of the very philosophical approach they advocated. As a result, soon after their arrival in America the Frankfurt theorists turned their critical eye to the culture of their temporary homeland. They were not impressed.

The Culture Industry

Generally in Marxism, the realm of culture and mass media has been relegated to the **superstructure**, that is, to secondary importance. At most, cultural analysis meant uncovering the class interests that could be found in various cultural forms. In the European novel, for example, social realism was progressive and proletarian because it exposed the evils of capitalism. For the Frankfurt theorists, understanding culture should never be reduced to a simple reflex of class interests. In a similar spirit, however, they sought to decode the ways in which the most powerful interests in society expressed themselves through the production of mass culture.[77]

Adorno distinguished among genuine art, folk culture, and mass culture. Genuine art had a deeper, social function; it was critical of domineering institutions and revealed the possibility of transcending, or going beyond, present-day society.[78] Folk culture was traditional and indigenous, expressed the daily lives of the masses, and had "rebellious resistance inherent within it." Mass culture in modern society, however, no longer originated from below; rather, peoples' consumption of culture was administered from above by the **culture industry**.[79] Never before had mass culture been subject to such a high degree of conscious manipulation. In Nazi Germany, propaganda had been manufactured by the government to mould public opinion and attract people to the regime. And in the United States, privately owned cultural industries played the same function.

Adorno and Horkheimer found American culture to be inferior to European high culture and dominated by big business. The culture industry comprises the big corporations that virtually monopolize the production and distribution of entertainment through media such as film, music, and popular writing. In the 1930s, for example, the film industry was controlled by a handful of big studios, such as MGM, Warner Brothers, and Universal, and the producers called the shots. These big studios ignored the independent fringes of the film industry, where innovations were developed, except to incorporate the most promising techniques into the studio system.

Like any business, the culture industry reflects the world of **instrumental rationality**. Art has been turned into a uniform commodity for mass manipulation. The industry generates products that are tailored for mass consumption and "manufactured more or less according to plan." Consumers are merely objects of calculation who obey "their master's voice," reinforcing their subservient mentality. "His master's voice" was the slogan that branded the products of the RCA-Victor electronics company. It appeared beneath the logo that pictured a dog listening intently to a gramophone record, presumably hearing her or his dead master's voice. For Horkheimer and Adorno, the image was ironic. The culture industry "hammers" the concepts of the prevailing society into human beings, who respond like well-conditioned dogs. The industry propagates social consensus and "strengthens blind, opaque authority."[80] As a result, according to Adorno, conformity has replaced critical thinking, the state to which most of humanity has been reduced in Aldous Huxley's dystopian novel, *Brave New World* (see Box 4.3).

Horkheimer and Adorner point out that just as standardized production prevails in the assembly lines of industry, under conditions of virtual monopoly in the culture industries all mass culture is identical.[81] Obviously, the film industry, the culture industry's central sector, does not produce films that are identical in their content. In this sense, then, industrial production is not the most suitable metaphor. Films are not identical like Ford motor cars are. Nevertheless, like the products of skilled crafts workers, films are produced to follow a small number of standardized plots or schema. The plot of *Star Wars*, for example, is a recycled Western. In general, the outcome of a film "can invariably be predicted from the start." Indeed, films and popular songs are strung together with a thread of "ready-made clichés."[82]

Once the culture industry finds a successful formula, Horkheimer and Adorno continue, it plugs it over and over again.[83] Soon, however, amusement turns into boredom. While the culture industry rejects anything that hasn't already been tried as being too risky, nothing can stay the same. The industry must appear, then, to be constantly changing. Paradoxically, the new is "what is both totally familiar and has never existed before."[84] The alien creatures in James Cameron's movie *Avatar*, for example, are imagined by recombining characteristics of ordinary animals, such as the heads of hammerhead sharks and the bodies of elephants.

❖ BOX 4.3 • THEORY IN CONTEXT ❖

Aldous Huxley—Technological Rationality Run Amok

In *Brave New World* (1931), novelist Aldous Huxley imagines a society where technology is employed to dominate human beings. Huxley's vision is similar to the One State in Zamyatin's earlier dystopian novel, *We*. Huxley envisages a future in which science and technology—the rational intellect—have come to dominate humanity. In the novel, society exists in a rigid and fixed hierarchy that is reproduced largely through human cloning: human beings are conceived and genetically engineered in a central hatchery, which produces 96 clones from one embryo. Several distinct castes of humans are created, fit for different kinds of work. From conception, each newly hatched being is conditioned in a Social Predestination Room to accept certain moral principles, such as social segregation and acceptance of their position in the social order.[85] Any anxiety felt by the inhabitants of Huxley's *Brave New World* is quickly stifled by Soma, the name Huxley gives to a fictional drug, taken for everything from reducing anxiety to suppressing emotions. Huxley claimed that his negative utopia was being increasingly, and frighteningly, realized in the modern world. In fact, the horror "may be upon us in a single century."[86]

The movie producers realized that the creatures (including the human-like Navi) had to be sufficiently recognizable that the audience would feel comfortable and unchallenged. Horkheimer and Adorno believed that the essence of mass viewing or listening was recognition of the familiar.

While there is some variety among the objects of cultural production and the differences are trumpeted through advertising, these differences are only "like Yale locks which differ by fractions of a millimetre." The culture industry recognizes, however, that not all consumers are identical in their purchasing power. As a result, consumers are identified, classified, and organized into target groups, and mass production is geared toward these quantifiable types. "Something is provided for everyone so that no one can escape," but the outcome of consuming any product is always the same: the body is given the superficial freedom of choice but the mind rots in intellectual powerlessness.[87] Even the form of jazz popular at the time and played on the radio, Adorno says, which was assumed to highlight spontaneous improvisation and individuality, had succumbed to standardization and commercialization.[88]

The main point of Horkheimer and Adorno's criticism is that mass culture has abandoned any intellectual purpose. Nothing is left of the original social function of art, which was to challenge society's claims and confront the social order with the deeper and "real interests of human beings."[89] The consumers of mass culture focus on the technology behind the production, which is the real seat of creativity, innovation, and social power. In contrast, the content of the entertainment is threadbare and stereotyped, offering little more than stale ideologies.[90] Given its lack of creativity, its shallow content, and the dullness of its ideas, mass culture causes intellectual growth to decline and even disappear.[91] Then, as the culture industry becomes more entrenched as big business, the meaning of entertainment becomes synonymous with society's apologia.[92] At the root of amusement, Horkheimer and Adorno believe, is powerlessness.

Assuming that all new technologies will be monopolized by the culture industries, Horkheimer and Adorno claim that in modern society technological progress makes it easier to introduce new illusions and cement old ones firmly in the minds of consumers. The technical domination of culture propagates mass deception and impedes "the development of autonomous, independent individuals who judge and decide consciously for themselves." Consequently, the industry undermines the most important precondition for democracy.[93] Those in control of the culture industries have entrenched themselves in advertising, which strengthens the glue that bonds consumers to big corporations.[94] The masses are conditioned to want and demand the goods that the culture industry—and through advertising, all industries—are selling.

Mass media, Leo Lowenthal says, offers only entertainment and distraction and thereby expedites "flight from an unbearable reality." Any notion that there may be a progressive solution to human problems is "cut short by a false fulfilment of wish-dreams, like wealth, adventure, passionate love, power, and sensationalism in general."[95] For Horkheimer and Adorno, entertainment is indeed escape, but it is not merely an escape from a bad reality but, rather, escape "from the last thought of resisting that reality." Amusement promises to free people, but it really means freeing them from thinking critically.[96]

The culture industry, however, does not have it entirely its own way. Its control of the consumer is mediated by people's need to be entertaining: "Demand has not yet been replaced by simple obedience." The film industry moguls pay attention to ticket sales. Entertainment has to fit in with the dual business process of fabricating needs among the consuming public and then appearing to satisfy those needs. It is not easy to keep the public in submission, although, "Even on those occasions when the public rebels against the pleasure industry it displays the feebleness systematically instilled in it by that industry." Perversely, perhaps, Horkheimer and Adorno claim that there are traces in American culture of something better than the sameness of the culture industry, found in any feature that is circus-like, "stubbornly purposeless," or physical rather than intellectual. Pure nonsense, they argue, such as farce and clowning, was a legitimate part of popular art, up to the time of Charlie Chaplin and the Marx Brothers: "[M]indless artistry . . . represents what is human against the social mechanism."[97]

It isn't that the culture industries are accepted uncritically. For Horkheimer and Adorno, however, standard criticisms of popular film and music reinforce the very tendencies they criticize. In the 1930s, the film industry was censored to prevent the overt display of such things as sexuality, nudity, illegal drugs, mixed-race relationships, and profanity. Even married couples had to have separate beds. But as liberal Europeans, the Frankfurt theorists did not see sexual desire as inherently evil.[98] The problem was that the culture industry promised happiness while delivering only a sad facsimile. American film had an important sexual subtext, but the audience was led to the altar and then left dangling; desire was aroused but had to be repressed and denied. The entire show of the culture industry, Horkheimer and Adorno believed, merely tantalized, endlessly cheating its consumers out of what it constantly promised: pleasure.[99]

The essential point is that the industry never wants to release its grip on the consumer, never "for a moment allowing him or her to suspect that resistance is possible."[100] That resistance was not futile was precisely the view of Walter Benjamin, who was a member of the Institute of Social Research in Europe. Benjamin saw something progressive even in art that was mass produced.

Walter Benjamin (1892–1940)

Benjamin was born in Berlin to a well-off, assimilated Jewish family. In the heady years of the German Revolution, Benjamin was introduced to **historical materialism**. He met Vladimir Mayakovsky in Russia and worked closely with the German playwright Bertholt Brecht. Brecht wrote and produced plays that were designed both to entertain and to challenge the thinking of his audience.[101]

Benjamin moved to Paris after the Nazi takeover in 1933, and was still in Paris in 1940 when the German occupation began. The United States government granted Benjamin an entry visa, but he was refused a French exit visa. In ill health from a heart condition, Benjamin made his way south, looking for an exit route through Spain. When he arrived at the border, however, he found that the Spanish authorities had closed the border. In the face of imminent arrest for attempting to leave France without a visa, Benjamin took an overdose of morphine and died an agonizing death at the age of 48.[102]

Benjamin's best-known essay is titled, "The Work of Art in the Age of Mechanical Reproduction" (1936). Benjamin argues that the technical ability to mechanically reproduce a work has fundamentally changed the meaning of artistic creation. *Reproduction* means the ability to make multiple, identical copies of an art work, such as copies from a photographic negative or records from a master disc. (In the digital age, the technical possibilities for copying have expanded exponentially.) Benjamin says that every reproduction is spawned from one original piece, which existed initially in one time and place. The original has a "unique existence" distinct from the "plurality of copies" that are made from it. Art originated historically in magical or religious rituals and was "embedded in the fabric of tradition." Consequently, every original work of art, Benjamin says, has a distinct "aura" or halo effect that is connected to its uniqueness, authenticity, and origin in ritual. Only a specific, unique piece can claim authenticity, which cannot be technically reproduced.[103]

All forms of original art continue to be surrounded by a sense of authenticity and a ritualistic aura that is connected to the origin and history of the piece.[104] When North American bus tourists approach the famous Louvre Museum in Paris on their lock-step march through Europe, they save time by asking the guard, "*Où est la Mona Lisa?*" They want to stand in front of the original, bask in the aura of authenticity, and imagine Leonardo da Vinci at work. To be shown a reproduction would be an outrage.

Making copies of originals is as old as art itself and may be done out of reverence or greed. Photography, however, was the first revolutionary form of visual reproduction. Photography put the ability to faithfully reproduce a scene into the hands of anyone with a camera and thereby precipitated a crisis in painting. The artistic response was to explore painting as a medium of line and colour, and to move from realism to abstraction. Ideologically, the result was the doctrine of art for art's sake, which denied any social function to painting.[105]

For Benjamin, mechanical reproduction has multiple effects on art. On the one hand, art becomes little more than a commodity having its value in exchange (money). As the commodity or exhibition value of the reproduction comes to dominate, the artistic function becomes merely incidental. On the other hand, photographic techniques reveal images that are unattainable by vision (for example, slow motion or the close-up). Unlike the single image of the painting, the cameraman's film consists of a montage or assembly of multiple fragments that can penetrate deeply into the web of reality. In addition, reproduction places the copy in social contexts that are not possible for the original: "it enables the original to meet the beholder halfway," in her or his particular situation.[106] The consumer decides how, where, and when the reproduction is viewed, such as watching a video at home rather than in a cinema.

Furthermore, "the total function of art is reversed." Art is emancipated from its original, conservative basis in ritual and tradition. Instead, the work of art becomes political. In modern society, according to Benjamin, film is a powerful agent of transformation. The film audience identifies with the camera and takes the position "of a critic," providing a perspective that undermines the values of cult and tradition. As in sport spectatorship, anyone who watches a film becomes "somewhat of an expert." Benjamin argues that people can appreciate film and sporting contests as knowledgeable commentators. With such things as letters to the editor—and today, the Internet—anyone becomes an author and the distinction between public and author is minimized.[107]

Benjamin disputes the common criticism that film spectacle merely creates a diversion for the uneducated; it requires no intelligence and permits no concentration. He says, "Clearly, this is at bottom the same ancient lament that the masses seek distraction whereas art demands concentration from the spectator." The question Benjamin asks of this commonplace criticism is "whether it provides a platform for the analysis of the film." Benjamin sees more room for optimism than either Horkheimer or Adorno. He suggests that "in some cases today's films can also promote revolutionary criticism of social conditions, even of the distribution of property." The films of Charlie Chaplin were socially significant and people responded progressively to them because they fused visual and emotional enjoyment together with the critical mind and the orientation of the expert.[108]

The critical potential of film is different from earlier artistic forms. The single painting, for example, invites contemplation whereas the quickly moving images in a film prevent contemplation at least while the film is being watched—think of the rapid cutting of a modern music video. On the other hand, film analysis deepens our perception of reality the way psychoanalysis deepens our perception of dreams and everyday speech: "[F]ilmed behavior lends itself more readily to analysis because of its incomparably more precise statements of the situation . . . because it can be isolated more easily." Film permits close-ups, slow-motion, the focus on hidden details, and "exploring commonplace milieus." The film medium, which consciously explores and penetrates space and creates physical shock effects, opens the world to new and different perceptions, within which "we calmly and adventurously go travelling."[109]

The Frankfurt School theorists analyzed the culture industry single-mindedly and ignored critical impulses and genres. They assumed that culture would follow the general capitalist trend of monopolization, through which technological innovations would only deepen domination and human alienation. They did not foresee that new technologies, beginning with the microchip, would create inexpensive forms of mechanical reproduction and make them widely available. The proliferation of content in terms of variety, source, and audience is the contemporary norm.

For the Frankfurt School theorists, however, the question was not just about monopoly but also ideological manipulation. Modern technology fundamentally altered the supply side of culture, both in terms of the multiplicity of amateur productions and mainstream industries. But the Frankfurt School theorists would likely be critical of the demand side. In their view, cultural production arose from and helped shape the desire for amusement and entertainment, and undermined the capacity for social criticism. They also did not foresee the incorporation of social criticism into the mainstream, as just one consumer preference among many. It doesn't matter to market capitalists whether you are eating, praying, or loving—or reading critical social theory—as long as you're buying something they're selling.

Today, production by the masses, as distinct from mass production, means there is no shortage of critical content on Internet sites. But Internet content is overwhelmed by pornography, personal tidbits, and every imaginable perspective. It is worth noting that the technological revolution that today makes production by the masses possible occurred in a period of neo-liberalism. Conservatism and reification was in the air the turn-of-the-century generation breathed. Since everything changes, however, it is possible that the impact of modern technology could take on a more leftist hue in the contemporary period of economic and social crisis.

Conclusion

World War II devastated Europe and the Soviet Union. The United States emerged from the war as a single dominant power possessing the atom bomb. As the world slipped quickly into a new Cold War between the US and the Soviet Union, social theory in the United States took a decidedly conservative form, whether in structural functionalism, development theory, behaviourism, or theories of equivalent exchange. These ideas are explored next, in Part II of this book, which describes the passage from the repression of the 1950s to the return of social rebellion and anti-colonialism in the subsequent decades. Chapter 5 examines social thought in the context of the post-war Red Scare.

Questions for Reflection

1. Why does fascism attract a mass following? Could fascism in some form become a mass movement in the West in the present time?

2. Debate the issue of blame: collective guilt versus the dangerous few. Do Western liberal democracies bear any responsibility for the rise of fascism in Europe?

3. As the Frankfurt School theory of the "culture industry" may suggest, are people today simply unthinking dupes of the mass media?

4. Why do you think contemporary cultural critics find Benjamin's analysis of culture more compelling than Horkheimer and Adorno's?

Timeline

1928	Anthropologist Margaret Mead publishes *Coming of Age in Samoa*; influential in 1960s.
1943	J.P. Sartre publishes *Being and Nothingness*; his play *The Flies* is performed in Paris.
1943	India and Pakistan win independence from Britain; decolonization underway.
1947	Jackson Pollock begins experimenting with "drip paintings" (American Expressionism).
1949	In France, Simone de Beauvoir publishes *The Second Sex* about women's oppression.
1949	The Chinese Communist Party comes to power led by Mao Zedong.
1950	US Senator Joseph McCarthy gives his Red Scare speech about communists in government.
1950	Harold Innis publishes *Empire and Communications*, applying his staples approach.
1951	Functional sociologist Talcott Parsons publishes *The Social System*.
1951	C. Wright Mills publishes *White Collar* about the US middle class.
1951	Albert Camus writes his essay *The Rebel* (*L'homme révolté*).
1951	Marshall McLuhan publishes *The Mechanical Bride*, a critique of media and advertising.
1952	The US detonates first hydrogen bomb, 1000 times more powerful than the atomic bomb.
1953	The USSR detonates a hydrogen bomb; the nuclear weapons race escalates.
1953	*Waiting for Godot*, Samuel Beckett's theatre-of-the-absurd play, opens in Paris.
1954	The Algerian Liberation Front begins the Algerian Revolution, an anti-colonial war.
1955	Rosa Parks refuses to sit at the back of the bus, the resulting boycott sparks a movement.
1956	Allen Ginsberg reads *Howl*, his controversial, defining Beat poem; he is charged with obscenity.
1960	The film *Spartacus* marks the end of the McCarthy-era blacklist in Hollywood.
1960	Daniel Bell publishes *The End of Ideology*; among other ideas, Marxism is dead.
1961	Frantz Fanon publishes *The Wretched of the Earth*, his attack on colonialism.
1963	Betty Friedan publishes *The Feminine Mystique*, the foundation text for second-wave feminism.
1963	George Wallace, governor of Alabama, makes his "segregation forever" speech.
1963	The civil rights march on Washington takes place, and M.L. King gives his "I have a dream" speech.
1964	Marshall McLuhan publishes *Understanding Media*: the medium is the message.
1965	The US has 75,000 troops in Vietnam, a major escalation of the anti-communist conflict.
1965	Malcolm X is assassinated in New York City; Martin Luther King is assassinated in 1968.
1970	Kari Levitt publishes *Silent Surrender*, about the US economic takeover of Canada.
1970	The Front de Libération du Québec (FLQ) precipitates the October Crisis in Canada.
1978	Edward Säid publishes the anti-imperialist book *Orientalism*.

II From Repression to Rebellion

For decades after World War II, the world was faced with the possibility of nuclear holocaust. In 1964, two years after the Cuban Missile Crisis, which appeared to bring the world to the brink of a nuclear war, two films were released that dealt with the nuclear threat. One was a tense drama and the other a satire.

In the film *Fail Safe* (directed by Sidney Lumet), a computer malfunction sends an attack code to the indoctrinated airmen on board a group of Vindicator nuclear bombers; the airmen believe that the United States is under attack. The president of the United States (played by Henry Fonda) phones the Russian premier on the hot line to explain that the attack is inadvertent. When neither the Americans nor the Russians can shoot down the bombers and Moscow is struck, the US president orders a bomb to be dropped on New York by the US Air Force to appease the Russians with equal damage and prevent all-out nuclear war.

Stanley Kubrick's *Dr. Strangelove* (subtitled *How I Learned to Stop Worrying and Love the Bomb*) deals satirically with the threat of nuclear holocaust. In Kubrick's film, a nuclear

---

Image: Major "King" Kong climbs into the bomb bay of his B-52 nuclear bomber to release the bomb by hand and thereby unleash nuclear holocaust. © Hawk Films Ltd / Ronald Grant Archive / Alamy

strike is deliberately launched by the wild-eyed General Jack D. Ripper, who believes the US will win—fewer Americans than Russians will die. Unknown to Ripper, the US has deployed a Doomsday Machine designed as the ultimate deterrent by an ex-Nazi scientist now in the US (played by Peter Sellers). If any country launches a nuclear attack, the machine will automatically detonate a barrage of nuclear bombs. Since total devastation is assured, no rational person would start a nuclear war. The attack is almost stopped until, against all odds, Major "King" Kong (played by Slim Pickens), onboard a B-52 bomber, demonstrates typical American ingenuity by climbing into the bomb bay to manually release the bomb. He straddles it like a bucking bronco as it falls toward Moscow, yelling and waving a cowboy hat. The film ends with a montage of multiple nuclear explosions engulfing the world.

The threat of nuclear annihilation becomes a predominant theme in culture, from *Godzilla* in Japan to American films about alien invasion. In the context of the Cold War, functionalism and behaviourism become dominant perspectives in American social science. Critical responses to the dominant theories arose in sociology, for example, in the work of C. Wright Mills and Irving Goffman, and in the culture of the Beats. Simone de Beauvoir and Betty Friedan reawakened a slumbering feminism. Marshall McLuhan recognized the complex importance of changes in the media of communications. In Europe, the response to the wars, cold and hot, emphasized the absurdity of the era and the need to take personal responsibility. The post-war world was marked by widespread anti-colonial struggles as European domination was challenged economically, politically, and culturally. Frantz Fanon, Che Guevara, and Edward Saïd responded to Western ideologies of development and imperialism, and contributed to theories of post-colonialism.

CHAPTER 5

Theory and Society in the Cold War

Learning Objectives

- To assess the responses of social theorists to the Cold War, the threat of nuclear annihilation, and the emergence of McCarthyism in the United States
- To assess the development of structural functionalism in sociology and ask whether a consensus model of society explains the main currents of development in the West
- To link the emergence of **macrosociology** with the dominance of behaviourism during the post-WWII decades
- To understand the emergence of social theories that emphasized individual choice as opposed to structural determination

For 30 years following Hiroshima, the world was a dangerous place. Overshadowing all was the threat of nuclear annihilation. Hiroshima changed virtually everything that came after it. The generation that came after 1945 lived under the mushroom cloud. The Cold War between Soviet Russia and the United States meant the arms race, nuclear proliferation, national paranoia, and global conflict. The two superpowers stored enough nuclear bombs to destroy the planet many times over. In an Orwellian twist, the accumulation of more weapons of war was defended as the best way to ensure peace. General Edgeways, a character in Sinclair Lewis's novel *It Can't Happen Here* (1935), explained, "For the first time in all history, a great nation must go on arming itself more and more, not for conquest—not for jealousy—not for war—but for *peace*!"[1] This sentiment was just as true in the 1950s, when the doctrine was called MAD—Mutually Assured Destruction.

This chapter begins by examining the Cold War through the eyes of intellectuals, such as George Orwell and Arthur Koestler, and in popular culture. At the heart of the American response was a policy of rooting out leftist dissent, known as McCarthyism. Senator Joseph McCarthy was the most visible and voluble antagonist of alternative thought in the United States. Other Western countries, such as Britain and Canada, adopted similar regulatory policies. Sociology has usually been a liberal discipline, inclined to social improvement and individual betterment; many sociologists then, as now, had left-leaning backgrounds and were targeted during the Cold War.

In American sociology, outside the Chicago School, the dominant theoretical traditions of the 1950s were developed at Columbia and Harvard Universities. Talcott Parsons was the most significant macro theorist in sociology. His approach, known as structural functionalism, dominated the discipline for 20 years.[2] According to Lipsett, most of the prominent sociologists at Columbia and Harvard, including Parsons, had at one time been left of centre. At Columbia, the principal functionalist was Robert Merton, who, as a student at Harvard, had been drawn to Parsons's work. Merton was one of seven Columbia academics denounced as leftists in 1952 by vice-presidential nominee Richard Nixon. There were, however, also sociologists who were dyed-in-the-wool conservatives, including Pitirim Sorokin, the founding chair of sociology at Harvard, who was an émigré from Bolshevik Russia.[3]

The Cold War and the Intellectuals

"Big Brother is watching you."

— George Orwell, *Nineteen Eighty-Four*, 1949

Many intellectuals had become Marxists and Communists during the Depression and the anti-fascist World War II. During the 1930s, much critical literature, particularly novels, espoused social realism—the depiction of social troubles to raise consciousness about the need for reform or revolution. Writing in the 1950s, however, differed from the critical realism of the Depression. By the fifties, many left-leaning intellectuals had abandoned or been pushed out of their radical phase. In Britain, the change in politics reflected the changing times that novelist Doris Lessing called "tight, suspicious, frightened." But the threat of Britain's own version of political paranoia was only part of this disillusionment. Lessing's character Anna in *The Golden Notebook* points out the other dilemma: "that the great dream [of socialism] has faded and the truth is something else— that we'll never be any use."[4]

But literature is socially useful one way or another. While many former socialists became apolitical, many others converted to the cause of anti-communism. The near-hysteria of the post-war leftist "witch hunts" in the United States and elsewhere drove many leftists underground for self-preservation or increasingly steered them in pro-capitalist directions. Although people had the right to walk to a different drummer, some percussionists were definitely taboo. The growing conservatism was grounded, however, in the return of American prosperity. What was to be enjoyed in what sociologist C. Wright Mills called the great American celebration of the 1950s was a rising standard of living for unprecedented numbers.

Increasingly, many European intellectuals turned away from Soviet-style socialism and from Marxism more generally. In eastern Europe, where Russian tanks suppressed rebellion in Hungary in 1956, the USSR seemed to be acting like any imperialistic great power, a far cry from the promised internationalism of Marx. Disillusioned ex-Marxists denounced the Soviet Union in the 1949 book, *The God That Failed*. Adopting the Romantic theory of individual freedom, they condemned what they saw as an over-emphasis on reason and rationality, and turned instead to subjectivity and often spirituality and mysticism. The most critical individuals, however, thought of organized religions as comparable in their hypocrisy to the Marxism of the Soviet Communist Party. Arthur Koestler was a Hungarian author and former Communist who had been a party member during the 1930s. He became one of the most articulate of the anti-Marxists.

In his novel *Darkness at Noon*, Koestler condemns Stalinism through the voice of a fictional old Bolshevik, Rubashov, who was tried and condemned to death for counter-revolution. Koestler's novel was based on the actual trial and execution in the 1930s of many of Russia's former revolutionary leaders. In his attempt to understand what went wrong with the revolution, Rubashov debates this fundamental theoretical question: does the means justify the end? If the end or final goal of a revolution is a just and equal world, is it acceptable to use any means to get there, even if these means are unjust or create inequality in the short run? George Orwell had satirized this doctrine in his novel *1984*, in which two subversives agree to do anything to weaken the power of Big Brother: to give their lives, to commit murder, "to cheat, to forge, to blackmail, to corrupt the minds of children," even, if it would somehow serve the interests of the revolution, "to throw sulfuric acid in a child's face."[5]

Koestler argues that the Soviet Communist Party under Stalin had focused so single-mindedly on the end—that is, the supposed creation of communism—that members believed that even evil means could be justified. Whatever harm had been done was in the name of preserving at all costs the Soviet Union, which was the fatherland and bastion of the revolution, from external and internal enemies. Koestler's dilemma was between personal morality and revolutionary violence. Like medieval popes who had undermined the Christian principles they supposedly avowed, Stalin "had besmirched the ideal of the Social State." The revolutionaries, similarly, had discarded all moral conventions; they were "sailing without ethical ballast."[6]

Western intellectuals compared the political forms of domination and the imposition of Party ideology on all aspects of culture and civil society in Nazi Germany under Hitler and in the USSR under Stalin. The most prominent intellectual voice that conflated Nazi Germany with Soviet Russia belonged to Hannah Arendt, a German exile from Nazism who found refuge in New York. In 1951 she published *The Origins of Totalitarianism*, analyzing the ideology and practice of Nazism and state socialism in the USSR as forms of a political and social system called **totalitarianism**.

Appearing during the depths of the Cold War, *The Origins of Totalitarianism* helped legitimize anti-Sovietism by equating it with resistance to Hitler. A new form of "radical evil" had replaced the old, but they were essentially similar kinds of regimes—US president Ronald Reagan would call Russia the "Evil Empire" in 1983. The two forms of totalitarianism had in common the rule of a single party and dominance of the institutions of the state over all other aspects of society, including culture, education, the mass media, politics, the economy, and social organizations. Conflating Nazism and the Soviet Union, however, ignored important and fundamental social and ideological differences between the two systems.

Dystopic Fiction: Orwell and Huxley

The most popular and biting Cold War satire on the Stalinist regime in Russia was George Orwell's *Animal Farm*. In this novel, the pigs lead the oppressed farm animals in a revolution and together, in the name of "animalism," they take over the farm. "All animals are equal," the pigs declare—certainly a revolutionary sentiment. Over time, however, the pigs who led the revolution become corrupt, giving themselves more and more privileges and monopolizing power. This reversal is symbolized by the degradation of the principles the revolution had stood for; for example, the pigs transform the original revolutionary slogan: "All animals are equal, but some animals are more equal than others." It is a deliciously ironic phrase, symbolic of the complete, cynical perversion of social theory. Later, the pigs move into the house that used to belong to the humans. When the other animals look through the window to spy on the pigs, they see them wearing clothes, feasting, and fraternizing with humans. In the end, the pigs are as tyrannical, elitist, and unjust as the human beings they had overthrown. And so, too, Orwell says, have the Communists in Russia been converted from revolutionaries to privileged bureaucrats and tyrants.

The short fable reflects Trotsky's theory of the *Revolution Betrayed* (1937), although Orwell's theory of counter-revolution in the USSR rests on the theory that the exercise of power is inevitably corrupting. In *Nineteen Eighty-Four* (1949), his most famous novel, Orwell imagines a negative utopian future society (a dystopia). This nightmare vision was constructed from myriad images drawn from Nazism and Soviet Russia but also, arguably, from the tendency of liberal democracies to degenerate into a world of mass manipulation, authoritarianism, and military tyranny.

In *Nineteen Eighty-Four*, Orwell imagines the world split among three superpowers. One is Oceania, a Western world under the heel of totalitarianism. In Oceania, the Party has perfected the science of surveillance. Under constant scrutiny by two-way telescreens that allow the State to peer into the bedrooms of the nation, Big Brother is always watching. The worst sin isn't breaking the rules; it's "thoughtcrime": *thinking* about breaking them. Fiction sometimes comes close to truth: technology moves so quickly that ethical decisions about data use are left far behind. As more and more information is collected about people in the Internet age, police are looking at ways to analyze the enormous amount of data to which they have access. The idea is to be able to predict the people who would be more likely to break the law so they can be detained and crimes stopped before they begin. It's called predictive policing, and it brings the film *Minority Report* and *Nineteen Eighty-Four* closer to actual practice.

In the novel, the dominance of the Party depends on control over the mind. For Orwell, mind control rests ultimately on the manipulation of language. In Oceania, words mean their opposite ("doublethink"): *freedom* is slavery; *war* is peace; *ignorance* is strength. The technique is used in advertising and in politics, for example, calling torture "enhanced interrogation." In *Nineteen Eighty-Four*, an important department of the so-called Ministry of Truth is busily "cutting the language down to the bones." Similarly, in the novel *Oryx and Crake*, Margaret Atwood comments that "When they're gone out of his head, these words, they'll be gone, everywhere, forever.

As if they had never been."[7] In Orwell's theory of language, once words and concepts such as *freedom, revolution,* and *independence* are eliminated from consciousness, resistance becomes unthinkable and the Party will have extinguished "once and for all the possibility of independent thought." Hitler, in a similar manner, had used the Big Lie as a propaganda tool. Orwell argues that if everyone believes a lie, the lie becomes truth. Sociologically, our opinions are shaped by what others tell us; in the absence of any other person to support our beliefs, we come to doubt our own memories: "Whatever happens in all minds, truly happens."[8]

In Aldous Huxley's *Brave New World* (1932), an earlier dystopic novel, free sexuality and liberal doses of mind-altering drugs worked the sociological magic of social control. Orwell's Oceanic nightmare of totalitarianism is far more Puritan. Any form of sexual expression outside of heterosexual marriage and procreation is labelled a "sexcrime." The Party suppresses sexuality not merely because a private bond between lovers creates loyalty outside Party control, but because sexual repression causes a bottling-up of energy (Freud's "libido") that the Party can then sublimate or redirect into hysterical war-fever, hatred, and leader-worship: "there was a direct intimate connection between chastity and political orthodoxy."[9]

Theoretically, free sexuality in this Puritan context appears to be a political act. One character, Julia, has apparently perfected the art of secret sexual, individual rebellion. Hiding behind the appearance of the most rigid orthodoxy, even becoming a stalwart member of the Junior Anti-Sex League, Julia is the clever rebel who simply learns to evade Party rules. Her individual rebellion is her indulgence in the "animal instinct" of sexuality, unashamedly and with abandon. Under the camouflage of keeping the small rules, she breaks the big ones and defies the Party. Orwell thought of Julia as "only a rebel from the waist downwards."[10]

When military governments in contemporary Latin America cause political opponents to "disappear," everyone understands why they were murdered and they become martyrs to their cause. In Oceania, they torture their victims until they surrender completely, in body and mind. Heretics are "washed clean" of thoughtcrime and come to believe the Party line is truth. They become mere shells of human beings, left with only sorrow, penitence, and love of Big Brother.[11] Returned to society, the former rebels become merely compliant non-entities. When they disappear, it's unnoticed, and the Ministry of Truth erases any evidence of their existence.

Orwell was equally blunt that the purpose behind the Party's persecution was a theory of power for its own sake. Big Brother's regime was "not interested in the good of others"; it was "interested solely in power. Not wealth or luxury or long life or happiness: only power, pure power." Orwell says the Communists in Russia had seized power pretending—perhaps even believing—that their ultimate aim was to create a world of freedom and equality. But, in Orwell's Oceania, "no one ever seizes power with the intention of relinquishing it. Power is not a means, it is an end. One does not establish a dictatorship in order to safeguard a revolution; one makes the revolution in order to establish the dictatorship."[12] Orwell sought to entomb the socialist experiment in Russia together with Nazism.

The Nuclear Arms Race

In 1949, 15 nations, including the United States and Canada, signed a military pact—the North Atlantic Treaty Organization (NATO)—to coordinate defense against potential Soviet aggression. In the Cold War context, it was easy to project onto Soviet foreign policy the drive for military expansionism and world conquest that had led Germany into World War II. Given the assumed parallel, a Soviet-led Third World War was immi-

nent. After Stalin's death in 1953, the Cold War intensified. The Soviets exploded a hydrogen bomb, heightening tension with the United States, expanding the arms race, and causing fear that a Third World War would result in the destruction of civilization. Americans frantically built bomb shelters in their basements, in which they would surely fry, and school children practised covering their heads under their desks, training that was absurd but increased public paranoia. In 1957, Canada and the United States established a coordinated air defence system (NORAD) headquartered deep in the Rocky Mountains in Colorado. Dozens of early-warning radar units were built in northern Canada to detect potential Soviet nuclear air strikes launched over the Canadian Arctic. Lester Pearson helped solidify Canada's reputation as a peaceful nation when he was prime minister by contributing Canadian troops to peace-keeping missions in such places as Egypt and Cyprus. He won the Nobel Prize for Peace. But in 1965, he agreed that American nuclear bombs could be mounted on Bomarc missiles on Canadian soil.

The potential for a nuclear holocaust could come about through deliberate strategy or through military recklessness or carelessness, as the Hollywood films *Fail-Safe* (1964) and *Dr. Strangelove* (1964) suggested. Many of the most brilliant German scientists were Jews, who had fled to the United States in the 1930s to escape Nazi persecution. Among the spoils of World War II that had been divided between the US and USSR were the scientists who had developed rocketry in Nazi Germany.

Wernher von Braun was one of the leading rocket scientists who had joined the Nazi Party in 1940. Although he exploited slave labour in his rocket factory, von Braun was not prosecuted for war crimes when he surrendered at the end of World War II to the Americans rather than to the Russians. "The next time," he said, "I want to be on the winning side."[13] This amoral expediency was based on the theory that science was politically neutral—scientists will build whatever technologies of destruction they're paid to produce, but they're not responsible for how they are used. In folk singer Tom Lehrer's view, this attitude is summed up in these lines: "Once the rockets are up, who cares where they come down? / That's not my department, says Wernher von Braun."[14]

In 1957, Australian Neville Shute (1899-1960) published *On the Beach*, a novel about nuclear Armageddon. The novel, which was filmed in 1959, takes place in the state of Victoria, in southeastern Australia, after the world has experienced a nuclear holocaust caused by the procurement of the atomic bomb by less well-developed countries. (Proliferation continues to be an issue in the twenty-first century, with Iran apparently posing the latest nuclear threat.) In *On the Beach*, a short, 37-day war takes place in 1963. Albania starts the war, which sets off a chain reaction involving all the nuclear powers.[15] The whole northern hemisphere is devastated by an exchange of about 5000 nuclear weapons, primarily "cobalt" bombs, which were designed to spread the maximum radiation. No one in the northern hemisphere survives. In Victoria, the survivors await the deadly radioactive clouds slowly drifting south on the prevailing winds. They know this radiation will inevitably cover the globe and wipe out life on earth.[16]

Shute explores a variety of ways that people might respond to certain death by describing the lives of several people who have to face the fact that there was "not so long to go."[17] A similar theme is addressed in the film *Melancholia* (2011), although in that film the earth is threatened by a comet. In *Melancholia* and in Shute's novel, everyone, in his or her own way, goes a bit mad. Some repress their fears by drinking double brandies and making public displays of excess. Most persevere until the end by going "through the motions,"[18] living "in the dream world of unreality." For others, the final answer is suicide. In *On the Beach*, druggists dispense "suicide pills" offering a quick death to avoid the prolonged agony of radiation sickness. The book, as well as the film, along with a spate of other apocalyptic fiction, contributed to the atmosphere of fear that pervaded the era. It also helped many people realize the absurdity and inhumanity of the nuclear arms race.

The "Red Scare"

"[Y]ou must understand, sir, that a person is either with this court or he must be counted against it, there be no road between."[19]

— Arthur Miller, *The Crucible*, 1954

Arthur Miller had been attracted to the fringes of the Communist Party in the 1930s, a connection that later made him a target of the post-war Red Scare. In the chilly atmosphere of the Cold War, Miller argued, artists were intimidated by the "atmosphere of dread" created by the anti-communist crusade that labelled even liberals enemies of the state.[20] Miller's 1953 play *The Crucible* examined the hysteria that had gripped seventeenth-century Salem, Massachusetts, during the witch trials, but Miller had a more contemporary witch hunt in mind. The play was a scathing critique of McCarthyism.

In Puritan New England, it was said, you either sided with God or with the devil; there was no other choice. In the post-1945 Cold War, conservative politicians generated a mass fear of "world-wide Communism" and largely invented a conspiracy within the very government of the United States to bring about communism at home. And in the politics that became known as McCarthyism, you either sided with the American system or you were a communist or a sympathizer—there could be no road between. Similarly, in the wake of the September 11, 2001, Al-Qaeda attacks on New York and Washington, President George Bush, Jr., had declared, "Either you are with us, or you are with the terrorists." In all of these either-or worlds, there is no room for dissent or criticism.

Hollywood responded to the Cold War in a number of ways. The danger of foreign invasion was a common theme in Hollywood films, although it was imagined as an attack by an alien species determined to enslave humanity. The theme appeared in such films as *It Came from Outer Space* (1953), *Invaders from Mars* (1953), *The War of the Worlds* (1953), and *Earth vs. the Flying Saucers* (1956). On the other hand, *The Day the Earth Stood Still* (1951) is an early and thoughtful anti-nuclear film. An alien arrives on earth in an advanced spaceship to warn of the catastrophic consequences that will befall humanity if we continue to develop nuclear weapons. But in a world of nuclear paranoia, who can trust an alien with such awesome power? Building more powerful bombs seems the only possible protection.

Invasion of the Body Snatchers is a Cold War film made in 1956 when the Soviet menace seemed even more threatening.[21] The film is susceptible to several interpretations. In the small town of Santa Mira, California, seedlings that had been drifting through space for years land in a farmer's field and grow into human-sized pods, like large, elongated watermelons. The seed pods have the power to reproduce themselves in the exact likeness of any human being. When people sleep, the pods replicate them, cell by cell. Their mind and memory are transferred to the duplicate, which then replaces the original host body except that the reproduced person has lost every attribute of his or her individual personality.

A few people in Santa Mira, who have not yet become pod-people, become aware that their family members are suddenly not themselves. But who will believe them? The local psychiatrist claims they are suffering from a "strange neurosis, evidently contagious, an epidemic mass hysteria." Their worry is attributed to "what's going on in the world." The theme of mass hysteria reflects 1950s politics, and the film's latent theme is the

erosion of individuality and humanity in the Cold War. Americans had, little by little, hardened their hearts and grown callous.

The manifest theory underlying *Invasion of the Body Snatchers*, however, is the threat of communism. The enemy is in our midst and looks just like one of us. The replicants claim to have been reborn into a better, untroubled world in which people no longer feel separated from one another: "There's no need for love, desire, ambition, faith. Without them, life is so simple." But they have lost any capacity for feeling or love. Replicants become assimilated conformists who lack any individuality and display no typical emotions, such as love, anger, compassion, or excitement. In the theory of Romanticism, humanity is defined by the need for love and everything that an emotional life entails. The original screenplay ended on a message of despair. Facing the inevitable, the last survivor in Santa Mira turns to the camera—to the audience—with a warning: "Look, you fools. You're in danger. Can't you see? They're after you. They're after all of us . . . everyone. They're here already. You're next."[22]

The centre of political gravity had moved to the left in the 1930s. In the post-war period, a right-wing resurgence was underway. In the United States, the principal target was the American Communist Party, but in Cold War politics, anyone who was critical of American society was liable to be branded a sympathizer and called to appear before the House Un-American Activities Committee (HUAC). In 1950, Senator Joseph McCarthy made a speech in which he claimed to have a list of 205 federal civil servants who were members of the Communist Party. It was a gross exaggeration, but highly effective. McCarthy was soon chairing his own Senate Committee and investigating alleged communists and radicals. His grandstanding, rhetoric, and prime-time media exposure made him the symbol of the witch hunters his committee and the HUAC had become. McCarthyism generated its own brand of American **dissidents** who clung to their First Amendment right to freedom of speech and expression (see Box 5.1).

One of the defining features of the right wing in the United States is hostility to intellectuals. Conservatives reject "all this highbrow intellectuality, all this book-learning."[23] Indeed, when Senator McCarthy found the hot-button issue of communism to advance his career, he said the threat to American democracy came from the intellectual class. Thirty thousand books were purged from US libraries because they had been written by "reds." The attack hit home in the elite universities. According to Halimi, agents sifted "minutely through curricula, bibliographies, exam scripts and remarks made in class, and issue[ed] certificates of patriotic loyalty."[24] Something of the flavour of the American right in the 1950s comes across in George F. Babbitt's speech in Sinclair Lewis's 1922 novel, *Babbitt*. The worst menace wasn't the socialists, but "the long-haired gentry who call themselves 'liberals.' . . . Irresponsible teachers and professors constitute the worst of this whole gang, and I am ashamed to say that several of them are on the faculty of our great State University!" Babbitt called these liberals

❖ BOX 5.1 · THEORY IN CONTEXT ❖

American Dissidents

[Major must be a communist because] "You never heard him denying
it until we began accusing him, did you?"[25]
— Joseph Heller, *Catch-22*, 1955

Joseph Heller's absurdist novel exposes as farce the loyalty oaths that many Americans were obliged to take during the Cold War as a condition of keeping their employment. The net that McCarthy cast had a mesh that was fine enough to catch many liberals. Most of the publicity surrounding McCarthyism focused on his attacks on celebrities, artists, and intellectuals—people already in the news. In 1947, the HUAC began to investigate Hollywood actors, directors, and screenwriters, claiming that they infused their films with anti-American values. Hundreds of people in the movie industry were investigated, obliged to name fellow leftists, and subsequently **blacklisted**. Among the banned writers was playwright Lillian Hellman. In her view, the radicals who were being condemned by McCarthyism had done little "more than sign protests, listen to the shocking stories of the few German émigrés . . . and given money to one cause or another."[26]

The big movie moguls, many of whom had emigrated from Eastern Europe early in the century to escape anti-Semitism, were eager to co-operate with McCarthy. The label "communist" undermined their identification with America and its dream of individual success, which had made their fortunes. Many people in Hollywood suspected of having radical views were called before the HUAC and given the choice of co-operating by naming others who, in their opinion, had been involved in left-wing politics. Failure to do so

snakes to be scorched and fired. And McCarthy was on the same page.[27]

The post-war Red Scare was fueled by the fear of internal enemies, communist agents, and spies operating within the heart of Western governments. In the United States, Julius and Ethel Rosenberg were charged and convicted of stealing atomic secrets and handing them over to the Soviet Union. Their sensational trial and execution by electric chair in 1953 is still controversial. In Britain, four Cambridge-educated academics connected to British intelligence, including Donald Maclean and Guy Burgess, were identified in the 1950s as Soviet spies. Maclean and Burgess defected to Russia after being tipped off by Kim Philby that they were about to be arrested. Philby was the head of counter-intelligence in Britain and another Russian spy. Making the British spy trials more sensational were allegations that the Cambridge Four were homosexual. Being gay was defined as an anti-social character weakness that made recruitment as a spy more likely. Since homosexual acts were still criminalized, governments believed gay people were open to blackmail and could be forced to reveal state secrets rather than having their sexuality exposed publically.[28]

meant a prison sentence for contempt of Congress. As a result, many people ended up naming others, and the number of people questioned snowballed. Over 350 actors, writers, producers, and directors were obliged to appear before the HUAC and become informants to preserve their livelihood. Those named included Charlie Chaplin, Pete Seeger, Richard Wright, and Arthur Miller. The Hollywood Ten refused to name names, claiming that the First Amendment gave them the right to remain silent. At a 1947 rally of progressive artists, Katharine Hepburn delivered a speech written by Dalton Trumbo: "Silence the artist, and you silence the most articulate voice the people have. Destroy culture and you destroy one of the strongest sources of inspiration from which a people can draw strength to fight for a better life."[29] The studios, the press, and the HUAC were deaf to this passionate speech. The studio bosses agreed not to hire anyone who didn't co-operate. Some refused to give in and suffered serious economic loss; some were imprisoned for contempt. Others continued to work, using pseudonyms to skirt around the exclusion list or moved abroad to work, including Ring Lardner, Jr., and Ian McLellan Hunter, who wrote *The Adventures of Robin Hood* series, filmed for TV in Britain.[30] The theme "rob from the rich and give to the poor" was patently anti-capitalist.

Finally, a growing backlash against McCarthyism grew stronger, with the film *Spartacus* (1960) marking the beginning of the end of the blacklist. Based on the novel by Howard Fast and with a screenplay by Dalton Trumbo, both of whom had been blacklisted, *Spartacus* tells the story of a slave revolt in Ancient Rome led by an ex-slave. When the slaves are finally captured by the Roman Army, they are asked, which of you is Spartacus? One by one each rebel in the film steps forward and declares, "I am Spartacus!" For their defiance of authority, all were crucified. The parallel to McCarthyism and the naming of names was deliberate.[31] In December 1954, McCarthy's reach had become so wide that he was subject to increasing criticism. His death in 1957 helped bring a political thaw to the country.

The anti-communist campaign in Canada was not as public or as sensational as in the United States. Canada established a Security Panel in 1946, "a small, secret committee of top civil servants" that investigated left-wing and homosexual activities among civil servants. Following the British spy trials, treason and homosexuality were closely linked. The RCMP conducted investigations into individuals' political affiliations as well as their assumed moral or character weaknesses. Hundreds lost their government jobs for security reasons. By the mid-1960s, the RCMP had compiled a list of over 8000 suspected homosexuals.[32]

The Security Panel supported research to develop technology that could identify homosexuals, resulting in what was homophobically referred to as the Fruit Machine project. The machine simultaneously projected pornographic pictures and took photographs of the subject's pupil at intervals of a half-second. If the pictures were sexually arousing, the subject's pupils would measurably dilate and the eyes would be riveted to the genitals, purportedly detecting homosexual responses. The Fruit Machine failed, however, for technical reasons and because the RCMP had difficulty recruiting people to act as so-called "normal" subjects for comparison purposes.[33]

Sociology during the Cold War

Under the theory of totalitarianism, American society was assumed to represent the democratic, capitalist alternative, which offered freedom with prosperity. Most sociologists adapted to the Cold War by accepting the political and economic system uncritically as a given. By the 1950s, American sociologists had taken one of three main paths.

One branch of sociology was concerned with making sociology a precise, empirical science—a type of sociology C. Wright Mills termed **abstracted empiricism**. Social researchers turned to increasingly sophisticated survey research

and mathematical models to relate people's attitudes to their social positions. Empirical sociologists abandoned theory altogether and became increasingly quantified, specialized, and focused on a narrow range of explanations and predictions. In many ways, these sociologists followed the path already well-worn by psychologists who, similarly, strove for the respectability that being recognized as "scientists" would give them.

The dominant theoretical perspective in sociology, however, was **structural functionalism**, which was another path that some American sociologists followed. Functional theory analyzed society as a complex, abstract, and unified system, an approach Mills called "Grand Theory." Finally, in response to empirical "quantophrenia" and the abstractions of functionalism, a third type of sociology concentrated on the concrete, everyday life of society and the social interactions that took place within it. Drawing inspiration from the Chicago School, this **symbolic interactionism**—a micro-level approach to sociology (**microsociology**)—sought to build theory from the bottom up (see Chapter 10). Where all three types of American sociology were similar was in the absence of concern for social criticism and social change.

Talcott Parsons and Structural Functionalism

Talcott Parsons (1902–1979) was the pre-eminent sociological theorist of the post-war era. Like many of the earlier generation of sociologists at the turn of the century who had deep roots in Protestantism, Parsons's father was a Congregational minister. As an undergraduate at Amherst College, Parsons studied biology, although he developed a new interest in social science. He would later apply biological analogies to his study of society as a system.[34] Lipsett says that, as a student in the 1920s, Parsons had been a reform socialist and a member of the Student League for Industrial Democracy.[35] Parsons also studied at the

London School of Economics with anthropologist Bronislaw Malinowski and completed a Ph.D. at the University of Heidelberg in Germany, where he studied the economic ideas of Max Weber and Werner Sombart. In 1927 Parsons became a faculty member at Harvard University.[36]

The central figure in the founding of sociology at Harvard was Pitirim Sorokin (1889–1968). Sorokin had been born in Russia and had roots in the revolutionary anarchist movement. After the October Revolution he became secretary to Alexander Kerensky, who had been the head of the provisional government before the Revolution. In 1918, Sorokin was arrested by the Bolsheviks; he was exiled from Russia in 1922 and accepted an invitation from Harvard University to establish a new department of sociology, which began in 1930 with Sorokin as chair.

Talcott Parsons, who was already at Harvard when Sorokin came, was induced to move from Economics into the new Department of Sociology. The two became bitter rivals for control of the department, a battle that Parsons won, transforming it into the Department of Social Relations. In 1937, Parsons published *The Structure of Social Action*, which introduced European classical social theory, Durkheim, Weber, and Pareto—but not Marx—to American sociology.

At Harvard, Parsons responded to anti-Communism by protecting deserving students with leftist backgrounds from the threats of administrators, who knuckled under political pressure and tried to purge radical students and faculty. In the 1940s, Parsons controversially recruited to the Harvard Russia Research Centre a number of former Soviet academics who had left the USSR when the Germans invaded and were living in Germany. They feared repatriation to the USSR, where they were considered traitors and Nazi collaborators.[37]

Social Systems within Structural Functionalism

Structural functionalists, such as Parsons, attempted to devise an all-inclusive, systematic (or macro)

theory that would "explain all the observed uniformities of social behavior, social organization and social change."[38] Parsons thought that the way to understand a society was to study it as you would a complex, living organism. Organisms have functional needs (to eat, to digest, to move, to procreate) and have evolved organs to meet these needs (systems of digestion, locomotion, etc.). All these bodily parts are functionally necessary to maintain the balance and health of the organism.

Similarly, a society has functional needs (to subsist, reproduce, maintain order, etc.) and it develops social institutions, such as the family and law, to maintain its stability and order. In *The Social System* (1951), Parsons lays out in detail a structural-functional model or paradigm for the analysis of social systems. His abstract model defines concepts and establishes patterns that can be applied to entire social systems or to sub-systems within a society, such as the family, socialization, and religion. Parsons says that his analysis is only a preliminary blueprint, which is left to future generations of sociologists to complete with all the details and complications of actually existing institutions. *The Social System* is only "a link in a much longer chain."[39]

And that chain begins with social actors. Actors are motivated to optimize their gratification in a given, physical environment, within which they interact "in terms of a system of culturally structured and shared symbols." A concrete system of social action is composed of four systems:

1. *Biological*: At the most basic level is the system of biological needs and dispositions, which motivate actors to gratify their needs or avoid dangers.[40]
2. *Personality*: Human nature is relatively plastic rather than instinctual, and elementary biological gratifications or aversions are never simple, genetic drives. The pursuit of an individual's goals is structured according to a

second system, the actor's personality system, which is the subject of psychology. Personality may result from some combination of genetics (nature) and experience (nurture), but Parson's interest is at the higher, social level of analysis.

3. *Cultural*: People's goal-oriented action usually involves interaction with other actors on the basis of a shared world of signs, symbols, meanings, and rules, which are part of the third system, the cultural system, and allow communication to proceed.[41]

4. *Social*: Parsons is concerned with personality and culture because of their bearing on the structure and functioning of the fourth system, the social system. An individual is born into a "normative order," a shared cultural tradition or system of patterning, which is imposed by the social system. Once they are learned through socialization, these cultural patterns are incorporated into the "action systems of individual actors." When a social actor makes decisions and takes action, she or he is aware of the given situation, evaluates options, and makes choices. By human nature, people are sensitive to the attitudes of others.[42] Social interaction entails a process of "double contingency" through which the actor's decisions takes into account the actions and reactions of others.

All four systems—the biological, personality, cultural, and social systems—are independent aspects of social action. Culture and personality, motivations and value-orientations are relatively independent of each other. One system can neither be reduced to nor be regarded as a fundamental cause of any of the other systems. Nevertheless, the systems are also interdependent and affect each other.[43] To be a system, the various parts must interrelate and more or less fit together symmetrically. Although the parts are never perfectly integrated, there is a systematic **pattern**

consistency among the personality, cultural, and social components of the system. In part, this relative although not complete integration of the parts is necessary for a social system to "function" in the first place.[44]

A structural-functional analysis provides an overall, static picture or snapshot of these interrelated parts that constitute a "system of structural categories." This structural analysis will permit systematic description and comparison of different systems. Analysis, however, also has a dynamic element, which entails understanding the motivational processes within the system. The dynamic aspect may either help to maintain stability or integration of the system, or produce disruption and change.[45]

Parsons concentrates on the structure rather than the dynamics. He specifies a number of basic or universal functional requirements that any social system must meet, specified as adaptation, goal attainment, integration, and pattern maintenance.[46] And social institutions are sub-systems within a society that enable it to meet these requirements. A society endures over time and is self-subsistent and self-recruiting through reproduction and socialization. A society requires a system that can adapt to meet the basic biological and other needs of the population through the production and distribution of resources. The economic system functions to meet this need for adaptation.

A social system requires relative stability and order. Stability is potentially threatened by an actor's selfish, goal-oriented pursuit of her or his own interest, termed the **Hobbesian problem of order**. A second prerequisite of society is that actors' motivations and goals must be shaped to reflect the normative value orientations of the cultural tradition. Various social institutions seek to channel people's goal activity to conform to the values of the social order. The most stable situation is one in which the actor has internalized the value standards of the culture.[47]

In addition, society is a functioning "system of complementary role expectations." In his structural analysis, Parsons focuses on the variety of roles within the system and the ways the roles are integrated to form a functioning system or a social structure. Roles are "the primary mechanisms through which the essential functioning prerequisites of the system are met." The relationship of roles and functions in society is analogous to that between organs and functions in a biological organism.[48] People play institutional roles in interrelated sets. When you play the role of parent, teacher, or administrator, you are part of a **role set** whose function is socializing children.

Given the variety of roles that meet the needs of a functioning system, the system must provide for the distribution of specific individuals to fill all the given roles and the allocation of rewards to these positions: who does what and who gets what in return. Different positions and rewards create a system of social stratification or inequality. The various roles in the division of labour require different levels of competence or skill, which can be graded by degrees of complexity and also ranked according to the amount of responsibility the role entails. The most important roles or occupations require high levels of skill and entail great responsibility. "It goes almost without saying," Parsons says, that there is an "inherent tendency" for greater rewards to be given to people whose occupations require higher levels of competence and responsibility.[49]

Parsons argues that unequal allocation is "a functional imperative of effectiveness and efficiency" and a necessary consequence for any society that values achievement. Marxist theory denied the necessity of paying unequal rewards for different jobs. In the USSR, for example, an official's salary was not supposed to be much greater than the pay of the average worker, although the need to employ technical experts from the old regime required pay differentials. As the Soviet Union industrialized, however, the gap in pay and other rewards widened between officials and workers.[50] The functional theory of stratification would later be elaborated by Kingsley Davis and Wilbert Moore, who argued that inequality or social stratification is functionally necessary for any society because the promise of receiving significantly higher rewards is the only reliable way to motivate people to undertake a job demanding higher levels of skill and responsibility.[51]

Another fundamental prerequisite for a society to exist, which Parson identified, is "pattern maintenance." A primary aspect of the integration of a social system is "the specific *commonness* of the value-orientation patterns of the participants."[52] In particular, a society must have a system of shared moral values if it is to survive. Inculcating common social values and norms is the function performed in the socialization process, whether socialization is primary (the family) or secondary (schools and religious institutions). Through the socialization process, "common values are internalized" in the individual's personality and individuals are integrated into the existing system of complementary roles.[53] For Parsons, pattern maintenance also entails the operation of institutions and processes that meet the functional need to manage conflict and tensions that arise in society.

Common or normative cultural patterns are established through many mechanisms, of which the socialization process is fundamental. Socialization, however, is never complete. Because of the potential for resistance to conformity, society requires mechanisms of social control to maintain appropriate boundaries and minimize the disruptive effects of non-conformity, bringing the social system back to **equilibrium**. Deviance is directly related to specific strains that arise in a given social system. For example, because men are initially socialized in a family, they develop a strong, dependent "love need." This need, however, conflicts with the detached and calculating social roles that men are expected to play in the public realm of work and politics, roles that cannot gratify their "love need." The resulting strain between this need and their social role results in a tendency to seek gratification in deviant sexual patterns.[54]

Although Parsons describes sex-role identification and erotic attachment as reflecting an "intricate geometry," he argues that all known societies institutionalize heterosexuality and, with few exceptions, define both homosexuality and incest as taboo. The mother provides the child with nurturing and love in the private family sphere; she is the child's first "central love object." Given that the father's primary social role is outside the family, the function of fathering is to help the child—particularly the male child—learn what Parsons describes as the higher level, more mature value orientations of prestige, responsibility, heterosexuality, and role status that operate in the wider society.[55]

In the area of erotic geometry, the price for growing up is the requirement, for both boys and girls, that they sacrifice their original erotic attachment to their mother. For the child, this early eroticism is connected to dependency on the mother. Maturity for the boy means renouncing this original infantile erotic status "in favour of an adult heterosexual attachment" outside the family. The main focus of socialization for a male is becoming a normatively "masculine" man and coming to identify with his father. Same-sex peer groups help the boy navigate this complicated adjustment process. For Parsons, forms of sexuality other than heterosexual are regressive; that is, they arise through a failure to develop according to the normal pattern. Consequently, "deviant" people should be readjusted. A man, says Parsons, "is 'worthy' to enjoy an erotic love relationship" if he "lives up to the general value pattern for the masculine role."[56]

For girls, maturing beyond their infantile status is more complicated. Not only must a girl renounce her initial erotic attachment to her mother, she must continue to identify with her as a role model and accept that she, too, will one day play the role of mother. Furthermore, she must abandon the "infantile erotic attachment to the father" in light of the incest taboo—which may be the source of "a fundamental focus of feminine resentment against men"; but then, she must develop the capacity "to form an adequate attachment to the opposite sex." Parsons said that a woman should "accept her familial role, her attachment to a fully masculine man . . . and the responsibility of socializing her children in terms of the general value system, as a condition of being loved."[57]

Pattern Variables within Structural Functionalism

Parsons calls his approach a theory of action, but this term implies more individual autonomy that his analysis delivers. For Parsons, actors are "authors" only insofar as they are *bundles of statuses and roles,*" which are to be understood as externally imposed norms that shape an actor's social action. The actor participates in an interactive relationship on the basis, first, of her or his *status* or location in the "social relationship system" and, second, according to her or his *role*. *Role* refers to "what the actor does . . . in the context of its functional significance for the social system." In playing a role, the actor is oriented to the roles and status of other actors. Roles are units of the social system rather than attributes of the actor.[58]

The process of acting, however, is not determined simply by existing statuses and roles. Actors must evaluate the meaning of the objects and cultural traditions, and the intentions of other role players they encounter. For Parsons, the intersection of role expectations and the institutionalized value patterns of a culture is the fundamental dynamic or "nodal point of the *organization* of systems of action."[59]

The cultural tradition imposes "value orientations" that mediate between the actor's choice of goals or interests (gratification/avoidance) and the social actions that she or he takes. The existing value orientations define a satisfactory solution to meet an actor's needs and also delineate the socially appropriate means to obtain them. Ultimately, these orientations are moral standards, "that aspect of value orientation which is of greatest direct importance to the sociologist."[60] Parsons identifies five pairs of alternative values, and he analyzes social action in terms of the choice between these polar opposites:

1. *Gratification vs. Discipline.* The first "choice dilemma" is between gratification and discipline. People may orient their action directly to optimize the gratification of their basic desires (their emotional needs or "affects"). Parsons terms this orientation *affectivity*. In a society, however, it is seldom possible to simply go ahead and expect to realize all your desires. You act in a world of other people and things over which you may have no control. Consequently, you have to learn to give up some desires or to express them only in socially approved ways. You control your desires by taking into account other people's needs and the standards of morality you have learned. You may calculate how to use these objects and people, that is, to use them **instrumentally** as a means to help you reach your goal, but you still have to take into account *their* needs, interests, and desires. In addition, since the cultural system imposes certain moral standards, you have to evaluate your actions according to the standards of morality you have learned. In either of these cases, Parsons says, you have to restrain your emotional needs in some fashion, a process he terms **affective neutrality**. Freely expressing your emotional needs versus reining them in is the first set of polar alternatives or "pattern variables" that Parsons defines.[61]

2. *Self-orientation vs. Collectivity Orientation.* The second dilemma distinguishes between private and collective interests: do you act according to your individual interests or according to the interests of the group to which you belong? If people orient their actions according to their own egocentric interests, they reflect *self-orientation*. If, on the other hand, they orient their actions according to the interests of the group to which they belong, they express a *collectivity orientation*.[62] The first two choice dilemmas have in common the expression of individual freedom versus subordinating action to the moral standards or interests of others.

3. *Universal vs. Particularistic Standards.* The third pair of alternative values refers to whether the standards by which an action is evaluated are universal or particular. If you help someone, for example, because he or she has a particular connection with you, such as a friend or relative, you play your role according to a *particularistic* standard. In Western society, to honour your mother means specifically honouring *your* mother, not anyone who happens to be a mother. Parsons thinks of this orientation as essentially emotional or appreciative. Alternatively, you may help people because the social role you play is guided by a set of norms or rules that are meant to apply universally, regardless of the particular situation. A doctor helps an unknown accident victim to the best of her ability because playing the role of a physician knowingly entails the *universalistic* moral rule that you help anyone in need and do not discriminate on any particular basis.[63]

4. *Ascribed vs. Achieved Status.* In the fourth pair, Parsons further defines alternative choices in terms of "the *characteristics* of social objects themselves"; that is, in relation to other social actors who are "the complementary member of a reciprocal role-orientation system." Human objects (other people) both "*are* such and such" and "*do* this and that." For example, they *are* their sex, their age, height, ethnicity, race,

and so on. Sociologically, they are assigned various types of *ascribed* status. Some of these attributes, such as race, are relatively permanent and difficult to change, although in contemporary society even sex has an element of choice, as expressed by the transsexual community. In addition, there is the question of what you have *done*—in Parsons's terms, what you have *achieved*.[64] In short, when you select an "object" as your focus of orientation, you treat people differently or expect different things from them according to whether the standard you apply is ascription (their status) or achievement (what they have done).

5. *Specificity vs. Diffuseness.* Finally, action may depend on the definition you apply to the role expectations of a specific relationship. On the one hand, the expectations may be quite specific. You expect your physician to diagnose your broken leg and set it but not to give you financial advice or loan you some money. Your relationship is marked by *specificity*. On the other hand, if that physician is your mother, you can expect her to fulfill a wider or more diffuse range of obligations and actions. This more personal relationship is marked by *diffuseness*.[65] In industrial societies, the division of labour narrows each relationship to more limited or specific definitions of role expectations. For example, the occupational role of the physician incorporates achievement values and is "universalistic, functionally specific, and affectively neutral."[66] In contrast, the roles people play in pre-industrial societies or in their families tend to be diffuse and non-specific.

A common criticism of structural functionalism, especially in Parsons's hands, is that it has an essential, conservative bias that assumes society has to be the way it is. Structural-functional sociology operated with a false, over-socialized conception of humanity. It assumes that people are mere puppets pulled by the strings of unknown forces

over which they have no control. Social problems are minor issues of imbalance or disequilibrium between various parts of the system, but they are temporary since the social system automatically adjusts to strain and returns to the state of equilibrium. Structural theory was largely ahistorical and could not account adequately for persistent conflict in society or for major social changes. Parsons's younger colleague, Robert Merton, would elaborate on structural incongruities in American society that contributed to destabilization and non-conformity.

Robert Merton: Culture and Social Structure

Robert King Merton (1910–2003) was born Meyer R. Schkolnick in Philadelphia to working-class Jewish immigrants from Russia. He went to Harvard in 1931 as a student of Pitirim Sorokin in the new sociology department. Talcott Parsons, who was eight years Merton's senior, became his most important influence. Merton's class and ethnic background shaped his initial left-leaning approach to social problems, a tendency that was reinforced when the Great Depression began while he was still an undergraduate. In 1938, Merton published an essay, "Social Structure and Anomie," that outlined an influential theory of forms of deviance. In 1941 Merton joined the sociology faculty at Columbia University in New York, where he retired 38 years later. His principal contributions to social theory appeared in his 1949 book, *Social Theory and Social Structure*, which he expanded and revised several times. Merton was married twice, the second time to sociologist Harriet Zuckerman. His son from his first marriage, Robert C. Merton, won the 1997 Nobel Prize in economics.[67]

Fundamentally, Merton argues that sociological analysis must primarily be structural. The ideas people have of their society "are themselves *products* of distinct social forces." Social change entails more than merely changing people's ideas or attitudes. Merton's argument asserts that social change must be directed at changing social structures and the pattern of people's relationships. Changing a structured situation takes more than good will and re-education. For example, no "'educational campaign' itself [will] destroy racial prejudice and discrimination."[68]

To understand the standards people use in making judgments about themselves and others, Merton employed the concept of the **reference group**. Individuals usually judge themselves according to the values, expectations, or standards of others. In general, people obtain their values and standards from a "normative" reference group and evaluate themselves and others according to a "comparison" reference group. When disaster strikes, people feel their loss deeply, but they feel *relatively* better off than the worst cases the media bring to their attention. In different situations and contexts, people have numerous reference groups with which to make evaluations. In these terms, nonconformity is often conformity with the values, expectations, and points of view of another, non-mainstream reference group.[69]

Functions and Dysfunctions in Merton's Theory

Parsons's theory of the social system was meant to describe processes in entire societies, but it could also be applied to subsystems within a society. Merton chose to focus on the latter. In his view, there hadn't yet been enough empirical work to construct a useful, total system of sociological theory. His analysis of forms of deviance is an example of what he terms "theories of the middle range" that are close enough to empirical reality to be tested.[70]

Anthropologist Bronislaw Malinowski said that "in every type of civilization, every custom, material object, idea and belief fulfills some vital function" for the culture. Merton's analysis of the forms of deviance and anomie suggests that cultural systems have contradictions and structural strains that may produce non-functional or disruptive consequences.[71]

A function is thought to contribute to the adaptation or adjustment of a social system. The most obvious function of the medical system is to maintain the population's health. While a given institution in society meets a functional need, Merton said, that need could equally be met by a range of possible alternative institutions or processes, such as holistic or alternative medicine in contemporary society. The Western romantic love complex, for example, is only one way to achieve the important social function of selecting a mate and reproducing the population. Different partnering arrangements or institutions could meet the socially necessary function of rearing children. For Merton, determining whether an alternative is in some fashion better or more functional than the existing, normative pattern is an empirical question.

On the other hand, a social practice or institution may produce consequences for an individual, group, or society that lessen social adaptation, adjustment, or integration.[72] In this case, the practice becomes a **dysfunction**. The conservative bias of functional theory arises from the assumption that existing institutional arrangements, which maintain the status quo, are socially beneficial. The ultimate question, though, is for whom are these arrangements functional? What is functional for one group may be dysfunctional for another. Your being a stay-at-home spouse, for example, may be functional for your partner's career, but playing that role is likely to be dysfunctional for your own occupational ambitions.

Further, according to Merton's paradigm, functions and dysfunctions may be either manifest or latent. **Manifest functions** are intended precisely for the purpose of maintaining the system or helping it adapt to change. **Latent functions** have similarly adaptive consequences, but they are neither recognized nor intended by participants.[73] In a sociologically well-known study of workers at the Hawthorne Western Electric Plant, experimenters manipulated training and pay rates to motivate workers' performance. The experimenters found that workers responded positively to *any* change in their situation. In addition to the manifest function of better pay, there were latent (unrecognized) functions that resulted from the experiment itself.[74] The concept of latent function has a critical element because it extends sociological analysis beyond what is expected and allows a researcher to uncover what is unintended or not recognized.

Dysfunctions may also be latent. Convicted felons are sent to penitentiary for the manifest function of punishing them for their unlawful conduct, to prevent them from harming society, and in the hope that they will be rehabilitated. In prison, however, they may be socialized further into a life of crime and may be subject to abuse by guards or other inmates, causing them to become worse than they were when they entered prison. These are examples of latent dysfunctions in the system, which have consequences that destabilize society and can lead to change.

Deviance and Social Structure in Merton's Theory

In his 1938 essay on anomie and social structure, Merton criticized the common assertion that deviance was caused by people acting on biological urges that broke through the normal social controls established by society. Parsons had interpreted deviance to be a consequence of role conflict or the malintegration of social institutions. Merton took this reasoning further, arguing that certain aspects of the social structure actually cause deviant responses that should be considered typical under the circumstances. In other words, "social structures *exert a definite pressure* upon certain persons . . . to engage in nonconformist . . . conduct."[75]

To explain his idea, Merton distinguishes between social and cultural structures. Cultural structures define people's goals and purposes—what people desire and seek to obtain—and they also define the acceptable and unacceptable social means to obtain these goals. In American society, the overriding cultural goal is to achieve success, which is measured by material prosperity. With regard to the means to obtain this dominant goal, American culture emphasizes using the most expedient or efficient methods. Valuing efficiency above all, as Durkheim had pointed out, leads to rapid innovation, but it also tends to engender crime. In the pursuit of expediency, people tend to disregard the norms that define the socially acceptable means to achieve the goal and, instead, use deviant ones.[76] In sport, for example, when the emphasis is on winning at any cost, deviant means of success are employed, such as cheating or doping. The end presumably justifies the means.[77]

In Merton's view, almost everyone in American society has been socialized to pursue the cultural goal of material success and ever-increasing wealth. To achieve this goal, many people do follow socially acceptable means. They seek more education to qualify for higher occupations; they are loyal to their employer and work hard to achieve promotions and higher pay; if they dream bigger dreams, they buy lottery tickets when they feel lucky. They are "conformists" in Merton's scheme.

Not everyone, however, accepts the goal of material success or agrees to follow the socially acceptable means. At the opposite extreme to the conformist are people who reject *both* the cultural goals and the acceptable means to achieve them—they are outsiders who become alien to their own society. Following this pattern of "retreatism" or escape from the requirements of society are vagabonds and tramps but also chronic alcoholics, drug addicts, and psychopaths.[78] Another set of individuals have actually given up the desire to acquire more, but they nevertheless continue to follow the rules scrupulously, as they are so well socialized to do. They are "ritualists" in Merton's theory, people for whom following the rules becomes a goal in itself.

Merton's primary concern is with what he terms the "illegitimacy adjustment," those who do believe the American dream but don't follow the rules about how to succeed in a socially approved way. The strain to deviance is caused when the population at large is thoroughly socialized into desiring the normative goal of ever-increasing material success in a society that is structured unequally. Many people don't have access to the socially approved means (such as higher education or a white-collar career) to obtain this goal: "there exist class differentials in the accessibility of these *common* success symbols." In this intolerable situation, people become frustrated and tend to adopt socially deviant means to obtain "at least the simulacrum of culturally defined success." Merton terms "innovators" those whose social situation induces them to employ deviant means to achieve the goal. For example, in neighbourhoods where there is only menial, low-wage work or high unemployment, people who aspire to the cultural goals of wealth and power have little opportunity to succeed following conventional patterns because of their low standing in the class structure. In this structural position, they may turn to various forms of innovation, such as gambling, prostitution, drug-dealing, or property crime, as effective means to achieve material success. What counts is how much money they have, not how they got it. Al Capone, the Chicago crime boss in the 1930s, was the model innovator.[79]

Merton's analysis might suggest the common-sense notion that there should be a close connection between poverty and crime. Empirically, however, social strain occurs at all levels of the stratification system because, with the American dream, there is no stopping point; people are socialized into wanting more than they have and they are judged by the standard of those who are better off. White-collar crime is similar to the innovations of the poor in that people adopt illegitimate means to obtain the goal of success. At some point, sharp business practices cross the moral and legal line into criminality, as Martha Stewart and Conrad Black discovered.[80]

The faith in the American dream—that anyone can rise to the top—Merton says, has become more myth than reality. The Dream survives mostly as an ideology, constituting "a useful sop for those who might rebel against the entire structure."[81] Rebellious nonconformists, who adopt the response of "rebellion" in Merton's culture/structure scheme, are distinct from the criminal because rebels reject both the socially approved goals as well as the conventional, normative means to achieve them. Beyond this negative position, they attempt to restructure both society's goals and its values in the interest of higher motives.[82] There was no shortage of rebellion in 1938 when Merton published his essay on "Anomie and Social Structure." In the 1950s, when he was building his reputation, the careers and future of many of these former rebels were facing official repression from the US government.

B.F. Skinner and Behaviourism

Alex: "What exactly is it, sir, that you're going to do?"
"Oh," said Dr. Brannon . . . "it's quite simple, really. We just show you some films."

— Anthony Burgess, *A Clockwork Orange*, 1962

In the decades that structural functionalism predominated in sociology, an approach known as behaviourism had taken precedence in psychology departments. The theory had been developed principally by John Watson in the 1920s. Although Freud had believed his work was scientific and that he was a scientist, Watson argued that inner subjective experience—the "mind" in general—could never be studied scientifically. Watson believed that science must restrict itself to observable behaviour that could be subject to experimentation involving measurement and prediction. According to behaviourist principles, the behaviour of any organism, including humanity, was a response to a stimulus. Persistent behaviour resulted from the rewards or punishments an individual associated with a particular stimulus. Watson had conditioned an infant to be fearful of a pet rat by pairing the rat with an unpleasant stimulus, a loud noise. Once the pairing was accomplished, the child reacted fearfully to the rat even in the absence of the noise. For Watson, even complex behaviours and emotions could be explained as conditioned responses to repeated stimuli.

The stimulus underlying the behaviourist perspective arose from experimental work on learning conducted among animals. Psychology was married once again to biology. Behaviourism was further developed in the 1950s by B.F. Skinner. Psychologists sought to predict behaviour and, more importantly, modify it by having it associated with specific rewards or punishments— positive or negative reinforcement. A simple phobia, such as a fear of rats, for example, might be interpreted by Freudians as a consequence of a frightening childhood experience that had been repressed from consciousness. The original source of the phobia had to be slowly uncovered through lengthy psychoanalysis, the causal event dredged

❖ BOX 5.2 • THEORY IN CONTEXT ❖

Anthony Burgess, A Clockwork Orange

A Clockwork Orange, which was written after Burgess had travelled to Russia, blends the cold, concrete, urban planning of the Soviet Union with the nighttime world of British delinquent mayhem. Burgess found that delinquent youth had become as intractable a social problem in the USSR as they were in Britain. The novel is set sometime in the near future in an indistinct, perhaps post-apocalyptic, Britain.[83] The government presides precariously over a chaotic and lawless state under a law-and-order mandate. Maintaining order entails recruiting "brutal young thugs" to the police force and utilizing "debilitating and will-sapping techniques of conditioning." Burgess warns that this path to state tyranny has been followed in other countries and represents the "thin edge of the wedge. Before we know where we are we shall have the full apparatus of totalitarianism."[84]

In the novel, 15-year-old Alex, from whose point of view the narrative is told, is the leader of an "ultra-violent" delinquent gang. Alex has two passions, which he feels equally strongly about: violence and classical music. In conventional understanding, each is the antithesis of the other—chaos and violence contrast absolutely with culture and sensitivity. In Burgess's vision, however, polar-opposite emotions are still essentially human. According to novelist Kurt Vonnegut, Jr., the cost of the high culture we enjoy is the concomitant propensity for self-willed destruction.[85] Good and evil are like day and night: one necessitates the other.[86]

Alex is on top of his little world, but his is a fragile dominance. Part Two of Alex's tale, he tells us, "is the real weepy and like tragic part." Alex—now 6655321—spends two years in Staja [State Jail]. His main focus is maintaining his individuality among the "leering like criminals" and the perverts who shambled "like a lot of broke-down apes."[87] Traditional

up to the conscious mind, and finally dealt with rationally. Not so, said Skinner. Regardless of how the fear response had been originally conditioned, it could be re-conditioned through the appropriate use of behaviour modification techniques. One could be re-conditioned far more quickly than through psychoanalysis to not fear rats.

Skinner used the novel as a device to explore some of the humanistic criticisms of applying behaviourism to control human beings. He published *Walden Two* at the same time Orwell was writing *Nineteen Eighty-Four*. Unlike Orwell's negative utopia, in Skinner's imaginary society,

violence is unnecessary. In *Walden Two*, the authorities have mastered the scientific modification of human behaviour, using only positive reinforcements (rewards) and never punishments. Everyone is so thoroughly conditioned that they not only fulfill all the functional necessities of society, they do so without crime or deviance and with complete satisfaction.

Critics complained that a society run by behaviourists would replace such human attributes as intelligence and initiative with "efficient co-ordination" and make society "as efficient as an anthill"[88] (see Box 5.2). Skinner argued that

social punishment dehumanizes, but Alex maintains his sense of self, his individuality. His body is behind iron bars, but not his mind. Alex's first reformation program consists of listening to classical music and reading the *Bible*. What Alex's vivid imagination lacks, the *Bible* provides. Like Mel Gibson's *The Passion of Christ*, Alex is caught up in "the scourging and the crowning with thorns and then the cross vesch [thing] and all that cal" [shit].[89]

After two years in the Staja, Alex is selected by the Minister of the Interior as an experimental subject. The bad is to be turned into the good by killing the criminal reflex. In two weeks, Alex will be reformed and released "out again in the big free world, no longer a number."[90] The experimental treatment involves forcing Alex to watch increasingly graphic scenes of violence with his eyes pinned wide open, while injecting a substance that makes him violently ill. Over time, the feeling of illness is so thoroughly conditioned with violence that the mere *thought* of violence makes Alex vomit, preventing him from acting in any violent way—even from defending himself.

The central critique "is whether such a technique can really make a man good. . . . Goodness is something chosen. When a man cannot choose he ceases to be a man."[91] Alex has been rendered unable to choose the bad and been transmogrified into the most passive of victims. What is more, and this is the fundamental argument, the technique violates the essence of humanity, which is free choice and creativity. But being free means having the ability to choose evil as well as good. Instinctive energy is responsible for both the most magnificent creations of culture and the worst acts of violence. They are inseparable. Curing one means destroying the other, turning people into objects. After the treatment, Alex is even more like a number, more a mechanical thing (a clockwork orange) than a choosing being. The more the Soviet Union attempts to condition the routine emotions of people, to transform them into the "new, socialist person," Burgess says, the more human nature revolts and the more creative energies are channelled in destructive directions. The problems of danger, disorder, and destruction are essential and necessary elements of human nature.

many people already use some of the technical abilities to manipulate and control the behaviour of other people, and they have the worst motives for doing so. Refusing to use the technology of behaviourism to create a new world would leave control in the hands of the "charlatan, the demagogue, the salesman, the ward heeler, the bully, the cheat, the educator, the priest—all who are now in the possession of the techniques of behavioral engineering." These techniques are now being used in psychological clinics, schools and churches, in politics, and in advertising: "Bring them all together and you have a sort of rule-of-thumb technology of vast power."[92] Negatively, then, Skinner draws attention to the misuse of behaviourism by those in modern society who intend to manipulate and control people for their own selfish ends.

There is a fundamental difference, Skinner argues, between the use of negative reinforcement—punishment—by governments throughout history, and the use of positive reinforcement techniques. The exercise of coercion by the state is only effective temporarily and can't even guarantee the power of the rulers, let alone, in the long run, create a humane, peaceful society. In society now, the "feeling of freedom" that people cherish is essentially negative; the feeling of being free to resist unjust authority. Whenever you feel forced into doing something, even if it is to your benefit, you resist and feel unfree. In the utopian community of Skinner's *Walden Two*, however, the members are free of coercion and fear. Negative reinforcements are never used. Positive **conditioning** does not take away people's freedom, Skinner says. People are free to complain, but there is no unjust authority to complain about. Furthermore, by utilizing only positive reinforcements, "We can achieve a sort of control under which the controlled, though they are following a code much more scrupulously than was ever the case under the old system, nevertheless *feel free*. They are doing what they [have been conditioned to] want to do, not what they are

forced to do." In Walden Two, Skinner says, "*the question of freedom never arises. . . . The question of freedom arises when there is restraint—either physical or psychological.*"[93] People can live in freedom and peace if we build a social structure that will satisfy the needs of everyone and in which everyone will want to observe the supporting codes because they have been conditioned to do so.[94] *Walden Two* represents Parsons's ideal situation of perfect socialization and complete consensus to society's values and needs.

Similarly, democracy is unnecessary in *Walden Two*. People will be content to allow the management of society to rest in the hands of the Managers. People don't care to understand how their automobile works; they're content to hand it over to the mechanics. Finally, Skinner refutes the argument that *Walden Two* replicates the social experiment in Russia. The early revolutionary experiments in child care, the family, and so on were all abandoned in the 1930s. The Russian government uses the techniques of capitalism, giving out extravagant and unequal rewards: "It obviously cannot operate for the *common* good. On the other hand the government also uses punishment or the threat of it. What kind of behavioral engineering do you call that?"[95]

Many of the criticisms of the existing society that Skinner expresses in *Walden Two* were developed further in other social theories, but they tended to be equally critical of Skinner's assumption that human beings could or, indeed, should be manipulated by behavioural conditioning. In the over-controlled society, human creativity and control is handed over to an elite. Critics objected, also, to Skinner's choice of title. The original nineteenth century *Walden*, written by the Romantic and naturalist Henry David Thoreau, was in many ways the antithesis of the image of the total domination of humankind by science in the dystopian *Walden Two* of Skinner's imagination.

George Homans and Exchange Theory

[Marriage] is a relation in which women serve men in the home in exchange for their security [and] . . . the means to care for and provide for themselves and their children, and in which they have no right to participate in the decisions which are consequential for their lives.[96]

— Dorothy E. Smith, *Feminism and Marxism*, 1977

The idea that society is organized according to reciprocal exchanges by people in relationships is the central idea of the aptly named exchange theory, developed by George Homans (see Box 5.3). Dorothy E. Smith, however, questions whether exchanges involving fundamental imbalances of power are ever actually reciprocal but, instead, come at a sacrifice for the subordinate party.

Anthropologists recognized the importance of exchange in maintaining relationships among individuals and tribes. In particular, the norm of exchange appears to be reciprocity: what you give and receive in some sense should be viewed as equal. For Homans, exchange theory "consists simply of behavioral psychology applied to the interaction" of individuals.[97] People, then, are "profit maximizers": they strive to optimize their adaptation to their environment by keeping their rewards high and their costs low, given the way they perceive their situation.[98] People, then, are rational decision-makers who choose between alternative actions.[99] The captain who chooses to go down with her ship is acting rationally because she is choosing to project the image of herself as being an honourable person, thereby deciding not to lose being seen as admirable. The cost of a dishonourable life is too high; death is exchanged for honour. On the other hand, acting emotionally, for example striking out in anger, may be "intrinsically gratifying" and therefore be consistent with profit maximization if the calculation

is immediate and not long term. In these terms, acting emotionally may be considered rational behaviour. In short, exchange theory is linked to rational-choice theory, but it is indifferent to the choice of rewards "and does not imply any conscious deliberation on the part of the actor." For Homans, the variables that shape the probability that a person will decide a certain action involve not just perception, but explicitly entail thinking and estimating.[100]

Homans believed that social behaviour, the subject matter of sociology, could ultimately be explained by (or reduced to) individual psychology. For example, people act in accordance with social norms because "they perceive it is to their net advantage to conform."[101] The fundamental axiom is that "People do not act unless it seems to them profitable to do so." It follows that whatever they do must somehow be profitable. So the altruistic act is identical to the egotistical act because in both cases it is the most profitable for the individual. You sacrifice your life for another or exchange your life for theirs, the ultimate act of altruism, because you value their life more than your own or you value your reputation as a hero more than you value your life. The Samurai commits ritual suicide exchanging death for honour because that is most profitable for her or him. But we don't know what is most profitable until someone chooses. People sometimes "change their values to accord with adaptations they in fact make."[102] So exchange theory fits any occasion after the fact and therefore offers little explanation of any of them.

It is through the experience of exchange that we learn the relative value of things, rather than having values established in some other way before exchange relations are entered. "What is in fact necessary in human affairs comes in time to be recognized as necessary . . . and what is regarded as necessary tends in time to be elevated to the status of a norm, particularly if the necessary runs counter to desires." The result is

✍ BOX 5.3 · BIOGRAPHY ✍

George Homans (1910–1989)

George Homans described his background as "a Republican Bostonian" who came from a wealthy and storied New England family. He was a descendant of John Adams, the second president of the United States. Homans became a junior fellow at Harvard in 1934 in the Harvard Business School. Under attack by Marxists in the 1930s, Ritzer says, Homans gravitated to the conservative, elitist theory of Vilfredo Pareto as a defense[103] and to sociology generally. He became a member of the Department of Sociology and then Social Relations, which Talcott Parsons had spearheaded. During his early period at Harvard, he met and befriended B.F. Skinner, who was also a member of the elite Harvard Society of Fellows.

Homans served in the Navy during World War II and then returned to Harvard. He published *The Human Group* (1950), in which he applied the systems approach, derived from Parsons, to the study of small groups. He renewed his friendship with Skinner, who had also returned to Harvard as a professor of psychology. Under Skinner's influence, Homans abandoned the application of social systems theory to group and individual behaviour.[104] He found behaviourism to be compatible with his ideas of human nature and the working of societies.

Homans elaborated his new sociological theory, which came to be called exchange theory, in *Social Behavior: Its Elementary Forms* (1961). In his view, social structures arise from and are perpetuated by the self-interested, rational actions of individuals, which can be explained by propositions that derive from behavioural psychology.[105] In this fashion, Homans believed that his approach brought the individual back into social analysis.

Homans retired from Harvard in 1970. Late in his life, he worried that his life's work had not had the influence he had hoped. Had he failed, "Just Like the Rest," which was the title of a poem he wrote in 1988? "My books were sound, but lacked the spell, / The confident presence, to compel / Their judgments on another mind." As Treviño argues, however, exchange theory was an influential theory in James Coleman's development of rational choice theory.[106]

institutionalization. Norms, then, do not underlie notions of fairness, justice, etc.; the norm of fairness "emerges from and rationalizes regularities of action." Rules may be given facts to the individual but not to the sociologist, who wants to understand their origin. When such qualities as sex, race, age, etc., are regularly linked with superior power, the connection will be assumed to be normal and become institutionalized.[107]

Exchange theory reduces explanation to individual choices and actions, assuming that people seek to maximize their benefits in social interactions and minimize their losses. In order for the rule of reciprocity to be sustained, each must value equally the items exchanged (whether they are material goods, reputation, prestige, or any other benefit that might be given or received). One common criticism of exchange theory is its circularity: it assumes people maximize their profit in an exchange, so if they exchange X for Y, the exchange is explained by claiming they received more profit from Y than X.

Ultimately the problem is that it is easy to reduce a social action to a choice; but sociology has generally sought to understand the choice by understanding the context and the forces operating in the context that make one choice more likely or possible than another. Sociology has been concerned to understand the consequences on people's actions of factors that are beyond their control and that they have given to them and do not choose themselves. George Homans was born an American Brahmin, a member of the Boston elite. A boy who is born to an alcoholic, uneducated, single mother in an urban ghetto may choose to sell drugs on the street corner rather than study in school to receive a scholarship to university, but for a sociologist, this choice must be understood within the context that shapes the decision; not only the attitudes or values the choice reflects but the relative powerlessness and lack of resources that being in that social situation imposes.

Abrahamsson points out that Homans's emphasis on overt behaviour rather than on an individual's subjective understanding is a serious limitation of his approach. Homans assumes that people feel certain sentiments simply from observing their overt behaviour. Buying roses for one's spouse may be assumed to be an expression of the sentiment of love, but the same objective act in the context of different subjective intentions can have quite different meanings. Abrahamsson considers, for example, the statement, "I love you," which is actually a question demanding in exchange the response, "I love you, too." His point, however, is that the identical claim can be made

by a lover or by an unscrupulous seducer out to exploit an unsuspecting victim. It is essential to understand the subjective meaning and intention of a statement.[108] Furthermore, the interesting point is not that different rational choices are being made at different times, but that the intentional and normative context within which decisions are made may have changed significantly. Understanding this context sociologically is key to understanding why people are more or less likely to make one choice or another.

Rational Choice Theory

"[F]or human reality, to be is to choose oneself."

— Jean Paul Sartre, *Being and Nothingness*, 1943

Humans choose to be who they are, Sartre asserts, expressing the idea that human action is a consequence of rational choice, which is foundational for many social theories. This idea assumes that people have options and weigh alternatives: that they are thinking, choosing, and, acting beings. In Adam Smith's eighteenth-century economic theory, individuals calculate and then act according to their material interests. When every person acts rationally to follow her or his individual interests, everyone is actually better off; these apparently selfish actions result, almost miraculously, in the best consequences for society as a whole. For Smith, humans had a natural tendency to truck and barter—buy and sell—and were basically profit maximizers, seeking to get the most from their dealings with others. The language of calculation and profit has been explicitly taken into sociology by theorists seeking to understand the mutual exchanges of goods and services that develop and maintain individual relationships. Rational choice theory is most easily applied to economic or political behaviour in which self-interest is an important calculation. Even in the Marxist movement, an approach that is primarily structural, the concept of "opportunism" is applied precisely to individuals who put self-interest ahead of the needs of the collective. Rational choice is applied more successfully at the micro level of analysis. In psychology, for example, cognitive therapy is predicated on the assumption that individuals can learn to perceive alternative behaviours and make better choices.

In American sociology, the idea that all personal interactions involve, in one way or another, the calculation of individual interests and entail an exchange of material and moral goods (love, attention, respect) is the central element of "exchange theory" developed by George Homans. Seeking a divorce, for example, is a decision or choice. Rational choice theory asserts that it is necessary to understand the reasoning that went into the decision, treating the decision as an "independent variable." How does someone rationally calculate that divorce is the most individually profitable choice? Generally speaking, sociological analysis seeks to understand the context within which individuals act: what are the factors outside the individual that have made the "choice" more or less probable? Considering divorce, among the most important would be changes in the institutional context within which the decision is made, such as the existence of laws that permit divorce easily (no-fault divorces), legislation that requires a fair distribution of the marital assets, as well as structural changes, such as the increase in the proportion of women able to earn an independent livelihood. From the point of view of rational choice theory, however, these legal and social changes do not *cause* an increase in divorce; rather, they influence the *choices* that individuals make. No longer, for example, must a woman feel trapped in a marriage. Now she is increasingly free to make a rational choice to stay or leave. If you are without a job, have had your self-confidence shattered by an emotionally abusive relationship, and quite rationally fear for your safety, your decision about staying or leaving is narrowly circumscribed. Nevertheless, from

the point of view of rational choice, there is still a choice to be made.

Choice, however, need not be "rational." Classical sociology took neither individual choice nor social action determined by biology as its subject. On the one hand, individual action was influenced by nonrational factors, such as values, beliefs, and emotions. People acted on the basis of custom, often in a taken-for-granted world, and often perceived that they acted without really having a choice. Studies of voting, for example, often reveal the extent to which people's choices are influenced by tradition or charisma. Large sums of money are expended on manipulating consumer behaviour, but the choice to buy a certain item is not always the consequence of rationally weighing the alternatives. Advertising is likely more concerned with imprinting brands, the authority of celebrity endorsement, or the unconscious manipulation of desires such as sexuality.

Perhaps rational choice explanations are most reasonable in specific types of micro situations, such as consumer decisions or voting behaviour, for example, although voting "choices" (and decisions generally) are influenced by a number of irrational factors, as well. Even in micro situations, the politics of rational choice theory becomes problematic. Denying that people make choices is to dehumanize them, to treat them as puppets of forces that only experts schooled in social science can understand. Nevertheless, claiming a decision is a rational choice risks blaming the victim (the party with the least power) for her or his situation. It makes sense to demand personal responsibility from the people who engineered the Holocaust; it makes little sense to blame Aboriginal peoples for the decay of their communities. Similarly, it is easier to claim that someone chooses to divorce than it is to say that someone chooses poverty or unemployment, or chooses to perform casual, part-time, insecure, and poorly paid work—even though each of these situations may be a rational choice for specific individuals. Too often, however, it's not a choice, or it's a choice made in the light of only worse options. Contemporary sociology tries to accommodate both approaches. Perhaps it is not a paradox that, at a time when remote, global processes impinge increasingly on an individual's field of possible choices, sociological theorists are focusing their attention on the role individuals play in the making of themselves and, in the process, reproducing or changing the world around them.

Conclusion

In 1960, sociologist Daniel Bell (1919–2011) published *The End of Ideology*, a book that thought to bury most of the grand, humanistic ideologies that society had inherited from the past, principally Marxism. In the United States, 25 years of unprecedented prosperity fed economic optimism and made Marxist theories seem increasingly irrelevant in a society that had apparently solved its economic problems. The 1950s and 1960s were the heyday of Keynesian economics and government intervention. The Cold War ensured high rates of government spending on the latest military technology; the space race was simply one of the rich government pots to stimulate American military industries and technology. Both structural functionalism and behaviourism reflected uncritical acceptance of the status quo and the end of ideologies.

Popular culture in the 1950s was also primarily conservative. It wasn't that the older generation accepted such inventions as rock and roll—the term derived from an inner-city slang expression for sexual intercourse; rather, popular culture of whatever kind became simply another commodity that could be bought and sold, another business opportunity. Popular music was just another diversion, another pastime. The entertainment industry seemed even more than in the 1930s to dominate consciousness and to undermine revolt and critical awareness.

Conservative thinking dominated even the popular expression of theory. In literature, the theory of the primitive origin of competition, aggression, and hierarchy underlay William Golding's *The Lord of the Flies* (1954). Golding's larger allegory suggests that "the darkness of man's heart" is revealed in the violence and destruction of modern warfare.[109] *Lord of the Flies* presented a pessimistic image of human potential, quite the contrary to the assumptions of the whole Enlightenment school, including Marxism, which put so much hope and expectation on the human ability to reason.

Konrad Lorenz's theory that humans are biologically aggressive was widely accepted in the 1950s and was compatible with the Cold War mentality. This view was the foundation for a spate of popular anthropology books with the same message: humans are innately aggressive, competitive, and violent. It was a return to the Hobbesian image of humanity as nasty and brutal. Robert Ardrey's *African Genesis* (1961), written in highly accessible language, claimed that competitive violence is embedded in humanity's deepest biological makeup. A similar story about humanity's animal origins was told in another bestseller, *The Naked Ape*, by Desmond Morris. Contrary to Bell, these ideas were highly ideological; rather than an end to ideology, it would be more accurate to say that what had emerged by the 1950s was a conservative ideological hegemony, a dominant ideology that supported the status quo and made fundamental change seem impossible.

Nevertheless, there *were* liberals, even left-leaning liberals, in the United States, which is the topic of Chapter 6. In Europe many intellectuals responded differently to the post-war world. Existentialists wondered if people were individually responsible for the evils of the world. In turn, European social theorists influenced artistic movements and social theory in the United States, a development that will be examined in the following chapter.

Questions for Reflection

1. Are we living now in a new Cold War in the age of terrorism? How is it different from the 1950s?

2. Thinking about your understanding of family relations and education, do they have more dysfunctions than functions?

3. Are there parallels between the "Red Scare" and the contemporary fear of radical Islam?

4. From your experience, do rational choice and exchange theories make sense? Are there reasons to reject them?

CHAPTER 6

Post-War Critical Social Thought

Learning Objectives

- To review forms of critical social thought that emerged in the early post-WWII decades
- To connect the literary critique of middle-class culture to the critical sociological analysis of the ideology and politics of the new middle class
- To link the early origins of second-wave feminism to women's dissatisfaction with traditional roles and their second-class status
- To contrast two responses of African Americans to the persistence of racialization: civil rights and black power

The radicalism of the 1930s had been submerged by the post-war forces of conservatism and conformity, which moulded post-war American opinion and social thought. The **American dream**—middle-class status, financial security, a late-model car parked in front of a bungalow in the suburbs with a white picket fence and 2.5 children—seemed within reach of the majority. Nevertheless, important critical currents in social theory and culture continued to exist on the margins. In American sociology, the acerbic C. Wright Mills described the emergence of a powerful elite in American society. The mass world of the new middle class and the dream of financial success seemed like a hollow joke.

Despite the trends to consensus and conformity, individualism was one of the fundamental values of the American system. The lifestyle rebellion of the "Beats" and the characteristically American art movement knows as **abstract expressionism** emerged as 1950s variants of

Romantic rebellion. Other groups were marginalized from the North American mainstream, including women and blacks. From their experiences of being "othered" emerged the critical perspectives and long-standing movement for change known as feminism and black power.

The dominant role of consumption in modern capitalism spawned a new critique of culture, which had begun with the Frankfurt School. Popularized in the 1950s, the emerging field of media and cultural studies generated a new culture industry among academics. Marshall McLuhan, the Canadian media theorist, was one of its earliest gurus. McLuhan believed the artist and the creative writer had the gift of the prophet and were able to anticipate emerging social trends. The contradictions of the American dream and the emptiness and vulgarity of lower middle-class culture had been recognized in literature before it became a critical, sociological outlook.

White-Collar Angst

Theoretically, it wasn't clear what to make of the new "middle-class" groupings in corporate capitalism, but by the 1950s, they were becoming the majority and the blue-collar proletariat was in numerical decline. From a Marxist perspective, the white-collar world of office workers was another stratum of the proletariat. They were property-less in the classical sense because they did not own businesses or make an independent livelihood. Like the proletariat, they were employees, working for other people.

From the time of Max Weber, however, sociologists focused on the differences between this new middle grouping and the working class. However modest their salaries, they felt "middle class": they consciously separated themselves from the working class and were more likely to identify with their bosses than with other employees. Even the forms of office work middle-class workers did—accounting, marketing, supervising—were tasks that employers had done themselves in the nineteenth century. They were apparently living the dream.

For many critics, however, white-collar employees were suffering from false consciousness. Critical thought probed the soft underbelly of the apparently contented middle mass. As long as there have been middle-class white-collar workers packed into the offices or salesrooms of corporate capitalism, creative writers have written their epitaphs. In *The War of the Worlds* (1897), for example, H.G. Wells had painted an early portrait of "all those damn little clerks" who spent their lives rushing every morning to catch a train or subway, clutching a little bit of breakfast in their hands. The middle mass, he said, was spiritless, without any proud dreams or even lusts, working at jobs they didn't care enough about to even understand. Life meant being insured, with a little set aside for accidents.[1]

When George Orwell returned to Britain from Burma in 1927, he saw that his homeland was being transformed—for the worse, he realized—by changes he summed up as **Americanization**. He defined the newly created mass society an "anti-culture." In 1939, Orwell described the new London institution of the milk bar that epitomized the modern world he found so sordid:

> There's a kind of atmosphere about these places that gets me down.
>
> Everything slick and shiny and streamlined; mirrors, enamel, and chromium plate whichever direction you look in. Everything spent on the decorations and nothing on the food. No real food at all. Just lists of stuff with American names, sort of phantom stuff that you can't taste and can hardly believe in the existence of. Everything comes out of a carton or a tin, or it's hauled out of a refrigerator or squirted out of a tap or squeezed out of a tube. No comfort, no privacy. . . . I order a large coffee and a couple of frankfurters. The girl in the white cap jerked them at me with about as much interest as you'd throw ants' eggs to a goldfish.[2]

One bite of the hot dog made him ill: "I'd bitten into the modern world and discovered what it was really made of."[3]

White-collar employees—small clerks, shop assistants, commercial travellers, insurance salesmen—were the typical twentieth century types, and the twentieth century was the worse for it, according to Orwell. For him, the white-collar masses were puppets who danced only when money pulled their strings. They were too busy working, getting married, buying furniture, begetting children, and dying to really care.[4]

So it was for George Bowling, Orwell's anti-hero in *Coming Up for Air*. Bowling is an insurance salesman who has what it takes to be moderately well off and "make a living." But Bowling is suffering from middle-class angst.

He senses that he's "just a dried-up seed-pod that doesn't matter twopence."[5] Nothing matters; nothing is real in his life "except gas-bills, school-fees, boiled cabbage, and the office on Monday."[6] He is suffocating and trying to come up for air, "But there isn't any air. The dustbin that we're in reaches up to the stratosphere."[7] The past doesn't exist, and the future will just happen, and there is nothing to be done about it.

Critical American authors had a somewhat different take. The images of the American frontier as a space of personal freedom and of the American dream as a destiny within the reach of the average person were part of the country's mythology. Sinclair Lewis had punctured these images in his 1922 novel *Babbitt*. Lewis's protagonist, the singularly materialistic George F. Babbitt, is a travelling salesman, a social type whose hidden insecurities are plastered over by brassy assurance. In the rhetoric of the travelling salesman, the modern romantic hero was "the great sales-manager . . . whose title of nobility was 'Go-getter,' and who devoted himself and all his young samurai to the cosmic purpose of . . . pure Selling." Next to selling, the most important idea Babbitt expresses is the importance of keeping blacks and immigrants "in their place."[8]

The premiere failure in American literature is Willy Loman, the travelling salesman who is the tragic protagonist of Arthur Miller's *Death of a Salesman* (1949). Willy Loman is becoming conscious of his own failings—as a businessman, as a father, as a husband, and as a human being. Willy is 64 years old, far too old to still be travelling, and he is coming to the end of his road. When we first see him, he's weighed down by the burdens of a lifetime, symbolized by the heavy sample cases that tug at his shoulders. Once, he made a reasonable living; now, he's had to borrow money to prop up the facade of success. In reality, he's lost his job and become the low man.[9] How do you admit failure or face the emptiness of the dreams you've always had? In the end, Loman

kills himself for the insurance money. He is worth more dead than alive, he thinks, a measure of his real failure in life. Everything has a dollar value, even human life.

Willy's failings are mirrored in his two sons. The elder, Biff, finds brief success on the high school football team and then tries to follow in his father's footsteps. But he finds that devoting his life trying to sell somebody something is "a measly manner of existence." Willy's second son, Happy, is making better money than his brother, but he is still the low man at work, putting in his time and waiting "for the merchandise manager to die." He knows the manager isn't content with his life, but Happy sees it as a personal failing, not a problem with the way of life itself. When the manager walks into the store, Happy says, "the waves part in front of him." He wants to feel that sense of being somebody. Happy still believes in Willie's dream: "It's the only dream you can have—to come out number one man."[10] His tragedy is just a little further down the road.

White male authors were still writing about white middle-class men. More fundamentally, not far from suburbia the American dream was out of reach for significant minorities marginalized by class, race, ethnicity, region, or some additional definition of otherness. It would take another decade before Michael Harrington would expose the persistence of actual material poverty in America. In the meantime, there was also poverty of the mind and spirit. In a competitive class system, all are ultimately losers because they never achieve all the aspirations set out for them. Success is brief and ephemeral; failure is chronic and permanent. In the white-collar worlds of Willy Loman and George Bowling, appearance, personality, and manipulation are everything. It is this image of the new mass society that was at the heart of the critique of American society, whether expressed in the new literature of alienation or in the scholarly work of a handful of critical sociologists.

The Middle Mass at Mid-Century

"[H]e who possesseth little is so much the less possessed! Blessed be moderate poverty!"[11]

— Friedrich Nietzsche, *Thus Spake Zarathustra*, 1917

Nietzsche says that we are owned by the things we possess. Tyler Durden, a character in the book *Fight Club*, expressed the identical point of view: "The things you used to own, now they own you."[12]

The United States differed from Europe by not having a traditional aristocracy and a long history of sharp class and status distinctions. In America, opportunity had always beckoned farther west or north to Alaska. The pioneering ideology fostered a view of America as largely classless and a belief that anyone can become wealthy by hard work or by striking it rich in the gold fields. Alienation was merely a matter of having less income, a dilemma that could be overcome without a change in economic systems. Not until the 1970s would a more sophisticated analysis of forms of alienation in twentieth-century capitalism become part of a revival of Marxism for the age of mass consumption.

The assumption that constant economic growth was inherently beneficial, which was part of the post-war consensus, was soon assailed. The Romantic tradition had long condemned the materialist success ethic at the root of capitalism for its emotional and intellectual shallowness. Mass consumption simply extended the banality and conformity of middle-class life to a larger proportion of the population. You were not what you did or what you thought; you were what you owned and could display to others. In the end, what you owned ended up owning you. Beneath the appearance of contentment, material prosperity was not all it appeared.

This anti-materialistic ethos would come to define a vocal segment of the youthful baby-boomer generation, being born precisely into these affluent conditions. They would be inspired by earlier thinkers who had anticipated the directions that modern society would take. Prominent among these otherwise-ignored theorists was Thorstein Veblen, whose ideas seemed quite contemporary again in the 1950s and 1960s.

Veblen's *The Theory of the Leisure Class* (1899) outlined his theory of **conspicuous consumption** in the United States. People judge themselves by the success of others and strive to be better than their neighbours. In modern capitalism, where people were mostly anonymous to one another, a claim of being better was based on displaying symbols of acquired wealth.[13] The need for conspicuous display extended from the rich and down the social ladder to the middle class, who had to display their incomes by making a "showing" in front of others. What mattered was the size of the paycheque and the quantity of goods that could be consumed in conspicuous ways, as the middle mass strove to keep up with the Joneses. When they don't have enough ready cash to buy respectability, they get into debt because the appearance of being well off is what counts. The display of opulence through conspicuous consumption is increasingly necessary the more anonymous and mobile society becomes.[14]

Veblen's theory of consumption influenced a new generation of social critics in the 1950s, a time when the tendencies Veblen observed at the turn of the century had multiplied infinitely. A popular, quasi-sociological literature found a market in the 1950s and 1960s, protesting the alienation, conformity, and shallowness of the new consumer masses (see Box 6.1). The corporate man or woman existed as a largely insignificant spoke in a vast enterprise, loyal to the company and to a career within it, and part of a vast suburban mass. Whether the collar was blue or white, the interest of marketers was drawn to the two-thirds of the population who occupied middle-level positions because they had disposable income and a proclivity to spend it.[15]

✤ BOX 6.1 · THEORY IN CONTEXT ✤

Advertising as Manipulation

Vance Packard exposed the mass manipulation of the advertising industry in his popular book, *The Hidden Persuaders*. The industry employed a modern army of psychologists and motivational experts to manipulate consumers in campaigns of persuasion. Mass consumption had become the new deity of capitalism. Marketing, rather than production, was "king," and advertising was its modus operandi, designed "to 'stimulate' consumer buying, by creating wants in people that they still didn't realize existed."[16]

The mass media, according to Packard, depicts Americans as rugged individualists, thoughtful voters, and shrewd, careful consumers. But the mass persuaders and "symbol manipulators" busily construct these images "with tongue in cheek." They see consumers "as bundles of daydreams, misty hidden yearnings, guilt complexes, irrational emotional blockages."[17] Packard was concerned that the same kind of practices had taken over the marketing of politicians. The large body of undecided voters was a "listless mass" waiting passively to be persuaded to prefer one candidate over others as they would wait to be enticed to try out a new candy bar.[18] In contemporary society, politicians are marketed like automobiles and advertisers have new ways to discover people's personal preferences and market directly on-line to targeted individuals.

C. Wright Mills (1916–1962)

In American sociology, C. Wright Mills critically analyzed the class and power dynamics of 1950s America. Mills felt that he didn't fit in with his times. Born in Waco, Texas, Mills was a difficult student who argued with his professors and later became a difficult colleague. Mills donned a black leather jacket and drove a motorcycle to work, where he told undergraduate students "like it was." Mills was married three times in Hollywood-style serial monogamy. Intellectually, he wanted to be a respected college professor with an appropriate status and salary and, at the same time, a popular political commentator, who took moral and political stands on controversial social issues. It was an impossible balancing act.

Sociologically, the dominant theme of Mills's work was power. He exposed the abuse of power in a supposedly democratic nation and urged ordinary people to rise from the prone powerlessness to which American society had reduced them. The United States may have once been a country of active, politically aware citizens who exercised some control over the economy and their government, but by the middle of the twentieth century, the reality had changed. American society was fundamentally divided between a small elite of powerful decision-makers and a great mass of alienated, disenfranchised, manipulated individuals. Two of Mills's most important books focused on each of these dimensions. In *White Collar* (1951), Mills examines the development and political passivity of the middle mass of white-collar workers. In *The Power Elite* (1956), Mills focuses his critique on the individuals in power at the top of the dominant social institutions.

Status Panic and the Work–Leisure Split

The white-collar mass, Mills writes, "slipped quietly into modern society."[19] Most of the work done by these white-collar workers—selling, accounting, supervising—was done in the nineteenth century by capitalist business owners themselves. As businesses became large bureaucratic corporations, these tasks were hived off to an army of specialists, including sales-workers, technicians, clerks, managers, and assistants. Mills still writes of the middle mass as masculine, although the feminization of the office was well underway by 1950.

An important theoretical question was the ideology that would be adopted by the new, middle mass. They might have felt independent, but the reality of their lives was precisely the opposite. Encompassing a broad range of occupations, the white-collar mass was split, fragmented, and dependent on larger social forces.[20] In a world dominated by big business and—as it appeared to the middle class, also by big labour—the white-collar worker, according to Mills, "is more often pitiful than tragic." Inflationary forces beyond these workers' control nibbled away their salaries and pushed out of reach their yearnings for the quick American climb. The white-collar worker was the "small creature who is acted upon but who does not act, who works along unnoticed in somebody's office or store, never talking loud, never talking back, never taking a stand."[21]

Perhaps the typical white-collar employee is the salesperson. Mills's father was a travelling insurance salesman. In one respect, Mills claims, the modern world has become a great salesroom, "the biggest bazaar in the world." The modern department store is "a factory of smiles and visions, of faces and dreams of life, surrounding people with the commodities for which they live, holding out to them the goals for which they struggle." For Mills, the great bazaar is a modern cathedral of consumption in which people worship the modern fetish of commodities and fashion:

"a curious blending of piety and the barking of the circus." Fashion in the "Big Bazaar" now extends to all types of commodities for all groups of worshippers. In the new "Religion of Appearance," the scenery of people's lives must be constantly renewed in trivial ways. Worshipping the new makes you ashamed of the old.[22]

In a world dominated by the marketing mentality, your personality itself becomes a commodity to be sold. In the new personality market, employees develop the skills of "'handling,' selling, and servicing people." One knows the sales-clerk not as a person but as a commercial mask. Kindness and friendliness become aspects of public relations, rationalized to further the sale of something. The successful salesperson makes an instrument of his or her appearance and personality: "The smile behind the counter is a commercialized lure." Under the ethic of salesmanship, people must learn to pretend to be interested in other people to better manipulate them. People "are estranged from one another as each secretly tries to make an instrument of the other, and in time a full circle is made: one makes an instrument of [one]self, and is estranged from it also."[23]

Salesmanship even entered into the lives of intellectuals. Mills was critical of the professional classes, especially the university social scientists who, he said, had abdicated any responsibility for critiquing, judging, and helping to reform society. University professors either abandoned any moral responsibilities in a pseudo-scientific objectivity or they became the trained handmaidens of the powerful. In fact, Mills argued, a new type of college professor had arisen: the academic entrepreneur living off research grants, for whom "academic careers are becoming dependent on the traits of the go-getter in business and the manager in the corporation."[24]

Sociologically, the new middle class must be understood in terms of striving for prestige. It was essentially status—their middling prestige—that had originally differentiated them from workers.

However, as the twentieth century wore on, Mills argues, the foundations of middle-class superiority were slowly eroding. Work became more routine, educational credentials became widespread, unionized wages nearly equalled salaries, and white-collar workers began to experience job insecurity.[25] As a result, the new middle class was faced with **status panic**.

Having leisure time, however modest it may be, is one of the chief characteristics of middle-class life. But, Mills says, mass leisure in the twentieth century became more frenzy than self-directed relaxation. Inevitably, the use of leisure time became big business, with myriad opportunities to consume amusement. For Mills, these were activities that "astonish, excite, and distract, but . . . do not enlarge reason or feeling, or allow spontaneous dispositions to unfold creatively." The result was the big split: the best and most important part of a person's life was spent in the grind of work, the meaning of which shrank to becoming only the necessary means to enjoy the consumption of leisure. The worse the grind of work, according to Mills, the more it became necessary to escape into the dream world of leisure: "Each day [people] sell little pieces of themselves in order to try to buy them back each night and week end with the coin of 'fun.'" Mills believed that people lived for Friday night and the weekend. Even their models of success changed. They anchored their sense of self—who they are, what they believe, and what they identify with—outside themselves, "in the spectator sports, the idols of the mass media, and other machineries of amusement."[26]

As Mills saw it, the dominant images of the new middle class were alienation and powerlessness; white-collar workers were "political eunuchs." As supervisors, they may have exercised some power over those beneath them, but it was a derived power representing those above them; at best, they were the assistants of authority.[27] Marxists had been quick to claim that white-collar workers were just another form of proletariat, but their middle-class consciousness, Mills argued, was defined precisely by their rejection of the working class. They felt superior to manual workers and identified with people higher on the occupational scale.

Politically, the new middle class had more often supported the right than the left; it "was one of the harps that Hitler played on his way to power."[28] For Mills, however, writing in the middle of the twentieth century, the real question was whether white-collar workers would take any political position at all. More than any other social strata, the new middle class expressed its politics negatively, in widespread public indifference and political apathy. The world seemed too distant, too powerful, too dominating. All that was really left was private life. And because people felt overpowered, they became "completely private and blasé, deep down and for good."[29] Politically alienated people do not become rebels, the active creators of their own realities. They become the silent partners of authority. If the white-collar mass (and people in mass society generally, Mills argued) were to adopt any politics at all, it would be the politics of conservatism, authoritarianism, even fascism.

For Mills, there really was no effective opposition from below and, therefore, no reason for optimism. In 1960, however, Mills believed the Cuban Revolution promised more. In the initial excitement of social change, he became the spokesperson for Cuba in his most polemical book, *Listen Yankee* (1960). Mills did not live long enough to face what, for him, would have been the betrayal of this revolutionary idealism. He lived and fought hard, and it took a heavy toll. In 1962, at the age of 45, Mills died of heart failure.

Neither, however, did he live to witness the new forms of radicalism that he had not foreseen. In the 1970s, the quiet, apolitical white-collar crowd he had written off politically erupted into militant unionism. The office and professional world had been significantly feminized, and the new spirit of the times reflected the experience of the feminist movement. At the same time, a new rebellion emerged among a generation of youthful rebels who, in the 1960s, would be inspired by Mills's critical legacy. He was more influential in death than in life.

Power Elites

Five years after publishing *White Collar*, Mills wrote another exploration of power in the United States, *The Power Elite* (1956). The major presupposition of Mills's contribution to the theory of elites and the sociological study of power is that formal democracy is an empty shell; the real wielders of power were becoming increasingly unified in a **power elite** of businessmen, high-ranking military officers, and members of the political executive. Each of these spheres of power were becoming increasingly centralized and beyond the control of people at lower and middle levels. Individual members of the American power elite came to move, easily, from the military command posts, to corporate boardrooms, and to the inner circles of the White House.

The members of this elite shared similar social origins and upbringing, had similar psychological dispositions, and existed in a social structure where their interests were increasingly common: "They accept one another, understand one another, marry one another, tend to work and think if not together at least alike." They were a distinct social stratum that enjoyed, simultaneously, power, wealth, and celebrity.[30] Popular versions of elite theory circulated widely among the public, such as William Domhoff's *Who Rules America?* Whether popular or academic, however, the single-elite theory exaggerates the unity of elites in the United States and ignores fundamental differences of interest. Differences include local and regional interests, differences among sectors of capital such as financial institutions, manufacturing, and oil companies, and the degree to which

elites are subject to influence from other social groups, including militant minorities.

In Canada, John Porter argued in 1965 that there existed in that country a plurality of elites: "The power of economic, political, bureaucratic, military and other institutions" tended to be separated and specialized, creating a number of elites. Wallace Clement demonstrated that, in 1972, the Canadian economic elite "is more exclusive in social origins, more upper class and more closely knit by family ties than in 1952."[31] Clement studied the corporate elite, "that set of positions known as senior management and directors within dominant corporations."[32] The membership of the Canadian economic elite was concentrated in finance, transportation, utilities, and the mass media, with less concentration in manufacturing and resources. Clement distinguished between indigenous elites and comprador elites. The latter operate branch-plants of US enterprises in Canada. Overall, there is overlap between the two groups: Canadian elite members are recruited to sit as directors of US branch plants and commit themselves to a continental rather than a national economy. These structured interlocks, combined with "common ideologies, class backgrounds and relationships" create a system of mutually dependent power holders.[33]

While the power elite model, including the analysis of social ties and family connections, seems applicable to Canada, Clement does not establish an equivalent set of connections between economic and political power. Instead, he adopts a structural argument. State policy decisions are matters of inter-elite negotiations that are designed to ensure the best conditions for capital accumulation. In the process, existing power relations are reinforced.[34] There is little direct participation simultaneously in state and corporate power. Nevertheless, there remains an affinity and community of interest between the two elite groups that is more than merely structural. Their connection is also rooted in "career-switching, kinship ties," regulatory and advisory bodies, and political-party fundraising.[35] Elite analysis strengthens the structural argument that the state functions to create the preconditions necessary for the successful accumulation of capital.

Post-War Feminism

The problem lay buried, unspoken, for many years in the minds of American women. It was a strange stirring, a sense of dissatisfaction, a yearning that women suffered . . . alone. . . . [T]he problem that has no name.[36]

— Betty Friedan, *The Feminine Mystique*, 1963

Beneath the apparently calm surface of the post-war American lagoon lurked many creatures: racial divisions, injustices, and personal troubles. Mills argued that for sociology the harm that someone experiences as an *individual* trouble has to be interpreted in terms of wider *social* issues. Women in the 1950s were on the verge of realizing that their personal problems were rooted in male oppression and dominance. The sordid reality behind the appearance of the orderly, tree-lined suburbs was painted graphically in the novel *Peyton Place*, reflecting the desperate sexual mores of suburban housewives—although not them alone—that were being documented in the 1950s.

Firestone argues that the 1950s was, for women, the bleakest decade, "perhaps the bleakest in some centuries." The fleeting liberation that had appeared when men temporarily vacated their domestic thrones to attend to the war was undermined in peace by the myth of domesticity cultivated by Parsons's functionalism. A woman's role as servant and helpmate offered respectability and upward mobility, borne on the shoulders of her husband's career in the full-employment economy of the Cold War. What American culture delivered, Firestone says, was "Disillusioned Romance, plenty of diapers and PTA meetings . . . family arguments, endless and ineffective diets, TV soap operas and commercials to kill the boredom, and, if the pain still persisted, psychotherapy."[37]

Simone de Beauvoir (1908–1986)

Simone de Beauvoir was a philosopher and novelist who developed the existentialist theme that, although the world is essentially absurd, individuals must seek to create meaning in their lives and are responsible for their actions. These themes are explored both in her novels and autobiographical works. Brought up by a devout Catholic mother, de Beauvoir abandoned her belief in a god in her early adolescence, seeking instead to find certainty and truth in learning. She also rejected the life of insignificance and drudgery that was the predetermined lot of women, who were obliged to accomplish nothing other than the endless round of housework and child care. Ascher quotes from de Beauvoir's autobiographical book *Memoirs of a Dutiful Daughter* to show the point where she decided that her life would have to be more meaningful. While washing the dishes, she was "filled with anguish," realizing this might be her fate: "All those hours, those endless recurring hours, all leading nowhere; could I live like that?" What was the point of continually improving herself if, at the end, there was only this "barren plateau?" She decided her life was "going to lead somewhere."[38]

By the age of 21, de Beauvoir was studying at the Sorbonne in Paris and associating with a group of philosophy students with a "bad reputation" that included Jean-Paul Sartre, who would become her lifetime companion, frequent lover, and early mentor.[39] Returning to Paris in September 1929, de Beauvoir experienced intoxicating freedom: freedom to come and go, freedom from the possession of things with a modest living and lifestyle, "on vacation forever."[40] She made her own living as an intellectual by tutoring and teaching part-time, as would a man; she lived independently, was surrounded by a circle of intellectual friends, and was taken seriously by her male colleagues; and she was wrapped tightly in an intellectual and sexual relationship with Sartre.[41] De Beauvoir and Sartre felt an unbound optimism. Humanity needed to be remade, and they were up for the challenge as long as it required writing only; they eschewed political activity. Their attitude, she wrote, was shared by much of the French Left in the fall of 1929.[42]

Under Sartre's influence, they established the terms of their relationship. Sartre was "not inclined to" monogamy, de Beauvoir said in her autobiography, and he had no intention, at the age of 23, of renouncing the "tempting variety" of women: "He explained the matter to me in his favourite terminology. 'What we have,' he said, 'is an *essential* love; but it is a good idea for us also to experience *contingent* love affairs.'" Only in other relationships would they be able to experience "the fleeting riches . . . of emotions—astonishment, regret, pleasure, nostalgia." Sartre believed they should, at some times, live apart, although in these early Paris years they took out a lease together and, de Beauvoir says, "intended to give ourselves wholeheartedly and without reservation" to their new relationship. They would maintain their "essential" love by being perfectly honest and open with each other about everything: "we would never lie to one another, but neither of us would conceal anything from the other."[43] The arrangement caused de Beauvoir considerable hardship and self-doubt. Sartre took lovers more easily and frequently than de Beauvoir did. Perhaps de Beauvoir felt something similar to the character Anna in Margaret Atwood's *Surfacing* (1972). In that novel, Anna says that David, her lover, has sex with other women,

> and tells me about it afterwards. . . . He says he is being honest. What a turd. When I get mad he says I'm jealous and possessive, it's a leftover from the property ethic, he thinks we should all be swingers and share it around. But I say there are these basic emotions,

if you feel something you should let it out, right? . . . He pretends he doesn't feel these things, he's so cool . . . but really it's just to show me he can do it and get away with it, I can't stop him; all that theorizing about it is coverup bullshit garbage.[44]

The de Beauvoir/Sartre relationship has been reinterpreted by contemporary feminists. In the film *Avenue Montaigne* (2007), the presumably aloof and controlled de Beauvoir was described as "sex-mad. . . . She went after [American novelist Nelson] Algren, seduced him, then dumped him." For his part, "Sartre was a lousy lay. . . . He was a little bourgeois. She was the wild one, the one who suffered inside, because she loved him. She let him screw around with a lot of bimbos supposedly with her blessing, suffering hell. Even posed as a lesbian to swipe girls who coveted him."[45] The magazine *La Nouvel Observateur* chose to recognize de Beauvoir's centenary by printing on their cover a 1952 nude photograph of de Beauvoir, taken from behind with her face appearing in Nelson Algren's bathroom mirror. Some feminists were scandalized by the objective sexualization of an icon; others claimed that the picture reinforced de Beauvoir's sexual freedom and independence.

During their early years as teachers, the two "essential" lovers worked in different locations and de Beauvoir made the difficult decision that they should not marry. She was very conscious that it was a choice, and an emotionally difficult one. By making this agonizing decision, she gave her life "a wholesome change of direction." She expressed the same attitude toward her career: it was her conscious choice and represented liberation. "To acquire a teacher's certification and have a profession" was something that made de Beauvoir "dizzy with sheer delight; it seemed to me far from enduring my destiny, I had deliberately chosen it." Their "anarchism was as deep-dyed and aggressive as that of the old libertarians, and stirred us, as it had done them, to withstand any encroachment by society on our private affairs."[46]

After Germany conquered France in 1939 and through the difficult experiences of the occupation and resistance, and then the tumultuous post-war period of the Cold War, both de Beauvoir and Sartre began to modify their earlier existentialism. The overwhelming pressure of world events in times of total war made it increasingly obvious that there were severe limits to action, constraints to freedom of choice. Faced with real-life hardships, de Beauvoir realized that her life was, in part, "a compromise between myself and the world at large."[47]

Politics became increasingly central to the life of de Beauvoir and to her intellectual circle in Paris, which included the painter Pablo Picasso, the surrealist sculptor Alberto Giacometti, and the novelist Albert Camus. De Beauvoir also became an active feminist. The most important issue in France, a largely Catholic country, was the illegality of abortion and birth control; de Beauvoir's most public act was to sign the *Manifeste des 343*, a document listing the names of women who admitted to having had abortions.[48]

Immediately after the war, de Beauvoir turned her attention to understanding women's oppression, beginning the writing of *The Second Sex* in 1946. The result was a remarkable book, written by a woman who was isolated from any woman's movement and, in fact, from any close connection with the lives of most women. Fundamentally, *The Second Sex* is written from a dialectical point of view—from the sociological perspective of the constraining effects of circumstances, and from the existentialist perspective of freedom of choice and ultimate individual responsibility. Individuals act in the world, developing "projects" that they then actively realize, in the process creating a sense of self and determining their own conditions of life and, to some extent, shaping the conditions of life of others.

Two things interfere with the creation of an individual's project. First, action is undertaken in relation to the actions of others, which can interfere with the realization of the project. Second, the recognition of human freedom imposes a great responsibility on people—they are responsible for the consequences of what they do. This knowledge imposes a burden from which humans try to escape. Through the exercise of **bad faith**, humans deny they are free and claim that forces over which they had no control caused their action or inaction.

The Second Sex
"Why can't a woman be more like a man?"

— "Hymn to Him," *My Fair Lady*, 1964. Lyrics by Alan Jay Lerner.

Lerner's lyrics, which reflect a traditional and sexist view of the difference between "irrational women" and "thinking, logical men," cannot justly be interpreted as representing the view of de Beauvoir. But in some ways, she did want women to have the same rights and ability to act freely and express themselves that, traditionally, had been monopolized by men. In her view, "the 'emancipated' woman . . . wants to be active and prehensile, and refuses the passivity the man attempts to impose on her. . . . The 'modern' woman accepts masculine values: she prides herself on thinking, acting, working, and creating on the same basis as males."[49]

Ultimately, surrounded by intellectual males, in the absence of a feminist movement or serious debate about the woman question, de Beauvoir seeks the liberation of women in *The Second Sex* by counselling that they choose to act freely as independent and autonomous individuals, competing with men on an equal footing. Mary Evans claims that de Beauvoir's brand of feminism reflects "women's assertion of their right to fulfil the very values society lauds for men." In this liberal feminist perspective, what is most important is equal access to education, the professions, and property: "equal opportunities and the formal emancipation of women into the public worlds of political control, meritocratic competition, and symbolic reward."[50]

In *The Second Sex*, Evans argues, de Beauvoir asserts that men have more freedom than women to make autonomous decisions.[51] It is male interests and actions that are most responsible for creating the social categories within which social norms and roles are defined. In particular, men define the norms of the roles that are assigned to women, thereby limiting women and judging them on the basis of their acceptance of these socially constructed categories. This situation is an obvious case of oppression—freely choosing to act in a way that tightly constrains an "other" (group or individual) from the exercise of freedom.[52]

The basic sociological premise from which de Beauvoir begins is that gender differences are not rooted essentially in nature, in hormones or instincts; rather, the category "woman" is socially constructed. The construction of masculinity and femininity, de Beauvoir claims, has assigned to men the possibility of **transcendence**—of acting creatively in the world, of defining and effecting his projects—while assigning women to the realm of **immanence**—passivity and inactivity. It is men who, historically, have created projects, transforming themselves and transcending their conditions of life. Men define themselves and become the superior "real"; women are defined in relation to men and come to see themselves as the inferior "other." For de Beauvoir, Ascher argues, women's nature appears to be part of the puzzle of their immanence. Giving birth, lactating, caring for children are all aspects of essential passivity, of immanence, in her view, rather than of creativity and transcendence.[53] Because women's immanence is rooted in their biology, the route to liberation entails a conscious decision—one de Beauvoir took for herself—of refusing to have children and thereby be a slave

to the internal "tenant" occupying her body and then her life.[54]

While women have been oppressed by circumstances beyond their control, de Beauvoir asserts, they are partly complicit in their enslavement, having made choices within these circumstances.[55] Choice derives from a woman's "dimension of liberty." In her words, "I believe that she has the power to choose between the assertion of her transcendence and her alienation as subject; she is not the plaything of contradictory drives; she devises solutions."[56]

Unlike other oppressed groups, then—such as children or slaves—the "feminine" woman makes of herself a docile thing.[57] She fights back using whatever methods are at her disposal: "All oppression creates a state of war. This particular case is no exception." Historically, de Beauvoir claims, women sought to dominate men, to deny their truths, and drag them into the prison of immanence in which "the mother, the wife, the lover are the jailers." Women play both sides; they want the esteem they deserve from their strength and success while simultaneously seeking the old-fashioned attention with which men reward femininity.[58] In this project, women submissively make of themselves things to be desired, with the object of capturing and enchaining men. This is still power, novelist Margaret Atwood explains. In Atwood's dystopic novel *The Handmaid's Tale*, power has been captured in the state of Gilhead by male religious fundamentalists. Sexuality is curtailed and regulated. The minority of fertile women—handmaids—are impregnated as surrogate mothers for upper class couples. With the repression of sexuality, the handmaids are able to exercise the relatively passive power of enticement. Walking down the street, the handmaid passes two young men, for whom sex is a forbidden fruit:

As we walk away I know they're watching, these two men who aren't yet permitted to touch women. They touch with their eyes instead and I move my hips a little, feeling the full red skirt sway around me. It's like thumbing your nose from behind a fence or teasing a dog with a bone held out of reach, and I'm ashamed of myself for doing it, because none of this is the fault of these men, they're too young.

Then I find I'm not ashamed after all. I enjoy the power; power of a dog bone, passive but there.[59]

Much social effort has gone into the oppression of women built on their immanence. The "monotonous burdens" of "housework and maternity" are shrouded by poetic veils as a woman exchanges her freedom for "the fallacious treasures of 'femininity.'"[60] Chief among these false treasures is irresponsibility. Not having to be responsible is an incomparable privilege—the bad faith argument of men avoiding responsibility and women escaping their liberty.

Ultimately in *The Second Sex*, de Beauvoir advocates a world that is androgynous but essentially more similar to the masculine than to the feminine. It is men who transcend existence by activity, such as through killing. In the present moment of history, however, women are claiming their own right; they seek "to emerge into the light of transcendence." In response, men, the privileged caste, refuse to accept women as equals, as their genuine companions.[61] Yet the socially constructed nature of woman is now inherently contradictory. She is spontaneously the "other," the role that has been imposed on her, and simultaneously an increasingly conscious "self," a potentially transcendent being. As man attempts to restore his dominance, woman resists with both the weapon of passivity and the weapon of activity. In *Force of Circumstances*, de Beauvoir recounts her own duplicity in using both masculine success and femininity:

Far from suffering from my femininity, I have, on the contrary, from the age of twenty one,

accumulated the advantages of both sexes; after *She Came to Stay* [her first novel] those around me treated me both as a writer, their peer in the masculine world, and as a woman; this was particularly noticeable in America: at the parties I went to, the wives all got together and talked to each other while I talked to the men, who nevertheless behaved toward me with greater courtesy than they did toward the members of their owns sex.[62]

The struggle between the sexes is not biologically necessary. If both sexes accept that each individual is free, each the expression of "pure liberty," then an agreement that is mutually beneficial could be reached. The problem, de Beauvoir claims, is rooted both in the nature of humanity and, specifically, in the social construction of femininity, the wish for submission that unconsciously shapes women's projects. Society is the instrument of this oppression: "Her whole education conspires to bar her from paths of revolt and adventure; all of society . . . lies to her in extolling the high value of love, devotion, and the gift of self." Both men and women are complicit in this situation; both are guilty by omission, by bad faith. But it is a bargain that is better for the man than for the woman. She is more oppressed. In her submissive relationship with a man, "he is the meaning, the justification of her existence." A man uses his time to add to his positive assets; a woman confined in passivity experiences time as idleness and boredom, as "a burden she aspires to get rid of."[63]

Implicitly, the social construction of masculinity is also at fault. In de Beauvoir's terms, men escape their essential freedom by "a dream of alienation" or identification. They seek their reality not in their liberty but in the "other" as a mirror. Man's identity is wrapped up in the image of himself projected by woman: "A husband looks for himself in his wife, a lover in his mistress . . . ; he seeks in her the myth of his virility, his sovereignty, his unmediated reality. . . . [M]an is consumed by the concern to appear male, important, superior."[64] Of course, de Beauvoir says, men cannot achieve their objectives unless women play their part. Women's potential freedom makes the maintenance of the male image fragile, making men fear and dislike women; men's success in maintaining the image of masculinity "is founded on the capricious freedom of women."[65] In surrendering autonomy, women choose the means of counter-dominance that are open to the inferior in a relationship. For men, the domination of the "other" comes at the cost of a dependency on women that in turn provides women with a weapon in the struggle for power.

In *The Second Sex*, de Beauvoir rejects the main theories that attempt to explain women's inferior social situation, principally Freudianism and Marxism. She traces the evolutionary social development of the oppression of women in considerable historical detail, providing more description than analysis. Her point is to demand the material conditions necessary for liberation: were women "endowed with an autonomous organism, were they able to fight against the world and wrest their subsistence from it, their dependence would be abolished: the man's also. Both would undoubtedly be much better off for it."[66]

Developing one's project becomes a very complex process for both men and women. Each must act on the material world and avoid being smothered or oppressed by another's project while, simultaneously, avoiding the tendency to define other's projects for them; that is, to oppress them. As de Beauvoir argued, women bear the brunt of this oppression. In North America, de Beauvoir was discovered in English translation in the 1960s and inspired the next generation of feminists who created second-wave feminism. One of the other inspirational leaders of the women's liberation movement was the anthropologist Margaret Mead.

Margaret Mead (1901–1978)

The attempt to study human gender differences and sexuality scientifically was a late-nineteenth century preoccupation, fuelled by Freudian theory and decadent culture. One of the consequences of Darwinism had been to root sexual behaviour in biology. From a Darwinian perspective, it could be argued, humans were "nothing but mammals," and rules of morality were merely social constructions designed to tame primitive passions. Anthropology contributed to the debate about sexuality by adopting a comparative perspective and demonstrating the degree to which sexual mores were relative to cultures, time, and space. In the process, however, it appeared that human nature was significantly different; humans were not just another mammal. Rather than having sexuality determined by cycles and hormones, human sexuality was always present, always active. The sexual drive was even more important in human life than among other mammals. As contemporary novelist Jim Crace puts it, "the sexual life of *homo sapiens* functioned in a state of disorder," a profligacy without pattern or natural regulation. Crace demonstrates this point of view in the dialogue between a husband and wife in his short story "In Heat":

> "Now that we are married we can make love," he told her, "at any time." "Like animals," she said, meaning to tease him but also, perhaps, to induce a little forbearance and composure when next his tumescence demanded her attention. "No, not like animals," he said. "The very opposite of animals, with their seasons, their ruts, their 'heats,' slaves to chemistry. No, it is this which separates us from the animals, our capacity to enjoy our bodies as the whim takes us, ever receptive to pleasure. Any place, any time. Now, for instance?"[67]

In place of chemical determination, human sexual regulation was a product of society. Since societies were different, however, a variety of sexual patterns could be expected: masculinity and femininity did not arise simply from biological genes. From the anthropologist Franz Boas, Ruth Benedict and Margaret Mead—two of Boas's most important students—had learned that culture, not biology, determined personality and behaviour. Both paid particular attention to socialization patterns and child-rearing. In *Patterns of Culture* (1934), Benedict attempts to show that different cultures produce distinct personality types. Where one culture might be boastful, wasteful, and hedonistic (Dionysian, in Nietzsche's terms), another might socialize people to become peaceful, co-operative, and mild (Apollonian). Each society had a particular cultural personality or ethos. This thinking suggested that character was socially created and could be understood through comparative anthropology rather than psychology.[68] It also tended to stereotype different peoples and nationalities, reinforcing some cultural biases and prejudices.

To prove this thesis of cultural variety in sex and temperament, at the age of 24 Margaret Mead took her anthropological training to the island of Samoa in 1925-6, where she spent nine months observing the behaviour of adolescents. Her intention was to show that adolescents behaved differently in different cultures and that, therefore, adolescent behaviour could not be explained by inborn biological drives or hormonal changes. In *Coming of Age in Samoa* (1928), Mead argued that Samoan culture did not experience the traumatic transition from childhood to adulthood that came to be called "teenage" in the West. In contrast to the North American anxieties over sexuality and the assumption that adolescence marked an abrupt hormonal transition in patterns of sexual behaviour, Mead claimed that Samoan children engage in sexual play freely, that intercourse

with more than one partner occurs normatively among them during young adolescence, and that the transition to adulthood is largely untroubled.

In the 1930s, Mead studied cultures in northern New Guinea. Her book *Sex and Temperament in Three Primitive Societies* (1935) challenged the assumption that masculine and feminine behaviours are biologically rooted in the male and female sex. This famous study argued that sex roles were socially learned. Among the Mountain Arapesh, Mead claimed, both men and women demonstrated behaviours that, in the West, would be defined as feminine. Both were nurturing, both parents participated equally in child care, and both men and women tended to be gentle and peaceful. In New Guinea, Mead also studied the Mundugumor, a tribe that included head hunting and cannibalism among its practices. Mundugumor men and women both displayed what would be described as stereotypically *masculine* behaviours; the women were "as assertive and vigorous as the men."[69] Both sexes were loud, aggressive, and competitive. Neither showed many signs of being nurturing to their children, who were treated roughly. Finally, Mead introduced the Tchambuli, who displayed what, from a Western perspective, would be an actual *role-reversal*. The women were the dominant sex, providing most of the food and playing the dominant roles in the society. They were "brisk, unadorned, managing and industrious." The men, on the other hand, were "decorative and adorned."[70] They carved, painted, and danced, were emotionally dependent, and gossiped among themselves. Mead argued that this evidence refuted the ancient beliefs in the West that biology was destiny, that gendered patterns of activity/passivity, dominance/subordination, and aggression/altruism were culturally, not biologically, based.

During World War II, Mead and her third husband, Gregory Bateson, worked with the US Office of War Information creating "white propaganda" to encourage intercultural understanding between American soldiers and their British hosts. After the war she hoped that the United Nations would foster multiculturalism world-wide. In the context of the Cold War, however, Mead's dream faded and the anthropologists were cleared out of the US State Department.[71]

While Mead's observations were elegantly constructed, as Levi-Strauss argued, other anthropological evidence suggested that her classification was oversimplified. For some anthropologists, Mead was more novelist than scientist. Her conclusions resulted more from *a priori* thinking than from her field work. Mead's were "hasty constructions" that reflected her own society more than the cultures in New Guinea.[72] In 1983, five years after Mead's death, Derek Freeman published a book, based on his extensive work in Samoa, in which he claimed that Mead's description of sexuality in Samoa was the result either of wishful thinking or of being misled by her informants. But much had changed in Samoan culture between Mead's field work and Freeman's. Ironically, by the 1960s the cultural side of sexuality, which Mead had championed, had been demonstrated in the United States by the women's liberation movement and the move to free sexuality, historical changes to which Mead had contributed through the popularity of her books and her public speaking.[73]

⁜ BOX 6.2 • THEORY IN CONTEXT ⁜

Margaret Atwood and The Edible Woman

The protagonist of Canadian author Margaret Atwood's novel, Marian McAlpine, rebels against the problem that has no name. She feels that her sense of personhood is not merely dissolving; she is being devoured by the men in her life. Marian is an unmarried working woman with a fiancé. She feels like a dish, an object to be consumed, like food. She struggles between the well-worn path of accepting the usual expectations for women and the more challenging feminist road of choice and independence.

Marian feels trapped, both in her working life and her personal life. She works for a company that is "layered like an ice-cream sandwich." The executives and psychologists, the upper crust, are on the top floor and all are men. Marian's place is in the sticky middle layer, which is virtually all female. Working under a glass ceiling, she feels bound by a future already mapped out and subject to rules she did not have a hand in making.[74] Marian's fiancé is the fastidious, over-organized, and very conventional Peter. Is that all life has to offer? Marian senses there has to be something else.[75]

As their relationship moves inexorably toward marriage, Marian realizes she has misgivings. As Isadora Duncan said, "Any intelligent woman who reads the marriage contract, and then goes into it, deserves all the consequences."[76] Peter objectifies Marian, feeling that he has property rights over her.[77] He treats her like a stage prop and she feels like a patient on an examination table. Marian is being consumed by him. Nevertheless, for Marian to strike out independently, alone, without a mapped-out future, requires an enormous and

Betty Friedan (1921–2006)

Before Simone de Beauvoir's *The Second Sex* was widely known in North America, post-war feminist consciousness was aroused by Betty Friedan's popular book, *The Feminine Mystique* (1963). Similarly, Canadian novelist Margaret Atwood put the new feminist consciousness to work in her first novel, *The Edible Woman* (1969) (see Box 6.2).

Betty Friedan grew up in a household in which her mother had, unhappily, given up a career to become a housewife and mother. She urged her daughter to go to college and become a career woman. During World War II, Friedan worked as a reporter, but she lost her job after the war when it was given to a returning soldier. When she again lost a job because her employer refused to give her a second maternity leave, Friedan assumed her mother's role as homemaker, but she carried her fight outside her household, first in her writing. *The Feminine Mystique* grew out of a survey she had conducted among her classmates. She found that most of the women from her graduating class were not using their education and felt unhappy and trapped in their lives.[78]

The Feminine Mystique documents the consequences of the "masculine and feminine" dualism and what Friedan believed was the complicity of women in their own oppression. In the 15-year period of post-war prosperity, women's

frightening leap. Simple acceptance is the path of least resistance. She is experiencing an inner split between her outward conformity to the feminine role and her inner values that this role denies.[79]

Once a woman is married, her husband expects her to play the feminine role. But this role is in opposition to her core, the centre of who she is and how she would like to see herself. One morning, Marian "discovers she doesn't have anything left inside, she's hollow, she doesn't know who she is anymore; her core has been destroyed."[80] As Betty Friedan put it in *The Feminine Mystique*, women must abandon passive dependency and child-like immaturity, which hollows out the self and is the definition of femininity. A woman's goal is to achieve humanization; each woman is alone and has to grow and create her own life and inner self.[81]

When Marian's rage pushes its way into her conscious mind, it is displaced by revulsion for consuming food. Fearing that she will be devoured, she begins to identify with dinner and finds it impossible to eat.[82] Her body is rebelling, unconsciously, against the passive feminine role that Peter and the man-made world impose on her. Gazing at her reflection in a spoon, she sees at first "a huge torso narrowing to a pinhead," symbolizing the shrinking of her mind. But then, by tilting the spoon handle, Marian is able to make the reflection of her forehead swell or recede at will.[83] Things are potentially under her control. She bakes a cake in the shape of a woman and invites Peter to eat it. She calls it her "substitute" and tells Peter he is destroying her as he would devour a cake. Peter escapes from the accusation. As soon as he is out of Marian's life, she is "immediately very hungry for nourishment."[84] Marian takes a fork to the legs of her cake and begins eating. She is alone and will have to make up her life as she goes along.

lives revolved around being dependent wives and mothers—the definition they accepted of feminine fulfilment.[85] Yet, Friedan found, suburban housewives felt surprisingly dissatisfied and silently asked themselves, *Is this all there is?*[86] Doris Day's 1956 hit record "Que Será, Será (Whatever Will Be, Will Be)"[87] didn't provide a satisfying answer. The "problem that had no name," Friedan argued, was rooted in the housewife role itself and in the mystique of femininity.

Suburban women felt empty, incomplete, and useless. They suffered from anomie, "that bored, diffuse feeling of purposelessness, non-existence, non-involvement with the world."[88] Women turned these feelings of dissatisfaction back onto themselves: something was wrong with *them* or their marriage. The **feminine mystique** counselled women that they could be fulfilled by sacrificing their own desires and by existing through and for their husbands and children. Instead of envying men, and trying to be like them, according to the feminine mystique, women should accept their own different and, in some ways, superior nature and accept "sexual passivity, male domination, and nurturing maternal love." Whole industries of psychotherapists, counsellors, self-help authors, talk-show hosts, and magazine publishers had grown up feeding off and perpetuating this anxiety. Women are bound to the household trap by chains of their own mind, chains of "mistaken ideas and misinterpreted facts, of incomplete truths and unreal choices. They are not easily seen and not easily shaken off."[89]

To change this situation, according to Friedan, women needed to listen to and act upon their inner voice, which demands something more than a home and family. Many women were well educated, but not enough of them had a worthwhile career outside the home. Just as sexual gratification had been stifled in the Victorian era, modern women were now restricted from reaching their full, human potential. The career woman

was ridiculed as being masculinized, as having sacrificed feminine fulfilment.[90] This conclusion was supported by the early results that came out of Kinsey's study of sexuality in the United States.

Alfred Kinsey, a zoologist by training, undertook a lengthy study of sexuality among Americans in the 1940s. His method, carried out by numerous trained researchers, involved in-depth interviews that probed extensively into people's sexual practices. His two main publications, *Sexual Behavior in the Human Male* (1948) and *Sexual Behavior in the Human Female* (1953), unleashed a storm of shock and criticism. Apparently, the more educated a woman was, the less likely it was that she had experienced sexual orgasm. Conservatives eagerly embraced this proof that the independent, career-oriented woman was sacrificing her femininity. As Friedan notes, however, in Kinsey's final report, he corrected this erroneous impression. The actual findings were the reverse: the number of women who reported reaching orgasm was actually higher for those with superior educational backgrounds.[91]

Friedan's solution for women was, first, to abandon the housewife role as defining the self. She doesn't imply abandoning rearing children or doing necessary household chores—she asserts that housework should not be seen as a career. Second, women must cease to see marriage and motherhood as their final fulfilment. Most importantly, women must find creative work of their own: not merely a job, but a career through which they can achieve self-actualization.[92] Without fully supportive partners who would share the double and triple burdens, however, independent, career-oriented women would be immersed in another set of social problems.

Friedan's book touched a barely concealed nerve and helped begin a transformation of consciousness, but the message was limited to middle-class women who had the opportunity to develop potentially rewarding professional careers.

Friedan's influence in the growing women's movement was strengthened when she was elected the first president of the National Organization of Women (NOW), founded in 1966.

What emerged was a movement for women's liberation, which expressed a variety of goals. Women had won the vote decades earlier. The new women's movement went beyond legal equality and demanded practical political and economic changes, including the following:

- Equal representation in party executives, in government, and in the Cabinet
- The enshrinement in law of women's equality
- The full integration of women into paid employment
- An end to discriminatory hiring and promotion practices
- Equal pay for equal work
- The opening of non-traditional occupations to women

And these were all goals that could be met within the current political and economic system and reflected a liberal type of feminism. In 1968, Shirley Chisholm (1924–2005) became the first black woman to win a seat in the US House of Representatives. Chisholm asserted that "Of my two handicaps, being female put many more obstacles in my path than being black."[93] Hilary Clinton and Barack Obama might now agree.

Divisions in the new women's movement emerged over questions such as the origins of the oppression of women, the necessary steps to overcome it, and the place of minorities in the movement. By the 1970s the movement had split into liberal, radical, and socialist branches (see Chapter 9). Friedan became a relatively conservative voice in the movement she had inspired, seeking to quell the rising attack on patriarchy and the emerging emphasis on women's sexual diversity. She believed that women should concentrate on

goals that could win the widest social support. Friedan's wish to accommodate change within the system was the reverse of a more radical rebellion that emerged among African Americans.

Post-War African-American Social Thought

"The war is over," I said. "You won and I didn't."

— Walter Mosley, *Bad Boy Brawley Brown*, 2002

In Mosley's novel, Brawley Brown is an African American World War II veteran.[94] His assertion that African Americans did not win the war speaks to the alienation blacks felt when they returned home from the European battlefield only to be faced with the same old-style racism in the heartland of the "democracy" they had fought to preserve. In the post-war era, the aspirations of African Americans were being awakened by a new social movement, inspired by the earlier generation of rebels. Tactically, the main division was between the advocates of peaceful, non-violent protest and those who believed that power grew out of the barrel of a gun. Should violence be met with violence or with peaceful, moral resistance? Strategically, what was the goal of black liberation? Was it full integration of black people into all aspects of American life—the dream of Booker T. Washington? Or was the goal the establishment of an African-American state, a nation within the nation for black people, abandoning as hopeless the aspiration for integration with whites? Within this multi-dimensional struggle, African-American leaders competed among themselves as they fought for the interests of blacks in America. "Black power" would emerge as the radical and nationalist slogan of the 1960s. Since the 1950s, however, the dominant movement had been rooted in religion, in non-violent tactics, and in the goal of civil rights legislation.

Civil Rights

"I draw the line in the dust and toss the gauntlet before the feet of tyranny and I say: Segregation now, segregation tomorrow, segregation forever."[95]

— George Wallace, Governor of Alabama, 1963.

Governor Wallace's blunt claim that racial discrimination was here to stay was not correct if he meant it in a legal sense. Among the African-American leaders who threw down the gauntlet of protest at the feet of tyranny, Martin Luther King, Jr., was the most distinguished. King was a Southern Baptist minister whose charismatic power was as influential from the pulpit as it was from his leadership of mass but tactically non-violent protests. King first came to prominence as the outspoken leader of the Montgomery, Alabama, bus boycott. This event was sparked by the refusal of a middle-aged black seamstress, Rosa Parks, to give up her seat to a white passenger when she was so ordered by the bus driver. Parks, a well-known activist, was arrested for violating a city law, was prosecuted, and was found guilty. In protest, an ad hoc group of 25 African-American ministers initiated an indefinite boycott. They expected that economic pressure would compel the bus company to accept a few demands, including the right of first-come-first-served on the buses.

To the struggle for black equality in the United States, King adapted the non-violent philosophy of Indian nationalist Mahatma Gandhi. Following this strategy, the civil rights movement practised civil disobedience: protesters would refuse to follow unjust laws and would allow themselves to be arrested without resistance. If a city government banned a peaceful demonstration, King's movement would march anyway. Blacks would enter whites-only restaurants and ask to be served. They would refuse to leave until the police were called, and they would have to be arrested and carried out. There weren't enough jails in the South to hold all the protesters. Sardonically, Langston Hughes said that bebop ("bop") was not just a style of jazz; it was the sound made by police billy clubs "beating Negroes' heads." White folks don't dig bop, he says, because they "do not get their heads beat *just for being white*. But me—a cop is liable to grab me almost any time and beat my head—*just* for being colored."[96]

In 1963, King brought his non-violent campaign to Birmingham, Alabama, the state of the nation's most outspoken racist: Governor George Wallace. Segregationists reacted violently to the peaceful tactics of the movement. Television brought nightly pictures of thousands of peaceful protestors, demonstrating for no more than the right to be treated equally, being beaten by clubs, bitten by dogs, tear-gassed, swept off their feet by fire hoses, and arrested by white police officers. This scene was repeated many times in other southern cities. In August 1963, a quarter of a million protestors—black and white—marched on Washington to demand equal rights and jobs.

The civil rights movement was counting on white, middle-class liberals to recognize that the demands of the black minority were fair and just, and that the response was violent and immoral. If the tide of white, majority opinion could be turned in favour of equal rights for blacks, then white governments would respond and change the laws. In 1964, the United States government, under President Lynden B. Johnson, passed the Civil Rights Act, which granted African Americans legal equality. Being legally equal, however, was some distance from being equal in fact. Black poverty and oppression persisted even though segregation was no longer legal. African Americans felt "othered"; in Ralph Ellison's view, they were still invisible as individuals (see Box 6.3).

In fact, toward the end of his life, King's politics went further left. He became more social in his demands—legal equality was not enough in a society where racial lines were also class lines.

✺ BOX 6.3 • BIOGRAPHY ✺

Ralph Ellison (1914–1994)

By 1950, neither Marcus Garvey's back-to-Africa movement nor Booker T. Washington's sly patience for social reform stirred either of the "two souls" of black people in America. Both approaches were critiqued explicitly in Ralph Ellison's celebrated first novel, *Invisible Man* (1952). Ellison had come to New York in 1936 and been inducted into the Harlem scene. He aspired to be a writer rather than only a "racial writer" and drew his inspirations as much from Dostoyevsky and European existentialism as from black history. Ellison included realism and biting satire in *Invisible Man*, but it is also a novel of despair, of pessimism of the intellect. There is only an individual and not a collective way out of the racial dilemma in America. *Invisible Man* was published before Rosa Parks refused to sit at the back of the bus and before Martin Luther King, Jr., began his non-violent protest movement for equal rights.

Ralph Waldo Ellison was born in Oklahoma City. His father, a construction worker, died when Ellison was three; his mother worked as a domestic. Ellison was named after Ralph Waldo Emerson and he carried his family's ambitions into the arts.[97] Drawn to the jazz and blues scene in Oklahoma City, Ellison played jazz trumpet and intended to be a musician. In 1933, he arrived at the Tuskegee Institute in Alabama, which had been founded by Booker T. Washington as a trade school to train African Americans for agricultural and industrial labour. Racial tensions had been inflamed in Alabama by the re-trial of the Scottsboro boys, who faced trumped-up charges of rape. Ellison survived in the South by hiding his wider ambitions and intellectualism beneath an external appearance of silence and self-control.[98]

After three years, Ellison was forced to leave the Institute for financial reasons and made his way to Harlem, the centre of black cultural renaissance and the New Negro. There, Ellison met Langston Hughes, who encouraged his writing ambitions. Ellison was able to penetrate deeply into the life of Harlem, collecting children's folktales and learning the speech patterns and idiom of the community. He moved uneasily, however, between the politics of the communists to which he was drawn and his passion for modern forms of literature and art.[99]

Ellison broke with the Communist Party because of their Jim Crow support for segregation in the US Armed Forces in World War II. Rather than enlist in the segregated army, Ellison joined the Merchant Marines to make his contribution to the war against fascism.[100] After the war, Ellison supported the African-American cause through his writing and speaking. His work, however, was criticized by radicals on the political left for being insufficiently "black" because he rejected radical politics and group violence—one reason that white critics admired his work, which assumed an artistic rather than political ethic.[101]

continued

In his award-winning novel *Invisible Man*, Ellison adapted Dostoyevsky's theme of alienation and underground invisibility to the plight of urban African Americans. The novel is a semi-autobiographical account of an African American who lives symbolically underground, holed up in a forgotten corner of a Harlem basement in a building rented exclusively to whites. "[A]ll life seen from the hole of invisibility is absurd,"[102] Ellison wrote, adapting a European, existentialist theme to black American experience. The narrator of the novel is socially invisible; he is not named and not seen by others as a person, an individual. Leaving the South and rejecting racial accommodation, the narrator finds work in New York, in the bowels of the Liberty Paints factory. His job is mixing white paint.[103]

In Harlem, the Invisible Man begins to understand the oppression of "white is right," and his black consciousness floats to the surface. He comes face to face with all the failed theories of African Americans.[104] He encounters black radicalism, modelled loosely after Marcus Garvey's movement. But "black is right" is not necessarily preferable to "white is right," he concludes, rejecting the politics of separatism and violence.[105] With the communists, he discovers just another organization that is dismissive of individual identity and is knowingly blind to the realities of everyday life in Harlem's streets, bars, barber shops, and beauty salons.[106] The narrator begins to glimpse that he is something more than a member of a race: he feels more human and experiences his individuality.[107] He has searched for a single identity, only to discover that his identity is plural, indistinct, multi-layered, acted upon, and changeable. The Invisible Man sits down to create his identity through the act of writing, as Ellison had done himself with *Invisible Man*.

King became a powerful voice against the Vietnam War and turned his attention to the issue of poverty in America, whether the poor were white or black. At the time he was assassinated, King was a more dangerous opponent of the American system than when he had addressed only the issue of black equality.

Black Power

Not all African Americans accepted the theory of non-violence. The Student Non-Violent Coordinating Committee (SNCC), for example, began to debate its commitment to non-violence following the brutality that had been directed against the voter registration campaign during 1964's Freedom Summer. SNCC became an all-black organization committed to black power and gave up on its program of non-violence.[108]

Unorganized mass violence broke out in many US cities in the mid to late 1960s. These riots were the visible manifestation of the frustration of black people in the face of the continuation of racism and discrimination despite the legal victories the civil rights movement had won. At the heart of this more militant response was a political party committed to armed self-defence—the Black Panthers—and an ideology of black consciousness and racial pride—black power. The Black Panther Party for Self Defense was formed in 1966. Known most widely for its armed defence of black communities, the Black Panthers were deeply involved in community organization and development, establishing a local socialist movement. The Panthers were systematically targeted by the FBI, which focused on arresting Panther leaders or forcing them into violent confrontations.

As Stokely Carmichael and Charles Hamilton—two of the most prominent voices of black power—put it, the theory of the movement of pacifists, such as King, was misguided. For King, integration was "a subterfuge for the maintenance of white supremacy." The goal for black people was emphatically "not . . . to assimilate into middle-class America, for that class—as a whole—is without a viable conscience as regards humanity." The middle class, they asserted, "*is the backbone of institutional racism in this country*."[109]

As Marcus Garvey foresaw, it was necessary for black people to define themselves and their heritage positively. Rejecting the term "Negro" as the invention of their oppressor, Carmichael and Hamilton recognized the new terms "African American" or simply "black." They associated both terms with a positive self-image, with "black people who are in fact energetic, determined, intelligent, beautiful and peace-loving."[110] They called for the unity of black people and for control by blacks where they were in a majority. Where they were in a minority, blacks must receive a proportional share of power. *Control* did not mean mere tokenism, more black faces in public offices, because most black politicians did not represent their own community but were connected, instead, to the white power structure.

To the white majority, however, black power was associated with violence. This was ironic, Carmichael and Hamilton argued, because the "black people of this country have not lynched whites, bombed their churches, murdered their children and manipulated laws and institutions to maintain oppression." The civil rights movement, they argued, spoke for whites, not for blacks, who became angrier and more determined the more white violence was used. Black power meant

fighting fire with fire, meeting violence with violence: "Black people should and must fight back. . . . *There can be no social order without social justice*."[111]

Malcolm X (1925–1965)

With respect to social theory, the most important militant black movement was led by Malcolm X (born Malcolm Little). His father was a Garvey supporter, but Malcolm had an inauspicious beginning as a political leader. His first career was as a petty criminal, for which he was imprisoned. The dominant black organization among prisoners was the Nation of Islam, a group that claimed Christianity was a white religion, part of the racist system of oppression. Malcolm Little converted to Islam and to the cause of black nationalism. And he changed his name to Malcolm X, rejecting "Little" as a name given his ancestors by slave owners. "X" represented the unknown African name he had lost.

According to the theory of the Nation of Islam, whites and blacks could never be integrated. The only possibility for black improvement and development was to be separate from whites. One way to achieve separation for blacks was to go back to Africa. An alternative solution was to create a black state in the United States out of territory in the South that had a majority black population. Ironically, the black nationalists and the white supremacists shared a common vision: the separation of the races. Both opposed the strategy of black/white integration, the goal of King and the civil rights movement.

Malcolm X did not subscribe to the territorial idea of nationalism; rather, black nationalism referred to the self-organization and self-determination of blacks within the United States. His energy, charisma, and organizing talents turned the Nation of Islam (also known as the Black Muslims) into a powerful political force for African Americans. As Malcolm X became more popular, a struggle ensued over the control of the Nation of Islam. In 1965, a faction of Black Muslims assassinated Malcolm X, although conspiracy theorists claim that the American government was involved in the murder.

Just prior to his death, and following his break with the Nation of Islam, Malcolm X had been slowly changing his theoretical orientation, as had Martin Luther King. Malcolm X became more conciliatory toward the civil rights movement and concluded that not all whites were enemies. The religion of Islam had ample room within it to embrace believers from all races and nationalities.[112] The Nation of Islam continues to be an influential force in black politics in the United States. It remains, however, a highly male-dominated movement.

Angela Davis (b. 1944)

Angela Davis is a radical activist with close links to the Black Panther Party. She was born in 1944 in Alabama, during the Jim Crow era of segregation. A precocious student, Davis finished high school in New York in the early 1960s, where she was influenced by Marxists. She studied at Brandeis University in Massachusetts and then in Paris, and was radicalized by the Vietnam War and the desegregation crisis unfolding in the US south. Davis also studied in Frankfurt with critical Marxist Theodor Adorno, and grew close to the German Students for a Democratic Society. Finally, she went to California, where Herbert Marcuse was then teaching and where the Black Panther Party was organizing in militant self-defence. Committed to socialism, Davis believed that Black Nationalism was too limited in its vision of liberation.[113]

Davis taught at the University of California while being a member of the Communist Party and maintaining ties with the Black Panthers. In 1969, the Board of Regents of the University of California, led by then-governor Ronald Reagan, fired Davis from her teaching position because of her affiliations. This resurrection of McCarthyism was short-lived, however, and, following popular protests, the decision was overturned.

The next year, Davis was implicated in an attempted breakout from a courthouse where three black men were on trial for the murder of a prison guard in Soledad Penitentiary. One of the prisoners was George Jackson, the author of *Soledad Brother*, written while he was in solitary confinement. Jackson's brother, Jonathan, stormed the courtroom with automatic weapons, seized the judge as a hostage, and demanded the release of the Soledad Three. He was shot and killed during the escape attempt, along with the judge. In 1971, George Jackson was shot and killed by prison guards, allegedly attempting to escape.[114]

Angela Davis was implicated in the escape attempt because the weapons that had been used were registered in her name. She was placed on the FBI's most-wanted list and was forced underground. Two months later she was arrested in New York and charged with conspiracy. Supporters in the Communist Party, black activists, and liberal intellectuals organized a "Free Angela Davis" movement.[115] She was celebrated in popular song: in "Angela" by John Lennon and Yoko Ono, and in "Sweet Black Angel" by the Rolling Stones. After a highly public trial in 1972, Davis was acquitted of the charges. Davis lived for a while in Cuba, where she linked the causes of black liberation in the United States with the Cuban Revolution. She is currently a professor of philosophy at the University of California.

Davis believed the key gains of the Black Panther and civil rights era were desegregation and the spread of black consciousness through such agencies as Black Studies programs. In the 1960s, simultaneously with the rise of the Black Panthers, certain cultural nationalist organizations were created in the black liberation movement. There was, for example, a black arts movement that, Davis says, was important in developing black consciousness. LeRoi Jones, who adopted the African name Amiri Baraka, argued for a time that black cultural nationalism, through which blacks identified with the cultures of their African ancestors, was the crucial step in solving the problems of racism in American economic and social institutions. The trend to adopt African names spread to black celebrities. Boxer Cassius Clay became Muhammad Ali; basketball star Lou Alcindor became Kareem Abdul-Jabbar.

At the time, the Black Panther Party debated whether to organize against police violence and whether they should begin wearing African clothes and adopt African names. Davis agreed that developing an Africa-centred cultural consciousness helped resist the long-standing effects of cultural genocide that, during the centuries of slavery and Jim Crow, had stripped black people of their languages and cultures. Nevertheless, in Davis's view, the cultural nationalists projected an "idealized, romantic image of Africa . . . and assumed that all we needed to do was to become African, so to speak, rather than become involved in organized anti-imperialist struggles."[116] This form of nationalism conflated cultural blackness and anti-racism.

As globalization has proceeded, black politics in the US has receded. Black liberation resulted in the growth of a black bourgeoisie or middle class, which has increasingly divorced itself from radical or progressive politics. Working-class communities have suffered economic collapse as blue-collar jobs are lost in the United States, and black communities have fallen into serious decline and disarray. The black community is fractured as the black bourgeoisie expands in tandem with the social disintegration of inner-city neighbourhoods and the rise in the number of incarcerated black youth.

In this social context, Davis argues, the movement withers for black liberation. Instead, young people tend to turn to cultural politics to express political issues.[117] Black role models are more likely to be rappers with a "gangsta" image

than militant, political activists. But cultural politics alone, Davis asserts, is not going to solve the problems of the black community.

Davis agrees there is an important place in black liberation for cultural resistance, identification with Africa, and black pride; but just appearing African is not enough. Cultural politics should be practised within a broader political struggle that is international in its focus, similar to the pan-African movement initiated by W.E.B. du Bois. The cultural side of black nationalism has continued to thrive, Davis claims, because "that is the aspect of the movement that was most commodifiable." For capitalist corporations, the commodification of blackness is profitable and clearly linked with the rise of the black middle class. Selling Afrocentric cultural artifacts may be pleasurable for many people,[118] but the crucial point is to maintain anti-imperialist and anti-capitalist struggles. Unlike commodification, these struggles do not happen spontaneously; they have "to be fought for and recrafted continuously."[119]

Conclusion

Critical social thought, feminism, and the movement for African-American liberation arose out of social movements and theories that developed in the early years of the twentieth century and that had roots that extended well back in Western history. All three have had continuing effects on contemporary social thought. Just as the foundations of black and women's studies were established in the critical response to the post-war world, a similar move was underway in cultural studies, in part inspired by the challenging thought of Marshall McLuhan, who is discussed in Chapter 7.

The end of both the empire in Europe and the Cold War between the US and the USSR book-ended a range of issues that challenged social thought. The horrors of the Holocaust had been exposed, demonstrating "barbarity" in the heartland of Europe. The rapidity with which American financial aid secured a new economic prosperity for its erstwhile enemies, Germany and Japan, embittered its former but now seemingly abandoned allies. For radicals, the view that the Soviet Union represented a better social system was undermined by revelations about ethnic repression and the archipelago of forced labour camps in Russia. As the world appeared to become an increasingly illogical and incongruous place, absurdity emerged as a dominant theme in European literature and in the social thought known as existentialism, including its close cousin, the American Beat counterculture.

Questions for Reflection

1. What is the American dream? Is it still alive in the contemporary world?
2. In what ways does your image of present-day white-collar work contrast with the analysis of C. Wright Mills? In what ways is it similar?
3. What is Friedan's "problem with no name," and has it been solved in the present day by eliminating the feminine mystique?
4. Do de Beauvoir's analyses of femininity, masculinity, and androgyny speak to men and women today? Why or why not?
5. Why is there no significant black power movement today?

CHAPTER 7

Existentialism, the Beats, and McLuhan

Learning Objectives

- To be able to explicate the distinctive features of existentialism in general and locate them in the theatre-of-the-absurd movement

- To summarize Jean-Paul Sartre's version of existentialism and its fusion with humanist Marxism

- To understand cultural rebellion in the 1950s as a response to the American dream

- To present an overview of Marshall McLuhan's ambiguous analysis of forms of mass communication

An introduction of social thought in the post-war years includes understanding an avant-garde movement known as existentialism, which flourished on the Left Bank of the Seine River in Paris in the post-war years. Significant affinities exist between this philosophical movement in Europe and a counter-culture associated with the Beats in the United States. Both rejected social conventions and sought meaning in action. Both were rooted in the fundamental Western value of individualism. And both sought to put the imponderable into words: for the Beats this meant **It**; for the existentialists "It" was the inexpressible concept of "nothingness" that represented the anguish and despair they found at the very centre of existence.

The theoretical analysis of culture had become a persistent theme of social thought since Western Marxism and the Frankfurt School. Marshall McLuhan continued this critical analysis of the media in the 1950s. With the publication of *Understanding Media* in 1964, McLuhan changed the terms of the debate. Rather than studying the ideology of the message embedded in forms of media, McLuhan argued that the medium *was* the message: the form of the medium itself had significant social consequences. In the contemporary age of digital communications, his argument— that the forms of media are themselves forces of change—is even more apparent.

Existentialism and the Absurd

"Above all things, I fear absurdity."[1]

— Salman Rushdie, *Midnight's Children*, 1981

The dominant philosophical view in France in the period before and after World War II was **existentialism**, a label that emphasizes the importance of immediate experiences more than complex, abstract, speculative thought. Rooted in Romantic subjectivism, existentialist ideas were developed further in the philosophies of Kierkegaard and Nietzsche, who "shared the same experience of loneliness, anguish, and doubt."[2] Similar views were conceived in the East, in Buddhist and Taoist writings. Many of the fundamental existentialist themes were expressed in the nineteenth-century novels of Fyodor Dostoyevsky. In *Notes from the Underground*, Dostoyevsky's anti-hero remonstrates against the perversity of the universe and what he sees as the ultimate self-destructiveness of human nature.

Nietzsche elaborated several themes that were later developed by modern existentialist theorists. Having rejected all contemporary standards for judging morality and rightness, such as science, **humanism**, or Christianity, Nietzsche asserted that humans had to face the fact that they were free to choose their own morality. Any systematic thought was merely a perspective, a choice of the acting person. In acting on their personal convictions, people express their individual will, the motive that compels the few to oppose the conformity demanded by the many. Humans must create their own meaning in the world and then act to realize it, as Frantz Fanon came to believe.

Phenomenology and Heidegger

In the world through which I travel, I am endlessly creating myself. . . .
I am my own foundation.

— Frantz Fanon, *Black Skin, White Masks*, 1952, p. 229

Philosopher Edmund Husserl (1859–1938) argued that philosophy had to begin with immediate experience. The focus was not an objective world of objects, existing independently and apart from our mind, which we simply perceive through our senses. The meaning of our experience of objects is created in the mind. Neither object nor consciousness is

primary; neither can be reduced to the other. The encounter with objects and the emergence of the mind are completely interrelated.[3]

Phenomenology assumes a correlation between the knowing subject and the world of objects. In *Being and Time*, Martin Heidegger called this correlation "being-in-the-world" (*dasein*). Freenberg and Leiss emphasize that the concept refers to a multiplicity of "worlds," which are neither entirely outside us (objective and independent) nor entirely in our minds (subjective and created). We act in a context that has meaning for us and must be understood in relation to our action. People act constantly in the present, but they do so in relation to an *anticipated* future.[4] This anticipated future "gives order and meaning to the present."[5] When we act, we cannot simply take the world as it is for granted. Instead, we interrogate "our world and ourselves" as we develop our intentions and put them into action.[6] In this way, we exist in a world that, over time, is partly of our own making.

In this sense, our world is *individually* constructed and, hence, we can reconstruct it. These acts of construction are what it is to be human. Experience is radically individualized: "[M]y experience belongs to *me* and is inseparable from *my* being."[7] For Heidegger, recognizing this philosophical truth creates an "authentic" relationship between the self and the world.

In ordinary consciousness, however, we don't always think or act as though we are continually constructing the world in which we live. In everyday experience, people act socially and conform to the average norms of others in their society. We are socialized through our participation with "the they" (*das Man*, or "the anonymous anyone" in Heidegger's terminology). People act following the views of others rather than according to the truth that they are "a questioning being, a being to whom experience belongs personally and inseparably." For Heidegger, "authentic" individuality is possible when an individual becomes "aware of his or her individuality beyond any and all mindless conformism."[8]

As Marcuse argues, Heidegger's notion of authenticity means "the return to oneself, to one's innermost freedom, and, out of this inwardness, to decide, to determine every phase, every situation, every moment of one's existence . . . ; to decide and to act according to your decision." But such inwardness ignores fundamental questions of whether the decisions, the goals expressed in action, are "morally and humanly positive."[9] What is left is only the purpose and meaning that the individual momentarily constructs and deconstructs for her- or himself. There are no abstract standards, such as rules of morality, that can be applied to guide one's action. The end result, it would seem, is **nihilism**, the anti-theory of those who have no guidelines for their conduct. Most existentialists who followed Heidegger, however, were not content to leave social theory in a state of absolute nihilism.

The Theatre of the Absurd and Beckett

Existentialist ideas influenced many art forms, from sculpture to theatre. The Cold War era was a time of great anxiety, a time when many artists felt the "anguish" at the heart of the existentialist experience. Italian sculptor Alberto Giacometti shared this feeling of despair and expressed a strong sense of human isolation through his sculpture. Earlier in his career, Giacometti had experimented with **surrealism**. During the war, he had worked long hours, creating smaller and smaller pieces, until his artistic vision almost shrank to nothingness. After the war he developed a style that satisfied him. His absurdly thin and fragile sculptures of the human body demonstrated the frailty and isolation of the human condition, an idea that was also illustrated in Samuel Beckett's play *Endgame*: an individual is merely a "speck in the void" surrounded by "infinite emptiness . . . like a little bit of grit in the middle of the steppe."[10] Beckett was one of the most important authors of the theatre of the absurd (see Box 7.1).

Perhaps the most influential works in the theatre-of-the-absurd movement were written by the Irish-born playwright Samuel Beckett. The unrelenting message that recurs in Beckett's plays is that life is futile and meaningless, yet people cling desperately to it out of the force of habit and the fear of the unknown. Being alone is the only thing that is worse than living with someone else, although any relationship is painful and frustrating and mutual communication is actually impossible. Beckett's most successful absurdist play was *Waiting for Godot*, first performed in Paris in 1953. Both the physical description of the main characters—two tramps—as well as the elements of slapstick comedy and farce are reminiscent of Charlie Chaplin, whose alienated *Little Tramp* character was an earlier victim of the absurdities of life. Time is the chief enemy as people have to endure the meaninglessness of their brief life in the vast sea of eternity. People are born "astride a grave, the light gleams an / instant, then it's night once more."[11] Beckett's plays become increasingly minimalist and absurd, until a single actor is reduced to a talking mouth. What is left? It is the theatre equivalent of painting a plain, white square. So the theatre of the absurd was, of necessity, short-lived.

For purely existential theorists, all humanly constructed systems of meaning were empty abstractions, "false gods" infecting individuals with what Ionesco called rhinoceritis, whether religious or secular. For most social theorists, however, nihilism is an unacceptable solution. What remains after existentialism and absurdity, as it was for social theorists such as Camus and Sartre, is to create meaning, to invent a purpose for art or for life. The weakness in the centre of the theory of nothingness became clear with the rise of Nazism and World War II. The Nazi terror brought the experience of "evil" to the forefront of existentialist consciousness. Logically, the concept of evil has

✣ BOX 7.1 · THEORY IN CONTEXT ✣

Theatre of the Absurd

The absurd made its reappearance in theatres in the late 1940s. In Paris, a new theatre movement emerged from the chaos and disillusionment of the early post-war world. Labelled the theatre of the absurd in 1961,[12] this latest generation of avant-garde playwrights and directors encapsulated the existentialist revolt against all conventions and certainties. Nurtured by the same extremities that had shaped the Cold War era, the theatre of the absurd was consistently nihilist in its intentions. Like its **Dada** predecessor, which flourished in Paris between 1918 and 1922, new theatre was "antirealistic, antipsychological, antiphilosophical, and apolitical."[13] Above all, it was antirational. The theatre-of-the-absurd playwrights were utterly alienated from contemporary bourgeois culture with no sense that any better future could be achieved. Their theatre was staged in a world of "rejection, isolation, and futility"—in a word, of absurdity.

Eugene Ionesco's *The Bald Soprano* opened in 1950, Gaensbauer tells us, to a crowd of three: the playwright, his spouse, and a "passerby taking refuge from the cold."[14] It was an inauspicious beginning for the theatre-of-the absurd movement. Ionesco's profound alienation from the world was rooted in his parent's divorce and his unhappy return in 1925, at the age of 13, under his father's custody, to Romania, a country becoming increasingly fascist. For the young Ionesco, his father, a former chief of police, became an anti-role model: "I was horrified by prosecuting attorneys; I couldn't lay eyes on a judge without wanting to kill him. I couldn't set eyes on an officer, a captain shod in boots, without giving way to fits of anger and despair. Everything that represented authority seemed to me, and is, unjust."[15] The politics in Ionesco's "apolitical" theatre, then, was a deeply rooted **anarchism**.

The Bald Soprano (1949) was the first of Ionesco's "anti-plays." It included inane dialogue, repetition, and long, uncomfortable silences. As the actors interchange roles, hurl insults, or chant meaninglessly, the anti-play, as Gaensbauer describes it,[16] "degenerates into savage linguistic anarchy." In 1957, Ionesco wrote his most obviously political play, *Rhinoceros*. A couple discover that a herd of rhinoceros have taken over political power. One by one, their friends, neighbours, and co-workers gradually become infected by "rhinoceritis" and begin to change physically—to undergo a surrealist metamorphosis—and join the frenzied herd of rhinos in the streets. *Rhinoceros* championed the individual rebel who resists, alone with his or her conscience, and does not give in to authoritarianism.[17]

no place in existentialist writing. Ultimately, each individual creates her or his own guidelines for acting in the world and there is no objective standard for determining good or bad—they simply *are*. In the midst of the struggle against tyranny, however, nihilism is not an acceptable position. What attitude could an individual human being adopt that would be compatible with existentialism yet also consistently battle evil? What ethics were possible in an utterly meaningless universe?

Existentialism did not have a single solution. Albert Camus and Jean-Paul Sartre were among the most influential existentialists in France.

Albert Camus (1913–1960)

We of the generation that has become mature from 1938 to 1945 have seen too many things.

— Albert Camus

Albert Camus was born in 1913 in Algeria, a French colony in the north of Africa. Within a year his father, who had been an agricultural worker, was killed in World War I. Young Camus and his mother, who worked as a charwoman, moved into a two-room apartment in a poor district of Algiers. Despite this background, Camus won a scholarship to a lycée (a public secondary school) and subsequently became a philosophy student at the University of Algiers. In the early 1930s, Camus supported himself with a number of jobs but became ill with tuberculosis. For a time he joined the Communist Party but he disagreed with their colonial policy. Instead, he expressed his politics by creating a theatre company dedicated to performing and writing plays with a social message for the working class and progressive (socialist and nationalist) intellectuals. At this point, his "revolt" had social, humanistic, and political aims.[18] When Northern France was occupied by the Germans in World War II, Camus worked as an underground journalist in Paris.

Prior to his experience with the French Resistance, between 1938 and 1941, Camus' writing had begun to reflect a wider sense of revolt against an absurd world in which human values had no solid foundation. Camus did not have a positive image of human nature. Humans are not social by nature, Camus believed, but are solitary and individualistic, naturally alienated from one another. Paradoxically, however, they simultaneously possess the desire to be sociable. Only society, "whose laws are necessary to his physical survival," makes life possible, Camus says, however artificial a creation is society.[19]

Camus reflects on the absurd through the Greek myth of Sisyphus. In Greek mythology, Sisyphus was condemned by the gods to repeatedly roll a heavy stone up hill. Each time the stone approaches the summit, it rolls back to the bottom again. Sisyphus symbolizes the absurdity of life because his prodigious efforts to achieve his goal always and forever come to nothing. The most basic absurdity, Camus claims in *Le Mythe de Sisyphe*, is that humans strive to understand the world, to make life coherent and understandable even though the world is essentially incomprehensible.[20] So the human mind tries, perpetually, to achieve an impossible task: to understand the incomprehensible, to invent a rationality in a world that is inherently irrational. For Camus, truth itself does not exist. The world is unknowable, by any means. Nevertheless, humans are cursed by consciousness and are driven to seek meaning where none exists.[21]

For Camus, a human is one who "instinctively wishes to be happy, who wants his life to continue indefinitely, who seeks close contact with other human beings and with the natural world, but who finds these desires frustrated by the nature of existence." What humans actually experience, then, is "anxiety, disappointment, a sense of estrangement and horror of death"—in a word, the absurd. The daily drudgery most people experience, especially in their work, is like a labour of Sisyphus.[22]

Faced with a realization of the absurdity of existence, Camus suggests, people can react in several ways. One is by committing suicide, but this is giving in to nihilism. Everyone faces the same predicament, but self-destruction, individually or collectively, is an unsatisfactory solution for Camus. The second possibility is to accept a belief on pure faith, such as humanism or socialism, but, at best, Camus believed they are merely myths; at worst, they perpetuate evil. The only alternative, according to Camus, is to continue to live despite the absurdity of the universe—to create your own purposes and meanings even though they may be doomed to failure.[23] Ironically, of course, accepting the absurdity of life means that the mind has actually arrived at one final truth: that the world is absurd. One must live one's life knowing that the world is absurd but also striving to understand (because humans have a need for explanation), while avoiding the two pitfalls of nihilism (giving up) or accepting false truths.

The Absurd and Existentialist Revolt

> *Then the angel, cruel as he was kind, / With giant hands twisted him till he wined; / But the damned soul still answered, "I will not!"*[24]
>
> — Charles Baudelaire, "The Rebel," 1957

In writing about such "somber subjects" as human isolation, self-estrangement, the failure of humanism, and death, Cruickshank argues that Camus "attempts to avoid the two extremes of nihilistic pessimism and facile optimism." As Camus commented, "With the rest of my generation I grew up to the drumbeats of the First World War, and our history since then has continued the tale of murder, injustice or violence." Camus's declared aim was not to trade on this "cruelty and infamy" but to seek "the means to transcend nihilism." Both easy optimism and absolute pessimism (nihilism) breed passivity and inaction. In their place, Camus emphasized the importance of active, individual revolt: "Meaning has to be created, not found, and it has to be created by the individual out of the actual experience of revolt." What kind of meaning makes sense for an existentialist? Camus explored this question in an essay, *L'homme révolté*. He championed *perpetual revolt*, an attitude of individual, moral rebellion.[25]

For Camus, all previous revolutions had failed largely because of the moral abstractions and theories that guided them, whether expressed as freedom, equality, socialism, or liberation. Revolutions begin as "revolt" and end in dictatorship. In Russia, for example, the 1917 workers' revolution "marked the dawn of real freedom and the greatest hope the world has known." But that revolution deteriorated into tyranny, became a police state, and denied freedom, until finally "the world's greatest hope hardened into the world's most efficient dictatorship."[26] When an individual moves from opposing evil (revolt) to committing evil (congealed revolution), that person has ceased to be in revolt. What is necessary, then, is perpetual revolt, not only against the evils of the existing world but also against the new evils brought about by those trying to remove the earlier evils. For Camus, the genuine rebel never demands "the right to destroy the person and freedom of someone else. He degrades no one. The freedom which he demands he claims for everybody; . . . He is not simply a slave opposing his master but a man opposing the world of masters and slaves."[27]

Revolt does not necessarily mean taking up arms. The authentic artist, for example, must be in perpetual revolt. The person who chooses revolt must walk a tightrope, balancing between simply abandoning hope (nihilism) or grasping false hopes (religion, humanism, Marxism). For Camus, freedom is, at its heart, "a perpetual risk." Ordinarily, however, people avoid this risk with its uncertain freedoms and "exacting demands," preferring "the comfort of conformism."[28]

Jean-Paul Sartre and Humanist Marxism

> *"Every existing thing is born without reason, prolongs itself out of weakness and dies by chance."*[29]
>
> — Jean-Paul Sartre, *La nausée*, 1938

Sartre was the long-time "essential" lover of Simone de Beauvoir. He had a more orthodox upbringing than his life companion. Sartre's

Victorian maternal grandparents were modestly middle class from Alsace, a territory over which France and Germany had fought for control. They taught their daughter Anne-Marie the conventional, feminine virtues: "She was taught to be bored, to hold herself straight, and to sew. She had gifts: it was thought refined to let them lie fallow; she had brilliance: it was carefully kept from her." In 1904, Anne-Marie married a naval officer, Jean-Baptiste Sartre, who soon died from a fever he had contracted in southern China. At the age of 20, Anne-Marie was widowed, and young Jean-Paul was fatherless. "Penniless and jobless," Sartre's mother returned to her parents' home, where she kept house under her parents' strict and intimidating supervision: she "returned . . . to her chains."[30]

Later, Sartre regarded the absence of his father as key to his free development: "If he had lived, my father would have laid down on me and crushed me. Fortunately, he died young." This left Sartre, according to his self-analysis, with no super-ego—no internal tyrant to deny his freedom. He was not "taught obedience" and would not willingly follow orders. But, Sartre concluded, he was also unwilling to *give* orders. In the absence of an authoritarian upbringing, he rejected both the imposition and the exercise of authority. Sartre concluded that, as a consequence of his upbringing, he "was not eaten up by the canker of power."[31]

Sartre studied philosophy in France and Germany in the 1930s and subsequently became a teacher. In 1938, he published his first existentialist novel, *La nausée* (*Nausea*). Heidegger had discussed authentic individuality as establishing connections between people that are not simply based on mindless social conformity. But for Sartre, human interaction is always fraught with conflict. Other people interfere with an individual's projects and undermine her or his sense of autonomy. To illustrate, in 1943 Sartre wrote *No Exit*, a play about three people who find themselves in hell. At first they assume there are no instruments of torture, but later they discover that each member of the triad will become the mental torturer of the other. The message that Sartre delivers is this: "Hell is other people." Each person tries to create his or her own self, but can only succeed to the degree that others accept the self that is projected. Consciousness, therefore, is awareness of one's self in a confusing universe in which others make you the object of *their* consciousness and their actions.

Freedom and Bad Faith

Hovstad: Call it what you like; we couldn't do otherwise.
Dr. Stockman: You dared not do otherwise! Isn't that what you mean?[32]

— Henrik Ibsen, *An Enemy of the People*, 1882

In Sartre's philosophy, an individual exists and is absolutely free; freedom is "very exactly the stuff of my being." But an individual is defined by her or his action; one is never free *not* to act. As Sartre expresses, "I am condemned to be free. . . . or, if you prefer, that we are not free to cease being free." Humans cannot simply "be" like an object that simply exists; rather, freedom "forces humanity *to make itself* instead of *to be*." Humans act to realize their "projects" in the world: "to be is to act."[33]

Freedom is human destiny, Sartre writes, but freedom implies responsibility. The logical consequence of being "condemned" to be free is that the individual "carries the weight of the whole world on his shoulders; he is responsible for the world and for himself as a way of being." We are the authors of our situations; nothing outside ourselves "has decided what we feel, what we live, or what we are." There are no accidents in life because everything comes from the inside. For example, Sartre argues, if his country goes to war, "this war is *my* war." He could avoid war through desertion or suicide, but if he takes neither action, "For lack of getting out of it I have *chosen* it." The choice will continually be repeated until the end of the war—every choice not to act is actually a choice to act. Consequently, human reality is to live without excuse. Sartre says, "I am abandoned in the world . . . in the sense that I find myself suddenly alone and without help, engaged in a world for which I bear the whole responsibility without being able, whatever I do, to tear myself away from this responsibility for an instant." Consequently, the consciousness of freedom causes people anguish; however, "most of the time we flee anguish in bad faith."[34]

And bad faith is, essentially, lying to yourself.[35] You make excuses to convince yourself that you had no choice; you could not have acted otherwise. Hence, the results of your action are not your responsibility. When you lie to yourself, you cannot recognize it as a lie. You must come to believe your own falsehood. Bad faith, therefore, perpetuates itself.[36] Acting in "bad faith" is a routine mental defence for people in all circumstances; as the character Gregory House says in the television medical-mystery drama *House*, "Everybody lies." Bad faith is especially prevalent in situations of oppression in which following orders, and denying freedom and responsibility, means self-preservation. This theme appears in Sartre's earlier works. During the war, the French Resistance fought a largely urban guerrilla war, killing German soldiers and destroying strategic installations. For every successful Resistance action, however, the Germans extracted a terrible revenge: they would execute a large number of otherwise innocent French civilians in retaliation. Indirectly, then, the Resistance guerrilla could feel responsible for the death of many innocent victims. Was it right to resist when there would be so much blood on one's hands? From Sartre's point of view (and de Beauvoir's as well, as indicated in her play *The Blood of Others*), it was necessary to resist evil even at such a terrible cost. An individual was responsible only for his or her own

actions. The death of innocent French civilians was the responsibility of the German soldiers who pulled the triggers. The existentialist doctrine of "bad faith" was never more apparent than during the Nuremburg Trials following World War II when many German officers and Nazi leaders claimed, "I was only following orders." For Sartre, this denial of responsibility is precisely bad faith.

Existentialism and Marxism: Search for a Marriage

> "[M]y Uncle Ted used to say that [life is what you make it]—until somebody dropped a bomb which took both his legs off. It changed his mind."[37]
>
> — John Wyndham, *The Day of the Triffids*, 1951

Through the war and its aftermath, some of the contradictions in Sartre's thinking became clearer. On the one hand, he was decidedly anti-capitalist and in favour of socialism. Yet his fundamental existentialist belief was in the autonomy and freedom of the individual—as capitalist a value as it was possible to find. But faced with evil, as represented concretely by Nazi oppression in Europe, any isolated acts of individual rebellion were utterly insufficient. Through his contacts with the French Communist Party in the Resistance, Sartre began to appreciate the limitations that the social order imposed on an individual's freedom of action. More and more, Sartre came to believe that Marx's theory—that people act according to a pre-existing social order—held some truth, despite its absolute contradictory point of view from existentialism. "[C]ommon sense," Sartre thought, "often belies the Existentialist platitude, life is what you make it," as a character in the novel *The Day of the Triffids* observed.

For an existentialist, what mattered was individual choice and responsibility. To talk about anything outside the individual that was responsible for a person's choices was to commit the sin of "bad faith." Like Uncle Ted's predicament in *The Day of the Triffids*, though, people make choices in circumstances that are encumbered by restraints, sometimes severe ones. For Marxism, on the contrary, people act under circumstances that appear to determine their actions. You can't have it both ways. Are individuals' actions freely chosen, or are they determined by historical forces over which the individual has no control? As he developed his ideas in the post-war world, Sartre wanted to combine both of these essential "truths" into a single theory, however contradictory they appeared to be at first.

In *Search for a Method*, Sartre offers a critique of Marxism as it was then generally understood, and a reinterpretation of Marxism that made it compatible with some of the basic tenets of his earlier existentialism. The result is a fusion of existentialism with the humanistic and philosophical "early Marx." At the very least, Sartre came to believe that the "resistances and obstacles" might play an important role, not in *causing* choices, but in *limiting* them. Sartre argued that both aspects of understanding are necessary. It would be an error to assume that either approach to reality is sufficient in itself. To study any concrete case adequately requires situating it in general categories—studying a single tree, for example, would be little help in understanding the concept "deforestation." However, it is equally an error to assume that you could understand any single part of a whole by applying generalizations to it—you also have to understand a thing in its specificity, its uniqueness and individuality.

Marx's early method, Sartre argued, had left room for both approaches. As an ideology that was made "official" by later Marxists after Marx's death, however, Marxism had become a dogma. What was necessary, Sartre said, was to return to Marx's actual method, the philosophical foundation of his work. The key principle that expressed the dialectical method of Marx was his observation that "men make their own history on the basis of prior conditions."[38] For Marx, humans

are born into conditions they do not create—the "given"—but then they consciously surpass and transform this "given." Humans *make* history, but not out of "whole cloth."

For Sartre, two essential conditions coexist. Humans possess free will, the ability to consciously direct their activities and attempt to achieve their aims. The world in which they act, however, is not their creation alone. People try to achieve their goals in a world as it is, which was constructed by the earlier activities of other people; at the same time anyone who tries to act in the world is affected and constrained by the actions of other people.

When Marxism is brought to the altar to be married with Sartre's existentialism, what it offers is an analysis of these "prior conditions," the concrete (structural) limitations placed on the activities of people in the world. An individual human being exists within a set of circumstances that Sartre called the "practio-inert" (really existing context within which humans act). The "practico-inert" includes "materiality," the physical objects in the world, whether natural or modified by humanity; it also includes the **praxis** (social actions) of other people, as well as social institutions, which are the solid structures that have been created by people's past praxis. Not everything is possible for humans to achieve in a given time and place. The "practico-inert" establishes boundaries to human action, even to what it is possible to think and imagine (although the limits to thinking are more vast than what is realizable in time and space). For Sartre, "Every [hu]man is defined negatively by the sum total of possibles which are impossible for him [or her]; that is, by a future more or less blocked off."[39]

Social science in general and Marxism in particular make a major contribution to knowledge in their analysis of the "practico-inert." It is never a case, however, that human actions can be said to have been "caused" by any externally existing component of the "practico-inert." Rather than establishing causal efficacy, an impossibility, Marxism helps in understanding the limitations that restrict the "field of possibles" in which people make choices and act. The future may be "more or less blocked off," but the field of possibles always exists—social science does not eliminate the free choices people make within their restricted horizons. The fundamental principle of human action, according to Marxism, is indeterminacy because humans are in essence free: "The field of possibles, however reduced it may be, always exists. . . . It is by transcending the given toward the field of possibles and by realizing one possibility from among all the others that the individual objectifies himself and contributes to making history."[40]

The 1950s Counter-Culture

In the post-1945 world, some of the most creative intellects had bound themselves intimately to corporate power, as the advertising industry became the animating power of consumer capitalism. Under the umbrella of this unprecedented prosperity and domination, the modern American avant-garde retreated into subjectivity, renouncing any artistic flirtation with social change. The Depression-era retreat—as it was deemed—back to artistic realism had been an aberration. Pure art was abstract and expressionistic. It had no message other than expressing the exuberance of creation, an artist's inner vision, and the immediacy of the here and now (see Box 7.2).

The generation that came of age in the early 1950s, as John Clellon Holmes writes, had been born in the Depression and weaned during the years of total war: "[T]hey had intimate experience with the nadir and the zenith of human conduct, and little time for much that came between. The peace they inherited was only as secure as the next headline. It was a cold peace." Typically, these post-war youth were fed up with going nowhere and with the loss of values and

faith. Their search for "somewhereness" took two related forms. Those whom Holmes characterized as Young Republicans sought stability in an unstable world. They embraced Richard Nixon in politics, and the suit and tie of a corporate career. The Beat generation, on the other hand, embraced instability: "Their own lust for freedom, and the ability to live at a pace that kills . . . led to black markets, bebop, narcotics, sexual promiscuity, hucksterism, and Jean-Paul Sartre."[41]

Part of the background to this cultural change was created by the Kinsey reports on sexuality. Alfred Kinsey's reports claimed that almost all men had masturbated; that slightly over one-third of American men had at least one homosexual experience at some time in their life; and that half of all married men and one in four married women experienced an extramarital affair. These figures were widely reported, challenged, and defended. It was no longer safe to assume that sexual behaviour took place predominantly in the bedroom of legally married men and women. Kinsey brought to light the existence of a closeted gay community, flourishing in the urban underground. It was parallel to this world of social and cultural transgression that the Beat generation flourished.

The Beats

"It's only after you've lost everything . . . that you're free to do anything."[42]

— Chuck Palahniuk, *Fight Club*, 1996

Unlike the 1920s lost generation, which was the name applied to the alienated American writers and artists who hung out in post-World War I Paris, the **Beats** were not obsessed with the loss and disillusionment that came in the wasteland. They were seeking a new faith, a new purpose. Two of the high priests of the beat generation were novelist Jack Kerouac and poet Allen Ginsberg, whose poem *Howl* set off a storm of controversy.

❧ BOX 7.2 • THEORY IN CONTEXT ❧

Expressionism in the Arts

Abstract expressionists, such as Jackson Pollock (1912–1956), adopted the earlier ideas of the Dadaists and the surrealists, and the stream-of-consciousness authors, and applied them to painting. What emerged in 1947 was spontaneous painting, without any preconceived idea of what would emerge. Pollock began his drip paintings, laying a huge canvas on the floor and applying colour spontaneously, or splashing it directly from the can, allowing patterns to emerge, until the canvas—or most of it—was covered with a dizzying array of blended and juxtaposed colours. This automatic painting was supposed to allow creativity free reign, diminishing the importance of the rational mind, and allowing an outpouring directly from the subconscious. If there was anything representational in the finished work, it was more by chance than conscious design and existed primarily in the mind of the viewer.

Abstract expressionism was the first essentially American visual art form to become fashionable in Europe. Many of the modern artists of the time were ex-leftists who had been disillusioned by the failure of the USSR. According to Frances Saunders, as artists created apolitical works of colour and design, the exuberant individualism and creativity of modern art became a useful political tool in the Cold War. The CIA clandestinely set up the Congress for Cultural Freedom and used it as a front to sponsor foreign exhibitions of American avant-garde, "free enterprise painting." At a time when the US president and public alike thought modern art was bunk, CIA funding was intended to foster American cultural freedom and expose Soviet socialist realism as an art of "un-freedom."[43]

The same spontaneous subjectivity celebrated by abstract expressionism also infected jazz, the first fundamentally American contribution to music, which had taken Europe by storm in the Roaring Twenties. Jazz was distinguished originally by spontaneous improvisation, punctuated by the long solo. In the 1940s and 1950s, jazz purists Dizzy Gillespie, Miles Davis, and Charlie Parker took jazz into the next plane, which became known as "bebop." Parker and company, playing at maximum tempo, pushed improvisation as far as it was possible to go, into the clouds of abstraction.

Both abstract expressionism and bebop were attempts at the subjective interpretation of sight and sound. They reflected social reality only indirectly. The written word is not so easily divorced from the rational and the real. But the same subjectivist impulse was felt by a new generation of writers. Holden Caulfield's penetrating gaze skewered adult hypocrisy in J.D. Salinger's subjective coming-of-age novel, *The Catcher in the Rye* (1951). And the high priest of spontaneous writing was Jack Kerouac, who wrote a draft of *On the Road* in less than one month, working on a single roll of teletype paper so that the outpouring of words would not be interrupted to change sheets of typewriter paper. Spontaneous prose, which was modelled after the writing experiments of some of the 1920s modernists, expressed the search for the self, adventure, free expression, and excitement. The automobile and the open road gave the illusion of freedom from social restraint.

The poem—and the passion of its delivery—put into words the alienation of the new seeking (rather than lost) generation and established the new poetic vision for which Ginsberg had been searching. If the poem's resonance with the anguish of the hipster crowd was not enough to propel Ginsberg into the national spotlight, a lawsuit against Ginsberg's publisher, City Lights Bookstore owner Lawrence Ferlinghetti, for distributing an obscene publication guaranteed *Howl* notoriety and lasting influence. As a self-consciously alienated pocket of rebellious intellectuals who did not fit into the "straight" world of conventional careers, marriages, and beliefs, the beat generation sought an identity for itself. The term was popularized in 1952 when John Holmes introduced it in an article in the *New York Times Magazine*.[44] At first, Holmes said, *beat* had a defeatist meaning; it implied being down and out, tired, and lost; it reflected the life of the small-time hustler and the hobo, those who had nothing in the conventional sense of having "things."

The Beats were alienated from the conventions of small-town America, but rather than giving in to despair and cynicism, they searched for new gods: the gods of extreme experience or ecstasy. They were all part of a loose, down-and-out subculture, in conscious or unconscious rebellion against the dominant values of hard work, conventional morality, and material success. In the argot of the times, these bohemians living on the margins of society were "hipsters." They were "with-it"; their precarious life was an incoherent rejection of the life of the grey flannel suit.

Novelist Norman Mailer referred to the hipster in "The White Negro" (1957) as "the American existentialist," living in the twin shadows of Auschwitz and the atomic mushroom cloud. For the older generation, the contradiction between individual impulses and social regulation had led nowhere except to **neurosis** and the psychiatrist's coach. Therapy merely tranquilized people's interesting vices, Mailer said, leaving them less than they were, not better. They were "less bad, less

good, less bright, less wilful, less destructive, less creative" and more able to conform to the society that had caused the neurosis in the first place. People conform to what they loathe because they lose the passion for intensely loathing anything.[45]

The new generation was passionate. Hipsters were like psychopaths, Mailer said, who sought "the liberation of the self from the Super-Ego of society." Hip morality, then, meant doing what you felt like doing ("do your own thing," in 1960s slang). Hip was nihilism, immoderation, rebellion against all forms of social restraint.[46] According to Mailer, "One is Hip or one is Square . . . one is a rebel or one conforms, one is a frontiersman in the Wild West of American night life, or else a Square cell, trapped in the totalitarian tissues of American society, doomed willy-nilly to conform if one is to succeed."[47]

The early Beats sought meaning in the romance of pure experience—and the more extreme, the better. Two years after Ginsberg's *Howl*, Kerouac published *On the Road*, the novel that defined the beat generation. In *On the Road*, Kerouac pictures his companion Neal Cassady (through the fictional character Dean Moriarty) as the model of "BEAT—the root, the soul of Beatific."[48] In Kerouac's words, they sought to find "It," to free the impulses of Freud's **id**. Finding "It" is always momentary. It will shine briefly and intensely, and then be gone, having to be sought once more. You could find It by getting lost in the playing of jazz, or in deep conversation, or in sex, but you couldn't hold onto It or understand It, and you couldn't explain It in words. The best jazz musicians, Kerouac thought, were the ones who really found It, time after time. It was through jazz that black culture merged with white alienation. Normal Mailer said jazz expressed the art of the primitive. It "gave voice to the character and quality of" black life in the United States, "to his rage and the infinite variations of joy, lust, languor, growl, cramp, pinch, scream and despair of his orgasm. For jazz is orgasm."[49]

Kerouac had written drafts of *On the Road* several years before it was published. Much of his time had been spent travelling the country by motor car. The United States had been strung together by a national highway system as the automobile culture came into full swing. The automobile symbolized more than the American dream of conspicuous consumption: the driver was the contemporary cowboy and the car, his horse. The automobile shrank the experience of space and distance, and expanded opportunities for an endless variety of experiences. Driving with the engine humming and the accelerator to the floor was itself an experience of freedom and exhilaration. The fast car, the game of chicken, and the dangers of reckless speed thrilled members of a young generation who wanted to live, not die, but live on the edge. People are most alive, it was believed, when nearest death. For Holmes, the new generation was represented by the hot-rod driver: "eating up the highway at ninety miles an hour and steering with his feet. . . . [He] invites death only to outwit it. He is affirming the life within him in the only way he knows how, at the extreme."[50] The lost generation contemplated death; the generation of the Beats defied it.

In the nineteenth century, the wanderer was immortalized in American culture by Walt Whitman. In the 1930s, it was the hobo who was romanticized as the American outsider, like the European gypsy. While riding the rails in the Depression had been more an act of economic desperation than a lifestyle choice, it also meant social protest, given a voice by American folk singers such as Woody Guthrie, who had done his own hard travelling. By the 1950s, however, the rebelliousness of wanderlust had shrunk back to the personal and individual. The search for experience had no meaning other than the experience itself. Dennis Hopper and Peter Fonda paraded that search in *Easy Rider* a few years later. The generation of the 1960s would extend the road to the Himalayas, to Morocco, to India via Turkey and Afghanistan, a time when exotic Far Eastern and Near Eastern cultures were much less threatening than they have become in response to twenty-first-century global hegemony.

From Counter-Culture to Pop Culture

The Beats did not have a long-lasting cultural presence. By the time Kerouac had published *On the Road* he was already off it. The book sold well, partly because the small market culture of the Beats was being transformed into the mainstream. Elements of jazz, blues, and soul were transmogrified into rock 'n' roll for white middle-class teenagers. Small-town DJs tried vainly to save the remnants of middle-class morality from the rock 'n' roll demons, such as the incestuous Jerry Lee Lewis and Elvis "the Pelvis" Presley. The parents of 1950s teenagers bemoaned the apparent loss of their children to new idols, but the decade turned out to be merely a dress rehearsal for the 1960s. In reality, however, the generation gap became less about differences in social values and more about differences in the style with which either generation expressed its conspicuous, mass consumption.

Indeed, American pop culture cashed in on the Beat generation. The Beats became "beatniks" (the suffix was taken from the name of the first successful satellite—Sputnik—that the Russians had rocketed into space in 1957). Black-turtle-necked college beatniks played bongo drums and recited angst-ridden free verse in coffee shops, to the thud of a bass fiddle. The alienated edge of Beat rebelliousness was filed down to fit the formula of the middle-class generation gap depicted in the 1955 movie *Rebel Without a Cause*, in which teen icon James Dean rebelled against social conventions just for the hell of it. Similarly, in *The Wild Ones*, the 1953 film of outlaw bikers, Marlon Brando is asked what he is rebelling against. He replies, "What do ya got?" The enigmatic figure of Marlon Brando straddled the artistic and the popular. Brando's method acting on Broadway and then in the film production of *A Streetcar Named Desire* established a new standard for naturalism in theatre and motion pictures. The beatnik character Dobie Gillis, who appeared in situation comedy books and TV, and the characters in the popular TV series *Route 66* were as far from the hipsters and Jack Kerouac as *I Love Lucy* was from radical feminism. Cultural rebellion begins in fury and ends in funds, as yesterday's anti-establishment stance becomes today's fashion and fad.

The migration of new forms of art from the margin to the mainstream became a fundamental theme in the critical analysis of popular culture. Marshall McLuhan was one of the first critics of popular culture to become an icon of the same culture, although his take on mass media became increasingly abstract and controversial.

Marshall McLuhan and Mass Media

"You know nothing of my work!"

— Marshall McLuhan

Marshall McLuhan (1911–1980) was at the tail-end of his celebrity media status in 1977 when he made a cameo appearance in Woody Allen's film *Annie Hall*. In the film, Allen (playing Alvy Singer) is in line waiting to enter a cinema when he is irritated by a loud-mouth professor of TV, media, and culture, who is spouting nonsense about McLuhan. An exasperated Allen then pulls the actual McLuhan on camera, and he quickly deflates the egghead: "I heard what you were saying. You know nothing of my work! You mean my whole fallacy is wrong." That his critics misunderstood him was McLuhan's trademark argument. "I am in the position of Louis Pasteur," he wrote in *Understanding Media*. Just as Pasteur could not convince other physicians of the existence of invisible germs they could not see, McLuhan was a prophet of the truth unheeded in his own time.[51]

Marshall McLuhan became a professor of literature at the University of Toronto in 1946, where he was influenced by the technological determinism of economic historian Harold Innis (see Box 7.3). Born in Edmonton, Alberta, McLuhan's father was a real estate agent and then an insurance salesman.[52] He first studied engineering and then switched to English literature, finishing a doctorate at the University of Cambridge.[53] Although engineering and literature might appear contradictory disciplines, McLuhan combined them in his study of communication technologies, as his career took flight from the formative work of Innis. In his mid-twenties, McLuhan converted to Catholicism. Marchand says that sometimes he claimed to be guided by the Virgin Mary with whom he had a "direct connection"—for McLuhan, the messenger *was* apparently a medium.[54]

The Mechanical Bride: The Folklore of Industrial Man, published in 1951, is McLuhan's ground-breaking study of **popular culture** that critically examines the content and ideology of the "mechanical agencies" of mass media. In no particular order, McLuhan skewers a wide variety of examples of media from the late 1940s and early 1950s, from comic strips and sports to advertisements and detective fiction. McLuhan provides two different messages about the purpose of his book. He says he writes to amuse, as a detached observer who is not suggesting strategies for change.[55] His objective is to use many points of view to get an overall sense of the constantly shifting popular imagery in American culture: "to the student of media structures, every detail of the total mosaic of the contemporary world is vivid with meaningful life."[56]

More critically, McLuhan said the purpose of *The Mechanical Bride* is to encourage critical consciousness, social harmony, and reasonable order. McLuhan's technique is to stop the endless stream of visual imagery created by popular culture so that it can be inspected and understood. The directors of big business, he says, hire thousands

⚜ BOX 7.3 · THEORY IN CONTEXT ⚜

Harold Innis and the Bias of Communication

Harold Innis (1894–1952) was a Canadian economic historian. He was 20 when World War I began and, as a soldier in the trenches of France, became a Canadian nationalist and a pacifist. After the war he studied at the University of Chicago and, from 1920 until his death, taught political economy at the University of Toronto. Most of his work focused on the social consequences caused by different types of economic industries, particularly **staple** products, such as the cod fishery, wheat farming, mining, and the fur trade. His argument was that the nature of the staple economy determines the social patterns and organization of the society that is built around the industry.[57] An economy dominated by one or two staples faces a potential trap should the price decline or the market for the staple fail. Furthermore, a staples-producing country would necessarily be dependent on large, manufacturing-based empires—in the case of Canada, first the French and British and now the American empire.

Toward the end of his career, Innis extended his thesis about the social consequences of technology to forms of communication. In 1950, he published *Empire and Communications*, which initiated media studies in Canada. McLuhan says that technological media are types of staples or natural resources that create "the unique cultural flavor of any society."[58] A new technological medium, Innis argues, will lead ultimately to structural and moral changes in society and in the types of knowledge that is disseminated. Oral discussion, for example, "involves personal contact and a consideration for the feelings of others," while science, technology, and the mechanization of knowledge produces too much knowledge, which leads to the decay of conversation, of creative thought, and ultimately, of Western civilization.[59]

In general, Innis argued, if the medium is heavy and durable, such as stone tablets or handwritten medieval manuscripts, it is suitable for (or biased toward) persistence over time, creating a culture marked by stability and tradition. If the medium of communication is less durable, but light and easily transported, such as paper, it creates a cultural bias toward rapid dissemination over large areas of space. Light, portable media are well-adapted to the spread of military communication. Printing presses and newspapers are biased toward rapid territorial expansion and thereby facilitate control over large areas. Newspapers also heighten nationalism and instability, which led to World War I.[60]

According to Innis, elites monopolize both knowledge and the exercise of force in a society. In response to centralized power, technological change takes place "in marginal regions which have escaped the influence of a monopoly of knowledge."[61] The Internet is the most relevant contemporary example. Although the Internet originated not at the margin but at the centre of military communication, its widespread and rapid dissemination has made control over digital communication a contested domain. Existing political and economic elites have yet to assert their monopolization of control over the new medium, which is the basis of many radical claims for its revolutionary character. The question of the relationship between knowledge as a source of power and dominant social elites, however, was only tangential to the work of McLuhan.

of the best-trained minds to create advertisements and forms of entertainment that "get inside the collective public mind . . . to manipulate, exploit, [and] control" their "intended prey."[62] At this point in his career, McLuhan says, he "loathed machinery." The industrial revolution and mass media, according to him, were equivalent to original sin and the fall. His criticism, however, was purely moralistic.[63]

In *The Mechanical Bride*, McLuhan assumes and morally condemns, rather than analyzes, the power structure behind the media. He is sometimes pessimistic, suggesting that little can be done to change the goals of those who control the modern media of communication.[64] In *Understanding Media* (1964), for example, he says that change does not come from people becoming conscious of the effects of technology and learning to control it: "not even the most lucid understanding of the peculiar force of a medium can head off the ordinary 'closure' of the senses that causes us to conform to the pattern of experience presented."[65] Overall, however, like the modern poets and symbolist artists he admired, McLuhan hoped to shatter people's preconceived view of the world and help them understand and perhaps control the effects of technology that otherwise work unconsciously.

The Medium Is the Message

The book of your revolution sits in your belly, young Indian. . . . Instead of which, they're all sitting in front of color TVs and watching cricket and shampoo advertisements.[66]

— Aravind Adiga, *The White Tiger*, 2008

By 1962 and the publication of *The Gutenberg Galaxy*, McLuhan had abandoned his moral criticism of media *content* to focus exclusively on the effects of the form of *technology* itself.[67] As Indian author Aravind Adiga suggests, reading

may inspire rebellion but watching TV may cool things down and have the opposite effect. McLuhan sought to understand the social and personal effects of a particular medium by focusing only on the characteristics of that medium. Just as a society built on manufacturing will produce a different type of life from one based on farming, a society in which the dominant form of communication is the newspaper will be fundamentally different from a society in which people watch TV. McLuhan's central thesis is that the medium of communication creates social consequences that shape the patterns of social life and community, irrespective of any specific content that is presented by the medium. It isn't the violent images shown on TV, for example, that is the real cause of change in society; it is the characteristics of the TV medium itself.[68] In McLuhan's words, "in operational and practical fact, the **medium is the message**." Like many theorists, McLuhan takes his central insight—that different forms of media cause different consequences in society—and applies it, not always successfully, to all aspects of society, past, present, and future.

New technologies are invented for specific purposes, but their consequences are far wider and deeper than those that were intended. They also introduce changes in the speed, the scale, and the pattern of human life—for McLuhan, this is their essential "message."[69] And these wholesale social changes are neither foreseen nor intended. The deeper effects of technology are unconscious or subliminal. Rather than changing people's opinions or understanding, they change people's experiences and perceptions.[70]

McLuhan distinguishes two kinds of media effects, caused by different forms of technology, that he calls "hot" and "cool." Paper, the radio, and film (movies) are "hot" media. A **hot medium** is one that extends a single sense, such as hearing or sight, in "high definition." A *high definition* hot medium is so well filled with data, like a photograph, that there isn't much left to be filled in by the audience. Therefore, the audience does not get to participate much in the act of communication—it is primarily one-directional.[71]

On the other hand, oral speech, the telephone, and TV are examples of "cool" media. A **cool medium** is one of *low definition* that gives a meager amount of information. With speech, and the extension of speech using a telephone, little is actually said, and the listener has to fill in a lot—as in contemporary texting. A cool medium is high in audience participation and completion. The hot excludes; the cool includes. A lecture is hot; a seminar is cool.[72]

Treating a complex field such as technology and media in terms of a binary distinction (hot versus cool) is inevitably controversial and fraught with contradictions. Film is a hot medium, but a film can present "casual, cool realism," which can undercut popular myths with doses of social reality—for example, a hot film can carry the cool message that economic success is "not only wicked but also the formula for misery."[73] The explicit message or content of the movie, then, is important, not just the fact that the medium being used is film. Furthermore, not all printing is the same. McLuhan says that the paperback is a "book in 'cool' version." Because of the paperback form, and regardless of its content, which could be philosophy or froth, readers now probe words and language "in depth."[74] But McLuhan doesn't mean "depth" in the sense of intellectual probing. The depth of a paperback is its portability, the expanded variety of topics that come, inexpensively, into more hands, and its potential for changing language and vocabulary. Once new media become popular, old media must attempt to adapt to the new demands. Paperbacks became popular, McLuhan says, only after TV. The introduction of printing itself, however, had been much more revolutionary than making a "cool" form of the book.

The Gutenberg Revolution

The first great technological innovation in communication was the invention of the alphabet, which led eventually to the mechanical reproduction of writing through printed books. The printing press was invented by Johannes Gutenberg in 1436, using a wine press to imprint ink on paper using moveable type. McLuhan attributes great social changes, including the rise of industrial society, to the invention of printing. The Gutenberg era lasted from the fifteenth century to the new age of electricity in the twentieth.

Originally, cultures were tribal, unified, traditional, and only oral. For McLuhan, speech is a cool medium because, "in speech we tend to react to each situation that occurs, reacting in tone and gesture even to our own act of speaking."[75] The invention of the alphabet fundamentally altered communication. Unlike speech, writing is careful, precise, step-by-step, detailed, and linear. Like rationality, it is "uniform and continuous and sequential." In the literate culture, sight predominates over the senses of touch, smell, and hearing. The alphabet is the "hidden cause of our Western bias toward rationalism and logic,"[76] which were first developed in the logical and scientific approach of the ancient Greeks. Print media opened a gulf between the human heart and the head, exalting the power of rationality and technology over feelings, "meaning and empathy."[77]

Reading, moreover, is an individual act, something requiring concentration that you do alone. The results are far-reaching, McLuhan claims. Modern individualism, personal freedom, specialization, the loss of spiritual wholeness, and our sense of time are all the consequences of mechanical writing. The individual separates her or himself from the family and clan—a process McLuhan terms **detribalization**. Both hot media and logic lead to intense concentration on small segments of reality, which leads to a fragmented and specialized view of the world. The Western individual comes to live in a world that demands the "rigorous separation and specialization of the senses, with the visual sense atop the hierarchy." In the process, the literate or civilized person becomes dissociated from her or his inner sensibilities, and loses any sense of "cosmic patterns" and the awareness of wholeness in the world. From the "visual, abstract, and uniform units" of the alphabet, McLuhan says, comes "our division of time into uniform, visualizable units" (hours and minutes on a clock). The result in the West is our feeling of time as duration and "our impatience when we cannot endure the delay between events." Even biological functions are made to accommodate to the clock more than to biological needs.[78] Training your toddler to eat and sleep on your "schedule" reproduces this historical transformation.

Gutenberg, or mechanical printing technology, burst the boundaries of medieval society. Somewhat paradoxically, literacy and print create individualism, detachment, and non-involvement, but they also bring centralization and uniformity. Since books were printed in local languages, by the sixteenth century the new technology had brought "political unification, nationalism, and religious wars." According to McLuhan, the population was pressured to think and speak alike, and to develop habits of uniformity. This homogenizing effect of print technology was an indispensable requirement for the most important outcome of the Gutenberg revolution, which was industrialism. The price system and market economy depended on predictability and uniformity of behaviour, which fundamentally transformed humanity's psychic, inner life. The ultimate expression of Gutenberg technology was the uniform and repeatable assembly line.[79] In the same way that the medium is what is important, rather than the message, it is the form of the machine that matters, not what it produces— whether Corn Flakes or Cadillacs. Under the domination of the mechanical assembly line,

McLuhan believed, people have automated and roboticized themselves.[80]

For McLuhan, the pressures of machine technologies led to demands in the West to abolish sex and race differentiation "along with the rest of human tradition and experience." Mechanical technology leads to the standardization of production, which tends to diminish differences in skill and creates cultural levelling. This technological change was accompanied by social demands for racial integration and gender equality. At the end of the nineteenth century, for example, the dream of integration led to demands for similar education and dress for both women and men. In the twentieth century, the machine economy had carried homogenization into mass education, "to the point where the same curriculum and the same room serve to prepare boys and girls alike for the neuter and impersonal routines of production and distribution."[81] This literate cultural strategy failed, however, McLuhan says, because it did not take into account actual human conditions. Women resisted gender homogenization because it robbed them of their distinctive roles and turned them "into fragmented citizens in 'a man's world.'" The contemporary electronic age rejected the false solutions of the uniform mechanical era and, instead, fostered uniqueness and diversity.[82]

The Electronic Age and the Global Village

Life at these speeds obliges everyone to discover a new career for himself every ten years, a new job and even a totally new personality.[83]

— Marshall McLuhan, "McLuhan Probes"

Since 1830 and the invention of the commercial telegraph, the electronic revolution has accelerated at the speed of light and perhaps beyond it. Young people today understand that they are more likely to have a succession of jobs rather than a single, life-time commitment to one career. As McLuhan suggested, they are also experiencing self-induced changes in their identity and personality.

Technological change causes changes in every other facet of human life, creating not just new jobs and careers, but a different psyche and novel ways to perceive the world. Since the creation of the alphabet, Western society has experienced centuries of change amounting to a technological *explosion*. The electric telegraph, however, began the opposite process of **implosion**, like beginning to play "a 2,500 year movie backward."[84] If the Gutenberg revolution created the mass assembly line, with its cookie-cutter products and mechanical human beings, the new, electronic age began to reverse all these effects. For McLuhan, modern electronic technologies *re*tribalize humanity; they decentralize and recreate diversity. Paradoxically, they also have the potential to recreate community and wholeness. In McLuhan's vision, the new, electronic technology can merge humanity into a single, global tribe.

Not all electronic forms of media, however, have identical effects. Radio displaced the print emphasis on the visual with an emphasis on sound, but it still focuses in depth on one sense only. Consequently, McLuhan says, radio is a hot, high-intensity medium. McLuhan uses Orson Welles's radio broadcast of *War of the Worlds*, the H.G. Wells classic, to show the "all-inclusive, completely involving scope of the auditory image of radio."[85] In 1938, Orson Welles had broadcast over radio a reading of the science-fiction novel about an invasion from Mars, which he presented as increasingly pressing and exciting news flashes that interrupted a musical program. The result was mass panic. Many people believed that radio news didn't lie.[86]

Unlike the hot medium of print, hot radio revives the traditional web of kinship and community and rekindles a sense of tribal involvement. Radio compresses space, McLuhan says.

People huddle around the radio and share the experience of story-telling. In the process, radio tends to reverse individualism. Fascism and communism in the 1930s, for example, were forms of retribalization that came about through the use of radio. American teenagers in the 1950s were retribalized by their embrace of radio. Hitler's use of radio, McLuhan says, reversed Western rationality and meaning because the "ear is intolerant, closed, and exclusive, whereas the eye is open, neutral, and associative." A cool, visual culture, such as print-based literacy, produces rationality and tolerance. Radio evokes "archaic tribal ghosts of the most vigorous brand."[87]

But a new medium does not have identical effects everywhere. The result of introducing a new medium, such as radio, into a society depends on the characteristics of that society. In the United States and Britain, literate, industrial culture had lasted so long that specialization and individualism were exceptionally deep. Consequently, radio did not have the same retribalizing effect that it had in Germany or Russia, which had had only brief or superficial experiences of literacy, industry, specialization, and rationality. But the literate West is not immune from "the tribal magic of radio." Indeed, according to McLuhan, in the 1950s teenagers turned to the radio for privacy but also for "the tight tribal bond . . . of song, and of resonance." They did so because radio created a remote sense of inaccessible isolation and "immunity from parental behest." Teenagers then listened to music while doing homework,[88] or now, with mobile devices at any time using earphones.

Film is also a hot medium for McLuhan, although he differentiates between silent and sound film (talkies). With silent film, we complete the scene in our mind by providing meaning, filling in the missing details; when the movie speaks, on the other hand, "there is very much less participation in the work of the image." With the movie medium, scenes pass by so rapidly that the spectator has no time to interpret the audio-visual impression, which then "standardizes thought." A movie, like the alphabet and the printed book, is an aggressive, imperial form of media that explodes into other cultures.[89]

Television, however, is the medium that has brought the greatest change to Western society. After the advent of TV, "America was not the same." If mechanical time was hot, "we of the TV age are cool." McLuhan argues that TV is anti-Gutenberg: it works against standardization and the homogenization of culture. Television "means the end of shopping itself, and the end of work as we know it at present." Furthermore, McLuhan says, the experience of television has changed the way people learn, and the gap is ever widening between the involved and connected form of learning that young people currently experience through their electronic devices, and the formal, literate style of learning they endure at home and in school.[90]

McLuhan disputes the common criticism that the TV experience creates passive viewers; rather, he says, television demands creativity and participation, although it does not excite, agitate, or arouse. Watching TV uses all of our senses—in McLuhan's terms, it is a "tactile" medium. In front of the screen, children "pore, they probe, they slow down and involve themselves in depth."[91]

Television has cooled down politics because it is not suited to the communication of hot, controversial topics. Radio, not TV, is the medium that induces frenzy. For example, McLuhan says, when Senator McCarthy's hearings were televised instead of being broadcast only over the radio, his influence declined sharply. TV is a cool, low-definition medium that rejects hot people and high-definition issues. What works politically on TV is mere posturing or appearance, a blurry and soft image rather than a precise and sharp one, although contemporary political attack ads suggest the opposite. Hitler's success would have been impossible in a TV era, McLuhan says. TV turns intensity into comedy, and it would have transformed Hitler into Archie Bunker (a bigoted

character in the TV comedy *All in the Family*). And, unlike radio, TV will not work as simply background because it is engaging: "You have to be *with* it."[92] Unlike radio or playing music while you work, you have to watch TV intently so that you don't miss what is happening.

McLuhan's argument about television, however, depends on an early form of TV transmission. Like a Seurat painting, if you got close enough to the early TV image, you would have seen that the electronic image was composed of a mosaic of light and dark spots that the viewer's automatic visual perception had to mesh together to make into a picture, like pixels in a JPEG image.[93] The TV image was low in data or definition and therefore it provided the viewer with a low degree of information. It was in this sense that McLuhan says that watching TV is a depth experience, one that demands audience participation. But this "active" participation is actually unconscious. McLuhan's argument, then, would have to change now that television is high definition and presents a great amount of information. He says that "improved TV would no longer be television."[94] In other words, the medium has changed and, therefore, so has the "message" of the new HD 3D TV technology—and electronic media generally.

With the electric power of instant information everywhere at once comes great social change. The effects of Gutenberg are being imploded or reversed. The electronic age recasts the ancient spell of traditional family and tribalism, forces to which people will submit almost unconsciously.[95] According to Jean Baudrillard, the message of TV lies in "the new modes of relating and perceiving it imposes, the alterations to traditional family and group structures."[96] The electronic age replaces the individualistic and fragmented idea of the "self" with a renewed sense of the "unity of the personality." This anti-individual effect diminishes the specialization of the senses, demands interrelation, and ends specialist learning and activities. Rather than linearity, the electronic age is marked by discontinuity and **nonlinear logics**, reflected in modern art and poetry, and in relativity and quantum physics.[97]

The electronic age changes our sense of time and space. Through the media of new, electronic technologies, our central nervous system has been extended, McLuhan argues, "in a global embrace" that involves "us in the whole of mankind" and incorporates "the whole of mankind in us." Electricity has contracted the globe until it has shrunk to village size. An event happening anywhere in the **global village** is known instantly everywhere and has widespread effects, "enabling us to react to the world as a whole." McLuhan hoped that the globalization of information technology and the contraction of time and space would create the basis for a new wholeness or unity among people worldwide. In this sense, McLuhan hoped for a new, global harmony. On the other hand, he said that contracting the world to village size also creates "insatiable village tastes for gossip, rumor, and personal malice."[98]

Electricity has an instantaneous characteristic that "is a way of thinking, as much as it is a way of doing." Rather than linear sequence, there is immediate "synchronization of numerous operations." Operating contemporary, integrated systems (whether electronic or social) requires feedback, which is a form of dialogue among the parts of the system. An information loop or circuit replaces the mechanical, one-way, linear flow of information. Automated technology integrates rather than fragments, and is decentralist in depth. In the electric age, human hands withdrew from industry and people became involved simultaneously in diverse jobs that entailed learning and computer programming. In this age of automation, McLuhan says, going to work will lose its present character, and the automobile, "in that sense, will go the way of the horse."[99]

Electronic technology now extends to the globe the instantaneous processing of knowledge that occurs in our central nervous system.

In addition to production, automation affects every aspect of consumption and marketing, which fuse together learning and information intake: "In the new electric Age of Information and programmed production, commodities themselves assume more and more the character of information." As a result, stockbrokers "have begun to look on the whole of society as a single unified machine for creating wealth." They manipulate shares and information for private profit, utilizing the electronic media of the press, radio and television[100]—and now the Internet. McLuhan was aware that technology always presented more than one possibility. When new technologies intrude into societies that use older forms, the resulting interface is fraught with contradictions. The electronic manipulation of markets brought the 2008 economic meltdown and ensured it had global consequences. The more we use social media to express self-identities, the more data we provide about ourselves and our tastes, allowing advertisers to target us ever more precisely as individual consumers.

McLuhan's ideas of media and the global village were popularized in the media and widely discussed academically in the 1960s and 1970s. He socialized among the artistic elite and was part of Andy Warhol's inner circle. McLuhan certainly had more than 15 minutes of fame. But single-minded analysis of the effects of different forms of communication technology, regardless of their content, became only a minor part of most contemporary studies of popular culture and the media. His work did, however, foreshadow the field of cultural studies in the later twentieth century, a branch of academic analysis that questioned the control over the media and the ideology of media content.

Conclusion

If McLuhan is right, existentialist angst was caused by the intrusion of new electronic and automated technology into the uncertain world of mid-twentieth-century employees. The next generation, however, was born into these conditions and began to live out the consequences of the TV age. The Beats of the 1950s may have been short-lived, but their influence extended into the next generation of middle-class rebels, the hippies of the 1960s. Their rebellion had wider political and social goals than those of the Beats, but the results were ambiguous. Contrary to McLuhan, the new age was more tied to consumerism than ever, even if it was highly diversified and specialized. The hippies outnumbered the Beats and, hence, were a greater potential market for new brands of consumption.

The middle-class radicalism of the post-1950s generation was fed by more than alienation from the staid and complacent authority figures in their lives, however. Global concerns had intruded into the West and inspired new forms of rebellion. A tsunami of independence movements had been unleashed that ushered in an era of decolonization. In India, for example, a nationalist movement inspired by spiritual leader Mahatma Gandhi had succeeded in 1947 in wresting independence from Britain for the separate countries of India and Pakistan. And British resistance to similar movements in Burma and Kenya had continued into the 1950s. The French fought to retain control of their territories in Southeast Asia and Algeria; the Dutch resisted independence for Indonesia. Portugal held on to power over Angola and Mozambique into the 1980s.

The following chapter examines post-colonialism as a movement and as a theory. Theories of global capitalism from the perspective of the so-called Third World emphasized the role of imperialism and dependency in creating the social problems that sparked the nationalist movements. Chapter 8 also presents an overview of the decolonization movement and the theories it inspired.

Questions for Reflection

1. Is the world ultimately meaningless and absurd, or does life have a meaning? If so, what meaning does it have and where does this meaning come from?

2. What are the strengths and weaknesses of Camus's existential hero? Do we need such heroes in today's world or has their time passed?

3. Is the doctrine of "bad faith" an accurate representation of social life in your experience, or is it too harsh?

4. Are the values of the Beats specific to their time and place, or are these values still relevant in the contemporary world?

5. Is it useful to think of world cultures now as being retribalized by electronic technology in a positive or negative way?

CHAPTER 8

Post-Colonial Social Thought

Learning Objectives

- To connect the theory of Frantz Fanon with the Algerian Revolution and the history of decolonization
- To distinguish theories of modernization and social evolution from theories of underdevelopment and dependent development
- To summarize Immanuel Wallerstein's model of globalization and the potential he perceives within it for an age of transition
- To understand Edward Saïd's concept of Orientalism in relation to continuing Western stereotypes of Arab and Muslim societies

After centuries of Western domination, the twenty-first century might belong to China. Such a reversal in global fortunes would turn history back on its head. In the fifteenth century, while Europe was an insignificant corner of the globe struggling out of the Dark Ages, China appeared poised for global power. The Ming Dynasty had expanded Chinese control beyond Asia. Decades before Columbus, Chinese Admiral Zheng He had explored the Indian Ocean and the eastern coast of Africa.[1] By that time, Europe had been connected for centuries to China by long-distance, overland trade routes. The most famous was the Silk Road, along which camel caravans carried silk, spices, cotton, and other exotic goods from Asia to the Black Sea, where goods were transferred to ships and sent to Europe. These slow, chain-link convoys of expensive commodities were vulnerable to raiding and piracy. By 1500, the powerful Ottoman Empire, centred in modern-day Turkey, was interfering with east–west trade, and use of the Silk Road was in decline.

The loss of the lucrative eastern trade motivated European merchants, such as Christopher Columbus, to find an alternative route. Western colonialism was the offspring of the search for profitable sea routes to the exotic products of Asia. Those who followed Columbus found enough riches in the Americas to excite their most extreme predatory impulses. According to Andre Gunder Frank, the Spanish mercenary Cortes, who led the invasion of Central America, said, "'The Spaniards are troubled by a disease of the heart for which gold is the specific remedy.'"[2] But gold is never a remedy for greed; it only feeds the desire. The Spanish committed the first modern acts of genocide, murdering and enslaving the Aboriginal populations, which were further decimated by the spread of imported diseases. This brutal conquest established the template for European empire building.

By the late nineteenth century, European nations had constructed a complex pattern of imperialist domination around the globe. In broad strokes, **colonialism** entails the military conquest of less economically developed territories and their subjection to political and economic domination by the economic and political elites of a ruling country. In the minds of some Europeans, colonialism was justified as a civilizing or "Christianizing" mission, bringing the benefits of Western enlightenment to the barbarians. The type of domination depended on the conditions in each colony. Large, traditional empires, such as in China, Egypt, and South Asia, became dependencies of European powers. In some cases, such as in the Americas and Australia, colonized territories had relatively small populations of Aboriginal peoples, who were overwhelmed by violence and disease. The present abysmal social and economic conditions of First Nations people in these white-dominated nations reflect this history of colonialism. Other colonies were established by white settlers in areas with large Aboriginal populations, in which the conquering Europeans became significant, privileged, land-owning minorities. These **settler colonies** included Algeria, Kenya, Indonesia, and South Africa. In Frantz Fanon's words, settler countries were the "citadels of colonialism" in which Europeans fought most ferociously to preserve their domination.[3]

Resistance to colonization took many forms. After World War II, intense decolonization occurred worldwide and the number of new nations overtook the number of older, established ones. Decolonization created new national identities and generated optimistic aspirations for social progress and industrialism as countries hoped to emerge from the depths of political domination and distorted economies. Progress, however, proved to be tortuously slow. The theory of underdevelopment analyzed the barriers to economic progress in the newly independent countries.

In this volatile atmosphere of social change, many Third World nations adopted forms of socialist development. Among twentieth-century revolutionaries, Che Guevara is perhaps the most recognized figure.

Colonization was not only political and economic; it also had profound effects on culture. In the view of Edward Saïd, Europeans had constructed a contemptuous and stereotypical image of the Middle Eastern and Asian "Other" in a discourse he called Orientalism. In the former colonies, native writers responded to disparaging Western representations by creating new national literatures, which drew from and contributed to post-colonial theories of identity, place, diaspora, and social transformation. Frantz Fanon, who was from the Antilles, was one of the early post-colonial theorists. He became a central figure in the Algerian movement for national liberation and, in the process, became a global spokesperson for decolonization.

Frantz Fanon and Decolonization

Frantz Fanon (1925–1961) was born in the French colony of Martinique in the Antilles. His father was a civil servant, a petit bourgeois of comfortable means. Social status on the island was conferred at least as much by race as by class. Fanon's relatives on his mother's side were from Alsace in France, making Fanon biracial.[4] In 1939, as the Germans blitzed toward Paris, 10,000 French sailors escaped to Martinique. For 14-year-old Fanon, the excitement of their arrival was short-lived because the French sailors exposed their overt racism and contempt for black Antilleans. From that time on, Fanon supported total decolonization.[5]

Aimé Césaire, a young black literature teacher at Fanon's high school, believed that Antilleans should fight for independence at home. Blacks in the colonies should stay out of World War II, and leave white Europeans to fight among themselves. Many young men from the French colonies did not agree with this view, however, because they felt that Nazism was the worst form of racism. In fact, Fanon paid money to be smuggled out of Martinique to join the anti-Nazi fight.[6]

Along with other Antillean recruits from all social classes, Fanon was transported to Casablanca, in North Africa, where an international and racially mixed force was being assembled. Eager to combat the Nazis and their doctrine of racial superiority, Fanon found the Free French Forces hierarchized by the same kind of racism he opposed.[7] Antilleans such as Fanon were classified as an intermediate group between the dominant white Europeans and the derided black Africans. Most Antilleans identified with the former and separated themselves from the Africans with the attitude that "all we need, [is] to be taken for niggers!"[8]

In Martinique, Fanon had been among the more privileged. He wanted to be seen as just one man among others and did not think of himself as a black, as an African. Once in Europe, however, he learned that the word *Negro* included him.[9] When the colonial army disembarked in France, Fanon was disillusioned by the racism he encountered. The non-white contingent of Free French soldiers felt only contempt from the army brass, civilians, and politicians alike. When the war ended, the colonials were to be dispatched *tout de suite* to whence they had come. As a youthful idealist, Fanon believed deeply in the cause of equality and justice. Brought face-to-face with hypocrisy and self-interest among ordinary people and their leaders, he felt angry and disillusioned.[10]

As an object of overt racism in Europe, Fanon felt completely dislocated, as though he had suffered an amputation. There, he said he discovered his blackness. He *was* his epidermis; his skin was his uniform. The world, Fanon

said, had slashed away his joy. At first, Fanon felt shame and self-contempt and was tormented by his blackness and by being locked into the circle of racism. Since racism was impossible to evade, Fanon says, "[T]here remained only one solution: to make myself known [and] assert myself as a BLACK MAN."[11]

There was no university in Martinique, so Fanon moved back to France where he became one of the "colonial subjects," as students from the colonies were disparagingly called. He studied medicine and philosophy in Lyon, being drawn to the typical array of post-1945 social thought, including existentialism, Marxism, and psychoanalysis. He was particularly drawn to the idea of action: of not just thinking or writing, but of doing.[12]

By his fourth year of studies, Fanon was specializing in psychiatry. An early article that he wrote, "The North-African Syndrome," reflected his experience of marginality as a black person in France. Fanon explained that the psychic troubles faced by immigrants in France derived from their social situation, from their life as a marginalized racial minority. Immigrants had been "thingified."[13] Cut off from their homeland, excluded, and treated as a racialized "other," black immigrants felt totally insecure and isolated socially, culturally, and emotionally.[14]

Fanon elaborated this theme in his first book, *Black Skin, White Masks*, published in 1952.[15] He had grown long, sensitive antennae for detecting racism. When his publisher began by praising the manuscript, Fanon curtly interrupted, "'Not bad for a Nigger!'"[16] For Fanon, it was important to deny the existence of an organic or constitutional component of **neurosis** because he was interested in doing something about the problem. In his analysis, neurosis should be understood structurally. Real-life experiences of racism shaped the unconscious minds of blacks in Europe and only a change in the existing environment could make a permanent difference.[17]

Fanon's *Black Skin, White Masks*

Yes *to life*. Yes *to love*. Yes *to generosity*. . . .
No *to scorn*. . . . No *to degradation*. . . . No *to exploitation*.[18]

— Frantz Fanon, *Black Skin, White Masks*, 1952

The aim of Fanon's book *Black Skin, White Masks* is to contribute to "the effective dis/alienation" of blacks.[19] *Black Skin, White Masks* was dictated orally to Fanon's wife while he paced back and forth. He wanted the book to be experienced emotionally not just intellectually.[20] In Fanon's analysis, white colonialism not only imposes discrimination and robs black people of their worth, it creates two opposite psychological complexes. Colonialism produces among whites a psychological complex of authority and superiority, and it imposes on blacks its correlate: a complex of dependency and inferiority. The psychological result among both races is the internalization—or, since it is synonymous with skin colour, the epidermalization—of this superiority or inferiority.[21] Black people do not make themselves inferior. From their first encounter with white people, they feel the full weight of being black in a white world; as a result, they internalize their subordination. They become preoccupied with comparison and negative self-judgment. Their ego is diminished. The norm becomes white, says Fanon, and colonized blacks judge themselves according to how closely they approximate whiteness. Rather than becoming an "*actional* person," blacks orient their behaviour to the other (the white), who alone gives them self-esteem. Blacks seek to imitate the dominant race and become "whiter" the more they renounce their blackness.[22]

Colonized people were caught in a perpetual twoness: their traditional, indigenous way of life was being destroyed by the "**master discourse**" of colonial ideology. Native languages were replaced by European ones, imposing a white-specific world and culture. From the European perspective, dark pigmentation was symbolic of ugliness and evil.[23] At a pivotal moment in the film *Malcolm X*, Malcolm learns the racialized meaning of *black* and *white*. Barely literate, he opens *Webster's Collegiate Dictionary* and looks up *black* ("soiled," "hostile," "wicked," "foul," "forbidding") and then *white* ("pure," "free from blemish," "innocent," "harmless," "honest," "honourable").[24]

Brought face-to-face with the dominating language and culture of the colonial power, the inferiority complex is created by killing and burying the local culture and all its originality. The young black child, socialized into a white-dominated culture, adopts the attitudes and values of whites, effectively enslaving him- or herself. The colonized mind becomes zebra striped, Fanon says.[25] In the 1956 essay "Culture and Racism," Fanon argues that cultural motifs routinely sexualized blacks. In the Antilles, for example, women competed to choose the man who was the least black, seeking to be acknowledged as white and to move from the class of slaves to the class of masters. The black man who married a white woman, says Fanon, felt revenge on becoming master of a white woman.[26] The "quest for white flesh," Fanon says, was "perpetuated by alienated psyches." Psychologically, whites experienced the cultural phenomenon of "Negrophobia," being paradoxically afraid of and enticed by blacks. The ambiguity became biological and sexual. White men longed unconsciously for sexual license and unpunished rapes, and then projected these desires onto black men. The black man, according to Fanon, was defined by the genitals. Jews could be killed or sterilized; blacks were castrated.[27] For Fanon, psychic phenomena such as neuroses have to be understood and combatted as products of social and economic realities. For blacks, liberation meant waging war on both the objective and subjective levels; people of colour had to free themselves from their internalized inferiority.[28]

The effects of the colonized mentality were similarly described by Howard Adams, a Canadian

Métis (French and First Nations ancestry), in *Prison of Grass: Canada from the Native Point of View* (1973). He described his own colonized personality. At the age of 21, Adams fell in love with Bonnie, "the most beautiful blonde girl I had ever seen." Her love made him feel worthy of white love: "I was a white man." Newly baptized in the "stream of whiteness," Adams felt crushed into inferiority. He began to hate everything "half-breed," to see Aboriginal girls as ugly, and began to extinguish the "hideous signs" of his "Indian-ness." To escape from his identity, Adams tried to destroy the characteristics that marked him as "Native." The white ideal spread from romance to dress, speech, manners, and dreams.[29] A colonized native wants to be a success as defined by white society. He or she adopts white ideologies of native inferiority, a contempt that is ultimately self-hatred. In writing his autobiographical book, Adams took the plunge into decolonization, identity politics, and social liberation.[30]

Fanon's theory of cultural domination became influential in the new post-colonial literature that took root as nations emerged from imperial domination. Post-colonial novelists depicted pre-contact cultures that had been suppressed or destroyed, exposed the evils of colonial rule, and revealed the monumental aspirations and disappointments of the post-independence era. In the process, world literature became genuinely global. Among the celebrated new national authors was Nigerian-born Chinua Achebe (see Box 8.1).

Achebe concluded that the problems in Nigeria were rooted in the country itself. In *The Trouble with Nigeria* (1983), Achebe explained that the country's natural wealth had been stolen by Nigerians who had taken over from the Europeans. They had squandered, embezzled, and consumed what otherwise could have transformed the lives of the poor and destitute.[31] In Fanon's view, this situation should not lead to pessimism or fatalism, however. Blacks had to overcome their alienation and not take the present situation as final. The

solution for exploited blacks was to take action, to fight back, and to change the social structure, which was the actual source of the problem.[32]

In creating a binary of two races and two worlds, Fanon accepted that his argument is essentialist; that is, that there are a set of characteristics that identify a whole category of people as fundamentally the same. Even though specific black societies and cultures have different social and historical realities, and Africans have been scattered all over the globe, Fanon believed they all face a universal situation. Whether he wrote about Antillean or African, he felt compelled to see them first as "Negroes." Since colonialism, "Wherever he [or she] goes, the Negro remains a Negro." Idealistically, however, Fanon believed in the possibility of love, of life, and of generosity. He wanted to rise above the absurd drama of race and embrace the universal.[33]

Fanon and Algeria

Until the philosophy which holds one race superior and another inferior
Is finally and permanently discredited and abandoned,
Everywhere is war. Me say war.

— Bob Marley "War," *Rastaman Vibration*, 1976

Once Fanon had completed his studies and internship in France, he hoped to return to Martinique to practise psychiatry. The authorities on the island, however, barred Fanon from returning home. Instead, he accepted a position in the psychiatric institution at Blida, Algeria. Fanon brought a left-leaning psychiatric practice to a highly conservative institution. He revolutionized psychiatric treatment using a technique known as sociotherapy, which included biweekly meetings where staff and patients engaged in open forums. Fanon believed that doctors must relinquish their monopoly of knowledge and integrate patients as equal partners in their cure. He became familiar

❧ BOX 8.1 • BIOGRAPHY ❧

Chinua Achebe (1930–2013)

Chinua Achebe was born in 1930, in Ogidi, an Igbo village east of the Niger River in what is now Nigeria. In his novels, Achebe provides vivid pictures of pre-colonial Igboland, including the masquerades in which village leaders would don elaborate masks and costumes, *becoming* spirits more than merely personating them, materializing after dark to expose wrongdoers and sustain village traditions and morality. By 1930, Igboland and its traditional culture had been subject to decades of colonization and dissolution.[34]

Before the 1880s, although Europeans had been in West Africa for centuries, they seldom ventured inland, into territory that became known as "the white man's grave" because of tropical diseases. Malaria was inescapable, but the widespread use of quinine to treat malaria in the latter nineteenth century opened the interior of West Africa to European penetration.[35] Christian missionaries began to arrive in Ogidi about 1892. Achebe's father was among the early converts, becoming a catechist or Christian teacher, perhaps "to learn the secrets of the white man's magic." Befriending white colonists, who exercised power, was a survival tactic for Aboriginal peoples.[36] Growing up in both worlds of traditional and Christian mythologies, Achebe developed a dual identity.

By the twentieth century, Britain began to establish administrative control over Nigeria, "singing the song of extermination." The missionaries were followed by the military, which attempted to root out tribal religions, masquerades, and oracles. The British imposed a system of chiefs on tribes in Igboland, which had lacked "Natural Rulers" and implanted a social order of hierarchy and exploitation.[37] In his first novel, *Things Fall Apart* (1958), Achebe vividly portrays the deeply rooted customs and idiosyncrasies of village life and their fateful encounter with colonialism. Two more novels completed his trilogy of Nigerian decolonization: *No Longer at Ease* (1960) and *Arrow of God* (1964).

The Nigerian experience played out the worst fears Frantz Fanon had anticipated. Corruption and regional conflicts began to tear Nigeria apart. In *A Man of the People* (1966), Achebe satirizes and critiques the debasement of Nigerian politics. Even more than his earlier trilogy, the novel is "an augury of the world's ruin."[38] The novel ends with a military coup, undertaken in the name of restoring order from "unruly mobs and private armies." Just as the novel was published, real life mirrored fiction in Nigeria. In 1966, the country's "young army officers seized the opportunity to take over."[39] Following a counter-coup, the country was plunged into a civil war that degenerated into a genocidal campaign against the Igbo people, as Achebe's homeland fought to secede and become the nation of Biafra. The army accused Achebe of being complicit in the first coup because of the accuracy of his prediction.[40] He and his family barely escaped alive. Achebe became an international spokesperson for his new country until starvation and slaughter in Biafra forced the capitulation of the independence movement.[41] His last publication, *There was a Country: A Personal History of Biafra* (2012), told the story of this perilous time in Achebe's national and political life.

with the cultures of Algeria, learned to speak local languages, visited villages, and witnessed traditional ceremonies.[42] Through these contacts Fanon became intimately involved with Algerian anti-colonialism.

Algeria's ten million people were about 90 per cent Muslim and Arab. Anti-colonial sentiments escalated after World War II. With the nationalist revolution in Vietnam underway, the nearly one million Europeans in Algeria worried about the dormant volcano on their doorstep. Blida was located about 45 kilometres from Algiers, the country's largest city. Algiers was rigidly divided, separating the Christian and Jewish populations from the majority Muslims. Hospital wards, clinics, schools, and sports teams were routinely segregated.[43] Most Europeans were habitually racist and conservative. In their view, Fanon said, "When it came to Arabs, the machine gun was a far superior tool to the word." On 1 November 1954, the Algerian National Liberation Front (FLN) proclaimed the beginning of armed resistance. The mountainous region near Blida was one of the first sites of armed resistance. In 1955, Fanon set up a clinic, which at times became a temporary refuge for Algerian militants on the run. Fanon's psychiatry and political work became closely linked.[44]

The conflict between the FLN and the French army accelerated in 1956. An FLN bombing campaign killed French civilians in Algiers; the French army massacred Algerian peasants and tortured Algerian militants to extract information. In 1957, Fanon applied the word *genocide* to the tactics of the French in Algeria.[45] He did not, however, condemn the bombings and assassinations perpetrated by the Algerian rebels.[46] For Fanon, every French colonial in Algeria was an enemy soldier. He criticized French intellectuals and leftists who abandoned their support for national liberation on the grounds that the FLN had resorted to "barbarism."[47] Fanon was blunt: "One cannot both be in favor of the maintenance of

French domination in Algeria and opposed to the means that this maintenance requires."[48] Precisely this point was made in the film *The Battle of Algiers*, commissioned by the Algerian government and made by Italian director Gillo Pontecorvo (see Box 8.2).

The French army won the Battle of Algiers, killing or capturing the urban guerillas and driving thousands of Algerian combatants out of the country. Fanon found that people in France were either indifferent to the conflict in Algeria or supported the emergency powers.[49] Even though white European liberals were unwilling to forgive Hitler, according to Fanon Europeans were actually using the same tactics against Algerian Arabs, Indian "coolies," and African "Negroes."[50]

As the battle raged, Fanon's position at Blida became untenable and he resigned his post. With FLN support, Fanon made his way to Paris and then to Tunis, where he became a member of and spokesperson for the FLN. He found the FLN leadership seriously divided over tactics and indifferent to his desires for a socialist and secular post-independence Algeria. Fanon grew increasingly concerned about the potential for post-independence conflict among clans and religious groups, about the rise of a new bourgeoisie, and about military domination by power-hungry colonels. He was also wary of the Islamic identity of the FLN and did not want to see a theocratic government in Algeria.[51]

Fanon warned against the emphasis on ethnic rather than national identity in Africa and any form of anti-colonialism that accepted half measures. Disguised forms of colonial domination were being implemented, and many African leaders were complicit in the sellout.[52] When it came to negotiating independence with liberation movements, the oppressor nations had shown their true colours. Gone were the concerns about their so-called civilizing mission. Negotiations were about economic interests: banking, monetary policy, commercial and trade

⚜ BOX 8.2 • THEORY IN CONTEXT ⚜

The Battle of Algiers

The Algerian Revolution was fought bitterly by both sides. The French used their air superiority to destroy villages with bombs and napalm. The National Liberation Front (FLN) used urban guerrilla tactics in the city of Algiers to assert national sovereignty, including assassinating French police officers and planting bombs that killed French civilians. Rural Algerians were moved to secure concentration camps to separate the guerrillas from the people. During the Battle of Algiers, the French tortured suspected FLN members to obtain information. For many French intellectuals, the use of barbaric methods so soon after World War II was a glaring contradiction for a country that claimed to be civilized and had recently suffered similar atrocities at the hands of the Nazis.

The view of the French military that torture was necessary for victory was vividly portrayed in the film *The Battle of Algiers*. In one scene, the military commander, Colonel Mathieu, gives a press briefing on the occasion of the capture of Ben M'Hidi, an FLN leader. In the scene, the reporters and the colonel skirt gingerly around the issue of torture. Finally, one reporter declares bluntly, "[L]et's talk about torture." Colonel Mathieu replies that the success of the French paratroopers "is the result of these methods." He defends torture as the only viable means for keeping Algeria French:

Reporter: "I'd just like more precise answers."

Mathieu: "Let's try to be precise. The word torture isn't used in our orders. We use interrogation as the only valid police method against clandestine activity. The FLN asks all its members in case of capture to remain silent for 24 hours. Then they may talk. This gives the FLN time to render any information useless. And us? What form of questioning must we adopt? Civil law procedures, which takes months for a mere misdemeanor?"

Reporter: "Legality can be inconvenient."

Mathieu: "Is it legal to set off bombs? . . . No gentlemen, believe me, it's a vicious circle. . . . The problem is this: The FLN wants to throw us out of Algeria and we want to stay. . . . We're here for that reason alone. We're neither madmen nor sadists. Those who call us Fascists forget the role many of us played in the Resistance. Those who call us Nazis don't know that some of us survived Dachau and Buchenwald. We are soldiers. Our duty is to win. Therefore, to be precise, it's my turn to ask a question. Should France stay in Algeria? If your answer is still yes, then you must accept all the consequences."[53]

concessions, and assurances that property would be untouched. The result was **neo-colonialism**: nominal sovereignty within the straitjacket of economic dependence. Neo-colonialism appeals to the middle classes and intellectuals, but nothing fundamental changes for ordinary people in the new, "castrated countries." The people were left without the essentials of adequate food, clothing, and shelter.[54] Post-colonialism, to Fanon, implied compromised governments, power struggles, ethnic identities, and corruption.[55]

In December 1960, Fanon was diagnosed with leukemia. His first thought was to die in battle for the Algerian people, but the FLN vetoed this idealism. With his health deteriorating and unable to pace back and forth, he dictated his last book, *The Wretched of the Earth*, mostly from his bed to a trio of typists. He completed the manuscript in July of 1961 and died in December in the United States, where he had been persuaded to go for one last round of treatment. The irony was apparent to him of seeking help in the country he viewed as the heartland of oppression and neo-colonialism.[56]

Fanon's *The Wretched of the Earth*

[A]s long as men are swayed by their hearts and stomachs and not their heads the Chief Nangas of this world will continue to get away with anything.[57]

— Chinua Achebe, *A Man of the People*, 1966

Fanon's last book, like his first, is as much an emotional appeal as an intellectual diagnosis of the problems of colonial revolution and post-independence. Fanon's critique is eviscerating, but he is still hopeful that "the people" will awaken and preserve the anti-colonial revolution in the interests of the nation and humanity. Two issues dominate the book. One is Fanon's belief in the necessity of violent action to overthrow colonial rule. In the context of oppression, degradation, and ingrained inferiority, violence is liberating for the nation and for the colonized individual. Second, the promise of national liberation has not been realized. Neo-colonialism triumphs on the backs of the native bourgeoisie and local politicians (like Chinua Achebe's fictional character Chief Nanga), who step into the shoes of the departing colonialists.

Colonialism was born of violence and is, ultimately, sustained by violence. Consequently, Fanon says, decolonization is necessarily a violent phenomenon. Violence is an unavoidable psychological reality in any society. Traditional societies experienced many forms of violence within and between clans and tribes. In all these societies, however, customs and the "magical superstructure" of terrifying spirits, masquerades, and other supernatural beings attempted to conjure away potential violence.[58]

Colonialism introduced an entirely different level of violence to traditional societies, according to Fanon. Colonialism "is violence in its natural state, and it will only yield when confronted with greater violence." Against the background of systematic exploitation, the "banner of revolt is unfurled" and guerilla warfare begins. The colonial regime survives by shunting violence into non-radical byways. When the settler or the police officer insults and strikes the native, he or she cannot directly strike back. Instead, the violent response is transferred to the native's own community.[59] Natives, novelist Chinua Achebe says, "have all accepted things from white skins that none of us would have brooked from our own people."[60] Quarrels, feuds, and tribal warfare ensue. National liberation still may not result until the people's spontaneous rebellion is directed at their settler oppressors.[61]

For Fanon, violence is the work of the colonized people, and they invest this work with "positive and creative qualities." Group violence unites the nation as a whole and integrates members of the group through shared responsibility. National and personal freedoms are both discovered through the use of violence. When despised and subjected colonized people arise and fight back, they experience newfound pride and dignity: "At the level of individuals, violence is a cleansing force. It frees the native from his inferiority complex and from his despair and inaction; it makes him fearless and restores his self-respect." For

Fanon, the person who has become a colonized "thing" becomes fully human through the fight for freedom.[62]

Once independence has been negotiated, the people's euphoria is quickly extinguished when they realize that their lives have not changed for the better. The moral dignity of being a citizen of an independent country wears thin; people come to believe that political independence is not worthwhile. No new values, no new society is being built and affirmed.[63] After independence, Achebe says, the smart and lucky—but seldom the best—scramble out of the rain into "the one shelter our former rulers left, and . . . barricade themselves in." They demand only the further extension of their privileges.[64] Completely divorced from the people, these new leaders construct a nationalism that is an empty shell: "The nation is passed over for the race, and the tribe is preferred to the state."[65] In his satirical novel *The White Tiger*, Aravind Adiga blames post-independence problems in India on the British *leaving* the country:

> See, this country in its days of greatness, when it was the richest nation on earth, was like a zoo. A clean, well-kept, orderly zoo. Everyone in his place, everyone happy. . . .
>
> And then, thanks to all those politicians in Delhi, on the fifteenth of August, 1947—the day the British left—the cages had been let open; and the animals had attacked and ripped each other apart and jungle law replaced zoo law. Those that were the most ferocious, the hungriest, had eaten everyone else up. . . .[66]

Economically, according to Fanon, the native bourgeoisie occupies the role of the well-heeled, neo-colonial intermediary, helping foreign capital continue to exploit the people. The bourgeoisie is not, however, in control of the national economy, which is still in the hands of the former imperial power; this group merely wants to be "part of the racket."[67] Public money is squandered on

the nepotism of clan and family, on prestigious expenditures, and on grandiose buildings. The police and the army, and their foreign advisors, become the pillars of the regime: "There is not a soul down to the simplest policeman or the customs officer who does not join in the great procession of corruption."[68] The goal is to become a member of the privileged class, symbolized by the ownership of an automobile.[69]

As the National Party degenerates into an organization to monopolize the spoils of government, says Fanon, it exercises an authoritarian, ethnic dictatorship, which is "organized like a gang, with the toughest person in at its head." The charismatic leader's prestige rests on his background as a "man of the people" and on the fading memories of the anti-colonial struggle. Privileges multiply, corruption escalates, morality declines, and politics degenerates into a type of fascism. While a new class thrives, it is surrounded by the majority of the population, which is ignored and continues to live in absolute poverty. Fanon indicts the native leadership for this situation: "These heads of the government are the true traitors in Africa."[70]

The Wretched of the Earth is less an essay of despair and more a call to arms. Through it all, Fanon clings optimistically to the hope that people will see through the mystifications of neocolonialism. Fanon believed that the rural peasant class alone retained the revolutionary spark and had the potential to bring about a genuine, just, and egalitarian social revolution:[71] "What counts today, the question which is looming on the horizon," he concluded, "is the need for a redistribution of wealth. Humanity must reply to this question, or be shaken to pieces by it."[72]

Theories of Modernization vs. Theories of Underdevelopment

The redistribution of the world's wealth is still a fundamental question of social justice in the early twenty-first century. Since the 1980s, the gap has widened between poor and rich countries, and between the poorest and richest people in each country. During the immediate post–World War II decades, however, the "Third World" had been expected to undergo modernization and to catch up with the advanced "First World" with the help of international agencies and the putative generosity of foreign aid from the developed countries. This period had been touted as the era of national development.

Evolution and Development

The term *modernization* implies many things. At its foundation is an evaluation of industrial capitalist societies as more civilized and better than traditional or backward societies.

According to social evolutionism, societies evolve through a fixed series of stages, from simple (backward) to complex (modern). The main difference between societies is that some, the preindustrial, are not as far along this evolutionary path as the industrial societies. The explicit value judgment embedded in this approach is that societies are "better" the further along the assumed evolutionary path they are. This perspective undergirds the theories of classical sociologists, such as Auguste Comte and Émile Durkheim. In the twentieth-century, Talcott Parsons sought to include evolutionary perspective in his otherwise static functional analysis of society. In 1960, Walt Whitman Rostow published *The Stages of Economic Growth*, a polemical generalization to the entire globe of the privileged economic experience of Britain and the United States.

W.W. Rostow sought to describe a universal process of social change through which all societies had to pass as they evolved from traditional to modern industrial nations. In *The Stages of Economic Growth*, with its provocative subtitle, *A Non-Communist Manifesto*, Rostow assumes that all countries are following an identical path

of economic progress, through five sequential stages: "the traditional society, the pre-conditions for take-off, the take-off, the drive to maturity and the age of high mass consumption."[73] He based this model on the history of industrialization in England and on the modernization of the United States. Rostow assumed that all societies had to follow the same stages, in an identical order, to arrive at an equivalent level of industrialization. The drive to maturity stage is more rapid than the final, mass-consumption stage. Consequently, as Third World societies go beyond the industrial take-off stage, their growth will be rapid, with the result, Rostow claimed, that economic disparities and global inequalities would diminish over time.

According to Rostow's sweeping generalizations, economically "backward" countries have limited economic potential. Their traditional cultures tend to be ideologically opposed to science, technology, and economic individualism. Agriculture dominates their economies and there is very little geographic or social mobility. The political system tends to be decentralized, and power is held by various local elites, hindering overall national development.[74]

The pre-conditions for economic take-off (industrialization) occurred first in Britain and Western Europe, where industrial growth required little direct government support. Elsewhere, economic developments were limited by the persistence of traditional social and political structures and values, and by the effects of colonialism, which stalled the emergence of a genuinely national political structure in the colonies.[75]

When these traditional and colonial barriers are overcome, the society reaches the great watershed moment. Rostow argues that the take-off depends on the rise of the entrepreneur and the emergence of a political elite, which regard the modernization of the country in question as an important state goal. India and China, for example, began their economic take-off in different ways in the 1950s. In this stage, growth proceeds quickly, the national economy finds its place in the international market, home manufacturing replaces imported goods, and new export commodities are developed. Within 60 years, although timing varies from country to country, these newly emerging economies will replicate the economic and political "maturity" of the United States. In a fully developed economy, multi-party democracy prevails, real incomes rise, the population moves to urban centres, the workforce is dominated by white-collar and skilled factory jobs in mass consumption industries, and the majority of people experience a rising standard of living. Rostow speculates that such a high-octane economy cannot, however, be sustained. In the future, Americans might become less consumer-oriented and even possibly turn to more cultural interests, perhaps reflecting a tendency for later generations to decline.[76]

Underdevelopment and Dependence

Rostow's "non-Communist manifesto" presumed that countries that were economically backward were temporarily lagging behind in the evolution to prosperity, which required capitalist development and Western-style government. Although much has changed economically since 1960, the world does not resemble Rostow's optimistic forecast. By the 1960s, it was clear to intellectuals in the Third World—particularly in Latin America—that the poor regions of the world were continuing to be poor and that development schemes seemed to benefit rich nations more than impoverished ones.

In the decades following the publication of *Stages of Growth* in 1960, American Marxists and radical economists in the Third World rejected the biased assumption that less developed societies would undergo convergence with the advanced societies and become increasingly modern economically, politically, and socially. Marxist economist Paul Baran (1909–1964), who had grown

into radicalism during the Great Depression, was an influential post-1945 critic of modern imperialism and neo-colonialism. He published *The Political Economy of Growth* in 1957. For Baran, capitalism is a single system that includes both the industrialized and the "underdeveloped" worlds. The fundamental issue facing the so-called backward capitalist countries is to explain why modern progress following the stages of capitalist development has, for them, been absent or, at best, extremely slow. The answer, according to Baran, is not found in the persistence of their traditional past but, rather, in the consequences of colonialism.

Generally, Baran argues, in most areas of the world prior to the emergence of industrial capitalism in Europe, traditional economies and social systems were actually beginning to break down as they followed a "common historical destiny." Everywhere, although at different rates, a class of merchants and traders was becoming more prominent economically and socially. This class expanded craft and manufacturing production, and accumulated wealth that could potentially be reinvested as capital rather than spent on lavish consumption. For a variety of historical reasons, Western Europe led this transformation from feudalism to merchant capitalism, and finally to industrialization by accumulating and investing the enormous profits derived from global colonialism.[77]

It was a path to progress that only the front-runners could take. "The violent, destructive, and predatory opening . . . of the weaker countries by Western capitalism" completely distorted the development of the colonized regions and prevented them from achieving their own capitalist revolution. Imperialism precluded these countries from developing the classical preconditions for economic growth that had occurred in Europe.[78]

Baran glosses over the conquest of Aboriginal societies in North America and Australia, which he claims were "virtually virgin" soil. In his words, Europeans "entered more or less complete societal vacua, and *settled* in those areas." In Asia and Africa, however, European "enterprisers" encountered a different world. Early colonization was entirely predatory, intent on transferring wealth from the non-European country to Europe, drastically affecting the subjected countries' course of development. Subsistence agriculture was destroyed and replaced by plantation economies producing specialized crops for export. As peasants were removed from their traditional land, an enormous pool of pauperized, urban labour was created. These migrants found little work because as industrial goods were imported from Europe and America, the fragile manufacturing sector in the colony was undermined.[79]

Imperialism breaks down the entire framework of the pre-capitalist, old-world society, Baran says, without creating a new world. It strangles the class of national capitalists that would otherwise have become the driving force of national **accumulation** and growth. In its stead, imperialism creates only a class of speculators, landowners, government agents, and village despots, whose privileges tie them to the strings of imperial power.[80] In the words of Jawaharlal Nehru, the first prime minister of India, all the problems of post-independence India were "'a direct result of British policy.'"[81]

Baran supports his argument that colonialism inevitably prevents industrialization by comparing the fate of the colonized countries with that of Japan. By the mid-1950s, Japan was the only Asian country that had attained an advanced state of industrial development. It was also the only Asian country that had not suffered direct colonial domination. The threat of Western economic penetration and military conquest had spurred Japanese elites to spearhead national development. Japan's commercial bourgeoisie allied with the traditional military caste and the governing elite to modernize the economy.

State-directed capitalist accumulation was the answer to both foreign competition, which threatened to foreclose Japan's industrial development, and to the need for advanced military power. The economic elite channelled investment into heavy industry, shipbuilding, transportation, communication, and armaments manufacturing with the assistance of the new industrializing government, which encouraged the adoption of Western technology and science.[82] The traditional warrior-class, the sword-wielding samurai, had to be liquidated as a hereditary status group and replaced by a well-equipped and trained national standing army, as depicted in the Hollywood film *The Last Samurai* (2003).[83] But the samurai spirit of emperor worship, hubris, and self-sacrifice was projected onto the world of business and the modern military, united by their joint mission of Japanese aggrandizement and colonial conquest.[84] When Tom Cruise became a samurai and represented the Japanese traditional warrior resisting Americanized military domination, irony collapsed into farce. James Cameron's film *Avatar* (2009) waded into the same waters despite its anti-colonial text (see Box 8.3).

Andre Gunder Frank and Underdevelopment

Baran's theory that imperialism permanently blocked economic growth influenced a group of South American scholars—known collectively as the *dependentistas*—who were developing their own critique of modernization theory.[85] According to Andre Gunder Frank (1929–2005), it was wrong to claim that the presently undeveloped societies were simply at an earlier historical stage and needed to catch up with the developed West. In the view of the *dependentistas*, **underdevelopment** was a consequence of the capitalist world economy through which the development of some parts of the system occurred at the expense of other parts.[86]

Frank's analysis of Latin America was influenced by Baran's theory of economic growth.

❖ BOX 8.3 • THEORY IN CONTEXT ❖

Avatar

In the movie *Avatar*, Jake Sully (Sam Worthington) is an alienated and disabled ex-marine. A mining corporation makes Jake an offer he can't refuse: in return for an expensive operation that will restore the use of his legs, Jake must infiltrate and spy on a native tribe known as the Na'vi. The Na'vi live on Pandora, a planet with an atmosphere that quickly kills any humans exposed to it. To overcome this difficulty, scientists have perfected the animation of a Na'vi body, which becomes an avatar controlled through brain energy channelled technologically. The Na'vi are simple, spiritual, graceful, and athletic people, but are neither rational nor scientific. The religion of Pandora is a form of transcendentalism, through which every creature and thing is connected physically and spiritually by mystical bonds that extend from the past into the future. The cultural clash on Pandora is shaped by typical Western dualities of the primitive and civilized, the spiritual and the rational, mind and body, innocence and original sin. The Na'vi are noble savages, an unspoiled Aboriginal group living with nature in a holistic, spiritual community. Anthropologist Grace Augustine (Sigourney Weaver) seeks to learn from Na'vi culture, but she represents the supposedly benevolent side of Western colonialism. She intends to implant Western institutions, such as schooling. The children of Pandora will learn to shut up and listen to Western authority while being decultured.

The other side of Western colonialism is imperialist exploitation, violence, and genocide. The motive for the military occupation of Pandora, for which Jake's avatar will provide the intelligence, is to extract a rare mineral, unobtanium, a rock that is more valuable than James Cameron's entire career of blockbuster movies. Unobtanium is buried deep within the bowels of Pandora, but not so deep that the gigantic earth-moving machines of the Parker Selfridge Mining Corporation can't dig it out—that is, once the Na'vi are driven off the land and the forest is uprooted for open-pit brutality. Military power on behalf of colonialism and corporate greed are the film's twin villains. The rape and destruction of a planet's delicate ecology are the consequences of corporate exploitation and imperialism. A mighty army of machines and heavily armed mercenaries is unleashed on the Na'vi, who

Through case studies of Chile and Brazil, Frank challenged the argument that industrial capitalist development was actually possible in the Third World.[87] According to Frank, the underdevelopment of Latin America could not be attributed to the survival of a feudal structure because no feudal structure had ever existed in the region. The large agricultural estates that continue to exist in the region were implanted by European settlers, and from their beginning they were tied into a worldwide system of commercial exploitation.[88]

Since the sixteenth century European capitalism has incorporated the globe in a single capitalist system. Capitalist expansion, however, is inherently uneven. The development of one part of the world (the **metropolitan-centre**) has

have only bows and arrows, guerrilla tactics, and their spiritual connections to their planet and its fauna to resist invasion. Their days appear to be numbered—that is, until Jake sides with the Aboriginal Na'vi and predictably goes native, like Kevin Costner in *Dances with Wolves*.

Jake's avatar survives Pandora, an environment with more ways to kill you than the Australian outback, through the help of a young Na'vi woman, Neytiri (Zoe Saldana). The colonizer–Aboriginal romance (think *Pocahontas*) follows the well-worn romantic script from initial dislike, through blossoming love, past a serious impediment, to a romantic conclusion. Through Neytiri's teachings, Jake's avatar becomes as physically and culturally skilled as a native. He learns to leap nimbly high in the branches and free-fall from limb to limb. Love sweeps Jake into the mental and spiritual world of Pandora, and he learns to "see" through the eyes of the Na'vi and to think using their concepts and world view, a hasty change of perspectives that would make any anthropologist blush.

More than just becoming one of the tribe, Jake's avatar becomes "the one." He tames the wildest thing on all Pandora, fulfilling an ancient Na'vi myth that names him the long-awaited messiah. Jake, the ex-marine, becomes the great white hope of the Na'vi, who would be leaderless without him. Jake's prophet-like avatar organizes the various tribes and inspires them with an impromptu battle-scene speech. The natives have to be saved by a Western warrior-king. Beyond the Aboriginal stereotypes that run throughout the film, this usurpation of native leadership reveals the explicit racism in Cameron's movie.

The game-like CGI battle is soon engaged in the floating mountain region of Pandora. In this Dr. Seuss-like skyscape (Grace used *The Lorax* in her English school), the battle un-folds according to the Hollywood script, although contemporary filmmaking is sufficiently self-consciousness to overturn some conventions. Typically, evil appears to have the upper hand until the battle comes down to a single combat between villain and hero. Ultimately, the villain is felled. With a wink to modern gender conventions, in *Avatar* he is killed by poison-tipped arrows shot by Neytiri, the hero's warrior mate: *she* saves *him*. Finally, rather than imposing Western laws and institutions to putatively civilize the natives, Jake's soul or life force is transferred from his human body to his avatar. When Jake becomes forever a living Na'vi, Cameron gives a marginally progressive twist to the cultural stereotype of Western leadership of Aboriginal peoples.

occurred as a result of the exploitation of the other part of the world (the **peripheral-satellite**). Both parts have changed; both have a history. But for metropolitan Europe and America, this history is one of industrialization, while for peripheral Africa, Asia, and Latin America, it is one of active underdevelopment. Over time, the gap between metropolis and satellite grows larger, internationally and within each country. Under-development, Frank concludes, was a "created" condition of European colonialism rather than an "original" condition of history.[89] Frank views the world capitalist system as consisting of a series of concentric circles or constellations, with the cen-tre the dominant world metropolis: Britain in the nineteenth century and the United States in the twentieth. The system extends outward through successive rings, incorporating regions that are at once peripheral to the world metropolis but that also become national, regional, and local metropolises relative to their own satellites, down to the most abject rural peripheral area. Each metropolis holds monopoly control over its respective satellites, and the whole is integrated into a single, world capitalist system.[90] Following the capitalist law of uneven growth, underdevelopment increases polarization between metropolitan and satellite countries while the urban and rural poor in the satellite countries grow poorer both relatively and absolutely.

The concept of *underdevelopment* is different from the modernization idea of *undeveloped*. *Undeveloped* suggests that a region's economy is essentially unchanged and traditional—not yet penetrated by modern capitalism. *Underdevelopment*, on the other hand, suggests that global capitalism has wrought fundamental changes in the economies of the satellites but that these changes actually prevent the periphery from being transformed into a highly industrialized, autonomous, mass-consumption society.

Throughout the colonial era, Western elites exported capital to finance mining, agriculture, and commercial businesses in the colonies. The result was a global division of labour in which the satellite transferred primary products to the metropolis in return for manufactured goods, such as luxury products. In this unequal trade, considerably more wealth was siphoned from the satellite and transferred to the metropolis than the value of the original investment. The colonial economy became over-specialized, producing one or two staple commodities for export.[91] When the staple industry was owned by foreign capitalists, most of their profits were shipped overseas and not reinvested to expand internal economic development in the periphery.[92]

Through this system of international capitalism, the urban commercial elites in Latin America became centres to (and exploiters of) peripheral regions and classes in their own nations. However, the underdevelopment of Latin America was caused not only by its insertion into worldwide capitalism, but by the political structure in the peripheral nation. Under the overall domination of neo-colonialism, economic and political power in Latin America was in the hands of a ruling alliance consisting of the agricultural, mining, and commercial bourgeoisie. They were united by common interests in the export market, free trade with the metropolis, and foreign investment. Rather than being oriented to the interests of the nation as a whole, this ***comprador* bourgeoisie**—Frank also calls them a "lumpenbourgeoisie"—was closely connected to the dominant metropolitan capitalists in the worldwide capitalist system.[93]

Many countries that are satellites in the world capitalist system have achieved periodic spurts of industrialization fostered by a small, national capitalist class. Brazil, for example, produced steel, textiles, and sugar in the early 1800s and developed some light industries and food-processing plants in the early twentieth century. During the Great Depression and World War II, when the concerns of world capitalism were diverted away from peripheral countries, some relatively autonomous industrial development occurred within local metropolises, such as São Paulo in Brazil and Buenos Aries in Argentina. Once the ties with the world capitalist system were restored, however, the pockets of autonomous development were soon misdirected or strangulated. The polarization between metropolis and satellite resumed, becoming particularly severe in the most peripheral regions of underdeveloped countries. What was left of the national bourgeoisie in the periphery was bludgeoned into submission by international economic forces or military coups supported by the armed power of the imperial metropolis.[94]

In general, under imperialism the forms of economic development that take place depend on the policies and interests of the metropolis. In the post–World War II era, Latin America experienced a new wave of investment from the advanced countries. Multi-national corporations (MNCs) began exporting technology to the periphery and established manufacturing industries intended to produce exports to the large, consumption markets in advanced capitalist countries. As MNCs increasingly penetrated into satellite nations, they often abandoned older manufacturing industries in the higher waged Western countries, leaving vacant factories and unemployed workers in their wake. In concert with the imperial powers, local governing elites ensured that government policies worked to favour foreign ownership and control in the satellite countries. The distribution of income grew increasingly unequal while the absolute income of the majority declined. Inflation and regressive taxes further diminished the actual income of the bottom three-quarters of the population.[95]

As the costs of importing equipment increased, including expensive licensing requirements for patented technologies, and as the world price for many primary products fell precipitously, satellite countries fell into a deepening debt spiral. Economic crises were staved off by additional private foreign investment and foreign aid to cover the deficit and finance further development. Foreign aid came with many strings, however, most of which were designed to benefit the donor countries more than the underdeveloped recipients. As a result, Third World countries were plunged deeper into the **debt crisis**. They were unable to pay back the money loaned to them; sometimes they couldn't even pay the annual interest charges. The consequence of these interconnected factors was **dependent development**, whereby only specific economic sectors are developed at the expense of constructing a fully integrated, internal economy. These countries became a haven for cheap labour, and international trade was carried on under fundamentally unequal conditions.

Only narrow interests benefited from such an arrangement, perpetuating "backwardness, misery, and social marginalization."[96]

Fundamentally, Frank pointed out in 1969, rather than being insufficiently integrated into world capitalist trade, a Third World country could be developed only "by taking it out of the capitalist system altogether."[97] Foreign interests exercise increasing influence not only on the economy of the Third World, but on its politics. When economic power is insufficient to protect the fundamental interests of the local elite and its international backers, according to Dos Santos, they resort to military power to preserve their interests. For the *dependentistas*, there were only two possible paths to take in Latin America. The region could remain wedded to international capitalism, which inevitably meant remaining mired in underdevelopment and being subject to brutal military dictatorships. This route, however, Dos Santos argues, opens the way to fascism. The alternative was deep radicalization that would break free of world capitalism altogether in a socialist revolution.[98]

Following World War II, in many parts of the world anti-colonial wars of national liberation were transformed into struggles for socialism. In 1949, China became the second great nation to begin an experiment in socialist development. Throughout the post-war period and into the 1980s, other Third World countries followed a similar path; in the view of the United States government, they were falling like dominos. For the Western powers, it was not just a matter of losing territory. What was at stake was the loss of their domination over the resources and economies of their former colonies. In this increasingly volatile world, the US responded with a multi-front, Cold War attack on "world communism."

Whether anti-colonial wars for national independence took a socialist direction, sought a "third way" between socialism and capitalism, or remained within the Western camp depended on conditions in each country and on the degree of support from the Eastern or Western blocs. In many cases, such as Vietnam, the struggle became a hot spot in the Cold War. Although the socialist tide seemed to be growing exponentially, under the surface the radical impulse was being slowly drained.

Dependent Development and Branch-Plant Economy

Canada's position resembles more closely that of a less developed nation than that of other developed countries.[99]

— B.W. Wilkinson, *Canada's International Trade*, 1968

The concepts *dependent development* and *metropolis/satellite* were employed in the 1970s in the analysis of Canadian political economy, a time in which nationalist and socialist sentiments grew in the country. Canada was originally a resource-producing satellite for Britain and France. Following World War I, New York had replaced the old imperial metropoles as the dominant power shaping development. Canadians lamented for a nation that had never been truly independent but had silently surrendered to American control. American domination of the Canadian economy had begun in the late nineteenth century under the misnamed National Policy. American capital was exported north as subsidiaries of US multinational corporations set up business north of the border. Canada adopted an early version of the import-substitution model of development through foreign investment.[100] American ownership and **Fordism** dominated Canada's development in such key growth industries as the automobile, rubber, chemicals, and electrical equipment, as well as in the resource sectors of mining and petroleum.[101] Direct foreign control was supplemented by technological dependency through joint ventures with Canadian capital and licensing agreements with American corpora-

tions. Canada had regressed, Kari Levitt said, "to a rich hinterland" with a powerless but comfortable business elite.[102] In fact, Laxer claimed in 1973 that 75 per cent of Canada's GNP was produced through foreign corporations.[103]

The American branch-plant economy brought prosperity to eastern Canada, but it was a dependent industrialization that proved to be fragile. American corporations sold to the small, northern market, but, more importantly, they exported manufactured goods back to the United States. The two national economies were increasingly inseparable, but Canada was the junior, vulnerable partner. In the 1970s, the United States faced international competition from Germany and Japan. As capital became global, US investment decisions led to the withdrawal of capital from Canada and to the expansion of economic speculation abroad in low-wage countries. The result for Canada was growing *de*industrialization.[104]

Canadian development, however, was not a one-way street. Carroll argues that at the same time that American domination was enflaming a new nationalism north of the border, Canadian capital was being invested in the global South. Within the country, local metropolitan centres developed to control regional satellites, originally in Montreal and Toronto and more recently in Calgary and Vancouver. Canada was not simply a dependant of the American economy; it was a middle-range semi-metropolitan centre with significant foreign investments of its own.[105] Canadian capitalists invested heavily in the financial sector and the transportation infrastructure, principally railways. Banking and finance remained the strongest capitalist sector although it was inextricably linked to the American market and US-based capital.[106] In short, Canada exists in a nexus of metropolis-hinterland relationships, occupying an advantageous, intermediary, and semi-peripheral position vis-à-vis global capitalism.

Within this nexus, Quebec has occupied a distinct place. Originally a colony of France, the territory was conquered by Britain in 1759–60, making Quebec a colonial satellite within the British Empire. Confederation in Canada created an unequal union between the two nations, the English and the French. Commercial enterprises and therefore wealth were largely in the hands of the English elite, which made Montreal the regional metropole for the hinterland of Quebec. French Canadians felt like a conquered and subordinate people, having to become anglicized to succeed in their own country. The national question in Quebec resurfaced during the conscription crisis in 1917. At the time, the nationalist movement was led by intellectuals such as Lionel Groulx (see Chapter 3) and was largely conservative and religious.[107]

By the 1950s and 1960s, the social and economic changes described by sociologists Everett and Helen Hughes were eroding the foundation of traditional Quebec society. The result was the growth of a more secular outlook in education and politics that has been called the Quiet Revolution. Many Quebec intellectuals, such as Pierre Trudeau, who had at first gravitated to the national cause converted to Canadian federalism. Under Trudeau's Liberal national government, Canada was defined as a bilingual and multicultural country. For Quebec nationalists, however, French Quebec had been invited into Canada only as second-class citizens, threatened by the power of gradual cultural assimilation by an English-speaking continent. In this context, Quebec nationalism assumed two forms. In 1960, a separatist party was formed to win electoral victory in the province of Quebec and to lead the nation to independence.[108] The Parti Québécois finally won the election of 1976 in Quebec. Since then, however, and most notably in the referendum of 1995, the nationalist movement has not succeeded in winning a majority vote to renegotiate sovereignty for Quebec.

Urban guerilla warfare was the second form of the independence movement in Quebec. Formed in 1963, the Front de Libération du Quebec (FLQ) conducted a campaign of terror in Montreal. The FLQ cells were largely isolated from the Quebec populace; they were not the military spearhead of a popular, anti-colonial movement, as the FLN had been in Algeria. The FLQ placed bombs in mailboxes in rich, Anglo suburbs and bombed an army recruiting office and other Anglo targets. Most members were arrested and imprisoned, including Pierre Vallières, who, in 1968, wrote an autobiographical call for a popular uprising entitled *White Niggers of America*. Distinguishing between the English elite and the Québécois working class, Vallières said that "without control over economic and social policy," Quebec's workers "will continue to remain for generations the 'white niggers of America,' the cheap labor that the predators of industry, commerce, and high finance are so fond of, the way wolves are fond of sheep."[109]

In 1970, an FLQ cell kidnapped British diplomat James Cross as well as Quebec Minister of Labour Pierre Laporte. Among other demands, the FLQ tried to bargain their hostages for the release of hundreds of Quebec nationalists. In an unprecedented move in peacetime, Prime Minister Trudeau imposed the War Measures Act, which removed Canadian civil liberties and deployed troops on the streets of Quebec. The Act was justified on the spurious grounds that a political insurrection was imminent. The police exploited the opportunity to cast a wide net, arresting without charges hundreds of activists, unionists, and nationalists with no actual links to the FLQ. The emergency and the FLQ were both finished shortly thereafter. Laporte was killed by his captors, who then negotiated the release of Cross in return for a flight to Cuba. Algeria had been their alternate choice.[110] The potential for Quebec independence remains a potent force in Canadian and Quebec politics. The 2014 referendum regarding independence for Scotland, which was lost by Scottish nationalists, was watched disappointedly by many in Quebec.

Since the 1980s, economic concerns have overshadowed questions of dependency and independence in Canada. Free trade with the United States furthered the decline of manufacturing in Ontario and Quebec. Deindustrialization in the east and oil production in the west have changed metropolitan-hinterland relations in Canada and abroad. New technologies and higher prices for petroleum products have made the Alberta oil sands a profitable venture, attracting US investment and returning Canada to a predominantly staple-producing economy. Oil-sand production has also put Canada in the forefront of the debate about climate change. Beyond only the consumption of oil-sand petroleum, its very extraction produces green-house gases and causes serious environmental degradation. The US-based oil industry and the Canadian government face significant opposition from environmentalists and First Nations peoples as they plan pipelines to connect Alberta oil to markets in the southern United States (Keystone) and to Asia via the Northern Gateway project through British Columbia.

Canada is increasingly a resource-producing nation within the contemporary international division of labour, which has created an essentially global economic system. Immanuel Wallerstein argues that the world has had a single economic system since the conquests of the Americas in the 1500s. That system is now in an age of transition to an uncertain future.

Immanuel Wallerstein's Model of Globalization

Immanuel Wallerstein was born in 1930 in New York City. As a teenager, he became interested in global politics and the anti-colonial movement in India. After receiving a BA degree from Columbia University in 1951, he then served two years in the US military. His master's thesis at Columbia (1954) was on McCarthyism. The following year Wallerstein went to West Africa with financial support from the Ford Foundation to study the rise of the nationalist movement. He received a Ph.D. in 1959 and taught first at Columbia, then at McGill in Montreal and at Birmingham in England, and is now a research scholar at Yale. He is best known for his analysis of global capitalism outlined in *The Modern World-System* (1974).[111]

While at McGill University, Wallerstein switched his analysis from national systems to world systems, a unit of analysis that encompassed an integrated zone of territories and cultural and economic institutions over a long duration of time. For Wallerstein, a world capitalist system was brought into being 500 years ago. At first incorporating Europe and the Americas, this single world system has since expanded to cover the whole globe. Capitalism is now fully global and mature. It is a system of many political units, cultures, and groups; the different zones are unified by a division of labour. Capital, labour, and goods flow unequally among the parts of the system. The fundamental feature of the modern world system is the ceaseless accumulation of capital. World-system theory incorporated the dependency concepts of core and periphery, which are regions existing in a relationship of unequal exchange vis-à-vis each other. Core economies tend toward monopoly (massive concentration of wealth) and produce high-profit goods; peripheral economies tend to be more competitive, are less profitable, and produce "peripheral products." Near-monopoly corporations require the support of strong political states, such as the United States, Japan, and Germany. In between the two poles of the system, Wallerstein identifies semi-peripheral states, such as Brazil, India, and South Korea.[112]

Production and consumption in the world system takes place in a number of locations, including firms, states, households, and among status or identity groups, such as religious structures or ethnic organizations. Status groups are defined by others; identities are self-inscribed. Wallerstein distinguishes between the value and norms of universalism—meritocracy, universal suffrage, equality before the law—and forms of anti-universalism, among which two of the most important are racism and sexism. Anti-universal practices incorporate various groups within the world system, but at inferior ranks. This binary is as fundamental to the world system as the distinction between core and periphery.[113]

New Age of Transition

The system has experienced many crises over the centuries. Ultimately, each crisis furthered the development and consolidation of the single world system. It was able to maintain capital accumulation by its ability to "de-ruralize" the world by incorporating increasingly low-paid, non-capitalist sectors into the global system. These new pools of cheap labour helped maintain production. Currently, there are no significant rural masses still be drawn into the ambit of capitalist exploitation. The world system is approaching an impasse at which "the pool [of rural labour] is diminished to the point where it no longer exists effectively."[114] As a result, postponing a final crisis in capital accumulation is no longer possible. Simultaneously, global capitalism has created an ecological crisis through "toxification" and the exhaustion of non-renewal resources. Capitalism is reaching the limits of its expansion; it is a world system with no new potential for growth.[115]

The crisis in the modern world system cannot be solved within the framework of the existing system. Wallerstein argues that, at such a moment of systemic crisis, the system is entering an age of transition, a chaotic and inherently unpredictable period in which the system oscillates wildly. For the first time in 500 years, there is a "real perspective of fundamental change" that will be permanent and global. Contrary to falsely optimistic Marxist expectations, there is no historical inevitability about a socialist transition following a systemic crisis of global capitalism. The actual

contours of a "successor system" to replace global capitalism are unknowable and will result from the struggles carried out over the next half-century. A systemic crisis creates a "chaotic ambiance" that offers opportunities for "creative action" and the operation of agency, highlighting the importance of the subjective factor (consciousness and theory) in a movement of transition.[116]

Over the last 150 years, there was only one dominant strategy for progressive transformation of the world, which, Wallerstein argues, was based on "two steps: first, gain state power; second, transform the world." This was the underlying strategy whether the form the political movement took was **social democratic**, Leninist, or anti-imperialist and socialist. By the end of the twentieth century, however, this strategy was in "tatters." State power movements were "probably the only one[s] possible at the time, since movements with any other kind of strategy could be simply crushed by the use of state power." Leninism was the only strategy to succeed in taking state power, but it failed to bring about the promised transition to socialism; it failed to achieve the "guarantees of 'shining tomorrows.'"[117] With the bugbear of world communism no longer present to shield capitalism from critique and condemnation, the global political spotlight can now shine directly on the existing world system.

In the contemporary age of transition between systems, no single class or group is the subject of modern revolution. In place of a single vanguard, such as the Marxist proletariat, there is a "world family of antisystemic movements" capable of a "rainbow coalition" or a "movement of movements" that would include working-class organizations. For these anti-systemic and anti-capitalist social movements, Wallerstein argues, weakness is strength: the overall movement is loosely structured, but this makes it "difficult to suppress," neutralizes the "centrist forces," and makes the state hesitant to repress it. The hybrid coalition and the political sentiments behind the uprising that erupted in Paris in 1968 appear to be the model for Wallerstein. Paris marked the beginning of a transition to a new kind of struggle that represented the future, based on the principles of spontaneous popular mobilization, non-hierarchical democratization, and the absence of structure.[118]

What is to be done? For Wallerstein, legal, parliamentary pressures within the system are necessary as defensive battles to preserve the remnants of the liberal state. More importantly, the "fundamental tactic is the use of loosely-structured, extra-parliamentary militant tactics," which were followed by the recent anti-globalization demonstrations in Seattle, Milan, and Quebec. Since earlier movements were "simply crushed by the use of state power," it is probable that Wallerstein underestimates the likelihood that the state will mobilize the powers of the police as the anti-capitalist tactics actually become effective. The so-called war on terrorism may be the next step in the mobilization of ideology, the "manufacturing of consent," for the suppression of popular manifestations of protest.[119]

Wallerstein's focus on ideology and consciousness alludes to the importance of culture for the maintenance and subversion of the global system. Frantz Fanon understood the importance of cultural hegemony for maintaining the power of a dominant regime. The emergence of a new society implied the importance of a revolution in culture to parallel the changes in economic and political life. Struggles over culture and identity were part of the revolutionary movement. In this battle of competing ideologies, post-colonial theory and literature played an increasingly important role. Edward Saïd's critique of the ideology he defined as Orientalism in Western social thought has shaped contemporary post-colonial theory.

Edward Saïd and Orientalism

Being a White Man, in short, was a very concrete manner of being-in-the-world, a way of taking ahold of reality, language, and thought.[120]

— Edward Saïd, *Orientalism*, 1978

Edward Saïd (1935–2003) challenged the Eurocentric view of First World scholars and politicians who epitomized the top-down, culturally biased, and hegemonic knowledge of the white world. Saïd was born to a Christian family in Palestine, a territory then under British domination. His father was a Palestinian-American businessman. Under a United Nations declaration in 1947, the Palestinian territory was to be divided into two separate nation states: one for Palestinians and the other designated as a national homeland for Israeli Jews. Many Arabs refused to accept the two-state solution, however. When British control of the territory ended in 1948, the State of Israel declared its independence, precipitating a war with neighbouring Arab countries. Edward Saïd's family became refugees and moved to Egypt, where Edward attended an elite private school. As a Palestinian in Egypt with a British first name and an American passport, fluently bilingual in Arabic and English, and a Christian in an Islamic culture, Saïd felt he "'was an uncomfortably anomalous student.'"[121]

This sense of multiple "two-ness" followed him when, in 1951 at the age of 15, Saïd was sent to a private school in Massachusetts. His American education followed a typically upper-class New England path. With degrees from Princeton and Harvard, Saïd joined the faculty of Columbia University in 1963, specializing in comparative literature.[122] As a Palestinian—a people without a state—Saïd experienced the "web of racism, cultural stereotypes . . . [and] dehumanizing ideology" that have fixed the Arab and the Muslim in time and space, making them, he said, the essential and dangerous Other in the contemporary world.[123]

Saïd's widely influential multidisciplinary book *Orientalism* (1978) became a tour de force in a wide range of intellectual fields, including post-colonial studies and sociology. For Saïd, colonialism is not only a matter of economic accumulation and the acquisition of territories. The culture of imperialism is also an important factor in colonialism; indeed, it is that culture that nurtures the rationale, imagination, and language of empire-building. The economic and political motives of imperialism are supported by (and perhaps driven by) ideologies that certain territories or people "*require* and beseech domination." And the language of nineteenth-century imperial culture is punctuated by such concepts as *inferior* and *superior, subject races*, and *dependency*.[124]

Orientalism refers to the ideology of an academic area of study that is widely defined as including all of Asia and the Middle East. The term also defines a set of dogmatic ideas and superficial generalizations that Europeans have constructed to define and describe the Orient (the East). Orientalism is rooted in the assumption that different regions are inhabited by radically different groups that "can be defined on the basis of some religion, culture, or racial essence proper to that geographical space."[125] In general, Orientalism is a discourse based upon a set of essential characteristics assumed to distinguish the Orient (the East) from the Occident (the West). As Rudyard Kipling wrote, "East is East and West is West, and never the twain shall meet."[126]

The assumption of a basic distinction between West and East is the starting point for broad generalizations about the people of the Orient, such as an assumed uniform "Oriental mind." Orientalism is a form of cultural hegemony that distinguishes a Western "us" from an Eastern "other" and rests on the assumption of Western superiority. In the nineteenth century, modern terminology and practices were created in Western literature, travel accounts, and political commentaries that established a dominant discourse about the Orient, which Saïd called **latent Orientalism**.[127]

Cultural discourse does not circulate truths; rather, discourse creates a systematic representation that constitutes and reinforces a set of social conventions and accepted codes of understanding. The Orientalist surveys the Orient from above, through a set of pre-formed categories that were meant to be rational and scientific, but were actually reductive and schematic. An Orientalist lens creates a fundamental gap between the misleading idea of "the Orient" assumed in Orientalist discourse and the actual "reality" of Eastern cultures and nations. The Orient is assumed to be as the European imagination has perceived it. Such a perspective is fundamentally conservative and is irrefutable within its own terms.[128]

In the nineteenth century, latent Orientalism converged with European economic and political conquest of the East ("manifest Orientalist experience"). The theory of innate racial inequality, stimulated by social Darwinism, nationalism, and imperialism, provided a pseudo-scientific cover to Orientalist discourse, promoting and justifying European colonialism. The Orientalist scholar of the nineteenth century assumed that races were inherently unequal and that the domination of the many by the few was an essential natural law. Discourses are never neutral, Saïd said; they must be studied in relation to "their configurations of power."[129] The discourse of Orientalism is shaped by unequal exchanges between various forms of power, including political, cultural, intellectual, and moral power.

As an intellectual discipline, Orientalism placed the scholar of the Orient on a pedestal as the authority on the East. Knowledge, however, is never disinterested; it is always political. As scholars of the Orient systematically accumulated knowledge about cultures, languages, and territories, they prepared the way for what colonial armies and administrators would later do on the terrain. Orientalism became an institution that dealt with the Orient; not just describing and teaching it, but "settling it, ruling over it," and restructuring it.[130]

Similar images and representations shaped the romantic and misleading version of the mysterious and exotic East. Exoticism was deeply sexual. In the West, sexuality was encumbered with Victorian authority and social and legal obligations. In French literature of the nineteenth century, the Orient was associated with escapist sexual fantasies and licentious sex, with harems, dancing girls, erotic balms, and enticing veils. Guilt-free, libertine sexual experiences unobtainable in the West could be bought in the East. Eastern women were presented as sensual and willing, Saïd writes. They became "creatures of a male power-fantasy."[131]

Despite its political and cultural consequences, Orientalism was not a nefarious Western plot. It was not in any "direct, corresponding relationship with political power in the raw." Nevertheless, Saïd argues, Orientalism was a form of cultural domination that aided political conquest. It "expresses a will or intention, in some cases to control, manipulate, even to incorporate, what is a manifestly different (or alternative and novel) world." As a cultural apparatus, "Orientalism is all aggression, activity, judgment, will-to-power and knowledge."[132]

For Saïd, the discourse of Orientalism continued to flourish throughout the 1990s in Western writing about Arabs and Islam. In contrast, scholarship in other specialist area studies underwent revision in the 1960s and 1970s through which various cultures and histories in the East were

---

⧼☙ BOX 8.4 · BIOGRAPHY ☙⧽

Salman Rushdie (b. 1947)

Salman Rushdie was born to a Muslim family in Bombay, India, in 1947. It was an auspicious year. Less than two months after his birth, the sovereignty of the British Empire came to an end in the subcontinent, which was divided between two hostile nations: India, with a majority Hindu population, and the Islamic Republic of Pakistan, born as two Islamic "chunks of land a thousand miles apart." East and West Pakistan were "sundered by the land-mass of its greatest foe."[133]

The first 14 vivid years of Rushdie's boyhood were spent in Bombay. Thereafter, he became an immigrant to two countries. He attended private school in England and then studied history at King's College, Cambridge, graduating in 1968. He was angry when his childhood home in Bombay was sold and his family moved, against his will, to Pakistan. Rushdie, however, never lived in Pakistan for more than six months.[134] He felt divided between the memory and imagination of his homeland and the ambivalent relationship he developed with the West. Migrants flee or fly from their place of birth. How far did Rushdie fly? "Five and a half thousand [miles] as the crow. Or: from Indianness to Englishness, an immeasurable distance."[135]

In 1981, Rushdie published *Midnight's Children*, his grand, award-winning novel of his homeland. The novel is set during three periods of Indian history, from the colonial past to the "moth-eaten partition that chopped up the old country," concluding with the creation of Bangladesh.[136] In the novel, he demonstrates how India had failed to achieve its

reinterpreted from the bottom up. No similar change occurred in the studies of Arabic or Islamic cultures: "Books and articles are regularly published on Islam and the Arabs by Middle Eastern area specialists that represent absolutely no change over the virulent anti-Islamic polemics of the Middle Ages and the Renaissance." For these specialists, "there are still such things as *an* Islamic society, *an* Arab mind, *an* Oriental psyche." The Orient, according to the standard dogma, is something to be feared or controlled.[137]

Saïd's *Orientalism* is a barbed, polemical indictment of Western racism and imperialism. He has been criticized, however, for holding an anti-Western bias, for making over-generalized judgments about the West, for making factual historical errors, and for selecting and misinterpreting evidence to support his claims.[138] In response, Saïd pointed out that his writings came from an "extremely concrete history of personal loss and national disintegration."[139] He was interested "in knowledge that is nondominative and noncoercive . . . produced in a setting that is deeply inscribed with the politics, the considerations, the positions and the strategies of power." Saïd sought knowledge, parallel to black or feminist or anti-imperialist studies, "all of which take for their point of departure the right of formerly un- or misrepresented human groups to speak for and represent themselves."[140]

---

early hope of becoming a multicultural nation that modelled tolerance and freedom ("one thousand and one promises of a numinous midnight"). Rushdie nevertheless remained hopeful for India's future. Pakistan, on the other hand, was born out of political and religious intolerance. Rushdie's third novel, *Shame* (1983), is a bitter account of public and private authoritarianism in Pakistan. In the modern world, when cultures and mythologies converge, the result is often disastrous. Rushdie concluded that politics is "a bad dirty business. . . . [P]rivacy, the small individual lives of men, are preferable to all this inflated macrocosmic activity."[141]

Although Rushdie claims to be secular, his books are replete with the people and lore of Muslim history. Religious themes often predominate.[142] Religion and secularism are a volatile mix. After the publication of Rushdie's *The Satanic Verses* in 1988, some Western critics claimed that his book disparaged Islam and was in fact Orientalist. Fundamentalist Muslims declared the novel blasphemous against the Prophet, Muhammad. The book was banned in many Islamic states and publicly burned by Muslims in Britain. On 14 February 1989, the supreme Ayatollah of Iran issued a *fatwa* against the author, offering a reward of 1.5 million pounds for his assassination. Rushdie went into seclusion for the better part of a decade.[143]

Rushdie weaves into his narratives the themes of diaspora, dispossession, and loss. Like anyone without "any fixed place, or space," Rushdie found nowhere that he could "rest the sole of his foot."[144] The migrant is forever caught between two worlds and lives unhappily and incompletely, never able to *be* fully one or the other. But the experience is intellectually exhilarating, according to Rushdie. Migrants are endowed with the advantage of multiple outside and inside perspectives. As they make life choices, they reject their old selves but create new selves, which all continue to exist as if in parallel universes.[145]

An essentialized and universal Arab society, Saïd argued, does not exist other than as a myth supported by various codes and discourses.[146] What does exist are numerous and different societies of Arabic-speaking people.[147] Scholarship should work "towards fragmenting, dissociating, dislocating and decentering the experiential terrain covered at present by universalizing" scholarship. The worse danger, Saïd argued, comes from ignoring differences and creating a grand synthesis, which could negate the counter-knowledge that has recently emerged. Saïd's **postmodern** perspective appears to reject any form of general theorizing about East–West differences in favour of concrete analysis. His general concept of Orientalism has become part of the theoretical language of contemporary social thought. These sensibilities are mirrored in the complex, nuanced, and controversial novels of the Indian-Pakistani-British author, Salman Rushdie (see Box 8.4).[148]

Conclusion

As the locus of historical world events shifted from the developed to the Third World, social theories from the South became globally influential. Like a map of the earth that is viewed from the perspective of the southern hemisphere, post-colonial theories turned Western thought upside-down. Frantz Fanon's defence of revolutionary violence shook Western notions of humanitarianism and peaceful change. Saïd's critique of Western stereotypes of Arabs and Muslims are especially relevant now in the post-9/11 era.

Part III of this book discusses more recent and contemporary theories that have arisen from the background presented thus far and that continue to be debated in social theory. The following chapters discuss the development of structural and post-structural theories, postmodern outlooks, and analyses of modernity. As noted in several places in earlier chapters, theoretical developments that occur over several decades emerge, develop, and change in relation to each other. The linearity of their presentation in print often obscures this complexity. As this chapter's discussion of Immanuel Wallerstein's social theory underscores, many of the most important foundational scholars of social theory today emerged from the heat of the 1960s. Their theories grew from New Left roots and inspirations, including the romantic image of Che Guevara, who still inspires youthful idealism worldwide. Chapter 9 examines some of the major cultural and theoretical moments that helped shape many of the dominant theorists of the contemporary age.

Questions for Reflection

———————•◆•———————

1. Fanon defended acts that would now be described as terrorism. Thinking of Algeria in the 1950s and the world today, is his defence of the necessity of revolutionary violence convincing?

2. Does dependency theory provide a sound foundation for understanding US–Canada economic relations?

3. Does Wallerstein's analysis of contemporary social movements offer a reasonable prospect for significant social change?

4. Is Orientalism an ideology of the past or is it still apparent, as Saïd claimed, in Western views of Islam and Arabs?

Timeline

1959   The Cuban Revolution succeeds; Che Guevara moves from guerilla to administrator.

1959   Erving Goffman publishes *The Presentation of Self in Everyday Life*.

1963   Timothy Leary is fired from Harvard University for experiments with psychedelic drugs.

1964   Free Speech movement at the University of California at Berkeley, sparks New Left groups on campuses.

1964   Herbert Marcuse publishes *One Dimensional Man*.

1966   Cultural Revolution begins in China; in the West, it is interpreted as a student-led revolt from below.

1967   Large-scale and sustained anti-war protests and demonstrations take place in the US.

1967   Che Guevara is executed by US-trained counter-insurgency troops in Bolivia.

1967   Jacques Derrida introduces deconstruction in *Writing and Difference* and *Of Grammatology*.

1968   USSR invades Czechoslovakia to suppress a move to "socialism with a human face."

1968   New Left zenith: student-worker protests in Paris almost topple French government.

1969   Riot at Stonewall Inn, NY: gay activists take militant action against repressive police.

1973   CIA-backed coup deposes socialist president of Chile; neo-liberal economics in charge.

1979   Conservative leader Margaret Thatcher, a neo-liberal, elected prime minister of Britain.

1979   Jean-François Lyotard publishes *The Post-Modern Condition: A Report on Knowledge*.

1979   Pierre Bourdieu publishes *Distinction: A Social Critique of the Judgment of Taste*.

1981   Socialist François Mitterand elected president of France; capitulates to neo-liberalism.

1981   Jean Baudrillard publishes *Simulacra and Simulation*.

1981   Jürgen Habermas publishes *The Theory of Communicative Action*.

1984   bell hooks publishes *Feminist Theory: From Margin to the Center*.

1984   Anthony Giddens publishes *The Constitution of Society*.

1990   Patricia Hill Collins publishes *Black Feminist Thought*.

1990   Judith Butler publishes *Gender Troubles: Feminism and the Subversion of Identity*.

1998   Hugo Chavez elected president of Venezuela; key victory for twenty-first century socialism.

1997   Tony Blair's New Labour elected to power in Britain; normalizes neo-liberal policies.

2001   Coordinated terrorist attacks in the US; begins era of restriction and surveillance.

2001   US and its allies, including Canada, invade Afghanistan to remove Taliban from power.

2008   Worldwide financial crisis occurs: the "Great Recession"; coincides with collapse of US mortgage market.

2011   Occupy Wall Street movement, proclaimed in *Ad Busters*, begins.

2014   Large demonstrations take place in New York and elsewhere for action on climate change.

III From Radicalism to Juggernaut

In the twentieth century, pessimism about the future of society was represented in a genre of dystopian science fiction, such as *We*, *1984*, *Brave New World*, and *Fahrenheit 451*. An all-powerful state dominated its subservient population through rational science, bureaucratic control, ideological manipulation, and military power. In the contemporary era, environmental destruction, climate change, and pandemic have largely replaced nuclear annihilation in the news headlines and in apocalyptic film scripts. Einstein had predicted that World War IV would be fought with sticks and stones, and the impending "end of the world as we know it" has generated a minor industry in post-apocalyptic and dystopian films (*Melancholia*, *Interstellar*, *The Day After Tomorrow*), television (*Falling Skies*, *Survivors*, *Revolution*), and literature (*The Road*, *The Hunger Games*, *Divergent*). Where authoritarianism doesn't rule, there is anarchy.

In the dystopian *The Hunger Games*, the police state of Panem is ruled by an oligarchic elite, which lives in the Capital, an opulent and leisured metropolis. The Capital maintains

---

Katniss Everdeen is escorted by "Peacekeepers" (Storm-troopers), who enforce the oppressive state-power of the dystopian regime in *The Hunger Games: Catching Fire*. © Pictorial Press Ltd / Alamy

a military occupation over 12 exploited, hinterland Districts, the poorest of which is the coal-mining District 12. To demonstrate its power and symbolize a failed rebellion, crushed years earlier, the Capital organizes a gladiatorial contest—the Hunger Games—between randomly chosen adolescent Tributes, who are obliged to fight in an elaborate arena, televised nation-wide, until only one victor survives. Through this spectacular blend of Roman circus and reality TV (*Survivor* with a vengeance), the populace is cowed anew and distracted from their daily oppression.

In American popular culture, resistance requires a savior who is reluctantly drawn into symbolic and actual leadership. In *The Hunger Games*, the recalcitrant leader is Katniss Everdeen (played by Jennifer Lawrence in the film). Everdeen's widespread popularity during the seventy-fourth Hunger Games catapults her into symbolic leadership of rebellion 2.0 when she defies the Capital by threatening to commit suicide with her fellow Tribute from District 12. There would be no victor, only two rebellious martyrs. When Everdeen's hero status is exalted in the seventy-fifth Hunger Games, she becomes the Mockingjay, the symbol and then actual leader of the rebellion, representing a compelling role model for adolescent women in our age when feminism may seem unfashionable.

Through the crisis-ridden 1970s and the neo-liberal 1980s, a new generation of academics faced disillusionment from the failure of radical politics and the privileged perspective of second-wave feminism. Against this backdrop, social thought took a variety of turns. Postmodernists and post-structuralists rejected fundamental elements of the enlightenment rationality and the centrality of the Western, autonomous subject. These perspectives engaged in a spiralling debate with theories of late modernity, which tried to overcome the binary between objective structure and subjective action but also tried to address the concrete threats of globalization and the perils that menaced the new millennium.

CHAPTER 9

The New Left and Feminism

Learning Objectives

- To distinguish between the aims and theories of the counterculture and of the New Left
- To connect the critical theory of Herbert Marcuse with both countercultural and leftist opposition in the 1960s
- To provide an overview of Che Guevara's life, his theory about socialism, and his iconic status among the New Left
- To distinguish between equal rights and radical feminism, particularly in terms of the important role of patriarchy as the basis of women's oppression
- To understand Dorothy E. Smith's feminist standpoint theory in the context of second-wave feminism.

[N]obody really knows . . . what actually occurred . . . or if, simply, I'm telling a truth which is only my truth.[1]

—Julio Cortázar, "Blow-Up," 1967

The swinging subculture of 1960s London forms the backdrop for Michelangelo Antonioni's film, *Blow-Up*, which reflects the view that reality is in the mind. *Blow-Up* deals with the basic questions of what is real, what is represented as real, what is "only my truth," and what is a fabricated unreality. The anti-hero of the film is a laid-back and bored fashion photographer in London, identified as Thomas and played by David Hemmings. He drifts from studio shoots to impromptu sex with groupies to drug-laced parties, without any particular aim or ambition. Thomas takes some random shots of a couple in a London park. His interest is sparked when the woman tries to se-

duce him in order to retrieve the undeveloped film. Intrigued, Thomas enlarges the picture several times. As the photograph becomes increasingly grainy and unfocused, Thomas sees what may be a man with a gun in the bushes behind the couple. Has he witnessed a murder? He returns to the park and finds a man's body, and the mystery deepens. But *Blow-Up* is a European art film, not a routine Hollywood murder mystery to be solved through CSI science. Thomas returns again to the park but the body has disappeared. Soon, the pictures go missing, and he can't find the mysterious woman. With everything vanishing, the line between what is real and what is simulated and virtual also disappears. At the end of the film, Thomas comes across some young people pretending to hit an invisible tennis ball, back and forth. When the "ball" is struck over the fence, Thomas hesitates but then pretends to pick up the "ball" and throw it back. It is ultimately impossible to sort out what is real from what is not. Thomas walks away across the field and then he, too, is just gone. There is no single meaning to be grasped. All you can do is play along with the uncertainty and absurdity of life as it flows around you and with you.

In the bell-bottomed, drug-inspired, free-loving lifestyle of the 1960s, society was on the verge of real transformation, or so it seemed. The sixties counterculture resembled nineteenth-century Romanticism in many ways, and was equally as complicated to analyze. During the sixties, several cultural currents that affected youth intersected in society. Interest in Eastern mysticism and other forms of mythology was widespread. As the rock musical *Hair* announced, the Age of Pisces was coming to an end and the world was entering the new Age of Aquarius. According to author Dan Brown, the Piscean ideal had reflected the dominance of faith and authority, the idea that humanity "must be *told* what to do by higher powers" because people were not capable of thinking for themselves. For the Western counterculture, the dawning of the Age of Aquarius marked an ideological shift from faith in obsolete institutions to an age of love and pleasure.[2]

The 1960s Countercultures and the New Left

Social conditions in the 1960s and early 1970s, which spawned the interest in love and peace as well as counter-hegemonic social criticism, gave rise to numerous but usually disconnected social movements. Socially oppressed groups, such as blacks, women, Aboriginal peoples, and sexual minorities, organized themselves to struggle for equal rights and just social conditions. Students were inspired by the critical theorists of the 1950s and by their own countercultural icons. African Americans turned to black power and cultural nationalism, and second-wave feminism moved from liberal toward radical, socialist, and revolutionary positions.

A desire for change also germinated among the new legions of young people exposed to the dull experience of bureaucratic education and coalesced for a time around opposition to the Vietnam War. As criticism of American society deepened, a **New Left** emerged that was rooted in Third World revolutions and theories of individual rebellion. In sociology, Herbert Marcuse's critical theory resonated among members of the New Left. Their goals and tactics overlapped with the widespread and amorphous counterculture that was less concerned about the struggle for power and more interested in alternative realities.

Countercultures

There was considerable affinity between the rebellious, youth counterculture of the 1960s and earlier generations of cultural rebels. The turn to spirituality and Eastern philosophy (Allan Ginsberg), the use of marijuana, the "drop out" mentality (Jack Kerouac)—all were defining elements of the Beat culture, and all had antecedents in 1890s bohemia. The 1960s counterculture was fuelled, perhaps ironically, by specific technological advances, such as the birth control pill and synthesized laboratory drugs, such as lysergic acid diethylamide (LSD). Ken Kesey's experimentation with hallucinogenic drugs and road trips on the Magic Bus bridged the 1950s and 1960s. With its capacity for creating imaginary worlds, if only temporarily, LSD symbolized the sixties generation of bohemia.[3]

Timothy Leary (1920–1996) was the principle, self-styled guru of the hippie counterculture. With his slogan of "Turn on, tune in, drop out," Leary advocated a cultural revolution through a drug-induced expansion of consciousness and lifestyle changes. Leary was his own model. He abandoned a career as a research scientist to become the media spokesperson of the hippie, psychedelic generation. Merging the hippie lifestyle of free sexuality with hard-rock music and psychedelic drugs defined the life of many cultural icons of the 1960s, including Jimi Hendrix, Janis Joplin, and Jim Morrison, who all died of drug overdoses. The hippie counterculture reflected the ideology of experience as the meaning of life, and the near-death experience (and ultimately death itself) as the ultimate trip, as reflected in Oliver Stone's 1991 film biography, *The Doors*. In the movie, Val Kilmer, playing Jim Morrison, says that he feels "most alive confronting death, experiencing pain. . . . Life hurts a lot more [than death]. When you die the pain's over."[4]

The physical centre of the countercultural movement in America was no centre at all, although the East Village in New York and the Haight-Ashbury district of San Francisco were its most recognizable poles. In January 1967, a music festival (called a be-in) was held in Golden Gate Park in San Francisco, featuring some 1950s Beat poets and 1960s psychedelic rockers, such as Jefferson Airplane. A few months later, on Easter Sunday, an even more spontaneous and unplanned be-in was held in Central Park, New York. The flamboyant celebration fused the hippy community in a quasi-spiritual unity under the influence of marijuana and other drugs.[5] In Abbie Hoffman's memory of the time, "Everybody [was] high on something: balloons, acid, bananas, kids, sky, flowers, dancing, kissing. I had a ball—totally zonked. People giving away free things—fruit, jelly beans, clothes, flowers, chicken, Easter eggs, poems."[6] It was the beginning of the "summer of love." As New York bohemian Anita Kushner proclaimed ecstatically in 1967, "The world was glorious. You could do anything. Magic was possible."[7]

The rhetoric of the movement was captured by a member of the San Francisco Diggers, who proclaimed that "Property is the enemy—burn it, destroy it, give it away. Don't let them make a machine out of you, get out of the system, do your thing. Don't organize the schools, burn them. Leave them, they will rot."[8] As the counterculture grew beyond the avant-garde and began to infuse mass culture, its luminaries and would-not-be leaders began to conceive **cultural politics** as revolutionary in itself. The new struggle was largely but not exclusively generational, pitting the with-it youth against the over-30s and the straights, a term that, at the time, suggested a conventional lifestyle in addition to compulsory heterosexuality.

The alternative culture developed little coherent theory about the world and how to change it. Most characteristic, perhaps, was the belief that all that was necessary was youthful vitality and idealism—that "all you need is love." If the times were going to change, the new world of love and peace would be brought forth by members of the younger generation, who were making lifestyle choices that were different from their parents. The sense that the new generation was escaping from deadly, life-long worship of materialism and dull conformity is captured in the popular song written by Malvina Reynolds that ridicules a lifetime of living in houses that resemble "Little Boxes" all built from "ticky-tacky" and each identical to the others.[9] She applies the description to suburban neighbourhoods, to university programs, and to the conventional middle-class lifestyle of golf, martinis, children, and death.

The rebelliousness of the generation of Aquarians was fertilized by a romanticized view of Third World revolutionaries and was fuelled by a generation gap between youth and their parents—one of the oft-repeated slogans summing up the attitude of youth was that no one over 30 could be trusted. And this slogan was presented as an in-your-face rejection of the very values the older generation stood for: material success, the American Dream, my country right or wrong, "don't talk back."

Whatever form this rejection took, the critical consciousness spawned by a deep sense of youthful alienation was widespread in the era of the counterculture. Like everything else in the era, these critical interests were met in the cultural marketplace by literally hundreds of books with a general theme of social criticism. Socially critical nonfiction books were widely read, such as Paul Goodman's indictments of US education, *Growing Up Absurd* (1960) and *Compulsory Miseducation and The Community of Scholars* (1966). Self-proclaimed radical books were as omnipresent then as the myriad self-improvement books and the *Chicken Soup for the Soul* franchise that currently crowd the shelves. The long-term irrelevance of this outpouring of social angst may be exemplified by Charles Reich's utopian *The Greening of America* (1970), a particularly vacuous but bestselling example of countercultural pastiche.

Social psychologist Erich Fromm offered a psychoanalytic critique of the "insane" society he found in the United States. The author of several popular books, Fromm provided some of the intellectual backdrop for the counterculture, as did Joseph Heller 1955 novel of the absurd, *Catch-22*, set in Italy in 1944. Heller's protagonist is Yossarian, a bombardier in the Air Force. Yossarian spends his time devising schemes he hopes will get him grounded so he won't have to face death by flying another bombing mission. He tries to convince the psychiatrist he is crazy: "They're trying to kill me,"[10] he says. The ploy doesn't work. Any sane person would be trying to avoid combat. If Yossarian were truly crazy, he'd *want* to risk his life flying more missions. That's the Catch-22. Ultimately, as Heller suggests, wrongs do not simply exist in the individual's mind or in her or his perceptions, but in society. Psychiatry is simply part of the problem, not part of the solution. For the New Left, which was the avant-garde of radical politics, the obsolete political solutions to the problems of society that had been tried by the old, Marxist left were also part of the problem.

The New Left

Hud (Reading from an underground newspaper): "The draft is white people sending black people to make war on yellow people to defend the land they stole from the red people."[11]

— Gerome Ragni and James Rado, *Hair*, 1969

The New Left was more explicitly political than the counterculture. The New Left was a movement largely of young people who opposed and confronted dominant institutions and the authorities in charge of them, such as the government, the university, the military, and Wall Street. Almost everything that was wrong with America was encapsulated in the Vietnam War. Anti-war actions, including draft resistance, were at the heart of much New Left social activity and protest. But only direct action would do. All political theories and methods of the past were equally worthless. The emphasis was on the new, the belief that the old radicalism associated with Marxism was either dead or had become authoritarian and obsolete. The proletariat had either disappeared or had surrendered to the spectacle and surfeit of contemporary capitalism. If the working class had ever been a revolutionary vehicle, it was no longer. Like the workers at the Goodyear plant described by novelist Walter Mosley in *Bad Boy Brawly Brown*, they lived "simple, straight-ahead lives" and enjoyed the fruits of economic success: "mindless labor and enough of anything they wanted to buy."[12] In the ideology of the New Left, the working class had become a bastion of racism, of right-wing patriotism, and of anti-youth bigotry. Archie Bunker, an intolerant blue-collar character in the TV series *All in the Family*, wasn't a caricature; he was the working man next door.

The New Left originated in student protests in the United States that condemned universities as education factories and drew inspiration from black nationalism. The organization Students for a Democratic Society (SDS) was formed in the

United States in 1960 and became an early ideological centre of the New Left, which was generally a more local and amorphous than centralized movement. The New Left was galvanized by the escalating war in Vietnam but also fed off the pervasive sense of alienation among youth in modern society. In the theory of the times, the generation gap had replaced class conflict as the fundamental fault line in society. The New Left felt like a rebellion *sui generis*, although the movement found its antecedents in anarchism, in the earlier cultural rebellion of Dada and surrealism, and in the bohemian lifestyle. Abbie Hoffman (see Box 9.1), one of the most flamboyantly visible specimens of New Left radicalism in the United States, tried to unite the more political New Left with the lifestyle rebellion of the Hippie generation.

By 1968, the New Left rebellion was in full swing. In early 1968, the Columbia University section of SDS began a protest against Columbia's active engagement in CIA-funded war research. The demonstration escalated into an occupation of university buildings. Within a week, the police attacked. The students reacted nonviolently and 700 were arrested. The SDS believed that students could be radicalized by confrontation and repression.[13]

New Left activism spread to many university campuses, inspired in part by these protests and by the Berkeley Free Speech Movement. The Student Union for Peace Action (SUPA) was formed in Regina in 1964. The group began by following the community organization movement among the poor that was underway in the United States. SUPA engaged in grassroots-organizing among blacks in Nova Scotia, among Aboriginal peoples, and among the urban and rural poor. Roussopoulos calls it a Sisyphean battle. The effective constituency for the New Left was among students.[14]

The New Left in Canada
In Canada, in 1967, students at Simon Fraser University (SFU) in Burnaby, British Columbia,

formed the Students for a Democratic University (SDU). Similar movements arose at the University of Toronto, the University of Regina, McGill University, and on other campuses. Karl Wolff, a spokesperson from the German SDS, spoke on the University of Alberta campus. He differentiated the old from the New Left and called for grassroots organizing and democratization. Students protested the dominance of American teachers in Canadian universities and rejected the "stifling, patriarchal character of what is taught, the absence of genuine self-learning . . . [and] the divorce between knowledge and action."[15]

Students at SFU—Berkeley North, as it was known—engaged in teach-ins, demanded fair admissions policies for the disadvantaged, confronted university authorities, and went on strike. Students desegregated the faculty lounge by staging a student occupation. They demanded, moreover, that SFU become a people's university and be renamed Louis Riel, after the Manitoba Métis leader who was hanged in 1885 by the Canadian state.[16] Social science students and faculty members were at the heart of campus protests. The university had hired Tom Bottomore, a British Marxist scholar, as the head of the Political Science, Sociology and Anthropology (PSA) Department. In 1967, he resigned in protest over the dismissal of five teaching assistants. Under Bottomore, the department had hired a cohort of activist, young scholars and, as a result, drew in many radicalized students. The department became a hotbed of New Left politics as students tried to link with working class organizations. In 1968, students and sympathizers occupied the SFU administration building to back demands for a democratic admission policy. The RCMP moved in at 3:00 a.m. and arrested 114 people.[17]

In 1968, the PSA department voted to give students parity on departmental committees and in faculty tenure, renewal, and promotion processes. The university administration refused to recognize the decisions of the PSA parity committees

---

৻৩ BOX 9.1 • BIOGRAPHY ৩৸

Abbie Hoffman (1936–1989)

I am my own leader. I make my own rules. The revolution is where ever
my boots hit the ground.[18]
— Abbie Hoffman, *Revolution for the Hell of It*, 1968

Abbie Hoffman's ancestors were Russian immigrants who settled in Worcester, Massachusetts. As a small businessman, Hoffman's father was socially conservative, patriarchal in the household, and voted Republican. His family resisted anti-Semitism passively and quietly, learning to avoid hotels and resorts that were advertised as accepting only Christians.[19] Economically well-off but subject to social discrimination, Abbie Hoffman was attracted to the plight of the underdog. In 1954, he began hustling in pool halls and listening to black musicians who were playing what became known as rock 'n' roll.[20]

Hoffman attended the University of California, Berkeley, one of the most radicalized campuses in the country. He supported the "Freedom Summer" of 1964, helping Mississippi blacks register for the vote in the face of violent opposition.[21] Within a year he had dropped acid (LSD) and his wife had divorced him; in 1966, Hoffman moved to a cheap "pad" in the Lower East Side in New York.[22] He helped create a "free store" where secondhand goods could be donated and recycled. He led hippie activists, who brought free clothes and tried to hand them out to the customers of Macy's department store.[23] He began to refer to his tactics as "monkey theatre" as distinct from guerilla theatre.

In August 1967, Hoffman brought his monkey tactics to Wall Street. With their pockets crammed with dollar bills, demonstrators climbed to the balcony of the Stock Exchange

---

and blocked the appointment of Andre Gunder Frank as a visiting scholar. In the fall of 1969, the administration threatened several PSA faculty members with termination. In response, the PSA students went on strike with the support of many faculty members. The BC courts issued injunctions against picketing. Eight professors were suspended by the university, some of whom were eventually dismissed. In early November, after five weeks, the strike was ended by a vote of students and professors, who were not willing to face possible arrest and imprisonment. Significantly, there had been no groundswell of support from the labour movement for the New Left students.[24]

The New Left in China and Europe

In Germany, student protests spread to the entire nation following the 1967 police shooting of a student who had been demonstrating against the visit of the Shah of Iran.[25] The generation gap widened into a chasm as children asked their parents how they could justify what they had done during the Nazi era. While the German economy had been rebuilt after 1945, making Germany the most powerful centre of resurgent European capitalism, the old generation had adapted itself to a politics that seemed more authoritarian and elitist than democratic—soft fascism, in the view of the Frankfurt School.

and threw money over the railing.[26] Some of the brokers stopped their trading to snatch at the money as it landed on the floor or floated through the air. Seeing hippies throw away money while capitalists grabbed it was exactly the image Hoffman wanted to publicize.[27] Also in 1967, during an anti-war demonstration, Hoffman announced that protestors would encircle the Pentagon, ritually attempt to exorcise its evil demons, and levitate the building in the air. The "happening" was memorable as propaganda, Hoffman wrote, and no crazier than the Vietnam War itself.[28]

Hoffman and his companions gave the name *yippie* to the movement they hoped to inspire. The yippies advertised a Festival of Life that would attract the hippie and anti-war crowds to Chicago in August 1968, to coincide with the National Convention of the Democratic Party. They nominated a pig—named Pigasus—for president.[29] Hoffman asked, "What would happen if large numbers of people really do decide to fuck the system? What would happen if large numbers of people who lived in slums moved into abandoned buildings, if office workers walked out and began panhandling or applied for welfare? What if people who wanted to get educated just went to a college classroom and sat-in without paying and without caring about a degree? Well, you know what? We'd have ourselves one hell of a revolution, that's what."[30]

The 1968 demonstration in Chicago ended in a large police riot. Hoffman and other leaders (the Chicago Seven) were arrested and put on trial for conspiring to cause the disturbance. Hoffman turned the court into a mock theatre, ridiculing the judge and the system. He was eventually acquitted of the charges. Diagnosed as bipolar in 1980, Hoffman died of an overdose of alcohol and drugs in 1989. His death was ruled a suicide. The legend of Abbie Hoffman follows the aphorism attributed to Jimi Hendrix: "Once you're dead, you're made for life."

In Berlin, a succession of New Left groups emerged that advocated protesting, provoking authorities, and resisting violence. The self-styled "cultural revolutionaries" were loosely organized in groups such as Subversive Action and traced their roots to the surrealists.[31] One radical student commune in Berlin, described by Rob Burns, distributed leaflets inciting people to commit arson in department stores to give the German public "'an authentic Vietnam feeling.'"[32]

In both North America and Europe, youth rebellion was inspired by the Chinese Cultural Revolution and the Prague Spring in Czechoslovakia. In China, schools and universities closed and youth were set loose to rebel against traditional authority and expose corruption and resurgent capitalism. In Czechoslovakia, Alexander Dubček, the reformist leader of the ruling Communist Party, began to introduce liberal measures into the country's politics and economics. The attempt to create socialism with a "human face," however, was suppressed in August by an invasion of troops and tanks led by the Soviet Union. Dubček's short-lived regime was overthrown and the status quo ante restored.

The climax of the international New Left rebellion was reached in Paris in May 1968, when widespread, popular demonstrations threatened to topple the government and appeared to pres-age a triumph of the New Left. The revolt began in the universities as students went on strike against the university system, inspired by a generation of young professors and radicalized graduate students. The police violently suppressed the protests, which caused the movement to spread into a general student strike. In response to the use of force by authorities and to their own political and economic grievances, French workers joined the strike movement. Younger workers in the newer technical and professional occupations and government employees tended to be among the most radicalized. The new-found unity of workers and students on the streets of Paris suggested that France was undergoing another revolution.

But uncontrolled rebellion from below threatened not only the government, but the established leadership of the dominant trade unions and the Communist Party in France. These leaders were committed to collective bargaining and achieving political office through the electoral system. When the government finally responded to the massive protests by calling for new elections to the National Assembly, the more conservative forces believed the movement had achieved its objective. They withdrew their support for the street demonstrations and for other forms of economic and political direct action. The return of unionized workers to their jobs exposed the absence of organization and leadership among the students and other protesters, and the events of May ended more abruptly than they had begun. In the June elections, the ruling party in France was re-elected with an even stronger mandate. The mythology of Paris 1968 celebrates what had appeared possible during a brief moment of exhilaration and blames the sold-out leadership of the old left for the failure. The tactics of the Paris rebellion, however, continue to inspire similar movements in the present time, from anti-globalization protests to the Occupy movement.

Vietnam and the Denouement of the New Left

Opposition to the war in Vietnam was the glue holding together the New Left and giving it some popular support. The anti-war movement had emerged from pacifist circles and the ban-the-bomb campaign. Early in the movement, the loose anti-war coalition of left, pacifist, union, and student organizations lacked cohesion and had only symbolic leaders (including Benjamin Spock, the pediatrician and author). For the counterculture, "flower power" was the cultural alternative to napalm. There was no deep connection, however, between radical actions for a political goal, such as ending the war, and a counterculture in which alternative lifestyle choice was its own theory of revolution.[33]

Late in 1966, *The New York Times* published a series of articles on the Vietnam War that began to undermine the government's version. Television coverage focused on civilian deaths and on the destructiveness of napalm bombings and defoliation.[34] It was difficult to reconcile the destructive images of the war with the American projection of itself as defender of democratic values fighting for Vietnamese freedom. People began to connect the violence against American blacks during the civil rights movement with the war in Vietnam. In 1967, Martin Luther King, Jr., strengthened that link by condemning the war. When mass anti-war demonstrations spread nationally and internationally, the leftists, hippies, and peaceniks were joined by many thousands of average, white, middle-class protestors.[35]

The strength of the anti-Vietnam war movement was its ability to unify a diverse set of interests and groups. Soon after the last Americans flew out of Vietnam in helicopters, the New Left effectively collapsed as a popular movement. The movement spawned myriad social movements and theories, however, and its legacy continues to the present. While the New Left eschewed theory as unnecessary and harmful—or, rather, adopted the action-oriented theory of anarchism—radical sociologist Herbert Marcuse, who had turned 62 in 1960, became one of the most widely known theoretical spokespersons for the much younger generation he taught.

The Critical Theory of Herbert Marcuse

Herbert Marcuse (1898–1979) was born to an affluent and assimilated Jewish merchant family in Berlin. During World War I, he was drafted into the German army but did not see combat. He was assigned to a Berlin stable where, he said, his job was "wiping horses' asses." Radicalized by the war, Marcuse was elected to the Revolutionary Soldiers' Council in 1918, but his experience in the German Revolution suggested that workers were not ready for revolution.[36]

In common with many intellectuals of his generation, Marcuse was attracted to Marxism. Capitalism in the 1920s was a more exploitative system than it had been in Marx's day, but still the working class had not been revolutionized.[37] In common with Marxist Georg Lukács, Marcuse investigated the cultural and ideological barriers that prevented the development of revolutionary consciousness in modern capitalism. Unlike Lukács, however, Marcuse did not see a party built on Leninist principles as the solution to the politics of revolution. In 1927, Marcuse read *Being and Time* (1927) by Martin Heidegger, a philosophy text that built upon Edmund Husserl's **phenomenology**. It "changed Marcuse's life."[38]

Husserl's crucial idea is that human beings actively create the world in which they live. Marcuse connected this concept with Marx's theory that people actively transform the world through their labour. To develop his understanding further, in 1928 Marcuse became an assistant to Martin Heidegger, Husserl's successor at the University of Freiberg. Marcuse wrote a dissertation under Heidegger's guidance, intending to combine phenomenology with Marxism.[39] One of the problems with phenomenology was its radically individualist view—that we each alone construct our own world. Marcuse agreed that we construct our world in relation to the objects we encounter that have meaning for us, but not that we construct it alone. In terms of microsociology, according to Marcuse, we construct our view of the world through **intersubjectivity**, in relation to and interaction with other people. The result is that people come to share, more or less, important elements of commonality in their experienced worlds.

For Heidegger, this commonality is expressed, over time, by developing and sharing "national communities of meaning," which are "carriers of tradition." In Marcuse's interpretation, however, Heidegger's theory wrongly suggests a national consensus rather than seeing society as radically divided between antagonistic classes. Marcuse uses Heidegger's concept of authenticity and applies it to collective rather than only individual action. In this context, authenticity implies grasping and acting in terms of the potential future that is available, not just for an individual but for a class. Human development is based on transcending the present and realizing this potential future.[40]

In 1933, the Nazi Party came to power in Germany. Marcuse was shocked to learn that Heidegger had become a Nazi. Despite his politics, Heidegger warned Marcuse to flee Germany.[41] Marcuse accepted the advice: "Don't wait to be hunted to hide."[42] In exile in the United States, he joined the Institute of Social Research (Frankfurt School).[43] In 1941, Marcuse published *Reason and Revolution*, his interpretation of Hegel as the foundational philosophy of critical theory. Marcuse said that he intended to make a contribution to "a mental faculty which is in danger of being obliterated: the power of **negative**

thinking."[44] Positive thinking, in his view, means accepting uncritically the way things are. Understanding the contradictions that exist within the present, critiquing the given state of affairs, and revealing the potential to change reality for the better is negative (or dialectical) thinking. Negative thinking is the role that social theory plays in changing society.

Eros and Civilization

One of the projects Frankfurt School members had pursued was the integration of Marxist thought with Freud. Marcuse's interest in this project culminated in *Eros and Civilization: A Philosophical Inquiry into Freud* (1955). Marcuse begins with Freud's idea that, at the level of instincts, the unconscious mind is ruled by the **pleasure principle**, which strives for the full and painless gratification of desires and freedom from restraint.[45] In the real world, however, the individual encounters barriers that prevent the full realization of desires: you can't always get what you want, any time, any place. Desires are constrained by the **reality principle**. Not only is gratification limited by the problem of scarcity but, more importantly, immediate gratification is incompatible with civilization. For society to exist, people must learn to rein in their desires, to control them, to keep them within boundaries; that is, to repress them.[46] Instead of achieving happiness by gratifying instinctual needs, the pleasure principle is confined and regulated by the reality principle, reflected in the demands of work, of the patriarchal family, of monogamous marriage, and of the established social order.

Any civilization requires some regulation of the instincts of life and of destruction. Of all the life instincts, Freud had emphasized sexual energy—**libido**. But for Marcuse, the life instincts were at the root of not just genital sexuality and reproduction, but the whole edifice of creative social action and overall human happiness and

freedom. When the life instincts and desires are controlled, they are not simply repressed and left to build up, as in a pressure cooker; they are released and channelled into other creative activities. Culture is created as instinctual life energy is deflected from original desires into "socially useful activities and expressions." But, Marcuse argues, Western industrial society is in a paradoxical position. Given modern industry's tremendous productive capacity, Western society is technically capable of ending scarcity and of providing necessary and useful consumption goods for all. Modern technology could reduce the actual time required for labour (through automation, for example), expand leisure time, and provide everyone with opportunities to fulfill their individual humanity. A society that is rationally organized to reduce the need for toil to its smallest amount has the (still unrealized) *potential* to bring about a truly human and free existence.[47]

This potential, however, is not being realized. Cultural progress has come at a price: instead of gradually expanding human liberation, Western technology has deepened the denial of human freedom and increased the domination of people. Capitalist society imposes restraints on people that are in addition to the regulations required for civilization generally. Technological and scientific progress makes comfort and luxury cheaper and more widely available, but it also perpetuates "toil and destruction." As a result, a world free from toil and want is denied by the organization of that very society. In industrial society, the very means that could bring human liberation—human reason and the development of advanced technologies—actually take a perverted form in which they deepen and perfect domination and control. Modern institutions rationalize their structures by downsizing, contracting out, or converting permanent, full-time jobs into temporary, insecure, casual positions. And the new technologies of communication provide a potent means of surveillance to control social dissent. Marcuse uses the term "surplus repression" for the additional controls that arise because of the specific needs of domination in capitalism, such as deepening the exploitation of labour and protecting private property.[48]

As the social rebellion of the 1960s rose around him, Marcuse found himself the spokesperson of sexual liberation. But it was not a mantle he wore comfortably. For Marcuse there was more involved in the advance of human freedom than the "mere release of sexuality." He dismissed William Reich's theory of self-regulated sexuality, advanced in *The Sexual Revolution* (1930—see Box 9.2).[49] If the time and energy devoted to work was minimized, Marcuse thought, the life instincts would flow beyond sexual gratification into other channels of creativity and self-expression; as a result, repressive institutions, such as monogamous marriage and the patriarchal family, would disintegrate.[50]

Contrary to Reich, Marcuse does not agree that the free expression of hyper-sexuality is the route to freedom, health, and happiness. Marcuse imagined that the libido would be transformed in the future from its overemphasis in modern society on mere genital sex. Freeing the libido would allow the full development of individual needs and abilities. The life instincts transcend or go beyond simple sexuality, according to Marcuse, and seek deeper gratification in aesthetics, in the beauty of knowledge, and even in spirituality. Life is brought to higher forms of development.[51]

Marcuse was critical of the modern sexual revolution, moreover, because it remained within the limits of genital satisfaction. Advanced industrial civilization already had a greater degree of sexual freedom than at any time in previous history. In his view, the free exercise of sexuality is gratifying in the short run for the individual, but it also serves "as a prop for the status quo." Compared to the past, the heightened sexuality that is rampant in theatre, film, and the modern novel "is infinitely more realistic, daring, uninhibited,

as well as wild, obscene, and virile." Precisely for this reason, however, it is perfectly harmless to the status quo. Such a heightened sexuality is "part and parcel of the society in which it happens, but nowhere its negation." It induces "voluntary compliance . . . generates submission and weakens the rationality of protest."[52]

Once reason is freed from its current "perverted" form, said Marcuse, in which it perfects modes of domination, people will be able to reach a general agreement on which forms of repression are liberating and which forms are "surplus" repression that can be abolished. Reason and happiness will then converge, and the distinction between play and work will largely disappear with the end of alienated labour and the move to self-realization.[53]

One-Dimensional Societies

In 1954, at the age of 56, Marcuse accepted a position at Brandeis University in Massachusetts. He published *Soviet Marxism* (1958), in which he argued that, after a brief heroic period, Marxism in the Soviet Union had been transformed into its opposite: a closed ideology had become the instrument of mass indoctrination and domination. Under the control of "the various ruling bureaucracies," the Soviet economy assumed a highly rationalized and efficient form. The more economic planning was able to expand consumption, the more it tied the population to the existing system of domination. The US and the USSR were undergoing a convergence in which their similarities increasingly outweighed their differences. Both were dominated by self-perpetuating elites who ruled through technological and political domination.[54] Marcuse did not reject the concept of totalitarianism for the USSR; he applied it to both Soviet and American social systems in *One Dimensional Man* (1964), his principal contribution to social theory in the 1960s.

Modern industrial society has never been more prosperous and has never had as high a

⁂ BOX 9.2 • THEORY IN CONTEXT ⁂

Wilhelm Reich and the Sexual Revolution

Wilhelm Reich (1897–1957) was born in what is now the Ukraine. Orphaned by the time he was 17, Reich fought with the Austrian army in World War I and, afterwards, attended medical college in Vienna. His interest in sexuality as the dominant instinct drew him to the work of Freud. For Reich, sexual energy governs the structure of both human feelings and thinking: genital "[s]exuality . . . is the life energy *per se*." As a clinical psychiatrist, Reich believed that libido—sexual energy—naturally builds up in the body and seeks release through orgasm. If the release of sexual energy is inhibited, the fundamental life functions are disturbed and patients suffer symptoms of mental disorder.[55] The best way to cure psychic disturbance in general, according to Reich, is to release individuals from the cultural regulations that inhibit sexual release.[56] The revolution that society needs, says Reich, is "a radical change in conditions of sexual living."[57]

For Reich, the difference between progressive and reactionary thinking did not follow class lines. Political revolution had definitely been played out. In place of class, the social struggles of his time were between the forces seeking the free release of sexual energies and the interests that demanded controls and suppressed life. In 1928, Reich founded the Socialist Society for Sexual Advice and Study in Vienna, dedicated to establishing the "genital rights of children and young people"[58] and furthering the sexual revolution.

Reich believed that the core of happiness was sexual. His basic concept is "sex-economy," the production, distribution, and consumption of the sexual drive. Free sexuality will not only prevent people from developing psychic disorders, it is the force that will ultimately transform society. The suppression of sexuality among young people, Reich argues, is also the basic mechanism through which individual character structures are produced

potential for solving human problems. Paradoxically, the way society is organized perpetuates the worst features of social repression. Never has society dominated the individual so thoroughly: "A comfortable, smooth, reasonable, democratic unfreedom prevails in advanced industrial civilization."[59] Capital and labour, the two primordial antagonists of early industrial society, have reconciled. Labour has been integrated into the bowels of the capitalist system and has traded any claim to create a more just and humane society for apparent improvements in the standard of living. Most people accept this society as it is, but they actually experience false consciousness because society as it is does not represent their "real interest." Society is dominated by "false" needs that are "superimposed upon the individual by particular social interests." The satisfaction of these needs appears gratifying— when we open a bottle of Coca-Cola, for example, we are told we "open happiness." Marcuse calls this satisfaction "euphoria in unhappiness" because meeting these needs undermines people's ability to see society as diseased, as perpetuating "toil, aggressiveness, misery, and injustice."[60]

that support political, ideological, and economic domination. Over thousands of years, religion and morality have suppressed natural living and natural sexuality, resulting in fear of authority and submission to it, "of incredible humility on the one side and sadistic brutality on the other." Authoritarianism and sexual suppression go together, as do "revolutionary 'morality' and gratification of the sexual needs." Compulsive morality must wither away.[61]

Sexual liberation, Reich argued, is a genuine and deep revolution in cultural living that goes to the root of people's emotional, social, and economic existence. The patriarchal-authoritarian family is being replaced by "*the natural form of the family*." Reich condemned both compulsive monogamy and Don Juanism (male sexual libertarianism) in favour of a relatively long-term monogamous sexual relationship based on love and genital sexuality, but rooted in women's economic independence and the socialized care of children.[62]

On the one hand, Reich defends the idea of monogamy as long as a monogamous relationship is established on the basis of the sex-economic principle of sexual harmony, which arises from "experiencing again and again vivid sexual pleasure and gratification with the same sexual partner." Reich prefers a long-lasting sexual relationship to a temporary one, such as the one-night stand. Only in the former do the partners have a "tender interest" in each other and is there a "complete sensual adaptation between the partners," brought about by the "harmonization of their sexual rhythms." Such a relationship is the basis for the fullest expression of sexual gratification.[63]

On the other hand, for Reich, "long-lasting" could be a matter of weeks, not just months or years, and he says that it is not necessary that "the relationship must or should be monogamous." Over time, as monogamous sexuality becomes an old habit and a stale duty, as dull and routine as wearing the same clothes every day, Reich suggests temporary sexual infidelity or permanent separation. Relationships collapse when "a new companionship promises higher pleasure."[64] For Reich, the liberation of genital sexuality—"genital gratification"—is the key to undermining personal and social repression, and thereby solving individual and social problems.

Individuals must identify their "true needs," according to Marcuse, but this free determination can occur only when they are no longer indoctrinated and manipulated by the power of the establishment. As the techniques of repression are perfected, however, people become less and less able to "break their servitude and seize their own liberation." It is not merely the delivery of mass consumption goods that is the root of people's acquiescence; equally important is the curtailment of intelligence. The false needs that society satisfies include not only goods, but people's thoughts, feelings, and aspirations. In such a situation, Marcuse asks, "why should they wish to think, feel, and imagine for themselves?" The result in the United States is "a pattern of *one-dimensional thought and behavior*." Ideas and aspirations for alternative modes of life that go beyond the established world of thought and action are either precluded or reduced to insignificance. The language of politics becomes the language of advertising and persuasion.[65]

The one-dimensional society is a society of total administration in which exercising political rights (free speech, demonstrations, and protests) actually strengthens the existing administrative system because the lawful expression of dissent becomes an apparent testament to the existence of democratic liberties. The progressive movement turns into its opposite.[66] The system permits modes of protest that do not challenge the fundamental terms of the institutional order. Religious movements, Zen, existentialism, and the Beats are not fundamentally contradictory to the status quo.[67] Private and personal rebellion are substituted for a deeper, more collective political opposition that recognizes the horrors of the whole system, which are reflected in private experiences of suffering and frustration.[68] The movement for the liberation of women, for example, understood that the private and personal sufferings of housewives were rooted in the patriarchal subsoil of traditional marriage and family life.

Since most people in one-dimensional society are conditioned to be content, it is unclear how society can move toward liberation. The proletariat had been Marx's historical subject, the class with the potential to develop revolutionary self-consciousness and transform society. If the working class has "sold out" however, Marcuse wonders which group in society could play the role of the "new subject" of history. There is a chance, Marcuse thinks, that social change may come if intellectuals, who possess "the most advanced consciousness of humanity," merge with society's most exploited groups, those having the greatest need to end their intolerable conditions. Marcuse defines the latter as "the substratum of the outcasts and outsiders, the exploited and persecuted of other races and other colors, the unemployed and unemployable." Even if their consciousness is not revolutionary, he says, their everyday opposition can be revolutionary if they begin refusing to play the game. Their participation in a "Great Refusal" may well mark "the beginning of the end of a period."[69] Third-World revolutions marked, perhaps, the greatest refusal

of the time. Of all the non-Western revolutionaries, Che Guevara provided the New Left with the most inspiration.

In 1989, with the collapse of the USSR, the United States claimed to have finally won the Cold War. A few persistent irritants remained, however. One of them was Cuba, an island in the Caribbean on the doorstep of the United States and, since 1959, a member of the socialist bloc. From its earliest days, the Cuban Revolution has been synonymous with the iconic name, Che Guevara.

Che Guevara and the Cuban Revolution

Ernesto "Che" Guevara (1928–1967) is identified with the Cuban Revolution although he was Argentinian by birth. He was born in June 1928 in Rosario, a city about 300 kilometres upriver from Buenos Aires. As a medical student, Guevara dreamed of being a famous researcher who would discover something that would be valuable to humanity and, at the same time, "would be a personal triumph."[70] In 1952, he drove around South America, an expedition of discovery depicted in the 2004 film, *The Motorcycle Diaries*. The movie represents Guevara's early politicization as he saw first-hand the living conditions of the poor of Latin America. He came "into close contact with poverty, with hunger, with disease . . . [and] with the numbness" that results. He resolved to dedicate his life to help the dispossessed.[71] Guevara stayed for a time at a leper colony in Peru where the hospital staff lived on the opposite side of the river from the patients, a physical separation that symbolized the social division between haves and have-nots.

In 1954, Guevara lived in Guatemala during the short-lived radical government of Jacobo Árbenz. He read Marxism and met exiled Cuban revolutionaries. When Árbenz's elected government was overthrown by a CIA-backed coup,

Guevara escaped to Mexico, where he joined a group of Cuban rebels. They gave him his famous "Che" nickname.[72] Guevara identified with the Cuban exiles, with whom, he said, he was tied "by a liking for romantic adventure and the thought that it would be well worth dying on a foreign beach for such a pure ideal."[73]

At first, the rebels were blindly confident that their return to Cuba would ignite "a rapid popular explosion" that would quickly bring down Cuban dictator Fulgencio Batista.[74] For the revolutionaries, "the people are like dry wood. . . . These sparks will start a fire."[75] Eighty-two revolutionaries, led by Fidel Castro, embarked from Mexico in December 1956 in a small cabin cruiser called the *Granma*, intending to incite the popular insurrection. The voyage to Cuba took seven days. The raw recruits had little food, suffered severe seasickness, and lost most of their supplies. After landing, the ragtag band of rebels was exhausted and ill, and their condition worsened as they trudged through coastal swampland. An exhausted Guevara had to decide whether to carry the remaining medical supplies or a box of ammunition: he chose the ammunition. Betrayed by their guide, the rebels were ambushed by the Cuban army. Guevara was shot in the chest and neck. At first he thought the wounds were fatal. The survivors made it into the shelter of the woods, but their force was almost destroyed. Three days after their landing the rebel force was reduced to 15 fighters.[76]

Nevertheless, what appeared at the time to be in inauspicious start to a revolution triumphed in two years. Abandoning the ill-conceived theory of a "spontaneous outburst throughout the island," the rebels recognized that the struggle would be long "and that it would need to have a large peasant participation." The rebels were originally from the cities; they had been neither workers nor peasants. They were uncomfortable among the rural people and, in turn, the peasants were at first unwilling to trust them. Having guerillas in

their territory made the peasants fear "barbarous reprisals from the government."[77]

Beginning with just a handful of serviceable weapons, the rebels followed the tactics of guerilla warfare and began to achieve small victories. Their respectful treatment of local villagers demonstrated that the guerillas were not just another military force out to take whatever they could get. Anti-government sentiment was widespread in Cuba and recruits rallied to the rebel cause. Support from the peasants was a necessary element in their success.[78] In the mountains the guerillas established the first liberated territory under control of their rebel army. The guerillas dispensed justice, established new civil and penal laws, collected taxes, and distributed food supplies.[79]

Guerilla Warfare

Guevara said that the revolution began "even without knowing theory." In the case of the Cuban Revolution, practice preceded and created theory, as the rebel leaders summed up their revolutionary experiences.[80] Guevara encapsulated the lessons of the revolutionary war in his book, *Guerilla Warfare* (1961). He challenged the view that it was "necessary to wait until all the conditions for revolution exist." On the contrary, even in the face of apparently disadvantageous conditions, it is the task of revolutionaries to work to create and accelerate these conditions.[81] First, revolutionaries must exhaust the possibilities of peaceful political reform and demonstrate to the people that change is impossible within the framework of ordinary politics. People will come into the streets and demonstrate peacefully, but their lawful demonstrations will be suppressed. Peace, according to Guevera, is broken first by the agents of authority. Provoked by this official violence, resistance crystallizes among the people. The arena of armed struggle in Cuba was the countryside. Urban guerillas in the city would be forced underground and faced enormous dangers. In the open countryside, the rebels and the people they protect can be "beyond the reach of the repressive forces."[82]

Rebels resort to guerilla warfare when they have popular support but are outgunned by a technically superior armed force. During the early, heroic period of the Cuban Revolution, guerilla fighters had been "their own generals" in that each was dedicated individually to the revolutionary cause.[83] But, as mentioned, guerilla warfare requires popular support, not just the heroic fighting of a handful of rebels who are "isolated from the popular masses." Through the struggle, the guerillas' revolutionary spirit is molded by close contact with the people and their everyday "instinctive wisdom."[84] Guevara stressed that guerilla warfare "is a mass struggle, it is the struggle of the people." The guerilla fighters are the armed vanguard of the people and "their great strength is rooted in the mass of the population." They become agrarian revolutionaries assisting the peasants to become owners of the land they work.[85]

Guerilla fighters carry out the struggle in rugged areas that are sparsely populated. Fundamental to guerilla warfare is that no battle or skirmish is fought unless it can be won. Otherwise, conflict with a superior force is avoided. Guerillas must rely on secretiveness, surprise, hit-and-run tactics that avoid direct confrontation, and even treachery. Such warfare differs "from the romantic and sporting conceptions with which we are taught to believe that war is fought." Guerilla warfare is, however, only a phase in the struggle; alone, it is not enough to accomplish victory. Through its success, the guerilla army grows into a large, more regular force. Then the battle is carried directly to the enemy.[86]

Rural guerilla tactics in the eastern highlands marked the beginning of the Cuban movement. Besieged by 10,000 armed troops with air support, the rebel army nevertheless held its mountain base.[87] And, as the rebel force grew in strength, numbers, and weapons, guerilla tactics gave way to a war of position. The rebels brought the offensive out of the mountains and, in 1958, began to sweep westward across the island. Guevara, now a commander, led decisive victories over Batista's army. Facing defeats on the battlefield and uprisings in the cities, Batista fled to Miami. In January 1959, Guevara, Castro, and their rebel comrades entered Havana, the capital city, and received an enthusiastic welcome.[88]

From Warfare to Bureaucracy

The Cuban Revolution, Guevara said, was "the hope of the unredeemed Americas," the vanguard of the world proletariat. The fate of the popular movements in Latin America would be shaped by Cuba's example. Once the rebels had seized power, the hard work began of transforming national liberation into socialist construction. Thousands of qualified technicians and professionals had abandoned revolutionary Cuba for exile in Miami. The new Cuban government was faced immediately with the need to fill government and economic posts with competent but revolutionary leaders (cadres). Guevara said that, at first, these posts "were filled simply by 'pointing a finger.'"[89] In this fashion, the revolutionary government assigned Guevara, a medical doctor, to several important posts, including president of the National Bank and head of the Ministry of Industry.[90] Guevara undertook his new revolutionary tasks with the same spirit of hard work, self-sacrifice, and concern for people's power that had led to victory in the guerilla campaign.

Thrust into leadership roles on all social, economic, and political fronts, the rebels-turned-administrators made many mistakes.[91] At first, the inexperienced administrators applied to management the lessons they had learned through guerilla warfare. Each guerilla fighter may have been his or her own general, but this approach to industry and government created chaos. The individualistic spirit was not lacking in zeal, but each "administrative guerilla" interpreted rules and decrees differently. As a result, there was constant friction between different enterprises as each operated in the absence of central organization. The failures of what Guevara termed "Guerillaism" required greater organization and discipline.

Economically, the principal difficulty Cuba faced, common to Latin America overall, was its almost complete reliance on a **monocrop**. Cubans were "slaves to sugarcane, the umbilical cord that binds us to the large northern market." The first task, then, was to diversify agriculture. The Cuban government embarked on an audacious agrarian reform, dividing the land held by the great land-owners into smaller, peasant-operated farms.[92]

In 1959 Guevara had said that the revolution was intended to support all classes, including small business owners, professionals, and Cuban industrialists.[93] Quickly, however, under the threat of direct American intervention and the ambiguous support of the Soviet Union, the Cuban Revolution became increasingly socialist. In the theory of neo-colonialism, national sovereignty is a fiction in the absence of economic independence: "If a country does not have its own economy, if it is penetrated by foreign capital, then it cannot be free from the tutelage of the country" on which it depends. Economic independence, Guevara claimed, required nationalizing the property of US monopolies. As American and, later, Cuban-owned industries were nationalized by the Cuban state, the US government responded with economic sanctions that culminated in a full economic blockade of the island. In 2015, US president Barack Obama took the first step to ending the American isolation of Cuba, foreshadowing economic and political changes on the island.

After the US-led blockade was imposed on Cuba, the Cuban economy and the fate of its revolution came increasingly within the Soviet sphere of influence. Indeed, the mainstay of the Cuban economy until 1989 was favourable trade relations with the USSR, exchanging sugar for oil.[94]

The administrative problems inherited by the Cuban government and the growing influence of the Soviet economic and political model on Cuba led to the centralization of both the economy and the political system. By 1965, Cuba was officially a one-party state led by a Communist Party. Cuba also copied models of rational planning from the existing socialist countries. Guevara supported these changes in principle. He concluded in 1963, however, that change had gone too far and had generated an overly centralized and bureaucratic structure that limited initiatives from below.[95]

The evil of **bureaucratism** had several causes. Even well-motivated cadres lacked the organizational skills to implement a rational plan. So many meetings were held trying to solve problems, Guevara said, that the Cadres succumbed to "meetingitis" and resorted to issuing directives and orders rather than consulting with the people affected. Central control should be balanced by initiatives from below, but the top-down style of organization had become one-way: leadership "simply sends directives to the ranks all the time and doesn't listen to anything they have to say."[96] Too much top-down authority had replaced too much local discretion.

In December 1964, Guevara came to New York to address the United Nations. Using blunt language, he condemned American imperialism and the Vietnam War. He then embarked on an extensive visit to Africa following in the footsteps of Frantz Fanon. In April 1965, Guevara resigned his government and military posts in Cuba to carry on active anti-imperialist struggles with liberation movements. After a few months of active engagement with liberation fighters in the Congo, in November 1966, Guevara led a small force to Bolivia to begin guerilla warfare against the military dictatorship. He had said in 1960 that "there are certain minimum requirements that make feasible the establishment and consolidation of the first [guerilla] center." Guevara underestimated both the minimum requirements for successful guerilla war and the new American-trained counter-revolutionary troops in Bolivia. He was seriously wounded in battle on October 8, 1967, and captured by the Bolivian army. Che Guevara was executed the following day. He was 39 years old.[97] In 1960, he had said this:

> I realized one fundamental thing: to be a revolutionary . . . there must first be a revolution. The isolated effort, the individual effort, the purity of ideals, the desire to sacrifice an entire lifetime to the noblest of ideals goes for naught if that effort is alone, solitary, in some corner of Latin America, fighting against hostile governments and social conditions that do not permit progress. A revolution needs what we have in Cuba: an entire people mobilized, who have learned the use of arms and the practice of combative unity.[98]

The rebels in Cuba had transformed revolutionary potential into a successful popular movement, but the Cuban-led insurrection in Bolivia was unable to establish a base for guerilla operations. Guevara's dream of creating "another Vietnam" in Bolivia was crushed before it could strike deep roots among the people.

The New Human Being

There is nothing that educates an honorable man more than living within a revolution.[99]

— Che Guevara, "Speech to Medical Students and Health Workers," 1960

Overthrowing an authoritarian ruler, such as during the Arab Spring that began in 2010, results in a great sense of euphoria that can be very short-lived. Change at the top is not a social revolution as the return to military rule in Egypt demonstrates. Deeply rooted revolutions, on the other hand, even if they eventually fail, can for long periods maintain that exceptional feeling of hope and expectation. Guevara's decision to leave Cuba in 1965 may have reflected his disappointment with aspects of the political and economic transition in Cuba. Guevara had made three diplomatic trips to the USSR and was impressed by many of the material advances that state planning had accomplished over 40 years, but he was critical of the absence of socialist consciousness among the people and its leaders. The overemphasis on economic growth had squandered the potential within the new Soviet system of production to develop a new society and to mould new generations of socialist-minded citizens.[100]

Through his practice and his writing, Guevara emphasized the active side of human history, the role of consciousness and practical activity. Marx's revolutionary theory stressed the importance of *transforming*, not just *interpreting* the world. Through conscious activity, people cease being the slave and the instrument of their environment and become architects of their own destiny.[101] Putting these ideas into practice is the difficult part. Just as the Cuban Revolution had not followed a pre-existing theory, there was also no established theory of the transition period from capitalism to socialism: "We are still in diapers,"[102] Guevara lamented.

Given the endemic problem of mal-development in Third World countries and the flight of capital away from a revolution, it is almost impossible to transition to socialism without deep sacrifices.[103] As a leader of the new economy, Guevara faced the dilemma of motivating people to work productively. How much attention should be paid to **material incentives**, such as monetary bonuses, unequal pay, and other tangible benefits to increase work productivity? How much effort could be induced by moral incentives that appealed to people's revolutionary spirit?

Guevara acknowledged the need for material incentives, but he believed these selfish motivations would diminish as socialism developed and that they would disappear under communism. They were a "necessary evil" during the period of transition but should not be "the main lever" of people's motivation to work. Under capitalism, material incentives dominate. While they continue to exist during the construction of socialism, they damage solidarity among the people. Such incentives reinforce old forms of competitive consciousness, individualism, and self-gratification through expanding consumption: "[M]aterial incentives and consciousness are contradictory terms." They were inimical to the new socialist consciousness and morality that had already emerged in Cuba despite the poorly developed economic conditions.[104] Popular enthusiasm and solidarity had carried the revolution through the early, difficult years; Guevara's aim was to find the means to "perpetuate this heroic attitude in daily life."[105]

When he had joined the Cuban revolutionaries in Mexico prior to the voyage of the *Granma*, Guevara realized "that a new type of human being should be created." The task of making a new type of person is the work of the whole social collectivity. The answer is not to have each individual merge into a shapeless, uniform mass but to have each person redirect her and his creative, individual capacities from self-aggrandizement toward accomplishing social goals for "the absolute benefit of the community." Socialist consciousness replaces concern for a good income with the pride of service and the rewards of gratitude from the people. The key to progress, according to Guevara, is to make "the individual feel more complete, with much more internal richness and much more responsibility." But "individualism . . . as the isolated action of a person alone . . . must disappear in Cuba."[106]

Changing people's manner of thinking is a matter of accepting the need for profound internal change through "a conscious process of self-education" while simultaneously acting to bring about external, social change.[107] The daily

battlefield for these internal and external changes is the workplace, where individuals contribute to the common life and fulfill a social duty. Work develops socialist consciousness when it is seen as a moral necessity and is applied with creativity and enthusiasm in the difficult struggle to build socialism.[108] In Cuba, the "opportunities for self expression and making oneself felt in the social organism are inherently greater," Guevara said, than in the formal democracy of capitalist countries.[109]

Above all, it is the responsibility of leaders to model socialist consciousness. Leaders must go among the people in a spirit of solidarity, "with an investigative zeal and with a humble spirit." Their purpose is not to showcase their own talents but to learn from the wisdom of the people.[110] Leaders are expected to give all to the revolution "from which one expects no material reward." In turn, they must be satisfied with the material standards of the common person. Their "magnificent and agonizing" task requires conscious self-sacrifice that is forged in daily actions for the betterment of the community.[111]

Guevara vested his hope for the construction of the new socialist human being in the next generation. Formal education was designed to be both practical and moral, intended to inculcate in young people the ethics of service to the country and willingness to sacrifice immediate benefits for social improvement. Youth, Guevara said, are "the malleable clay" from which that new person can be built. Schooling was integrated with work in the expectation that Cuban children would learn that labour is dignified and necessary. The message Guevara hoped to imprint on Cubans, young and old, was that, although the "present is a time of struggle," the future was theirs.[112] The difficulty was to prevent the message from becoming threadbare as the benefits of the revolution materialized slowly and the sacrifices were not shared equally.

Guevara had promised to "be faithful up to the final consequences" of his acts.[113] After his death in 1967, the Cuban government fashioned Che Guevara into an iconic model of the new socialist person he had envisaged. His relative youth and the circumstances of his martyrdom solidified his aura. Guevara lives on as a model revolutionary and also as an ironic symbol, as his image has been transmogrified into a cultural object of Western mass consumption. His image on T-shirts and tourist trinkets reflects youthful rebelliousness but not the revolutionary consciousness he had hoped to inspire.

Feminism, Equal Rights, and Radicalism

Five lonely women. . . . The phrase they all used: "there must be something wrong with me." . . . This country's full of women going mad all by themselves.[114]

— Doris Lessing, *The Golden Notebook*, 1962

In advanced capitalism, the "Great Refusal" that Marcuse sought came from oppressed minority groups and from women who were at the centre of the system of social reproduction. British novelist Doris Lessing's comment, above, about lonely women echoed Betty Friedan's assertion that women were filled with self-doubt and guilt "because they were not happy." They were lonely, not in spite of having husbands and children but because of them.[115] By the 1920s, **first-wave feminism** had been successful in many Western countries at winning political rights for women. More women were being educated and finding paid employment and professional work. But Friedan's judgment that for any woman born after 1920, "feminism was dead,"[116] seemed reasonably accurate. Shulamith Firestone described the period between the age of the suffragettes and the rise of the new women's movement in the 1960s as "the fifty-year ridicule."[117] Although women such as Virginia Woolf, Margaret Mead, and Jane Addams carried the feminist torch, sometimes

self-consciously, there was no widespread women's movement.

The major twentieth century socialist revolutions had brought substantial improvements for women and the early optimism about the liberation of women spread well beyond the boundaries of these new states. In the West, however, radicalism in its various forms influenced women's consciousness in a more negative way. New Left organizations of many kinds had emerged in the 1960s, to struggle against the bureaucratization of society and the Vietnam War and in favour of black emancipation and anti-colonial revolution. Membership included men and women, but women were increasingly alienated within and from these organizations. There was no greater contrast than between the rhetoric of the New Left and black power male leadership and their continuation of male chauvinism and misogyny. Stokely Carmichael, for example, was widely condemned for defining the position of women in his movement as "prone." As radical women became alienated in these struggles, they theorized that patriarchy was a deeper oppression than capitalism.

From the ashes of the New Left and the counterculture arose a second wave of feminism. Like the first wave, the new feminists defined many objectives, from achieving equality in the workplace to ending violence against women. Unlike first-wave feminism, however, this movement did not coalesce around a single over-riding objective. Instead, the ideal of sisterhood was sometimes overshadowed by significant divisions within the movement, as liberals, radicals, and socialists worked out common and different positions within and among themselves.

Kate Millett (b. 1934)

Insofar as Marxism was taken seriously by this second generation of feminists, these women also suggested that Engels, Marx's collaborator, had made important observations about the necessity for economic independence before women could be equal. In capitalism, however, women found they were consigned to second-class status even in the economic sphere. Furthermore, the Marxist assumption that there could be no liberation of women without socialism had been refuted by the continuation of patriarchy in the Soviet Union. Certainly, more women were employed in the USSR, but they had only limited representation in politics and upper management, and men and women did not share domestic burdens including child care. The conclusion was that the root of women's oppression was not primarily in the economic sphere.[118]

For Kate Millett, writing in *Sexual Politics* (1969), the source of women's oppression—in fact, the root of all forms of oppression—is the existence of patriarchy, a system through which men exercise incomparable power over women. Patriarchy pre-dated capitalism; it was perpetuated by capitalism; it characterized male-dominated struggles against capitalism; and it persisted in post-revolutionary socialist societies. The ideology of patriarchy undergirded the system of values and norms that women had taken for granted. These values were expressed in literature, in the division of labour at work, and in sexual relationships. Marxists had overemphasized the importance of the role women played in production; they had neglected the equally (or more) important role women played in *reproduction*, particularly in child-bearing and child-rearing. Male domination, however, is not rooted in nature or biology, as postulated by Freud.[119] Patriarchy is essentially a matter of the social power of men over women; it has a sociological, not a biological, foundation. This power is recreated, generation after generation, through the socialization practices of the patriarchal family.[120] Women are, first and foremost, psychologically dominated.

The root of women's oppression is in the psyche, in consciousness, and in the habits of mind of both men and women. The oppression of women is much deeper than mere exclusion from formal politics (the limited aims of the early suffragette movement), or even the exclusion of women from the economic sphere, although these are important. It is based, according to Millett, in women's femaleness, in their sexuality. And because men have dominated women sexually, women's liberation must extend to sexual politics, to the liberation of women's sexuality. It must challenge the socialization practices of the patriarchal family and liberate women's psyche, with its deep roots in the past.

Identifying patriarchy as the foundation of women's oppression was a central characteristic in the theory of **radical feminism**. Millett's analysis that the source of the problem is in ideology, in ideas and consciousness, suggests that the solution is to be sought in "liberating" consciousness. One of the practical consequences of Millett's feminism was the development of the "consciousness raising" movement. Women met together, exchanged stories of their experiences of oppression ("speaking bitterness," as the Chinese put it), and came to recognize that their own private hell of "sleeping with the enemy" was widely shared by their sisters. They labelled these experiences patriarchal domination, and they began to take steps to liberate themselves practically from their oppressors. In the politics of consciousness-raising, first comes liberation of the mind; then actions follow. Juliet Mitchell adds that structural changes in society must also be made. Most of these changes, such as equal rights, daycare centres, free contraception, equal parenting, and sexual liberation, could, at least theoretically, be achieved within capitalist society.[121]

Shulamith Firestone (1945–2012)

Shulamith Firestone had a more radical vision of the future of feminism. Firestone was born in Ottawa to a Jewish family and raised in the United

States. Her mother had fled Germany to escape the Holocaust. Her father was a travelling salesman from Brooklyn who fought with the US Army in World War II and witnessed the liberation of the Bergen-Belsen concentration camp. He had converted to Orthodox Judaism in his teens and raised his children in his faith. Theirs was a thoroughly traditional, patriarchal household in which women were expected to know their place, and men ruled. Violating religious rules would lead to being banished from and disowned by the family. Firestone fought bitterly with her dominating father. In 1967, she fled to New York to get away from a physically abusive boyfriend. She co-founded the feminist group New York Radical Women. Firestone defined herself as an intellectual and, conscious of this status, she refused to perform menial labour. The women's movement which she helped shape was primarily middle class and white in its membership and sentiments. For decades, Firestone contended with schizophrenia. When she died in August 2012, she was alone and living on social assistance.[122]

Firestone poured her invectives into a book, *The Dialectic of Sex: The Case for Feminist Revolution* (1970). Radical feminism, Firestone asserts, is the descendant of a long-standing tendency toward militant action in the women's movement, going back to the pioneering work of Susan B. Anthony, Elizabeth Cady Stanton, and the Women's Party. Feminist issues are central to any revolutionary analysis, and fundamental to radical feminism is the claim that the essential form of oppression is sex, an antagonistic relationship Firestone defines as **sex class**. Sex replaces the Marxist category of economic-class in the determination of the principal contradiction, or fault line, in society. The time has come, Firestone claims, to reject the assumptions of biological determination of gender roles and "develop a materialist view of history based on sex itself."[123]

Similar to Millett, Firestone asserts that the reality that lies beneath economics is psychosexual.

Understanding reality requires an analysis of history, but not economic history (as with Marx); rather, Firestone claims, understanding reality requires an analysis of the materialist history of sex. She recognizes a fundamental dualism in the human species, the division into male and female, that is biological in origin: "Men and women were created different, and not equally privileged."[124] While difference does not inevitably mean that one sex necessarily dominates the other, the origins of male power did result from a biological fact: before the advent of effective birth control, women were at the mercy of their biology. They could not control their own reproduction and they became, historically, dependent on males "for physical survival." As well, biologically, human children are dependent for long periods of time and this biological need conditioned the "basic mother-child interdependency." These biological facts, and the spontaneous social organization to which they gave rise, determined the first division of labour, which was between men and women, "as well as furnishing the paradigm of caste (discrimination based on biological characteristics)." For Firestone, then, the economic class system has "its origin in the sexual class system."[125]

Firestone based her psychosexual theory on Freud, but an adulterated Freud, reinterpreted in terms of political power. Sexual repression in childhood, according to Firestone, "is the basic mechanism by which character structures supporting political, ideological, and economic serfdom are produced." Since the structure of sexuality is co-existent with the structure of the family, Firestone concluded, to liberate sexuality requires the abolition of the family as we know it.[126]

Biological facts determined the first oppressive "class" relationship between the sexes. The gendered division of labour then created a fundamental cultural division between technology, which is the male form of culture, and aesthetics, the female mode. Modern technology, however, has evolved to the point where sex-class duality and inequality is no longer necessary. The symbol and reality of the coming liberation of women was found in "the pill," which represented freedom from domination by biology. Firestone correctly anticipated a future technology of artificial insemination and test-tube babies, but she also imagined artificial wombs. Pregnancy, Firestone asserted, was "*barbaric . . . the temporary deformation of the body of the individual for the sake of the species.*" Artificial reproduction, on the other hand, is not inherently dehumanizing, and, according to Firestone, only when it was available as an option would it be possible to honestly evaluate motherhood, around which so much of the ideology of sex distinction revolves. It was nature that needed to be interrogated. The first order of business, for Firestone, was to free women from the tyranny of biological reproduction.[127] For her, giving birth was like "shitting a pumpkin."[128] The feminist revolution Firestone hoped to inspire would integrate "the Male (Technological Mode) with the Female (Aesthetic Mode), to create an androgynous culture surpassing the highs of either cultural stream."[129]

For Firestone, the "elimination of sexual classes requires the revolt of the underclass (women) and the seizure of control of *reproduction*: not only the full restoration to women of ownership of their own bodies, but also their (temporary) seizure of control of human fertility." Women and children must achieve "*full self-determination, including economic independence*" and be fully integrated into all aspects of the larger society. One of the preconditions of this economic and social revolution was the widespread adoption of the technology of cybernetics, through which increasingly complex machines take over routine work functions. In a world where machines worked and people did not, the class system would be destroyed. Machines would become "the perfect equalizer, obliterating the class system based on exploitation of labor."[130]

Furthermore, just as the goal of the socialist revolution was a "classless society," similarly "the

end goal of feminist revolution must be . . . not just the elimination of male *privilege* but of the sex *distinction* itself." By eliminating the sex distinction, Firestone did not imagine a physical change in anatomy as much as a social change: "genital differences between human beings would no longer matter culturally." The feminist revolution would establish the "*freedom of all women and children to do whatever they wish to do sexually.*" After the revolution, sexuality would become "polymorphous," fully liberated human sexuality, in which genital and orgasmic pleasure would be only one part of a total relationship that was both physical and emotional. In fact, relations between children and other children, as well as adults and children, "would include as much genital sex as the child was capable of—probably considerably more than we now believe."[131]

Without uprooting the biological family, Firestone believed, "the tapeworm of exploitation will never be annihilated." When technology had advanced to the point where artificial reproduction was a realistic choice, children would become the responsibility of a small group of people who were not necessarily or even primarily related biologically. Child-rearing would be diffused to "the society as a whole" and women and children would both be fully integrated into the larger society. Children would have full legal, sexual, and economic rights. In short, "the tyranny of the biological family would be broken" and with it "the psychology of power." Firestone declared that either this feminist revolution would occur over the next century, or society would fall into the abyss, "the creation of a hell on earth, followed by oblivion."[132] Firestone's apocalyptic revolutionary rhetoric complements her singular analysis of sex-class and feminist revolution. Radical feminists differed in their analysis of the relative importance of patriarchy and of capitalism in the oppression of women. Dorothy E. Smith argued that it was necessary to understand the intersection of both kinds of subjugation in the daily, lived experience of women.

Dorothy E. Smith (b. 1926)

In the many letters we had written in those years neither of us knew much more than the bare terms of each other's life, nothing of the daily stuff that is the real truth, the importance.[133]

— Lillian Hellman, *Pentimento: A Book of Portraits,* 1973

For sociologist Dorothy E. Smith (see Box 9.3), the stuff of women's daily life was the place to begin developing a sociology for women. Women's sociology meant abandoning the intellectual and cultural world of male-dominated sociology, which reflected men's point of view, and starting instead from the direct, everyday experience of women in their actual lives.[134] A feminist position is distinctive, Smith says, because it actively opposes women's oppression and recognizes sisterhood; that is, feminists identify as women. Sisterhood relocates a woman's space and reorients her understanding of oppression: "It becomes clearer whose side you are on." Oppression is not simply external; it is part of women's interpersonal lives and their sexuality. Women should understand their oppression not just in personal terms but "located in a political and economic process."[135]

◦◦ BOX 9.3 • BIOGRAPHY ◦◦

Dorothy E. Smith (b. 1926)

Dorothy E. Smith was born to a working-class family in England in 1926. She studied in the United States and built an academic career in Canada. Smith found employment after grade school as a secretary in the publishing industry. At the age of 26, she realized that, as a woman, she had no future with the company and would never move "upstairs" with the men. She studied sociology at the London School of Economics and went to graduate school at the University of California, Berkeley, where she gave birth to two children and wrote a dissertation. She was drawn to **ethnomethodology**; her sociology would be addressed first to the world of the everyday, especially the everyday world of women. She developed an approach that investigates the organization of "a lived world in which we are active and in which we find and make ourselves as subjects."[136]

Soon divorced and a single mother, Smith taught at the university in a non-tenured position, almost the only woman in a department of 44 people. She experienced the discrimination faced by academic women, which played a considerable role in igniting the fires of second-wave feminism.[137] Smith lived what she would later describe as a double life with a "bifurcated consciousness." As an academic, she entered a predominantly male world, structured around ideas and concepts that represented that world as genderless. In fact, it was structured by a male subtext through which men took for granted the ordinary, everyday reality of gender inequality in the university. Smith, however, also lived and worked in a second world. When she went home, she crossed a gender divide in which

Relations of Ruling

Smith intended to develop a new way of thinking sociologically. The work of women was as instrumental as the work of men in the construction of society, but women had been systematically excluded from the production of forms of thought. Only men's experiences counted as knowledge. Women had difficulty asserting their own authority and finding their own voices in a discourse and culture in which they were silenced and excluded. They were deprived of the most important means to create general theories that explained their own experiences and helped them understand their own situation and interests.[138]

People learn to think about their world through a structured set of social practices, ideas, and everyday explanations, which shape how they understand their lives. As the women's movement critiqued the institutions that alienated women, from sexism in advertising to phallic-centred psychiatry, it revealed that the structure of social controls emerge from **the relations of ruling**, an apparatus that is dominated by upper-class men. Power is organized and exercised through this apparatus, including in government, in businesses, and in the professions. Ruling is not conscious manipulation; rather, it arises from the common perspectives,

she returned to "a local and particular world" as a busy, single mother, the telling of which "is a potentially endless detailing of particulars."[139]

Encountering the women's movement caused a profound transformation in Smith's consciousness and life, and she became an activist in the movement. Feminism taught her that the troubles women experienced as personal were, in fact, "aspects of an objective organization of society." One of the effects of becoming a feminist, Smith says, is you "become very angry and . . . become angry with men."[140] For Smith, feminism also meant discovering "sisterhood." Women, she wrote, were "my people . . . the people I stand with . . . the people whose part I take."[141] For Smith, sociology was never armchair but always value-driven, involved, and action-oriented.

Smith accepted a regular position in sociology at the University of British Columbia and began teaching one of the first women's studies courses in Canada. She re-read Marx and sought to incorporate Marxist analysis and methods into her feminist sociology. For Smith, Marxism offered a way of understanding the world by connecting the everyday— the immediately observable and known—with the social and economic relations that go beyond people's direct knowledge of the everyday.[142] As Smith and most feminists discovered, however, men avowedly on the left were just as anti-feminist as "the 'upstairs' people." Unlike the US and Canada, she said, Marxists in Britain were more open to feminism and more closely connected to the working class. Marxists had done little to understand women' oppression and did not recognize that it had a distinct basis in patriarchy.[143]

Smith left British Columbia in 1977 to teach at the Ontario Institute for Studies in Education (OISE). There, she developed a distinctive, women's centred (and later "people-centred") approach to sociology that influenced many graduate students, who took Smith's methodology and ideology into the women's movement and into academia.

interests, and experiences that develop among men who occupy superior positions in social organizations. Women, Smith says, "have learned to set aside as irrelevant, to deny, or to obliterate our own subjectivity and experience. We have learned to live inside a discourse" and general culture "that is not ours."[144]

In these male-dominated relations of ruling, gender is socially constructed. Patriarchal rule is expressed not just in sexual relations but in all hierarchical social institutions and structures of power. Furthermore, the relations of ruling shape the thinking of marginalized and oppressed groups within the society, such as women and working-class men. The result, for women, is an absence of ideas and concepts to describe their own experience and to formulate self-knowledge. Thinking is dominated by the authority of the expert, inevitably organized in a male-dominated tradition of thought, such as psychiatry or sociology. Women discovered a fundamental rupture between their lived experiences and the ideological modes that interpreted these experiences. Smith says that women, as a result, had to develop their own expressions, concepts, and methods of analysis.[145]

Women's Standpoint

The aim of an alternative sociology would be to explore and unfold the relations beyond our direct experience that shape and determine it.

— Dorothy E. Smith, *The Conceptual Practices of Power: A Feminist Sociology of Knowledge*, 1990

In mainstream sociology, women's voices have been marginalized by "a discourse that we did not have a part in making, that was not 'ours' as women." Thinking about sociology from women's standpoint calls into question not just the conceptual apparatus that organizes thinking, but the way sociology is practised as a supposedly objective science. Established sociology excludes

"the presence and experience of particular subjectivities," especially women's. The basic error in sociology, for Smith, is that it operates within the traditional scientific framework according to the principles of "[a]nonymity, impersonality, detachment, impartiality, and objectivity," which structure the relationship between knowers and known.[146] Women, therefore, become objects of study. In fact, however, the knower (the sociologist) is "a member of a definite social category occupying definite positions in the society." Sociology understands society and social relations, therefore, from the subjective standpoint of men who rule.[147] Typically, (mostly male) sociologists begin their research by looking at society and people's lives from the outside, ignoring the local places in which they actually live.

The major forms of mainstream sociological theorizing have in common the assumption that people act in a rational manner and exercise individual control over their conditions of life. Women's experience of the world, in contrast, cannot be understood according to these assumptions because they don't conform to women's experience. In response, Smith intends "an alternative to standard sociology" that adopts women's standpoint. The place to begin a sociology of women is with a language that expresses women's experiences[148] and with a method of working that begins "from where women in general are, doing the type of work with which we are a sex identified." Smith understands that women are skilled and knowledgeable social actors in their everyday worlds, but she rejects the idea that they are autonomous agents. Rather, the organization of women's daily experience, their work routines, and the structure of their lives through time have been powerfully shaped by processes that are external to, and beyond, their everyday world. Hence, a sociology of women would not be **voluntaristic** or based on the idea of agency. Women learn to subordinate the self and focus on others, not to act "in terms of a project of their own."[149]

Smith argues that the forms of consciousness that develop from a position of dominance are different from the types of consciousness that arise among those whose work produces the actual conditions that enable ruling to proceed, day to day. Domestic labour fulfills the concrete, practical, and "routine aspects of bodily maintenance," which are the everyday, material means necessary for working in the managerial and professional circles that constitute the positions of ruling. Men are largely liberated from this domestic work and, for them, it is largely invisible and taken for granted. Women's consciousness, on the other hand, begins precisely in this material and local world.[150]

The method of understanding society from the point of view of the ruling apparatus must be turned on its head, and the everyday world must become "the locus of a sociological problematic." Sociology has to be built from the inside out and from the bottom up. Smith distinguishes between the knower (the sociologist) and the known (the person or group that is the "object" of study). But the sociologist is a member of the same society she or he is studying, and the people who are studied have their own knowledge and subjectivity. The object of **standpoint sociology** must begin with the knowledge people have of their "directly experienced everyday world."[151]

This approach is employed in microsociology. Erving Goffman, for example, investigates the everyday world as a self-contained phenomenon, with its own rules and features. Beginning with an actual social situation, microsociology develops a conceptual apparatus that discovers the social organization that is unrecognized and implicit in the world of the everyday. Smith's method, she says, relies "entirely on what women tell us." Each woman's story is equally valid and each opens to view a different understanding of the world, "as women who have not yet spoken now speak. Each speaker from a new site discloses a new problematic of inquiry." As posited in **microsociology**,

people actively create and recreate their world in common through intersubjectivity.[152]

It is essential to validate women's experiences and their discourse about them. For Smith, though, this approach is incomplete because it confines the inquiry "to the concepts of the everyday world." An alternative sociological account must "go beyond the reporting of experience to the development of a knowledge of the social relations within which we work and struggle as subjects." These social relations, however, are not immediately observable from within the everyday world. While a sociology for women would preserve subjects as both knowers and actors, Smith argues that subjects are located in particular historical settings that are neither obvious nor transparent. Their everyday world is embedded in a socially organized context that may not be directly known.[153] But the two worlds increasingly interpenetrate. The forms of social organization, ideologies, and other social forces are not simply outside the everyday; rather, "the local and directly known world is extensively and increasingly penetrated" by larger forces of the ruling social organization. It is the work of the social scientist to disclose the social organization that is implied or presupposed in the everyday.[154] Smith argues that sociology must see the world as "problematic"; that is, sociology must come to understand the complex relationships involved in studying people who are knowledgeable actors in a world in which they are embedded and which they continually re-make in their everyday activities.

When Smith argues that everyday understanding has to be "transferred . . . to the level of sociological discourse," she does not imply that women are dupes; rather she asserts the following:

Within our everyday worlds, we are expert practitioners of the quiddity, of the way they are just the way they are. Our everyday worlds are in part our own accomplishments. . . . But how they are knitted into the extended social relations of a contemporary capitalist economy and society is not discoverable within them.[155]

Sociology, then, must connect the micro with the macro in a methodology Smith terms "institutional ethnography." This methodology is a complex research activity that has to be seen as open-ended, that discloses and connects a variety of different viewpoints and relationships, and attempts to reveal or explicate "how these relational processes work."[156]

The institutional ethnography is a difficult balance. The sociologist must give up the privilege of substituting her or his understanding of the world "for those whose stories instruct us in their experience of lived actualities." The point is not to collapse differences into one overall version but to establish the matrix of these differences.[157] At any time, the ideas we advance about the world and how it works must be assessed in terms of the world that is actually happening and that can be observed.

At the same time, the sociologist is "a member of the same world she explores, active in the same relations as those for whom she writes." The sociologist who is active in research enters and, in part, structures the very social situation she or he is studying, helping to shape the experiences within it.[158] Consequently, sociology must become self-critically **reflexive**. The sociologist and the subject are "cosubjects in a world we make—and destroy—together." The point of sociology is not to not to extract knowledge from the subjects to benefit the researcher, but to further the knowledge of the people involved: "we want to know more so that she can also."[159] Smith's activist research method was consciously *interested*, not disinterested. She practised a kind of "action research" that addressed the issues raised by the women with whom she worked. She integrated her "subjects" into all aspects of the research process and produced results that were shared by the participants and were aimed at addressing the issue that sparked the research. Smith's method is applicable to research generally, and, in her own terms, Smith now advances a type of sociology for "people" rather than specifically only for women.

Conclusion

The principal irony of the white countercultures and the New Left was that both sprouted among the more privileged youth: among the white middle-class who had attended university. It is easy to exaggerate the extent of the rebelliousness of these privileged youth. Most university students accepted their parents' world and sought only the paper keys to enter it. For every long-haired radical with a peace symbol around his or her neck, there were many commerce students with string ties. And if these ties soon became paisley, their shirts coloured, and their hair grew past their ears, it was only fashion and the Friday-night thrill of looking a little different. Popular novelist Peter Benchley recognized that most privileged white youth weren't Aquarians. The teens who lay "serried in tight, symmetrical rows" on the beach of Amity, the fictionalized Cape Cod holiday resort in his novel *Jaws*, were secure even from the economic upheavals that worried their parents. Nothing touched them, he wrote, not race riots, water pollution, police corruption, the rise in murders, "or revelations that hot dogs contained insect filth" and chemicals that were linked to brain damage.[160]

It was also common in the 1960s to substitute the struggle for cultural freedom for political change or, at least, to assume that mass participation in a culture of rejection would itself constitute this social change. The 1970s appeared to deal with serious political issues that demanded more organization, more theory, and more commitment than New Left anarchism could provide. As a result, many former New Leftists became active in the green and feminist movements, as well as in the anti-globalization politics that define current social protests. The 1970s, however, were in many respects another "pink decade." Anti-colonial struggles and the spread of versions of socialism inspired new socialist movements. In the West, new versions of Marxism took root, although the offshoots of the 1960s were most long-lasting in the universities, where **neo-Marxist** theories allowed young intellectuals simultaneously to feel both successful and progressive. Neo-Marxism in the 1970s was marked by an emphasis on the analysis of structure rather than on consciousness. The next chapter, Chapter 10, reviews structuralist theory and introduces post-structuralist responses.

Questions for Reflection

1. Are the goals and strategies of the New Left still relevant for today's movements of social change?
2. Are Herbert Marcuse's theories still useful for analyzing the world, or are they obsolete in the post–Cold War era?
3. People continue to wear Che Guevara T-shirts. Does Guevara still speak meaningfully to people today?
4. Are liberal, radical, and/or socialist versions of feminism still important in the twenty-first century, or are we in a post-feminist age in which feminist struggle is no longer necessary?

CHAPTER 10

Structuralism, Microsociology, and Foucault

---◆---

The student-worker rebellion in Paris in May 1968 and the Woodstock music festival of 1969 marked the end rather than the triumphant beginning of an age. At the time, the denouement of the counterculture and the New Left was not immediately obvious. Globally, the rise of socialism appeared to coincide with the decline of the American Empire. The United States withdrew from the Vietnam War in 1973; revolutionary movements took power in Zimbabwe, Angola, and Mozambique; in Central and South America, guerilla forces opened fronts in Nicaragua, El Salvador, and Colombia. Che Guevara's dream of many Vietnams seemed to have been realized.

In the West, New Left radicalism grew beyond its student roots. Women's liberation mushroomed into an international movement for equal rights and, some claimed, feminist revolution.

Racialized divisions in the United States continued to generate sporadic violence. Aboriginal groups took up arms against the state in defence of land claims and self-government. The gay community in New York resisted police oppression with counter-violence in the Stonewall Riot of 1969, a date that symbolizes the beginning of an activist phase of LGBTQ (lesbian, gay, bisexual, transgender, queer) liberation. The number and variety of social movements at the time suggested a deepening of radicalization. It appeared that single-issue political groups could be united into a comprehensive social movement for change.

In the 1950s, radicals in New York had joked that you could fit all of the Marxist economists into a taxi cab. By the 1970s, they would need a jumbo jet. As inflation eroded workers' actual pay and undermined the living style of the new middle class, strikes increased in number and intensity, particularly among newly unionized government employees. Marxism became a serious although not dominant academic study in Western universities in such disciplines as sociology, political science, social and labour history, cultural studies, and radical political economy. The idea of revolution was being intellectualized in relatively comfortable careers. Left-wing journals and newspapers were mass-produced, and conferences were organized to debate themes in Marxist scholarship. Bookstores stocked and sold popular versions of books offering a radical analysis of the hot-button issues of the day to an expanding literate and socially conscious middle-class market. Hollywood produced some serious, critical, and realistic dramas about current social problems, such as the Vietnam War (*Coming Home* [1978]), nuclear power (*The China Syndrome* [1979]), and political scandals (*All the President's Men* [1976]). Politics and culture reflected a critical turn.

Under the surface of cultural radicalism, however, the cracks in the welfare state and social democracy were becoming increasingly visible in continuing inflation, relatively high unemployment, and government indebtedness. In the wider society, people gradually abandoned the dream of a peaceful, anti-materialist counterculture in the 1970s. Those who had once been caught up in the New Left tried to introduce leftist politics to existing social democratic parties or, in the United States, joined the liberal wing of the Democratic Party. Hippies drifted back to straight society and conventional jobs; socially conscious folk and rock music faded into disco; communes were abandoned or followed a routine devolution into petty production and small retail. Some alternative individuals and groups survived on the margins of corporate culture as icons of nonconformity and difference in new-age religions, non-traditional medicine, progressive education, and early environmentalism.

The crises in late capitalism culminated in a wholesale economic, political, and social change in the West with the rise of neo-liberalism, discussed in Chapter 11. Some of the contours of debate in social thought during this period can be understood by examining the differences between a structural and an interactionist orientation to social thought. Interaction (or action) theories, which were initially rooted in American social psychology, focus attention on people's ability to interpret, make choices, and decide on actions. Interactionism in the 1950s and 1960s was a reaction against the then dominant school of structural and functional thought in social science. Structural analysis eschewed consideration of individual interpretations and consciousness, and emphasized the importance of the existing social order into which people are born and which shapes their thinking and actions. The dominant figure in structuralism in France was anthropologist Claude Lévi-Strauss.

Claude Lévi-Strauss and Structuralism

To say that a society functions is a truism; but to say that everything in a society functions is an absurdity.[1]

— Claude Lévi-Strauss, *Structural Anthropology*, 1958

Born in Belgium, Claude Lévi-Strauss (1908–2009) was brought up in France and studied philosophy at the Sorbonne. As a student, he was drawn to socialist politics, psychoanalysis, and the writings of Marx. His life was decisively changed when he accepted a post at the University of São Paulo in Brazil. From 1935 to 1938, Lévi-Strauss undertook anthropological fieldwork in the interior of Brazil. He sought to uncover the underlying but unconscious principles that channel marriage patterns and kinship relationships along structured lines.[2] He had begun to develop the structural approach to the social sciences that would be one of the two poles between which much so-cial thought would oscillate in the second half of the twentieth century.

Lévi-Strauss, who came from a Jewish back-ground, joined the French army in 1939. Follow-ing France's defeat by the German army, he was removed from his academic position after the new pro-Nazi French government enacted anti-Semitic laws. He migrated to the United States in 1941 and taught at the New School of Social Research in New York. In 1959, Lévi-Strauss was appointed to the social anthropology chair at the prestigious Collège de France. In *La Pensée Sauvage* (*The Thought of Primitive Peoples*), Lévi-Strauss argues that the social thinking of so-called primitive peoples, which is full of myths, stories, spirituality, and magic, is no less sophisticated than modern systems of thought.[3]

In France, the dominant philosophy in the post-war era was the version of existentialism es-poused by Jean-Paul Sartre. For Lévi-Strauss, Sar-tre gave too much credit to the individual as the subject of her or his own destiny. On the contrary, from the point of view of structural anthropology, it was necessary to abandon concern with peo-ple's subjectivity—their ability to think, interpret, choose, and act. Instead, attention should focus on pre-existing social structures, which pattern people's thoughts and actions. In addition to structure, analysis necessarily included a culture's history. Without historical study, it was impossi-ble to *evaluate* a society's elements and functions.[4] Lévi-Strauss was well aware that not everything in a society functions well.

Structural theorists argue that underlying the explicit social rules that people consciously know and follow are hidden structures that pattern and organize people's thoughts and actions. People in society are not generally aware of this implicit structural arrangement and do not consciously understand it.[5] The idea of an implicit, underlying structure parallels the psychoanalytical notion of an unconscious mind. To apply this notion to social

structure, Lévi-Strauss required a methodology that would parallel psychoanalysis. He found this model in the theories of communication and language.[6] Speakers are generally able to speak their native language correctly even though they are unable to articulate the actual rules of grammar and syntax they are using properly.[7] This idea was formulated by Ferdinand de Saussure (1857–1913), one of the founders of modern linguistics. His systematic study of language signs is at the root of twentieth-century structuralism (see Box 10.1).

Structural analysis involves a two-stage pro-cess. The first is the observational level, at which point, Lévi-Strauss says, the details of concrete reality are described carefully without using any theoretical preconceptions. Drawing from a pleth-ora of concrete examples from a wide range of cultural mythologies, Lévi-Strauss sought to detect any pattern found in different cultures and mythol-ogies that employed a binary opposition. A culture typically favours one of the binary alternatives (for example, dark or light, good or bad, male or female, raw or cooked) over the other. Binaries may be interrelated. In the mythologies of many tribal so-cieties, for example, heavenly bodies are commonly sex-typed, such as moon (female) and sun (male).[8]

The second stage of analysis entails the search for structures that underlie these concrete reali-ties. A society's mythologies, customs, and norms exist in a complex, interdependent set of systems, and any single system can only be understood in relation to others in that society. Each system in-fluences its neighbour as the whole society evolves and changes. Social relations are played according to certain rules, which may be analogous to the rules of a game. In this sense, Lévi-Strauss says, individuals and groups engage in "normal" social relationships by trying to maximize their own advantage at the expense of others. Structuralism studies *rules* and the play (or social action) that "is being patterned after these rules."[9]

The methodology by which Lévi-Strauss moves from real details to structural models is

❖ BOX 10.1 • THEORY IN CONTEXT ❖

Ferdinand de Saussure and Semiotics

Semiotics is the study of the meanings of signs and symbols. A green light, for example, is commonly a symbol for "go" and a red light is a symbol for "stop." We can easily imagine the traffic chaos that resulted when, in the 1960s, revolutionaries in China decided to switch these meanings because the colour red was associated with revolution. Verbal signs (words and their meanings) are far more important and complex than street lights, however, and linguistics, the systematic study of language, is the most complex branch of semiotics. Saussure believed that language should be studied as a system of existing rules that people follow in everyday use.[10]

For Saussure, a word such as *pig*, is a linguistic *sign* that coveys meaning in several ways. Linguistic signs unite two, inseparable mental components: (1) a mental concept that is signified and (2) a sound-image, which is the signifier of the concept. The concept "pig" (signifier) is associated with a particular image or picture (signified) in our mind. Both elements are inseparably associated in the sign.[11]

A fundamental characteristic of language is that signs, in almost every case, are arbitrary. *Pig* (English), *cochon* (French), or *schwein* (German) are illogical sounds (signifiers) that have no natural connection with the object being signified.[12] Furthermore, the sound-images that are formed in peoples' minds upon hearing a sound are not always identical. When an American says "pig," this signifier may elicit a mental image of a specific kind of snouted domestic animal—or it may not. Is a pig someone who overeats? A male chauvinist? A police officer? Or just someone who, like the *Peanuts* character Pigpen, is permanently untidy?

The most important contradiction in language, Saussure argues, is between change and permanency. On the one hand, language is bound by timeless tradition. It is immutable or unchangeable for the linguistic community that uses it. If we want to communicate within a single community, we have to use existing, meaningful signs (words, gestures, and so on). Society, he asserts, is naturally inert, making it a basic force for conservatism. The underlying set of linguistic habits and rules of grammar and syntax, which is necessary for mutual understanding, constitutes language or **langue**, in Sassure's terms.[13]

While successful communication demands that language remain unchanged, the contradiction inherent in language is that it is mutable. Language both stays the same and changes constantly over time, a process Saussure terms a "radical duality." He uses the term **parole** to indicate an individual act of speech that unfolds over time. Constant evolutionary changes are made in the relationship between signifier and signified. This *parole* continually modifies the language as it is practised through individual usage.[14] The most obvious change comes from adding new vocabulary. Recently, the *Oxford English Dictionary* listed *selfie* as a new word because of its widespread use.

somewhat vague. In his view a single structural scheme undrrlies what appears to be a chaotic set of rules and customs.[15] By analyzing the empirical descriptions of living reality, structural anthropologists seek to isolate these stable elements, classify them and then compare them to each other. Social structure is an abstract model formulated by the analyst to make the empirical facts understandable.[16] By singling out some but not all aspects of each case, utilizing what Lévi-Strauss

calls "a kind of straining process . . . the faint outline of a structure does begin to appear."[17]

Unlike classical Marxism, economic factors are not the sole base of a social structure; rather, society is composed of an entire network of different types of orders: kinship systems, social organization, and social stratification provide different ways of ordering individuals that operate within the total model.[18] For Lévi-Strauss, the basic forms of social organization that structure the

---

♣ BOX 10.2 • THEORY IN CONTEXT ♣

Campbell, the Hero's Journey, and Star Wars

George Lucas claims that Campbell's monomyth helped him shape the plot of the 1977 movie *Star Wars*, a medieval-inspired western set in space. According to Campbell, the journey of the hero in world mythology follows a general pattern that resembles a rite of passage: separation from the world, initiation into a source of power, and a triumphant return.[19] Campbell identifies 11 stages in the hero's journey. Cultural studies have frequently pointed out that *Star Wars* follows these stages although, in some cases, the storyline has to be shoe-horned into the formula, or the analysis must encompass other films in the *Star Wars* trilogy. Rather than revealing an unconscious, underlying structure, the monomyth in the film is a consciously employed trope.

The journey begins with a call to adventure, initiated by a chance meeting between the hero-to-be and a herald-figure. In *Star Wars*, Luke Skywalker purchases R2-D2, who reveals the existence of an unanticipated world and brings the call to adventure involving an important historical purpose. The hero is drawn "into a relationship with forces that are not rightly understood."[20] At first, the hero-to-be refuses to follow the call. Luke says that his uncle needs him to work on the moisture farm. When his aunt and uncle are killed by Empire Stormtroopers and the farm is destroyed, there is no going back. The hero sets forth to the threshold of adventure. At this point, the hero-in-the-making receives supernatural aid, encountering a protective figure, often an old man and teacher, who represents the hero's destiny and provides some amulets to protect against the powers that the hero is about to face.[21] Obi-Wan Kenobi becomes Luke's ageless guardian, mentor, and father-substitute. He provides Luke with a light sabre and introduces him to the mysterious "force," the "protective power [that] is always and ever present within the sanctuary of the heart and even immanent within." The hero also acquires other helpers in the adventure.[22]

The hero then crosses the first threshold, "going beyond the hero's present sphere" toward darkness, danger, and the unknown. The hero and his elderly mentor meet and overcome

unconscious minds of all people are fundamentally the same for ancient and primitive, as well as modern and civilized societies. The ultimate object of anthropology is to identify the basic structures that are universal; that is, ones that are common to and found in all societies.[23]

Structural analysis has been employed to understand modern mythologies in popular culture that are structured around a set of stereotyped storylines and conventional narratives or tropes. Joseph Campbell (1904–1907) argues in *The Hero with a Thousand Faces* (1949) that almost every hero myth in any culture follows a similar structure: beneath its variety of appearance or costumes, myths are the same everywhere. He used the term "monomyth" to define the constant, underlying story of the myth of the hero that survives into the modern era, the characteristics of which are essentially the same.[24] The idea of the hero's journey influenced the storyline of the original *Star Wars* film (see Box 10.2).

the threshold guardians in the "desert place outside the normal traffic of the village," which is peopled "with deceitful and dangerous presences." The hero encounters violent threats but also dangerous delights.[25] In a shady and dangerous bar in the frontier town of Mos Eisley, a wretched hive of villains and scum, Luke and Kenobi negotiate their flight from the planet Tatooine with the smuggler Han Solo, and escape the dangers of the guardian Stormtroopers.

The hero is then swallowed into the unknown "belly of the whale . . . and would appear to have died."[26] A tractor beam drags Luke and Solo into the Death Star and, ultimately, they find themselves in the garbage compactor of the spaceship, where they are threatened by a dangerous, though often unseen, presence. Luke is dragged underwater. At this point in the film, he has already begun the stage of initiation, moving through "a fluid, mysterious landscape . . . where he must survive a succession of trials." Initiation teaches the young hero the techniques and duties of his vocation, and radically readjusts his emotional relationships. The hero is aided by the amulets and the supernatural helper he had met before entering the sphere of danger (the light sabre, the force, and Kenobi). The hero has to be purified but also humbled, and achieves moments of enlightenment.[27] The hero faces temptations (toward the dark side of the force) that potentially deter him from the trail laid out by destiny.

While he is in the belly of the Death Star, the hero meets with the goddess (Princess Leia). She "is the paragon of all paragons of beauty, the reply to all desire, the bliss-bestowing goal of every hero's earthly and unearthly quest. She is mother, sister, mistress, bride, ... the incarnation off the promise of perfection."[28] The hero then faces the ultimate trial (the attack on the Death Star), during which he requires assistance and receives rescue from without.[29] Han Solo joins the battle just in time to save Luke from being shot down by Darth Vadar. Luke's precise volley destroys the Death Star and defeats the forces of evil, finally bringing the blessing of freedom back to the world.

Lucas's *Star Wars* condenses the final stages in Campbell's monomyth, which involve the hero's miraculous passage back across the threshold and his return to the world. Not until *Star Wars Episode VI: Return of the Jedi* does Luke go through the stage of atonement, where he removes Darth Vader's helmet, "beholds the face of the father," and the two are atoned. The hero is now competent to become an initiator, guide, and mentor—in Luke's case, a future Jedi.[30]

Lévi-Strauss is aware that it is essential to avoid applying categories of thought that come from the anthropologist's own culture.[31] But, he argues, a group's understanding of its own culture is also not to be trusted. All social groups construct inaccurate models to interpret or justify their customs and mythologies. For Lévi-Strauss, only social scientists are capable of constructing *scientifically valid* structural models. The natives' conception of their own social structure is different from what Lévi-Strauss calls the real structure of their society.[32] The social group does not try to *explain* a phenomenon, generally and abstractly; rather, the group justifies the existence of norms and does not question them. The culture generates merely a surface understanding that becomes a screen to hide and perpetuate the existing customs or norms. Nevertheless, understanding these homegrown explanations, even if they are inaccurate, is likely to provide insight into the underlying structure.[33] The structuralist interpretation itself, however, may reflect a Eurocentric conception of the world in which social phenomena are interpreted as emanating from deep, unconscious forces that reflect the operation of a single and universal human mind.

Structuralism as a theory of social causation became a dominant theory among Marxist academics in the 1970s. A decade-long debate ensued over basic Marxist concepts, such as state power; modes of production; changes in the class structure of capitalism; the place of race, gender, and ethnic divisions in the social formation; and so on. Louis Althusser argued that Marx had a structural theory of social change. He analyzed the social formation as a whole, including its economic base, to make sense of the Marxist theory that the system of production determined other aspects of the society, such as the form that the political or religious systems would take.

Louis Althusser (1918–1990)

Louis Althusser was born in Algeria and was drafted into the French army in 1939 at the start of hostilities. Captured by the Germans shortly afterwards, he was interned in a prisoner-of-war camp until 1945. During his incarceration, Althusser began to experience symptoms of psychological disorder. Subsequently, he suffered periodic bouts of deep depression and spent time in psychiatric institutions. After his release from the concentration camp, Althusser became a Marxist and joined the French Communist Party. He is best known for his structuralist interpretation of Marx, formulated in essays published in *For Marx* (1965) and *Reading Capital* (1968).[34]

In 1969 Althusser published an influential essay entitled "Ideology and Ideological State Apparatuses." Marxists think of the state as a machine that functions to protect and maintain the power and wealth of the dominant class. The armed forces, police, courts, and prisons are all, in Althusser's terms, elements of the **repressive state apparatus** that function to maintain the status quo in society.[35] Antonio Gramsci had argued that the power and interests of the dominant class are also strengthened by ideological hegemony exercised through such institutions as religion, education, law, politics, and the mass media. For Althusser, these institutions constitute the **ideological state apparatus**. Ideological institutions are multiple, volatile, and relatively autonomous from ruling class control. Consequently, they become sites of resistance for exploited classes.[36]

For Althusser, the various apparatuses—"the State, the dominant ideology, religion, politically organized movements, and so on"—generally reinforce hegemony and contribute to the temporary solidity of the structure as a whole. In Althusser's terms, the structure is **overdetermined** in the direction of social stability. At other times, the conflicts and contradictions that exist in every part of the structure may reinforce each other and deepen social conflict. In Althusser's terms, this situation produces overdetermination in the direction of a rupture, putting society in a *potentially* revolutionary situation.[37] Finally, social contradictions may explode and cause a restructuring of the whole society on a qualitatively new basis (social revolution).

The "ever pre-given complex structure" of a society is independent of the individual wills of the people who live within it. For Althusser, people occupy positions in the structure of society; they perform the functions and act out the roles assigned them by their respective locations. Whether the individual capitalist is a reforming Robert Owen or a selfish Ebenezer Scrooge does not matter; what matters is that, in the given conjuncture (time and place), the capitalist is compelled by the logic of her or his position to take certain actions: lay off workers; close a factory; bring in new technology; or move production to a poor, Third-World country. For Althusser, the true subjects are not concrete individuals but, rather, the structures that define their functions and positions.[38] (Althusser's student Michel Foucault later theorized the "death" of the Western idea of the individual, autonomous, rational subject.) Althusser chose not to analyze the subjective side of Marx's dialectical theory. People are not the makers of their social structure. His omission of the role of consciousness and theoretically guided practice among individuals and collectivities is the most glaring omission in his social theory.[39]

In 1981, a French court ruled that Althusser had been in a psychotic state the previous year when he had strangled and killed his wife, Hélène Rytmann. Althusser was not prosecuted. He claimed to have no conscious recollection of the event. He was not the active, choosing, and responsible subject of a murder. Rytmann's death resulted from the deeply disordered structure of

his unconscious mind of which he was the unwitting agent. The homicide added dramatic notoriety to Althusser's already controversial image as a structural theorist. He died in 1990 in a mental hospital in Paris.[40] Structural Marxism became a significant force in Western social theory in the 1960s and 1970s, displacing structural functionalism from the centre of the stage. At the same time, microsociology emerged as an alternative to both forms of structural theory.

Microsociology: Goffman, Interactionism, and Garfinkel

The microsociological approach has its roots in the Chicago School. It focuses attention on individuals and small groups, and on the way social order is negotiated through the interactions of the people who construct this order. While Althusser had been taking structuralism to new theoretical heights in France, in the United States Erving Goffman, who was working out of an interactionist historical tradition, brought social analysis down to the more minute aspects of social life.

Erving Goffman (1922–1982)

Little wonder I looked upon my life and the lives of others as a kind of theatrical impromptu, self-knowledge as a matter of improvisation, and moral injunctions . . . whether high-minded or wicked, as so many stage directions.[41]

— John Barth, *Giles Goat-Boy*, 1966

Erving Goffman was born in 1922 in Mannville, Alberta, and raised near Winnipeg in a traditional, Jewish Ukrainian small business family. His father was a shopkeeper while his mother did not work outside the household. The parents had immigrated to Canada around the turn of the twentieth century. Erving Goffman had one sibling, a sister, who became an actress. As a student, Erving Goffman was drawn to the natural sciences and studied chemistry at the University of Manitoba. In 1943, Goffman left Manitoba and moved to Ottawa, where he worked with the National Film Board of Canada, which sparked a life-long interest in the social world. He enrolled at the University of Toronto in sociology and anthropology and then left in 1945 for Chicago to undertake graduate studies.[42]

Under the influence of the Chicago School of social psychology, the University of Chicago was a premier research institution in the social sciences. Fine and Manning claim that in graduate school Goffman's tendency for sarcasm earned him the nickname "the dagger." Over the next four years, Goffman became disenchanted with quantitative research and was drawn, instead, to social psychology and the work of Everett Hughes and the tradition of ethnographic research. After completing a master's program in 1949, Goffman lived in the Shetland Islands off the northeast coast of Scotland. For the next year-and-a-half he studied daily life in a static, rural community. Posing as a student of agriculture, he began collecting ethnographic observations of daily life and interpersonal interactions, winning the trust of the islanders who, in the early post-war years, first suspected that he might be a spy. From living virtually at the margins, Goffman moved to Paris, the centre of cosmopolitan Europe. He wrote a dissertation focusing on the face-to-face interactions of the villagers he had studied. He married Angelica Choate in 1952, joining an upper class, American family.

In 1955, relocated to Washington, DC, Goffman began observations in another closed community, the Saint Elizabeth's psychiatric institution, which led to the publication of *Asylums* (1961) based on his observations in the mental-health system in Washington. In 1958, Herbert Blumer, another Chicago School second-generation sociologist, invited Goffman to join the expanding Department of Sociology at the University of California, at Berkeley. Goffman published *The Presentation of Self in Everyday Life* (1959). At Berkeley, Goffman played the stock market and gambled. He became a blackjack dealer and pit boss in a Las Vegas casino, intending to write an ethnographic study of casino life. Goffman's wife, Angelica, suffered from a serious mental disorder and committed suicide in 1964. Goffman's second marriage in 1981 was even shorter; Goffman died of stomach cancer the next year.

Total Institutions and Stigma

Goffman was intimately connected with mental disorder through his marriage and through his ethnographic studies at Saint Elizabeth's Hospital. In *Asylums: Essays on the Social Situation of Mental Patients and Other Inmates*, Goffman popularized the concept of a total institution.[43] A total institution is a place in which large numbers of similar inmates are confined, live, and work in isolation from the wider society for a considerable time, under the close supervision of a staff that enforces a regimented and closely regulated existence. The term encompasses mental institutions, prisons, and POW and concentration camps.[44] In such institutions, staff and inmates develop contradictory cultural and social worlds. Brought into the institution involuntarily, the inmate undergoes ceremonies of degradation and humiliation through which his or her "self is systematically . . . mortified." Earlier beliefs concerning the self and significant others are undermined, and degraded ones are substituted. Inmates are forced into close social relationships with people beyond their control and choice. The most extreme forms of such interpersonal contamination are rape and murder.[45]

People have dealings with one another according to specific frameworks or models, such as high caste/low caste or mental patient/psychiatrist, which provide identity, the rules of interaction, and a basis for solidarity or social distance and ranking.

In *Asylums*, Goffman examined the doctor–patient relationship, which has special points of strain. People tend to identify with their body. It is a "possession" that can't be separated from the person, unlike the way a car is left with a mechanic. Physicians develop a practice in which they treat the body mechanically, as if it were not inhabited by a thinking person. For a mental patient, the relationship among client, bodily possession, and server is radically changed when the patient is brought to the medical gaze not as a free, self-admitted client but as an "object" committed to the asylum by someone else, often a close kin.[46]

The nature of psychiatric disorders and particularly the functional kinds, such as schizophrenia, is that they are notoriously difficult to diagnose and to treat. Nevertheless, inmates must be given a legally sanctioned label. Goffman is skeptical about these labels, however. Initially, diagnosis begins with a non-expert defining a person's behaviour as troublesome, a judgment that may reflect the ethnocentric views of a particular subculture. Such decisions tend to become political in that they express the interests of some over the interests of others. "[T]he patient's symptomatic behavior is an integral part of his [or her] interpersonal situation," which is inseparable from the trouble being experienced. Once released, a patient is discharged back into that situation of which the "psychotic response is a natural part."[47]

The psychiatrist, however, acquires the power over the inmate "to pass fatefully on everything that the inmate succeeds in obtaining and everything" he or she is deprived of. "The patient's life is regulated and ordered according to a disciplinarian system" through which a small staff can control a large population, as in a prison. Living in closed worlds subjects inmates to severe kinds of stress that make psychiatric observations of their behaviour particularly unreliable. Most such observations simply record patients' transgressions. Ultimately, Goffman concludes, the probability

is high that hospitalization will "damage the life chances of the individual" patient.[48] Part of the damage is caused by stigmatization.

Goffman points out in his book *Stigma* that the term originally referred to bodily signs signifying that the individual was a blemished person. In early modern Europe, criminals were branded to show publically the type of transgression they had committed, as Jean Valjean, the protagonist in *Les Misérables* (1862), was branded with the letter *V* for *voleur* ("thief"). Sociologically, the term *stigma* applies when an individual is assigned an undesirable status, which reduces her or him in the minds of others "from a whole and usual person to a tainted, discounted one." Stigmas include "abominations of the body, . . . blemishes of individual character [and] mental disorder."[49] Entire groups of people may be subject to stigmatization on the basis of such factors as ethnicity (the Roma) or religion (Muslims in the West).

Through the life course (or "moral-career"), these stigmatized individuals learn about and incorporate the point of view of the wider society vis-à-vis their difference, which negatively affects their self-concept. "The fully and visibly stigmatized . . . must suffer the special indignity of knowing that they wear their situation on their sleeve, that almost anyone will be able to see into the heart of their predicament." One may seek to cover or disguise the sign or learn to compensate for it, as a stutterer avoids using certain words and phrases. Learning to pass as a "normal" is an important adaptation to living with a stigmatized identity (managing a spoiled identity, in Goffman's terms).[50] In these situations, people work to manage the reception of their stigma using various techniques of information control.

Dramaturgy and the Presentation of the Self
Stigmatization is an element of the world over which people have limited control. In his study of total institutions, Goffman focused attention

on the way that social institutions tend to shape the formation of certain types and conceptions of "self." His interest in the management of "spoiled identities" in *Stigma*, however, reflects his greater interest in the ways individuals negotiate their responses to the social order and actively shape the environment that surrounds them. The opportunity to exercise such agency is most severely restricted in total institutions, but it is never absent anywhere. One's identity and sense of self evolve in the complex interplay between freedom and constraint.[51]

Goffman is best known for his analysis of the complex way people manage their identities. For Goffman, all the world's a stage and everyone is a player. The dramaturgical perspective he employs in *The Presentation of the Self* (1959) is that social interaction should be understood as a theatrical performance. In everyday situations, individuals present themselves to others and try to shape the impression others form of them. Unlike a stage performance, in which the script is laid down in minute detail before the performance, in life the parts one plays are continually tailored to the parts played by others—actual interaction has an improvised rather than an entirely scripted character.[52]

When people interact with others, they express certain signs that are meant to create impressions for others. Regardless of what perspective people want to convey in their interaction, they intend to manage the impressions they give of themselves and shape others' definition of the situation. In this work of impression management, people engage in performances that involve trying to stage successfully a particular image of their character. They consciously convey both verbal and non-verbal cues and unconsciously give off other cues, which may undermine the impression they had intended. In Goffman's terms, the intended impression is the one the individual *gives*. In addition, there is the impression that an individual *gives off*, by which he means "the more

theatrical and contextual kind, the non-verbal, presumably unintentional kind."[53] For example, in a restaurant, you say you are interested in what I am saying, but your attention keeps straying to observe someone else at another table.

Both verbal and non-verbal cues, however, are subject to conscious manipulation by social actors. Social interaction entails an information game through which people play a cyclical sport of "concealment, discovery, false revelation, and rediscovery." Throughout Goffman's account, interaction is seen as a calculated game in which authenticity is more an act that is put on than an actual description of an actor's intent. He describes how young women in college conceal their intellectual abilities in the presence of datable young men. In this complex game, it is impossible to consistently avoid discrediting yourself through the impression you give off. Consequently, individuals learn corrective or defensive practices through which they attempt to hide or deflect these embarrassing lapses.[54]

In analyzing interaction in terms of drama, Goffman understood that, just as actors in a play form a cast, much interaction involves a "team of performers" who collude together to manage impressions. He also distinguished between the front stage and backstage. In theatre, the front stage is what the general audience is intended to see, but not everyone is invited into the backstage, where the actors let down their hair and play roles more consistent with their self-conceptions. The front of an everyday performance consists of the physical setting in which the action takes place, the appearance that is given, and the manner with which the performance is conducted (for example, politely or sarcastically). It is important that a performance be given as if it were spontaneous and uncalculated, for example, by managing one's face and voice (tone and manner).[55] Goffman does not elaborate on the importance of objects in the presentation, such as the style of clothes or automobiles, and other consumer attributes of status. In backstage areas, actors perform "out of character" and collude to prepare the front-stage performance. The audience is generally barred from backstage areas. In the real world, for example, customers are not allowed in the garage bay while their automobile is being repaired. Thin apartment walls, on the other hand, make maintaining a backstage difficult.[56]

Part of a performance involves concealment. People hide activities that are profitable to them but incompatible with the responsibilities of their job, such as doing personal work during company time. They try to conceal their mistakes as well as any "dirty work" that is necessary for their performance to succeed. Maintaining a performance for a certain audience can be difficult when outsiders view the action, especially if they have a different definition of the situation.[57] People are skilled role players who play differently to different audiences, as the language of the locker room changes once outside the locker rooms. Problems arise when audience segregation breaks down and people who think they know a person in one setting witness different, perhaps inappropriate behaviour in another.

Backstage behaviour can frequently consist of derogatory comments about the front-stage audience, as teachers gossip about their pupils in the common room. Similarly, police talk in the office, which often includes racial and gender slurs, is very different from what the public is allowed to hear. Group insiders, such as teammates or professional colleagues, often scheme or discuss (gossip about) absent people.[58]

Since everyone is basically engaged in the same game of impression management, knows they are, and knows that others know they are, complex mechanisms of saving face are employed, which Goffman calls defensive practices. In-group solidarity prevents cracks from appearing in the impression that is to be given. Retail managers, for example, develop means to prevent store clerks from accurately revealing the

weaknesses of products they sell.[59] At the same time, in the knowledge that everything is, in fact, a performance, audience members exercise tact in how much they will reveal of their understanding of the performance and how they will react to an obvious faux pas. If privacy is impossible, tact entails acting as though you do not have knowledge that you think you are better off without. Audience members exercise tact when they forgive a known beginner or try to avoid making a scene. And they act as though they were blind to a front-stage mistake or they placate the performer by appearing to accept the excuse she or he makes.[60] In these ways, an individual or team performance establishes a working consensus or agreed definition of the situation.

The dramaturgical perspective, Goffman concluded, should be added to other points of analysis in social psychology, such as the analysis of structure, politics, or culture. He gave social theory a wide vocabulary to discuss the conscious and unconscious tactics employed in interpersonal interactions, which most people use in their everyday encounters. People recognize themselves and others in Goffman's account of dramaturgical encounters, although his deep skepticism about people's motives and actions may have been painted with a sometimes too heavy brush. Particularly in his work on institutions and stigmatization, Goffman adopted an underdog approach to sociology that critiqued the exercise of power and took the side of those not defined as normal.

Herbert Blumer and Symbolic Interactionism

I was adored, therefore I was adorable.[61]

— Jean-Paul Sartre, *Words*, 1964

Sartre's recollection of being adored in his childhood parallels a central tenet in G.H. Mead's social psychology that one's sense of self is a social product that arises through social interaction. When

Mead died in 1931, his successor at the University of Chicago was Herbert Blumer (1900–1987), who went on to develop a distinctly American interactionist approach in sociology.

Blumer was born in St Louis, Missouri, in 1900. His early years were spent on a small farm and he attended a one-room schoolhouse. He went to business school and worked as a stenographer. Blumer thought of himself as a humanitarian and was drawn to the socialist movement. In 1918 he began studies at the University of Missouri, writing a master's thesis on the theory of socialist revolutions. In 1924 Blumer entered a Ph.D. program at the University of Chicago, where his interest in socialism waned after studying with Robert Park. Blumer played professional football with the Chicago Cardinals. A knee injury in 1933 ended his playing career, although he coached for a few years at the college level.[62]

In the 1930s, Blumer was fascinated by the differing views of the world held by a variety of groups defined as socially deviant, which included notorious figures in the Chicago criminal underworld.[63] He began to developed a distinctive approach to sociology he called **symbolic interactionism**. Blumer later said the term was "a somewhat barbaric neologism that I coined in an offhand way" but that it had "caught on." In 1952, Blumer accepted an offer to become chair of the department of sociology at the University of California at Berkeley, then undergoing an ambitious expansion to become a dominant department in the United States. He retired from Berkeley in 1972 and died in 1987. Blumer had a distinctly outsider perspective at a time when sociology was dominated by abstract structural-functional theory and quantitative empiricism.[64]

Blumer's main interest at Chicago was social psychology and the Chicago School. His approach was influenced by Cooley's idea of the looking-glass (mirrored) self, through which a person's sense of self arises through reflexive social interaction with other people. The tradition of research in Chicago was rooted in **ethnography** and long-term immersion in fieldwork. Blumer stressed the need for extensive empirical methodology that took into consideration unique human attributes, such as minded (thoughtful) activities.[65] He rejected any theory of cultural determinism, which regards the individual as simply a passive recipient of biology or of the cultural patterns of his or her group. As a symbolic interactionist, Blumer argued that everyday, co-operative activity proceeds because members of a group possess a set of common symbols and shared understandings. These common understandings reflect the definition of the situation, which defines the view individuals take of a given situation and how they are expected to act within it.[66]

Blumer said that both functionalism and structuralism made the error of seeking knowledge by elaborating ideas and concepts without any reference to the real world. Factual data do not speak for themselves. No situation in society carries "its own meaning; the meaning is conferred on it." The researcher must get to know the interpretations, definitions, codes, rationalizations, or models that are used by the group under study. Interpretation, not mere fact-finding, is the formative and creative process. And such interpretation entails perception, cognition, evaluation, assessment, and decision-making about the cues and definitions that arise from the individual and others.[67]

Meanings and Interpretive Action

What were Bloom's thoughts about Stephen's thoughts about Bloom's thoughts about Stephen?[68]

— James Joyce, *Ulysses*, 1922

As novelist James Joyce realized, people possess the unique ability of sympathetic introspection, which Blumer defines as "the ability to project oneself imaginatively into the position of another and to experience vicariously his [or her] feelings and state of mind." The individual tries to assess a situation from her or his particular point of view, but each person also engages in the continuous process of perceiving, defining, and judging the conduct of the other from what they believe to be the other's standpoint. In this way, social interaction actually shapes human conduct because people orient their own action by taking into account what others are doing as well as their beliefs about what other people are likely to do. Interaction, then, is a continuous, ongoing process of back and forth, call and response. As individuals take others into account, and develop joint actions, interaction becomes thoroughly reflexive. Through symbolic interaction, human group life is actually formed and re-formed as a communicative process.[69]

From Blumer's symbolic interactionist perspective, the social world is the everyday, ongoing life experience of people facing situations that arise in their daily life. Interaction involves more than just other people, however. Physical objects in the environment, abstract ideas such as honour, and other people are all "things," and people act toward things according to the meaning they have for them. The meaning of things comes from the way each member of the interaction defines them. Different people, even those who occupy the same space, may have quite different interpretations of their social situation or milieu—they may, in fact, live in different worlds.[70]

People respond to the world of objects by taking note of them, assessing and interpreting them, giving them meaning, mapping out particular lines of conduct, and then directing their action accordingly. Each person has a self-conception and interacts with others according to the kind of self she or he intends to portray, which is typically modified by the way others respond to it. The self may become an object on which one consciously works. When people interact with themselves, for example, they communicate to themselves consciously as people and respond to this communication. Through self-reflection,

people take into account their desires, their goals, their image of themselves, the anticipated actions of others, and the means of action that are available to them. In most cases, however, self-directed action is undertaken in interaction with others, who must also be assumed to have their own interpretations and meanings, which must be appreciated and responded to as the individual constructs and guides her or his own actions.[71] The empirical world exists for humans only in their perceptions of it and conceptions about it. But these conceptions are not all equally valid. A perception is subject to modification because the empirical world may challenge our view of it. Reality has an "obdurate character" that allows us to test the relative accuracy of our conceptions.[72] For example, we may believe a mushroom to be edible. If we test its properties by eating it and the mushroom is poisonous, we become ill and the obdurate character of the empirical world becomes apparent.

In any given encounter, unless the object is entirely new to the individual's experience, people begin with a meaning that has been created through previous interactions. Not only is this pre-given meaning socially created, but it has to be reinforced through subsequent interaction. If it is not, the meaning may begin to shift as a result of the encounter with other people's definitions and interpretations. There is always the potential, however, for a stable pattern to be disrupted and to be changed. Group rules and norms, which are created initially through interaction, are sustained or changed through subsequent interaction. When faced with new experiences or situations, the definitions are altered and new stable meanings develop, which then change the repertoire of actions and the social structure they constitute. Changing an objective factor depends, in the first instance, on applying some new orientation or viewpoint.[73]

Human life entails both an objective (empirical) situation and a subjective experience, the interpenetration of which makes social psychology unique among the sciences. For Blumer, an adequate social theory must place the subjective factor at the centre of analysis, focusing on the change that interaction entails. Interactionism can explain features of social life that are usually taken to be structural aspects of social existence, such as the way institutions are organized and the way people's relations are stratified. The limitless, ongoing interpretive process is the chief means through which social activities are patterned and social institutions are constituted. Once definitions are stabilized, the resulting interactions become regularized—like "a vast digestive process"—making institutions lasting. What have been defined as social structures are generated, reinforced, or transformed through symbolic interaction. People interpret and act meaningfully in relation to their position and status, to their material interests, and to the resources they control. These pre-existing elements of social structure shape and influence their self-reflection, decision-making, and interaction.[74]

Blumer's symbolic interactionism has only a rudimentary theory of social organization, but it has a well-developed conception of methodology. An adequate social psychology must incorporate change and social transformation. Researchers are almost always outsiders who lack intimate acquaintance with and first-hand knowledge of the area of life they are investigating. The key to research is to secure reliable observations that do not ignore the actual character of social life. According to Blumer, researchers ought to spend considerable time becoming intensively and extensively familiar with the area they are studying and assess carefully any applicable theoretical schemes. They form dependable judgments through "the slow and tedious manner of developing a rich and intimate familiarity with the kind of conduct that is being studied and in employing whatever relevant imagination observers may fortunately possess." The researcher must

freely explore the area and get close to the people involved, noting their difficulties and observing the ways they handle them.[75]

Respecting this world requires that the guiding conceptual scheme of the researcher is not imposed from outside but is faithful to this ongoing world. Different people and groups "build up separate worlds, marked by an operating milieu of different life situations and by the possession of different beliefs and conceptions for handling these situations." The delinquent, for example, lives in a different social world from the clergyman or military officer. Naturalistic research requires careful and imaginative life study of the concrete, empirical world. Nothing can substitute for developing a flexible familiarity "with what is actually going on in the sphere of life under stud."[76] For Harold Garfinkel, understanding daily life entails grasping the various everyday methods people use to make the world comprehensible and negotiate their way through it, an approach to micro-sociology he labelled ethnomethodology.

Harold Garfinkel and Ethnomethodology

Harold Garfinkel (1917–2011) was born in New Jersey, the son of a small businessman. At first he studied accounting, but he was soon drawn to sociological enquiry. Garfinkel studied race relations in the US South as a research fellow at the University of North Carolina. His first publication was the short story "Color Trouble" (1941), which was published in *Opportunity*, a journal of Negro life.[77] The story recalled an incident that Garfinkel witnessed in which an African-American passenger refused to sit at the back of the bus when it passed below the Mason-Dixon Line that had once separated slave and free states.[78]

Garfinkel enlisted in World War II but did not see combat. After the war, he studied with Talcott Parsons at Harvard and was influenced by European **phenomenology**, which focuses on how people perceive and act in their immediate experience. On this foundation, he concentrated on the everyday world and the unnoticed background conditions that make social action possible. Garfinkel developed his approach at the University of California (Los Angeles), where he taught from 1954 until 1987. In his first decade at UCLA, Garfinkel defined his approach using the term **ethnomethodology**, which means the methods people use to understand their daily life.[79] Ethnomethodology elucidated the often unconscious rules of behaviour and the common-sense way people go about understanding their everyday lives.

When people are faced with a situation, they respond to it by following social rules and conventions, but these rules in turn depend on common-sense assumptions that everyone shares but that operate beneath the conscious level. Garfinkel argued that the ability of a person to act rationally in the conduct of everyday matters requires that person to rely on and take for granted a vast amount of both conscious and tacit knowledge about her or his social wold.[80] Following the phenomenologist Alfred Schutz, Garfinkel argues that, if scientific rationality (the rational human) is used as a model with which to compare the decisions and actions people actually make, it is clear that actual persons, even actual scientists, rarely match up to the model.[81] Rationality is like the tip of an iceberg in comparison with the importance of the unquestioned, taken-for-granted, "unstated and *essentially unstatable* . . . background" matters that shape social action.[82] The ethnomethodologist seeks to uncover these deeply rooted assumptions and ways of thinking that allow everyday interaction to occur.

Taken-for-Granted Features of Routine Life

Garfinkel conceived his approach to research when he was interviewing jurors about their deliberations and decision-making during trials. Individuals enter the jury room as socially competent people who have a well-developed sense of the ethics and morals that guide their personal decision-making in the outside world. In daily life, for example, people are inclined to act on the basis of what, for them, seems to be fair and reasonable in the circumstances. Once people become members of a jury, however, they are asked to replace these common-sense rules of decision-making with a legalistic set of rules that define the way jurors are expected to arrive at verdicts. Jury members learn the rules of legal deliberation from a number of sources, including directly from judges' instructions. They are expected to put aside other considerations and decide their verdict solely on the basis of law: not whether the law is fair or unjust, but only whether, in the given circumstances, the individual is guilty because she or he broke the letter of the law.[83]

During the trial, jurors experience some ambiguity between the formal requirements of judicial decision-making they are asked to apply and the common-sense rules they use in daily life. Their verdict is heavily weighted by their everyday understanding of how people typically act in daily-life situations, the ordinary motivations they have, and of what they believe is commonly known to be true. In this sense, 95 per cent of their understanding as a juror is carried in with them when they enter the courtroom. Nevertheless, when they are asked to explain their verdict, the jurors claim that their decision has been reached by following the official court rules. Garfinkel concludes that, in general, people's decisions result from the application of routine rules that are simply assumed and not consciously deliberated. Only when people have to supply reasons to clarify their choice do they formulate an explanation that makes their decision-making appear to be legitimate.[84]

At UCLA in the 1950s, Garfinkel collaborated with physicians at the university Medical Center in a study of people with pronounced "anatomical sexual irregularities." Garfinkel presumed that most people take their sex status for granted as "an invariant but unnoticed background among the relevant things that comprise everyday life." The Medical Centre studied people who were then defined as "intersexed" and did not fit the assumed natural sexual binary. Garfinkel investigated the social definition of transgender and transsexual people, who cannot take their gender or sexual status for granted. They are acutely aware and knowledgeable about socially constructed gender roles because, for them, sex status is not assumed to be automatic or routine.

Garfinkel reported extensively on one young woman, identified as Agnes. She was described as a girl who had been brought up as a boy because she had male genitalia. Agnes said that she had always felt female, that her external genitalia were a gross error of nature, and that she wanted her body to conform physically to the female sex she knew she had always been. She accepted the binary of male/female and claimed to have been assigned the wrong gender (male) on the basis of external appearance while, inside, she was a natural and normal female. Agnes had levels of estrogen that were typical for women despite having no internal female organs. Most doctors assumed the estrogen was being produced by her testes.[85]

While in school, Agnes developed breasts at puberty and had an hour-glass figure although others identified her as a boy. At the age of 17, she left her hometown and went to a large city, where she changed her gender from masculine to feminine. In 1959, at the age of 19, Agnes changed her sex, undergoing transsexual surgery at the UCLA Medical Center. Over this period, Garfinkel recorded 35 hours of interviews with Agnes.[86]

Garfinkel argues that Agnes "achieved" her status as a desirable female because, in the circumstances of her original genitalia, it was not assigned at birth. Her female status was achieved because she also had to consciously acquire the skills and capacities of femaleness. Through careful "management work," Agnes had to learn to display and perform her female status and mobilize feelings and purposes appropriate to the situation. When she was a transgender person, Agnes had rehearsed feminine actions consistent with her new female appearance. She had to learn the female role while she was actually playing it, learning the rules while participating in gendered interaction and risking being found out.[87] In 1966, Agnes casually revealed to her physician that she had been taking estrogen pills since the age of 12, using her mother's prescription.[88]

Garfinkel was interested in Agnes's case because he believed that, for most people, gender-appropriate actions become more or less automatically matters of common-sense knowledge. For Agnes, however, they were matters that required "active and critical deliberation." For Garfinkel, everyone is a practical methodologist in everyday life but, for Agnes, the process was uncommonly visible and conscious. Agnes was "constantly involved in the work of passing" as she tried to live a typical life.[89] In Garfinkel's terms, her sexual status was a **managed achievement** in the face of the social demand that people must comply with sexual norms.[90] Her claim to being a "natural female had to be bolstered and managed by shrewdness, deliberateness, skill, learning, rehearsal, reflectiveness, test, review, feedback, and the like." Understanding this work required more than applying a game-like analysis of strategy because it consisted of an ongoing and complex process of constructing and maintaining a skilled and biased past.[91]

Agnes's performance made it clear that so-called normally sexed persons are also cultural events. Her conscious methods brought to light the ways socially defined "normals" make their sexuality "commonplace . . . obvious, familiar, recognizable, [and apparently] natural." The visible order of everyday, practical activities is socially produced. Just as was the case with Agnes, so-called normally sexed people are equally "a contingent, practical accomplishment."[92]

Ethnomethodology

The studies of jurors and of Agnes's gender helped to make visible the standardized background features of commonplace situations that went unnoticed. To explore these background features further, Garfinkel designed unusual **breaching experiments** in which the life-as-usual features of everyday interactions were exposed by deliberately disrupting them. In one experiment, Garfinkel asked his students to engage a close acquaintance in a typical conversation but to insist that the person clarify her or his common-sense remarks. One participating student was asked by a friend, "How are you?" The student didn't reply with the expected, "Fine, how are you?" Instead, the student asked, "How am I in regard to what? My health, my finances, my school work, my peace of mind . . . ?" The friend grew red-faced and angry, and replied, "Frankly, I don't give a damn how you are."[93]

Other students were instructed to engage in conversations in which they would doubt the truthfulness of the other person's statements; that is, they would assume that the other person's choice of words was actually hiding their real motives.[94] In another experiment, Garfinkel assigned students the task of going home to their families and acting for up to an hour as though they were polite strangers who were boarding in the house. The emotional outbursts that each of these breaching experiments elicited revealed that the experimenting student had violated the standard rules of everyday behaviour and the underlying moral code that actually make routine conversations possible. Actors know their everyday world and their social and bodily place within it. They act on the basis of a set of assumed natural facts of life and morally enforceable rules that everyone in the group is expected to share. In short, people assume they live in a common, intersubjective world.[95] From his breaching experiments, Garfinkel concluded that when these unspoken moral rules and expectations are breached, people react with moral indignation and try to enforce the unstated rules.

It is not just that members know, use, and take for granted the ordinary methods through which they accomplish their everyday life. For the ethnomethodologist, it is important to analyze these methods that members use for making these everyday activities accountable—that is, visible, rational, and reportable.[96] People not only produce and manage the settings of their everyday actions, they reflexively create accounts of and justifications for what they are doing.[97] It is a remarkable phenomenon through which members use "everyday activities as methods with which to recognize and demonstrate . . . the rational properties of their" contextualized actions.[98]

Explaining everyday actions not only maintains the stable routines of everyday life; the stable and practical activities in which people engage, as well as their accounts of these activities, actually produce the social structures within which they conduct their everyday activities.[99] What appears to be objective reality is actually a continuing accomplishment of the interconnected activities of people as they go about daily life and produce the circumstances of their own actions. People interact and engage in the process of socially constructing the world in which they live, a perspective on reality that was developed in the United States by two Austrian-born sociologists, Thomas Berger and Thomas Luckmann.

The Social Construction of Reality

Thomas Berger (b. 1929) and Thomas Luckmann (b. 1927) were post-war immigrants to the United States from Vienna, Austria, who met at the New School for Social Research in New York. The New School was an extraordinary institution for graduate students staffed by European intellectuals who had escaped fascism in Europe. In collaboration, they published *The Social*

Construction of Reality in 1966, a book in which they developed a sociological approach they called social constructionism that reflected the dialectical nature of social life: people actively create the society they inhabit; their "subjective meanings *become* objective fact[s]."[100] Their perspective derives from American interactionism and the work of Alfred Schutz, whose philosophy focused on understanding the common-sense world of everyday life. Berger and Luckmann were critical of functional and structural sociology, and were sympathetic to the importance the interactionist perspective placed on everyday background knowledge for the working of society.[101]

For Berger and Luckmann, common sense "constitutes the fabric of meanings without which no society can exist." Individuals act on the basis of a taken-for-granted reality that is transmitted and maintained within social situations. In this sense, knowledge is socially constructed. As the reality of everyday life is interpreted by people, it becomes meaningful to them subjectively and is perceived as a coherent world. Berger and Luckmann place theoretical priority on consciousness or subjectivity: the world originates in people's thoughts and actions and their subsequent actions maintain them as "real."[102]

Although Berger and Luckmann claim that the perspective of each person is not identical with another—each person's sense of reality is somewhat distinct—people believe they share with others a common world and a common-sense knowledge about the normal, routine activities of everyday life. Through back-and-forth negotiations, a routine situation becomes defined as typical. Everyday reality is composed of a great number of these **typifications** that are shared with others. For Berger and Luckmann, "Social structure is the sum total of these typifications and of the recurrent patterns interaction established by means of them. As such, social structure is an essential element of the reality of everyday life."[103]

The closer the situation is to the individual's experience, the more the typical knowledge or recipe is taken for granted. The more remote the situation, the less the recipes of knowledge work, and the more the individual is aware of "**multiple realities**" beyond her or his own perception. Knowledge is possessed differently by different individuals and types of individuals, and the social world is perceived differently by people in distinct cultures.[104] People involved in a social institution, such as a marriage, have somewhat different senses of reality. What a husband imputes to his wife as representing *her* views or definitions (what he thinks she thinks) may not be congruent with the views and meanings the wife actually holds (what she actually thinks), and vice versa. Symbolic interactionism is an appropriate research technique to uncover multiple realities coexisting in an apparently common situation.

Society as Objective Reality

Society is a human product. Society is an objective reality. [Hum]an[ity] is a social product.[105]

— Berger and Luckmann, *The Social Construction of Reality*, 1966

For Berger and Luckmann, society should be understood in terms of an ongoing dialectical process. People's activity originates in their subjectivity; when they act, subjectivity becomes manifest in physical products that exist objectively. In other words, what they have produced becomes part of the physical reality or common world lived in by themselves and others. Finally, this newly produced reality is internalized by its producer and by others as objective reality, appearing to exist independently of human subjectivity. Knowledge about this objective reality is a *realization* in the double sense of the word: people continually *realize* (produce) the reality they inhabit, and they come to *realize* (apprehend) what they have produced *as* objective social reality.[106]

While people experience the social world and its institutions as a massive, objective reality, society, in fact, "is a humanly produced, constructed objectivity." Paradoxically, humans produce the social world through their actions but they then experience it as though it was a natural rather than a human product.[107] The process of continually producing this world becomes obscured. This tendency to regard something that is a human creation as, instead, a natural and non-human "fact" is termed *reification*. In people's consciousness, the social world becomes a thing with its own obdurate existence that neither appears to have been produced by human action nor to be continuously reproduced by this continuing action.[108]

When social actors reciprocally share habitual actions over time and develop a common history, Berger and Luckmann claim, they create institutions. Institutions are solidified typifications, which control human conduct and direct it in predictable channels. Institutionalization becomes relatively permanent as it is transmitted through socialization from one generation to the next. The world becomes firmly fixed in consciousness and confronts the new generation as an objective world, having a given reality that is assumed to be similar to the reality assumed for the natural world. Institutions are experienced as external, persistent, and coercive. Human existence appears regularized and stable because the social order always precedes an individual's introduction into it. A given social order imposes itself and shapes an individual's conduct in specific ways, enforcing a sense of inflexibility. Social order is the result of past activity, but it "exists only and insofar as human activity continues to produce it."[109]

In the process of transmission to the next generation, the institutional order requires **legitimation**—it must be explained and justified. Legitimation tells an individual "why things *are* the way they are" and why he or she "*should* perform

one action and not another." Through legitimation, the reality of the socially constructed universe is maintained.[110] The social construction of reality points to the need for ongoing reproduction of social institutions. Institutions exist because people continuously act to sustain them. In principle, institutions are precarious and can be changed if people refuse to follow the scripted recipes that reproduce them. The university, for example, continues to be socially (re)constructed as long as students continue to enroll, and they do so as long as they understand that their future careers depend on employers' demands for formal qualifications.

If society is to be understood dialectically, it is necessary to understand the multiple realities people differentially inhabit. And those who are defined as "mad" produce perhaps the most profoundly different counter-knowledge in society (see Box 10.3).

While Erving Goffman was studying psychiatric patients in the United States and writing *Asylums*, Michel Foucault was coming to somewhat similar conclusions in France. Foucault claimed that psychiatrists asserted specialized knowledge that allowed them to perpetuate their power over people they diagnosed. With psychiatry, social control was no longer only an external force compelling the individual to obey authority; it had become an internal power under which the individual acted to control him or herself.

Michel Foucault's Social and Biopolitical Critique

Paul-Michel Foucault (1926–1984) descended from a wealthy family in the provincial town of Poitiers, France. His father was a surgeon and anatomy professor. In 1940, when Poitiers was occupied by the German Army, Paul-Michel attended secondary school under the shadow of the Gestapo, the German secret police. Teachers who were suspected of working with the French

⁂ BOX 10.3 • THEORY IN CONTEXT ⁂

Anti-Psychiatry

Randle P. McMurphy: "You ain't crazy that way. I mean—hell, I been surprised
how sane you guys all are. As near as I can tell you're not any crazier
than the average asshole on the street."[111]
— Ken Kesey, *One Flew over the Cuckoo's Nest*, 1962

Ken Kesey's novel *One Flew over the Cuckoo's Nest* is a critique of the regime of control imposed on those labelled mentally ill. It is also a broad critique of the abuse of power by people in authority, a widely influential theme among college-educated youth in the 1960s. Kesey says that the inmates in a mental institution are no less sane than the people outside. According to the theory of anti-psychiatry, mental illness is a label imposed by people who hold positions of power on those they deem deviant nonconformists to make them knuckle under and obey authority. The arbitrary nature of psychiatric diagnoses was highlighted in an article by David Rosenhan entitled "On Being Sane in Insane Places." In an experiment, eight pseudo-patients who falsely reported hearing voices sought admission to psychiatric hospitals in the United States. All were admitted and none was defined by the professional staff as "sane." Although they immediately claimed to no longer have delusions, all were labelled with a psychiatric disorder (usually schizophrenia) and held for an average of 19 days. Rosenhan argued that his results demonstrate the unscientific and arbitrary way that mental disorders are diagnosed and treated. The labelling theory in sociology, ironically, would suggest that the pseudo-patients would likely *become* mentally ill if they experienced a prolonged stay in the institution.

Are psychic disturbances only in the mind, in the sense that they are the result of social experience? Or are they organic in origin, resulting from malfunctions of the brain or from chemical imbalances? The psychoanalytic movement relies on the former assumption. In contrast, twenty-first-century psychiatry is heavily invested in the pharmaceutical drug revolution and in altering body chemistry.

The anti-psychiatry movement categorically rejected both logics; rather, it is society that is sick and needs a cure. In the view of radical psychiatrist R.D. Laing (1927–1989), a psychotic episode is "real" and not merely a construction of a psychiatrist. In *The Divided Self: An Existential Study in Sanity and Madness* (1960), Laing viewed madness as

Resistance were arrested and disappeared.[112] Foucault was admitted to the Lycée Henri IV, an elite school in Paris dedicated to preparing students for university. The young recluse from the provinces did not fit well into the communal boarding school.

Eribon described him as "fragile and unstable . . . unsociable, enigmatic, and withdrawn."[113]

In 1946, Foucault passed the exams to enter the prestigious École Normale Supérieure, where he read philosophy and the theories of Hegel

an individually creative and expressive act. It is meaningful in terms of the individual's confused effort to cope with conflicts in her or his environment. In this sense, Sam Lowry's escape into blissful madness in the face of imminent torture in Terry Gillian's Kafkaesque film *Brazil* (1985) is an act of creative resistance against oppressive reality.[114]

Unlike psychoanalysis, Laing assumed that the psychotic episode is a valid if confused expression of the individual's objective, external dilemma. With the guidance of a sensitive analyst, who helps the individual live through and understand the confused symbolism of the episode, the "patient" emerges with a deeper appreciation of his or her experiences and dilemmas. Laing's approach was connected to the therapeutic community movement, in which "patients" and "analysts" lived together, learned from each other, played each other's roles, and helped each other interpret the world differently and live within the world they mutually created. Such an arrangement presupposed that everyone's view of the world was essentially valid and that, through democratic interaction and power-sharing, a workable, commonly defined view of reality could be produced that would function as a form of practical sanity.

Erving Goffman's investigations into total institutions, such as mental hospitals, reported in *Asylums* (1961), alerted the critics of psychoanalysis to the stigmatization caused by mental diagnoses. If there was no single, objective reality but, rather, different perceptions of reality and a variety of points of reference—in effect, multiple realities—then the dichotomy between being mentally ill and mentally normal was a social construction. For those in the anti-psychiatry movement, a condition such as schizophrenia was neither an organically based illness nor a specific form of psychic disturbance that required a cure. It was a label and condition that was imposed on the patient by psychiatrists.[115] As the Italian movie *The Best of Youth* (2003) points out, schizophrenia means that a person is split in two. But the film then asks the question, "who isn't?" If patients really are sick, the film claims, their illness is induced by being locked in an institution; they are suffering from "asylum sickness."[116]

Thomas Szasz (b. 1920) claimed, in *The Myth of Mental Illness* (1960), that schizophrenia is a label imposed by physicians in positions of power for the purpose of control. For Szasz, Freud's theory is the most complete example of an essentially religious doctrine (to be accepted on faith alone) that psychoanalysts try to pass off as scientifically objective. Mental illness is a social construction of the powerful psychiatric establishment. Unlike real diseases, which can be explained organically, mental disturbances are merely forms of behaviour disapproved of by those in power.

and Marx. In the highly competitive milieu of the École Normale, life for Foucault was often unbearable. He responded to his schoolmates with ridicule, scorn, anger, and aggression. His fellow students thought of him as partially mad, a verdict he helped confirm by his bizarre behaviour, which culminated in 1948 in a suicide attempt. Foucault underwent analysis, through which he first encountered institutional psychiatry. Foucault's doctor attributed his patient's obsessions and behaviour to symptoms of difficulty he had accepting his homosexuality. Homosexuality in France during the 1950s and 1960s was condemned legally and morally. Feeling himself balanced on a precarious mental tightrope, Foucault began an intensive study of psychology and psychiatry, the better to understand himself and his social experiences. He became fascinated with authors who dealt with transgression, "limit experiences," and excess.[117] Foucault took groups of his students—including Jacques Derrida—to observe his work at the psychiatric Hôpital Sainte Anne. He sought "something different from the traditional grids imposed by the medical gaze."[118] Foucault's thesis on the mental-health establishment was substantially abridged at the behest of R.D. Laing and the anti-psychiatry lobby to about one-third of its length and translated into English in 1965 as *Madness and Civilization*.[119]

Foucault's *Madness and Civilization*

Only our concept of time makes it possible for us to speak of the Day of Judgement by that name; in reality it is a summary court in perpetual session.[120]

— Franz Kafka, attributed

Foucault argues in *Madness and Civilization* that the dichotomy of sanity/madness was a social construction that became common sense only with the rise of modern society. The modern attempt to suppress all forms of "unreason" imposed a world of narrow moral rules and subjugated desire, and created a regime of oppression disguised as scientifically progressive. In the classical works of Shakespeare and Cervantes, for example, fools spoke truths that ordinary people were forbidden to utter. Even as the mad roamed the world, shaking their fists at destiny, they remained part of the social fabric. Wisdom and madness were equivocal and reversible. The modern dichotomy of sanity/truth, insanity/falsehood had not yet

been constructed. On the contrary, madness, in a way similar to death, revealed the limits of human experience but was still part of that experience.[121]

During the Enlightenment age, humanity was defined solely by the ability to reason. All forms of non-reason became inferior and were silenced and subjugated by reason, most thoroughly in the "monologue of reason *about* madness" that became modern psychiatry. Foucault's task, he claimed, was to uncover the moment when madness and reason began to move apart.[122] In barely 50 years, madness was separated from its "dark freedom" and "bound to Reason, to the rules of morality and to their monotonous nights." Nervous diseases were invested with undesirable moral values that resulted from deep, socially unacceptable desires that society both solicited and condemned.[123] Those defined as mad were judged and denounced by the standards of reason, classified, and locked away in asylums and madhouses. Suppressing madness and other forms of unreason denied important elements of the human experience and what could be imagined beyond the limits of rationality.[124]

In the asylum, the insane were defined as "other" and subordinated to those in authority, who claimed to represent reason and morality. The insane had to acknowledge their status as objects until, through their acceptance of guilt and personal responsibility, they could be returned to themselves as free and responsible subjects. The asylum imposed both surveillance and judgment. It was not mere repression, a faceless exercise of power; it imposed the authority of reason over unreason. Those defined as mad were silenced and expected to gaze as if into a mirror and define themselves as insane. Thereby, the mad were obliged to become their own judges even while they were perpetually judged from outside "by a sort of invisible tribunal in permanent session."[125]

By the close of the eighteenth century, the confinement of those deemed mad required certification by a physician, and the asylum was converted into a medical space. What Foucault identifies in the development of the psychiatric and medical establishments is a discourse rooted in the principles of scientific knowledge that confers power on its bearers. Difference is defined as madness, as abnormal, and knowledge is imposed on the mad to judge them, subject them to the professional **gaze**, and impose **normalization**. The birth of the asylum glorified the power of the expert, medical practitioner. Freud's talking cure (psychoanalysis) vested the physician with a divine-like status.[126] Physicians monopolized the knowledge and power to diagnose and treat illnesses based on the medical gaze. Medical science not only distinguished between health and illness, but between normality and pathology, which implied judgments about the character of the ill and their responsibility for their own condition.

Archaeology of Knowledge

The post-thesis Foucault was a changed man from the early troubled student. The new Foucault was "radiant . . . relaxed and cheerful" although he retained his penchant for sarcasm. He dressed the role of a dandy, complete with a green cape.[127] In 1960, Foucault met Daniel Defert, with whom for almost 25 years he shared a passionate and sometimes stormy relationship. In 1966, Foucault published his influential *Les mots et les choses* (*The Order of Things*). In 1970, Foucault's academic career reached its apex when, at the age of 43, he was chosen for a chair in the Collège de France, an institution Eribon calls "the holy of holies in the French university system."[128]

In *The Order of Things* (1966), which can literally be translated as *Words and Things*, Foucault explained the analytical approach (**archaeology**) that he had begun to employ in his studies of the birth of the asylum and the medical clinic. The structuralists had argued that language is shaped by unconscious rules of grammar and

logic. Similarly, Foucault claimed, entire systems of thought are also governed by rules that do not enter the consciousness of writers. These rules shape the framework of thinking, the classifications, and the concepts that are employed in understanding phenomena and thereby establish the boundaries of thought—what can and cannot be thought or expressed in the given universe of meaning.[129] The fundamental codes of a culture (such as embedded in its language, values, forms of exchange, etc.) establish for everyone the empirical orders with which they deal every day.

Unlike structuralism, which seeks to locate uniformities and similarities, Foucault argues that archaeology uncovers the apparent inconsistencies and contradictions within a given set of discourses.[130] Archaeology seeks to discover the foundation of knowledge, which Foucault terms the *episteme*. A given *episteme* makes possible both the ordinary, everyday categories that people use to order their world and also the abstract systems of thought that make this order appear to be the only reasonable form of knowledge.[131] Fundamental ruptures in society are linked to often sudden and fundamental transformation of one dominant discourse to another. The change of *episteme* is a radical event that transforms what is defined as knowledge. Foucault claims his archaeology reveals several "great discontinuities in the *episteme* of Western culture." The pre-Classical age came to an end near the middle of the seventeenth century (~1650). The succeeding Classical Age opened a new space of knowledge that lasted for about 150 years until the beginning of the nineteenth century (~1800) when it was superseded by the modern age. While it is possible to perceive similarities in the ideas of all three periods, Foucault claims that, on the archaeological level, in each case the dominant discourse was "transformed in a wholesale fashion."[132]

It is only during the modern age that humanity rather than god or nature became the centrepiece of Western knowledge. But, for Foucault, the modern *episteme* is already being transcended. He explicitly rejects its central elements, such as its focus on the reasonable, knowing subject and foreshadows a new, postmodern era. Along with the singular focus on the subject, the "I" who is thinking, Foucault abandons the dualisms that have dominated Western philosophy since Descartes. His archaeology is attentive to the objects of thought, those texts in which discourse is embedded, but he eliminates consideration of the actual writers in his interpretation of these texts.[133] In a similar vein, Foucault claims he is not the discoverer or creator of the archaeological framework of understanding; he is only the object of its appearance. The death of the subject is the foundation of the emerging and radically new postmodern or post-structuralist *episteme* (see Chapter 11).

Genealogy of Knowledge/Power

For also knowledge itself is power.

— Francis Bacon, "Of Heresies," *Meditationes Sacrae*, 1597

Francis Bacon said that knowledge is a form of power. The philosopher Nietzsche argued that power determines what is taken for knowledge. Foucault explores the intricate connections between power and knowledge. From archaeology, Foucault turned to **genealogy** as the descriptive term for his analytical method. Genealogy, in Foucault's sense, analyses the formation of specific discourses and their functions within a system of knowledge and distribution of power. Knowledge and power are inextricably intertwined, both in terms of domination and of resistance to dominating power.

Foucault employed genealogy in his book *Discipline and Punish* (1975). The book opens with a detailed description of the extreme bodily torture to which Robert-François Damiens was subjected in 1757 after he had attempted to assassinate Louis XV. A similar description appeared in Peter Weiss's play, *Marat/Sade* (1964). Weiss contrasts the public torture that constituted the festival of the execution of Damiens, which was passionate, personal, and singular, with the cold and utilitarian execution by guillotine. The guillotine represented a mode of killing that was mechanical, "inhuman . . . dull / and curiously technocratic."[134] Foucault's purpose is to contrast the extreme punishment of the body with the strict discipline imposed on the mind within the modern prison regime.

By 1800, according to Foucault, the public festival of inflicting torture and death on the body of the condemned was dying out.[135] People condemned as criminals were exiled to closed institutions called penitentiaries, where punishment was hidden from public view. A trace of torture persisted in the form of food rationing, sexual deprivation, and solitary confinement. The body of the convict continued to be involved in the punishment of confinement, but modern punishment now includes an entire array of technicians who base their techniques on new, scientific discourses, such as criminology, psychotherapy, and rehabilitation.[136]

For Foucault, modern punishment is directed to the "soul" through the body of the convict. The modern penal system passes judgment less on overt acts and more on offenders' passions, sexual "perversions," instincts, drives, and desires: "It *is* these shadows lurking behind the case itself that are judged and punished." The soul, in Foucault's terms, becomes the prison of the body. Courts now make judgments on "something other than crimes, the 'soul' of the criminal."[137] Meursault, the anti-hero of Camus's novel *The Outsider* (1942), said he was condemned to death, not for his actions, but based on the prosecutor's judgment of "what he called my 'soul.'"[138]

For Foucault, knowledge is produced by power; power and knowledge imply one another: "there is no power relation without the correlative constitution of a field of knowledge, nor any knowledge that does not presuppose and constitute at the same time power relations." Power-knowledge is properly hyphenated because each term presupposes the other. Punitive methods are specific techniques of control that operate along with other ways of exercising power. In the new techniques of correction in the prison, authority surrounds and acts upon the convicts, turning them into obedient subjects who must follow automatically and habitually the institutional rules and orders. The prison becomes a system of total power that is anonymous and secretive, subjecting the body to discipline and training.[139]

Putting an end to public torture appeared to be lenient and humane, but it was actually a change in the techniques of power that transformed humanity into an object of scientific discourse and knowledge.[140] Like those defined as mad or ill, the prisoner became an object pinned in time and space for the scientific gaze of authority. Prison administrators, supervisors, governors, chaplains, and instructors are given the power to make judgments about individual convicts through techniques of "observation, diagnosis, characterization, information, [and] differential classification." The confined become docile objects of knowledge. Power is reconstituted in the hands of those who supervise and administer the punishment, based on the monopoly of knowledge they possess.[141] The penitentiary becomes a place for the further development and application of this clinical knowledge about the inmates.[142] The contemporary power to punish offenders derives its rules and justifications from scientific and legal discourses. Knowledge-power is not merely imposed externally; the mind is enlisted in its own supervision and control. The focus of supervision, constraint, and punishment has shifted from dominating the external body to controlling the inner consciousness and mind. Punishment is directed at the will and the essentially criminal character of the delinquent subject.[143] The mind is taught to imprison the body.[144]

Because ordinary people, the masses, were perceived by authority as potentially dangerous and rebellious, delinquency became a relatively generalizable social phenomenon. Penitentiary techniques were diffused beyond the prison and implanted in the entire social body, creating a widespread and subtle "carceral archipelago."[145] The power to control and regulate was to be rendered regular, effective, and constant through "stricter methods of surveillance, a tighter partitioning of the population, [and] more efficient techniques of locating and obtaining information." The Classical Age created the modern machinery of justice, including the police as an organization of public surveillance.[146]

Intervention by the agents of authority extended to potential as well as actual criminals, constituting a general formula for exercising power over people.[147] The original goal of normalizing delinquents was broadened to apply widespread and perpetual policing and surveillance not just to those who had transgressed the law, but to include those who departed only slightly "from a rule, an average, a demand, a norm." The power to regulate and punish began to operate at every level of the social body, although even the smallest coercions were made to appear legitimate and natural.[148] For Foucault, the body is directly involved in political power relations that "have an immediate hold upon it; they invest it, mark it, train it, torture it, force it to carry out tasks, to perform ceremonies, to emit signs." Individuals subject their bodies, actions, attitudes, and achievements to the domination of the universally normative, subject to the judgment and regulation of innumerable people in supervisory positions, such as doctors, teachers, legal officials, and social workers. In Foucault's terms, individuals are subject to biopower.

Disciplinary techniques became general formulas of domination, creating a new "microphysics of power" that spread from one institution to another: the army, the factory, the school, and the penitentiary.[149] In these institutions, the continuous concern with perpetual surveillance was expressed in their structure and architecture, which permitted an unprecedented degree of control. The exercise of biopower rendered visible those inside it, regulated their conduct, and carried "the effects of power right to them, to make it possible to know them, to alter them."[150] Jeremy Bentham's design of the Panopticon, a circular prison in which prisoners are never free from surveillance by authorities they cannot see, was generalized to the modern penitentiary.[151] If not continually under surveillance, as in the modern closed-circuit TV cameras, prisoners are aware that they *could* be under surveillance and, as a result, have to self-regulate their actions. In the contemporary world, the widespread, voluntary use of social media makes a vast amount of personal data available for authorities to analyze.

The micro-physics of power that operate throughout modern institutions is not simply a rational mode of domination. It entails a relationship of power that is understood as a perpetual battle, an activity and network that is constantly in tension. Someone does not possess power; rather, they exercise it. As power exerts pressure upon people, they resist its hold on them and struggle against it. Just as cruel, public executions created space for resistance and rebellion, penitentiaries produce rather than reform delinquents by subjecting them to an "unnatural, useless and dangerous existence."[152] Power relations entail multiple points of instability, confrontation, conflict and struggle. At risk, at least temporarily, is the potential for existing power relations to be inverted.[153] Individual transgression becomes the most viable form of resistance in the face of normalizing power.[154]

In the 1970s, Foucault became a politically engaged intellectual, active against the Franco regime in Spain, in favour of the revolution in Iran, and protesting the crackdown in Poland against the Solidarity union movement. He was principally interested in prisoners' rights and formed the *Groupe d'Information sur les Prisons* (GIP) in early 1971. The intent was to expose and criticize the official discourse on the system of imprisonment when it was defended with words such as *justice* or *objectivity*. Rather than intervening in the name of higher values, the GIP focused attention on intolerable realities. Investigations into concrete prison conditions were specific and detailed, and were meant to unite academics and prisoners, with the intention of empowering the latter.[155] In 1972, Foucault visited the New York prison at Attica, the site the previous year of the most serious prison riot in US history, during which sexual offenders were targeted by other prisoners.

Foucault's anarchist-influenced politics were apparent in the controversy he initiated over the idea of "people's courts" to dispense revolutionary justice. For Foucault, a court was a court, and even a people's court was not a form of genuinely popular justice; rather, it was the embryonic beginning of a state institution.[156] Normalization from the point of view of the wider public gaze rather than the official one would not be better, and perhaps it would be worse. Revolutionary change required the radical elimination of all judicial and repressive apparatuses and practices, institutional and personal. The role of intellectuals in the present conjuncture was to intervene in specific, local struggles, on specific points with the objective of combating "all the controls and constraints that everywhere provide a new version of the same power."[157]

By the eighteenth century, problems arising from the life of populations as composed of living beings, such as "population health, hygiene, birthrate, life expectancy, [and] race," challenged governmental practices. The new fault line of resistance became issues of the body in relation to state regulation and control. It was the beginning of biopolitics, or the politics of life.[158] Foucault began to examine discourses around the political and economic concerns that were raised by the focus on life-process politics.[159] In 1976, the year following the publication of *Discipline and Punish*, the first volume of Foucault's multi-volume *History of Sexuality* was published. The study of sexuality and the "self" took Foucault back to the sexual practices of ancient Greece and Rome. *The Use of Pleasure* (1984) and *The Care of the Self* (1984) were published after his death.[160]

In 1979, Foucault delivered a set of lectures at the Collège de France entitled "The Birth of Biopolitics." Biopolitics emerged from his analysis of liberalism, which Foucault saw as a practice, "a way of doing things" that rationalized the exercise of government. In contrast to German history, which emphasizes the concern with too little government and establishes the need for rules, order, and administration, English liberalism was grounded in the principle of opposition to too much government. The necessity and usefulness of government must always be questioned.[161] Power designates a domain or grid of relations that Foucault termed "governmentality," which connects his idea of micro-powers to procedures of control. Micro-power is not a question of scale; it is not simply local and interpersonal but extends techniques of power to the entire society.[162]

Foucault frequently lectured abroad. He had given his first lecture in the United States in 1970 and in 1983 he agreed to lecture annually at the University of California at Berkeley. By that time, he had attained a cult-like status in the United States. Foucault liked America for many reasons, not the least of which was the many pleasures it afforded. There was a thriving gay culture on both east and west coasts, and Foucault threw himself into this environment with gusto.[163] It was an inopportune time for sexual excess and experimentation, however. By the end of 1983 and during the first half of 1984, Foucault was persistently ill. He suspected that AIDS was at the root of his ill health, but the symptoms were not clearly defined. He died suddenly on 25 June 1984.[164]

Conclusion

By the 1960s and 1970s, sociologists had stampeded decisively away from the previous dominant orientation of functional and organizational theory. Structuralism and interactionism developed as binary opposites, but the theoretical status of binary divisions was quickly being called into question. Overcoming the opposition between interpretive and structural explanations had already begun with the notion of the social construction of reality. A fusion of the two would be featured in a great deal of late-modern theorizing.

Although many varieties of Marxism had sprouted in the fertile soil of social activism in the 1970s, neo-Marxism soon spawned its negation. A critical new generation of academics, including Foucault, emerged from the entanglements of New Left activism, which had shaped their theorizing, whether structuralists or post-structuralists. They rose to prominence in the last decades of the twentieth century, seeking to reorient social thought from the path it had taken since the Enlightenment. Interactionism may be considered a form of post-structural social thought. Structuralism and interactionism have fundamentally different orientations to the modern concept of the autonomous subject. Individual identity and negotiated action are central to the interactionist understanding of the social world, as they are to existentialism. Structuralism eschews a consideration of the subject as such because the determinants of action are structures rather than individual subjects. Foucault developed his theory in reaction to and with some affinity for structuralism. Post-structuralism and the idea of the decentring of the role of the subject shaped social thought in the latter decades of the twentieth century.

Questions for Reflection

1. What aspects of the myth of the hero are still applicable for interpreting contemporary action or super-hero films?

2. Dramaturgy, interactionism, and ethno-methodology seek to uncover the hidden or unconscious background conditions of social life. Are these perspectives useful for understanding present-day social life?

3. Berger and Luckmann claim to have developed a social theory that combines Durkheim's emphasis on objective social facts with Weber's focus on subjective meaning and interpretation. Is one perspective better than the other for understanding the contemporary world?

4. Foucault's theory of power-knowledge connects to his interest in transgression and limit experiences. What role does transgression play in bringing about social change in the present time?

CHAPTER 11

Post-Structuralism and Third-Wave Feminism

Learning Objectives

- To describe the historical and theoretical context in which post-structural and postmodern thought has developed

- To outline Baudrillard's view of the dissolution of politics and society, and the replacement of the "real" by the "hyperreal" in the contemporary era

- To recognize the critiques made by contemporary feminists of second-wave feminism and the characteristics distinguishing third-wave feminism

- To reflect on the intersection of class, racialization, and gender as interpreted by black feminists

- To understand the social construction of gender and sexuality and consider the radical possibilities of transgressive politics

The coordinated terrorist attacks on the United States on 11 September 2001 (9/11) have been imprinted indelibly on the American psyche. However, there was an earlier 9/11 that is less often remembered but marked the beginning of the contemporary neo-liberal age. On that date in 1973, the Chilean Army, with the support of the United States and the CIA, overthrew the elected socialist government of Salvador Allende, ushering in decades of military dictatorship under General Augusto Pinochet. The military coup was the climax of a long campaign to destabilize Chile by intensifying internal conflict and undermining social reform. The Pinochet dictatorship embarked on an economic and political program that established the first **neo-liberal** regime.

Chile was the economic harbinger of a new era in global capitalism. Under the glitter of the affluent society and its radical-seeming 1960s culture lurked a number of structural crises that were eroding the glue holding together the welfare state. When the 1970s began, the United States was riding high on the unprecedented prosperity of what C. Wright Mills had termed the great American celebration, which was underwritten by a militarized economy and remarkable levels of peacetime government spending. In other developed countries, politics was dominated by **social democracy**, a political movement that reformed capitalism in favour of workers' rights, welfare-state policies, and restrictions on the power of capital. Generally in the West, the economic policy of **Keynesianism** was supposed to smooth out the capitalist business cycle.

In practice, Keynesianism came at the cost of a persistent level of inflation and deepening government debt. The costs of the welfare state were met by regressive new taxes on working- and middle-class incomes and consumption. Large businesses and corporations complained that they had lost too much of their potential profit to taxes and were fettered by too many government regulations. In addition, and anomalously in a high-inflation economy, unemployment remained relatively high.

The hidden burden of sustaining Western affluence rested on the weary shoulders of the underdeveloped world. While the United States had a domestic supply of oil, the advanced economies generally were greased by a plentiful supply of relatively cheap primary products, principally oil, from **neo-colonies** in Africa and the Middle East. Oil-producing states in the Third World possess an essential commodity and so they flexed their independence by creating the Organization of the Petroleum Exporting Countries (OPEC) to reduce the supply of oil and force a rise in the world price. The effects were instantaneous. The sudden jump in the cost of gasoline, heating oil, and other petroleum products had an impact on every oil-dependent Western economy, causing a jump in inflation and affecting peoples' lifestyles. OPEC was a dramatic illustration of the extent to which Western affluence depended upon access to cheap resources and inexpensively produced commodities from the global South. Feelings of impending doom signalled that the good times were coming to an end for the Western middle class. The political, economic, and social crises culminated in the rise of neo-liberalism in the 1980s.

With the Keynesian solution to global crisis itself in crisis, the road to unbridled power for laissez-faire capitalism was open. The success of neo-liberalism in electoral politics was preceded by counter-hegemonic strategies employed against the welfare state. Unlike unemployment, which is more likely to hit the industrial working class, inflation eats away at everyone's real incomes. As public services were disrupted by strikes and other industrial actions, those who sought these services were defined as victims. Public services were funded by taxes, which were paid by people who demanded the services. In this complex situation, neo-liberal political parties took advantage of the fault lines between taxpayers and government employees, between service providers and clients, and between the unionized and non-unionized sectors.

Ironically, neo-liberalism in the West was espoused by conservative governments, creating a **New Right**. In 1979, Margaret Thatcher was elected prime minister in Britain, bringing a commitment to re-make the economy along neo-liberal lines. Ronald Reagan won the 1980 presidential election in the United States on a similar, free-market, deregulation platform. In Canada, Brian Mulroney was an ideological, free-trade cousin. Under neo-liberal governments, nationalized industries are sold to private-sector buyers; regulations on capital are eliminated; restrictive labour legislation is imposed, limiting the right to organize and to strike; and government service departments have their budgets slashed, resulting in severe cuts to public services and public sector job losses. Under the New Right, class struggle was initiated from above. In Britain, Thatcher took on the powerful National Union of Miners in 1984–5. In the US, Reagan fired air-traffic controllers nationwide after they walked off the job.

While neo-liberal governments use the mantra of the dangers of public debt to shrink the welfare state, budgets expand for prisons, police, and the military. In this sense, the New Right regimes of power also adopted policies that were fundamentally neo-conservative. "Laissez-faire" had originally been a liberal slogan. In the 1980s, *liberal* came to mean the welfare state, and conservatives took on the old liberal mantle of small government and free trade. New Right governments practised stern law-and-order tactics at home and were consistently militaristic abroad. As Russian state-socialism was being hollowed out from within, preparing the way for its quick collapse in 1989, pressure on socialist regimes continued through a variety of modes. For almost 30 years, the Berlin Wall was the visible symbol of the Cold War, of the division of the world into capitalist and Soviet spheres. As the Soviet system collapsed in 1989, Berliners from east and west took sledgehammers and began to break down the wall, which was flattened in 1990. The destruction of the wall became as significant a symbol as its existence had been, but with opposite connotations.

Postmodernism and Post-Structuralism

I used to care, but things have changed.

— Bob Dylan, *Things Have Changed*, 2000

The rise of **postmodernism** and post-structuralism paralleled the ascendancy of neo-liberalism in social, political, and economic policy. Postmodernism began as an artistic and literary movement that tried to blur the barrier between elite culture and mass or popular culture. Through the apparently endless succession of "new" styles and genres of modern art and literature, each supposedly going beyond the previous one, artists reflected on art itself. Writers became increasingly self-conscious about their craft, producing a genre that claimed to be postmodern. Novelists addressed the reader directly and mused about composition, as did John Fowles in *The French Lieutenant's Woman* (1960), a novel that crosscut between a modern and historical storyline.[1] In the fine arts, postmodernists began to assemble elements from a variety of previous styles in an eclectic fashion and juxtapose them

in unexpected ways. The result is a pastiche that refers back to and reiterates previous styles or works, more in homage than in parody.

Pop art, which emerged in Britain in the 1950s, was an early form of visual art that reflected postmodern tendencies. Pop art represented a rebellion against abstract expressionism and broke down the barrier between "high" and "popular" art, a rebellion that Dadaism had begun earlier in the century. By the 1950s, artists of all stripes were well entrenched in the advertising industry, creating designs, writing jingles to sell products, and producing radio and TV commercials. Pop artists took images from popular culture and commercial design and fashioned them into "art" (that is, items that were set apart as artistic expression and were not commissioned as sales gimmicks) as paintings or directly into collages. Andy Warhol popularized the genre in the United States, mass-producing silk screen prints of celebrities, such as Marilyn Monroe; comic strip characters; and typical objects of consumption, such as Campbell's Condensed Tomato Soup.

Pop art took consumer culture for granted and dropped any critical edge other than undermining the divide between high- and low-brow art, which brought pop art into line with a postmodern perspective. Pop art deals ironically or humorously with the distinction between commercial design and art. The trajectory of avant-garde art has always been from the alleys and garrets of individual artists to mainstream galleries and commercialization. Pop art jumps directly from mass production to commodification. But commodification in the context of postmodernism is not a critical concept; it doesn't reflect the modernist distinction between authentic artistic creation and selling out. Art ceases to reveal hidden social realities and truths.

Postmodern is a term that has been applied to the contemporary era of globalization to emphasize the differences that distinguish contemporary developed societies from their recent past. Within the overall framework of contemporary thought, postmodernism suggests theories of cultural production and opposes the fundamental tenets of rationality and progress that defined modernity. Post-structuralism is a theoretical reaction against twentieth-century structural theories that assumed societies operated like integrated, normative systems. The typically binary categories of structural theory, such as male/female and progress/backwardness, actually constituted and reproduced the taken-for-granted social system. But these categories obscured or denied marginalized groups and the contradictory knowledge they produced about themselves and about the system as a whole. Post-structuralists, then, seek to uncover the way dominant categories and the dominant reality is constructed by shining new light on its limits and boundaries, and on those who live beyond its margins.

Postmodernism and post-structuralism share many affinities. They emerged in the same milieu of mid-twentieth century Marxism, existentialism, and structuralism, with close ties to the New Left. These two labels can be applied only tentatively to the theorizing of a wide range of late twentieth-century and contemporary theorists. As labels are developed and imposed, those who are classified reject them. Their self-consciousness about language use and the power of definitions compel these theorists to eschew labels or taxonomies that link bodies of work together. And, as with most intellectual currents, contemporary theorists are often in serious disagreement with one another. Theories are constructed and revised in a complex interaction with other perspectives and approaches. The theoretical orientations of those variously identified as postmodernists or post-structuralists became new avant-garde perspectives in European and North American social thought in the late 1980s and 1990s. To simplify discussion, the most significant division in social thought is between these contemporary avant-garde theorists, generally labelled post-structuralists, and social theorists who discuss contemporary society as being in a state of *late* modernity. Both bodies of thought developed simultaneously; both responded to the positions and critiques of theorists identified with the other approach. This chapter deals with them separately, in a linear fashion that does not reflect the cross-fertilization of ideas that make up contemporary social thought.

Postmodern and post-structuralist theorizing also express common elements. They reject modern social theories that imply a separately existing objective world that can be understood through the methods and theories of positivistic science. Post-structuralists are fundamentally anti-Enlightenment in their orientation and declare the search for objective truth to be mistaken. Just as there is no way to talk about language without using language, it is impossible to find some position outside the world from which to understand the world objectively; indeed, anthropologists have produced culturally biased accounts of pre-industrial societies.

Post-structuralism and postmodernism appear to be fueled by four contemporary developments: (1) the decline of the left with its corollary of intellectual despair; (2) the rejection of the Western philosophical tradition of industrialism, scientism, and liberalism; (3) a principal focus on language and language games; and (4) what Jean-François Lyotard has defined as incredulity toward metanarratives.

The Failures of the Left

Post-structuralism is fueled by the failure of state socialism, social-democratic Keynesianism, and New Left radicalism. Many individuals who had defined themselves as Marxists, at many different crisis points over the course of the twentieth century, had abandoned the view that the Soviet Union represented a desirable form of "socialism."

Although many post-structuralists came out of a past that bore some relationship to **neo-Marxism**, they quickly distanced themselves from Marxist politics and theory. State socialism in all its guises was condemned, both practically and theoretically.

The real failure that is reflected in the abandonment of politics is not in the East but in the West—the failure of both New Left radicalism and social democracy. The collapse was most spectacular in France, where much of the new theorizing theorizing originated. For neo-Marxists, the "new working class" of technicians and intellectuals, including radical students, had appeared to be the modern "subject" of revolution, a force for democratization and change. The fantastic anticipation that fueled the May 1968 revolt in Paris brought about a large firestorm that was quickly burned out.

Social democracy, a form of government premised on some state regulation of private capitalism, a non-negligible degree of taxation on the rich, and welfare-state policies, has been reduced by neo-liberalism to a ghost of itself. Ironically, while the welfare state may have temporarily reduced the polarization of poverty and wealth, it also deepened social control and regulation of the population. Underneath the consumer dazzle of the post-welfare state era was a powerful, ever more coercive and authoritarian state. As neo-liberalism captured both the political spotlight and governmental power, social democrats beat a fast retreat to the right. If neo-liberals were partly responsible for killing the welfare state, then it could also be said that social democracy was committing suicide. As the whole political spectrum shifted to the right, social democracy became one more political party of deficit reduction, balanced budgets, and globalization. Tony Blair's New Labour in Britain, the Socialist Party in France, and the Canadian New Democratic Party represented the demise of social democracy, not its renaissance. Social democracy has been transformed from an ideological alternative to capitalism and become a more humane managing of the dismemberment of the welfare state.

The Rejection of Enlightenment Rationalism

I am apt to think that men, when they come to examine them, find their simple ideas all generally to agree, though in discourse with one another they perhaps confound one another with different names.[2]

— John Locke, *An Essay Concerning Human Understanding*, 1689

For Locke, all minds were essentially alike; therefore, the same ideas could be understood and accepted by all if language could be made common. Both Marxism and social democracy, which are equally discredited in post-structuralist thought, rest on Locke's philosophical foundation, which they had inherited from the Enlightenment. Both Romanticism and rationalism are based on what, for post-structuralists, is an untenable myth: that there exists, within each person, an essential "self" that is a real, fundamental core of the individual. For rationalists, the self is a reasonable, autonomous, willing subject, the captain of one's fate. For Romantics, the self is a feeling and passionate being who approaches the world with intuitive knowledge and natural sympathies. Post-structuralists, however, reject the binary notions of the rational or the feeling subject. For them, there is no core self; the self is multiple and complex, decentred. There is no one identity; there are many identities, and they are fluid, mobile, and tactical.

Despite rejecting the classical idea of the subject, post-structuralists and postmodernists reiterate many of the concerns that have persisted in the Romantic traditions of modern social thought. Fundamentally, both approaches critique Enlightenment universalism and scientific positivism. The *philosophes* of the Enlightenment argued, with Locke, that the world could be understood rationally and that both "truth" and "justice" could be discovered on the basis of the universal principle of reason. Indeed, universal reason was the foundation of Western science. In sociology, positivists assumed that science would uncover the laws of society, making human life predictable and social engineering of society both practical and possible.

In the 1880s, Nietzsche turned the scientific principle of doubt on science itself. Every system of thought is self-referential in the sense that there are no acceptable standards outside the given system of thought that can refute or legitimate it. Consequently, no truth claim, and certainly not Enlightenment scientism, rests on any more secure foundation than any other. No knowledge claim is privileged. Scientists, for example, are typically skeptical about spiritual claims, but science has to bracket the spiritual—set it aside on the grounds that science cannot deal with the truth or falsity of supernatural claims because it has no way to disprove them. Each claim rests ultimately on philosophical assumptions, axioms, and values that cannot be easily refuted. For Nietzsche, all claims were equivalent and it was the exercise of power that conferred legitimacy on a particular point of view.

Truth and falsity, for the post-structuralist, are purely relative; each culture has its own standard for judging truth that is not inherently superior to any other. Post-structuralists argue that the Enlightenment claim for the universality of reason and truth was ethnocentric in that it privileged a Western view of the world while discounting other views, including alternative voices in the West as well as views that originated in non-Western societies. Cultures that differed from those of Europe were defined as culturally backward.[3]

Following Kant, Enlightenment thought distinguished among three distinct kinds of knowledge and truth-claims: (1) science (how we gain true knowledge of the world), (2) morality and values (right and wrong), and (3) **aesthetics** (standards of beauty): what was "true" was distinct from what was moral, and both were distinct from what was or was not beautiful.[4] A key postmodernist claim, however, is that these three spheres are not distinct. For example, one cannot separate science from questions of values or ethics. Whether pipelines should carry crude oil is not simply a question of economic rationality; it involves ethical, moral, and even aesthetic concerns.

A Focus on Discourse and Deconstruction

Language, a thoroughly social system, and language use are fundamental to the post-structuralist view. You cannot say that the world is experienced or perceived through the senses because experience and perception require apprehension, the way that the mind conceives, organizes, and interprets the sensations it receives. In between perception and apprehension stands language, the symbolic systems through which experience is filtered through concepts, knowledge, and values to produce an understanding. Different cultures apprehend the world in quite different ways, and different symbolic systems produce different claims to knowledge. Different branches of knowledge, moreover, develop conceptual schemes and understanding requires access to the language they use. For example, understanding a social theorist requires familiarity with the words or terminology she or he uses and the meaning that is intended by their use.

Given the premise that the social world is socially constructed, one of the tasks of critique is to go beneath the surface appearances of reality and uncover the structures and practices that compose it. Logically, such critique entails **deconstruction**, like peeling off the rings of an onion to uncover its core. The object of critique is to take a text—or a film, an advertisement, a painting, and so on—and reveal the context of its production, the assumptions and biases underlying it, and what is ignored or missing in its presentation. Feminists, for example, frequently argue that beneath classical sociology's claims to objectivity is an underlying masculine bias that is at the root of gender inequality and oppression. In this sense, *de*construction is rooted in critical theory. In the approach to post-structuralism presented by Jacques Derrida (1930–2004), deconstruction is as interested in what a text does not say explicitly but assumes or elides (slides over and obscures). Deconstruction, then, goes beyond critique to reveal not only what is present in a text but also what is absent: which groups are privileged to be heard, for example, and which groups are ignored and silenced.[5]

Deconstruction of texts draws attention to the multiple interpretations that can be derived from them. The intention of the text's creator becomes unimportant; its reception becomes more important, that is, the way consumers interpret the text and the meanings they derive from it. Foucault tried to efface himself from his texts as if the main question was not the author who produced them but the underlying contextual forces that call for such texts at a particular time and place. Rather than seeing mass, popular culture as a culture industry or a grand scheme for inculcating dominant values into the minds of the population, contemporary cultural studies attempts to uncover the interpretations people actually take from the "texts" produced by mass culture. Furthermore, alternative cultural productions are developed at the margins of society and therefore have an effect on dominant values and cultural productions.

It is not just that language and symbolic systems are instrumental in forming the world we live in. That will always be the case. The problem is that the conceptual schemes according to which we think and act have shaped the social world unequally. These schemes, including the taken-for-granted assumptions about the world explored in ethnomethodology and critical

theories, were constructed on the basis of binaries or opposites, such as male/female, body/mind, black/white. These binary concepts were not merely different. They were assumed to be hierarchical: one was dominant and one subordinate. These hierarchical distinctions are embedded in language, in the very concepts people use to understand and act in the world. They are part of the way society is constructed, interpreted, and enacted. Deconstruction exposes these binaries; demonstrates that social reality cannot be so simply dichotomized; reveals their inherent biases and consequences; and demonstrates the existence of multiple, intersecting frameworks, not simply a binary.

By the late 1960s, Derrida was challenging modernist social thought at its most fundamental point: the rational, logical, and linear form that undergirded what counts as knowledge and how understanding is produced. Deconstruction resurrected the anti-Enlightenment perspective as its own genealogy. It was a Nietzschean moment in literary studies except that Nietzsche had been a lone wolf. While structuralism and neo-Marxism appeared to presage a new political and social revolution, deconstruction developed a counter-academic movement that spread from literature to cultural studies and then to sociological theory. Foucault, Baudrillard, and other theorists in the French milieu began to re-orient social thought away from the politics of the past toward a post-modern sensibility of exposing the boundaries of social categories, transgressing them, and thereby undermining the conceptions with which the modern world had been constructed. As a strategy of social change, the post-structuralist idea was to undermine the foundation on which the house of cards rested, which was presumed to be the concepts and discourse that created and sustained the social structure.

Deconstruction as a critical technique has been applied to discourse. In its simplest meaning, a discourse is an act of communication. More

⚜ BOX 11.1 · THEORY IN CONTEXT ⚜

The Incredulity of Metanarratives

In his influential *The Postmodern Condition: A Report on Knowledge* (1979), Jean-Francois Lyotard states, "simplifying to the extreme, I define *postmodern* as 'incredulity toward metanarratives.'"[6] Metanarratives refer to large-scale and comprehensive explanations of the world that give history a meaning, a purpose, and an ultimate goal. Christianity and Marxism are examples of metanarratives. Other examples are the nineteenth-century doctrine of progress and what is sometimes termed the "Enlightenment" project—the attempt to construct a world of justice and social equality based on human reason. Romantics, in common with postmodernists, reject such views. In response to a schoolmaster's modernist, ethical claim that it is necessary to be "just," Stephen Dedalus, a character in James Joyce's *Ulysses*, replied, "I fear those big words . . . which make us so unhappy. . . ." For Stephen, history "is a nightmare from which I am trying to escape."[7] For the postmodernist, metanarratives are works of selective fiction that are passed off as grand truths. As truth claims, however, they are significant because they privilege some perceptions or discourses and silence others, thereby conferring power on specific interests or groups.

What actually exists, Lyotard says, are "clouds" of heterogeneous language games or language particles. An individual is positioned at the intersection of numerous of these "clouds of sociality."[8] In his perambulations about Dublin, Leopold Bloom, another character in Joyce's *Ulysses*, reduces liberal and socialist claims about reform to clouds of nonsense:

widely, *discourse* refers to the system of language and conceptual schemes through which the world is experience and apprehended. Broadly speaking, for example, the religious and spiritual discourse of the Middle Ages has been overlain and largely obscured by a modern discourse of logic, science, rationality, and subjectivity. Foucault analyzed the production of discourses and the great leaps in society that occurred as one discourse became newly dominant.

Discourse analysis is a central feature of post-structural thought. Enlightenment thinkers had criticized the tradition of religious authority, but both religion and its alternative, rational science, had erected a body of essential and universal truths that could not be proven outside their own

discourse. These so-called truths were merely sophisticated stories or **metanarratives** of the past, present, and future. Post-structuralists sought to deconstruct metanarratives and undermine their claim to knowledge by critiquing their essential or foundational presuppositions (See Box 11.1).

If the social world is constituted through symbolic systems such as language with embedded conceptual schemes, which form the way we interpret the world and the meanings we find in it, then reality is essentially rooted in discourse. Consequently, understanding society entails analyzing the discourses that produce it. Equally importantly, if the social world is formed by discourse, it can be changed by discourse. Social theories and the theorists who present them become

I stand for the reform of municipal morals and the plain ten commandments. New worlds for old. Union of all, jew, moslem and gentile. Three acres and a cow for all children of nature. Saloon motor hearses. Compulsory manual labour for all. All parks open to the public day and night. Electric dishscrubbers. Tuberculosis, lunacy, war and mendicancy must now cease. General amnesty, weekly carnival, with masked license, bonuses for all, Esperanto the universal brotherhood. No more patriotism of barspongers and dropical imposters. Free money, free love and a free lay church in a free lay state.[9]

Those whom Lyotard calls decision makers "attempt to manage these clouds of sociality," allocating certain language games to the realms of justice and truth, thereby legitimating their own power, while exercising a degree of "terror" over other individuals' language games.[10] Knowledge and power, as Foucault had argued, are two sides of the same coin. For Lyotard, there is no distinction between the kind of language games that are called science and those that are called politics or ethics. Those who have the power to assert the right to decide what is true also have the power to decide what is defined as just.[11]

Modernist culture used techniques of parody, satire, and irony to criticize society. Postmodernist cultural forms often adopt similar styles while abandoning the critical underpinnings. Post-structural social thought, in contrast, is often self-consciously political. In the discussion of social theory, it is useful to consider the strategies for social change that emerge from post-structuralist and, indeed, late-modernist theorizing. Jean Baudrillard occupies a central place within the complex interchange of contemporary ideas that are still being debated.

central not just to understanding the world but to changing it—by changing the way people think about it and, presumably, the way they act within it. This perspective animated the surrealists in the early decades of the last century. Jean Baudrillard's wide-ranging and often deliberately provocative writings challenge conventional ways of thinking about the world in a similar way. His writings have been influential in post-structural thought and culture.

Jean Baudrillard's Social Theory

Jean Baudrillard (1929–2007) was born in Reims, France.[12] He said he was from an upwardly

mobile family, which followed a normative postwar path. His grandparents were petty bourgeois peasants; his parents, new middle-class civil servants. With the third generation Baudrillard, the path of success culminated in university degrees and a career as a professional philosopher.[13] In his early thirties, Baudrillard translated into French works by Peter Weiss and Bertolt Brecht, and began publishing essays on literature in *Les Temps modernes*, a left-wing journal closely linked to Sartre. Baudrillard came to political awareness and action in the context of the Algerian Revolution, the French and American intervention in Vietnam, and Paris in 1968.

Baudrillard taught German in a French lycèe in the 1950s and arrived late at university as an academic outsider.[14] In 1966, Baudrillard studied at the University of Nanterre, a new campus that quickly became one of the centres of the French radical left, revolving around Daniel Cohn-Bendit. Cohn-Bendit was a New Left activist in 1968 who was a leader of the students' movement that occupied the University of Nanterre as well as of the May 1968 protest in Paris, an action in which Baudrillard also participated.

Baudrillard's first book was derived from his dissertation, for which he worked closely with Henri Lefebvre, who had been a Marxist in the 1960s. Baudrillard worked as Lefebvre's assistant at Nanterre, where he worked through his break with Marxist theory, publishing *The Consumer Society* in 1970 and *For a Critique of the Political Economy of the Sign* in 1972. By the time he published the provocatively titled *Forget Foucault* (1977), Baudrillard had abandoned any direct relationship with Marxism and, indeed, with academic sociology, developing his own version of critical and ironic social theory. According to Gane, "Baudrillard retired from university teaching at the first available opportunity."[15]

Marx had analyzed economic forces and political power, relegating ideology and culture to secondary importance. Antonio Gramsci had later studied the role that culture plays in shaping revolution or counter-revolution. Modern global capitalism was characterized by a division of labour that increasingly relegated the production of objects as commodities to the developing world. In this division of labour the advanced West played the roles of technological innovation, financier, and mass market, all of which were necessary for the re-production of the system. To understand Western society, then, it was necessary to focus on the sphere of consumption and culture, which was increasingly dominated by the mass production of the culture industry.[16]

Baudrillard's *The Consumer Society*

What then constitutes human wisdom or the path of true happiness? . . . . If our desires were at the same time increased to a greater extent, we would only become more miserable.[17]

— Jean-Jacques Rousseau, *Emile*, 1762

The subtitle of Baudrillard's *The Consumer Society* (1970) is "Myths and Structures," which acknowledges the influence of structuralism. From the vantage point of advanced, urban, middle-class capitalism, modern society is characterized by the enormous profusion of goods and services for sale, which creates a fantastic environment of conspicuous consumption and abundance. For Baudrillard, underneath the profusion of commodities, society had changed fundamentally.[18]

Baudrillard refutes the putative claims of social democracy to have achieved an actual redistribution of income and life chances. Despite the welfare state, inequalities of living standards and health persisted in affluent societies. Among Western countries, this gap was particularly wide in the United States, where there was a great discrepancy between private consumption and collective (state) expenditure and where the welfare state was least developed. Baudrillard said that the system was not actually failing; rather, the false claim of redistribution was a part of the power system, functioning to preserve privilege.[19]

In previous ages, humans were surrounded by the face-to-face presence and speech of other people. Now, in the modern world of mass consumption, humans are surrounded more by things than by people: by the endless succession of objects, signs, and messages. The great profusion of objects for consumption produces a frenzy of buying and acquiring. In shopping centres, goods are put on tantalizing display and shoppers wander among them, "flirting with objects."[20] Flirting, however, is a quite different undertaking from utilizing, a term that suggests Marx's concept of use-value.

Marx analyzed commodities in terms of their use-value or utility (people consume cars as a means of transportation) and its exchange-value (how much money it costs). In a typical exchange, an individual finds an object that has potential use-value, purchases it for its appropriate exchange-value, and then reconverts it to use-value by consuming (that is, using) it.[21] Capitalists make rational decisions to produce goods only if they will sell for a profit. Millions of people may need (have use-value for) low-cost housing, but capitalists do not provide cheap housing because it is not profitable. But an endless variety of novel, competing goods are produced for an affluent, middle-class market.

Baudrillard argues that the contrast between use- and exchange-value is obsolete. In advanced capitalism, scarcity is a thing of the past and capitalist production is unlimited. It has been clear since the 1930s that the real problem in the system is finding a consumer market for disposing the goods that are manufactured so prolifically. Part of the solution is the ratcheting up of desire through an increasingly sophisticated advertising industry. Advertising is nothing more than an ingenious trick that "has pulled the world into a phantasmagoria, and we are all spellbound victims."[22]

Baudrillard had no time for the moral criticism that modern consumer advertising creates false or artificial desires to stimulate unnecessary consumption. It thereby leaves people unsatisfied and wanting more rather than providing authentic satisfaction—an idea reflected by Rousseau in *Emile*. People desire and enjoy, at least momentarily, the things they buy. But they no longer buy things principally for these reasons. Fundamental to the modern social structure is the growing importance of status differences, organized around the demand for signs that reflect and produce these status distinctions. As the punk/alternative rock band Billy Talent put it, "We got a counter-culture you can buy off a shelf / If you're losing your identity, try somebody else."[23] In a world of status seekers, the basis of consumption is not to consume an object for need or satisfaction or for its use-value but to buy it as a symbol of status, for its sign-value. Symbolic consumption has no such practical limit.[24] The value of consumption objects is detached from the objective factors that determine their value (use and exchange), just as souls are severed from children in *The Golden Compass*.[25]

Sign-value refers to the production of signs, particularly through advertising, that confer value. The highest values are assigned to the most unnecessary uses, such as waste, conspicuous consumption, idleness, and so on. Objects of consumption are produced with an eye to their expiration, through planned obsolescence and changes in fashion. What is symbolically important is consumption beyond what may be essential: consumer society requires and perpetuates this waste. In the consumer age, the cultural celebrity—rather than the self-made entrepreneur—is the icon who becomes a hero through excessive consumption.[26]

Objects are embedded in a **code**, like a language or communication system, that signifies the value of the signs the objects embody.[27] When you consume, you purchase a sign through which you claim that your status is superior to some groups and that you belong with other high-status group. The sign confers social caste privilege. Baudrillard argues that the sign-values of objects and the status differences they reflect are parts of the human condition. Objects have always conferred the attribute of social distinction on their possessors. In the modern affluent society, a commodity's sign-value has become its social and economically dominant form.[28]

The code of signs and differences not only confers status, according to Baudrillard, it also integrates and regulates society. The modern ideology of egalitarianism, justice, and so on, cannot integrate society because these values are too obviously contradicted by the actual workings of the system. Instead, the system is integrated and regulated by the unconscious mechanism of a code of signs and differences. People are socialized into the code and taught to play by its rules. Within this system, only fashion revolutions can take place.[29] Like makeup on the face, the media of advertising obscures the real features of objects and substitutes a code that signifies their sign-value.

For Baudrillard, the change from use and exchange to sign-value reveals that society is changing its form fundamentally: "A neo-reality has everywhere been substituted for reality, a neo-reality entirely produced by combining elements of the code." Throughout all aspects of daily life, **simulations** are taking the place of what used to be assumed to be real. As mass communications expand and present the world to us, that presentation assumes the cloak of reality. As the simulated or the virtual replace the real with the neo-real, reality is abolished and obliterated. There is no longer any way to peer through the veils and see an actual reality beyond.[30]

In denying reality, Baudrillard is not concerned with distinguishing between what is real and what is only a simulation, as if the former had pride of place. The real, he says "is what it is, but it no longer makes sense to think or reflect upon it as such."[31] For example, in the nineteenth and twentieth centuries, what had once been a purely utopian project (socialism) was brought into real existence but, in the process, it was revealed to be false. This simulation of socialism (based on a model that never existed) has hollowed out the meaning of *reality*, leaving only a **hyperreality** devoid of any single meaning.[32] As the real disappears behind the proliferation of signs, it is resurrected, then, as a caricature of itself.[33] The western

frontier is long gone in America, but it is brought back to life in numerous ways through consumer culture, from films to simulated western decor in restaurants.

Baudrillard's *Simulacra and Simulation*

> *The furniture in [the Georgian-style house] was called* reproduction. . . . *[F]or each reproduction item, there was supposed to be an original somewhere. Or there had been once. Or something.*[34]
>
> — Margaret Atwood, *Oryx and Crake*, 2003

There is a widespread view among post-structuralists that there is a crisis of representation in contemporary discourse. Empirical science and Enlightenment theories suppose a realistic theory of knowledge (epistemology), Frederic Jameson says, which "projects a mirror theory of knowledge and art, whose fundamental evaluative categories are those of adequacy, accuracy, and Truth itself."[35] The key to understanding the contemporary world, Baudrillard writes in *Simulacra and Simulation* (1981), is to see it as a vast field of simulations that have less and less connection with anything that is or might have been real. A simulacra is, generally, a copy of an object that had once existed, such as a Georgian-style house. When copies are made of copies, in endless repetition, the link is broken between the original and the copy.

In Ridley Scott's science fiction film *Blade Runner* (1982), "replicants" are virtually indistinguishable from humans. Rick Deckard (Harrison Ford) uses a retinal scan—a 2019 "Fruit Machine"—to detect Rachael's emotional responses, which separate authentic humans from robotic simulacra (replicants). Since the development of artificial intelligence, authentic humanity can be defined only by empathy and not rationality. Rachael is a replicant but doesn't know it; Deckard is attracted to Rachel, but, as a hardened replicant hunter, is he actually less human than Rachael or equally inhuman?

If the real is defined as "*that for which it is possible to provide an equivalent representation,*" Baudrillard says, then the real has been effaced. We are left with models of something that no longer have an origin or a real history.[36] Indeed, there need not even be an original in the sense that the origin of a copy might be in the imagination. Social life is regulated by the simulation principle, not the reality principle; the search for some final truth or meaning reveals only models that have been divorced from any grounding in reality.[37] An idol, which is the graven images of a God, does not simulate something final and real; it is a perfect simulacrum because it has no underlying truth or reality. A simulacrum is not "unreal" because that word would imply the possibility of being real. A simulacrum refers endlessly, in a circular or revolving way, only back to itself.

Consumer culture endlessly reproduces a manufactured environment that is signified, Baudrillard says, by the phenomenon of pop art. Pop art was mechanically, artificially, and serially reproduced, eliminating the distinction between the original or the real and the representation. For Baudrillard, pop art signified "the end of the subversion of the world and of the curse of art." It conflates the existing society with models and colludes with the status quo.[38] We live, therefore, in a world that is defined, not as real, but as "*the desert of the real itself,*"[39] a phrase that has entered popular culture (see Box 11.2).

For Baudrillard, the real has dissolved into something that is "always already reproduced," a model of the real that has no longer any original and therefore no actual link to the real. In his terms, as mentioned earlier, it has become hyperreal; and hyperrealism never leaves the realm of simulation. Hyperreality eradicates the contradiction between the real and the imaginary.[40] Mass media is the prime mechanism for generating

hyperreality. For example, the reality TV show *Cops* purports to show real police work. It doesn't show cops in their mundane, everyday, repetitive routines that make up the vast majority of their policing time.

The idea that the hyperreal has come to overshadow the real can be exemplified by Baudrillard's response to the Gulf War (1990–1). The war was waged primarily by the United States following Iraq's invasion of Kuwait, an important oil-producing kingdom. Baudrillard, however, declared that "the Gulf War Did Not Take Place." In his view, the war was presented by the media much like a video game or simulation. Spectators experienced the war as a media scrum, through the commentary and gloss of CNN talking heads. The media promoted the war and gave people an outlet for their desire for spectacle. Information or pseudo-information about the event, endlessly repeated, overwhelmed the event. The simulation became more real than real. No one interrogated the fraud behind the war or the illusion of actual battle. Through the distorted media lens, it was impossible to see beyond "the systematic manipulation of data [and] the artful dramatization" of the event.[41]

Once the hyperreal has established its dominance, it is difficult to see any way to bring back the "real" or to imagine any politics that could fulfill the now-dead claims for truth or justice. In *The Consumer Society*, Baudrillard said that the Achilles heel of the system is the need for increasing consumption. People could attack the system through boycotts and acts that destroy consumption goods. The consumer, like the Third Estate in France in 1789, represents nothing, Baudrillard asserts, but might come to be everything.

The idea of a consumer revolt does not hold Baudrillard's attention for long, however, because it does not negate the system as a whole. A real rupture from capitalism must entail a total break that originates from outside the system. Before capitalism, pre-modern societies produced and

✣ BOX 11.2 • THEORY IN CONTEXT ✣

The Matrix

Jean Baudrillard's ideas make several cameo appearances in Andy and Lana Wachowski's 1999 film *The Matrix*, about a future dystopian social order that is run by humanly-created AI. Humans are kept unconscious in pods while their inert bodies are enslaved for the purposes of creating a gigantic, interconnected power grid to maintain the AI robots. To keep the human battery cells in a healthy state, their minds are stimulated by a computer program, the matrix, generating a common dream-state that appears to their minds as their reality. Their programmed dreams are more vivid, pleasurable, and less dangerous, than the actual apocalyptic wasteland that is the Earth—they are more real than real. Nevertheless, a rebel faction is intent on liberating the human energy slaves and reconstituting society. The matrix recreates social life pretty much as it exists in the turn-of-the-century world. The AI overlords might have done better by fulfilling simulations of conscious desires, as depicted in such television shows as *Fantasy Island*. They had created an earlier matrix 1.0 designed to simulate happiness, but human nature is perverse and functions well only in a world that also produces unhappiness, as simulated in the matrix 2.0 reboot, which is the dream reality of the film.

The hero of the film is a hacker whose code name is Neo. The leader of the real-world rebel movement is Morpheus. When Neo is rescued from the dream-state and introduced to the world-as-it-is, Morpheus paraphrases Baudrillard by welcoming Neo to "the desert of the real."[42] *The Matrix* implies that the simulation of reality produces a false consciousness, which is intentionally generated to hide from people the actual, desolate reality of their existence. Neo is brought back to actual reality and to a rebel army intent on replacing the simulacrum with the real. He travels, with increasing difficulty, between the matrix and the real, aware of the difference between them. For Baudrillard, however, the distinction between the two in the late twentieth century had been effaced and only the hyperreal remained.

In another episode of the film, Neo is visited (in the matrix) by a contact, Troy, who purchases contraband software. Neo keeps the CD and the money hidden in a copy of Baudrillard's book, *Simulacra and Simulation*—although it only appears to be a book because it's hollowed out. The existence of a void within Baudrillard's book, however, brings to mind the long-standing paradox that a claim that there is no truth cannot be true because truth itself is denied. What is the relationship between Baudrillard's iconic book and the replacement of reality by hyperreality? Is Baudrillard's book only self-referential and circular?

exchanged goods in the form of gifts. The form was symbolic exchange, which was a self-limiting cyclical event that imposed the social obligation to reciprocate the gift. In the act of gift-giving and in festivals of **symbolic exchange**, Baudrillard perceives "the *transgression* of the economic" and the potential to bring the system to an end. Although the code is ubiquitous and generates symbolic order, this order is precarious. It can be breached through symbolic disorder.[43]

The Death of the Political and the Social

The dialectic is definitively over. The grand Marxist promise has ended.[44]

— Jean Baudrillard, *The Divine Left*, 1985

Marx had moved critical theory beyond religion to political economy, engaging, Baudrillard says, in theoretical violence. His critique of political economy has similarly reached its limits. Marx merely substituted a new religion of meaning that reproduced the dominant codes of capitalism and universalism.[45] The Marxist dialectic was embedded in capitalist relations: "It never stopped being on the side of capitalism." The bourgeoisie accomplished a through-going social revolution by putting an end to the total feudal order, its status groups (estates), and its "code of social relations (birth, honour, hierarchy)." In place of the feudal order, the bourgeoisie substituted a radically new conception of social relationships (classes) and a new code based on "production, economy, rationality, progress." The proletariat is a necessary part of capitalist relations and does not offer a radical alternative. Trapped in the struggles of classes, it is doomed to remain within the bourgeois code.[46]

Politically, the division between the left and the right represents only a simulation of disagreement, the twin poles between which the existing system oscillates. Each is the mirror image, not the negation, of the other and each needs the other to exist.[47] Even Western Communist parties have abandoned their Leninist shells and accepted capitalism as a permanent system. What the left has abandoned, Baudrillard claims, is the threat of political violence. The left has "lost the immoral and excessive aspects of revolution, which would have challenged capital on the field of its virulence." The phantom of a real enemy sustains the whole system. Without its more threatening political binary, the Western political system is more vulnerable to disaffection. Communism appeared to threaten the social order and stimulated its apparent defence. The end of substantive division removes the false binary that otherwise keeps the social from dissolving.[48]

Similarly, Baudrillard asserts, "power, a real power, no longer exists."[49] There is no power in the sense of the lack of ability to control the future based on rational planning and predictability: "Power is still what it is, but it no longer makes sense to speak about what it represents, nor to represent it as 'real.'" Indeed, power is more a form "whose contents are unpredictable and whose stakes can be reversed." Power has disappeared, according to Baudrillard, along with social classes and class struggle. For Baudrillard, just as reality has collapsed into hyperreality, the social is imploding, collapsing inward into an undifferentiated mass. The masses are indifferent, bored, apathetic, and passive. In its ascending phase, capitalism had created the sphere of the social—civil society—in which people acted and exercised agency. Baudrillard does not see civil society as a potential source of counter-power to capital. In fact, with the collapse of power and the "Moribund real," the social also collapses. Society is evolving toward soft technologies and increasing simulation, making it "fluid, tactile, tactical, and psychedelic."[50]

In the world of the hyperreal, political power is replaced by spectacle. The masses do not want rational administration or social change. They neither want to be represented politically nor to represent themselves, as in self-management. They do, however, want spectacles, preferably ones that are grotesque and derisive. The modern is a world where "everyone floats, where everyone is left to his own desires, in the agony of doing and thinking what one wants at the moment" even as the will to act disappears.[51]

As a result of the death of the political and the social, it is necessary to move to a third, radically different level: that of symbolic exchange.[52] Marx defined humanity as being made up of essentially productive beings who make things and, in the process, make themselves. Baudrillard, in contrast, sees productive labour as in itself alienating: actual liberation is freedom *from* labour. Symbolic wealth makes a mockery of rational, material values and revels in "destruction, the deconstruction of value, transgression, or discharge." What is radically different from productive work is the seduction of play, pleasure, "pulsating, libidinal" bodily enjoyment, "a gratuitous and festive energizing of the body's powers."[53] Ultimately, change requires a new code, the equivalent of a revolution in "form, space, and colour . . . [similar to] the deconstruction of the object in painting." Politics, the real, the social are all ending with a whimper, not a bang. But, as the principles of reality and sociality dissolve, they might open into an unpredictable conflagration.[54]

Paradoxically, the more complete the system of meaning that is constructed, the more fallible it is and the easier it is to deconstruct; such a system can be reversed instantaneously. Change is not dialectical; it is catastrophic. Once things are pushed to the limit, they decompose. Simulation pushed to its limit, Baudrillard says, can only be destruction and death. But Baudrillard is not talking about the actual death of a human subject. What dies is the modernist idea of the subject, of economic value, power, and the social. In a world that is hyperreal, only the strategy of reversibility is fatal; purely symbolic exchange and the seduction of enjoyment and play are the negations of modernity.

Symbolic exchange derives precisely from the societies that had been colonized by Western imperialism. As a form, symbolic exchange is cyclical and reversible: production ends in destruction; life, in death; a gift demands a counter-gift. The culture of symbolic exchange is different from modern society, which entails economic exchange, linear time, and power. These modern principles dissolve in the hyperreal, however, opening space for a new, "radical utopian version" of symbolic exchange to spring into being in all areas of society.[55]

The notion of reciprocation recurs throughout Baudrillard's analysis of the 2001 attack on the World Trade Center in New York. American society, he says, was deeply complicit in the event. As power accumulates in the centre, it generates the will to destroy it, particularly among the exploited and disinherited. Popular culture had rehearsed and prepared for such an attack through numerous films, discussions, and small-scale rehearsals.[56] The event was not unimaginable; it was, in fact, routinely imagined. Like the Gulf War, the attack on the Twin Towers was worse than real; it was symbolic.

When a concentrated system of power completely dominates technically, militarily, and ideologically, the only response to it is the "absolute weapon of death," the singular act that can challenge such power. The "ghostly enemy" of globalization is not simply Islam; the conflict is not a clash of civilizations. Once a system has expanded to its limits and become the epitome of power, it becomes so internally fragile that it can "be ignited by the slightest spark." Terrorists shift the battle to the symbolic realm in which death is much more than merely real; it is a pure, "symbolic and sacrificial" form of defiance. Death is a "gift" for which only the death of the system is the reciprocal answer. One infinitesimally small action can cause incalculable consequences. Just as the Twin Towers were the simulacra of global power in their symmetrical twinness, their sudden and unexpected collapse, which Baudrillard likens to their own suicide, foreshadowed the fragility and potential collapse of the system they represented.[57] In a simple and realist interpretation, as the West reacts to the 2001 attacks and the 2014 threat of the Islamic State in Syria and Iraq by increasing surveillance of its own population and further empowering spy agencies—making everyone who travels a potential suspect, increasing police powers of detention without charges, and taking away civil liberties—it responds to the symbolic deaths of the terrorists with its own suicide. Freedom is slowly killed while constraints and regulations expand, mirroring in the West the fundamentalism it supposedly combats.

Not everything in the new surveillance society is turning to the right. For example, gay marriage has become lawful in Canada and in several US states, and transgender and transsexual persons have greater visibility and acceptance. Within the women's movement, third-wave feminists took to task the relatively privileged position of second-wave, white, middle-class feminists. Feminism had to come to grips with the complex intersection of competing identities: gender, colour, class, sexuality, ability, and so on. On the other hand, some third-wave feminists argue that anything that empowers individual women within the existing social system is by definition feminist. The meaning of feminism has become an increasingly contested terrain.

Third-Wave Feminism

By the 1990s, many of the goals of second-wave feminism appeared to have been achieved. The generation of girls that grew up as daughters of second-wave feminists inherited a world that was significantly changed from their mothers' childhood, largely through the efforts of their parents' generation. For middle-class women, only the most hidebound professions and workplaces remain primarily male-dominated, such as engineering, primary industries such as mining and fishing, and computer science. Women are now well-established in law, medicine, and academia. More university students are women than men, with the exception of some graduate programs. Growing up in families that often pay more than only lip service to female empowerment and the sharing of household tasks, today's young, middle-class

women often take for granted a level of equality that their parents could not. It is easy for them to assume that feminism has achieved its goals. Caught up in lifestyle concerns, common sense suggests that feminism is passé and that identifying as a feminist has more negative than positive consequences.

As second-wave feminists become grandparents, they often lament that the feminist agenda has stalled and that many gains of the past are being lost. Symbols of decline include the return of makeup, taking on the male partner's surname, the evolution of sexually alluring clothing for women that emphasizes a succession of exposed body parts, and a general return to feminine identity, however redefined. In second-wave feminism, controlling one's body meant more than just reproductive rights; it meant liberating sexual expression, symbolized by sexualized clothing. Burning bras was meant to be symbolic of removing restraint. But sexuality was a problematic form of empowerment. Second-wave feminists had generally condemned the sexualization of women that made them objects of male domination. Pornography and prostitution were forms of patriarchal oppression. Escaping objectification appeared to mean de-emphasizing sexuality rather than flaunting it. In a world shaped by the sexual double standard, multiple sexual partners did not carry the same connotations for women and men. Sexual freedom seemed to demand freedom *from* sexuality. These issues persist today, despite culturally produced models of sophisticated, single, urban women in control of their personal and sexual lives, such as Carrie Bradshaw (Sarah Jessica Parker) in *Sex and the City*. To punctuate the point that what was once a male preserve was open to women, Hollywood concocted the raunchy female comedy (*Bridesmaids* [2011], *The To Do List* [2013]).

In this sense, the contemporary age is sometimes seen as post-feminist. Feminism was rooted in legal inequality and second-class status. In the new world of equality of opportunity, legal boundaries have been erased and women have been empowered, as individuals, to define their identities and sexualities. Feminism is normalized and difference is commodified. During the 2014 Video Music Awards, for example, Beyoncé performed in front of a large sign labelling the artist "Feminist." Beyoncé is in charge of her life, her sexuality, and her corporate empire. As well, the mainstreaming of what used to be pornography offers specific models that purport to represent female, sexualized emancipation that serve only to stimulate the consumption of clothing, makeup, accessories, and lifestyles. Celebrity emancipation comes from money and status. It doesn't translate to the legions of imitative fans who can model the same image, gestures, and attitudes, but not from the high plane of distant stardom. Camille Paglia worries that hypersexualized young women are making themselves easy prey in a male-dominated world. Rather than culture, as suggested in the notion that we live in a "rape culture," Paglia attributes the danger to male instincts. In her alternative and essentialist version of feminism, the world is still a wilderness and rape arises from males' "savage nature."[58]

Women continue to be predominant in traditionally female occupations, such as nursing, clerical work, and school teaching. They also make up the majority of low-paid, part-time, and casual employees in the mushrooming service and retail industries. The glass ceiling that had frustrated women such as Dorothy E. Smith still prevents most women from moving in significant numbers into management and administration. And, despite important exceptions, politics is still a male domain. When women do break into positions of corporate or governmental power, they have to adapt to male cultures and reproduce hierarchical ways of administering things and people. As Virginia Woolf suggested, the institutional cultures that women enter change women entrants more

than women are able to transform these cultures in progressive, feminist ways.

Over the decades, what feminism is, how it is defined, and what its goals and methods are have divided women and their movement. Feminists who are now secure in their academic footholds and have gone beyond the conceptions of the previous generations of women activists often use the label "third-wave feminism" to differentiate their views from those who went before them. Their evaluations of the feminist agenda and what the emancipation of women entails differ from second-wave feminism. Issues surrounding sexuality are at the forefront of the debates among contemporary feminists, including sex work as a legitimate occupation, sexuality as empowerment, the proliferation of transgender and transsexual identities, and new means and politics of reproduction.

Perhaps most fundamentally, contemporary feminists recognize that earlier feminist movements were deeply marked by their white, middle-class, Western origins. Despite the rhetoric of inclusion, women who were "othered" by racialization, ethnicity, sexuality, ability, and class were excluded, or they were included only at the price of whitewashing their differences. Critical social theory demands the ability to harness an outsider's perspective to help contextualize intimate, inside knowledge, which is regularly demonstrated by post-colonial and feminist literature. Things not only look different from the outside, they *are* different. The perspectives of black, working-class women not only expand feminist analysis to excluded groups but open new ways to understand what has been assumed to be normative. Judith Butler has a widespread following among graduate students, which is similar to Dorothy E. Smith's influence on an earlier generation. One of the differences between second- and third-wave feminism is that black feminist thought now has an established place in the canon. Patricia Hill Collins and bell hooks, for example, are making significant contributions to black feminism and to social theory generally.

Patricia Hill Collins (b. 1948)

Patricia Hill grew up an only child in a black working-class family in Philadelphia. A diligent student, Hill began attending Brandeis University in 1965 at the age of 17.[59] At first, the experience was overwhelming, and she gradually felt silenced by the daily assaults that came from being socially denigrated as an African-American, working-class woman.[60] In between earning degrees from Brandeis (in sociology) and Harvard (in teaching) and her 1984 Ph.D. from Brandeis, Hill married Roger Collins and worked as a schoolteacher in Roxbury, a racially and culturally diverse community in Boston. Her experiences as an inner-city teacher and in developing curricula for black studies inspired her investigation into the history and social thought of black women. She began her professional academic career in African Studies at the University of Cincinnati. Capping a series of firsts, Collins became the one-hundredth president of the American Sociological Association in 2009, the first African-American woman to hold that position.[61]

Hill Collins elaborates standpoint theory and methodology, asserting that the task of the feminist writer is to give a voice to the voiceless and learn to see things through their eyes. Hill Collins's book *Black Feminist Thought* (1990) integrates issues of race, gender, and social class seen though the experiences of women. The book places black women at the centre of the analysis, privileging their voices and their standpoint and highlighting their difference from the dominant discourse. The voices Hill Collins represents are diverse, demonstrating that theory and intellectual creativity are not the province of a select few but instead emanate from a range of people. She inserts her experiences into the book, speaking for the many who have been silenced. By 2000, Hill Collins recognized that empowerment for black women necessarily had to occur in the context of the struggle for social justice, and that this struggle includes issues of sexuality and culture.[62]

Hill Collins's aim is not just to produce analysis but to produce critical social theory that, by definition, empowers its subjects. A **dialogical** relationship exists whereby for black feminists "action and thought inform one another." She recognizes that intersecting forms of oppression have to be targeted simultaneously. Black women exist within a multi-dimensional **matrix of domination**, within which institutionalized racism is especially visible. In the United States, racism and racial segregation remain basic features of the landscape. This entrenched social inequality is buttressed by an ideology of colour blindness: the idea that racial differences can and should be ignored.[63]

In the post–civil rights era, when legal barriers were removed, it was sometimes suggested that colour blindness had replaced racialization. In a situation in which structural racism persists, treating everyone as though they are the same perpetuates the inequalities. In this sense, colour blindness is another form of racism. African Americans experience a new form of duality: invisibility and hyper-visibility. Blacks in positions of celebrity status, such as musicians, hip hop artists, actors, and including Barak Obama, present one image of blackness that reinforces colour blindness. At the same time, black inner-city neighbourhoods deteriorate, sinking deeper into invisibility, neglect, and poverty.[64]

For Hill Collins, most black women in the United States have certain common experiences and "live in a different world from that of people who are not Black and female." Their standpoint includes common struggles, which have long historical legacies and reflect the dangers of everyday life. Black women from different social classes, for example, often experience the same discriminatory treatment in stores. This specific position, undergirded by racial segregation, stimulates a distinctive consciousness. Black women create a collective body of wisdom and practices that allow them to survive in white-dominated America.[65] Their interpretation of their own lives is valid, as is the oppression they experience. If oppressed groups are not politically active, it is not because they accept dominant views or have a false, flawed consciousness about their own oppression.

Nevertheless, common challenges do not necessarily foster a group consciousness or standpoint. "[I]ndividual Black women neither have identical experiences nor interpret experiences in a similar fashion," nor do they respond to core themes in a similar way. Black women may respond to dominant images by deconstructing them, internalizing them, or transgressing them. These varying responses in the US are shaped by social class, sexuality, ethnicity, and citizenship statuses. Consequently, there is no homogeneous or unifying black women's standpoint. To claim such a standpoint suppresses difference and applies a normative, essentialist understanding to individual women. Nevertheless, Hill Collins asserts, there is still a black women's *collective* standpoint. Transnationally, women of African descent "encounter recurring social issues such as poverty, violence, reproductive concerns, lack of education, sex work, and susceptibility to disease."[66]

Critical social theory is critical because of its commitment to justice not just for one's own group, but for others as well. It is tied to lived experience and the everyday thoughts of black women, but it aims to improve these experiences. Such theory is a form of specialized knowledge produced by black women intellectuals that has to be grounded dialogically in black feminist practices and everyday knowledge. Black feminist thought does not raise consciousness but "affirms, rearticulates, and provides a vehicle for

expressing in public a consciousness that quite often already exists." It aims to empower its subjects and to stimulate resistance.[67] This aim is exemplified in theory and practice through the work of bell hooks.

bell hooks (b. 1952)

Gloria Watkins, who later adopted the pseudonym bell hooks, was born in Kentucky in 1952. Her father worked as a custodian while her mother raised seven children. In her book on feminist theory, hooks wrote that she grew up in a "southern, black, father-dominated, working-class household" in which she experienced "various degrees of patriarchal tyranny." She was angered by these experiences and, by the age of 13, was critical of male domination and patriarchal politics. Women in her racially segregated community had an unacknowledged history of being strong mothers and active spiritual leaders in the church. She "had not known a life where women had not . . . helped, protected, and loved one another deeply."[68]

As a black, working-class, feminist activist, hooks imagined the importance of integration in a close, loving community for overcoming class distinctions, racism, and sexism. By the mid-1950s, schools in the American south had been desegregated and hooks was plunged into a cauldron of personal and public racial politics when she attended a school where the majority of students and teachers were white. After graduating, Watkins attended Stanford University in California and received an MA in English from the University of Wisconsin (Madison). She then became a lecturer in Ethnic Studies at the University of Southern California and received a Ph.D. in 1983.[69]

Watkins first used the pseudonym bell hooks in 1978 in a small book of poems. Bell Hooks was her grandmother's name; the decision not to use capitals in the pseudonym was meant symbolically to help efface the (postmodern) author from the text. hooks believed that the readers' focus should be on the words and ideas rather than on the person who wrote them.[70] Ironically, this idiosyncratic use of capitals tends to draw *more* attention to the author's name than otherwise.

Her book *Ain't I a Woman? Black Women and Feminism* (1981) has become a key text in what has become known as third-wave feminism. Critical of the unacknowledged race and class blindness indicative of most second-wave feminist writings, hooks uncovered a systematic oppression in the United States in which class subjection is linked inextricably to patriarchal oppression and white supremacy. In *Feminist Theory: From Margin to the Center*, hooks condemns the implicit and often explicit racism she found in the writings of white feminists. Their exclusive focus on gender prevented them from understanding the diverse positions of women and the interrelationships among race, class, and gender. Both white women and black men can be oppressed (in the sense of having limited choices), but they can also act as exploiters and oppressors. When poor men express male chauvinism, they give vent to their own sense of powerlessness rather than privilege. Simplistic definitions of feminism, such as the movement to achieve equality with men, ignore differences of class and colour. Poor or, in most cases, black women could not define feminism this way because the men in their experience were themselves oppressed and exploited.[71]

In addition, hooks resists seeing feminism as a lifestyle choice or a question of personal identity, a perspective that is privileged for white middle-class women. Minority women, she argues, do not feel an absence of a community of women because they do not live in the splendid and lonely isolation of the white suburban housewife. The focus of the feminist movement on male domination privileged women over men and too often amounted to a war between the sexes. An authentic feminist movement that ends sexist oppression would have a positive effect on both men and women. It "offers a new ideological meeting ground for the sexes, a space for criticism, struggle and transformation" that brings the war of the sexes to a halt and creates "intimacy, mutuality, and camaraderie." Women should not assert that they *are* feminists, which implies a politics of identity and lifestyle; instead, they should assert that they *advocate* feminism.[72]

Focusing on ending oppression rather than seeking equality, hooks believes, calls attention to systems of domination and the interconnections among all forms of group oppression, including race, class, and gender. Within this struggle, however, sexist oppression is fundamental—not because patriarchy is the basis of all other forms of oppression, as second-wave feminists often believed, but because it is the form of domination that most of us experience directly in our lives and are socialized to accept as normal. But all systems of oppression are interconnected because they are maintained by similar institutional structures. To resist one is necessarily to fight against all.[73]

Much feminist theory, from Engels through second-wave feminism, viewed the family as a key site of patriarchal domination and talked of abolishing family relations. Even female-headed families may teach children to accept dominant authority, hooks argues. The family may be a "setting of intense suffering and pain." But oppression is not endemic to family relations and devaluing family life reflects the perspective of privilege. Middle-class women, hooks generalizes, may have experienced material well-being but their family lacked the attributes of long-term, unconditional care and love. From the perspective of many black women, family "is an important kinship structure . . . an environment of care and affirmation, especially for the very young and the very old." Many black women find the family the least oppressive social institution. It provides a necessary support system in the face of the exploitation people experience from other social institutions, such as schools and work. Rather than focusing on helping to destroy the family, feminism should inject family life with the ethics of "communalism, shared responsibility, and mutuality."[74]

As an educator, hooks practises critically engaged pedagogy. She argues that schooling does not have to be an agency of oppression and authority. Teaching can be a subversive act that challenges wrongs and encourages people to transgress oppressive roles and rules.[75] In her many roles as educator, journalist, poet, and activist, hooks is an insurgent black intellectual who makes waves when she writes or talks.

Postmodernists, hooks says, with few exceptions, have not recognized black cultural presence and appear not to know that black women exist. This absence is particularly ironic when postmodernists claim to have "opened up a theoretical terrain where 'difference and Otherness' can be considered legitimate issues in the academy."[76] Postmodernism is mired in the inaccessible language of the **master narratives** it purports to challenge, and it excludes the voices of "displaced, marginalized, exploited, and oppressed black people." Feelings of hopelessness are expressed both by the black middle-class in response to continuing racism and by the rapidly growing black underclass, mired in despair, nihilism, and addiction. They are all, also, yearning for a voice. In response, hip hop and rap provided a means for expressing the critical voices of underclass black males. In contrast, the postmodern deconstruction of the "subject" denies anyone an authentic, transcendent identity. It contradicts the very search for a subjective voice through which African Americans can express their conditions. From this perspective, postmodernist strategies do not transform or change circumstances.[77]

On the other hand, the postmodern critique of essentialism, which challenges the idea of universality and the idea that identity is basically determined by mass culture, opens new grounds for constructing the self and affirming agency.

There exist multiple black experiences and black identities. The struggle of African Americans to develop and express "radical black subjectivity" constructs an identity from the authority of these experiences that is oppositional and liberating.[78]

Part of the struggle for black identity is over representation in the media, hooks says, an area in which there has been little progress and few revolutionary interventions. Dominant representations in the culture reflect and reproduce white, patriarchal supremacy. Such images are negatively seductive; they colonize and dehumanize African Americans, who internalize white values and come to see themselves through white eyes. In the context of the history of racist representation, deconstructing the category of whiteness and loving blackness is necessary.[79] White ideology has sexualized blacks as forbidden delights as part of their "othering." Blacks are seen as more exciting, intense, and somewhat more dangerous and therefore more alluring. But hooks detects a subversive possibility in the desire for the "other." Openly expressing this desire for the "other" indicates a break from a white supremacist past, although not necessarily a break from class or patriarchy.[80]

White culture has an ambiguous relationship with black culture, which it has commodified and neutered of its critical potential. The inappropriate and ultimately colonizing perspective of white society on black culture is reflected in Jack Kerouac's *On the Road* (1957). Sal Paradise, the Beat protagonist of the novel, wishes he were African American, not a bored, disillusioned white. Strolling "through the dark mysterious streets" of the black section of Denver, Sal said that he was "wishing I were a Negro, feeling that the best the white world had offered was not enough ecstasy for me, not enough life, joy, kicks, darkness, music; not enough night. . . . All my life I'd had white ambitions." In that "unbearably sweet night," Sal wishes he "could exchange worlds with the happy, true-hearted, ecstatic Negroes of America." In the black neighbourhood, "there was excitement and the air was filled with the vibration of really joyous life that knows nothing of disappointment and 'white sorrows' and all that."[81] Kerouac's description can be read as irony or parody. What Sal does immediately afterwards is look up a rich, white woman he knows who gives him a 100 dollars to go back to San Francisco to have fun.

The role of the insurgent black intellectual is to intervene in all sites of struggle in everyday life and critique the interlinked domination that reproduces class-divided, racist, and sexist cultures. In her interventions, hooks speaks of oppression, patriarchal domination, and racialization more than happy, "Negro" ecstasy. She brings her radicalizing message to the wider audience through poetry, journalism, and public speaking. She addresses university graduates and small local groups in churches and neighbourhoods. David Horowitz, a neo-conservative, considers bell hooks to be one of the most dangerous intellectuals in the United States.[82]

Judith Butler (b. 1956)

Judith Butler was born in Cleveland Ohio in 1956 to Jewish parents. Most of her family on her mother's side had been killed in the Holocaust. Butler attended Hebrew school and, by the age of 14, developed an interest in philosophy and Jewish ethics. She said the rabbi had complained that she talked back in class and was not well-behaved. He assumed she was not serious about her studies and, as a punishment, began one-on-one tutoring in philosophy and ethics with his wayward pupil. Butler, however, said she "was thrilled" by the opportunity to study more deeply.[83] She attended Yale University, from which she received a Ph.D. in philosophy in 1984. She was trained in European philosophy, studying Kant, Hegel, Marx, and the Frankfurt School, later turning to postmodern French thought, including Foucault. Butler became professor of Comparative Litera-

ture and Rhetoric at the University of California, Berkeley.[84]

Butler said that her Jewish background is not incidental to her interpretations of sex and gender. She said that, as a youth, she had been troubled by Jewish exclusiveness and what she later defined as the policing of identity. The first question her family would ask about someone was whether that person was Jewish. When she was in graduate school, Butler became part of a lesbian community where she found the same tendency to assume binary identities: lesbian or not lesbian, gay or straight. When the AIDS crisis hit the gay community in the 1970s and 1980s, many gay men had kept their relationships secret from their families. They "were unable to get access to the hospital to see their lover, unable to call their parents and say, 'I have just lost the love of my life.'"[85] In this context, Butler began developing her ideas about sex and gender, which she expounded in her book *Gender Trouble: Feminism and the Subversion of Identity* (1990), a text which has become influential in contemporary feminism and queer theory.

Butler questions one of the most fundamental assumptions in feminism: that women can be viewed as the subject of their own emancipation. The idea of the "subject" is basic to modern society. People assumed that the individual was a rational and conscious being who could use her or his mind to understand the world as it actually was. The individual subject could grasp her or his true interests in relation to this objective world and seek enlightenment and liberation from illegitimate constraints. The point of critical analysis, Butler says, is to critique "the categories of identity that contemporary juridical structures engender, naturalize, and immobilize."[86]

The idea of a subject is based on political and linguistic criteria that are established in discourse and that then create the frame within which a subject (individual self) is defined. As Foucault argued, "systems of power *produce* the subjects they subsequently come to represent." Power, in this sense, is a political structure that regulates, limits, and controls individual subjects. In particular, the political system that rests on dominating power constructs "gender" and gendered subjects, but the basis of this construction is concealed by a discourse that takes this construction to be natural and normative.[87] The category "woman," then, is not simply a pre-existing given but is actually a social construction that emerges from existing relations of power that are written into law. Our ideas of gender have been developed through a process that is fundamentally shaped by power inequalities: the law produces the discursive formation of a legal subject and then conceals this act of construction behind the premise that the subject is naturally pre-existing (foundational). The result of this reification of the subject is to naturalize and legitimate the hegemony of existing regulations. Consequently, gender identity is not something fixed in the physical body but is variable according to different discursive formations.

The category "women" does not connote a common identity within which all those designated women may be subsumed: "[G]ender is not always constituted coherently or consistently in different historical contexts." Furthermore, gender intersects with a number of other political and cultural categories, such as class, race, ethnicity, and sexuality, that are equally the result of discursive formation and, hence, no less socially constructed than gender. The search for a universally valid form of patriarchal domination in feminist thought has tended to sweep away cultural differences and reproduce dominant Western definitions of gender and oppression and thereby contribute to rather than resist colonization. Assuming a stable and universal subject separates identity from intersecting categories. It also excludes those who refuse to accept the category or those "who fail to conform to unspoken normative requirements of the subject." Consequently, feminism has become fragmented and the idea

that there is a universal "woman" misrepresents many of those whom feminists claim to represent. As a result, a new sort of feminist politics is required that contests the way gender and identity have been normatively constructed.[88] Cultural theorist Stuart Hall similarly argues that black identity has to be built through the recognition of diversity and difference rather than by seeking a single black identity (see Box 11.3).

In theories related to Freud, sex was defined as related to physical difference (male or female anatomy). Freud's idea was that biology is destiny, that being born male or female necessarily entails gender behaviours that are either masculine or feminine: the gendered subject was split into two binary categories. Butler, however, disputes "the immutable character of sex"; that is, that sex is essentially a biologically determined desire generated by "natural, anatomical, chromosomal, or hormonal" forces. In feminist theory, *gender* is used as a term to distinguish biologically given sex from socially constructed behaviour. *Sex* becomes "a politically neutral surface *on which* culture acts."[89] *Gender* refers to the culturally variable meanings that are assigned to the "sexed body."

Gender does not simply mirror the assumed binary sex differences. For Butler, "the constructed status of gender is theorized as radically independent of sex." As a result, "gender itself becomes a free-floating artifice" according to which there is no necessary connection between men and masculinity and women and femininity; either term could equally signify a male as a female body. Further, Butler argues that the category "sex" is also a cultural construct; hence gender cannot simply be "the cultural inscription of meaning on a pre-given sex." More deeply, she argues that sex is a discursively formulated category and not an objective, **prediscursive** biological fact. As such, sex categories are produced by the "matrix of power relations"[90] but the differences thereby produced are then assumed to be objectively existing differences, making the sexual binary appear natural

✒ BOX 11.3 • BIOGRAPHY ✒

Stuart Hall (1932–2014)

Stuart Hall was born in Kingston, Jamaica, into a middle-class family in thrall to what he called "the colonial romance": his family identified closely with Britain and with white Jamaicans. Both of Hall's parents were mixed race (including white, black, and East Indian). He says that he was the darkest member of his family and knew it from the moment he was born. His sensibility about racial distinctions was honed early in his life when his status-conscious parents told him he was not to bring home black friends from school. Hall's sister fell in love with a black medical student but was barred from seeing him by her mother. After 1945, while still in school, Hall became interested in Jamaican independence. His family, however, was not a part of the movement.[91]

In 1950, Hall went to England to attend Oxford University as a Rhodes Scholar. He was part of a large, post-war migration of black people from the West Indies to Britain. As he searched for an identity in England, he experienced the typical sense of cultural twoness. He was drawn into the West Indian Society at Oxford and developed a strong sense of being black in a very white (and upper middle-class) world. As civil rights became an issue on both sides of the Atlantic, Hall consciously identified as a "black intellectual." In 1958 he abandoned a Ph.D. he was writing on the American novelist Henry James and became a founding editor of the radical academic journal the *New Left Review*. The *Review* opened debates about immigration and the politics of identity.[92]

In 1964, Hall married Catherine Barrett, 13 years his junior, whom he met on a Campaign for Nuclear Disarmament (CND) march. As a mixed-race couple in Birmingham, they experienced daily prejudice but watched it fade over time. Catherine became a post-colonial historian and wrote a book about the free-slave movement in Jamaica.

When, in 1964, Raymond Williams and Richard Hoggart established the first Cultural Studies program at a British university in Birmingham, Hall became a founding member, bringing concerns with political and social change into the study of popular culture. At the foundation of cultural studies at Birmingham was an insistence on taking popular, low-status cultural forms seriously and tracing the interweaving threads of culture, power, and politics.

Hall examined the way that colonialism expropriated indigenous peoples from their culture and identity, substituting a deformed and crippling sense of otherness. The attempt to construct an anti-colonial black identity rooted in Africa helped create a sense of unity, but it ignored the numerous cultural differences that had developed during the **diaspora**, in the centuries of enslavement and post-slavery oppression. Identity has to be constructed within the centrality of diversity and heterogeneity. There is no essential Caribbean, for example: only a pastiche of skin colours, musical genres, cuisines, and dialects.

and legitimate. Power, according to Butler, is the generative mechanism shaping language and all subsequent discursive categories.

Performativity

Don't be a drag just be a queen . . . I'm on the right track baby / I was born this way.

— Lady Gaga, "Born This Way," 2011

Lady Gaga's progressive message in "Born This Way" is her assertion that it does not matter what colour your skin is or what your ethnic background is; everyone is beautiful and should express self-love. She extends her argument to gender differences: "No matter gay, straight or bi / Lesbian, transgendered . . ." When people reveal their homosexuality, one strategy of acceptance is to state that their sexual preferences are inborn and natural to them. Their homosexual identity is who they are inside. It is a useful, legitimating argument because it exposes homophobia as a violation of human rights that is equivalent to racial and ethnic discrimination and, therefore, demands emancipation and equality. Perhaps ironically given the title of her song, Lady Gaga plays with a variety of gender categories and expressions in a transgressive way that suggests that gender is performed.[93]

Butler, however, disputes the basic notion that sex, gender, and sexuality should be understood as being "born" one way or another. For Butler, the body is not a "taken-for-granted ground or surface upon which gender significations are inscribed, a mere facticity . . . prior to significance." The body is not the original source of identity, or desire, or meaning because it is always interpreted in the context of culturally imposed meanings. But her argument does not mean that gender as an attribute is simply free-floating or that gender is simply the attributes one chooses. Nor does her argument mean that "all gendered possibilities are open" at any time. Seeing sex, gender, and sexuality as attributes of social constructions implies

that what is socially done can be undone. Gender is contextualized within hegemonic cultural discourses that shape the limits within which gender can be imagined and constructed. For example, our understanding of gender is moulded by the normative view that the male/masculine and female/feminine binaries reflect a necessary link between sex and gender. Gender identity, for Butler, is a disciplinary production, generated in a society within a masculine-dominated domain along the taken-for-granted lines imposed by an idealized and compulsive heterosexuality. Gender, sex, and sexuality are assumed to reflect each other, making gender identity a falsely stable phenomenon that conceals and repudiates actually existing gender discontinuities.[94]

The dominant discourse of **compulsory heterosexuality** and the norms of gender it constructs impose a rigid, regulatory frame that persists over time through endless repetition. In so doing gender norms appear to be a real substance with "a natural sort of being." In this process, attributes that are socially constructed undergo sedimentation, becoming seemingly permanent. Bodies are configured into two sexes that are naturally in a binary relation to each other, a categorization that is made to seem natural and to reflect common sense. This naturalization thereby consolidates and strengthens the hegemony of power that engendered them. Compulsory heterosexuality is the regulatory practice within which gender identity is formed. These regulatory practices actually constitute "the internal coherence of the subject, indeed, the self-identical status of the person."[95]

Butler argues that regulatory practices actually constitute this identity, which is then thought to be substantive, independent, and autonomous. For Butler, gender is not a thing (a noun) or a state of being; it is something that people *do*, a performance that, through repetition, comes to be seen as natural. The cultural discourse of compulsory heterosexuality shapes the gender performances people enact, which both create their sexual identity and consolidate their sense of being a coherent self. Rather than attributing actions to a subject, for Butler, "the performance founds and consolidates the subject." These **performative** acts and gestures repeatedly stylize the body through various discursive means. They create the illusion of springing from an authentic, interior gender core ("a seemingly seamless identity") but, on the contrary, they are merely "*performative* in the sense that the essence or identity that they otherwise purport to express are *fabrications* manufactured and sustained through corporeal signs and other discursive means."[96] The gendered body is performative and has no "reality" apart from these constitutive acts.

Genders that are politically constituted within the regulatory mechanisms of compulsory heterosexuality are neither true nor false. Hegemonic cultural discourse is believed to produce primary and stable gender identities, but identities, so constituted, are actually tenuous. They can come into existence or dissolve "depending on the concrete practices that constitute them." The fragile, constructed nature of gender identities is revealed by the appearance of "'incoherent' or 'discontinuous' gendered beings who appear to be persons but who fail to conform to the gender norms of cultural intelligibility by which persons are defined."[97] Therein, for Butler, lies the possibility of going beyond the constraints and injustices of compulsory heterosexuality.

Radical Resignification

The power of language to work on bodies is both the cause of sexual oppression and the way beyond that oppression.[98]

— Judith Butler, *Gender Trouble*, 1990

Because *woman* and *gender* are ongoing discursive practices, they are "open to intervention and **resignification**." Power regulates, bringing about restrictive repetition, but these acts may also be subversive. They also "enable the assertion of alternative domains . . . new possibilities for gender. . . . [I]t is only within the practices of repetitive signifying that a subversion of identity becomes possible." Certain possibilities of doing gender through hyperbole or parody, such as transvestism or transsexualism, for example, create dissonance and confusion, which potentially call identity into question and expose its otherwise normalized regulatory practices. Within "the repetition of heterosexual constructs within sexual cultures both gay and straight may well be the inevitable site of the denaturalization and mobilization of gender categories."[99]

Sex is "a performatively enacted signification" that can be detached from heterosexual constructs. As normative notions of gender are represented through self-parody, self-criticism, and playfulness, these categories may be subverted and displaced "to make gender trouble." "Drag" performances, for example, represent identity as fluid and contingent, which opens a space for "resignification and recontextualization." Failing to repeat compulsory identities reveals the arbitrary relationship among sex, gender, and performance. Dissonant performances reveal that the assumed natural is no less a performative status than the parody.[100]

Butler's approach is central to a relatively new body of thought called **queer theory**. The term is an appropriation and reassigning of what had once been a derogatory term applied to gay and lesbian people. Rooted in the social construction of gender and gender identities, queer theory understands socially assigned categories and discourses from the point of view of the socially marginalized, from those who are defined as varieties of "other." Deconstructing identity, as mentioned earlier, demonstrates that identity in general is articulated through the politics of power. Since there are no pre-made subjects and therefore no fundamental interests of such subjects, politics does not derive from these interests. Contemporary politics can arise instead from the new configurations of sex and gender that are already proliferating.[101] Ultimately, when the sexual binary is unmasked as a political construction, other equally constructed binary social categories can be brought under the same lens and then be subverted performatively. Critical race theory, for example, argues that racial categories are social products. From the point of view of performativity, racial binaries are enacted through discourse and conventions, which sustain the hierarchy of power but are susceptible to transgressive and transformative practices. Queer theory theorizes social change rooted in concepts, discourse, and performance that is meant to go beyond transgression and positively construct everyday alternatives by developing not-so-ordinary social practices.

Conclusion

Self-declared action [that] modifies only the word, not things, the external gesture and not the [hu]man inside . . . only creates a superior kind of puppet . . . which will collapse into nothingness the moment the strings are cut.[102]

— Antonio Gramsci, *Selections from the Prison Notebooks*, 1929–35

Gramsci draws a sharp distinction between modifying words and symbols, and between changing people and material things. There is, however, a dialectical connection between changing the way things and people are conceived and changing the physical world. Marxism prioritized changes in reality and being over consciousness, while post-structuralism privileges words and symbols. Social life and understanding are constituted through language and discourse. Thinking differently about the world is changing it. Butler argues that repeated locutionary acts become entrenched social practices and, ultimately, become naturalized and regulated as institutions. Social order is, therefore, ultimately founded on discourse. Con-

sequently, language use also has the power to alter these practices and institutions. Emphasizing the importance of words and ideas makes intellectuals the contemporary political subjects of social change.

Among the litany of "posts" that have become contemporary social thought, post-structuralism challenges social theory on its most basic grounds. Ultimately, no claim to even relative truth can be sustained. In this sense, post-structuralism rests on a radical relativism. All claims are valid and all social practices are merely cultural variations, neither inherently inferior nor superior to any other. Keily argues that relativism "at its worst . . . simply ignores, or even becomes an apology for, all kinds of oppressive practices." As the twist on Descartes puts it, for postmodernists, "I think, therefore, whatever."[103] The word *oppressive* implies that there is a way to validate in some objective fashion the claim of being oppressed. But if every form of evaluation or judgment is the same, then there is no basis on which to act to end the practice. If all resorts to power, not as repressive but as productive, necessarily end by reproducing oppression, then we are left not with "whatever" but only with discourse, endless deconstruction, and transgression. In the post-structuralist view, globalization poses enormous challenges to any possibility for a radical restructuring of the world.

Post-structural ideas are important critically but less so constitutively. Deconstructing discourse; revealing false premises; uncovering the power consequences that underlie claims about justice, truth, progress, equality: these are what critical social theory does. The social world is constructed through discourse and language use, and thinking differently and critically is necessary for social change. Ultimately, however, the practices of violating norms, transgressing rules, deconstructing theories, and challenging authority as a strategy for social change never fundamentally touch the actual power that is always talked about but seldom theorized in any substantive foundation. Reality does have an obdurate character, as Blumer pointed out. Margaret Atwood said that men are afraid that women will ridicule or laugh at them, while women are afraid that men will kill them.[104] This is not a post-feminist, post-racial, post-class world.

Third-wave feminism reflects a focus on global women's issues. Women in the West, however, still need to organize for the goals of second-wave feminism. Particularly for disadvantaged women, but not exclusively, the post-feminist assumption of autonomy has been deconstructed. The women's movement is now global, and third-wave feminism taps into the needs and demands of women worldwide. The wave-like, social-movement character of present-day feminism in the West may be threadbare, but academic feminists, such as Hill Collins and hooks, are activists and not just theorists. Ultimately, that combination of theory and practice, concrete struggles, and uncompromising tenacity define political practice today.

Post-structuralist ideas are common intellectual currency in the early twenty-first century. At least among critical social theorists, thinking and writing should eschew concepts that reflect Orientalism, heteronormativity, and racialization or that reify and obscure the socially constructed nature of social life. Of all of the most obdurate of problems in social theory is social change, which must assume a conceptual and discursive form, as well as a practical and material content. Theorists who focus on the continuity in our fundamental underlying structures, such as global capitalism, have an equal difficulty in finding alternatives. Chapter 12 discusses the views of three significant theorists of high, or late, or fluid modernity: Jurgen Habermas, Anthony Giddens, and Pierre Bourdieu.

Questions for Reflection

1. Is there a relationship between the crises of late-twentieth-century capitalism and the ideas that are reflected in postmodern thought?
2. Is Baudrillard's social thought basically nihilistic, and can it be the foundation for a "real" transformation of society?
3. In the post-apocalyptic scenario in the film *Cloud Atlas* (2012), the survivors distinguish between what is "true" and what is "true true." In light of the arguments in this chapter, can this distinction make sense?
4. Is it possible to develop a single social movement for change that unites class, gender, and racialized groups, or are identity politics necessarily single-issue?
5. Are sex and sexuality socially constructed performative acts, or are they essentially inborn?

Social Theory in Late Modernity

Ulrich Beck, a German-born sociologist, argues in *Risk Society* (1986) that modernity has entered a second phase. Classical industrial society is being dissolved, yielding to a "second modernity" that is coming into being. He calls the new modernity a **risk society**.[1] Modern capitalist society (first modernity) entailed risks, but the risks were largely individualized. Now, risks involve global dangers resulting from the rapid growth of the system. What used to be seen as progress is being superseded, Beck says, by global risks, "which are revealed as irreversible threats to the life of plants, animals, and human beings." Modern hazards do not just affect individuals: they threaten everyone.[2]

Beck enumerates many of the basic changes that are occurring as modernity expands and the risk society emerges: a new capitalism and economy, a new kind of society and global order, and a new kind of personal life.[3] In the West, family relations in industrial society, for example, were based on feudal-like gender roles, which were beginning to crumble as women moved into the workforce and exercised their reproductive and relationship rights. As a result of these transformations, other changes are brought into being that alter parenting, love, and sexuality. In the world of employment, rigid and standardized industrial work is being changed as the line is blurred between work and non-work through flexible work times and the networking of multiple worksites, even from the household. While Western governments are still liberal democracies, beneath the level of national politics, power relations arising from business and technology multiply social risks and shape society in ways that national politics cannot control. And as society is increasingly differentiated, skepticism about modernity itself develops. People lose a sense of certainty about their way of life and become anxious about the future.[4] Not only is unemployment a persistent and, frequently, growing problem in advanced capitalism, youth unemployment is much higher.

Young adults in the West face a likely uncertain future as "generation rent" that is personal as well as national and global.

Beck argues that the modern welfare state has redistributed wealth to the point where the major social issue is no longer the problem of scarcity. Consequently, the old distribution conflicts, which occurred in the face of scarcity, are diminishing. But simultaneously, knowledge grows about the destructive and hazardous effects of this immense wealth production. Deforestation, for example, has become a global problem; nuclear power threatens full-scale desolation; food is laden with toxins. Contemporary problems are global in their scope and fundamental in their scale. The unintended, negative consequences of modernity are beyond the risk calculations of insurance companies, says Beck, because the dangers are incalculable.[5] The forces of globalization develop in all societies, but not identically, so that there are different or plural modernities developing in different places and times.[6]

While modernity has, certainly, bequeathed a number of positive changes to the contemporary world, including multicultural societies and the idea of tolerance, as well as legal pluralism and multiple sovereignties, Beck enumerates additional negative changes, including the **deregulation** of work and production, a decline in the legitimacy and power of nation states, rising underemployment, the increase in the power of private corporations, high rates of violence, and potential meltdowns of the global capitalist financial system. Risks are global, but they are not equally global. Environmental risks, for example, affect the poor more than the rich; poverty, along with its consequences for health, housing, and malnourishment, has intensified in the global South. In the north, the poor are increasingly marginalized and excluded. Countries that are the least wealthy spend more money paying interest on their loans from Western governments and banks than they spend on health and education for their own people.[7]

Neo-Liberal Globalization

The growing inequality in wealth that characterizes late capitalism was the focus of the Occupy Wall Street movement's simplistic but politically effective class analysis of the "one percent." Large amounts of surplus funds are present in the system with few opportunities for high-profit investments. Traditional economics in agriculture and manufacturing, for example, yield relatively low profits. One exception may be to invest in new communication platforms and Internet companies, but these are volatile and tend to be overrated and, hence, as in the case of Facebook, become less valuable than on first offering. The highest and the fastest returns can be found in the financial sector itself. As a result, late capitalism is rife with stock market speculation, currency speculation (buying and selling foreign currencies), risky mortgages, and expanding consumer loans. Perhaps personal debt, even more than state debt, keeps the capitalist market afloat. It is also an important Achilles heel of the system.

One problem with debt financing is that there has to be enough actual money kept on reserve to support a realistic percentage of the loaned money in case of default. Arguably, the risky financial system is kept afloat by the trust that people have that the money values that appear on paper are sufficiently tied to real, material wealth to make them safe. Over time, however, the value of investments has been based less on real, tangible property than on trust that repayments can be made and the system can continually refinance itself. High profits can be made by speculatively buying stocks that then inflate beyond their reasonable value, gambling that they can be sold just before the market makes a "correction" and brings down their price to the market value.

Following the radical deregulation of markets by neo-liberal governments, by the 1990s and early 2000s, financial speculation ratcheted up the stock market to unprecedented heights.[8] Much of the apparent prosperity was in the housing market. The American dream had by that time shrunk for the working and lower middle classes: "owning" one's own home was possible, although it was mortgaged to the hilt by the bank. To realize this truncated dream for more people, regulations restricting mortgage loans were relaxed. People were able to receive a home mortgage without a cash down payment. Interest-only loans were granted to reduce monthly payments. Even lower "teaser" rates were offered for a short period to entice more buyers. Consumers were offered sub-prime mortgages—interest rates that were lower than the rate at which banks themselves could borrow money. Overall, interest rates were kept artificially low. The dream of home ownership appeared within the reach of people ever further down the class structure.

The result was that the price of houses began to increase markedly—more money was available to buy housing, so demand pushed prices higher. The gap increased between what was otherwise a relatively realistic value for property and the ever-rising house values that speculation had wrought. Real estate became less "real"; the housing market became a sandcastle with a weak, shaky foundation. Too many people with insufficient cash flow were getting deeply in debt to the point where they began to default on their loan payments. To amplify both risk and profit, financial institutions downloaded their unsecured debts along the chain to smaller banks and other investors, turning a profit as quickly as possible. Additional money could be squeezed out by betting accurately on which companies would default.[9] When

---

⚜ BOX 12.1 • THEORY IN CONTEXT ⚜

Margin Call

Are you a wolf, / warm in your pinstripes?
Is your pen a bootknife, / drawing red and dollar green?
— Hey Rosetta, "Handshake the Gangster" from *Into Your Lungs*, 2012

The 2011 film *Margin Call*, written and directed by J.C. Chandor, covers a day-and-a-half of frantic activity in a Wall Street investment firm. Eighty per cent of the firm is being downsized, including Eric Dale (Stanley Tucci). He slips a flash drive to Peter Sullivan (Zachary Quinto), a young broker. Dale had been working on something important, he says, warning Sullivan to be careful. At first, the firm tries to carry on business as usual. Sam Rogers (Kevin Spacey), a long-time manager, addresses the remaining 20 per cent of the firm as the fittest survivors. Eighty per cent of the people standing between them and their bosses' jobs have suddenly vanished: "This is your opportunity. . . . Get back to work."

The characters in the film talk about almost nothing but money, on and off the job. They speculate how much erotic dancers make a night and how much their supervisor makes. They are impressed that one boss spent $76,520 on hookers, booze, and dancers, but claimed most of it back as entertainment. Despite their obsession with money, the brokers realize there should be more to life than money. One had been an engineer and had once built a bridge—something real and tangible. On one level, all they do is "push numbers around on a computer screen," like "a bunch of glorified crack addicts," and try to "outbid

this complex bubble burst in 2008, it sent the stock market into a serious spiral and brought about the worst recession since the 1929 crash that had led to the Great Depression. The result was the spectacular failure of some long-standing banks and investment firms, such as Lehman Brothers. Ultimately, the banking sector was stabilized on the basis of a massive bailout of billions of federal (and therefore taxpayer) dollars. Conspiracy theorists could not have imagined a better example of the complete collusion between capital and the state.

Some recent Hollywood films have tried to capture the ethical vacuum that appears to underlie the pursuit of speculative profit in financial markets. *The Wolf of Wall Street* (2013), for example, suggests that stockbrokers fraudulently induce unsuspecting investors into risky ventures.

But the obvious greed of the brokers is matched by the greediness with which average investors expect to gain a quick, financial windfall. Their get-rich-quick dreams are about as improbable as winning the state lottery. Stock values are more like fairy dust, the film says. They depend for their virtual existence purely on the trust that values are worth what they are said to be worth. The film *Margin Call* (2011) offers a less sensational and flamboyant depiction of Wall Street, but it packs a weightier punch. This film exposes the moral cynicism and self-seeking ideology of the financial system, and reveals some of the inner workings of the 2008 meltdown. The CEO in *Margin Call* may not know the details of how his billions are actually squeezed out of gullible investors, but he certainly knows when to run (see Box 12.1).

other jackasses on information" they only pretend to understand. "It's fucked up," Sullivan says. "Does that seem right to you?" His partner, Seth Bregman, replies, "Right is . . . Right is . . . ," but he doesn't know what is right; it's a sentence he can't complete.

That night, Sullivan stays behind and begins going over the figures on the flash drive Eric Dale had given him. The firm's assets are primarily in mortgages, and they have pushed the risk profile far beyond the normal limits. The firm's projected losses are greater than the total value of the company. Bankruptcy is one click of the mouse away. Panic sets in and staff meetings go on all night. Finally, the local executives call in the top gun, John Tuld (Jeremy Irons), the company CEO. He doesn't understand the details, but he gets the big picture: "So what you're telling me," he sums up, "we're going to be left with the biggest bag of odorous excrement ever assembled in the history of capitalism."

One executive climbs onto the ledge of the roof and looks down. He wouldn't be the first investment banker to commit suicide during a financial crash. Jumping is exactly what Tuld has in mind. The brokers are told to get on the phones as soon as the market opens and start selling company shares for as high as possible for as long as possible. The sell-off will be profitable only until buyers realize that the stock they are being sold is about to be worthless; they're drawing dollars that are green but are also blood-red. The first firm to liquidate its assets makes the most money and wins. In the process, it starts a system-wide financial meltdown in which the firm's own customers take the first hit. Near the end of the film, we learn why Seth Bregman could not finish his sentence. The philosophy of global capitalism says, "*It's not wrong*, and it's certainly no different today than it's ever been. . . . It's always the same thing, over and over. We can't help ourselves. . . . And there always have been and always will be the same percentage of winners and losers, happy fucks and sad sacks, fat cats and starving dogs in this world."

In the contemporary world, the problems and risks are substantial and material; they are "real" in the common-sense meaning of the term. Many contemporary sociologists, however, propose means to bring runaway globalization to heel in the interests of humanity. For Beck, change requires individual and collective action within new, cosmopolitan public spheres that are opening outside corporate and state control. Jürgen Habermas believes that positive change requires open and free dialogue and discussion among equals, and that contemporary society has the potential to realize this communicative ideal. Anthony Giddens argues that self-conscious individual actions have global consequences that can be understood and directed to global change. In the last decades of his life, Pierre Bourdieu, one of the most widely cited contemporary social theorists, became an active opponent of globalization and its effects.

Jürgen Habermas and His Critique of Modernity

Jürgen Habermas was born in Germany in 1929 and grew up in a small town east of Cologne. He was a child when Hitler captured power. His father, who was director of the local Chamber of Commerce, "pragmatically" co-operated with the Nazi Party.[10] Habermas dutifully joined the Hitler Youth movement. At the age of 15, he was drafted into the German army and sent to the Western Front. Like many Germans of his generation, Habermas was horrified by the post-war revelations about Nazi death camps and the shocking details about the regime that became publicly known during the Nuremburg Trials. He reinterpreted the Nazi regime as morally evil, and rooted in narrow and destructive customs and ideas.[11] Following the war and the reintroduction of parliamentary democracy in Germany, Habermas became committed to the liberal democratic ideal, although he was critical of the ease with

which old German leaders slid into positions of power in the new Germany.[12] As a philosophy student after the war, Habermas critiqued Martin Heidegger, the dominant German philosopher of the 1930s, for not abandoning his earlier sympathy for Nazism.[13]

After receiving his Ph.D. in 1954, Habermas became an assistant to Theodor Adorno at the Institute for Social Research and was greatly influenced by critical theory. Habermas read deeply into the works of Marx, Freud, and the Frankfurt School, finding Adorno's critical theory "electrifying."[14] Adorno and Horkheimer had argued that the foundation of social domination in the modern world could be found in the destructive over-emphasis on rationality that had shaped European philosophy since the Enlightenment. For them, social domination was rooted in humanity's exploitative relationship with nature; in the basic principles of capitalist profit-making; and in the emerging elite of technical-rational experts, scientists, and officials who imposed narrow rules of efficiency that disregarded ethical values or concerns.

In the end, the critical theory of Adorno and Horkheimer led them to intellectual despair. The technical domination of humanity was so pervasive that there was no longer any realistic possibility for progressive change. They saw no future in Western democracy other than domination and manipulation. Habermas, however, was not satisfied with this conclusion. The modern Enlightenment principle of human reason was a necessary part of human liberation. This critical legacy had to be revived in the face of a return in the twentieth century to irrationalism and arbitrary authority. The Nazi regime had played upon deep-seated prejudices and fears. Reason and logic were not the foundation of Nazism; they were its antidotes.

Habermas's intention is to theorize the key principles necessary for democratic decision-making through which people can communicate equally and determine the most rational course of action to benefit everyone. He has spent his life in academic pursuits as a publically committed intellectual whose ideas are widely influential in philosophy and social science.

In 1962, Habermas published *The Structural Transformation of the Public Sphere*. He depicted the salons and coffee houses of the eighteenth century as spaces within which individuals discussed, as equals, issues of public concern and attempted to arrive at rational, logical, and mutually acceptable understandings.[15] The salons were both the fruit of and the instrument for realizing capitalist liberties, such as freedom of speech, of the press, and of assembly.

The salons gave to a small number of intellectuals the public space to engage in political critique of traditional society; they stimulated the modern projects of political liberalism and representative democracy. Utilizing the liberal freedoms of assembly, speech, and conscience, citizens (at least elite citizens) were able to confer, debate, and critique ideas and shape opinions. For Habermas, the public sphere represents a potential model of free, open, and co-operative discourse that should be replicated on a mass scale. In the actual world, however, discourse at the time was increasingly shaped by dominant institutions and powerful interests, which undermined the promise of egalitarian communication and decision-making. By the mid-1800s, the emergence of mass, print-based media had commercialized and commodified information and ideas, making them instruments of domination rather than of liberation.[16]

Habermas was a university professor in the 1960s. At first, he supported the radicalization of German students, but he later distanced himself from the movement as it evolved into anarchism.[17] Habermas wanted the student movement to become a model of reasoned discourse and democratic decision-making, and he warned of the danger of what he termed "left fascism": democratic in rhetoric, but authoritarian in action.[18]

A splinter group from the German students' movement became the Red Army Faction, an underground New Left formation that undertook a campaign of bombings and assassinations in Germany in the 1970s.

Early Critical Theory

In his early work, *Theory and Practice* (1963) and *Knowledge and Human Interests* (1968), Habermas presents a critique of positivist social science (in sociology and also Marxism), and presents an alternative critical theory. Critical theory, Habermas claimed, was implicit in Marx's "scientific socialism." The natural sciences assume that there is an absolute distinction between the object studied (a rock or plant, for example) and the subject who studies the object (the "scientist"). Western science adopted a technical and manipulative approach to science in which the scientist is supposed to be a neutral or value-free observer of the object, seeing nature as it really is, not as he or she would like it to be. Scientists perfected various forms of technology to dominate and transform nature and bracketed (set aside as irrelevant) any questions about whether they should develop the technology, or transform nature in specific ways. For example, scientists who invented the atomic bomb had viewed splitting the atom as a value-free activity and had not asked the necessarily unscientific question of whether this technology should have been developed.

Assuming a sharp object/subject dichotomy in the natural sciences was a serious flaw of the scientific method. Perhaps more serious was applying the same scientific model to the study of human societies. Positivist sociology had adopted the identical stance on value neutrality and objectivity. The consequence was that the subjects of the social sciences—actual people—were studied as objects. Social scientists adopted the same type of technological and manipulative approach to studying society as the natural scientists had adopted for studying nature, with the same negative consequences for humanity. Technological rationality had come to prevail in the social as well as the natural sciences.

In both forms of "science," in natural and especially in social science, Habermas claimed, it is not possible for a human subject to observe any phenomenon objectively or free of values. Marx had argued that the attempt to be value-neutral was not only impossible, it was in principle undesirable. Marxism understood society from the point of view or standpoint of the proletariat, just as positivist social science (despite its claim to neutrality) expressed the interests of the capitalist class.

For Habermas, Western social science's claim to value neutrality is, in Sartre's terms, an act of "bad faith" since values are implicit in all aspects of the research, affecting not only the choice of research subjects, but the very way that subjects are perceived and understood. The social scientist operates within a whole complex of values, including a pre-given body of scientific concepts and laws rooted in the belief in the value of science itself and even in the specific language used to understand the world. Knowledge of nature always comes coded by human understandings and interests. As a tradition, Western social science is carried out by groups of experts who communicate only among themselves and, in principle, maintain their "object" (the people being studied) in an assumed state of ignorance—the less the "object" is aware of the purpose and intention of the experiment, the less such awareness will contaminate the scientifically verifiable results.

Habermas argues that empirically grounded, scientific knowledge is only one type of knowledge that corresponds to the fundamental human interest of controlling nature. A second type is knowledge derived from inter-subjective interpretation, utilized in the study of society and culture. In the everyday world in which we interact with others, our mutual interest in understanding each other is dependent on our nuanced ability to interpret what others mean when they communicate. Interpretation depends on our experiences and on our implicit knowledge of language and cultural practices.

Emancipatory knowledge went beyond empirical and interpretive knowledge. Since the Enlightenment, Habermas argues, people in general had become more knowledgeable and rational. On the basis of this potential for rationality, Habermas proposes constructing a critical theory that would further the long-term goal of human emancipation that had begun with the Age of Reason. The essential problem in the world could no longer be understood in terms of economic production and distribution—capitalists had managed to contain the contradictions of the economic system. Now, the basic problem was one of consciousness and awareness.

While people in post-Enlightenment society are potentially more rational than in previous social systems, they live in a world shaped by the ever-expanding manipulative capacities of technological rationality.[19] The manipulative character of technical (or functional) rationality "can only by altered by a change in the state of consciousness itself, by the practical effect of a theory which does not improve the manipulation of things . . . but which instead advances" critical reason.[20]

Critical theory, Habermas contends, would transcend the manipulative, one-way flow of knowledge from the theorist to the largely unknowing "object" and, instead, promote a reciprocal flow to and from social agents who are all conscious and knowing subjects, with the aim of promoting self-liberation. Unlike the positivist sciences, which have explicitly disavowed any philosophical underpinnings (making them simply blind to the philosophy they necessarily contain), critical theory goes beyond moral condemnation and demands intervention and conscious praxis. The critique would "constitute a challenge to everyone to transform his causally explainable behaviour through self-reflection into understandable action."[21] The aim of critical theory is to liberate individual consciousness through open communication, thereby minimizing if not entirely negating the possibility of manipulation.

Communicative Action

In 1981, Habermas published his two-volume *Theory of Communicative Action*. **Communicative action** is, first, rational communication (discourse) among a linguistic community of people. It is action insofar as the communication is oriented to the goal of establishing a consensus of understanding among the participants. Ultimately, communicative action is the mechanism through which rational people can freely discuss, mutually understand, critique, and collectively resolve their differences. It is the means necessary for a changed practice aimed at establishing a morally just and equitable future: the unrealized goal of the Enlightenment.

Communicative action can best be understood in the sociological tradition because it is the only discipline that is oriented to the problems of society as a whole. The disciplines of economic and political science attempted to become specialized sciences, focusing respectively on two subsystems of modern society: the analysis of the market-regulated economy (money) and of the nation state (power). Economics and political science restrict their study to purposeful, rational action that either maximizes profit or acquires and uses political power. In contrast, sociology is concerned with the everyday practices of people in what Habermas terms the **lifeworld** (the world of everyday life), which is intimately connected to community and culture.[22] Communicative action takes place in intimate settings, such as within the family, as well as in public places.

Habermas distinguishes among types of rationality. One is cognitive-instrumental rationality—the goal-oriented, profit-maximizing, or power-grasping type. Historically, modern capitalist society was rooted in the practical and self-interested calculations of individuals who employed rational means to acquire specific ends, such as money or power. The domination of such manipulative and individualistic rationality is at the root of the troubles of modern society. In contrast to instrumental rationality is communicative rationality, which is the basis of Habermas's theory. Communicative rationality connotes "[t]he unconstrained, unifying, consensus-bringing force of argumentative speech, in which different participants overcome their merely subjective views." Ideally, a participant acts like the autonomous subjects of Enlightenment theory. They are "competent to judge facts and [act] in a purposeful-rational way." They are "morally judicious and practically reliable," and evaluate with "sensitivity and an aesthetically open-mind."[23]

In this ideal situation, the participants bring to their communication a motivation to reach mutual understanding and agreement (consensus) and therefore enter into discourse with one other. In the course of their argumentation, people make cognitive-instrumental claims or descriptions for which they provide substantial reasons that can be judged on their validity. They also make three other types of statements: (1) moral-practical assertions or *ought* claims that should be "reliable and insightful" and argue the rightness of actions or rules; (2) evaluative statements (arguments about value judgments that should be "discerning or illuminating"); and (3) expressive statements that are truthful and sincere, as well as "candid and self-critical in the expressive dimension."[24]

Consensus-building through communicative action is especially problematic in the actual rather than the ideal world. Lyotard regards talk as less an attempt to reach communicative agreement and more as a competition or contest—a struggle for control.[25] To succeed in consensus-making, Habermas says, the participants have to recognize the limitations and self-interests that are inherent in their individual subjectivities (their personal motivations and interests) and emphasize common or universally shared interests and views.

Communicative action in its undistorted form of seeking mutual understanding can be understood as an **ideal speech situation**. This situation is an ideal type, following Weber's usage of the idea, which presents a model that is not found in its pure state in the real world. This ideal type can be used to measure how actual practices deviate from the model. In an ideal speech situation, then, the evidence on which an argument is based determines its truth-claim and validity. In **distorted communication**, truth or validity is determined by relationships of power (as Nietzsche held that they were in all circumstances). The ideal speech situation becomes a goal for which to strive and a concept with which to critique language-use that is less than ideal.

Habermas differentiates three principal spheres within which we make claims and to which we orient our actions:

- *The objective world in which we live*: Claims about the objective world are truth-claims.
- *The world of interpersonal interaction*: Intersubjectively, we make claims about the correctness or rightness of our beliefs or actions in terms of a general social consensus about social norms and rules.
- *An individual's internal, subjective world of feelings and desires*: When we express our intentions or feelings, we make claims about their sincerity and authenticity.

These acts of communication are rational insofar as they can be questioned, critiqued, and defended using reasons and grounded arguments.[26] The object of this discourse is to reach mutual understanding and, if possible, agreement. In each sphere, cultural traditions of validity checking have been established: science has procedures for determining the validity of statements about the objective world. Legal institutions shape understandings about the rightness of actions and social rules.[27] Institutions regulating expression are less formalized, although institutions involved with producing and consuming art shape discourses about their authenticity or expression.

Furthermore, mutual discourse depends upon (and reproduces) a common view of the objective world and reinforces common intersubjective understandings. People in society possess a common store of background knowledge that is necessary for any social interaction to take place. Their interaction reinforces and solidifies these common views and understandings. It is within this community of interacting members that the validity and apparent truth of statements can be tested, examined, and modified. In this rational interaction, people's actions, personal expressions, and statements of value and truth should be "oriented to achieving, sustaining, and renewing consensus" through reasonable argument and the use of evidence. People who act rationally will "willingly expose themselves to criticism" and "participate properly in argumentation."[28]

The Lifeworld and Systems

People live, experience, and mutually interact within the world of everyday life. Our understanding of and actions in this everyday world are underpinned by taken-for-granted, implicit knowledge that guides our daily activity but is largely outside our conscious mind. For Habermas, this partly unconscious site of human action is the lifeworld. The bedrock of the lifeworld is, in part, composed of the overall cultural world view into which we have been socialized and that shapes our beliefs, values, and actions. The lifeworld, however, can be understood rationally, although we must penetrate below the surface to understand the structures that sustain and reproduce it. In this sense, critical theory—the theory of communicative action—parallels Freudian interrogation of the unconscious. For Habermas, a full understanding of society also entails understanding the overall system in which the lifeworld is embedded.

People's actions and communications within the lifeworld are conducted within the framework of a mutually shared world view. This world view in turn provides the framework of concepts with which people interpret the things in their world. While world views cannot be deemed to be true or false, they can be compared "from the standpoint of *cognitive adequacy*."[29] For Habermas, mythological and religious claims to knowledge are less valid or adequate than modern, scientific ones. So, Habermas argues, scientific rationality can "claim validity beyond the context of particular cultures." But he is particularly interested in understanding the "losses" that we incurred on the Western path to modernization. The problems in the West are not to be found in scientific rationality specifically, but in the way instrumental rationality achieved a one-sided dominance. The contemporary capitalist system has been constructed on the basis of unregulated self-interest and egotistically centred rationality. In this context, language has been used by individuals as a medium to achieve success (goal-oriented action) by bringing opponents to take actions that are not in their interest. For example, capitalists convince their employees to accept wage reductions by claiming that capital and labour are "in the same boat" and have identical interests. On a broader social canvas, language has been used to transmit and reinforce a consensus of normative regulations and values that benefit some but not all.[30]

Pre-modern societies on the other hand operated on the basis of deeply rooted, traditional world views, which became so taken for granted that people did not distinguish between what was humanly constructed and what was assumed to be natural. Their beliefs and values were reified and were not open to criticism or disbelief. There was little differentiation among descriptions of

the objective world, valid norms of behaviour, and people's subjective feelings and expressions.[31]

With modernity, an egocentric reference system develops that distinguishes the worlds of objectivity, interpersonal interaction, and internal subjectivity. People come to contrast their own internal world with "the subjective world of others, [and] with the external world." Modern societies are decentred in the sense that people and groups within them advance different claims about what is defined as objectively real (cognitive), what is normatively and morally right, and what is an expression of their individual, subjective experiences. Rather than unquestioned truths, in modern society people reflect critically on their own traditions in relation to actual changes in the world and their experience of it. In addition, as Weber stressed, modern society embeds the requirement for purposeful-rational action in legally grounded social institutions or subsystems, particularly those designed to control rational economics (money) and rational government (power).[32] Both subsystems impose constraints on the ability of actors to communicate.

Habermas is not content, however, to enumerate world views pluralistically and have them stand equal to one another. The whole emphasis on rationality implies the importance of establishing standards for judging and evaluating different forms of life as "more or less failed, deformed, unhappy, or alienated."[33] Modern, capitalist societies, for example, should be critiqued on the basis of what they have lost from the past as well as on their one-sided emphasis on cognitive-instrumental rationality. For Habermas, societies should seek to balance the cognitive with the moral and the aesthetic-practical.[34]

The ideal of communicative action (mutual understanding) is frequently distorted in language use. Systematically distorted communication relates to structures of domination and power that exist in the world. For Habermas, action is oriented either to success (especially action that entails acquisition or retention of money and power), or it is oriented to reaching understanding, in the broad sense of communicative action. Money and power reflect the capitalist economy and state power; they become two forms of "steering" mechanisms or media that deform communication in the lifeworld. Many acts of communication, such as advertising or political propaganda, are *not* oriented to achieving mutual understanding. The same manipulative end may be achieved through the use of language to harness an individual to one's ulterior purposes. These manipulative or instrumental uses of communication, which are oriented to success rather than to shared understandings, are "parasitic."[35]

In short, for Habermas, humanity is sustained "through the socially-coordinated activity of its members." Such coordination is achieved through communication—in particular, communication that is oriented to reaching agreement. This agreement, in turn, is predicated on sustaining rationality in this communication. Integration of members of humanity takes place through reaching understanding, but integration is affected by the strength of various competing interests, including economic and political ones.[36]

Integration is also affected by objective, systemic factors, such as capital and power, that influence social actors involved in communication. These objectively existing, structural imperatives comprise the "system." The institutional order of modern society evolves according to the principles of functional rationality, which become increasingly differentiated and separate from the lifeworld. These principles are embodied in the growth of money and power, which impose objective conditions on the lifeworld and shape the ideas and interests within it. In Habermas's terms, the lifeworld comes to be colonized by the system and begins to erode. Communicative action in the lifeworld comes to duplicate the functional reason that saturates the system, causing

communication to be less rational and more uncritically normative.

The administrative and economic action systems invade the lifeworld through such practices as imposing the norms of competition and performance in elementary schools. Similarly, in middle-class families, children are enrolled in innumerable competitive activities. When a system invades the lifeworld it may be called colonization, which imposes consumerist goals and standards on lifestyle definitions and converts to money exchanges services that were once voluntary or shared. The public sphere is saturated by opinion-forming and voter-inducing mechanisms originating from formal party politics and privately owned media empires.[37]

The possibility for progressive social action arises from the relationship between lifeworld and system. Crises originating either in the economic or the political sphere can induce crises of legitimation in personal and family relations. Communicative action can contest the legitimacy of practices that establish system-down colonization. In the family, for example, progressive forms of child-rearing and egalitarian familial relations model the potential of communicative action to replace normative and dominant discourses. The modern equivalent of the eighteenth century salon is the open space that develops in civil society, such as the free press and voluntary organizations, which allow for countervailing communication, debate, and discussion.[38] The Internet has the potential to create such a public space for reasonable discourse, although it is usually overshadowed by trivia, pornography, and self-promotion.

Communicative action should entail rational social critiques and critical theory, formulated on the basis of a human interest in emancipation, freedom, and justice. Rather than the old politics of reform or revolution, Habermas proposes "new politics" centred on the uncoupling or separation of lifeworld and system. The colonization of the lifeworld by various systems produce contradictions that are felt in families and by individuals, and give rise to a range of protest movements beyond the labour–capital contradiction. Conflicts in the welfare state were based on the distribution of resources, and they were managed through increased compensations within the system. The new conflicts are arising in other domains, such as culture, socialization, sexuality, and the environment. New protests involve conflicts over "restoring endangered ways of life" that cannot easily be diverted into quiescence by the usual steering mechanisms of money and power.[39]

A "silent evolution" of attitudes and values is occurring in contemporary society that undergirds the rise of "new politics" concerned with the "quality of life, equal rights, individual self-realization, [and] participation." New politics animates young people, the new middle class, and the better educated. Diverse social movements have arisen that have in common the overall complaint about growth, which is the backbone of late capitalist societies. In his enumeration of this set of protest movements, Habermas lists a number of disparate groups with potential for "resistance or withdrawal." Among them is the women's movement, which retains, according to Habermas, its emancipatory and offensive character. Other protests are defensive in the sense of restoring threatened ways of life. Some defend traditional social rank and the distribution of property, such as religious fundamentalists, groups struggling for individualistic autonomy, and tax protesters.

The new politics arise in the seam between the colonizing system and the lifeworld.[40] Among the most important new movements are those that have been sparked by demands for ecological security, peace, and protection from the misuse of private data. They "operate on the basis of a rationalized lifeworld." Ecological protests focus on fundamental issues involved in the imposition of system requirements, such as clear-cutting of forests, pollution, the side-effects of pharmaceutical products, the industrialization of the food supply,

and so on. Groups seek to find their identity on the basis of their basic characteristics, such as gender, age, locality, skin colour, or religion. In a protected subculture, they seek to shield themselves from the forces that are undermining their everyday ways of life. In the process, groups have sought to revitalize possibilities for self-expression that have been buried; that is, to develop spaces for communicative action.[41]

In the widening gap between system and lifeworld, and in the face of the pressures of colonization, Habermas believes there may be space for localized and communicative counter-institutions to arise. To be socially progressive, however, such institutions must find, within the lifeworld, a central place for rational discourse and planned action.[42] Reciprocal knowledge flow among all groups, involving all areas of knowledge and, ultimately, between lifeworld and system, will allow humans to *consciously* make their own history. Ultimately, the lifeworld must shape and determine the institutions of the system.

In contrast to Habermas's concern about the dangers inherent in the colonization of the lifeworld by dominant groups and their spokespersons, Anthony Giddens developed a theory that claimed that dominant groups may use their power in ways beneficial to the globe and to its citizens.

Anthony Giddens and Structuration

Anthony Giddens was born in North London, England, in 1938, the son of a middle-class clerk. Educated at Hull University and the London School of Economics and Politics (LSE), Giddens began lecturing at the University of Cambridge in 1969 and received his Ph.D. from Cambridge in 1974. Between 1997 and 2004, Giddens was the director of LSE. During this time, he became a principal advisor to Britain's New Labour prime minister, Tony Blair. On his retirement from LSE, Giddens was rewarded for his political support by being elevated to the English peerage as a baron, complete with a seat in the House of Lords. Giddens is a prolific author and one of the most influential sociologists of his generation.[43] In 1971, Giddens published *Capitalism and Modern Social Theory*, a critical analysis of Marx, Durkheim, and Weber. The questions raised by classical social theorists are essential to Giddens's reconstruction of theory as the duality of structure.

Class Structuration

Weber's influence is apparent in Giddens's *The Class Structure of the Advanced Societies*, published in 1973. Giddens avoided the typical dichotomy of defining objective class positions and then relating this structural category to the emergence of subjective class consciousness. He argues that the subject/object dichotomy should be combined in a theory of structuration. In this view, a class is by definition a self-conscious entity, not in Marx's sense that it is aware of its generic or "real" long-term interests, but in that its membership manifests a common consciousness. This distinct consciousness may actually consist of the denial of the existence of classes, which Giddens claims characterizes the new middle class.[44]

Class emerges due to the possession of unequal resources. Actors mobilize these resources to use in market encounters with others in the pursuit of their interests. In the theory of class **structuration**, classes are groups of people who share similar life chances but also share common consciousness. The theory begins with the encounter of actors on the basis of their prior conditions and then builds a theory of systems of interaction, which they continually reproduce. Structuration, then, is an ongoing process of social class. Some of the differences between the class structure of European and North American societies, such as the existence of a conscious and historically

constituted working class in the former, can be understood in terms of class structuration.

While societies on both sides of the Atlantic may have relatively similar occupational distributions, class structuration is more complete in Europe because of the importance in North America of other-than economic factors, such as ethnicity, racialization, and national differences. Such factors provide competing and often more immediately salient identities. The tenacity of the idea that American society is classless follows from the relatively low degree to which occupational groupings are structurated as distinct classes. By the late twentieth century, in advanced capitalism generally, the factors that condition structuration were weakening and, as a result, the working class was losing its distinctive consciousness as a class. The potential for working-class revolution had been present only in the early stages of industrial capitalism, as the proletariat was forced into the factory system. In late capitalism, the working class is no longer a collective social agent capable of progressive change.

The Duality of Agency and Structure

> *Human history is created by intentional activities but is not an intended project; it persistently eludes efforts to bring it under conscious direction.*[45]
>
> — Anthony Giddens, *The Constitution of Society*, 1984

By the later 1970s, Giddens had broadened his analysis of social theory, incorporating a wide range of social thought into a comprehensive theory of society. His work in this period may be defined by the duality of **agency** and structure. Agency relates to the theory of the acting subject, as developed by interpretive sociology and ethnomethodology. Rather than seeing these micro perspectives and structuralism as dichotomous paradigms, useful for analyzing different levels of society, Giddens intended to reconstruct sociological theory as a single theory of structuration that supersedes this binary. Structuration theorizes the relationship between the actions of individual actors and the existence of a socially constituted structure.

Giddens begins his overview of structuration theory with the activities of individual agents endowed with the capacity for skilled, self-reflective action. In their routine activities, individuals interact with others with whom they are co-present through an ongoing sequence of encounters. In these situated encounters, individuals orient their body physically, judge the effects of interactions with others, and express their selfhood. When people engage successfully in routine actions that occur in repeated circumstances, they experience a necessary sense of trust in the continuity of the world as it is and in the continuity of their sense of self.[46]

Above all, people are knowledgeable agents and social theory must take into account their purposive, reasoning behaviour. Because humans come at the world face-first, the face becomes "the dominant area of the body across which the intricacies of experience, feeling and intention are written."[47] Social actors are reflexive insofar as they monitor and adjust their purposeful actions to their circumstances and situations. They do not act blindly; rather, individuals are skilled actors with knowledge of the world they inhabit. In part, actors can articulate reasonable explanations for what they are doing, demonstrating discursive consciousness.

Often, this mutually shared knowledge is not explicit and conscious; rather, it is tacit and inferred. In their habitual and practical everyday activities, people are often unaware of the grounds for what they do or how they do it. They display, instead, what Giddens terms practical consciousness. Knowing what to do in most everyday situations is so routine as to be unacknowledged, an idea that was elaborated by ethnomethodologists. Whether they are able to explain their actions discursively or not, people are agents insofar as they act and produce effects, although the effects are often not the ones they intended.[48]

That point that many unintended social consequences result from people's recurring actions is central to structuration theory. According to the "duality of structure," the activities of social actors are **recursive** in the sense that people's activities continually recreate "the conditions that make these activities possible." When people act purposefully, their behaviour always takes place within social and material contexts that constrain or enable their actions.[49] Agents respond to these contexts reflexively by interpreting and taking these external situational factors into account. As they perform a set of similar social practices over varying times and spaces, they create and reproduce specific patterns of social relations. In so doing, they simultaneously respond to and actively reinforce (or change) the structural properties of the contexts in which they act. Structures exist only because people create and sustain them through their reflexively monitored activities, which have a range of intended and unintended consequences.[50]

Practices that have the most extensive structuring properties over time and space are referred to as social institutions. Structural properties are perceived by the agent as having an external, objective existence that places contextual limits on the options open to actors. Actors are constrained by the material environment, by the physical nature of their bodies, by punitive social sanctions, and by what Giddens calls structural constraints. However, actors likely know little of the many, structuring consequences of their activities.[51] Routine activities endure over extended periods of time and space, as do the virtual social structures that are continually reproduced by these actions. Structure, then, is a process rather than a thing.

These regularized social practices, which reproduce relations between individuals or groups and have unintended structuring properties, form social systems. A social system does not so much *have* structures as have structural properties. Social systems exist only through the recursive properties of structuration. Actors do not create social systems; "they reproduce or transform them, remaking what is already made in the continuity of *praxis*."[52]

Power is one of several elemental concepts of society "clustered around the relations of action and structure." For Giddens, power is not just a relationship of domination and constraint; power is also "at the very origin of the capability of agents to bring about intended outcomes of action." To have an effect or make a difference, agency requires using some form of power or transformative capacity. Institutions involve sets of rules and resources that actors employ in their actions. Power is exercised through the agent's ability to have access to and manipulate resources ("structured properties of social systems"); the agent is then able to draw upon these resources and reproduce them.[53]

In addition to the typical recursive action of everyday life, Giddens recognizes that some actors, particularly those who are "strategically placed," self-consciously seek to either maintain or change the conditions through which the social system is reproduced. All actors, even subordinate ones, have access to some resources through which they can influence their situations, a reciprocity Giddens terms the **dialectic of control**. Power is enabling, but it is also contested. Power struggles involve the division of resources and the control of social systems. The dialectic of control is operative in power struggles.[54]

Structures of domination are constituted by two types of resources: allocative and authoritative. *Allocative* refers to material resources, including the raw materials of production, technological instruments, and the goods that are produced through the combination of the two. *Authoritative resources* refer to the structures within which people are organized. They include the organization of life chances, by which Giddens means different opportunities for self-development and self-expression. Structures of domination are reproduced through the employment of all of these resources.[55]

A social system entails a variety of structures and patterned relationships that function within the terms of each other. These various structures, however, may also operate in contradiction with one another. Such disjunctions in systems express the fault lines in the system's structural constitution and tend to coincide with conflict among groups. People living within the same structured conditions, however, may be unaware of the structures that constrain them, or they may feel unmotivated or unable to change them.[56]

Social science, Giddens argues, should be understood in terms of a double hermeneutic, that is, a double process of interpretation. Sociological knowledge is drawn from ("is parasitical upon") the concepts utilized by social actors in their everyday lives. Once these ideas are transformed into more abstract, sociological concepts, they are brought back into the social world, where they have consequences for daily life.[57] Expert knowledge, as a result, becomes ever more specialized and complicated, but "in a dialectical interplay," this "technical expertise filters back" to ordinary people (lay agents). They continuously reappropriate this knowledge "as part of their routine dealings with abstract systems." This process of reflexive ordering and reordering is a double spiral because experts then draw upon this new, everyday usage. The result is that knowledge has, in principle, an indeterminate quality since it depends in part on what people do with the knowledge that is created and brought back to them, and how they transform it. Recent generations, for example, have learned to assemble and up-grade computer hardware and have developed varying degrees of expertise in the use and diagnosis of modern software. People are also able, for example, to treat their own physical maladies and become knowledgeable about child-rearing practices and dieting.[58]

In contrast to postmodern social thought, Giddens argues there are still some "viable methods of sustaining knowledge claims." The key to understanding "the erratic character of modernity" is *"unintended consequences* and *the reflexivity or circularity of social knowledge."* New knowledge does not simply accumulate to make the world increasingly comprehensible and predictable, as Enlightenment thinkers had supposed. New knowledge and, particularly, the technical application of new knowledge alter the nature of the world, "spinning it off in new directions."[59]

To emphasize the importance of the need to continually reproduce the properties of various structures and institutions is to emphasize their rootedness in human activities and to demonstrate that they are not necessarily permanent. Since human actions constantly reproduce these virtual structures, they are susceptible to being changed precisely by changed human practices.

Late or Radical Modernity

Giddens argues that we are not entering a new period of postmodernity. We are in a high modern age during which the consequences of modernity are more radical and global, foreshadowing a new and different social order beyond modernity. While some continuities persist from past to present, modernity is radically post-traditional in that it sweeps away *"all* traditional types of social order."[60] In Zygmunt Bauman's terms, modernization liquefies everything that had been solid and permanent in society, bringing about rapid change and instability (see Box 12.2).

Among the unprecedented discontinuities of the modern age are its global extension and its effect on personal intimacy and on the day-to-day features of life. Modernity is marked by extreme rapidity of change. For Giddens, modernity entails distinct but interrelated dimensions, including the world capitalist economy, widespread commodification, new sources of technical power, a global military order based on the industrialization of warfare, an international division of labour, and the nation-state system, which includes the potential for totalitarian governments.[61] Behind each of these institutional dimensions lies cultural globalization expressed in the new technologies of communication that form "an essential element of the reflexivity of modernity." There are more opportunities for people to live secure and rewarding lives, but modernity is also double-edged in that it has not necessarily led to a happy and secure social order. Indeed, modernity has a darker side that is "fraught and dangerous."[62]

A fundamental feature of the modern world is what Giddens terms time-space **distanciation**, which refers to "how social life is ordered across time and space." Ordinarily, social activities are embedded in particular contexts that entail co-presence, such as in face-to-face interactions that are shaped by local habits and customs. Local interaction, in which actors are co-present, is made progressively more complex as more interaction involves people at a distance. What is physically present is increasingly connected with what is absent. It is not just that modern institutions have a global span; rather, they are situated differently in time and space. All modern societies are interwoven with connections that extend beyond their present boundaries. While interaction still takes place in a locale, a physical and geographical setting in which people experience their "presence,"[63] such presence is often virtual rather than face-to-face.

In addition, locales are not simply "local" in time or space; they are thoroughly shaped and

⤚ BOX 12.2 • BIOGRAPHY ⤙

Zygmunt Bauman (b. 1925)

Zygmunt Bauman was born in 1925 into a working-class Jewish family in Poznan, Po-land, near the border with Germany.[64] When the German army invaded in 1939, Bauman's family escaped to Russia, thereby avoiding the Holocaust. Bauman joined the Soviet-led Polish Army, studied Marxism, and in 1954 became a lecturer in sociology at the University of Warsaw, Poland. He was married in 1948 to Janina Lewinson, who had survived the destruction of the Warsaw Ghetto by the German army.

Although he was a Communist Party member, Bauman was attracted to a new, critical sociological circle in Poland that was critical of Stalinism and the rigidity of Eastern European communism. He advocated a humanistic version of socialism at odds with both. In 1968, as the Soviet Union sent troops to suppress the movement for socialism with a human face in Czechoslovakia, and as Polish students sought to join the rising international student rebellion, the Polish government cracked down on academics, especially Jewish ones. An anti-Semitic purge forced Bauman and his family out of Poland. Exile in Israel was not a solution because Bauman was unwilling to trade one form of ultra-nationalism for another. In 1972, he accepted a professorship at the University of Leeds, his final place of exile.

One of Bauman's enduring preoccupations is the Holocaust. His influential book *Modernity and the Holocaust* was published in 1989. Rather than blaming the Holocaust on German nationalism or on cultural romanticism, Bauman claimed the Holocaust was a product of modern technology and bureaucracy. Modernity created the material instruments of the Holocaust and simultaneously provided its necessary ideological foundation by undermining humanistic ethics and denying the importance of individual moral responsibility. Bauman was fascinated by the realization that the people who perpetrated the day-to-day horrors of the Holocaust were ordinary men and women, who otherwise were dedicated family members, parents, and co-workers. On the other hand, some people did resist evil, fought to save victims, and put their lives at risk in the process—and they were no less ordinary, everyday people. The difference, Bauman concluded, was whether or not the individual took seriously the ethic of personal responsibility. The problem of acting morally in an unjust world is at the core of Zygmunt Bauman's sociology. In his view, socialism was initially an ethical movement that was corrupted.[65]

In Bauman's terms, modernity is characterized by "liquidity." As the modern world dissolved the glue holding traditional society together, everything, including ethics, became fluid instead of solid, with the unintended consequence of producing widespread insecurity and anxiety. Fluidity drives people to search for forms of solidity, which lead them to new forms of authoritarianism, such as fascism or religious fundamentalism. In other terms, fluidity exposes the dark side of *anti*-modernity. In the contemporary era, Bauman says, people in the West have traded their freedom for the hope of security. In his sociological work, he raises the question of taking personal responsibility for making things better.[66]

penetrated by social influences that connect them to distant locations. Modern institutions stretch time-space relations. They "connect the local and the global . . . and in so doing routinely affect the lives of many millions of people." Distanciation tends to undermine local customs and practices. Social relations are **disembedded** or lifted out from local contexts and reconstructed. The use of money as a medium of exchange is an example of disembedding because it permits transactions between agents who are widely separated in time (post-dated cheques) and space (wiring money). The disembedding tendencies of modernity caused by the global extension of modern institutions bring about countertrends, such as religious fundamentalism or other "forms of reactive traditionalism." Disembedding tendencies also elicit demands for local autonomy or regional cultural identities,[67] for example, the sovereignty claims of francophones in Quebec.

Giddens suggests that the appropriate image for modernity is a juggernaut: "a runaway engine of enormous power" which humans can steer to some extent "but which also threatens to rush out of our control." Rather than postmodernity, the era is characterized by drawing out all the positive and negative implications of modernity. The course of globalization is often erratic and unpredictable, and it threatens to crush those who are in its path. Consequently, life is full of high-consequence risks, including global calamity in a world where the nuclear threat has been pushed off the front pages by concerns over climate change and environmental desolation.[68]

Utopian Realism

Politically, Giddens argues that globalization is permanent and irreversible. Social classes have largely disappeared and class politics are increasingly irrelevant in the world. But, in contrast to postmodern thought that considers political engagement increasingly impossible in the modern world, Giddens argues that coordinated political activity is necessary and possible, globally as well as locally.[69] He calls his vision "utopian realism," which would appear to be a contradiction in terms. Being able to imagine a different future, however, is a crucial characteristic of modern reflexivity and is an ingredient for actually bringing about change; that is, "we can envisage alternative futures whose very propagation might help them be realized." To be a realistic option, a utopian image of the future must be an "institutionally immanent" possibility; it must be practically achievable in the given circumstances.[70]

Giddens's vision of a progressive era beyond modernism supposes a time of post-scarcity. *Post-scarcity* can no longer mean what it used to mean: the global achievement of a contemporary Western lifestyle, which is impossible. In the face of the enormous inequalities that exist on a global scale and the finite nature of earth's resources, there is no alternative but to redefine *post-scarcity* by lowering expectations to what is sustainable. Sociologically, scarcity depends on needs that are socially defined. Therefore the key is, first, to redefine lifestyles in the developed world, with the objective of effecting a global redistribution of wealth. The post-scarcity system would have to be "globally coordinated."[71]

Because the world is divided by inequalities of power and different value positions, change still requires **emancipatory politics**, which are those "radical engagements concerned with the liberation from inequality or servitude." But there is no privileged agent in terms of social change, as Marx conceived the revolutionary role of the proletariat. In general, contemporary social movements of various kinds offer important models of radical engagement and offer guidelines for social transformation. They allow glimpses into the future and are part of the means through which change may be realized. Labour movements, for example, continue to be important in the increasingly narrow sphere of capitalist (or industrial) relations.[72] In addition, struggles for political rights, such as freedom of speech and popular sovereignty, are generally significant in all societies. In the contemporary world, moreover, new social movements have emerged around peace, ecology, and women's rights. Feminist movements have gone beyond emancipatory movements to achieve political and economic equality, and have brought gender relations into question. These movements are sources of counterfactual thinking that can contribute to social change. Presently, state surveillance is an important issue of struggle.[73]

Social movements, however, are only collective agents that can exercise pressure on the seats of power. There is no revolutionary strategy that can overthrow power. Giddens argues that "beneficial social changes often demand the use of differential power held only by the privileged." Power differentials are inevitable, but the use of power can be socially beneficial. For Giddens, "Hierarchical power is not inevitably oppressive any more than all authority is inherently exploitative." Given the problems caused by accelerating globalization, "the coordinated use of power," including "the politics of business corporations and national governments, are fundamental to the achieving of basic reforms." Corporations and national governments would have to control aspects of the international flow of money and goods toward the realization of a post-scarcity system.[74] Short of a global economic catastrophe of epic proportions that compels the privileged in their own self-interest to make changes, this argument expresses Giddens's most utopian idea.

Emancipatory politics are fundamental to any narrowing of the economic gap, but **life politics** in the West must induce radical lifestyle changes as part of the process. In late modernity, life politics takes over larger areas of the political agenda in terms of both individuals and nation-states.[75]

Identity and Life Politics

"My body, like my life, is a work in progress."

— Weight Watchers Advertisement, 2014

In the 1990s, Giddens focused on questions of identity and politics. Social actors are situated in relation to others in a network of social relations and positions, within which they have a specific identity. Cross-culturally, age and gender are the most important criteria for defining social position, the practices they entail and, consequently, social identity.[76]

One of the fundamental differences between traditional and modern society, as it developed centuries ago, was the emergence of individualization. Modernity has given individuals increased opportunities to make choices that affect their life and their way of living. Choice, then, is related to the growth of reflexivity and self-awareness. The individual is to be understood as a self-created but reflexive self; that is, an individual develops a self-definition or narrative that responds to circumstances and to others' reactions. In this sense, a self undergoes structuration. In other words, self-identity is created through interaction but becomes a relatively stable entity in the mind of an individual, and this structured self is something that has to be remade and sustained over time and throughout one's various interactions. The agent, for Giddens, is "the overall human subject" existing through the duration of the lifespan. Over this lifespan, the agent constructs a self that is intimately related to physical existence (the body) and is reflexively structured through memory.[77] In late modernity, the self becomes a "project"—something that is worked on and sculpted, a reflexive project of the individual. We make ourselves as persons reflexively. In life politics, the body becomes a central focus of reflexive action, as Weight Watchers suggests. The body is not so much disciplined and docile, as

Foucault theorized; rather, individuals develop strategies of bodily development over time, which would include issues such as dying with dignity.[78] Maintaining a consistent projection and awareness of one's self-identity is a problematic process in a world fraught with anxiety, anguish, and uncertainty.

Many of the indices of identity, such as race, ethnicity, and even gender, are less salient as the fulcrums on which individuals in late modernity orient their actions. Living in a post-scarcity society, people focus instead on personal lifestyle choices and self-definitions. In such a society, what kind of progressive politics are possible? For Giddens, the answer is life politics. Individuals struggle in the world to shape their lifestyles and sustain their reflexively produced identities. In the process, they do not simply sustain existing institutions and structures, but modify them over time. For Giddens, the modern "ethos of self-growth" is at the heart of subversive potential in the modern world. The feminist movement for emancipation, for example, succeeded in establishing the basics of equality in law for women. Now, it is up to individual women to develop their own identities and use their new powers to break into male-dominated occupations and transform traditional patterns of relationships, thereby changing the social structures that have hitherto restrained them.

The key to understanding the subversive potential of lifestyle politics is that "personal decisions also effect global considerations," linking the person to the planet. The contemporary environmental crisis is the most significant intersection between lifestyle choices and global influence. For Giddens, "reversing the degradation of the environment depends upon adopting new lifestyle patterns."[79] In this way, personal activities are intimately bound to planetary problems. Giddens argues that overcoming the environmental threats will demand "coordinated global

responses on levels far removed from individual action. On the other hand, these threats will not be effectively countered unless there is reaction and adaptation on the part of every individual."[80] There is also reflexivity between the environment and the global systems that are transforming the global ecology; in their reflexive self-project and lifestyle choices, individuals have to become reflexively aware of the personal–global connection and change their actions accordingly. Ultimately, what is necessary is to redefine self-actualization away from ever-expanding consumption. Giddens suggests that "personal growth" in terms of "self-expression and creativity" may be a reasonable substitute goal for lifestyle choices.[81] Used in this way, life politics refers to "radical engagements which seek to further the possibilities of a fulfilling and satisfying life for all, and in respect of which there are no 'others.'"[82]

Life politics assumes generative power (i.e., the power to do and make choices) rather than coercive, hierarchical power (i.e., power over others). Giddens argues that a key environmental/ life-politics risk comes from the dangers of nuclear energy and nuclear weapons, although in the latter case, it would seem that the existence of nuclear weapons is largely outside the lifestyle decisions of everyday people. Life politics is a politics of choice. It is conceivable that individuals could choose to not live in communities in which electrical services were provided by nuclear energy. In terms of life politics, ending the threat of nuclear warfare entails not only reflexive knowledge of the threat, but collective action to pressure hierarchical power to liberate humanity from the risk. Collective action undertaken by committed individuals on behalf of present and future generations might be characterized as the type of emancipatory politics that are still important in late modernity.

In this context, Jürgen Habermas's theory of communicative action is an example of emancipatory politics. The more that communication approximates a situation in which there is complete understanding, the more free and equal individuals will be, and the more autonomy they will have in making life decisions.[83]

Giddens's theory of the duality of structure and agency was rooted in the primacy of agency. In contrast, Pierre Bourdieu theorizes the structure of fields within which interests are constituted and expressed.

Pierre Bourdieu and Social Distinction

Pierre Bourdieu (1930–2002) was born an only child in a small village in southwestern France to a family with its roots in the local peasantry. The independent farming economy in the region was being marginalized and transformed by industrial capitalism. His father worked in the post office. Bourdieu was an exceptional student. He was granted admission to elite education in Paris, first at the Lycée Louis-le-Grand and then the École Normale Supérieure, a mecca for young French intellectuals, such as co-student Louis Althusser. Bourdieu became a philosophy student at a time when the dominant approach was French existentialism.[84] As a student from the provinces who spoke a French dialect at home and as an outsider in the elite, Parisian environment, Bourdieu was daily aware of the disagreeable effects of class and status distinctions. He later said that he was horrified by the intellectual world of the École.[85] After graduating, Bourdieu taught philosophy in a small-town high school in central France.

Bourdieu was conscripted into the French army and was sent to Algeria during the war of independence waged by the Algerian Liberation Front. In 1958 he became a lecturer at the University of Algeria. The experience of living in a French colony undergoing insurrection radicalized Bourdieu and inspired him to investigate the society first-hand. Influenced by the structural

anthropology of Claude Lévi-Strauss, Bourdieu undertook an ethnographic study among the Kabyle, an indigenous group in Algeria referred to as the "Berbers." He published *The Algerians* in 1958. Following his return to Paris in the early 1960s, Bourdieu became an academic. He sought to develop a theory that overcame the division in sociology between an objective, structuralist approach and the subjectivist, social construction perspective. He was elected to the prestigious Collège de France in 1982. Bourdieu died of cancer in 2002.[86] In 1979, he had published his influential book *Distinction: A Social Critique of the Judgment of Taste*.

Distinction: A Social Critique of the Judgment of Taste

They had never had to defer and polish themselves and win favor in the world, they never would have to, and that was because they were rich.[87]

— Alice Munro, "The Beggar Maid," 1977

France had a centuries-long tradition of aristocracy that the French Revolution of 1789, despite its liberal use of the guillotine, had not completely severed. Even without the trappings of royalty and titles, which continue to exist, for example, in Britain and Spain, an aristocratic "high culture" has persisted in France into the present. This elite culture, as reflected in the social disposition that Alice Munro detects among the rich, is distinct from "popular" or lower-class culture. While it is useful to distinguish, as had Max Weber, between status and class—an individual may have high social status but not be wealthy or powerful— Bourdieu sought to understand the complex relationship between status and culture, as reflected in different consumption "tastes," and social and economic classes. In France, class awareness and difference continue to shape people's ideas and practices. Each social class has a distinct system of classifying cultural objects that is rooted in the structure of the French class system. American critics have argued that distinct class preferences and tastes are less common in the supposedly classless United States. Bourdieu suggests, however, that systematic differences in social status, which are expressed in cultural distinctions, can be found in all societies.

Popular taste in literature or theatre, which is linked closely to the functions and purposes of daily life, is distinct from what Bourdieu terms the "pure taste" that elite classes exercise. Working-class people, for example, want realistic-seeming stories with happy endings and characters with whom they can identify. They focus on the content of the art and reject any of the experiments with form and presentation that are undertaken by the modern, avant-garde. Moreover, according to Bourdieu, working-class people are not interested in artists working in theatre or in the visual arts who seek to overturn the normative conventions of what is deemed appropriate in playwriting or painting. Some avant-garde art is presented intentionally as an affront to common sense and, therefore, to common people. These kinds of games, Bourdieu says, deliberately exclude working class people. It is precisely such forms of "high" art that the elite identifies with as a mark of distinction. Their "pure" rather than common gaze is detached and evaluative. Such a cool point of view is connected to the general disposition concerning the world, which is found among prosperous people who live "a life of ease."[88]

Taste classifies people, and a person's demonstration of taste (deciding whether something is beautiful or ugly, distinguished or vulgar) is what classifies them, thereby expressing or betraying their social status. Expressions of taste unite some people and separate them from others. Taste is, above all, distaste "of the tastes of others." Bourdieu found that people commonly rejected the tastes of groups that were beneath but socially close to them, the better to distinguish themselves

from near competitors.[89] Bourdieu notes three broad zones of taste, which correspond to educational levels and to social class:

1. Dominant classes express "legitimate taste," a term that implies a preference for serious literature, modern art, classical music, and high cuisine. Nothing classifies people more infallibly than taste in music.
2. The middle-class zone of taste is, appropriately, "middle-brow" (for example, light classical music).
3. The working classes have "popular taste" as defined, for example, by contemporary pop music.

These sets of tastes from different areas of cultural consumption interconnect and form general **dispositions**, which distinguish groups of people and "forge the unconscious unity of a class."[90] Poverty is not only an absence of money, not just wretchedness or deprivation, author Alice Munro says; it also means owning ugly things and being proud of them or being jealous of other people's ugly things. It means "being able to hear every sound from the bathroom" while pretending to be oblivious.[91]

Understanding the principles that underlie people's tastes is like decoding the grammar underneath spoken language. People's dispositions, which are expressed in their taste and, therefore, their consumption patterns, are shaped by their conditions of existence. Bourdieu sought to uncover the economic and social determinants of taste. A person's social position is strongly correlated with that person's dispositions.[92] Tastes vary "in a necessary way according to their social and economic conditions of production, and the products on which they confer their different social identities." There are also important differences in dispositions and tastes among different fractions of classes, for example, between skilled tradespeople and clerical workers.[93] Socialization embeds both a common linguistic world view and different representations, significations, and ways of taken-for-granted thinking and living in various social classes, which serve to reproduce them over time. As a result, dominated classes develop a sense of inferiority similar to the experience of colonized people.

It is typical of class societies for specific forms of inequality to be reproduced over time, so that a person occupies the same class as her or his parents. On the other hand, there is often a difference between one's social place of origin and the present place he or she presently occupies, a feature of modern social life known as social mobility. Bourdieu, whose father was a postal worker, refers to this movement as "class trajectories," which may be upwards or downwards. Within a class, there is a set of more or less typical paths (trajectories) that lead to more or less similar positions. Bourdieu calls this set of paths an objectively existing "field of possibles." Some people within a class will deviate from these common paths, a tendency that is more common among the middle class. Trajectories can also reflect long-term changes in society that often go unnoticed in the short run, such as the slow decline of the family farm. Moving from one trajectory or another, being upwardly or downwardly mobile, is also often influenced by external events, such as wars or economic crises, or by a contingent event, such as a divorce. Often in situations of social mobility, the expectations and dispositions to which an individual has been conditioned no longer fit the new circumstances. The result may be the Don Quixote effect: acting inappropriately in new situations based on beliefs that reflect the obsolete circumstances.[94]

Bourdieu investigated education and schooling, and the effects they have on both the acquisition of tastes and dispositions, and the acquisition of social positions. Fundamentally, educational institutions work to reproduce the social system. Trajectories aside, it is most likely that people will find occupations within the economic system that are equivalent to those of their social origins (i.e., their parents). Nevertheless, the educational system is putatively a means for upward mobility. In general, however, schooling simply confirms the status and the pre-existing dispositions with which people enter the system. Disposition is a product of history, but it also has to be endlessly reproduced though education.[95]

Bourdieu argues that students are allocated to different institutions and streams, within which the institution manipulates different aspirations and demands. These streams affect students' self-image and self-esteem "by channeling pupils towards prestigious or devalued positions." In different streams, such as academic or vocational, students acquire distinct cultural accomplishments that have unequal images associated with them, helping to make these differences real. The prospect for employment that each stream offers is "objectively inscribed" in it. Schooling simultaneously reinforces the belief in the differences between the people who are assigned to those streams. Beyond students' employment prospects, the cultural accomplishments and dispositions that are represented by the educational qualifications students receive (credentials) function as a condition of entry to the world of high culture.[96] Through schooling, students acquire the linguistic skills and the knowledge necessary for them to express high-brow aesthetic preferences, and these preferences are actually constituted or established through this expression. An aesthetic disposition is dependent for its existence upon specific material conditions, past and present, which are the preconditions both for its formation and its continued application.[97]

In North America, there is somewhat less overt streaming than in Europe, where decisions about academic futures are often made quite early. Bourdieu comments that, by the 1960s, schools in France were becoming more open, increasing the apparent possibilities for working-class students to acquire both credentials and "high-brow" tastes.

He found, however, that opening school admissions to working-class children tended to intensify competition in which the well-off and the middle classes have the greater opportunity to ensure social reproduction. Perhaps more importantly, the result of opening schooling to a wider range of classes is to create a kind of "diploma inflation" through which qualifications are worth less than they were in the past, a consequence Bourdieu calls "the cheating of a generation." Nevertheless, the Don Quixote effect is also at work here. People subjectively continue to value educational titles (such as a Bachelor's degree) even when these credentials are losing their connection to privileged positions in the labour market.[98]

Working-class students who were drawn into schooling on false promises have become disillusioned as they discover that schooling structures life chances unequally. Diploma inflation widens the gap between aspirations for positions and the probabilities of actually attaining them. Consequently, working-class students have difficulty accepting their actual social destiny (they were told to aspire above their origins). Frustration and disillusionment follow. Among middle-class students, the situation results in downclassing (downward trajectory). In this case, the result is protest, escapism, or total rejection of the system and the development of "an anti-institutional cast of mind."[99] In England, Paul Willis argued that working class "lads" contribute to their own class reproduction. They understand they have a limited employment future and that schooling is of no use. As they resist schooling by being disruptive, they actively fail themselves and reproduce their working-class origins.[100]

Volume and Structure of Capital(s)

The concept of "capital" as an economic value is generally well understood. Max Weber had argued that economic class—the amount and source of a person's wealth—is not necessarily the same as the social status someone has or the amount of power he or she can exercise. Similarly, Bourdieu argues that people can acquire other kinds of resources that, like wealth, allow them to claim status or to use power. Acquiring an advanced degree in engineering, for example, inculcates an individual into a specific field of cultural and linguistic competence, and thereby gives that person "educational capital." Like wealth, educational capital (or one's "cultural pedigree") can be profitable in the sense that it is marketable and its use can improve life chances.[101]

Bourdieu refers to a number of kinds of "capital," such as "literary, scientific, economic or political" capital, each of which can bring a profitable return, using the term *profit* to include a wide range of resources and benefits.[102] Similarly, someone may have social capital, which is the network of connections they have with other people. Whether the volume of social capital is high or low depends on the total capital possessed by the people in the network. The *structure* of someone's capital, then, can include a number of different indices. Like wealth, the types of capital can differ in amount or in *volume*.

In general, many of these types of capital are represented as **cultural capital**, which includes the dispositions and tastes that create (and establish the criteria for) distinctions and unequal social status. Educational qualifications tend to be closely connected to cultural capital. On the other hand, cultural competence can be obtained outside formal schooling, as in the case of the self-taught person. In Bourdieu's terms, having identical volumes of educational capital does not mean having equivalent volumes of "socially profitable cultural capital" because there are other ways than schooling of obtaining cultural capital. Similar to taste and disposition, cultural capital is routinely inherited from a person's social origins. The older generation embodies and enacts high-brow cultural capital and becomes a familiar model. The next generation benefits from a head-start and begins from birth to acquire the basic elements of this culture.[103]

It might be presumed that economic capital is always connected with cultural capital. Bourdieu argues that the distribution of economic capital is frequently opposite to that of cultural capital. Cultural capital tends to be highest among those classes that have to use credentials (educational capital) for access to positions and income. Middle classes, for example, may be most heavily invested in education, from which cultural capital may be acquired. It is the middle class, not the rich, that needs to learn, as Munro said, how to "defer and polish themselves and win favor." But even within the middle class, as economic capital increases (for example, among skilled trade's workers), the volume of cultural capital declines.[104] That is, different *fractions* of classes may be distinguished by the structure of the kinds of capital they possess.

Furthermore, at the lower economic levels, individuals acquire dispositions objectively related to higher positions, "towards which they 'tend' and 'pre-tend.'" Cultural capital and the dispositions it constitutes and reproduces becomes a stake fought over in social struggles. Cultural capital can open access to economic capital.[105] In addition, access to political capital frequently paves the way for the acquisition of economic capital. Among the dominant classes, fractions struggle with each other for dominance (dominant capital), and these struggles over resources and positions occur in various fields.

Habitus and Field

Bourdieu uses the term **habitus** to refer to the systems of dispositions that social actors acquire and express through such phenomena as the exercise of taste and distinction. The term refers to the mental constructions through which people interpret their social world and within which they organize their actions. Just as they occupy different positions in social space, different classes and fractions of classes have different systems of dispositions and different habitus.[106] Class habitus is "the internalized form of class condition and of the conditioning it entails." While habitus is basically a subjective element, it is constituted through the structuring or objective principle of social class. A class, in this sense, is a set of agents (acting individuals) who are placed in similar conditions, express similar dispositions, and generate similar actions (practices). The class of agents possesses a set of common, objective properties that are either guaranteed in law, such as legal ownership of property or positions of power, or are embodied as habitus.[107]

Habitus is socially constructed. The primary conditions of its production are the volume and composition (structure) of the various forms of capital objectively existing in a particular **field**. A field is a structured social network of agents, individuals or groups, which shape the habitus of individuals within it. There are numerous fields in society, from literary or artistic to industrial. There are also fields involving personal relationships. Fields are the sites within which unequal resources and powers are activated. They become the site within which individuals struggle over the distribution of resources (forms of capital).[108] Habitus and field are mutually conditioning: the dispositions that constitute the habitus are formed within, and function within, fields.

In relation to the agency/structure debate, habitus refers to mental constructs while field refers to the multiplicity of structures within which various dispositions that constitute the habitus are formed. The mutual relationship between habitus and field is expressed through practice. Practice mediates between and recreates the connection between field and habitus.[109] Structures (fields) create dispositions (habitus), which shape practices (action) which react back on structures.

Bourdieu is at pains to explain that he does not have in mind some kind of linear causality through which classes simply express their interests in fields of struggle. In general, the relationship between class and practice arises from a particular configuration within a field that is defined by "the whole set of factors operating in all areas of practice—volume and structure of capital, . . . sex, age, marital status," residence, and so on. The key is to understand the system within which the field operates, what is at stake within it, "the type of capital needed to play for it," and the conditions under which this struggle takes place.[110] The analyst has to superimpose determinants and consider them together, not see them in a liner fashion. Their relationship should be understood in terms of the structural causality of a network.

This "multiplicity of determinations" does not lead to simple indeterminacy whereby factors cancel each other out. Instead, structural causality leads to over-determination in the direction of unity, just as biology, psychology, and sociology intersect in the construction of sexual identity. In an argument that resembles Althusser's model of structural causality, for Bourdieu, some factors in this complex determination have more functional weight than others: "Thus the volume and composition of capital give specific form and value to the determinations which the other factors (age, sex, place of residence, etc.) impose on practices." In each field, agents are assigned a social rank and a specific power that "depends firstly on the specific capital they can mobilize."[111]

The system of objective relations operates in a "field of struggles" within which social positions and also dispositions are defined. Individual or collective agents occupy spaces in the "game," which they seek to either reproduce or redefine and transform. It is in relation to the configuration of this space that it is possible to understand strategies that are employed by social agents in their struggles. Actors do not struggle uninhibitedly in the name of their specific self-interest. They tend to rely on a personal, charismatic quality that hides self-interest behind another form of capital that Bourdieu labels **symbolic capital**. It consists of the intangible quality of an individual's

reputation, skills at argument, or personal vigour that compels others to believe and develops a following. According to Suzanne Collins, "If you appeal to the crowd, either by being humorous or brutal or eccentric, you gain favor."[112] Since this manipulation of reality disguises the substantive forms of capital that are behind it, Bourdieu claims that **symbolic violence** results from the use of symbolic capital.

In his consideration of struggles, Bourdieu says it is necessary to move beyond "thinking in pairs," such as *either* perpetuating *or* overturning the established order. Social contradictions and struggles may not contradict the continuation of the status quo; they may in fact be the conditions under which continuation becomes possible. Specific kinds of changes can ensure permanence. For example, one way to shock the middle class is to transgress ethical censorship by violating normalized rules of morality. Another form of resistance is to claim high aesthetic value for objects or representations that the dominant aesthetic defines as vulgar or worthless. These seemingly radical attacks do not necessarily undermine the status quo, however. When they are combined with political neutrality or radical aestheticism, they become only "the antithesis of petty-bourgeois moralism."[113]

Changes in formal politics, even apparently radical ones, can similarly strengthen the existing system. In 1981, the social-democratic French Socialist Party under François Mitterand was elected to power in France. Mitterand undertook some progressive, welfare-state measures early in his term, but, in the face of economic crises, he changed policies in mid-stream and advocated austerity and cutbacks in services. In this political environment, in which neo-liberalism became dominant in Western politics, Bourdieu became a public intellectual, speaking and writing in opposition to the new economics represented by Mitterand, British prime minister Tony Blair, and the other political handmaidens of contemporary globalization. He also criticized television talk shows for providing "cultural fast food" instead of serious analysis.

When Bourdieu played the role of a social critic opposed to the depredations of globalization and neo-liberalism, he made use of his symbolic capital as an expert qualified to speak and inform the public. He had said that symbolic capital obscured the interests of a particular group behind the claim of meeting universal interests. Bourdieu's use of his prestige and reputation to become a social critic, however, demonstrates that various kinds of capital can be "expended" in more than one way. Symbolic capital need not produce symbolic violence.

Conclusion

> *"Sometime they'll give a war and nobody will come."*[114]
>
> — Carl Sandburg, *The People, Yes*, 1936

By the 1960s, Carl Sandburg's line, which in his poem was delivered by a little girl, had become popularized as an anti-Vietnam War slogan: What if they gave a war and nobody came? In the context of the US policy of drafting young American men to fight in Vietnam, the slogan implied that the everyday choices made by individuals could have a profound effect on national and global society. This idea of the global significance

of individual choices is basic to Giddens's view of life politics.

Common to all the theories of high modernity discussed in this chapter is the aim of reconciling interpretive and structural theories into a single theoretical perspective. Such an amalgamation requires a fine balance. Typically, the theorist is critiqued on the grounds that the theory is weighted toward individual consciousness (Giddens) or structural determination (Bourdieu). Habermas's wish that individuals or groups could come to approximate the ideal speech situation puts him in the position of advocating discursive action, tending to emphasize interpretation and communication more than structure.

One way to approach sociology that allows for maximum diversity of theories is to argue that sociology requires and benefits from multiple paradigms and that shoe-horning all possible perspectives into one paradigm distorts social analysis more than it illuminates it. George Ritzer argues that different levels of understanding are useful to grasp social issues and that some approaches are more appropriate than others for the analysis of particular levels of social life and particular sociological questions.[115] In the conclusion to this book, it is useful to consider the plans for social action that emerge from contemporary social theory in relation to the problems that Beck had outlined in the risk society.

Questions for Reflection

1. What connects the social problems that emerge in the risk society to the social theories that have arisen in late modernity?
2. What are the strengths and limitations of Giddens's view that global social change ultimately relies on personal life-choice decisions?
3. Is the colonization of the lifeworld beyond repair, or do contemporary social movements

of various kinds have the capacity to go beyond preservation and defence, and create new identities and institutions that reflect a world free of the negative effects of Bourdieu's steering mechanisms?

4. To what extent is Bourdieu's discussion of taste, disposition, and distinction relevant to an analysis of North American society?

Conclusion

—◆—

Rudyard Kipling (1865–1936) is the author of many stories, poems, and novels, including *The Jungle Book*. Kipling was born in Bombay (now Mumbai), India. He is remembered in social theory primarily as an ideologue for British imperialism, which he called the "white-man's burden." Kipling's briefly-titled poem *If—* is full of advice and homilies that, Kipling believed, defined a "true man," to whom the whole earth belonged "and everything that's in it." In the era of anti-globalization and the critique of Orientalism, of third-wave feminism, and "gender trouble," the masculinist jingoism in Kipling's writings has been discredited. But the idea that people should aspire to more than only thought for its own sake is relevant to the consideration of the implications, intended and unintended, of social theories.

Marx claimed that philosophers only interpreted the world differently; the point is to change it. Changing requires that the world first be interpreted, but Marx demanded that the aim of social analysis be to foster substantive transformation. The social thought that developed from Marx was, at first, intimately connected with social change. In the concept of praxis, Marx argued that thinking and doing, theory and practice were intimately related, and each transformed the other. Marx was active politically in Europe. He helped organize and was closely involved in the daily workings of the First International Workingmen's Association. Until the 1930s, most Marxists, whether they were reformists or revolutionaries, were active leaders in labour and revolutionary movements, a legacy that continued through a variety of twentieth-century social revolutions.

Durkheim and Weber shared with Marx the aim of changing society. Weber had been more pessimistic than Durkheim about the potential to make the world better in the future, but neither theorist only thought and wrote. In his writings about society, Durkheim advocated social reforms that would result in a less unequal distribution of wealth and open access to all important positions to the most talented, a system known as meritocracy. He was actively involved in combating the social injustices of his day. Weber warned of the negative consequences of the domination of instrumental rationality and tried to bring a form of liberal democratic, parliamentary government to post-World War I Germany.

Not all social theories aim to foster social change, however. Georg Simmel, for example, one of the sociologists of the classical era, said that the task of sociology was "only to understand." He meant that the purpose of sociology was not to make judgments—neither to accuse nor to pardon—but his approach to the discipline was less concerned with social reform than his contemporaries. It is one of the ways in which Simmel is the most "postmodern" of the classical generation of sociologists.

This book is concerned primarily with the development of "critical" social theories over the last century. The book attempts to contextualize ideas in time and space. From Virginia Woolf through to Bourdieu and beyond, social thinkers have been closely linked to and more or less influential within the major events of their era. The tradition of active engagement and leadership continued through the great movements for emancipation involving women's liberation, gender/sex-based struggles, anti-colonial movements, and movements for social equality among people of African descent in the West. Activists involved in these movements keep sociological analysis vital, contemporary, and relevant. The canon of recognized social theory, however, is still predominantly white, Western, and male.

Between the Russian Revolution of 1917 and the fall of Russian state socialism in 1989, the dynamic of substantive social change, which radicalizes and emancipates politics, economics, and culture, passed from the developed West to the global South. The revolutionary movements spawned in the twentieth century appear to have run their course, drowned in the liquidity of modernity. The West won the Cold War, but the initiative for change has not returned to Western consumers, or to ecologists, cultural rebels, or the sexually transgressive. Theories of agency, lifestyle subversion, communication, discourse deconstruction, and gender transformation still have a Western sheen, despite globalization and the change in time/space configurations.

Of the generation of social theorists deemed contemporary because of the significance of their work for analyzing late modernity, many have died (Foucault in 1984, Bourdieu in 2002, Baudrillard and Habermas in 2007). Part of an influential cohort of social theorists, these four were born within a few years of each other between 1926 and 1930. They were children during the Depression and adolescents during World War II; they came to intellectual awareness during the Cold War and were establishing academic careers in the raucous 1960s. They developed their distinctive versions of thought against the foils of structuralism and neo-Marxism, and within the theoretical space opened by the move in social thought to the analysis of language and discourse (the "linguistic turn").

Few of the theorists discussed in this book sought to make thought their *sole* aim. Many were active in various ways as public intellectuals, a European tradition that is seldom matched in North America except among third-wave feminists—Noam Chomsky is a singular exception. Nevertheless, most of these active academics are not "organic intellectuals" in the sense meant by Antonio Gramsci. Organic intellectuals are closely integrated with the people for whom they write and with whom they struggle. It is a difficult calling; bell hooks comes closest to playing this role now.

Primarily, however, social thought is the preferred instrument of social change among contemporary theorists, and Patricia Hill Collins comes close to making this claim explicit. Einstein said that it isn't possible to bring change without changing people's thinking. Deconstructing the dominant discourse, helping give the "subaltern" a voice, championing the transgression of normative and naturalized identities and ways of life, making lifestyle choices that reflect alternatives to the risk society—all of these strategies have some progressive potential here and now. In the contemporary period, Giddens's "utopian realism," Habermas's "communicative action," Foucault's sexual transgressions, Baudrillard's seduction of play and festivals, and Bourdieu's multitude of disconnected and singular social movements have been advanced as strategies for social change originating primarily in the West. As we face the prospect of some form of apocalypse, the decline and fall of the third rock from the sun, post-structural playfulness, excess, and irony take on the appearance of temporary coping strategies in the face of impending doom.

In the litany of posts that designate intellectual genres today, perhaps post-colonialism deserves particular attention. Late modernist and postmodern perspectives tend to reflect Western experiences and troubles more than global ones. The impetus for social transformation in the last 100 years, however, has been strongest in the global South. It is precisely economic growth that is at the root of the "risk" society and of the impending dangers that threaten the globe. Ulrich Beck points out that these risks and dangers are not spread equally among countries over the globe or among social groups within countries. French economist Thomas Piketty has analyzed the changes in income distribution over time. He argues that the returns to capital investment are growing faster than the actual economy while other incomes are not keeping pace. The resulting imbalances are not sustainable in the long run. To avoid the inevitable crises that will ensue, in *Capital in the Twenty-First Century* Piketty recommends that governments should tax wealth, not just income. There are few prospects for such a global version of the Keynesian welfare state.

In the global South, resistance to globalization and the economic, cultural, and military domination of the West has spawned ethnic identity politics and violent separatist movements, religious and traditional fundamentalism, and real and symbolic acts of terrorism. The West responds with state violence, which reiterates power and domination at great cost but with little long-term success. One of the key tenets of modern social theory is that the national state is increasingly unable to control the conditions of its economic growth. In this light, contemporary attempts to develop a nation-state along socialist lines, as in Venezuela and Ecuador, face insurmountable odds.

Twenty-First-Century Socialism

In 1994, in the state of Chiapas, Mexico, an insurrection broke out largely among indigenous people struggling for land reform and human rights. The militant, armed movement was led by the Zapatista Army of National Liberation.[1] The Zapatistas raided and occupied a number of towns in Chiapas and tried to initiate local control and land reform. The Mexican army soon counter-attacked and pushed the rebels back into the jungle. The movement survived underground and brought international attention to the plight of Mexico's poorest people and to the Zapatistas. Images of guerillas carrying submachine guns and masked with balaclavas were splashed across the international media. To get their message out to the international community, the educated and sophisticated leaders of the Zapatistas spread communiqués through the Internet, demonstrating the progressive potential of modern means of mass communication.[2] The two-faced nature of the Internet is readily apparent, however, in the dissemination of atrocity videos and recruitment appeals by the Islamic State (ISIS).

Latin America has a long revolutionary history. In 2009, the Cuban Revolution turned 50 years old, and it persists as one of the few explicitly socialist states. The Cuban example spurred numerous guerilla movements throughout Central and South America. The FARC (in English, the Revolutionary Armed Forces of Colombia—People's Army) in Colombia continued its rural guerilla campaign into the second decade of this century. For many socialists, however, FARC represents an outdated form of Marxism. In this view, what Latin America needs is a new, democratic, and popular socialist movement—that is, twenty-first-century socialism. In Venezuela, Bolivia, and Ecuador, leftist parties were elected into government. Of these, only the late Hugo Chavez, the Venezuelan leader, openly proclaimed his revolution to be socialist.

Contemporary socialism in Latin America explicitly wants to avoid the disastrous policies of state socialism as practised in the USSR but Latin America also wants to be much more than merely a capitalist-led welfare state. Twenty-first-century socialism must be constructed on the basis of the specific conditions found in each country. In general, however, socialism must be democratic and participatory. In Venezuela, popularly elected communal councils based in neighbourhoods are designed to realize local self-government and support movements that go beyond only legislating equal rights by putting equality rights in practice. Venezuela is a multi-party state and not a one-party monopoly. Beyond simple elections for state and national governments, Chavez utilized referenda to allow the population to vote directly on policy changes. Economically, socialism entails nationalizing, at least in part, major industries such as oil (compensating the owners) and regulating the private sector. In agriculture, land reform divides agricultural land among the rural population and encourages the development of co-operatives. In addition, Petras says that Chavez "funded a plethora of programs designed to raise living standards of 60% of the population that include[d] the working class, self-employed, poor, peasants and female heads of households."[3]

The Venezuelan example is not essentially a model of socialism, but an example of a political and social praxis that attempted to change society, peacefully and democratically, in an increasingly socialist direction. In a multi-party democracy, in which most industries are still in private hands, including the mass media, and in which the elite survives intact, any socialist-leaning experiment is precarious and uncertain.[4] Twenty-first-century socialists want to avoid repeating the negative lessons of the past. Without a comprehensive theory of the failures of twentieth-century Marxism, however, it is difficult to know what can be learned positively from the revolutionary century that has passed.

Giddens says that emancipatory politics—aimed at equalizing conditions and overcoming injustice and oppression—is at the top of the agenda for less developed countries. This kind of new politics, however, appears to be overwhelmed by more conservative or reactionary responses. Globalization ignites ethnic and tribal rivalries, religious fundamentalism, intolerance, and apocalyptic nightmares. Caught up in the machinery of westernization, many people had generally taken for granted that the problems of the world could be solved by bringing everyone's standards up, not by levelling down. Giddens argues, however, that making standards of living more equal must entail a diminution of consumption in the West. Although many middle-class living standards are under threat, the number of people who count as relatively privileged is large, particularly in the West. Privileged groups tend not to give up their privileges unless real circumstances oblige them to do so.

The decade of modernization and development was supposed to close the gap between rich and poor nations by raising the global standard of living. The social changes occurring now in China, India, Brazil, and to a lesser extent in other countries, which are thoroughly integrated into globalization, are not simply the adoption of a Western model. Each of those countries is modernizing in its own way, but each is still tied to a global economy that runs on the principles of capitalist growth and accumulation. The average Chinese urbanite, for example, aspires to the way of life of the average Westerner, however impossible it will be to reach such a high standard of living globally. Political passivity in China is related at least as much to the success of rapid economic growth—what Herbert Marcuse referred to as "delivering the goods"—as it is to Chinese political repression.

Ecology

One fundamental problem with the contemporary globalization strategy is the physical impossibility of levelling social conditions by raising living standards globally. The world that has been socially constructed has an obdurate, fundamentally material character that goes beyond concepts and discourses. Physical changes in the globe have consequences that a reflexive social science can understand and attempt to address. Most obdurate of all in the contemporary world is climate change, which rests on an established political and economic power base that is wedded to fossil fuels. The enormous amount of wealth being amassed globally by the one per cent is well known. Even redistribution of this wealth, assuming that it is something tangible that can be divided in a substantial way, will not do enough to level upwards. More importantly, the Western, middle-class lifestyle is unsustainable physically in a resource-strapped globe. Global sustainability is very close to an absolute limit. Worse, the attempt to attain this ideal is destructive and dangerous. The ecological damage wrought by global industrialization is widely acknowledged, with the exception of the New Right, which is tied to globalization, capital accumulation, and the carbon industries. Although the risks of industrialization are global and will affect everyone, ecological crises and climate change are likely to hit the poorest regions of the world particularly hard. The supply of food and fresh water are particularly at risk, and the world's poor are the most threatened. Capitalist resource development is the primary cause of these deeply real social problems, and there will inevitably be blow-back. In North America, such an analysis entails understanding the history and social conditions of First Nations peoples. Environmental destruction turns their land into waste and underscores the importance of demands for native sovereignty and land claims.

Given global threats to food security, employment, sources of fresh water, ecology, climate, the global economy, and social justice, it is likely that we are heading into a period of discord and strife unprecedented in its global scope. On a given weekend, hundreds of thousands of people can be mobilized to demonstrate against climate change in New York, but there is as yet no sustained, large-scale, grass-roots movement. Cracks in the ruling class are still relatively small although there is a limited move to divest from the carbon industry.

In additional to being comprehensive, historical, and comparative, as in the best tradition of classical theory, an adequate social theory for this era would also be global in its vision. In this context, the lessons of the aborted attempt to construct state socialism, the contradictions of national Keynesianism, the proliferation of weapons of mass destruction, the dangers of incipient fascism, and, above all, the threat posed by climate change are all aspects of recent history that we must understand and analyze. Einstein said that no problem can be solved within the consciousness that created it. Critical theory adds that a changed consciousness requires changes in practice. While none of the theories reviewed in this book measure up to an effective theory of social change for the present age, perhaps the most utopian of needs, many of their insights allow us to better understand the difficulties we are facing and the blind alleys that have got us to this point.

Glossary

abstract expressionism An American form of painting from the late 1940s and 1950s that ignores realism in favour of colour and design, and emphasizes spontaneous creation.

abstracted empiricism The application of advanced statistics to the analysis of quantitative data that is usually decontextualized and applied to determine correlations between variables.

accumulation Wealth that is not consumed but is reinvested in further economic development; can be private or public.

aesthetics The branch of knowledge that is concerned with questions of beauty and artistic form, not content.

affective neutrality Parsons's idea that modern industrial society requires that people handle situations and other people according to objective and rational standards, rather than on the basis of emotional attachments or preferentially because of personal connections.

agency Relates to the theory of the purposively acting subject, as developed by interpretive sociology. Agents' actions recreate or can change the social structures that set the limits of their agency.

American dream The myth that anyone, regardless of social background, could "make it" (become rich) in the United States—the land of opportunity—by dint of hard work, initiative, and an enterprising spirit.

Americanization The process through which American culture becomes globalized; for example, through dissemination of American pop culture and fast-food restaurants.

anarchism A radical political movement that demands individual freedom and workers' control, and that opposes all forms of authority.

androgynous Describing a person whose definition of gender typically includes both conventionally defined masculine and feminine elements.

archaeology For Foucault, the methodology through which he sought to uncover the generally hidden preconditions that structured the discourse of any given age and the boundaries of its possible thought.

assimilation The process through which newly arrived immigrant groups lose their distinctive cultural attributes (language, customs, etc.) and assume the values, practices, and attitudes of the dominant group.

Auschwitz One of the most well-known German concentration camps, built in Poland, and connected to the extermination camp at Birkenau.

bad faith In Sartre's existentialism, the tendency to deny responsibility for the choices people make and the consequences of those choices; the denial of essential human freedom.

Beats A group of cultural rebels in the 1950s, connected to avant-garde artists and writers, who abandoned conventional, middle-class values and sought free expression especially in extreme experience.

blacklisted To be excluded from some benefit, such as employment or education, on grounds such as political activity or opinion. During the McCarthy era, people suspected of leftist ideas were identified and fired from their jobs.

Bolsheviks The Lenin-led revolutionary Russian Marxist (Communist) Party that was composed of relatively few professional revolutionaries and characterized by centralized power; opposed reformists.

bourgeois revolution The revolution that takes place in a feudal, aristocratic system that brings the capitalist class, or bourgeoisie, to political power, after which capitalism becomes the dominant economic system.

breaching experiments Harold Garfinkel had students violate, in everyday interaction, the assumed and taken-for-granted conventions of polite society to reveal the hidden rules and morals that are the foundation of common sense and common beliefs.

bureaucratism When the government of a revolutionary regime deteriorates into top-down, over-centralized, and undemocratic form that prevents the exercise of popular power.

code For Baudrillard, an underlying system, like a language or communication system, that signifies the value of the signs and significations that objects embody.

collective guilt The belief that millions of Germans participated in, benefited from, or acquiesced to the Holocaust in World War II, and therefore share a portion of the blame.

colonialism The military conquest of less economically developed territories and their subjection to political and economic domination by the economic and political elites of a ruling country.

colour line The geographic and symbolic separation of black and white races in the US; historically, crossing the Mason-Dixon Line meant crossing from northern free states to southern slave states.

communicative action For Habermas, the situation through which people discuss and debate, and potentially come to mutual recognition and understanding; opposed to **distorted communication**.

comprador bourgeoisie Elites in Third World countries whose interests are tied to the imperialist power; contrasts with **national bourgeoisie** who seek independent capitalist growth.

compulsory heterosexuality Enforced patterns of socially constructed gender relations within which the binary male/female is assumed to be natural and is subject to regulation and enforcement.

conditioning In behavioural psychology, the idea that the behaviour of all animals, including humans, is determined by the application of positive rewards (benefits) or negative ones (punishments). Excludes concern with cognitive processes or consciousness.

conspicuous consumption Veblen's idea that we demonstrate our social status through the visible consumption of expensive consumer goods, such as houses, automobiles, and fashion.

cool medium For McLuhan, a medium of communication that provides little information, such as ordinary speech or texting, so that the audience actively has to participate in the act of communication; the opposite of a **hot medium**.

critical theory The name applied to the main ideas held in common by theorists of the Frankfurt School, fundamentally stressing the importance of making judgments about society using critical reason.

cultural capital The skills, knowledge, and dispositions that individuals acquire, principally from their family and education, that become resources for their struggles for status, wealth, and power.

cultural politics The theory that changes in culture, such as lifestyle changes, once sufficiently widespread, are the means to social transformation; rejects the need for political organization or for seeking state power.

cultural relativism Boas's term for studying a culture in its own terms instead of ethnocentrically, which means interpreting it in terms of one's own cultural biases.

culture industry Just as manufacturing industries were being increasingly monopolized, artistic production was becoming an industry dominated by a few big businesses intent on entertaining, distracting, and controlling the masses rather than engaging them in critical thought.

Dada A modern artistic and literary movement that expands the definition of art so broadly that the art/non-art distinction becomes meaningless; a nihilistic art form.

debt crisis Occurs when the cost of borrowing money from the West for economic development grows beyond the ability of Third World countries to pay back, causing social crises.

deconstruction The post-structuralist approach to analysis that reveals as socially constructed the underlying concepts and modes of understanding of a text and/or exposes its suppositions, gaps, limitations, silences, and bias.

definition of the situation To understand the effects of a social phenomenon it is necessary to go beyond its objective characteristics and understand the complex of meanings it has for all the people involved.

dependent development Whereby the amount and kind of economic development in a Third World country is dictated by and in the interests of dominant Western nations.

deregulation Policies of neo-liberalism that remove government constraints and regulations on the movement and utilization of capital; a return to laissez-faire.

detribalization McLuhan's term for the result of printing technology, which created nationalism, uniformity, and specialization, destroying tribal clans and communities. The reverse effect is retribalization.

dialectical The form of understanding through which a phenomenon is analyzed in terms of the contradictions within it, the interrelationship among elements making up the social whole, and its potential for change. For example, Enlightenment can be liberating as critical reason, but it has the opposite potential to become an instrument of domination.

dialectic of control Giddens's term to refer to the fact that all actors, even subordinate ones, have access to some resources through which they can influence their situation; no social actors are entirely powerless in a social situation; control always elicits forms of reactive resistance.

dialogical A relationship, commonly employed in pedagogy, in which action and thought influence one another; the roles of teacher and student are integrated.

diaspora The wide dispersal of a people from their homeland; refers to the forced migration of African people to the Americas beginning with the slave trade.

disembedded When relations between people are lifted out from local contexts and reconstructed in light of globalized imperatives.

dispositions For Bourdieu, the set of factors shaping an individual's sense of taste, which is activated in consumer choices that claim and establish that individual's social status and class membership.

dissident A Russian intellectual suppressed by the Soviet state for opposing the regime; the term may be applied to US intellectuals during McCarthyism.

distanciation Refers to the ways "social life is ordered across time and space" (Giddens). Globalization changes the speed with which time is experienced and brings widely separated people into communication with one another.

distorted communication The practice of manipulating communication through the exercise of power to deflect it from consensus-building and to exert the will of the powerful over social action.

dysfunction In structural functional theory, a term applied to a process or institution that has disruptive consequences for social integration and order.

emancipatory politics For Giddens, social movements and other types of political engagements designed to bring about social equality or end servitude, such as labour movements or campaigns for civil rights.

émigré A refugee from Russia after the 1917 Bolshevik Revolution; supported the anti-Communist cause.

Enlightenment An eighteenth-century intellectual movement that inspired the French Revolution. Stresses the singular importance of human reason and science as a source of knowledge rather than intuition, authority, instinct, or spirituality.

Enlightenment rationalism The modern idea that social life should be understood rationally and all aspects of society should be judged according to their rationality.

episteme The underlying structure that establishes the conceptual framework and rules of truth, which operate within the many different discourses that coexist in any given age.

equilibrium In structural-functional sociology, the idea that a social system has an in-built mechanism that helps it cope with social strains or conflicts, automatically returning society to its previous or normative state.

ethnography A qualitative research method developed in anthropology and designed to understand a culture from the inside by revealing the knowledge and meaning of cultural insiders.

ethnomethodology The everyday methods people use to make sense of their world and their actions within it, and to explain these actions to themselves and others.

eugenics A movement to forcibly sterilize and thereby eliminate from the population groups and individuals deemed to be genetically inferior.

existentialism A philosophy centred on the freedom of the individual to self-define her or his existence in an otherwise meaningless and absurd world.

Fascism (and fascism) Fascism (capitalized) refers to the Italian totalitarian state, while fascism (lower case) refers to extremely right-wing, authoritarian, intolerant views and politics (in general).

feminine mystique For Friedan, the ideology of femininity, by which women were naturally suited to and gained fulfilment from homemaking and motherhood and were unsuited for professional careers.

field A structured social network of individuals or groups, which shapes their habitus and becomes the site within which individuals struggle over the distribution of resources.

fin-de-siècle The waning of the nineteenth century and dawning of the twentieth, during which concepts of the arts and society were in transition.

first-wave feminism The Western movement for women's rights that began in the 1850s and culminated in the 1920s after women won the vote and other political rights. *See* **second-wave feminism**.

Fordism Modern production methods pioneered by Henry Ford, such as product standardization, the assembly line, relatively high pay linked to mass consumption, and (later) accommodation to modern union demands.

futurism An artistic movement that condemned all previous art, including architecture, as well as middle-class (bourgeois) customs and manners; looked toward a new future of dynamism, speed, and technological power. In Italy, Futurism supported nationalism and fascism.

gaze For Foucault, the act of observing and ultimately judging the "other," as by a physician or other authority figure, that constitutes that person as an object.

genealogy Foucault's method of analyzing the formation and career of specific discourses and their functions within a system of knowledge and distribution of power.

global village McLuhan's idea that contemporary electronic communications are so rapid and widespread that they, effectively, reduce the globe to village size so that anything that happens anywhere has consequences everywhere.

Greater Germany The political and military idea of expanding the German nation to include territory with a significant number of German-speaking people.

habitus For Bourdieu, the systems of dispositions that social actors acquire from their objective social positions and express through such phenomena as the exercise of taste and distinction.

Harlem Renaissance An African-American cultural movement in literature and the arts in the 1920s centred in Harlem, New York; it was central to the development of black pride, independence, and nationalism.

historical materialism The term Marx applied to his theory of historical change; it implies a theory that history evolves through economic stages.

Hobbesian problem of order Hobbes's argument that humans were naturally selfish and sought always to increase their power. In this case, society always faces the problem of controlling these impulses and preventing the breakdown of social order.

hot medium For McLuhan, a medium of communication that extends only one sense, such as sight, with so much information that the audience does not participate in the act of communication; the opposite of a **cool medium**.

humanism The tendency within Marxism to emphasize the importance of subjective consciousness and direct action to explain social consequences. Opposed to economic determinism.

hyperreality The point at which simulations eradicate the contradiction between the real and the imaginary; things become more real than reality, which pales alongside the simulation.

id Freud's term for the part of personality that is driven by inborn desires, such as for food or sexuality, that society teaches us must be repressed and controlled.

ideal speech situation Habermas's ideal type in which communication is free from any distorting effects of power and within which consensus is possible.

ideological state apparatus For Althusser, the ensemble of institutions that maintain the ideological hegemony of the capitalist class but are relatively autonomous from that class. These institutions include education, religion, and the mass media.

immanence For de Beauvoir, the state of subservient passivity forced upon subservient groups, such as women and slaves, by dominant groups.

imperialism The control by an industrialized nation of a less-developed region, to which the industrialized nation exported capital, and from which it imported large profits and raw materials.

implosion To contract; the opposite of *explosion*. For McLuhan, printing technology led to the expansion of Western control and uniform culture over vast territories. With electronic technology, the process is imploding or reversing, creating diversity, wholeness, and harmony.

industrial unionism A militant union movement among North American industrial workers in the 1930s that combined workers in most trades, as well as unskilled workers, in a single union; distinct from craft unions that organized workers in only one trade.

instrumental rationality The narrow use of reason to find the most efficient means to a desired end; avoids questioning the ends themselves.

instrumentally When you treat other people as objects to help you attain your desires rather than as individuals whose interests and needs have to be taken into consideration.

intersubjectivity The idea that our consciousness and our understanding of the world around us come from our interactions with other people and the development of more or less shared perceptions and understandings.

"It" For Kerouac, an indescribable but exquisite experience. The search for *It* motivated the Beats (capitalized by Kerouac).

Jewish conspiracy The fantasy that there is a Jewish world conspiracy to dominate the world, through any means, including ownership of big business and banks, and leadership of socialist parties.

Keynesianism Economic policy opposed to laissez-faire, giving the government responsibility for regulating the economy by managing the money supply, interest rates, public works, and state spending to prevent economic crises from developing into depression.

Labour Party A reform party in England rooted in the trade union movement. Elected to government in 1946, it began to implement reforms creating the welfare state.

langue For Saussure, the set of linguistic rules, such as grammar and syntax, that exists largely as a structure beneath the consciousness of individuals who use it.

latent function Merton's term for the consequences of an action that is *not* intended by the actor. The latent function of schooling is to promote passive acceptance of authority.

latent Orientalism The ideology of discourse of Western superiority over the East; influences actual colonial conquest and domination, known as manifest Orientalism.

legitimation For Berger and Luckmann, values and "knowledge" that represent the existing state of things as "normal" and thereby justify its existence.

libido Freud's term for basic sexual desire or energy. The sexual drive has to be controlled by society and may be diverted into other forms, such as creative arts.

life politics Describes how through an individual's choices and lifestyle decisions, in which the personal become political, it is possible to affect global polices and contribute to social change.

lifeworld The everyday world that is underpinned by taken-for-granted, implicit knowledge that guides our daily activity but is largely outside our conscious mind (Habermas).

lumpenproletariat The chronically unemployed, career criminals, and the down-and-out, who are excluded from the capitalist system and become a dangerous class of potential anarchists and fascist thugs.

macrosociology A sociological paradigm that focuses attention on societies as a whole system, concentrating either on the processes that integrate the social order or on systematic contradictions and conflicts that fracture the society.

managed achievement For Garfinkel, when social roles reflect people's cultivated, practised, and knowledgeable actions through which they accomplish goals and achieve socially recognized statuses; they are engaged in "management work."

manifest function Merton's term for the consequences of an action that is intended by the actor. The manifest function of schooling is to pass on a cultural heritage.

master discourse The language and culture of domination that is imposed from a position of power and causes the deculturation of a subordinated other.

master narratives Stories that explain the world and embody the ideology and perspective of dominant groups that, in turn, shape the perceptions and thinking of subordinate groups.

material incentives In a socialist economy, giving unequal pay and benefits to different groups to motivate hard work; inculcates individualism and undermines social solidarity.

matrix of domination A concept used by Hill Collins to designate the interconnectedness among a variety of types of social inequality, including class, racialization, and gender.

the medium is the message McLuhan's central thesis that the form of a medium (radio, TV, Internet) has profound social effects regardless of the content that is actually broadcast via the medium.

metanarratives Grand theories of social totalities that claim universal validity (Marxism, Christianity) and are deemed incredulous in postmodern thought.

metropolitan-centre Part of Frank's model of colonial domination, in which the capitalist system extends outward through successive rings from a metropolitan centre; each ring represents an exploited satellite of the larger metropolis that exploits its own peripheral regions.

microsociology A sociological paradigm that focuses on the ideas, decisions, and interpretations of individuals and their interactions with others.

modernization The ideology that all countries should emulate the political, economic, and cultural characteristics of developed Western nations, which mirror their future.

monocrop Refers to a single crop or product that many countries are trapped by colonialism into producing, making them economically vulnerable; for example, a "banana republic."

multiple realities Schutz's idea, adopted by Berger and Luckmann, that differentially situated people "see" and interpret the world differently and construct different conceptions of what is real.

negative thinking Marcuse's term for thinking critically about the present society, revealing the potential for change within it, and inspiring this change.

neo-colonialism The term used for the period after a Third World country becomes politically independent but its economy is still under the domination of First World economies; its independence is an illusion.

neo-liberalism A return to laissez-faire capitalism in the late twentieth century; the political side of globalization.

neo-Marxists A diverse group of Marxist theorists in the 1960s and 1970s who attempted to update Marxist theory in the light of social and economic changes in the capitalist mode of production.

neurosis In psychoanalysis, a character tendency or irrational anxiety that interferes with a person's ability to achieve happiness; often brought on by failing to or fearing to address personal problems constructively.

New Economic Policy (NEP) Implemented in Russia by the Bolsheviks after the Civil War, the NEP allowed capitalism to grow in many businesses; and agriculture, to increase productivity. The NEP was controversial because it seemed to strengthen capitalism at the expense of socialism.

New Negro The new generation of African Americans post–World War I, who, Alain Locke argued, rejected both violent resistance and passive assimilation, creating instead a proud, black cultural heritage in the US.

New Left A movement largely of youth in the 1960s that demanded revolutionary change in society but eschewed the politics of organized unions and Marxist political parties in favour of spontaneous, anti-authoritarian, mass, direct action.

New Right Late twentieth-century conservative politics combining neo-liberal economics with conservative social policies and militarization (neo-conservatism).

New Woman A member of the generation of young women who, in the 1890s, sought meaningful careers and rejected the norms of traditional marriage.

nihilism The view that, since life is meaningless and absurd, no standards of morality or ethics are valid other than those defined by the individual for herself or himself.

nonlinear logics The idea that ordinary logic is orderly and step-by-step, and focuses on small parts. If thinking is nonlinear, it is free to be spontaneous and disconnected, and to embrace wholeness; expressed, for example, in symbolic poetry and abstract painting.

normalization For Foucault, the attempt to bring someone who is transgressing social rules within the bounds of normative judgments.

overdetermined For Althusser, the total effect of the contradictions in society, which reinforce each other and tend toward either social stability or a revolutionary break.

paradigms The basic assumptions and supposed truths of a particular view of scientific knowledge that are foundational for theory but are subject to change.

parole Saussure's term for an individual act of speech that unfolds over time and that utilizes **langue** (embedded rules) but can slowly modify language usage.

patriarchal Refers to the dominating role of the father/husband in a family; more generally, to male dominance in society.

pattern consistency Parsons's idea that the roles people play in a society and the value orientations they have must be congruent for society to function; the parts of a society have to be integrated for social stability.

performative   Hill Collins's term to describe gender, which is neither inborn nor only an identity that is produced through discourse; rather, gender is an accomplished identity that arises through actions that embody gender physically and socially.

peripheral-satellite   Part of Frank's model of colonial domination, in which the capitalist system incorporates exploited regions that are peripheral to the world metropolis but that are also national, regional, or local metropolises relative to their own satellites.

phenomenology   A philosophy that begins with phenomena as individuals experience them, assign meaning to them, and construct their conscious world in interaction with them; pays attention to the appearance of objects rather than making assumptions about something's "inner essence."

pleasure principle   Derived from Freud, the theory that the unconscious mind is ruled by instinctual desires for pleasure that demand fulfillment or gratification, but that have to be controlled by society in order for civilization to exist.

polygenism   In biology, the theory that different races of human beings evolved from separate ancestors, justifying racist assumptions of inborn racial inferiority; opposed to monogenism, the theory of one single line of descent for all humanity.

popular culture   Varieties of mass-produced forms of commercial entertainment disseminated by the mass media, unlike folk or grass-roots culture; it inspires alternative cultural expressions, but then tends to incorporate such alternatives into its nexus.

positivism   A scientific approach to understanding society that seeks the underlying laws that determine human action and thinking, and ignores the role of conscious action in bringing social change.

postmodernism   Contemporary rejection of broad theoretical generalizations in favour of fragmented, localized, and experiential perspectives and knowledge.

power elite   Mills's term for the coordination of economic, political, and military groups in power at the top of American society, held together as a self-conscious and socially insular sub-community.

praxis   In Marxism, implementing change in society by putting theoretical ideas into practice, assessing the results, and changing the theory as appropriate.

prediscursive   An essential element, such as an instinct, that exists as a foundation of social life but is not created by or influenced by social discourse.

primitive accumulation   The brutal early period of capitalist industrialization, extended over centuries, during which capital was amassed in Europe through various forms of severe exploitation, including colonialism and slavery.

queer theory   Built on the social construction of gender, an approach that understands categories and discourses from the point of view of the socially marginalized and envisages change through both discursive and performative practices.

radical feminism   A tendency in **second-wave feminism** that argued that the root of women's oppression was found in patriarchy, which originated prior to capitalism and persisted in post-capitalist societies; women's liberation demanded widespread cultural change beyond politics and economics.

reality principle   Derived from Freud, the theory that the body's instinctual demand for the gratification of instincts is constrained by scarcity and must be placed under the control of social regulations and controls to maintain an orderly society.

recursive   Similar to **reflexive**; people's activities continually recreate the conditions that make their activities possible (Giddens).

reference group   The idea, applied by Merton, that people make judgments about others and social situations according to the standards of a group with which they identify.

reflexive   The idea that a social actor reflects upon the consequences and effects of her or his action and then takes this reflection into account for subsequent actions.

reformists   Marxists opposed to the Bolshevik Party and its strategy of revolutionary insurrection and immediate socialist development.

regulations   Social rules and enforcement practices that control people's behaviour externally and become naturalized internally.

reification The process through which people come to regard something that is actually a human creation as being an independent, natural force that controls people from outside rather than being produced by people in the first place.

relations of ruling Dorothy E. Smith's term for the way power in society is organized and exercised through dominant social institutions and the way it arises from the common perspectives, interests, and experiences that develop among men who occupy superior positions in these organizations.

repressive state apparatus For Althusser, the ensemble of government institutions that use force to maintain social order and the power of the ruling class.

resignification Challenging dominant definitions of signs and discourses so that the significations they are meant to convey are interrogated and, through discourse, overturned.

risk society The new stage of modernity in which industrial society is being dissolved, producing a world in which progress is overshadowed by dangers that have spread globally.

role set The roles that people are assigned to in society; usually part of a set of connected and interacting roles—in education, for example, people play roles as students, teachers, administrators, guardians, etc.

Romantic subjectivism The modern idea that rejected Enlightenment rationality in favour of the mystical, intuitive, irrational, and subjective.

scapegoating The practice of blaming social problems on marginalized and oppressed groups, who are actually victims themselves but who often become the target of violent repression.

second-wave feminism The movement for the liberation of women that arose in the 1960s and divided into liberal, radical, and socialist versions of feminism. *See* **first-wave feminism**.

semiotics The study of the meanings of signs and symbols; linguistics is the scientific study of language, which is a system of signs and symbols.

Settlement Movement A residential and service centre built near a city core dedicated to helping and educating disadvantaged women and the dispossessed.

settler colonies Colonies established by conquering, white migrants who settled in areas with large Aboriginal populations; these settlers became significant, privileged, land-owning minorities.

sex class Adopting Marx's idea of class division to feminism, Firestone's argument that the primary division in society is between men and women and that what is required is an androgynous feminist revolution that will eliminate the social significance of gender division.

simulations For Baudrillard, systems of representation, reproduced through media; simulations have come to so overshadow the "real" that they effectively become indistinguishable and replace the "real."

social constructionism A sociological approach in which the world we experience as real and apparently objective is actually the result of our daily interactions, through which we actually create and maintain the social institutions we inhabit.

social democracy The liberal democratic form of social reform politics that created the welfare state and opposes neo-liberalism.

social facts Collective habits; common ways of feeling, thinking, and acting that have real consequences.

social realism A genre in the creation of works of art that singles out for critical presentation negative characteristics of society for the purpose of stimulating criticism and change.

soviet A Russian form of worker's control; an organization through which workers democratically controlled and managed their own factories, workplaces, neighbourhoods, etc.

Spanish Civil War Spanish fascists, with help from Nazi Germany, overthrew an elected, republican government in Spain. Liberals and radicals from abroad joined an International Brigade to resist the fascists.

standpoint sociology Coined by Sandra Harding, the claim that ways of understanding social reality stem from specific positions; for example, women's and men's understandings of the world are fundamentally opposed.

staples Basic, natural, or raw commodities around which economic activity is built; these include fish, farming, mining, lumber, but also, according to Innis and McLuhan, modes of communication.

status panic Mills's term; occurs when members of the new middle class fear the loss of their hard-won success and are especially afraid of losing their status by falling back into the working class.

structural functionalism A sociological paradigm that examines society as though it were an organism made up of various structures (like an animal's organs) that perform necessary functions for the survival and reproduction of the society.

structuration Giddens's term for the process through which individual actions recreate, through repetition, virtual structures that become perceived as factual and determining phenomena.

superstructure In Marxist theory, those secondary parts of society—such as politics, ideas, and culture—that are held to be powerfully shaped or determined by the basic economic system of capitalism that is the structural foundation of a given society.

surrealism A modern artistic movement that seeks to express the unconscious mind and reveal a deeper reality that problematizes realistic perception.

symbolic capital The intangible quality of an individual's reputation, skills at argument, or personal vigour that compels others to believe and follow.

symbolic exchange A form of exchange among people that was fundamental to pre-capitalist societies; included prevailing norms of reciprocity, gift-giving, and circularity of obligations.

symbolic interactionism Herbert Blumer's term for his methodological approach to social research involving ethnographic details of the cultural understandings and interpretations that shape social life and are re-shaped through people's relationships with each other.

symbolic violence The violence done to society through the exercise of symbolic capital, which distorts reality and compels individuals to accept a reality that is not in their interests.

syndicalism A radical economic and political movement that demands workers' control over factories as well as

direct democracy at work and in public affairs; it pursues its ends aggressively.

totalitarian A term employed to condemn a society in which all activity—political, economic, ideological, and social—is under the direction and control of a centralized, authoritarian state.

totalitarianism An authoritarian governing regime in which political power dominates all other areas of society, including the economic system and culture.

transcendence In existentialist thought, the ability of the free individual to act creatively and realize her or his projects in the material world.

typifications Recurrent patterns of interaction including recipes of knowledge that are based on common understandings through which people reproduce social situations and institutions that reinforce these patterns.

unanticipated consequences When social change that is initiated, usually from above, produces results that were not originally desired by the reformers, many of which have deleterious consequences that mitigate the reform.

underdevelopment The idea that Third World countries have been prevented from genuine social development because of their exploitation by rich Western nations.

voluntarism The theory that people's actions are self-directed (voluntary) rather than arising from or being significantly shaped by their social conditions, circumstances, or environment.

woman question The debate among socialists over the role of women's organizations in the workers' revolution and in the movement for the emancipation of women; for some, fighting for women's equality before the revolution contradicted the solidarity of the worker's movement.

Yellow Peril The racist belief that European civilization and supposed racial purity were threatened by the growing number and territorial expansion of Asians (principally Chinese and Japanese).

Notes

Preface

1. Anthony Thomson, *The Making of Social Theory: Order, Reason, and Desire*, 2nd edn. (Don Mills, ON: Oxford University Press, 2010).

Introduction

1. Günter Grass, *The Tin Drum* (New York: Vintage Book, 1964 [1959]), 337.
2. Hermann Hesse, *Siddhartha* (New York: New Directions, 1951), 115.
3. For further discussion of Freud, see Thomson, *The Making of Social Theory*, 318–33.
4. *A Room with a View*, directed by James Ivory, screenplay by Ruth Prawer Jhabvala (1986; Merchant Ivory Productions).
5. Peter Nicholls, *Modernisms: A Literary Guide* (Berkeley, CA: University of California Press, 1995), 47–8.
6. Abbie Hoffman, *The Best of Abbie Hoffman*, Daniel Simon, ed. (New York: Four Walls Eight Windows, 1990). [Selection from *Revolution for the Hell of it*], 44.
7. For further discussion of Nietzsche, see Thomson, *The Making of Social Theory*, 192–205.

Part I

1. Biography.com, "Charlie Chaplin." BIO, www.biography.com/people/charlie-chaplin-9244327#awesm=~oGPptLX4QOrA87. Accessed 10 June 2014. Chaplin returned to the US in 1972 to receive a special Academy Award and the adulation of his peers.

Chapter 1

1. In *Collected Essays*, Vol. 1 (London: Hogarth, 1967), 320.
2. Bertrand Russell, *The Autobiography of Bertrand Russell, 1914–1944*, Volume II (London: George Allen & Unwin, 1968), 20. Russell was sentenced to a six-month imprisonment in 1918 for a pacifist article he published in *The Tribunal* (p. 33).
3. Guillaume Apollinaire, "The Cavalier's Farewell," *Calligrammes: Poems of Peace and War 1913–1916*. Translated by Anne Hyde Greet (Los Angeles: UCLA Press Berkeley, 1991), 221.

4. H.G. Wells, *The War of the Worlds* [1897] (Harmondsworth: Penguin, 1946), 48.
5. Russell, *Autobiography* Volume II, 17.
6. Ibid., 16.
7. Rupert Brooke, "Peace" [1914] in Geoffrey Keynes, ed., *Poetical Works*, 2nd ed. (London: Faber & Faber, 1970), 19.
8. Mann quoted in Barbara Tuchman, *The Guns of August* [1962] (New York: Ballantine Books, 1994), 311.
9. Barbara Tuchman, *The Guns of August* [1962] (New York: Ballantine Books, 1994), 31.
10. John Davidson, "Thirty Bob a Week" in Oscar Williams, ed., *Immortal Poems of the English Language: An Anthology* (New York: Washington Square Press, 1966), 482.
11. Guillaume Apollinaire, "To Italy," *Calligrammes: Poems of Peace and War 1913–1916*. Translated by Anne Hyde Greet (Los Angeles: UCLA Press Berkeley, 1991), 269.
12. Ibid., "Festival," 189;"Battery of Heavy Guns," 171.
13. Ibid., "Festival," 189.
14. Ibid., "War," 161, 163.
15. Wilfred Owen, quoted in Edmund Blunden, "Memoir," in Edmund Blunden, ed., *The Poems of Wilfred Owen* (London: Chatto & Windus, 1969), 12.
16. Owen, "The parable of the Old Men and the Young," in *Poems*, 57.
17. From Owen, *Poems*, 63.
18. D.H. Lawrence, *Lady Chatterley's Lover* (New York: Penguin Books, 1965), 11.
19. Ernest Hemingway, "The Natural History of the Dead," in *The Short Stories of Ernest Hemingway* (New York: Charles Scribner's, 1966), 2–3. Hemingway experienced the horror of the Great War, but he believed that fighting honourably was an essential aspect of masculinity.
20. Quoted in Carol Ann Howells and Eva-Marie Kröller, *The Cambridge History of Canadian Literature* (Cambridge UK: Cambridge University Press, 2009), 231.
21. Owen, "Anthem for Doomed Youth," in *Poems*, 80.
22. Owen, quoted in Blunden, ed., *Poems*, "Memoir," p. 25. "He'd seen men shoot their hands on night patrol, / Their people never knew. Yet they were vile. / "Death sooner than dishonour, that's the style!" / So father said" (Owen "S.I.W," in *Poems*, 70–1).
23. Blunden, "Memoir," 38–9.
24. Günter Grass, *The Tin Drum* (New York: Vintage Books, 1964 [1959]), 42.
25. H.H. Arnason, *History of Modern Art: Painting, Sculpture, Architecture* (Englewood Cliffs: Prentice-Hall, 1968), Fig. 482, 310.

26. Erich Maria Remarque, *All Quiet on the Western Front*, A.H. Wheen, trans. (Boston: Little Brown, 1957), 176. In the 1930 movie version, directed by Lewis Milestone, the people who profit by the war are identified as the "manufacturers. They get rich."
27. G. Santayana to B. Russell, December 1917, in Russell, *Autobiography* Volume II, 51. Santayana adds that his philosophy reconciled him to pessimism: "How else could I have lived for forty years in America?"
28. Erich Maria Remarque, *All Quiet on the Western Front*, 16.
29. Ibid., 166.
30. Ibid., 191.
31. Alden Nowlan, *Ypres: 1915* in *Alden Nowlan: Selected Poems* (Concord, ON: House of Anansi Press, 1995), 65.
32. Anthony Giddens, "Durkheim's Political Sociology," in *Politics, Sociology and Social Theory* (Stanford: Stanford University Press, 1995), 92.
33. Stephen Lukes, *Emile Durkheim; His Life and Work, a Historical and Critical Study* (New York: Harper and Row, 1972), 551, 547.
34. Ibid., 544–58.
35. Ibid., 549, 555-8.
36. Ibid., 87, 41, 88, 87, 88. Consequently, revolutions, "taking the word literally, are as impossible as miracles."
37. Ibid., 543-4, 545, 546.
38. Ibid., 350, 118, 350.
39. Ibid., 543-4, 545, 546.
40. Ibid., 102, quoted.
41. Ibid., 533-4.
42. *The Crowd*, directed and co-written by King Vidor (1928; MGM).
43. Lukes, *Emile Durkheim*, 530-3; quoted.
44. H.H. Gerth and C.W. Mills, "Introduction" to *From Max Weber: Essays in Sociology* (New York: Oxford University Press, 1946), 7. In the film *Jaws*, the three shark hunters pass the time below decks in their too-small boat by displaying their various scars in a ritual of masculine one-upmanship.
45. Dirk Käsler, *Max Weber: An Introduction to His Life and Work* (Chicago: University of Chicago Press, 1988), 4-5.
46. Heinrich Mann, *Man of Straw* (New York: Penguin, 1984 [1918]), 70-1.
47. Dirk Käsler, *Max Weber: An Introduction to his Life and Work* (Chicago: University of Chicago Press, 1988), 18–22.
48. Ibid., 18-22.
49. Alan Sica, *Weber, Irrationality, and Social Order* (Berkeley, CA: University of Berkeley Press, 1988), 113-6.
50. Anthony Giddens, *Politics and Sociology in the Thought of Max Weber* (London: Macmillan 1972), 58.
51. Max Weber, "Religious Rejections of the World and their Directions" [1915], in Gerth and Mills, *From Max Weber*, 340-1.
52. Ibid., 341-3.
53. Ibid., 343-5.
54. Ibid., 346-7.
55. Ibid., 348-9. Weber cites Tolstoy's *War and Peace* and Nietzsche's *Will to Power* precisely in this context (349n).
56. Rogers Brubaker, *The Limits of Rationality* (Boston: Allen & Unwin, 1984), 78.
57. Ibid., 79-80.
58. Margaret Atwood, *The Handmaid's Tale* (Boston: Houghton Mifflin, 1986), 231.
59. T.S. Eliot, "The Rock" (1934), in *The Wasteland and Other Poems* (London: Faber & Faber, 1968), 74-5.
60. T.S. Eliot, "III The Fire Sermon," in *The Wasteland*, 36-7.
61. Peter Nichols, *Modernisms: A Literary Guide* (Berkeley: University of California Press, 1995).
62. André Breton, *What Is Surrealism?* David Gascoyne, trans. (New York: Haskell House, 1974), 45.
63. Hermann Hesse, *Siddhartha* (New York: New Directions, 1951), 64.
64. In *The Da Vinci Code* (New York: Anchor Books, 2003), novelist Dan Brown noted that English-language critics of the cubist movement had realized "that Picasso's masterpiece, *Les Demoiselles d' Avignon* was a perfect anagram of *vile meaningless doodles*" (p. 99).
65. Howells and Kröller, *The Cambridge History of Canadian Literature*, 229-30.
66. Breton, *What Is Surrealism?* 48-51.
67. Antonio Gramsci, *Selections from the Prison Notebooks*. Quinton Hoare and Geoffrey Nowell Smith, trans. (London: Lawrence & Wishart, 1971), 299.
68. Berkeley Digital Library, "The Life and Times of Emma Goldman." The Emma Goldman Papers, http://sunsite.berkeley.edu/Goldman/Curricula/timeline.html. Accessed 3 July 2003.
69. Fiona McCarthy, "Signs of the Future Writ Large." *Guardian Weekly*, 2–8 July, 2004, 23.
70. F. Scott Fitzgerald, *The Great Gatsby* (New York: Scribner, 1953 [1925]), 78, 47, 43.
71. Shulamith Firestone, *The Dialectic of Sex: The Case for Feminist Revolution* (St. Albans: Paladin, 1970), 32-3.
72. Fitzgerald, *The Great Gatsby*, 17.
73. Isadora Duncan, *My Life* (New York: Liveright, 1927), 115, 75.
74. Quoted in Fredrika Blair, *Isadora: Portrait of the Artist as a Woman* (New York: McGraw-Hill, 1986), 327.
75. The other four women were Henrietta Muir Edwards, Louise McKinney, Emily Murphy, and Irene Parlby. "The Persons' Case (1929)." Global Perspective on Personhood: Rights and Responsibilities, http://people.ucalgary.ca/~gpopconf/person.html. Accessed 7 October 2014.
76. Andrew McNeillie, "Bloomsbury," in Sue Roe and Susan Sellars, eds., *The Cambridge Companion to Virginia Woolf* (Cambridge: Cambridge University Press, 2000), 8.
77. Ibid., 7.
78. Virginia Woolf, *A Room of Her Own* (New York: Harcourt Brace, 1929), 4.
79. Virginia Woolf, "Modern Fiction," in *Collected Essays, Volume Two* (London: Hogarth Press, 1966), 105.

80. S.P. Rosenbaum, *Aspects of Bloomsbury: Studies in Modern English Literary and Intellectual History* (London: Macmillan, 1998), 8. In her diary, Woolf described her technique in *To the Lighthouse* as "oratio oblique" (p. 8).

81. Julia Briggs, *Virginia Woolf: An Inner Life* (New York: Harcourt, 2005), 402.

82. Virginia Woolf, *To the Lighthouse* (London: Granada, 1977 [1927]), p. 27.

83. Laura Marcus, "Woolf's Feminism and Feminism's Woolf," in Sue Roe and Susan Sellars, eds., *Cambridge Companion to Virginia Woolf* (Cambridge: Cambridge University Press, 2000), 212.

84. Woolf, *To the Lighthouse*, 10, 13; Virginia Woolf, *Three Guineas* (New York: Harcourt Brace Jovanovitch, 1966 [1938]), 58.

85. Woolf, *Three Guineas*, 6, 107.

86. Ibid., 107–9.

87. Virginia Woolf, "Professions for Women," in *Collected Essays, Volume Two*, 286.

88. Woolf, *Three Guineas*, 6.

89. Woolf, "Professions for Women," 285-6.

90. Virginia Woolf, *To the Lighthouse*, 9.

91. Ibid., 10, 158, 12. Mrs Ramsay complains that her daughters begin being critical too early (p. 13).

92. Ibid., 17, 38, 163.

93. Ibid., 79.

94. Marcus, "Woolf's Feminism and Feminism's Woolf," 211-2.

95. Woolf, *Three Guineas*, 18, 54, 65.

96. Ibid., 67, 66.

97. Ibid., 94, 80, 143.

98. Ibid., 101–3.

99. Ibid., 106–7.

100. Briggs, *Virginia Woolf*, 135, 90.

Chapter 2

1. Gleb Struve, *Russian Literature under Lenin and Stalin, 1917-1953* (Norman: University of Oklahoma Press, 1971), 24–5.

2. Mirra Ginsberg, "Introduction," Yevgeny Zamyatin, *We* (New York: The Viking Press, 1972), vi–vii.

3. Struve, *Russian Literature*, 43–4.

4. Zamyatin, *We*, 3–15, 167.

5. Struve, *Russian Literature*, 162–4.

6. Mikhail Bulgakov, *Heart of a Dog* (New York: Grove Press, 1968 [1925]). When Philoppovich's House Management Committee attempts to assert its authority by reallocating his dining room, they tell him that "nobody has a dining room in Moscow. . . . Not even Isadora Duncan" (p. 26).

7. Ibid., 58, 60, 62.

8. Ibid., 103.

9. Joseph Conrad, *The Secret Agent: A Simple Tale* (New York: Cambridge University Press, 1990 [1907]), 37–9, 43.

10. E.H. Carr, *The Bolshevik Revolution 1917–1923*, Vol. 3 (Harmondsworth, UK: Pelican, 1966 [1953]), 113–14.

11. Isaac Deutscher, *The Prophet Armed: Trotsky 1879–1921* (New York: Oxford University Press, 1954), 5, 7, 26, 36–7, 55–7.

12. Leon Trotsky, *Our Political Tasks*, Part II "Tactical Tasks" (1904), Trotsky Internet Archive, www.marxists.org/archive/trotsky/1904/tasks/ch03.htm. Accessed 22 April 2012.

13. Karl Marx to Friedrich Sorge, 1 September 1870, *Collected Works*, Vol. 44 (New York: International Publishers, 1975), 57.

14. Deutscher, *The Prophet Armed*, 246–7, 286–8.

15. Carr, *The Bolshevik Revolution 1917–1923*, Vol. 3, 114–15.

16. Elżbieta Ettinger, *Rosa Luxemburg: A Life* (Boston: Beacon Press, 1986), 244–6. Luxemburg's body was dumped into the River Spree and recovered months later.

17. Vladimir Mayakovsky, "Left March," *For the Voice* (Cambridge, MA: MIT Press, 2000 [1924]), 8.

18. Ibid., 8–9.

19. Struve, *Russian Literature*, 5.

20. Ibid., 17.

21. Ibid., 178.

22. Ibid., 33.

23. Charles Lipton, *The Trade Union Movement in Canada 1827–1959* (Toronto, ON: NC Press, 1973 [1967]), 185–9.

24. "Winnipeg General Strike." Canadian Museum of History, www.historymuseum.ca/cmc/exhibitions/hist/labour/labh22e.shtml. Accessed 5 November 2014.

25. Lipton, *The Trade Union Movement in Canada*, 193, 199–201.

26. "Winnipeg General Strike," Canadian Museum of History.

27. Mayakovsky, "Scum: Nailed by Verse," 19.

28. Ibid., 24–5.

29. "Vladimir Mayakovsky Biography." IMDB, www.imdb.com/name/nm0562194/bio. Accessed 5 June 2012.

30. Struve, *Russian Literature*, 37.

31. E.H. Carr, *The Interregnum 1923-4* (London: Macmillan, 1965), 4–16.

32. Carr, *The Bolshevik Revolution 1917–1923*, Vol. 2, 311–15.

33. Carr, *The Interregnum 1923-4*, 80–2.

34. Doris Lessing, *The Golden Notebook* (New York: Bantam Books, 1973 [1962]), 114.

35. Isaac Deutscher, *The Prophet Outcast: Trotsky 1920-1940* (New York: Oxford University Press, 1963), 503–8.

36. Struve, *Soviet Literature*, 284.

37. Leon Trotsky, *The Revolution Betrayed* (Detroit: Labor Publications, 1991 [1937]), 210-14. While the elite "had long ago forgotten how to shine their own shoes," Trotsky wrote, too many labourers "go barefoot" (p. 203).

38. Trotsky, *The Revolution Betrayed*, 215.

39. Clara Zetkin, "German Workers Women's Movement" (1909), Marxists.org, www.marxists.org/archive/zetkin/1909/10/09.htm. Accessed 2 May 2012.

40. V.I. Lenin, *On the Emancipation of Women* (Moscow: Progress Publishers, 1965), 16, 18.
41. Maria Meis, *Patriarchy and Accumulation on a World Scale* (London: Zed Books, 1986), 107-8.
42. Ibid., 108
43. Sheila Rowbotham, *Women, Resistance and Revolution* (Harmondsworth, UK: Penguin, 1974), 142-3.
44. Lenin, *Emancipation*, 60.
45. Rowbotham, *Women, Resistance and Revolution*, 147-51.
46. Zetkin, "Recollections of Lenin," 114-5.
47. Lenin, *Emancipation*, 63-4.
48. Ibid., 78-9.
49. Ibid., 84.
50. Rowbotham, *Women, Resistance and Revolution*, 159-60.
51. Zetkin, "Recollections of Lenin," 101.
52. Marxists.org, "Korsch, Karl (1886–1961)." Encyclopedia of Marxism: Glossary of People, www.marxists.org/glossary/people/k/o.htm#korsch-karl. Accessed 13 April 2012.
53. Zetkin, "Recollections of Lenin," 105.
54. Ibid., 107-8.
55. Marxists.org, "Korsch, Karl (1886–1961)."
56. Interview with Hedda Korsch, 1972: "Memories of Karl Korsch." *New Left Review*, No. 76, www.marxists.org/archive/korsch/memories-korsch.htm, 1972. Accessed 13 April 2012.
57. Ibid.
58. Ibid.
59. Ibid.
60. Karl Korsch, "Marxism and Philosophy," *Monthly Review Press*, www.marxists.org/archive/korsch/1923/marxism-philosophy.htm, 1970. Accessed 13 April 2012.
61. Ibid.
62. Max Horkheimer and Theodor H. Adorno, "The Culture Industry: Enlightenment as Mass Deception" [1944] in Horkheimer and Adorno, *Dialectic of Enlightenment: Philosophical Fragments* (Stanford: Stanford University Press, 2002), 121.
63. Max Horkheimer and Theodore W. Adorno, "The Concept of Enlightenment," in Horkheimer and Adorno, *Dialectic of Enlightenment: Philosophical Fragment* (Stanford: Stanford University Press, 2002), 25.
64. John Steinbeck, *Grapes of Wrath* (New York: Viking Press, 1967 [1939]), 385.
65. Ibid., 316-17, 43-9.
66. Ibid., 387.
67. A. Thomson, *The Making of Social Theory: Order, Reason, and Desire* (Don Mills, ON: Oxford University Press, 2010), 347-50.
68. For further discussion of Gramsci, see Thomson, *The Making of Social Theory*, 347-63.
69. Antonio Gramsci, *Selections from the Prison Notebooks*, 302-3.
70. Ibid., 302. The reference to training an "intelligent gorilla" was made by Frederick Taylor in his 1911 book, *The Principles of Scientific Management* (p. 302n).
71. Ibid., 280-5. In America, Gramsci concludes, hegemony "is born in the factory and requires for its exercise only a minute quantity of professional political and ideological intermediaries" (ibid., p. 285).
72. Richard Bak, *Henry and Edsel: The Creation of the Ford Empire* (Hoboken, NJ: John Wiley & Sons, 2003), 1–17.
73. Ibid., 19–30, 38–52.
74. Ibid., 61–2, 68.
75. Gramsci, *Selections from the Prison Notebooks*, 311–12.
76. Bak, *Henry and Edsel: The Creation of the Ford Empire*, 141-7, 193-9, 122-8, 247.
77. Gramsci, *Selections from the Prison Notebooks*, 310–11.
78. Ibid., 300–4.
79. Ibid., 302–3.
80. Ibid., 304–6.
81. Ibid., 308–9. This freedom to think while working was the source of worker resistance, Gramsci added. As workers receive no immediate satisfaction from their work, and as they become aware of this alienation, they will respond to being treated as a trained gorilla and develop non-conformist thinking.
82. Ibid., 286–7. American workers, Gramsci said, were in a "backwards state" (pp. 286–7).

Chapter 3

1. Lewis Coser, "American Trends," in Tom Bottomore and Robert Nisbet, eds., *A History of Sociological Analysis* (London: Heinemann, 1979), 290-1, 312.
2. "Dr W.I. Thomas Held in Chicago: Registered in Hotel with Woman as Man and Wife: Well Known as Sociological and Sex Lecturer: Was Former Knoxville Resident and U.T. Graduate: Married Miss Hattie Park," *Knoxville Journal and Tribune*, 13 April 1918. Mead Project, www.brocku.ca/MeadProject/KnoxvilleJournal/KJT_1918_04_13.html. Accessed 22 August 2012. The fraudulent registration was an offence. Thomas was also charged with violating the Mann Act, which prohibited crossing state borders for the purpose of illicit sex. The original intention of the act was to prevent prostitution or "white slavery." Thomas was found not guilty, but he was fired anyway.
3. Coser, "American Trends," 313. Thorstein Veblen had also been sacked from Chicago 14 years earlier for marital infidelities.
4. William I. Thomas and Florian Znaniecki, *The Polish Peasant in Europe and America* (New York: Dover Publications, 1958), 38, 19, 30–1.
5. Ibid., 31-6.
6. Ibid., 40-1, 72.
7. Ibid., 68-9.
8. Ibid., 69-70.
9. Ibid., 71.
10. Coser, "American Trends," 315-16.

11. "Robert E. Park: Sociology." The University of Chicago Centennial Catalogues, www.lib.uchicago.edu/projects/centcat/centcats/fac/facch17_01.html. Accessed 22 August 2012.

12. Lee Harvey, "Myths of the Chicago School." *Quality and Quantity* 20 (1986): 181-216.

13. Coser, "American Trends," 316-17.

14. Robert E. Park, Ernest W. Burgess, and Roderick D. McKenzie, *The City* (Chicago: University of Chicago Press, 1925), 115.

15. Ibid., 63-4, 55.

16. Ibid., 6, 10, 9.

17. Ibid., 1, 23-7.

18. Ibid., 121.

19. Ibid., 12-14, 40.

20. Ibid., 40-5.

21. Ibid., 117-18.

22. Ibid., 158-9.

23. Helen MacGill Hughes, *News and the Human Interest Story* (Chicago: University of Chicago Press, 1940), 263-5.

24. Ibid., 274.

25. Ibid., 267-9.

26. Christian Heath, "Review Essay: Everett Cherrington Hughes (1897-1983): A Note on His Approach and Influence," *Sociology of Health and Illness*, 6, 2 (28 June, 2008): 218-37, 219-20. Wiley Online Library, http://onlinelibrary.wiley.com/doi/10.1111/1467-9566.ep10778393/pdf. Accessed 19 October 2014.

27. Everett Hughes, *French Canada in Transition* (Chicago: University of Chicago Press, 1943), v.

28. Heath, "Review Essay," 221-2.

29. "Helen MacGill Hughes," Women in Media Research, http://outofthequestion.org/Women-in-Media-Research/News-and-Journalism-Studies.aspx#MacGill_Hughes. Accessed 19 October 2014.

30. Heath, "Review Essay," 224-6.

31. Lionel Groulx, *The Iron Wedge* (Ottawa: Carleton University Press, 1986 [1922]), 170.

32. Hughes, *French Canada*, 190-201.

33. Claude-Henri Grignon, *The Woman and the Miser* (Toronto, ON: Harvest House, 1978 [1936]), 45.

34. Groulx, *The Iron Wedge*, 4.

35. Ibid., 6-7, 17-18, 169, 174.

36. Ibid., 115-18, 176-7.

37. Hughes, *French Canada*, 1-5.

38. Ibid., 20, 39.

39. Ibid., 44-7.

40. Ibid., 88-91. Women first exercised this right in Quebec in 1944.

41. Ibid., 210-11.

42. Hugh MacLennan, *Two Solitudes* (Toronto: McClelland & Stewart, 2003 [1945]).

43. Nick Spitzer, "The Story of 'This Land Is Your Land.'" NPR.org, www.npr.org/2000/07/03/1076186/this-land-is-your-land, 15 February 2012. Accessed 7 July 2014.

44. Doris Lessing, *The Golden Notebook* (New York: Bantam Books, 1973 [1962]), 42-3, 60. The middle class in Britain reads novels about "the lives of working people, and vice-versa . . . [which] are read as if savage tribes are being investigated."

45. Alice Dunbar-Nelson, "The Proletariat Speaks," in Venetria K. Patton and Maureen Honey, eds., *Double-Take: A Revisionist Harlem Renaissance Anthology* (New Brunswick, NJ: Rutgers University Press, 2001), 148-9.

46. Jonathan Reban, "American Pastoral," *New York Review of Books* (19 November 2009), www.travel-studies.com/sites/default/files/American%20Pastoral%20by%20Jonathan%20Raban%20%7C%20The%20New%20York%20Review%20of%20Books.pdf. Accessed 25 September 2012.

47. Walter Mosley, *Bad Boy Brawley Brown* (Boston: Little, Brown, 2002), 165.

48. John Steinbeck, *Grapes of Wrath* (New York: Viking Press, 1967 [1939]), 383, 335-6, 280.

49. Ibid., 266-7.

50. Ibid., 372.

51. Robert Brym, "Canada's Regions and Agrarian Radicalism," in James Curtis and Lorne Tepperman, eds., *Images of Canada: The Sociological Tradition* (Scarborough, ON: Prentice-Hall, 1990), 127.

52. Ibid., 126.

53. Ibid., 127-8.

54. "The Regina Manifesto (1933): Co-operative Commonwealth Federation Programme." Socialist History Project, www.socialisthistory.ca/Docs/CCF/ReginaManifesto.htm. Accessed 28 October 2014.

55. John Smart, "Populist and Socialist Movements in Canadian History," in Robert M. Laxer, ed., *[Canada] Ltd: The Political Economy of Dependency* (Toronto, ON: McClelland and Stewart, 1973), 197-212.

56. Brym, "Canada's Regions and Agrarian Radicalism," 121-2.

57. Jean-Paul Sartre, *The Condemned of Altona*. Sylvia Leeson and George Leeson, trans. (New York: Vintage Books, 1963 [1959]), V, 172.

58. Joseph Heller, *Catch-22* (New York: Dell Publications, 1968 [1955]), 85-6. In novelist William Styron's phrasing, *Catch-22* is "a taut, searing book, eviscerating the military in a tragicomedy of the absurd" (*Sophie's Choice*, New York: Bantam Books, 1979, p. 548).

59. C. Loring Brace, *Race is a Four-Letter Word* (New York: Oxford University Press, 2005), 104-5.

60. Sinclair Lewis, *It Can't Happen Here* (Garden City, NY: Doubleday Doran, 1935), 389-90.

61. Thomas Hylland Eriksen and Fins Sivert Nielsen, *A History of Anthropology* (London: Pluto Press, 2001), 39-40.

62. Ibid., 41.

63. Boas, quoted in Thomas C. Patterson, *A Social History of Anthropology* (New York: Berg, 2001), 49.

64. John Monaghan and Peter Just, *Social and Cultural Anthropology: A Very Short Introduction* (New York: Oxford University Press, 2000), 99.

65. "Biography: Booker T. Washington." The Progress of a People, http://lcweb2.loc.gov/ammem/aap/bookert.html. Accessed 4 April 2013.

66. Richard Wright, "How 'Bigger' was Born," in Richard Wright, *Native Son* (New York: Harper and Row, 1940), xii.

67. W.E.B. Du Bois, "Strivings of the Negro People" (1897), in Meyer Weinberg, ed., *W.E.B. Du Bois: A Reader* (New York: Harper & Row, 1970), 20, 25.

68. The Maroons were a group of escaped slaves who lived in independent settlements in the remote hills of Jamaica. They resisted British colonialism fiercely until they were finally subdued and transported to Nova Scotia in 1796. In 1800, most Maroons agreed to immigrate to Sierra Leone in West Africa.

69. Richard Wright, *Native Son* (New York: Harper and Row, 1940), 109–10.

70. Marcus Garvey, "The Image of God" in *Philosophy and Opinions of Marcus Garvey or Africa for the Africans*, compiled by Amy-Jacques Garvey (London: Frank Carr & Co. Ltd., 1967), 34.

71. *Pressure Point*, directed by Hubert Cornfield, co-written by Robert Lindner, Hubert Cornfield, and S. Lee Pogostin (1962; MGM Studios Inc.).

72. "Marcus Garvey." The Marcus Garvey Library, 19 June 2003, www.hartford-hwp.com/archives/45a/420.html. Accessed 4 February 2015.

73. Effie Lee Newsome, "The Bronze Legacy (To a Brown Boy)" in Venetria K. Patton and Maureen Honey, eds., *Double-Take: A Revisionist Harlem Renaissance Anthology* (New Brunswick, NJ: Rutgers University Press, 2001), 243.

74. W.E.B. Du Bois, "The Negro in Literature and Art" (1913) in Meyer Weinberg, ed., *W.E.B. Du Bois: A Reader* (New York: Harper and Row, 1970), 235.

75. Ibid., 253.

76. A. Philip Randolph and Chandler Owen, "The New Negro—What Is He?" [*The Messenger*, August 1920], in Patton and Honey, eds., *Double-Take*, 7.

77. Ibid., 7–9.

78. Alain Locke, "The New Negro," in Patton and Honey, eds., *Double-Take*, 3–5.

79. Ibid., 6.

80. Fenton Johnson, *Tired* (*The Book of American Negro Poetry*, 1922) in Patton and Honey, eds., *Double-Take*, 270.

81. Ruth Whitehead Whaley, "Closed Doors—A Study in Segregation" (1923), in Patton and Honey, eds., *Double-Take*, 19.

82. Richard Wright, *Black Boy: A Record of Childhood and Youth* (Cleveland: World Publishing Company, 1945 [1937]), 160, 49.

83. Ibid., 68.

84. Ibid., 88.

85. John Reed was a US radical journalist. The John Reed Club was a literary organization for writers and activists and was tied closely to the American Communist Party.

86. "Richard Wright." Spartacus Educational, www.spartacus.schoolnet.co.uk/USAwrightR.htm. Accessed 24 February 2005.

87. Snally Gastor, "Richard Wright: Biography." www.math.buffalo.edu/~sww/wright/wright_bio.html. Accessed 24 February 2005.

88. James Baldwin, "Many Thousands Gone," in Abraham Chapman, *Black Voices: An Anthology of Afro-American Literature* (New York: St. Martin's Press, 1970), 594.

89. Patton and Honey, "Introduction," *Double-Take*, xxii.

90. Ibid., xxiv–xxv.

91. Ibid., xxii.

92. Alice Dunbar-Nelson, *"You! Inez!"* in Patton and Honey, eds., *Double-Take*, 147.

93. "The Negro Artist and the Racial Mountain." *The Nation* (1926), www.english.uiuc.edu/maps/poets/gl/hughes/mountain.htm. Accessed 24 February 2005.

94. Langston Hughes; Arnold Rampersad, ed., *The Collected Poems of Langston Hughes* (New York: Alfred A. Knopf, 1997), 426, 548.

95. "Good Morning Revolution—Langston Hughes (1932)." The Workers Dreadnought, http://theworkersdreadnought.wordpress.com/2008/12/13/good-morning-revolution-langston-hughes-1932/. Accessed 6 November 2014.

96. Doris Lessing, *The Golden Notebook* (New York: Bantam Books, 1973 [1962]), 69.

97. Roland Stromberg, *An Intellectual History of Modern Europe*, 2nd edn. (Englewood Cliffs, NJ: Prentice Hall, 1975), 446.

Chapter 4

1. Quoted in J.H. Whitfield, *A Short History of Italian Literature* (Westport, Conn.: Greenwood Press, 1976), 273.

2. Marjorie Perloff, *The Futurist Movement: Avant-Garde, Avant-Guerre, and the Language of Rupture* (Chicago: University of Chicago Press, 1986), 103. In George Bernard Shaw's play *Man and Superman* (1903), the character described as a "revolutionist" made a similar claim about London (Harmondsworth: Penguin, 1973), 262.

3. Joseph Conrad, *A Secret Agent: A Simple Tale* [1907] (New York: Cambridge University Press, 1990), 61.

4. Perloff, *The Futurist Movement*, 92.

5. Perloff, *The Futurist Movement*, 89.

6. Ibid.

7. Wyndham Lewis, quoted in Jeffrey Meyers, *The Enemy: A Biography of Wyndham Lewis* (London: Routledge & Kegan Paul, 1960), 60–1.

8. Antonio Gramsci, "Serial Novels," *Selections from Cultural Writings* (trans by William Boelhower, edited by David Forgacs and Geoffrey Nowell-Smith (Cambridge, MA: Harvard University Press, 1985), 249n.

9. Perloff, *The Futurist Movement*, 89. H.H. Arnason, *The History of Modern Art* (Englewood Cliffs, NJ: Prentice-Hall, 1968), 212.

10. Meyers, *The Enemy*, 61.

11. Perloff, *The Futurist Movement*, 92.

12. Marinetti, quoted in Peter Nicholls, *Modernisms: A Literary Guide* (Berkeley: University of California Press, 1995), 91.

13. Antonio Gramsci, *Selections from Cultural Writings*, 51.

14. Nicholls, *Modernisms*, 103.

15. "Fascist Manifesto, 1919." Conservapedia, www.conservapedia.com/Fascist_Manifesto,_1919. Accessed 6 May 2012.

16. Jonathan Jones, "Visual bombardment." *Guardian Weekly*, 14–20 January 2005, p. 21.

17. Wyndham Lewis, quoted in Meyers, *The Enemy*, 62.

18. Heinrich von Treitschke, "Politics," Vol. 1 (1870), in Carl Cohen, ed., *Communism, Fascism, and Democracy: The Theoretical Foundation* (New York: Random House, 1967), 316-17.

19. Conrad, *The Secret Agent*, p. 226. "They are our sinister masters—the weak, the flabby, the silly, the cowardly, the faint of heart, and the slavish of mind. They have power. They are the multitude. Theirs is the kingdom of the earth. Exterminate, exterminate!"

20. Alfred Rosenberg, *The Myth of the Twentieth Century*, in Cohen, *Communism, Fascism, and Democracy*, 398-9.

21. Walter Mosley, *Devil in a Blue Dress* (New York: Pocket Books, 1990), 138.

22. Houston S. Chamberlain, "Foundations of the Nineteenth Century" (1899), in Cohen, ed., *Communism, Fascism, and Democracy*, 327, 330-1.

23. Adolf Hitler, *Mein Kampf* (New York: Reynal and Hitchcock, 1940 [1925]), 67, 73.

24. Ibid., 83-4, 75, 78.

25. Alan Bullock, *Hitler: A Study in Tyranny* (Harmondsworth, Middlesex: Pelican Books, 1962), 40.

26. Hitler, *Mein Kampf*, 56-8.

27. Ibid., 468, 313.

28. Ernst R. Huber, *Constitutional Law of the Greater German Reich*, in Cohen, *Communism, Fascism, and Democracy*, 401.

29. Ibid., 402-3.

30. *The Avengers*, directed by Joss Whedon (2012; Marvel Studios and Walt Disney Studios Motion Pictures).

31. Bullock, *Hitler*, 46.

32. William L. Shirer, *The Rise and Fall of the Third Reich* (New York: Simon & Schuster, 1960), 68; Bullock, *Hitler*, 75.

33. Bullock, *Hitler*, 135-6.

34. For Bullock, though German industrialists may increasingly have paid Hitler—the title of German steel baron August Thyssen's memoirs was *I Paid Hitler*—they could not "call the tune he was to play" (Bullock, *Hitler*, 175).

35. Quoted in Shirer, *Rise and Fall*, 197-201.

36. Quoted in Bullock, *Hitler*, 215.

37. Lillian Hellman, *Watch on the Rhine*, in Lillian Hellman, *The Collected Plays* (New York: Macmillan, 1972), 249.

38. Paul Sweezy, *The Theory of Capitalist Development* (New York: Monthly Review Press, 1970 [1942]), 333.

39. Shirer, *Rise and Fall*, 259, 265.

40. Sweezy, *Capitalist Development*, 334-5.

41. Peter Weiss, *The Investigation* (New York: Atheneum, 1966), 108-9.

42. Ernest Rhys, ed., *Heine's Prose and Poetry* (New York: Random House [Everyman's Library], 1934), 95.

43. Günter Grass, *The Tin Drum* (New York: Vintage Books, 1964), 588. Ironically, not until 2006 would Grass reveal his own involvement with Hitler's notorious SS, after 60 years of demanding that Germans speak up about their Nazi pasts.

44. Jean-Paul Sartre, *The Condemned of Altona*, Sylvia Leeson and George Leeson, trans. (New York: Vintage Books, 1963 [1960]), I, 28.

45. William Styron, *Sophie's Choice* (New York: Bantam Books, 1979), 400.

46. Weiss, *The Investigation*, 264-5.

47. Alan Moore and David Lloyd, *V for Vendetta* (New York: DC Comics, 2005), 117.

48. Weiss, *The Investigation*, 190-2, 156-7.

49. Elisabeth Young-Bruehl, "Origins of Totalitarianism," in David E. Wellbery and Judith Ryan, eds., *A New History of German Literature* (Cambridge, MA: Harvard University Press, 2004), 818.

50. Quoted by Gustav Jonouch, *Kafka m'a dit* (Paris: Calmann-Lévy, 1952), in R.M. Alberes and Pierre De Boisdeffre, *Kafka: The Torment of Man* (London: Vision Press, 1968), 80.

51. Ritta Jo Horsley, "'This number is not in service': Destabilizing identities in Irmgard Keun's novels from Weimar and exile," in *Facing Fascism and Confronting the Past: German Women Writers from Weimar to the Present*, edited by Elke P. Frederiksen and Martha Kaarsberg Wallach (Albany: State University of New York Press, 2000), 38.

52. Fritz Giese, quoted in Horsley, "This number is not in service," 38.

53. Ibid., 38.

54. Quoted in Ian Buruma and Avishai Margolit, *Occidentalism: A Short History of Anti-Westernism* (London: Atlantic Books, 2005), 5. Women (specifically, grandmothers) would be, in the words of Dr Zoidberg, a character in the animated series *Futurama*, "subjugated, yet honoured" (*Futurama*, "The Cryonic Woman," Fox Broadcasting Co., 2000).

55. Grass, *The Tim Drum*, 175.

56. Horsley, "'This Number Is Not in Service,'" 38.

57. Crista Wolf, quoted in Elaine Martin, "Victims or Perpetrators? Literary Responses to Women's Roles in National Socialism," in Frederiksen and Kaarsberg Wallach, eds., *Facing Fascism and Confronting the Past*, 71.

58. Martin, "Victims or Perpetrators?" 71-2.

59. Ibid., 73.

60. John Wyndham, *The Day of the Triffids* [1951] (Harmondsworth, Middlesex: Penguin, 1954), 86.

61. Naomi Wolf, "Fascist America, in 10 Easy Steps." *The Guardian*, 24 April 2007, www.theguardian.com/world/2007/apr/24/usa.comment. Accessed 3 May 2012.

62. David Held, *Introduction to Critical Theory: Horkheimer and Adorno* (Los Angeles: University of California Press, 1980), 29–30.

63. Max Horkheimer, "The Social Function of Philosophy" (1939).Marxists.org,www.marxists.org/reference/archive/horkheimer/1939/social-function.htm. Accessed 4 May 2012.

64. Tom Bottomore, *The Frankfurt School and its Critics* (London: Routledge, 2002 [1984]), 12.

65. Max Horkheimer and Theodor W. Adorno, "The Concept of Enlightenment," in Horkheimer and Adorno, *Dialectic of Enlightenment: Philosophical Fragment* (Stanford, CA: Stanford University Press, 2002), 29.

66. Horkheimer and Adorno, "The Concept of Enlightenment," 25.

67. Martin Jay, *The Dialectical Imagination: A History of the Frankfurt School and the Institute of Social Research, 1923-1950* (Los Angeles: University of California Press, 1996 [1973]), 35–6.

68. Max Horkheimer, "The Social Function of Philosophy" (1939). Marxists.org, www.marxists.org/reference/archive/horkheimer/1939/social-function.htm. Accessed 4 May 2012.

69. Jay, *The Dialectical Imagination*, 22–3, 175–6.

70. Horkheimer and Adorno, "The Culture Industry," 107.

71. Jay, *The Dialectical Imagination*, 4.

72. Horkheimer and Adorno, "The Concept of Enlightenment," 73–4.

73. Ibid., 1–7.

74. Jay, *The Dialectical Imagination*, 62–3.

75. Horkheimer and Adorno, "The Concept of Enlightenment," 20.

76. Jay, *The Dialectical Imagination*, 60–1.

77. Ibid., 178.

78. Ibid., 178–9. In contemporary society, avant-garde art is the culture industry's adversary (Horkheimer and Adorno, "The Culture Industry," 101).

79. Theodore Adorno, "The Culture Industry Reconsidered," in S.E. Bronner and D.M. Kellner, eds., *Critical Theory and Society: A Reader* (New York: Routledge, 1989), 128.

80. Ibid., 134.

81. Horkheimer and Adorno, "The Culture Industry," 95.

82. Ibid., 98.

83. Jay, *The Dialectical Imagination*, 192.

84. Horkheimer and Adorno, "The Culture Industry," 106.

85. Aldous Huxley, *Brave New World* (Harmondsworth: Penguin, 1967), 33.

86. Huxley, "Preface," Brave New World, 14. Huxley died in 1963 after a deliberate overdose of LSD, coincidentally on the same day that John F. Kennedy was assassinated.

87. Horkheimer and Adorno, "The Culture Industry," 125, 97, 106. "Being nothing other than style, it [the culture industry] divulges style's secret: obedience to the social hierarchy" (103–4).

88. Adorno, "Perennial Fashion—Jazz," in *Critical Theory and Society: A Reader*, S. E. Bronner and D. M. Kellner, eds. (New York: Routledge, 1989), 200–1.

89. Adorno, "The Culture Industry Reconsidered," 133.

90. Horkheimer and Adorno, "The Culture Industry," 108–9.

91. Horkheimer, "The Social Function of Philosophy."

92. Horkheimer and Adorno, "The Culture Industry," 115.

93. Adorno, "The Culture Industry Reconsidered," 135. While formal freedom is guaranteed, "all find themselves enclosed from early on within a system of churches, clubs, professional associations, and other relationships which amount to the most sensitive instrument of social control" (Horkheimer and Adorno, "The Culture Industry," 120).

94. Horkheimer and Adorno, "The Culture Industry," 131.

95. Leo Lowenthal, "Historical Perspectives on Popular Culture," in *Critical Theory and Society*, 195.

96. Horkheimer and Adorno, "The Culture Industry," 116. Both the cartoon character Donald Duck and the unfortunate victims in real life "receive their beatings so that the spectators can accustom themselves to theirs" (p. 110).

97. Horkheimer and Adorno, "The Culture Industry," 108–9, 114–16.

98. Jay, *The Dialectical Imagination*, 180.

99. Horkheimer and Adorno, "The Culture Industry," 111–12. In Greek mythology, as a punishment from the gods, Tantalus was immersed to his neck in a river in Hades. Fruit was suspended above his head, but it was just out of reach. When he tried to drink, the water receded from him. So he suffered thirst and hunger but, also, unfulfilled desire and anticipation: hence the verb "to tantalize."

100. Horkheimer and Adorno, "The Culture Industry," 113.

101. Jay, *The Dialectical Imagination*, 201.

102. Ibid., 197–8.

103. Walter Benjamin, "The Work of Art in the Age of Mechanical Reproduction," in Meenakshi Gigi Durham and Douglas M. Kellner, eds., *Media and Cultural Studies: Key Works* (Malden, MA: Blackwell, 2001), 50–3.

104. Ibid., 50–3.

105. Ibid., 52–3.

106. Ibid., 59, 50–1.

107. Ibid., 53–8.

108. Ibid., 59–60.

109. Ibid., 60–2. Photographs are similarly manipulated in the film *The Girl with the Dragon Tattoo*, directed by David Fincher (2011; Sony Entertainment Pictures).

Chapter 5

1. Sinclair Lewis, *It Can't Happen Here* (Garden City, NY: Doubleday, Doran & Co., 1935), 3.

2. Herbert Blumer commented, in 1969, that structural-functionalism was "so popular today." *Symbolic Interactionism: Perspective and Method* (Englewood Cliffs, NJ: Prentice Hall, 1969), 57.

3. Seymour Martin Lipsett, "The State of American Sociology," *Sociological Forum* Vol. 9, No. 2 (1994), 202–3.

4. Doris Lessing, *The Golden Notebook* (New York: Bantam Books, 1973 [1962]), 159, 53.

5. George Orwell, *Nineteen Eighty-Four* (Harmondsworth: Penguin Books, 1975 [1949]), 140.

6. Arthur Koestler, *Darkness at Noon* (New York: Scribner [Simon & Schuster], 1968 [1940]), 264–5.

7. Margaret Atwood, *Oryx and Crake* (Toronto: Vintage Books, 2009 [2003]), 68.

8. Orwell, *Nineteen Eighty-Four*, 156, 173, 223.

9. Ibid., 109.

10. Ibid., 104, 127.

11. Ibid., 205.

12. Ibid., 211–12.

13. Quoted in Paul Boyer, "Dr. Strangelove," in Mark C. Carnes, ed., *Past Imperfect: History According to the Movies* (New York: Henry Holt, 1996), 267.

14. Tom Lehrer, "Werner Von Braun." *That Was the Year that Was* (Reprise Records, 1965).

15. Nevil Shute, *On the Beach* (New York: Ballantine Books, 1974 [1957]), 76–8.

16. Ibid., 10, 3, 73, 239. A parody, perhaps, of the capitalistic ethic, the "neutron bomb" maximized the spread of radiation while minimizing physical destruction and was conceived as a weapon that would kill only people and other living things but leave property intact for the eventual use of the victors.

17. Ibid., 6, 8.

18. Ibid., 182, 35, 61, 240.

19. Arthur Miller, *The Crucible* (New York: Bantam Book, 1959 [1952]), 90. For a time, Miller was married to Marilyn Monroe.

20. Leonard Moss, *Arthur Miller* (New York: Twayne Publishers, 1967), 27.

21. *Invasion of the Body Snatchers*, directed by Dan Siegel and written by David Mainwaring (1956; Allied Artists Picture Corporation). The latest remake, *The Invasion*, was released in 2007 (directed by Oliver Hirschbiegel and written by David Kajganich, Warner Bros. Pictures). This time, the transformation is caused by an infection. The infected people promise a future society without violence. But violence is the price we have to pay for being human—it is not possible to eliminate violence without destroying the individuality that American society values—as Anthony Burgess argues in *A Clockwork Orange* (1971).

22. Before releasing the film, however, the producers added a Hollywood ending. Miles convinces the authorities he is not insane, and the police and army move in to save freedom, love, and individuality from the alien invasion.

23. Lewis, *It Can't Happen Here*, 8.

24. Serge Halimi, "US: Phoney Culture Wars," *Le Monde Diplomatique* (June, 2006): 14–15. In the contemporary period, when conservatives rail against the new "one-party classroom," they lump together a variety of different political positions and threaten to chill intellectual debate in a way that McCarthy would have appreciated.

25. Joseph Heller, *Catch-22* (New York: Dell Publishing 1968 [1955]), 117–18.

26. Lillian Hellman, *Pentimento: A Book of Portraits* (Boston: Little, Brown & Co., 1973), 122.

27. Sinclair Lewis, *Babbitt* (New York: Harcourt, Brace & Co., 1922), 187–8.

28. Gary Kinsman, "'Character Weaknesses' and 'Fruit Machines . . .'" *Labour/Le Travail* 35 (Spring 1995): 133–61, 137–8.

29. Ed Rampell, "Remembering the Hollywood 10," *Third World Traveler*, www.thirdworldtraveler.com/McCarthyism/Remembering_Hollywood_10.html. Accessed 21 December 2008.

30. Dan Georgakas, "The Hollywood Blacklist." Modern American Poetry, www.english.uiuc.edu/maps/mccarthy/blacklist.html. Accessed 21 December 2008. The phenomenon of using phony names and surrogates became the basis of *The Front* (1976), a film that involved many formerly blacklisted artists.

31. "Hollywood 10," Spartacus Educational, http://spartacuseducational.com/USAhollywood10.htm. Accessed 21 December 2008. Humphrey Bogart was reputed to have said, in reference to the HUAC, "They'll nail anyone who ever scratched his ass during the National Anthem." He organized a delegation to appear before the HUAC but eventually recanted when the producers decided to blacklist suspected leftists.

32. Kinsman, "Character Weaknesses," 138, 140–2.

33. Ibid., 156–8.

34. Ruth A. Wallace and Alison Wolf, *Contemporary Sociological Theory*, 6th edn. (Upper Saddle River, NJ: Pearson Prentice Hall, 2006), 25.

35. Lipsett, "The State of American Sociology," 203.

36. "Talcott Parsons, 1902–1979." Bolender Initiatives, www.bolenderinitiatives.com/sociology/talcott-parsons-1902-1979. Accessed 2 August 2012.

37. Dennis H. Wrong, "Truth, Misinterpretation, or Left-Wing McCarthyism?" *Sociological Forum*, 11, 4 (1996). Wrong says the charge that Parsons recruited Nazi collaborators is a form of left-wing McCarthyism that ignores the totalitarian and expansionist nature of Stalinism.

38. Merton, *Social Theory and Social Structure* (New York: Free Press, 1968), 39.

39. Talcott Parsons, *The Social System* (New York: Free Press of Glencoe, 1951), 555.

40. Ibid., 4–7.

41. Ibid., 32, 4–5.

42. Ibid., 19, 11, 16, 7, 33.

43. Ibid., 14–15.

44. Ibid., 17, 27.

45. Ibid., 21–2.

46. Talcott Parsons and Neil J. Smelser, *Economy and Society* (Glencoe, Ill.: Free Press, 1956), 53.

47. Parsons, *The Social System*, 36–7.

48. Ibid., 114–15, 208, 167. The "distribution of role types is itself the basic structure of the social system as a system" (p. 116).

49. Ibid., 114–15, 158, 160.
50. Ibid., 160–1.
51. Kingsley Davis and Wilbert Moore, "Some Principles of Stratification," *American Sociological Review*, Vol. 10 (1945): 242–9.
52. Parsons, *The Social System*, 96. Parsons's term is "*latent pattern maintenance*" because the processes that hold society together are often done without the conscious knowledge of social actors.
53. Ibid., 211. See pp. 214–26 for Parsons's analysis of socialization and sexuality.
54. Ibid., 249–51, 269.
55. Ibid., 221–2.
56. Ibid., 223–5. Parsons says that men are more likely to be erotically attracted to younger rather than older women as a reaction against unconscious incestuous wishes and dependency.
57. Ibid., 224–5.
58. Ibid., 25.
59. Ibid., 42, 541.
60. Ibid., 12–14.
61. Ibid., 60.
62. Ibid., 60.
63. Ibid., 62–3.
64. Ibid., 63–4.
65. Ibid., 66.
66. Ibid., 434.
67. "Robert K. Merton," Management Library: Vector Study Group, www.vectorstudy.com/management_gurus/robert_merton.htm. Accessed 12 August 2012.
68. Robert K. Merton, *Social Theory and Social Structure*, 1968 Edition (New York: Free Press, 1968), 478–9. American workers were racist because African Americans acted as strike-breakers; but structurally, they were excluded from union membership and unemployed, so their actions should be understood structurally.
69. Ibid., 337, 313, 413.
70. Ibid., 45.
71. Ibid., 84, 90. Malinowski quoted by Merton and italicized.
72. Ibid., 104–6.
73. Ibid., 105–6.
74. Ibid., 120–1.
75. Robert K. Merton, "Social Structure and Anomie," *American Sociological Review*, 3, 5 (October 1938): 672. Emphasis in original.
76. Ibid., 673, 673n, 674.
77. Ibid., 681.
78. Ibid., 676–7. It is not so much that mentally ill people choose illness, but they feel the strain of their situation to be overwhelming and fall prey to an individually dysfunctional response.
79. Ibid., 678–80.
80. Merton, *Social Theory and Social Structure*, 190, 195.
81. Merton, "Social Structure and Anomie," 679n.
82. Merton, *Social Theory and Social Structure*, 414–15.
83. Anthony Burgess, *A Clockwork Orange* (Harmondsworth, Middlesex: Penguin, 1972 [1962]), 28, 30–1.
84. Ibid., 125.
85. Kurt Vonnegut, Jr., *Mother Night* (New York: Avon Books, 1967), 163.
86. Burgess, *A Clockwork Orange*, 36. Kurt Vonnegut, Jr., remarked on a similar absurd juxtaposition in the death camp at Auschwitz, where Rudolf Hoess, the Commandant, "could alternate over the loudspeakers . . . great music and calls for corpse-carriers" (*Mother Night*, 163).
87. Ibid., 61, 65, 67.
88. B.F. Skinner, *Walden Two* (New York: Macmillan, 1962), 253.
89. Burgess, *A Clockwork Orange*, 64.
90. Ibid., 74–5.
91. Ibid., 67. Alex's speech is scattered with Nadst, a vocabulary Burgess invented, partly from Russian slang.
92. Skinner, *Walden Two*, 256–7.
93. Ibid., 262.
94. Ibid., 263.
95. Ibid., 264–76.
96. Dorothy Smith, *Feminism and Marxism: A Place to Begin, A Way to Go* (Vancouver: New Star Books, 1977), 50.
97. Harry C. Bredemeier, "Exchange Theory" in Tom Bottomore and Robert Nisbet, eds., *A History of Sociological Analysis* (London: Heinemann, 1979), 423; quoting George Homans (unattributed).
98. Ibid., 424.
99. Ibid., 424. Cites George Homans, *Social Behavior: Its Elementary Forms*, rev. ed. (New York: Harcourt Brace Jovanovich, 1974), 43.
100. Ibid., 426–9.
101. George Ritzer, *Sociological Theory*, 7th edn, (New York: McGraw-Hill, 2007), 416–17.
102. Bredemeier, "Exchange Theory," 431–5.
103. Ritzer, *Sociological Theory*, 209.
104. A. Javier Treviño, "George C. Homans, the Human Group and Elementary Social Behaviour." *the encyclopaedia of informal education*, www.infed.org/thinkers/george_homans.htm, 2009. Accessed 8 November 2014.
105. Ritzer, *Sociological Theory*, 209–10, 414–15.
106. Treviño, "George C. Homans."
107. Bredemeier, "Exchange Theory," 431–6.
108. Bengi Abrahamsson, "Homans on Exchange: Hedonism Revived," *American Journal of Sociology*, 76, 2 (sep. 1970), 283.
109. William Golding, *The Lord of the Flies* (Harmondsworth: Penguin, 1967 [1954]), 191.

Chapter 6

1. H.G. Wells, *The War of the Worlds* (Harmondsworth: Penguin, 1967 [1897]), 165–6.

2. George Orwell, *Coming Up for Air* (Harmondsworth: Penguin, 1969), 25–6.

3. Ibid., 27.

4. George Orwell, *Keep the Aspidistras Flying* (London, 1954), 293, quoted in Alex Zwedling, *Orwell and the Left* (New Haven: Yale University Press, 1974), 127.

5. Orwell, *Coming Up for Air*, 12.

6. Ibid., 231.

7. Ibid., 216.

8. Sinclair Lewis, *Babbitt* (New York: Harcourt, Brace & Co., 1922), 139–40, 143, 145. Babbitt admires advertising copy as "the poetry of industrialism," the place to find "really *the* American genius" (p. 120).

9. Arthur Miller, *Death of a Salesman* (New York: Bantam Books, 1949), 18, 150.

10. Ibid., 151.

11. Friedrich Nietzsche, *Thus Spake Zarathustra* (New York: Modern Library, 1917), 52–3.

12. Chuck Palahniuk, *Fight Club* (New York: W.W. Norton, 1996), 44. "The teacher who clears all possessions from my path will set me free" (p. 110).

13. Thorstein Veblen, *The Theory of the Leisure Class* (New York: New American Library, 1953 [1899]), 42.

14. Ibid., 72.

15. Vance Packard, *The Hidden Persuaders* (New York: Pocket Books, 1969 [1957]), 98.

16. Ibid., 1, 15, 153. Packard is skeptical of subliminal advertising, which he terms "subthreshold effects" (p. 35). "Hidden" refers to psychological manipulation of nonrational factors in behaviour.

17. Ibid., 4, 135. Riesman offers the following analysis of the bestselling children's story *Toodle, the Engine*: "The main lessons taught are you should always stop at a red flag and never get off the track" (p. 174).

18. Ibid., 157–8.

19. C. Wright Mills, *White Collar: The American Middle Classes* (New York: Oxford, 1956 [1951]), ix.

20. Ibid., ix.

21. Ibid., xii; Box 9-A, 161.

22. Ibid., 166–9.

23. Ibid., 182–3, 188.

24. Ibid., 134.

25. Ibid., 240, 249.

26. Ibid., 236–8.

27. C. Wright Mills, *The Power Elite* (New York: Oxford University Press, 1956), xvii, 74.

28. Ibid., xviii.

29. Mills, *White Collar*, 328–9.

30. Mills, *The Power Elite*, 19–20, 11, 3–4.

31. John Porter, "Foreword," in Wallace Clement, *The Canadian Corporate Elite: An Analysis of Economic Power* (Toronto, ON: McClelland and Stewart, 1975), xiv, xi.

32. Wallace Clement, *The Canadian Corporate Elite*, 5.

33. Ibid., 5, xxv, 16, 354–5, 339.

34. Ibid., 361.

35. Wallace Clement, "The Corporate Elite, the Capitalist Class and the Canadian State," in *Essays in Canadian Society* (Toronto: Methuen, 1983), 89, 102–4.

36. Betty Friedan, *The Feminine Mystique* (New York: WW Norton, 1963), 15, 19.

37. Shulamith Firestone, *The Dialectic of Sex* (St Alban's: Paladin, 1970), 33–34.

38. Quoted in Carol Ascher, *Simone de Beauvoir: A Life of Freedom* (Boston: Beacon Press 1981), 142.

39. Ibid., 20.

40. Simone de Beauvoir, *The Prime of Life* (New York: Lancer Books, 1962 [1960]), 11–12. "So we went our way without let or hindrance, unembarrassed and unafraid," with "no external limitations, no overriding authority, no imposed pattern of existence" (pp. 16–17).

41. Ascher, 1981, 129.

42. De Beauvoir, *The Prime of Life*, 14.

43. Ibid., 22–4.

44. Margaret Atwood, *Surfacing* (Toronto: Paperjacks, 1973 [1972]), 106.

45. *Avenue Montaigne*, co-written and directed by Danièle Thompson; co-written by Christopher Thompson (2007; Image).

46. De Beauvoir quoted in Ascher, 1981, 24–6.

47. Ibid., 32.

48. Ascher, *Simone de Beauvoir*, 45.

49. Simone de Beauvoir, *The Second Sex*, Constance Borde and Sheila Malovany-Chevallier, trans. (New York: Vintage Books, 2011 [1949]), 754–5.

50. Mary Evans, *Simone de Beauvoir: A Feminist Mandarin* (London: Tavistock, 1985), xi–xiii.

51. Ibid., 34.

52. Ibid., 34.

53. Ascher, *Simone de Beauvoir*, 137.

54. Evans, *Simone de Beauvoir*, 62–4.

55. Ascher, *Simone de Beauvoir*, 130.

56. De Beauvoir quoted in Ascher, 130.

57. De Beauvoir, *Second Sex*, 745.

58. Ibid., 754.

59. Margaret Atwood, *The Handmaid's Tale* (Boston: Houghton Mifflin, 1986), 22.

60. De Beauvoir, *Second Sex*, 756.

61. Ibid., 754.

62. De Beauvoir quoted in Evans, 58.

63. De Beauvoir, *Second Sex*, 757–8.

64. Ibid., 756.

65. Ibid., 756.

66. Ibid., 760.

67. Jim Crace, "In Heat," in *Continent* (New York: Harper and Row, 1986), 64.

68. Thomas Hylland Eriksen and Finn Sivert Nielsen, *A History of Anthropology* (London: Pluto Press, 2001), 62.

69. Margaret Mead, *Male and Female: A Study of the Sexes in a Changing World* (New York: Dell, 1968 [1949]), 77.

70. Ibid., 77.

71. Peter Mandler, "Culture War" *Cam Magazine*, 69 (Easter Term 2013): 32-5. The *Washington Post* in 1943 named Mead one of eight outstanding women in the world (p. 33).

72. Claude Lévi-Strauss, *Structural Anthropology*, Claire Jacobson and Brooke Grundfest Schoepf, trans. (New York: Basic Books, 1963), 15. Lévi-Strauss makes the same point about Mead's ethnocentric classification of "North American tribes as competitive, cooperative, and individualistic" (p. 15).

73. Eriksen and Nielsen, *History of Anthropology*, 62.

74. Margaret Atwood, *The Edible Woman* (Toronto: McClelland & Stewart, 1969), 19-21; "you get adjusted to that at school," Atwood explains (p. 21).

75. Ibid., 243.

76. Isadora Duncan, *My Life* (New York: Liveright, 1927), 187.

77. Atwood, *The Edible Woman*, 17.

78. Jone Johnson Lewis, "Betty Friedan: Key Second Wave Feminist." About.com, http://womenshistory.about.com/od/bettyfriedan/p/betty_friedan.htm. Accessed 9 July 2012.

79. Friedan, *The Feminine Mystique*, 308.

80. Atwood, *The Edible Woman*, 235-6.

81. Friedan, *The Feminine Mystique*, 305-6, 290.

82. Atwood, *The Edible Woman*, 151, 155, 177-8.

83. Ibid., 146.

84. Ibid., 271.

85. Friedan, *The Feminine Mystique*, 18.

86. Ibid., 15.

87. Jay Livingstone and Ray Evans, "Que Será, Será (Whatever Will Be, Will Be)," Columbia Records, 1956. Another hit record, sung by Peggy Lee in 1969, asked Friedan's question, "Is That All There Is?" (Jerry Leiber and Mike Stoller, Sony/ATV Music Publishing LLC, Warner/Chappell Music, Inc., 1969). The song's answer, however, was just to keep dancing, "break out the booze and have a ball."

88. Friedan, *The Feminine Mystique*, 181.

89. Ibid., 47, 43, 31.

90. Ibid., 32, 77, 120-1.

91. Ibid., 193-4. Friedan cites Alfred C. Kinsey et al., *Sexual Behavior in the Human Female* (Philadelphia and London: W.B. Saunders, 1953), 378f. Kinsey says, explicitly, that the data reported earlier "now need correction."

92. Friedan, *The Feminine Mystique*, 342-5.

93. Harold Jackson, "Shirley Chisholm: Obituary." *Guardian Weekly* (7-13 January 2005): 25.

94. Walter Mosley, *Bad Boy Brawley Brown* (Boston: Little, Brown, 2002), 107.

95. Gary Young, "Alabama Clings to Segregation." *Guardian Weekly* (3-9 December 2004): 7.

96. Langston Hughes, "Bop," in Joyce Carol Oates, ed., *The Best American Essays of the Century* (Boston: Houghton Mifflin, 2000), 191-2. In 2015, English football hooligans prevented a black man in Paris from entering a subway car, shouting, "We're racists, we're racists, and that's the way we like it!"

97. Norma Jean Lutz, "Biography of Ralph Ellison," in Harold Bloom, ed., *Ralph Ellison* (Philadelphia: Chelsea House, 2003), 11.

98. Ibid., 24-25.

99. Ibid., 30-1.

100. Ibid., 32.

101. Thomas Heise, "Race, Writing, and Morality," in Bloom, ed., *Ralph Ellison*, 56-7.

102. Ralph Ellison, *Invisible Man* (New York: Random House, 1952), 437.

103. Ibid., 189. Being defined as "other" causes invisibility for women, as well, as the fictional character Diana realizes in Ken Follett's *Night Over Water*: "She knew that Mervyn [her husband] loved her, but he did not *see* her. In his vision there was just a person marked 'wife'" (New York: Penguin Signet, 1992), 90.

104. Ibid., 194-5.

105. Ras the Destroyer, as he becomes in the riot, leads the mob on a big, black horse "dressed in the costume of an Abyssinian chieftain," with a lion skin cape "stretched out behind him," and carrying a shield and a spear, "the kind you see them African guys carrying in the moving pictures" (pp. 420, 425).

106. Ellison, *Invisible Man*, 355, 414.

107. Ibid., 267-8.

108. Mary Jezer, *Abbie Hoffman: American Rebel* (New Brunswick, NJ: Rutgers University Press, 1992), 64.

109. Stokely Carmichael and Charles V. Hamilton, *Black Power: The Politics of Liberation in America* (New York: Vintage, 1967), 54, 40-1.

110. Carmichael and Hamilton, *Black Power*, 37-8.

111. Ibid., 47-53. Like Booker T. Washington, the civil rights leaders had accepted the basic lie of white society: be patient and work hard and you will gradually achieve integration and success (p. 52).

112. Malcolm X, *The Autobiography of Malcolm X* (New York: Grove Press, 1965), 328, 344-7. Malcolm X said that his pilgrimage to Mecca "was the start of a radical alteration in my whole outlook on 'white' men" (p. 328).

113. "Angela Davis." Spartacus Educational, http://spartacus-educational.com/USAdavisAN.htm. Accessed 14 July 2010.

114. Ibid.

115. Angela Davis, interviewed on PBS *Frontline*, 1987, PBS.org, www.pbs.org/wgbh/pages/frontline/shows/race/interviews/davis.html. Accessed 15 July 2010.

116. Ibid.

117. Ibid.

118. Ibid.

119. Ibid.

Chapter 7

1. Salman Rushdie, *Midnight's Children* (New York: Alfred A. Knopf, 1981), 11.

2. Hayden Carruth, "Introduction" to Fyodor Dostoyevsky, *Notes from Underground* (New York: Dell, 1964), viii.

3. Andrew Freenberg and William Leiss, "Introduction," in Herbert Marcuse, *The Essential Marcuse: Selected Writings of Philosopher and Social Critic Herbert Marcuse*, Andrew Feenberg and William Leiss, eds. (Boston: Beacon Press, 2007), xii–xiii.

4. Ibid., xiii–xiv.

5. Ibid., xvii.

6. Ibid., xiii–xiv.

7. Ibid., xiv. "'What is important in phenomenology is less the study of a large number of instances than the intuitive and deep understanding of a few individual cases.'" (Karl Jaspers quoted in Frantz Fanon, *Black Skin, White Masks* [London: MacGibbon & Kee, 1968 (1952)], 169).

8. Ibid., "Introduction," xiv.

9. Frederick Olafson, "Heidegger's Politics," in Freenberg and Leiss, eds., *The Essential Marcuse*, 123.

10. Samuel Beckett, *Endgame* (New York: Grove Press, 1958), 36.

11. Samuel Beckett, *Waiting For Godot* (New York: Grove Press, 1954), 58.

12. Deborah Gaensbauer, *The French Theatre of the Absurd* (Boston: Twayne, 1991), xv.

13. Ibid., xvi.

14. Ibid., 43.

15. Ionesco quoted in Gaensbauer, *The French Theatre of the Absurd*, 44–5.

16. Gaensbauer, *The French Theatre of the Absurd*, 46–7.

17. Ibid., 56–8.

18. John Cruickshank, *Albert Camus and the Literature of Revolt* (New York: Oxford University Press, 1959), 11–14.

19. Albert Camus, "Reflections on the Guillotine," in Albert Camus, *Resistance, Rebellion, and Death* (New York: Alfred A. Knopf, 1960), 178.

20. Albert Camus, *The Myth of Sisyphus* (Toronto: Penguin, 2000), 41.

21. Ibid., 50–2. For Camus, "If I were a tree among trees, a cat among the animals, this life would have meaning, or rather this problem would be without meaning because I would be part of this world."

22. Ibid., 43–4, 54–5.

23. Ibid., 44.

24. Charles Baudelaire, "The Rebel," Jackson Mathews, trans., in Charles Baudelaire, *The Flowers of Evil*, Marthiel and Jackson Mathews, eds. (New York: New Directions, 1989), 193.

25. Cruickshank, *Camus*, 2–7, 18.

26. Camus, "Bread and Freedom," in Camus, *Resistance, Rebellion, and Death*, 91.

27. Cruickshank, *Albert Camus*, 113; quotation from Camus, *L'homme révolté* (Paris: Gallimard, 1951), 351.

28. Albert Camus, "Create Dangerously." Lecture given at the University of Uppsala, Sweden, in December 1957, in Camus, *Resistance, Rebellion, and Death*, 268–9.

29. Jean-Paul Sartre, *Nausea*, Lloyd Alexander, trans. (New York: New Directions Publishing, 1964 [1938]), 133.

30. Jean-Paul Sartre, *Words* (London: Hamish Hamilton, 1964), 12–15.

31. Ibid., 15–17. With no father, and a neglected mother, Sartre also concluded that he had "a very incomplete Oedipus complex," claiming that he therefore learned little of jealousy, violence, and hatred (p. 20).

32. Henrik Ibsen, *An Enemy of the People*, in *Plays: Two* (London: Methuen, 1984), 215.

33. Jean-Paul Sartre, *Being and Nothingness: A Phenomenological Essay on Ontology* (New York: Pocket Books, 1966), 566, 558, 567, 613.

34. Ibid., 707–11.

35. Ibid., 89.

36. Jean-Paul Sartre, *Condemned of Altona*, Sylvia Leeson and George Leeson, trans. (New York: Vintage Books, 1963), III, 105, 113.

37. John Wyndham, *The Day of the Triffids* (Harmondsworth: Penguin, 1954), 248.

38. Hazel E. Barnes, "Introduction" in J.P. Sartre, *Search for a Method* (New York: Vintage Books, 1968), xviii.

39. Sartre, *Search for a Method*, 95.

40. Ibid., p. 93.

41. John Clellon Holmes, "This Is the Beat Generation." *The New York Times Magazine* (16 November 1952), Literary Kicks, www.litkicks.com/Texts/ThisIsBeatGen.html. Accessed 17 February 2015.

42. Chuck Palahniuk, *Fight Club* (New York: W.W. Norton, 1996), 70.

43. Frances Stonor Saunders, "Modern Art was CIA 'Weapon.'" *The Independent* (22 October 1995), www.independent.co.uk/news/world/modern-art-was-cia-weapon-1578808.html. Accessed 25 July 2012.

44. Holmes, "This Is the Beat Generation."

45. Norman Mailer, "The White Negro" (1957), in *Advertisements for Myself* (Cambridge: Harvard University Press, 1992), 346.

46. Ibid., 354.

47. Ibid., 339.

48. Jack Kerouac, *On the Road* (New York: Viking Press, 1959), 115.

49. Mailer, "The White Negro," 341.

50. Holmes, "Beat Generation."

51. Marshall McLuhan, *Understanding Media: The Extension of Man* (New York: McGraw-Hill, 1964), 18. McLuhan increasingly adopted an aphoristic and contradictory style of writing that made his argument frequently obscure. His use of the word *fallacy* in *Annie Hall* suggests self-mockery.

52. Philip Marchand, *Marshall McLuhan: The Medium and the Messenger* (New York: Ticknor & Fields, 1989), 4, 6.

53. Thomas L. McPhail and Brenda M. McPhail, *Communication: The Canadian Experience* (Toronto: Coop Clark Pitman, 1990), 64. McLuhan studied under F.R. Leavis, whose approach to literature was known as "new criticism."

54. Marchand, *Marshall McLuhan*, 45.
55. Marshall McLuhan, *The Mechanical Bride* (Boston: Beacon Press, [1951] 1967), v.
56. McLuhan, *Understanding Media*, 70, 195.
57. McLuhan, *Understanding Media*, 21.
58. Ibid., 21.
59. Harold A. Innis, *The Bias of Communication* (Toronto: University of Toronto Press, 1951), 190–2.
60. Ibid., 33, 187n, 188, 82.
61. Ibid., 4.
62. McLuhan, *Mechanical Bride*, 11, 78, v–vi, 3. McLuhan uses the Nazi term *Gauleiter* to refer to the stratum of sub-managers in big companies. "Whatever fosters mere passivity and submission is the enemy of this vital activity [freedom]" (p. 22).
63. Marshall McLuhan, "A McLuhan Mosaic," in George Sanderson and Frank Macdonald, eds., *Marshall McLuhan: The Man and his Message* (Golden, CO.: Fulcrum, 1989), 2.
64. McLuhan, *Mechanical Bride*, 22.
65. McLuhan, *Understanding Media*, 329. "The voice of reason is audible only to the detached observer." But "everyone is intellectually and emotionally a patchwork quilt of occupied and unoccupied territory" (*Mechanical Bride*, pp. 3, 144).
66. Aravind Adiga, *The White Tiger* (New York: Free Press, 2008), 261.
67. Dennis Duffy, *Marshall McLuhan* (Toronto: McClelland and Stewart, 1969), 11–12.
68. McLuhan, *Understanding Media*, 127. The medium is the message "or the basic source of effects" (p. 314).
69. Ibid., 7.
70. Ibid., 18, 318.
71. Ibid., 22–3.
72. Ibid., 22–3, 27, 319.
73. Ibid., 293.
74. Ibid., 325.
75. The ideogram (e.g., Chinese logographic writing) "is an inclusive," holistic form, a *gestalt* (McLuhan, *Understanding Media*, p. 84).
76. McLuhan, *Understanding Media*, 15, 84–5.
77. Duffy, *Marshall McLuhan*, 27, 30.
78. McLuhan, *Understanding Media*, 315, 124, 88, 145–6. The passing of Japanese time, McLuhan said, was marked by different types of incense, so that time was associated with a scent.
79. Ibid., 323, 334, 23, 300, 221.
80. Ibid., 8, 279.
81. McLuhan, *Mechanical Bride*, 72, 53.
82. McLuhan, *Understanding Media*, 316.
83. Marshall McLuhan, "McLuhan Probes," in Sanderson and Macdonald, eds., *Marshall McLuhan*, 89.
84. McLuhan, *Understanding Media*, 270. "Electricity does not centralize, but decentralizes" (p. 36).
85. Ibid., 298–300.

86. Gilbert Cruz, "Orson Welles' *War of the Worlds*." *Time*, www.time.com/time/arts/article/0,8599,1855120,00.html, 30 October 2008. Accessed 20 July 2012.
87. McLuhan, *Understanding Media*, 300–6.
88. McLuhan, Ibid., 301, 298, 303.
89. McLuhan, Ibid., 286–7, 294–5; McLuhan, *Mechanical Bride*, vi.
90. McLuhan, Ibid., 221, 27, 219.
91. McLuhan, Ibid., 336–7, 309, 308.
92. McLuhan, Ibid., 310–12, 329, 299. "Potentially, it [TV] can transform the presidency into a monarchic dynasty" (p. 336).
93. McLuhan, Ibid., 317.
94. McLuhan, Ibid., 313–14.
95. McLuhan, Ibid., 304, 185.
96. Jean Baudrillard, *The Consumer Society* (London: Sage, 1998 [1970]), 123.
97. McLuhan, *Understanding Media*, 289, 315, 85; McLuhan, *Mechanical Bride*, 3.
98. McLuhan, Ibid., 3–5, 294–5, 306.
99. McLuhan, Ibid., 348–9, 354–5, 8, 279, 218.
100. McLuhan, Ibid., 350, 36, 354.

Chapter 8

1. Charles A. Parker, *Global Interactions in the Early Modern Age, 1400–1800* (New York: Cambridge University Press, 2010).
2. Andre Gunder Frank, *Capitalism and Underdevelopment in Latin America* (New York: Monthly Review Press, 1969), 124.
3. Frantz Fanon, "Accra: Africa Affirms Its Unity and Defines Its Strategy," in Frantz Fanon, *Toward the African Revolution (Political Essays)*, H. Chevalier, trans. (New York: Monthly Review Press, 1967), 156.
4. Alice Cherki, *Frantz Fanon: A Portrait* (Ithaca: Cornell University Press, 2000), 6–7. The local term, which is now archaic, was "mulatto."
5. Ibid., 78.
6. Ibid., 9–10.
7. Ibid., 11. Fanon found the trans-Atlantic crossing disturbingly similar to the slave trade.
8. Frantz Fanon, *Black Skin, White Masks*, C.L. Markmann, trans. (London: MacGibbon & Kee, 1968 [1952]), 26.
9. Ibid., 148.
10. Cherki, *Frantz Fanon*, 13–14, 12.
11. Fanon, *Black Skin, White Masks*, 112–16. "I was overdetermined from without" (p. 116).
12. Cherki, *Frantz Fanon*, 15–16.
13. Frantz Fanon, "The 'North African Syndrome'" [1952], in *Toward the African Revolution*, 10, 13–14. Expatriation, Fanon said, was a morbid phenomenon.
14. Cherki, *Frantz Fanon*, 17.
15. Fanon, *Black Skin, White Masks*, 48. Cherki says that Fanon submitted the manuscript to his thesis supervisor, who found it unacceptable (*Frantz Fanon*, 18).

16. Cherki, *Frantz Fanon*, 24; Frantz Fanon, "Racism and Culture" [1956], in *Toward the African Revolution*, 37. For Fanon, "Look, a Negro!" translated precisely into "Dirty Nigger." Racism, he said, "stares one in the face" (*Black Skin, White Masks*, 109–12).

17. Fanon, *Black Skin, White Masks*, 80–1.

18. Ibid., 122.

19. Ibid., 11–13, 184.

20. Cherki, *Frantz Fanon*, 27.

21. Fanon, *Black Skin, White Masks*, 14, 29, 93, 99.

22. Ibid., 149–54, 215, 47, 18.

23. Cherki, *Frantz Fanon*, 21–2; Fanon, *Black Skin, White Masks*, 17, 23, 38, 180, 189.

24. *Malcolm X*, written and directed by Spike Lee (1992; Warner Bros. Pictures).

25. Fanon, *Black Skin, White Masks*, 147–9, 191–2, 63, 38, 151.

26. Ibid., 47, 58, 83, 69, 63.

27. Ibid., 81, 165, 162, 216. Scientifically, racial differences such as penis sizes have been disproven (p. 170).

28. Ibid., 152, 13, 10.

29. Howard Adams, *Prison of Grass: Canada from the Native Point of View* (Toronto: New Press, 1973), 163–7. Adams quotes feelings similar to those expressed by Black Panther leader Eldridge Cleaver in *Soul on Ice* (New York: McGraw-Hill, 1967): "I love white women and hate black women. . . . [A white woman] is like a goddess. . . . I worship her. I love a white woman's dirty drawers" (quoted, p. 168).

30. Adams, *Prison of Grass*, 169, 212–21 6.

31. Chinua Achebe, *The Trouble with Nigeria* (London: Heinemann, 1983), 3.

32. Fanon, *Black Skin, White Masks*, 82, 100, 226.

33. Ibid., 172 179–80, 197. He would always be a man who questioned (p. 232).

34. "The white person is the masked spirit of today." Chinua Achebe, *Arrow of God* (London: Heinemann 1964), 190.

35. Ezenwa-Ohaeto, *Chinua Achebe: A Biography* (Indianapolis: Indiana University Press, 1997), 17.

36. Achebe, *Arrow of God*, 155, 51, 55.

37. Ibid., 52, 67, 69.

38. Ibid., 8.

39. Chinua Achebe, *A Man of the People* (London: Heinemann, 1966) 162, 165.

40. Jonathan Kandell, "Chinua Achebe, Writer Who Reclaimed a Continent, Dies at 82." *New York Times* (22 March 2013), C8.

41. Ezenwa-Ohaeto, *Chinua Achebe: A Biography* (Oxford: James Curry, 1997), 116–18, 127, 134–42.

42. Cherki, *Frantz Fanon*, 23, 67, 35–6, 74. The experiment did not work well with Muslim men (p. 69).

43. Ibid., 54–5, 41, 46–7.

44. Ibid., 43, 75, 77, 79, 82. A black African was "'almost identical to a lobotomized European'" (p. 77).

45. Ibid., 84; Frantz Fanon, "French Intellectuals and Democrats and the Algerian Revolution" [1957], in *Toward the African Revolution*, 78.

46. Cherki, *Frantz Fanon*, 110.

47. Fanon, "French Intellectuals and Democrats and the Algerian Revolution," 81, 79.

48. Frantz Fanon, "Algeria Face to Face with the French Torturers" [1957], in *Toward the African Revolution*, 66.

49. Cherki, *Frantz Fanon*, 95.

50. Frantz Fanon, "Racist Fury in France" [1959], in *Toward the African Revolution*, 166.

51. Cherki, *Frantz Fanon*, 90, 101–2, 112, 124, 137.

52. Ibid., 147.

53. *The Battle of Algiers*, directed and co-written by Gillo Pontecorvo (1966; Rizzoli, Rialto Pictures).

54. Frantz Fanon, "First Truths on the Colonial Problem" [1958], in *Toward the African Revolution*, 121–2.

55. Cherki, *Frantz Fanon*, 147.

56. Ibid., 155, 161, 164–5.

57. Achebe, *A Man of the People*, 73.

58. Frantz Fanon, *The Wretched of the Earth*, C. Farrington, trans. (London: MacGibbon & Kee, 1965 [1961]), 40, 32, 29, 44–5, 56.

59. Ibid., 48, 31, 93, 42–3.

60. Achebe, *A Man of the People*, 49.

61. Fanon, *The Wretched of the Earth*, 43, 73.

62. Ibid., 73, 30.

63. Ibid., 59, 64.

64. Achebe, *A Man of the People*, 42.

65. Fanon, *Wretched of the Earth*, 121.

66. Aravind Adiga, *The White Tiger* (New York: Free Press, 2008), 53–4.

67. Fanon, *Wretched of the Earth*, 134, 122–4.

68. Ibid., 133–4, 139.

69. Achebe, *A Man of the People*, 122.

70. Fanon, *Wretched of the Earth*, 147, 135–8.

71. Cherki, *Frantz Fanon*, 148.

72. Fanon, *Wretched of the Earth*, 77–8.

73. W.W. Rostow, "The Five Stages of Growth," in M.A. Seligson and J. Passe-Smith, eds., *Development and Underdevelopment: The Political Economy of Global Inequality* (London: Lynne Rienner, 2003 [1962]), 124.

74. Ibid., 124–5.

75. Ibid., 125–6.

76. Ibid., 127–31. Rostow points out that in Thomas Mann's novel *Buddenbrooks: The Decline of a Family*, the first generation of a family pursues money. The second, born to money, seeks social status. For the third generation, born to social privilege, the Buddenbrooks phenomenon sets in, through which the family degenerates into decadence (p. 131n).

77. Paul A. Baran, *The Political Economy of Growth* (New York: Monthly Review Press, 1957), 140–1, 162.

78. Ibid., 162–3.

79. Ibid., 141–4.

80. Ibid., 148–9.

81. Nehru, quoted in Baran, *Political Economy of Growth*, 149.

82. Baran, *Political Economy of Growth*, 156–7.

83. *The Last Samurai*, directed and co-written by Edward Zwick; co-written by John Logan (2003; Warner Bros. Pictures).

84. Baran, *Political Economy of Growth*, 161.

85. The earliest spokesperson for a new interpretation of Latin American economic underdevelopment was Raúl Prebisch, head of the UN's Economic Commission for Latin America and the Caribbean.

86. Theotonio Dos Santos, "The Structure of Dependence," *American Economic Review* Vol. 60 No. 2 (May 1970): 231.

87. Andre Gunder Frank, *Capitalism and Underdevelopment* (New York: Monthly Review Press, 1969), 146.

88. Ibid., 116. Aboriginal communities in Latin America were gradually integrated into the capitalist system and transformed into a rural **lumpenproletariat** (p. 142).

89. Ibid., 116-7, 8-9.

90. Ibid., 95, 146-7, 87.

91. Dos Santos, "Structure of Dependence," 232.

92. Frank, *Capitalism and Underdevelopment*, 284.

93. Ibid., 67, 285.

94. Ibid., 160, 170, 159-60, 185-6.

95. Ibid., 177-8, 310-12, 107-9.

96. Dos Santos, "Structure of Dependence," 233, 286-7. In addition, the internal market was restricted because of the low wages paid to industrial workers employed in capital-intensive technology.

97. Frank, *Capitalism and Underdevelopment*, 97. Frank challenged the strategy of internal, national development advocated in 1964 by Chilean politician Salvador Allende (pp. 97-8).

98. Dos Santos, "Structure of Dependence," 236.

99. Quoted in Kari Levitt, *Silent Surrender: The Multinational Corporation in Canada* (Toronto, ON: Macmillan, 1970), 118.

100. Mel Watkins, "The Political Economy of Growth," in Wallace Clement and Glen Williams, eds., *The New Canadian Political Economy* (Montreal: McGill Queens University Press, 1989), 23.

101. William K. Carroll, "Dependency, Imperialism and the Capitalist Class," in James Curtis and Lorne Tepperman, eds., *Images of Canada: The Sociological Tradition* (Scarborough, ON: Prentice-Hall, 1990), 175-6.

102. Levitt, *Silent Surrender*, 77.

103. Robert Laxer, "Foreword," in Robert M. Laxer, ed., *[Canada] Inc.: The Political Economy of Dependency* (Toronto: McClelland and Stewart, 1973), 21.

104. Jim Laxer, "Introduction to the Political Economy of Canada," in Laxer, ed., *[Canada] Inc.*, 36-7.

105. Carroll, "Dependency," 177.

106. The continuing strength of financial capital in Canada (banking) was foregrounded in the 2008 recession, which affected Canadian banks significantly less than those in the US and other nations.

107. Henry Milner, *Politics in the New Québec* (Toronto, ON: McClelland and Stewart, 1978), 27-30.

108. Ibid., 37.

109. Pierre Vallières, *White Niggers of America* (Toronto, ON: McClelland and Stewart, 1971 [1968]), 19.

110. Mitch Abidor, "La Front de Libération du Québec." Canada History Archive, www.marxists.org/history/canada/Québec/flq/introduction.htm. Accessed 29 October 2014.

111. Mathew Booth and Sarah Yowakim, "Immanuel Wallerstein." Prezi, http://prezi.com/b6s9wkryoopk/immanuel-wallerstein/, 15 Feb. 2013. Accessed 29 October 2014.

112. Immanuel Wallerstein, *World-Systems Analysis: An Introduction* (Durham NC: Duke University Press, 2004), 17, 23-4, 28.

113. Ibid., 36-9, 41.

114. Ibid., 32.

115. Immanuel Wallerstein, "A Left Politics for an Age of Transition," *Monthly Review* Vol. 53, No. 8 (January 2002): 17-18.

116. Ibid., 17, 22-3.

117. Ibid., 17-18.

118. Ibid., 19.

119. Ibid., 20.

120. Edward Saïd, *Orientalism* (New York: Pantheon, 1978), 227.

121. The European Graduate School, "Edward Saïd: Biography." The European Graduate School, www.egs.edu/library/edward-said/biography/. Accessed 28 January 2013.

122. Ibid.

123. Edward Saïd, *Culture and Imperialism* (New York: Alfred A. Knopf, 1994), 27, 110. The Oriental "lives a life of Oriental ease, in a state of Oriental despotism and sensuality, imbued with a sense of Oriental fatalism" (Saïd, *Orientalism*, 102).

124. Ibid., 9, 12 (emphasis in original).

125. Ibid., 322.

126. Rudyard Kipling, "The Ballad of East and West," in *Rudyard Kipling: The Complete Verse* (London: Kyle Cathie Ltd, 1998), 190. In the poem, however, Kipling accepts that both Eastern and Western men can recognize individual equality, regardless of race, in the shared masculine virtues of bravery and self-reliance. In this sense, Kipling evades absolute Orientalism.

127. Saïd, *Orientalism*, 2-3, 156, 221. The "lamentably alien" identity of the Orient thereby joined another set of internal "others" in the West—"(delinquents, the insane, women, the poor)"—to be analyzed as "problems to be solved or . . . taken over" (pp. 206-7).

128. Ibid., 202-3; 22, 5, 122, 239. The intellectual result is "paradigmatic fossilization" (p. 349).

129. Ibid., 223, 133, 5-7.

130. Ibid., 122-3, 5.

131. Ibid., 115, 190, 207. The Orient became a surrogate or an "underground self" through which European culture created its own identity, "a fecund night out of which European rationality developed" (p. 349).

132. Ibid., 12, 100, 204.

133. Salmon Rushdie, *Shame* (Toronto: Vintage, 1997 [1983]), 57, 186.

134. Ibid., 84, 66.

135. Salmon Rushdie, *The Satanic Verses* (New York: Viking Penguin, 1988), 41.

136. Rushdie, *Shame*, 57.

137. Said, *Orientalism*, 287, 300-1. For the contemporary Orientalist, "Islam is an irrational herd or mass phenomenon ruling Muslims by passions, instincts, and unreflecting hatreds" (p. 317).

138. See, for example, Bernard Lewis, "The Question of Orientalism" in A.L. Macfie, ed., *Orientalism: A Reader* (Washington Square, NY: New York University Press, 2000), 249-70.

139. Edward Saïd, quoted in Macfie, "An Elaborate Account," *Orientalism: A Reader*, 87.

140. Edward Saïd, "Orientalism Reconsidered," in Macfie, *Orientalism: A Reader*, 347.

141. Salmon Rushdie, *Midnight's Children* (New York: Alfred A. Knopf, 1981), 422, 425, 419.

142. Arthur Bradley and Andrew Tate, *The New Atheist Novel* (London: Continuum, 2010), 82-3.

143. Ruvani Ranasinha, "The Fatwa and its Aftermath," in Abdulrazak Gurnah, *The Cambridge Companion to Salmon Rushdie* (Cambridge: University Press, 2007), 62. The blood-reward included a sum for killing the publisher of the book.

144. Rushdie, *Satanic Verses*, no page number. The quotation is from the opening epigram of the book, taken from Daniel Defoe's *The History of the Devil*.

145. Ibid., 523. In *The Satanic Verses* Rushdie writes, "To be born again, first you have to die," which he calls an "old Gramsci chestnut" (pp. 84-5).

146. Said, "Orientalism Reconsidered," 348. The Middle East defies definitions that are neutral or disinterested.

147. Edward Saïd, "Shattered Myths" [1975], in Macfie, *Orientalism: A Reader*, 89.

148. Saïd, "Orientalism Reconsidered," 359. In this connection, Saïd refers positively to the work of Antonio Gramsci.

Chapter 9

1. Julio Cortázar, "Blow-Up" in *Blow-Up and Other Stories*, Paul Blackburn, trans. (New York: Pantheon Books, 1967), 116.

2. Dan Brown, *The Da Vinci Code* (New York: Anchor Books, 2003), 268. Actually, Brown claims, the Aquarian ideal was reason: in the new Aquarian age, people would learn to think for themselves.

3. In the 1950s, the Unites States Central Intelligence Agency (CIA) sought to find ways to use LSD as a chemical, psychosis-producing weapon against individuals or whole civilian populations. CIA agents took the drug in order to recognize its effects when Soviet agents, so the notion went, would use it against them. Marty Jezer, *Abbie Hoffman:*

American Rebel (New Brunswick, NJ: Rutgers University Press, 1992), 69n.

4. *The Doors*, directed and written by Oliver Stone (1991; Tri-Star Pictures). Morrison's countercultural girlfriend, Pam (Meg Ryan), on the other hand, was turned on by "Experience. Freedom. Love. . . . [T]he secret of everything [was]: We're all one, the universe is one, and that everything is beautiful."

5. Marty Jezer, *Abbie Hoffman: American Rebel* (New Brunswick, NJ: Rutgers University Press, 1992), 81-3.

6. Abbie Hoffman, *The Best of Abbie Hoffman*, Daniel Simon, ed. (New York: Four Walls Eight Windows, 1990), 14.

7. Quoted in Jezer, *Abbie Hoffman*, 85.

8. Emmett Grogan, San Francisco Digger, quoted in Hoffman, *The Best of Abbie Hoffman*, 23. The Diggers was the name of an anarchistic, community-action group that began as street theatre and organized grass-roots services for the disadvantaged.

9. Malvina Reynolds, "Little Boxes" (Columbia Records, 1967).

10. Joseph Heller, *Catch-22* (New York: Dell Publishing, 1968 [1955]), 17.

11. Gerome Ragni and James Rado, *Hair: The American Tribal Love-Rock Musical* (Richmond Hill: Pocket Book, 1969), 74.

12. Walter Mosley, *Bad Boy Brawly Brown* (Boston: Little, Brown, 2002), 129.

13. Jezer, *Abbie Hoffman*, 142.

14. Dimitrios J. Roussopoulos, *The New Left in Canada* (Montreal: Black Rose Books, 1969), 43, 9–10.

15. Ibid., 31, 47, 106.

16. Ibid., 33–34, 99.

17. Ian Milligan, "Coming off the Mountain," *BC Studies*, Vol. 171 (Autumn 2011): 74–9. OnLine: http://ojs.library.ubc.ca/index.php/bcstudies/article/view/2046. Accessed 8 November 2014.

18. Hoffman, *The Best of Abbie Hoffman*, 65.

19. Jezer, *Abbie Hoffman*, 2–8.

20. Ibid., 14.

21. Ibid., 62–4.

22. Ibid., 75–7.

23. Ibid., 88–90.

24. Milligan, "Coming off the Mountain," 80–1.

25. David Roberts, "Transformations of the Literary Institution," in David E. Wellbery and Judith Ryan, eds., *A New History of German Literature* (Cambridge, MA: Harvard University Press, 2004), 892.

26. Hoffman, *The Best of Abbie Hoffman*, 21.

27. Jezer, *Abbie Hoffman*, 112.

28. Hoffman, *The Best of Abbie Hoffman*, 28.

29. Jezer claims that Hoffman hoped to acquire an actual pig from the Hog Farm, a hippie commune in New Mexico led by Hugh Romney, a former Greenwich Village Beat poet turned hippie. Jezer, *Abbie Hoffman*, 153. The word *pig* was a multilayered inspiration. Among its many uses, the Black Panthers had begun to call policemen "pigs," but

the symbolism went to the core of American capitalism and power politics (pp. 123–4).

30. Hoffman, *The Best of Abbie Hoffman*, 94–5.

31. Roberts, "Transformations of the Literary Institution," 892–3.

32. Rob Burns, "Dramaturgies of Liberation," in Wellbery and Ryan, eds., *A New History of German Literature*, 886.

33. Jezer, *Abbie Hoffman*, 97.

34. Ibid., 101–2.

35. Ibid., 102.

36. Andrew Freenberg and William Leiss, "Introduction," in *The Essential Marcuse: Selected Writings of Philosopher and Social Critic Herbert Marcuse* (Boston: Bacon Press, 2007), vii–viii.

37. Ibid., ix–x.

38. Ibid., xi.

39. Ibid., xv.

40. Ibid., xvii. At this point in time, Marcuse's views on the human potential to create and recreate the world were similar to those Marx had expressed in his early writings, which became available in 1932.

41. Harold Marcuse, "Biographical Notes on Herbert Marcuse." Herbert Marcuse Short Biography, UC Santa Barbara, www.history.ucsb.edu/faculty/marcuse/herbert.htm. Accessed 28 August 2012.

42. Herbert Marcuse, *One Dimensional Man* (Boston: Beacon Press, 1964), 243.

43. Freenberg and Leiss, "Introduction," xviii–xix.

44. Herbert Marcuse, *Reason and Revolution: Hegel and the Rise of Social Theory* (Boston: Beacon Pres, 1960 [1941]), vii. Marcuse is parodying *The Power of Positive Thinking* (1952), a popular self-help book written by preacher Norman Vincent Peale that basically promoted self-hypnosis and faith as means to individual success.

45. Herbert Marcuse, *Eros and Civilization: A Philosophical Inquiry into Freud* (New York: Vintage, 1962 [1955]), 17.

46. Ibid., 3, 74, 12–13.

47. Ibid., 4,178.

48. Ibid., 90, 34.

49. Ibid., 218.

50. Ibid., 218, 184. Reich's sex-politics ("sexpol"), the idea that the sexual revolution is the necessary forerunner of the socialist revolution, foreshadowed "the wild and fantastic hobbies of Reich's later years."

51. Marcuse, *Eros and Civilization*, 218, 184, 193.

52. Marcuse, *One Dimensional Man*, 74–7.

53. Marcuse, *Eros and Civilization*, 205. What appears within the repressive society to be sexual perversions, such as homosexuality and sadism/masochism, reflect an instinctual substance that "may well express itself in other forms" in a future society in which people act within free libidinal (but not just sexual) relationships (p. 185).

54. Marcuse, *One Dimensional Man*, 42–3. For real qualitative change or revolution to take place in the USSR, "the State, the Party, the Plan, etc." would have to disappear.

55. Wilhelm Reich, *The Sexual Revolution: Toward a Self-governing Character Structure* (New York: Octagon Books, 1971 [1930]), xxx.

56. "The Biography of Wilhelm Reich." Wilhelm Reich Infant Trust, www.wilhelmreichtrust.org/biography.html. Accessed 18 September 2012.

57. Reich, *The Sexual Revolution*, xix.

58. Ibid., xiii; italicized in original.

59. Marcuse, *One Dimensional Man*, 1, ix.

60. Ibid., 6.

61. Reich, *The Sexual Revolution*, xxvii–xxx.

62. Ibid., 119.

63. Ibid., 119–21, 6–7.

64. Ibid., 6–7.

65. Marcuse, *One Dimensional Man*, 50, 102–3.

66. Herbert Marcuse, "Repressive Tolerance" [1965] in *The Essential Marcuse*, 34. In education, by default, students are drawn into "the predominant framework of values." Consequently, students must learn "to think in the opposite direction" (p. 52).

67. Marcuse, *One Dimensional Man*, 15. Marcuse, "Remarks on a Redefinition of Culture," 25.

68. Marcuse, "Repressive Tolerance," 53–4.

69. Marcuse, *One Dimensional Man*, 255–7. Critical theory "wants to remain loyal to those who, without hope, have given and give their life to the Great Refusal" (p. 257).

70. Che Guevara, "Speech to Medical Students and Health Workers" in David Deutschmann, ed., *Che Guevara Reader* (New York: Ocean Press, 1997), 95. Sigmund Freud had a similar impulse early in his medical career.

71. Ibid., 96. *The Motorcycle Diaries* (2004; Focus Features) was directed by Walter Salles.

72. David Deutschmann, "Ernesto Che Guevara" in Deutschmann, ed., *Che Guevara Reader*, ix, 7. *Che* is "a popular form of address in Argentina."

73. Che Guevara, "Episodes of the Revolutionary War" [1958] in Deutschmann, ed., *Che Guevara Reader*, 22.

74. Che Guevara, "Notes for the Study of the Ideology of the Cuban Revolution" in Deutschmann, ed., *Che Guevara Reader*, 110.

75. Salman Rushdie, *Shame* (Toronto: Vintage, 1997 [1983]), 277.

76. Guevara, "Episodes of the Revolutionary War," 25–8.

77. Ibid., 110.

78. Ibid., 28, 33, 54.

79. Guevara, "Ideology of the Cuban Revolution," 112.

80. Che Guevara, "Socialism and Man in Cuba" [1985] in Deutschmann, ed., *Che Guevara Reader*, 199.

81. Guevara, "The Essence of Guerilla Struggle" [1960] in Deutschmann, ed., *Che Guevara Reader*, 66–7.

82. Ibid., 66–7.

83. Guevara, "Socialism and Man in Cuba," 199.

84. Guevara, "What We Have Learned and What We Have Taught" [1958] in Deutschmann, ed., *Che Guevara Reader*, 65.

85. Guevara, "Essence of Guerilla Struggle," 68–9.

86. Ibid., 69–1

87. Guevara, "Episodes of the Revolutionary War," 49–51.

88. Deutschmann, "Ernesto Che Guevara," 8–11.

89. Che Guevara, "The Cadre: Backbone of the Revolution" in Deutschmann, ed., *Che Guevara Reader*, 127.

90. Deutschmann, "Ernesto Che Guevara," 10–12.

91. Guevara, "The Cadre," 128.

92. Guevara, "Episodes of the Revolutionary War," 61–2.

93. Guevara, ""What We Have Learned," 65.

94. Che Guevara, "Political Sovereignty and Economic Independence" [1960] in Deutschmann, ed., *Che Guevara Reader*, 80, 79, 85, 88–9.

95. Che Guevara, "Against Bureaucratism" in Deutschmann, ed., *Che Guevara Reader*, 157.

96. Ibid., 163.

97. Deutschmnn, "Ernesto Che Guevara," 13–15, x.

98. Guevara, "Speech to Medical Students," 96.

99. Ibid., 100.

100. Guevara, "On the Budgetary Finance System," 178, 202.

101. Guevara, "Ideology of the Cuban Revolution," 108.

102. Guevara, "Socialism and Man in Cuba," 206.

103. Ibid., 202. *Mal-development* is Samir Amin's term.

104. Guevara, "On the Budgetary Finance System," 180, 185, 176–8.

105. Guevara, "Socialism and Man in Cuba," 198.

106. Guevara, "Socialism and Man in Cuba," 97–8, 101, 211; Guevara, "Speech to Medical Students," 99. The professional must become a person "among the masses . . . within the community."

107. Guevara, "Socialism and Man in Cuba," 201; "Speech to Medical Students," 99.

108. Che Guevara, "A New Culture of Work" [1962] in Deutschmann, ed., *Che Guevara Reader*, 119, 206, 124–5. For Weber, work as a moral necessity expresses both the Protestant ethic and the spirit of capitalism.

109. Guevara, "Socialism and Man in Cuba," 207.

110. Guevara, "Speech to Medical Students," 101.

111. Guevara, "Socialism and Man in Cuba," 212, 211, 214.

112. Ibid., 210, 209.

113. Che Guevara, "To Fidel Castro" [1965], in Deutschmann, ed., *Che Guevara Reader*, 354.

114. Doris Lessing, *The Golden Notebook* (Harmondsworth: Penguin, 1962), 167.

115. Ibid., 167.

116. Betty Friedan, *The Feminine Mystique* (New York: W.W. Norton, 1963), 100.

117. Radical sociologist Marlene Dixon, who taught at McGill University in Montreal after being fired from the University of Chicago for her political activities, wrote an article in 1969, published in the radical *Ramparts* magazine, that analyzed the forces that contributed to the re-emergence of feminism.

118. Kate Millett, *Sexual Politics* (New York: Avon, 1971 [1969]).

119. Ibid., 182–9.

120. Ibid., 35.

121. Juliet Mitchell, *Women: The Longest Revolution* (New York: Pantheon Books, 1984 [1966]), 26, 49–50.

122. Susan Faludi, "Death of a Revolutionary." *The New Yorker* (15 April 2013), www.newyorker.com/magazine/2013/04/15/death-of-a-revolutionary. Accessed 9 November 2014.

123. Shulamith Firestone, *The Dialectic of Sex: The Case for Feminist Revolution* (New York: Bantam Books, 1970), 37, 8, 5.

124. Ibid., 5, 8.

125. Ibid., 9, 37.

126. Ibid., 55–6.

127. Ibid., 198–9, 206.

128. Firestone, quoted in Faludi, "Death of a Revolutionary."

129. Firestone, *Dialectic of Sex*, 190.

130. Ibid., 198, 207–8, 201. Italics in original. Firestone refers to this stage as "communistic anarchy." The feminist revolution would also establish "a new ecological balance" (p. 202).

131. Ibid., 11, 209, 240.

132. Ibid., 12, 239, 11, 242.

133. Lillian Hellman, *Pentimento: A Book of Portraits* (Boston: Little, Brown & Co., 1973), 107.

134. Dorothy Smith, "Dorothy Smith." Institutional Ethnography, Department of Sociology, Syracuse University, http://faculty.maxwell.syr.edu/mdevault/dorothy_smith.htm. Accessed 23 August 2012.

135. Dorothy Smith, *Feminism and Marxism: A Place to Begin, a Way to Go* (Vancouver: New Star Books, 1977), 13–15, 17.

136. Dorothy E. Smith, *The Everyday World as Problematic: A Feminist Sociology* (Toronto: University of Toronto Press, 1987), 6.

137. Dorothy Smith, "Dorothy Smith."

138. Smith, *The Everyday World as Problematic*, 18, 30, 35–6.

139. Smith, *The Everyday World as Problematic*, 7.

140. Smith, *Feminism and Marxism*, 34.

141. Ibid., 11. Smith recognized that "the category of women in general had its own class and racial subtexts" (Smith, *The Everyday World as Problematic*, 56, 9) but she did not develop the theme in her early work.

142. Ibid., 142. Smith moved into the faculty office that had been vacated by Lionel Tiger, the author of *Men in Groups* (1969), a book that argued, by analogy from animal species, especially monkeys, that women's inevitably secondary status derives from the inherent masculine propensity to bond and exclude women.

143. Ibid., 12, 33, 13.

144. Smith, *The Everyday World as Problematic*, 54–7, 36.

145. Ibid., 3–4, 58–9.

146. Ibid., 52, 74, 2, 73.

147. Ibid., 74, 2.

148. Ibid., 64–5, 2, 36, 58–9.

149. Ibid., 86, 65–6.

150. Ibid., 80–4.

151. Ibid., 88–9.

152. Ibid., 122–3.

153. Ibid., 140–1, 89–91, 108.

154. Ibid., 95, 110.

155. Ibid., 120, 110.

156. Ibid., 177.

157. Ibid., 127, 134, although "the practice may at time prove more complicated."

158. Ibid., 142, 134.

159. Ibid., 140–1, 127.

160. Peter Benchley, *Jaws* (Garden City, NY: Doubleday, 1974), 49–50.

Chapter 10

1. Claude Lévi-Strauss, *Structural Anthropology,* Claire Jacobson and Brooke Grundfest Schoepf, trans. (New York: Basic Books, 1963 [1958]), 323, 13.

2. "Claude Lévi-Strauss: Biography." The European Graduate School, www.egs.edu/library/claude-levi-strauss/biography/. Accessed 12 September 2013.

3. Ibid.

4. Lévi-Strauss, *Structural Anthropology*, 9, 12.

5. Maurice Golelier, "System, Structure and Contradiction in *Das Kapital*," in Michael Lane, ed., Philip Brew, trans., *Introduction to Structuralism* (New York: Basic Books, 1970), 344–5.

6. Lévi-Strauss, *Structural Anthropology*, 308.

7. Ibid., 19–20. Boas formulated this idea eight years before Ferdinand de Saussure's ideas were published as *Course in General Linguistics*, Wade Baskin, trans. (New York: Philosophical Library, 1959 [1916]).

8. Clause Lévi-Strauss, "The Sex of the Heavenly Bodies," in Lane, ed., *Introduction to Structuralism*, 330, 336–7.

9. Lévi-Strauss, *Structural Anthropology*, 291.

10. Ferdinand de Saussure, "On the Nature of Language," in Lane, ed., *Introduction to Structuralism*, 54. [From: *Course in General Linguistics*.] There was also a separate history of how these rules came to exist. The complete study of language entailed both dimensions.

11. Ibid., 45.

12. Ibid., 46.

13. Ibid., 47, 50. Consequently, it is useless and unnecessary to give any amount of consideration to the origins of language. As a science, linguistics must begin with signifiers and "signifieds" as they presently exist.

14. Ibid., 50–4.

15. Lévi-Strauss, *Structural Anthropology*, 21.

16. Ibid., 297, 271–2.

17. Lévi-Strauss, "The Sex of the Heavenly Bodies," 336.

18. Lévi-Strauss, *Structural Anthropology*, 305–6. Anthropological findings about economic co-operation and competition among various groups, Lévi-Strauss says, parallel some aspects of Marx's theory (p. 290). Marx's famous phrase that people "make their own history, but they do not know they are making it" justifies structural anthropology (p. 23).

19. Joseph Campbell, *Hero with a Thousand Faces* (Princeton, NJ: Princeton University Press, 1968 [1949]), 30, 35.

20. Ibid., 51. The herald is often dark or terrifying, and "judged evil by the world" (p. 53), a description that hardly fits R2-D2.

21. Ibid., 69–73. In *Star Wars Episode V: The Empire Strikes Back*, the figure is Yoda.

22. Ibid., 73, 246.

23. Lévi-Strauss, *Structural Anthropology*, 22, 21.

24. Campbell, *Hero with a Thousand Faces*, 15.

25. Ibid., 77–9.

26. Ibid., 90–2.

27. Ibid., 97, 136, 101, 109.

28. Ibid., 109–11. "The meeting with the goddess . . . is the final test of the talent of the hero to win the boon of love" (p. 118).

29. Ibid., 207.

30. Ibid., 147, 137.

31. Lévi-Strauss, *Structural Anthropology*, 274–5.

32. Lévi-Strauss, "The Sex of the Heavenly Bodies," 328.

33. Lévi-Strauss, *Structural Anthropology*, 273–5.

34. "Biography: Louis Althusser." The European Graduate School, www.egs.edu/library/louis-althusser/biography/. Accessed 15 September 2013.

35. Louis Althusser, "Ideology and Ideological State Apparatuses" in *Lenin and Philosophy and Other Essays* (London: New Left Books, 1971 [1969]), 131–2.

36. Ibid., 140–2.

37. Louis Althusser, *For Marx*, Ben Brewster, trans. (New York: Vintage Books, 1969), 106.

38. Louis Althusser, "Part II: The Object of *Capital*," in Louis Althusser and Etienne Balibar, *Reading Capital*, Ben Brewster, trans. (Bristol, UK: New Left Books, 1971), 181.

39. E.P. Thompson, *The Poverty of Theory and Other Essays* (London, UK: Merlin Press, 1978).

40. "Biography: Louis Althusser."

41. John Barth, *Giles Goat-Boy* (Greenwich, CN: Fawcett Crest, 1967 [1966]), 117.

42. Goffman's biography is derived from two sources: (1) Gary Alan Fine and Philip Manning, "Erving Goffman," Center for Democratic Culture, University of Nevada, Las Vegas, http://cdclv.unlv.edu//archives/interactionism/goffman/fine_manning.pdf. Accessed 22 March 2014; (2) Philip Manning, "Goffman, Erving," in George Ritzer, ed., *The Encyclopedia of Social Theory* (Thousand Oaks, CA: Sage, 2005), 333–5.

43. Erving Goffman, *Asylums: Essays on the Social Situation of Mental Patients and Other Inmates* (New York: Doubleday, 1990 [1961]).

44. Ibid., xiii.

45. Ibid., 9, 14, 23.

46. Ibid., 323, 341–4, 342n.

47. Ibid., 360–4.

48. Ibid., 357–62.

49. Erving Goffman, *Stigma: Notes on the Management of Spoiled Identity* (Englewood Cliffs, NJ: Prentice-Hall, 1963), 3–4.

50. Ibid., 127, 32, 48, 73.
51. Erving Goffman, *Frame Analysis* (New York: Harper and Row, 1974), 269.
52. Erving Goffman, *The Presentation of Self in Everyday Life* (New York: Doubleday, 1959), xi.
53. Ibid., 2–4.
54. Ibid., 8, 39, 13.
55. Ibid., 22–8, 217.
56. Ibid., 113–5, 119.
57. Ibid., 43–4, 137.
58. Ibid., 170, 175–6.
59. Ibid., 214.
60. Ibid., 232.
61. Jean-Paul Sartre, *Words* (London, UK: Hamish Hamilton, 1964), 21.
62. Thomas J. Morrione, "Herbert Blumer: A Biography," in Morrione, ed., *George Herbert Mead and Human Conduct* (Walnut Creek, CA: AltaMira Press, 2003), 179–80. The Chicago Cardinals of the NFL became the St Louis Cardinals in 1960. The Cardinals now play out of Phoenix, Arizona.
63. Herbert Blumer, "The Methodological Position of Symbolic Interactionism," in Morrione, ed., Herbert Blumer, *George Herbert Mead and Human Conduct*, 182.
64. Morrione, "Herbert Blumer: A Biography," 1n, 183.
65. Ibid., 180–1.
66. Herbert Blumer, "Social Psychology," in Emerson P. Schmidt, ed., *Man and Society: A Substantive Introduction to the Social Sciences* (New York: Prentice-Hall, 1937), 157, 159, 165.
67. Herbert Blumer, *Symbolic Interactionism: Perspective and Method* (Englewood Cliffs, NJ: Prentice-Hall, 1969), 168. Seeking conceptual knowledge without reference to the empirical world is a mistake that philosopher Immanuel Kant had labelled "conception without perception:" the conceptual structure "is as hollow as an empty shell."
68. James Joyce, *Ulysses* (Harmondsworth, UK: Penguin, 1968 [1922], 602.
69. Blumer, *Symbolic Interactionism*, 167, 114, 109, 7–10, 171.
70. Ibid., 102, 2, 11.
71. Ibid., 12–15.
72. Ibid., 22.
73. Ibid., 2–5, 18–20, 194, 118.
74. Ibid., 118, 35.
75. Ibid., 117, 120, 36, 181, 37.
76. Ibid., 38, 152.
77. Keith Doubt, "Garfinkel before Ethnomethodology," *The American Sociologist* (Fall 1989): 253, http://link.springer.com/article/10.1007%2FBF02697831#page-1. Accessed 11 July 2013.
78. Michael Lynch, "Harold Garfinkel Obituary," *The Guardian* (13 July 2011), www.guardian.co.uk/education/2011/jul/13/harold-garfinkel-obituary. Accessed 11 July 2013.
79. Ibid.
80. Harold Garfinkel, "Passing," in Garfinkel, *Studies in Ethnomethodology* (Englewood Cliffs, NJ: Prentice-Hall, 1967), 172–3.
81. Garfinkel, "The Rational Properties," in Garfinkel, *Studies in Ethnomethodology*, 280.
82. Garfinkel, "Passing," 173. Italics in original.
83. Garfinkel, "Some Rules," in Garfinkel, *Studies in Ethnomethodology*, 107–9.
84. Ibid., 110–11, 104, 114.
85. Garfinkel, "Passing," 121–2, 154n–155n, quoting from a description written by Robert Stoller, Agnes's Los Angeles physician. Stoller in Garfinkel, *Studies in Ethnomethodology*, "Appendix," 285.
86. Ibid., 131, 120–1.
87. Ibid., 134, 144, 135, 147.
88. Stoller, in Garfinkel, "Appendix," 287. A resident at the UCLA Medical Center had suspected that Agnes had an external source of estrogen. Garfinkel first believed the resident was biased because he disliked Agnes and because he had argued that the sex-reassignment "operation was neither necessary nor ethical" (p. 160).
89. Garfinkel, "Passing," 176, 137.
90. Harold Garfinkel, "Passing and the Managed Achievement of Sex Status in an 'Intersexed' Person: Part 1," in Garfinkel, *Studies in Ethnomethodology*, 118.
91. Garfinkel, "Passing," 178.
92. Ibid., 180–1.
93. Harold Garfinkel, "Studies of the Routine Grounds of Everyday Activities," in Garfinkel, *Studies in Ethnomethodology*, 36.
94. Ibid., 44, 50–1.
95. Garfinkel, "The Rational Properties," 273, 275.
96. Harold Garfinkel, "Preface," in *Studies in Ethnomethodology*, vii; Garfinkel, "What Is Ethnomethodology?" Garfinkel, *Studies in Ethnomethodology*, 4, 8.
97. Garfinkel, "Appendix," 288.
98. Garfinkel, "What Is Ethnomethodology?" 10.
99. Garfinkel, "Passing," 185.
100. Peter L. Berger and Thomas Luckmann, *The Social Construction of Reality* (Garden City, NY: Anchor Books, 1967), 18. Italics in original.
101. Ibid., 16, 186–7. "[A] purely structural sociology is endemically in danger of reifying social phenomena [confusing] . . . its own conceptualizations with the laws of the universe."
102. Ibid., 15–20.
103. Ibid., 22, 29–33.
104. Ibid., 21.
105. Ibid., 61 (italicized in original).
106. Ibid., 34, 129, 66. The authors derive the term *objectification* from Hegel (p. 198n).
107. Ibid., 60–1. They refer here to Marx's conception of "reification" (p. 198n). "*Society is a human product. Society is an objective reality. Man is a social product*" (p. 61).
108. Ibid., 89, 62, 78.
109. Ibid., 51–9.
110. Ibid., 61, 93–4, 114.
111. Key Kesey, *One Flew Over the Cuckoo's Nest* (New York: Signet, 1962), 61.

112. Didier Eribon, *Michel Foucault*, Betsy Wing, trans. (Cambridge, MA: Harvard University Press, 1991 [1989]), 4–10.
113. Ibid., 13–16.
114. *Brazil*, directed and co-written by Terry Gilliam (1985; 20th Century Fox): "He's got away from us, Jack." / "'Fraid you're right, Mr. Helpmann. He's gone."
115. Eli Zaretsky, *Secrets of the Soul: A Social and Cultural History of Psychoanalysis* (New York: Alfred A. Knopf, 2004), 317.
116. *Nos Meilleures Années*, directed by Marco Tullio Giordana, screenplay by Sandro Petraglia and Stefano Rulli (2003; Océan Films).
117. Eribon, *Michel Foucault*, 16–29. He read, for example, Bachelard, Kafka, Gide, Genet, and Sade.
118. Ibid., 50, 72.
119. Ibid., 252, 125.
120. Kafka, quoted in Philip Rahv, "Introduction" to *Selected Stories of Franz Kafka* (New York: Modern Library, 1952), x.
121. Michel Foucault, *Madness and Civilization: A History of Insanity in the Age of Reason* (New York: Random House/ Vintage, 1988 [1961]), 31, 30, 31.
122. Michel Foucault, "Preface" in *Madness and Civilization*, ix. Some of the quotations from the text were originally italicized.
123. Foucault, *Madness and Civilization*, 64, 156–7.
124. Ibid., 35–6, 49. On the one hand, Foucault notes, houses of confinement had a clearly repressive function. Confinement "constituted one of the answers the seventeenth century gave to an economic crisis that affected the entire Western world." *Confinement* acquired a specific, bourgeois meaning (p. 51).
125. Ibid., 246–7, 251–2, 265.
126. Ibid., 277–8. Freud had, also, ended the silencing of the mad.
127. Eribon, *Michel Foucault*, 138.
128. Ibid., *Foucault*, 141, 209–10, 213.
129. "Michel Foucault." Stanford Encyclopedia of Philosophy, http://plato.stanford.edu/entries/foucault/#1, 2 April 2003. Accessed 10 May 2007.
130. Michel Foucault, *The Order of Things: The Archaeology of the Human Sciences* (New York: Pantheon Press, 1970), xix–xx.
131. Ibid., 58.
132. Ibid., xxii, 75. "[T]he mode of being of things, and of the order that divided them up before presenting them to the understanding, was profoundly altered."
133. Eribon, *Foucault*, 305–6, 218. Foucault was interested in Zen Buddhism because, unlike Christianity, which sought "further individualization," Zen tends "'to obliterate the individual.'" Foucault quoted in Eribon, p. 310.
134. Peter Weiss, *The Persecution and Assassination of Marat as Performed by the Inmates of the Asylum of Charenton under the Direction of the Marquis de Sade* (London, UK: Calder and Boyars, 1970 [1964]), 57.
135. Michel Foucault, *Discipline and Punish: The Birth of the Prison*, Alan Sheridan, trans. (New York: Random House/ Vintage, 1979 [1975]), 7, 8.
136. Ibid., 9, 11, 22–3.
137. Ibid., 17, 19.
138. Albert Camus, *Outsider* (Harmondsworth: Penguin, 1966), 127.
139. Foucault, *Discipline and Punish*, 128–9, 131.
140. Ibid., 23–9.
141. Ibid., 247.
142. Ibid., 249
143. Ibid., 100–01.
144. Ibid., 110–12. There will be "hundreds of tiny theatres of punishment" (p. 113).
145. Ibid., 281, 297.
146. Ibid., 77–81, 96, 101.
147. Ibid., 110–12.
148. Ibid., 298–303, 216.
149. Ibid., 137, 139, 141. There was, Foucault notes, "a military dream of society" that referred fundamentally to "the meticulously coordinated cogs in a machine . . . to permanent coercion . . . to indefinitely progressive forms of training . . . to automatic docility" (pp. 168–9).
150. Ibid.,172–3. "[T]he offender becomes an individual to know" (pp. 255–6).
151. Ibid., 249
152. Ibid., 265–6.
153. Ibid., 25–7.
154. Ibid., 304.
155. Eribon, *Foucault*, 234; Deluze interviewed, 1986, 228.
156. Ibid., 244. Foucault, interview, *Les Temps modernes*, No. 310 (February 1972): 336–6.
157. Ibid., 246, 259; Foucault quoted from 1972.
158. Michel Foucault, *The Birth of Biopolitics: Lectures at the College de France, 1978–79*, Michel Senellart, ed.; Graham Burchell, trans. (Houndhills, UK: Palgrave Macmillan, 2008 [2004]), 78.
159. Ibid., 317.
160. "Michel Foucault." Stanford Encyclopedia of Philosophy.
161. Foucault, *The Birth of Biopolitics*, 317–19.
162. Ibid., 186.
163. Eribon, *Foucault*, 313–16.
164. Ibid., 324–7.

Chapter 11

1. The style was not new. When Laurence Sterne began publishing *The Life and Opinions of Tristram Shandy, Gentleman*, in 1759, he was already parodying the new "novel" form of prose; for example, the book began in the middle of the story, and the beginning of the narrative was in the middle of the book.
2. John Locke, *An Essay Concerning Human Understanding*, Books I and II, in J.A. St. John, ed., *The Philosophical*

Works of John Locke, Vol. I (London: George Bell & Sons, 1894 [1689]), 298.

3. Ray Kiely, *Sociology and Development: The Impasse and Beyond* (London: UCL Press, 1995), 153–4.

4. Richard Rorty, "Habermas and Lyotard on Post-Modernity," in James Farganis, ed., *Readings in Social Theory: The Classical Tradition to Post-Modernism*, 3rd edn. (New York: McGraw Hill, 2000), 436.

5. Ben Agger, "Critical Theory, Poststructuralism, Postmodernism: Their Sociological Relevance." *Annual Review of Sociology* (1991), www.artsrn.ualberta.ca/courses/Political-Science/661B1/documents/BenAggerCriticalTheoryPost-structPostMod.pdf. Accessed 10 November 2014.

6. Jean-François Lyotard, "The Post-Modern Condition: A Report on Knowledge" in James Farganis, ed., *Readings in Social Theory*, 419.

7. James Joyce, *Ulysses* (Harmondsworth, UK: Penguin, 1968 [1922]), 37, 40.

8. Jean-François Lyotard, *The Post-Modern Condition: A Report on Knowledge* (Minneapolis: University of Minnesota Press, 1984 [1978]), xxiv.

9. Joyce, *Ulysses*, 462.

10. Lyotard, *Post-Modern Condition*, xxiv.

11. Ibid., p. 8.

12. "Jean Baudrillard." Stanford Encyclopedia of Philosophy, http://plato.stanford.edu/entries/baudrillard/, 22 April 2005. Accessed 23 December 2008.

13. Mike Gane, ed., *Baudrillard Live. Selected Interviews* (London: Routledge, 1993), 1.

14. Ibid., 1.

15. Ibid., 2.

16. Douglas Kellner, *Jean Baudrillard: From Marxism to Postmodernism and Beyond* (Stanford: Stanford University Press, 1989), 8.

17. Jean-Jacques Rousseau, *Émile* (Geneva, 1780) quoted in Steven Lukes, *Émile Durkheim: His Life and Works* (New York: Harper Row, 1972), 126.

18. Jean Baudrillard, *The Consumer Society: Myths and Structures* (London: Sage, 1998 [1970]), 25.

19. Ibid., 37–8.

20. Ibid., 25–30.

21. Jean Baudrillard, "For a Critique of the Political Economy of the Sign," in Mark Poster, ed., *Jean Baudrillard: Selected Writings* (Stanford, CA: Stanford University Press, 2001), 61.

22. Baudrillard, "Barbara Kruger," in Gary Genosko, ed., *The Uncollected Baudrillard* (Thousand Oaks, CA: Sage, 2001), 134.

23. Billy Talent, "Surprise, Surprise," *Dead Silence, Red Distribution*, 2012.

24. Baudrillard, *The Consumer Society*, 71–4.

25. Philip Pullman, *The Golden Compass* (New York: Dell Laurel-Leaf, 2003 [1995]).

26. Baudrillard, *The Consumer Society*, 45.

27. Ibid., 93.

28. Baudrillard, "For a Critique of the Political Economy of the Sign," 62.

29. Baudrillard, *The Consumer Society*, 94.

30. Baudrillard, Ibid., 126.

31. Baudrillard, "The Divine Left," in Genosko, ed., *The Uncollected Baudrillard*, 101.

32. Baudrillard, "Barbara Kruger," in Genosko, *The Uncollected Baudrillard*, 134.

33. Baudrillard, *The Consumer Society*, 99–100.

34. Margaret Atwood, *Oryx and Crake* (Toronto: Vintage Books, 2009 [2003]), 26. Italics in original.

35. Frederic Jameson, "Preface," Jean-François Lyotard, *The Postmodern Condition: A Report on Knowledge* (Minneapolis, MN: University of Minnesota Press, 1984 [1978]), viii.

36. Baudrillard, "Simulacra and Simulation," in Poster, ed., *Jean Baudrillard: Selected Writings*, 169–70.

37. Baudrillard, "Symbolic Exchange and Death," in Poster, ed., *Jean Baudrillard*, 123.

38. Jean Baudrillard, *The Consumer Society*, 115–16.

39. Baurillard, "Simulacra and Simulation," in Poster, ed., *Jean Baudrillard*, 169–70.

40. Baudrillard, "Symbolic Exchange and Death," 147–9.

41. Baudrillard, "The Gulf War Did Not Take Place," in Poster, ed., *Jean Baudrillard*, 236, 246, 253.

42. *The Matrix*, directed by Andy and Lana Wachowski (1999; Warner Bros.). This phrase, derived from Baudrillard, is also the title of a 2002 book by Slavoj Žižek.

43. Baudrillard, "Symbolic Exchange and Death," in Poster, ed., *Jean Baudrillard*, 124–5.

44. Jean Baudrillard, "The Divine Left" in Gary Genosko, ed., *The Uncollected Baudrillard* (Thousand Oaks, CA: Sage, 2001), 95.

45. Jean Baudrillard, "The Mirror of Production," in Poster, ed., *Jean Baudrillard: Selected Writings*, 119.

46. Baudrillard, "The Divine Left," 95–6.

47. Ibid., 96–7. The Left is "the historical prosthesis of the Right."

48. Ibid., 116, 93–5, 109. The Socialist Party in France under Mitterand (1981) was "already in Allende's skin, committed to suicide" (p. 105).

49. Ibid., 92.

50. Ibid., 99–101.

51. Ibid., 105–6, 112. Like women, in Nietzsche's view, the mass resists any kind of representation.

52. Baudrillard, "The Mirror of Production," 119.

53. Ibid., 107, 115.

54. Baudrillard, "The Divine Left," 101.

55. Baudrillard, "Symbolic Exchange and Death," 122–7.

56. Jean Baudrillard, *The Spirit of Terrorism and Requiem for the Twin Towers*, excerpted, in Sean P. Hier, ed., *Contemporary Sociological Thought* (Toronto: Canadian Scholars Press, 2005), 307–8.

57. Baudrillard, *The Spirit of Terrorism*, 308–16.

58. Camille Paglia, "The Modern Campus Cannot Comprehend Evil," Time.com, 29 September 2015, http://time.com/

3444749/camille-paglia-the-modern-campus-cannot-comprehend-evil/. Accessed 4 November 2014.

59. Elizabeth Higginbotham, "A New Perspective with Patricia Hill Collins." American Sociological Association, www.asanet.org/about/presidents/Patricia_Hill_Collins.cfm. Accessed 5 May 2014.

60. Patricia Hill Collins, *Black Feminist Thought: Knowledge, Consciousness and the Politics of Empowerment*, 2nd edn. (New York: Routledge, 2000), vi.

61. Higginbotham, "Patricia Hill Collins."

62. Collins, *Black Feminist Thought*, vii–x.

63. Ibid., 29–30, 22–3.

64. Patricia Hill Collins, *From Black Power to Hip Hop: Racism, Nationalism and Feminism* (Philadelphia, PA: Temple University Press, 2006), 3.

65. Collins, *Black Feminist Thought*, 24.

66. Ibid., 25–30.

67. Ibid., 31–2.

68. bell hooks, *Feminist Theory: From Margin to Center*, 2nd edn. (London, UK: Pluto Press, 2000), 11–12.

69. "bell hooks—Biography." The European Graduate School, www.egs.edu/library/bell-hooks/biography/. Accessed 16 February 2014.

70. Ibid.

71. hooks, *Feminist Theory*, 3, 15–19. bell hooks's works are, necessarily, under the copyright of Gloria Watkins.

72. Ibid., 29–36.

73. Ibid., 36–7.

74. Ibid., 37–40.

75. "bell hooks—Biography."

76. bell hooks, "Postmodern Blackness," in *Yearning: Race, Gender, and Cultural Politics* (Boston, MA: South End Press, 1990), 24.

77. Ibid., 28.

78. Ibid., 29.

79. bell hooks, *Black Looks: Race and Representation* (Boston, MA: South End Press, 1992), 1–2, 6, 10.

80. Ibid., 23–6.

81. Jack Kerouac, *On the Road* (New York: Viking Press, 1957), 180–1.

82. D. Horowitz, "Top 10 Most Dangerous Professors in America." The Human Events Group: Powerful Conservative Voices, www.humanevents.com/2006/02/21/top-10-most-dangerous-professors-in-america/, 21 Feb 2006. Accessed 29 March 2015. .

83. Udi Aloni, "Judith Butler: As a Jew, I Was Taught It Was Ethically Imperative to Speak Up." *Haaretz*, 24 Feb 2010, www.haaretz.com/news/judith-butler-as-a-jew-i-was-taught-it-was-ethically-imperative-to-speak-up-1.266243. Accessed 15 May 2014.

84. "Judith Butler." NNDP (Notable Names Database), www.nndb.com/people/639/000095354/. Accessed 15 May 2014.

85. Aloni, "Judith Butler: As a Jew I Was Taught It Was Ethically Imperative to Speak Up."

86. Judith Butler, *Gender Troubles: Feminism and the Subversion of identity* (New York: Routledge, 1999), 8.

87. Ibid., 4–5. Italics in original.

88. Ibid., 6–9.

89. Butler, *Gender Troubles*, 10–11. Italics in original.

90. Ibid., 39.

91. Tim Adams, "Cultural Hallmark." *The Guardian*, 23 Sept. 2007, www.theguardian.com/society/2007/sep/23/communities.politicsphilosophyandsociety. Accessed 25 March 2014.

92. Ibid.

93. Lady Gaga's video production meshed together a variety of modernist styles and movements in a typical, postmodern pastiche.

94. Butler, *Gender Troubles*, 165, 33, 12, 15, 19, 172–3.

95. Ibid., 43–4, 177–9, 23–4.

96. Ibid., 43, 179, 173. Italics in original

97. Ibid., 22–3.

98. Ibid., 148.

99. Ibid., 41–3, 185.

100. Ibid., 44, 179, 180, 186.

101. Ibid., 189–90.

102. Antonio Gramsci, *Selections from the Prison Notebooks*, Quinton Hoare and Geoffrey Nowell Smith, trans. (London: Lawrence & Wishart, 1971), 307.

103. Kiely, *Sociology and Development*, 155.

104. Margaret Atwood, "Writing the Male Character," *Second Words; Selected Critical Prose* (Toronto: House of Anansi Press, 2011), 413.

Chapter 12

1. Ulrich Beck, *Risk Society: Towards a New Modernity* (London, UK: Sage Publications, 1986), 9–10.

2. Ibid., 11, 21.

3. Ulrich Beck, *World Risk Society* (Cambridge, UK: Polity Press, 1999), 2.

4. Beck, *Risk Society*, 13–14.

5. Ibid., 20–2.

6. Beck, *World Risk Society*, 2–3.

7. Ibid., 3–6.

8. See Walden Bello, "A Primer on Wall Street Meltdown." MR Zine, 3 Oct. 2008, http://mrzine.monthlyreview.org/2008/bello031008.html. Accessed 19 May 2014.

9. Ibid.

10. William Outhwaite, *Habermas: A Critical Introduction* (Stanford, CA: Stanford University Press, 1994), 2.

11. "Jürgen Habermas: Biography." The European Graduate School, www.egs.edu/library/juergen-habermas/biography/. Accessed 25 January 2014.

12. Outhwaite, *Habermas*, 2.

13. "Jürgen Habermas: Biography."

14. Michael Pusey, *Jürgen Habermas* (London, UK: Tavistock, 1987), 14.

15. "Jürgen Habermas." The Stanford Encyclopedia of Philosophy, 17 May 2007/4 Aug. 2014, http://plato.stanford.edu/entries/habermas/. Accessed 25 January 2014.

16. Ibid.

17. Pusey, *Habermas*, 14. The outspoken leader of the German student's movement (SDS), Rudi Dutschke, advocated acts of civil disobedience and militancy. Dutschke believed that Germany was heading for another totalitarian government, which would use the threat posed by student protest as an excuse to introduce a new emergency law to establish authoritarian power in Germany.

18. "The Attack on Rudi Dutschke: A Revolutionary Who Shaped a Generation." *Der Spiegel International*, 11 April 2008, www.spiegel.de/international/germany/the-attack-on-rudi-dutschke-a-revolutionary-who-shaped-a-generation-a-546913-2.html. Accessed 25 January 2014. Dutschke was gunned down in the street in 1967 but survived to become an important member of the German Green Party.

19. Jürgen Habermas, *Theory and Practice* (Boston: Beacon Press, 1973), 210–11.

20. Ibid., 256.

21. K.O. Apel, "Scientism, Hermenutics, and Critique of Ideology: An Outline of a Theory of Science from the Point of view of an Anthropological Theory of Knowledge." Mimeo. F. Bail, trans., *Wiener Jahrbuch für Philosophie* (1968), 27.

22. Jürgen Habermas, *The Theory of Communicative Action, Vol. 1, Reason and the Rationalization of Society*, Thomas McCarthy, trans. (Boston, MA: Beacon Press, 1984 [1981]), 4–5.

23. Ibid., 10, 21.

24. Ibid., 1, 23, 39, 43.

25. Frederic Jameson, Preface, in Jean-Francois Lyotard, *The Postmodern Condition: A Report on Knowledge* (Minneapolis, MN: University of Minnesota Press, 1984 [1978]), xi.

26. Thomas McCarthy, "Introduction," in Jürgen Habermas, *The Theory of Communicative Action, Vol. 1*, x.

27. Ibid., xi.

28. Habermas, *Communicative Action, Vol. 1*, 11–18. Habermas would describe his own theorizing in these terms.

29. Ibid., 58.

30. Ibid., 55–6, 95, 99.

31. Ibid., 70–1.

32. Ibid., 69–72.

33. Ibid., 73.

34. Ibid., 73–4.

35. Ibid., 286–8.

36. Ibid., 397–8.

37. Jürgen Habermas, *The Theory of Communicative Action, Vol. 2, The Critique of Functionalist Reason*, Thomas McCarthy, trans. (Cambridge, UK: Polity Press, 1987 [1981]), 395.

38. William Outhwaite, *Habermas: Critical Introduction* (Stanford, CA: Stanford University Press, 1994), 105–6.

39. Habermas, *Theory of Communicative Action, Vol. 2*, 392.

40. Ibid., 392–4.

41. Ibid., 395.

42. Ibid., 396.

43. Shaun McMann, "Anthony Giddens: A Biography." The Open University, 14 Nov. 2007, www.open.edu/openlearn/society/politics-policy-people/politics/anthony-giddens-biography. Accessed 6 March 2014.

44. Anthony Giddens, *The Class Structure of the Advanced Societies* (London: Hutchinson, 1973), 111.

45. Anthony Giddens, *The Constitution of Society: Outline of a Theory of Structuration* (Berkeley, CA: University of California Press, 1984), 27.

46. Ibid., 64–6.

47. Ibid., 67.

48. Ibid., 4–5, 9.

49. Ibid., 2–3, 179. Giddens argues that in the duality of structure, neither macro nor micro processes have priority over the other (p. 139).

50. Ibid., 13, 83, 212.

51. Ibid., 17, 176–7, 25–7.

52. Ibid., 25, 83, 170–1.

53. Ibid., 177, 173, 14–15.

54. Ibid., 27, 16, 283.

55. Ibid., 258–9.

56. Ibid., 193, 198–9.

57. Anthony Giddens, *The Consequences of Modernity* (Stanford, CA: Stanford University Press, 1990), 15–18.

58. Ibid., 144–6. 15–18.

59. Ibid., 151–3. Italics in original.

60. Ibid., 3–4. Italics in original.

61. Giddens, *The Consequences of Modernity*, 4, 71, 6, 9.

62. Ibid., 77, 7–10.

63. Giddens, *The Constitution of Society*, 64, 14, 17, 118.

64. Madeleine Bunting, "Intellectual Appetite: Zygmunt Bauman," *The Guardian*, 3 April 2003, http://libcom.org/library/poland-1956-vladan-v. Accessed 2 March 2014.

65. Ibid.

66. Ibid.

67. Giddens, *The Consequences of Modernity*, 14–21, 65, 158.

68. Ibid., 139, 149, 146.

69. Ibid., 150.

70. Ibid., 154–5.

71. Ibid., 165–6.

72. Ibid., 154–61.

73. Ibid., 160–1, 162n.

74. Ibid., 155, 212–13, 162, 166.

75. Giddens *Modernity and Self-Identity*, 230.

76. Giddens, *The Constitution of Society*, 83–5.

77. Ibid., 51.

78. Ibid., 351–3.

79. Giddens *Modernity and Self-Identity*, 221.

80. Ibid., 222.

81. Ibid., 223.

82. Giddens, *The Consequences of Modernity*, 156.

83. Giddens, *Modernity and Self-Identity*, 213–14.

84. Etienne Ollion, "Pierre Bourdieu." Oxford Bibliographies, www.oxfordbibliographies.com/view/document/obo

-9780199756384/obo-9780199756384-0083.xml. Ashley Crossman, "Pierre Bourdieu." About.com, http://sociology .about.com/od/Profiles/p/Pierre-Bourdieu.htm. Both accessed 25 May 2014.

85. Alan Riding, "Pierre Bourdieu: 71, French Thinker and Globalization Critic." *New York Times*, 25 January 2002, www.nytimes.com/2002/01/25/world/pierre-bourdieu-71-french-thinker-and-globalization-critic.html. Accessed 25 May 2014.

86. Ollion, "Pierre Bourdieu"; Crossman, "Pierre Bourdieu."

87. Alice Munro, "The Beggar Maid," in *My Best Stories* (Toronto, ON: Penguin, 2009), 36.

88. Pierre Bourdieu, *Distinction: A Social Critique of the Judgment of Taste*, Richard Nice, trans. (Cambridge, MA: Harvard University Press, 1984), 4–5, 32–3.

89. Ibid., 56, 66.

90. Ibid., 18, 16, 77. "Aesthetic stances . . . assert one's position in social space" (p. 57).

91. Munro, "The Beggar Maid," 27–8.

92. Bourdieu, *Distinction*, 67, 56, 110.

93. Ibid., 100–1, 69.

94. Ibid., 109–10. Sartre used the term "field of possibles" to indicate the range of possible choices for an actor.

95. Ibid., 29.

96. Ibid., 25, 28.

97. Ibid., 53–4. Schooling is one of the mechanisms "which channel towards positions individuals who are already adjusted to them" (p. 110).

98. Ibid., 131, 141, 140.

99. Ibid., 142.

100. Paul Willis, *Learning How to Labour: How Working Class Kids Get Working Class Jobs* (Aldershot, UK: Gower, 1977).

101. Bourdieu, *Distinction*, 64.

102. Ibid., 115.

103. Ibid., 13, 80, 71.

104. Ibid., 119, 121.

105. Ibid., 114, 121–2.

106. Ibid., 5–6.

107. Ibid., 101.

108. Ibid., 114.

109. Ibid., 94. "[I]n accordance with the formula: [habitus (capital)] + field = practice" (p. 101).

110. Ibid., 112–13.

111. Ibid., 107, 113.

112. Suzanne Collins, *The Hunger Games* (New York: Scholastic Press, 2008), 116.

113. Bourdieu, *Distinction*, 154, 162, 47–8.

114. Carl Sandburg, "The People, Yes" in *The Complete Poems of Carl Sandburg* (New York: Harcourt Brace & Jovanovich, 1969), 464.

115. George Ritzer, *Sociological Theory*, 7th edn. (New York: McGraw Hill, 2008), A13–16.

Conclusion

1. The movement was named after Emiliano Zapata, a national hero of the 1910 Mexican revolution who had indigenous roots.

2. Thomas Olesen, *International Zapatismo: The Construction of Solidarity in the Age of Globalization* (London: Zed Books, 2005).

3. James Petras, "Latin America's Twenty-First Century Socialism in Historical Perspective." Dandelion Salad, 12 Oct. 2009, http://dandelionsalad.wordpress.com/2009/10/12/latin-america%E2%80%99s-twenty-first-century-socialism-in-historical-perspective-by-james-petras/. Accessed 29 June 2012.

4. Ibid.

Acknowledgements

Grateful acknowledgement is made to the following persons or companies for kind permission to reproduce material in this book.

Chapter 1

Epigraph on page 12: Apollinaire, Guillaume. 'The Cavalier's Farewell' in *Calligrammes: Poems of Peace and War 1913–1916*. Translated by Anne Hyde Greet. (Los Angeles: UCLA Press Berkeley, 1991), p. 221. Copyright © 2004, The Regents of the University of California.

Chapter 3

Epigraph on page 62: THIS LAND IS YOUR LAND. Words and Music by Woody Guthrie. WGP/TRO-© Copyright 1956, 1958, 1970 and 1972 (copyrights renewed) Woody Guthrie Publications, Inc. & Ludlow Music, Inc., New York, NY. Administered by Ludlow Music, Inc. Used by Permission.

Block quote on page 71: From PRESSURE POINT © 1962 METRO-GOLDWYN-MAYER STUDIOS INC. ALL RIGHTS RESERVED. Courtesy of MGM Media Licensing.

Chapter 4

In-text quote on page 82: From *The Avengers* (2012). Used by permission of Marvel Entertainment.

Chapter 5

Epigraph on page 104: From THE CRUCIBLE by Arthur Miller, copyright 1952, 1953, 1954, renewed © 1980, 1981, 1982 by Arthur Miller. Used by permission of Viking Penguin, a division of Penguin Group (USA) LLC.

Chapter 6

Epigraph on page 137: A HYMN TO HIM (from "My Fair Lady"). Words by FREDERICK LOEWE. Music by ALAN LERNER. © 1956 (Renewed) CHAPPELL & CO. All Rights Renewed.

In-text quotes on pages 137–9: Excerpt(s) from THE SECOND SEX by Simone de Beauvoir and translated by Constance Borde and Sheila Malovany-Chevallier, translation copyright © 2009 by Constance Borde and Sheila Malovany-Chevallier. Used by permission of Alfred A. Knopf, an imprint of the Knopf Doubleday Publishing Group, a division of Penguin Random House LLC. All rights reserved.

Chapter 8

Epigraph on page 179: Words and Music by Allen Cole and Carleton Barrett. Copyright © 1976 Fifty-Six Hope Road Music Ltd. and Odnil Music Ltd. Copyright Renewed. All Rights in North America Administered by Blue Mountain Music Ltd./Irish Town Songs (ASCAP) and throughout the rest of the world by Blue Mountain Music Ltd. (PRS). All Rights Reserved. Reprinted by Permission of Hal Leonard Corporation.

In-text quotes and epigraph on pages 196–9: Excerpt(s) from ORIENTALISM by Edward W. Saïd, copyright © 1978 by Edward W. Saïd. Used by permission of Pantheon Books, an imprint of the Knopf Doubleday Publishing Group, a division of Penguin Random House LLC. All rights reserved.

Chapter 9

Epigraph on page 205: Excerpt(s) from END OF THE GAME AND OTHER STORIES by Julio Cortazar, copyright © 1963, 1967 by Random House LLC. Used by permission of Pantheon Books, an imprint of the Knopf Doubleday Publishing Group, a division of Penguin Random House LLC. All rights reserved.

In-text quote on page 207: ALL YOU NEED IS LOVE. Written by: John Lennon & Paul McCartney. ©1967 Sony/ATV Music Publishing LLC. All rights administered by Sony/ATV Music Publishing LLC, 424 Church Street, Suite 1200, Nashville, TN 37219. All rights reserved. Used by permission.

Chapter 11

Epigraph on page 265: Lyric from Bob Dylan, "Things Have Changed." Copyright © 1999 by Special Rider Music. All rights reserved. International copyright secured. Reprinted by permission.

In-text quote on page 273: SURPRISE, SURPRISE. Written by: Ian D'Sa, Jon Gallant, Ben Kowalewicz, & Aaron Solowoniuk. ©2012 EMI April Music (Canada) LTD and Dudebox Music. All rights on behalf of EMI April Music (Canada) LTD and Dudebox Music administered by Sony/ATV Music Publishing LLC, 8 Music Square West, Nashville, TN 37219. All rights reserved. Used by permission.

In-text quotes on pages 285–90: From Judith Butler, *Gender Troubles: Feminism and the Subversion of Identity*, copyright © 1989, CCC Republication.

Epigraph on page 288: From "Born This Way," Words and Music by Stefani Germanotta, Jeppe Laursen, Paul Blair and Fernando Garibay. Copyright (c) 2011 Sony/ATV Music Publishing LLC, House Of Gaga Publishing Inc., Universal Music Corp., Warner-Tamerlane Publishing Corp. and Garibay Music Publishing. All Rights on behalf of Sony/ATV Music Publishing LLC and House Of Gaga Publishing Inc. Administered by Sony/ATV Music Publishing LLC, 424 Church Street, Suite 1200, Nashville, TN 37219. All Rights on behalf of Garibay Music Publishing Administered by Warner-Tamerlane Publishing Corp. International Copyright Secured All Rights Reserved. Reprinted by Permission of Hal Leonard Corporation.

Chapter 12

Epigraph on page 294: Lyrics from Hey Rosetta, "Handshake the Gangster," *Into Your Lungs* (2012).

Epigraph on page 310: Weight Watchers Advertisement (2014).

Index

Friedrich Sorge, 37; on socialist revolution, 36; on use-value, 273; on women, 43; on workers, 47

Marxism, 32, 125, 261, 290; Baudrillard on, 277; development of European, 44–8; disillusionment with, 100; feminism and, 224–5; Frankfurt School and, 88, 89; Korsch on, 46–7; Marcuse on, 213; as metanarrative, 270; opportunism and, 123–4; reformists and, 36, 43, 331; renewed interest in, 234–5; revolution and, 36–7; Sartre on, 161, 162; scientific, 44; social change and, 319; "soviet," 53; varieties of, 33; in western Europe, 33–4; workers and, 47

masculine/feminine binary, 5, 288

masculinity, 141; de Beauvoir on, 138, 139–40; Friedan on, 143

mass culture, 90, 92; counterculture and, 207

master narratives, 284, 329

material incentives, 222, 329

Matrix, The (film), 276

matrix of domination, 281, 329

Mayakovsky, Vladimir, 38–40, 93; "It's Good," 38; "Vladimir Ilyich Lenin," 38

Mead, G.H., 55, 245–6

Mead, Margaret, 140–2; criticisms of, 142. Works: *Coming of Age in Samoa*, 141, 142; *Sex and Temperament in Three Primitive Societies*, 141

meaning: Blumer on, 246–7; Camus on, 158

Mechanical Bride, The (McLuhan), 166–8

media: hyperreality and, 275; Innis on, 167; mass, 92, 275; McLuhan on, 168

Medicare, 65

medium is the message, 168–9, 329

medium/media: cool, 168–9, 325; hot, 168–9, 327

Mein Kampf ("My Struggle") (Hitler), 81

Melancholia (film), 104

Memoirs of a Dutiful Daughter (de Beauvoir), 135

men: de Beauvoir on, 139–40; marriage and, 17–18; socialization and, 111–12; transcendence and, 138; Woolf on, 29–30

mental disorder, 242, 243, 254

Merton, Robert, 100, 114–17; deviance and social structure and, 116–17; functions and dysfunctions and, 115–16. Works: "Social Structure and Anomie," 114, 116, 117; *Social Theory and Social Structure*, 114

Merton, Robert C., 114

metanarratives, 270, 329

metropolitan-centre, 188, 190, 192, 329

Mexico, Zapatistas in, 321

Meyers, Jeffrey, 78

micro-powers, 261

microsociology, 108, 213, 241–51, 329; ethnomethodology, 248–51; Goffman and, 241–5; standpoint sociology and, 231; symbolic interactionism, 245–8

middle class, 128, 132–3, 174, 316

Midnight in Paris (film), 24–5

Midnight's Children (Rushdie), 153, 198–9

Miller, Arthur: *The Crucible*, 104; *Death of a Salesman*, 129

Millett, Kate, 224–5; *Sexual Politics*, 225

Mills, C. Wright, 98, 100, 108, 127, 131–5, 263. Works: *Listen Yankee*, 133; *The Power Elite*, 131, 134; *White Collar*, 131, 134

Les Misérables, 243

Mitchell, Juliet, 225

Mitterand, François, 317

modern, as term, 22

modernism, 329; art and, 21, 22–3, 24–5; dance and, 27; doubt and, 20–2; Habermas on, 301; poetry and, 20–1; scientific uncertainty and, 21–2; varieties of, 22–3; women and, 24–5, 26–7

modernity: Bauman on, 308; Giddens on, 307, 309; identity and, 310; impact of, 292–3; late or radical, 307–9; second, 292; self and, 310

Modernity and the Holocaust (Bauman), 308

modernization, 185, 322

modern society: capitalism and, 3; change and, 11–12; Thomas on, 56; transition to, 3; Weber on, 19

Modern Times (film), 9, 49

monocrop, 221, 329

monogamy, 217

monogenism, 67

monomyth, 238, 239

Montgomery, Lucy Maud, *Rilla of Ingleside*, 24

Montreal, 60

morality, knowledge and, 268

moral-practical assertions, 299

Morris, Desmond, *The Naked Ape*, 125

Morrison, Jim, 207

mortgage crisis, 294–5

mortgages, sub-prime, 294

Mosley, Walter, *Bad Boy Brawley Brown*, 145, 208

Motorcycle Diaries, The (film), 218

Les mots et les choses (The Order of Things) (Foucault), 257

Mountain Arapesh, Mead and, 141

Mrs. Dalloway (Woolf), 29

Mulroney, Brian, 264

multi-national corporations (MNCs), 191

multiple realities, 252, 253, 329

Munch, Edvard, 23; *The Dance of Life*, 23; *Puberty*, 23; *The Scream*, 23

Mundugumor, Mead and, 141

Munro, Alice, 313, 316; "The Beggar Maid," 312

music, African Americans and, 71; *see also* jazz

Mussolini, Benito, 80, 84

Le Mythe de Sisyphe (Camus), 157

Myth of Mental Illness, The (Szasz), 255

Napoleon, 3

narratives, master, 284, 329

nationalism: black, 75, 149, 150, 151; Canadian, 15–16; Durkheim on, 16–17, 18; German,

16, 82; Quebec and, 60, 61, 193; Woolf on, 30; World War I and, 12, 14–16

National Labour Relations Board, 51

National Organization of Women (NOW), 145

National Policy, 63

National Social Christian Party, 87

Nation of Islam, 149–50

Native Son (Wright), 69, 74

NATO. *See* North Atlantic Treaty Organization (NATO)

Nazi Party, 46, 81, 82–3

Nazism, 15, 80–6; anti-Semitism and, 81; death camps, 83; Habermas on, 296; opposition from Antilleans, 177; patriarchy and, 86; responsibility for, 84–5; sexuality and, 84–5, 86; women and, 84–6

needs, true and false, 216–17

negative thinking, 213–14, 329

Negro, as term, 73, 149

Nehru, Jawaharlal, 187

neo-colonialism, 182–3, 221, 264, 329; Fanon on, 183–4

neo-fascism, 87

neo-liberalism, 235, 317, 329; in Chile, 263; policies of, 264; political success of, 264; social democracy and, 267; Western, 264

neo-Marxism, 233, 261, 267, 329

neo-reality, 274

Neumann, Franz, 88

neurosis, 164, 177, 329

new criticism, 345n53

New Deal (US), 54, 66

New Democratic Party (NDP), 65, 267

New Economic Policy (NEP) (Russia), 40–1, 329

new human being, 222–3

New Labour Party (UK), 267

New Left, 32, 206, 208–13, 224, 232, 261, 266, 329; in Canada, 209–10; in China and Europe, 210–12, 272; collapse of, 212–13; denouement of, 234; failure of, 267; student protests and, 208–9

New Left Review, 287

New Negro, 71, 72, 329

New Right, 264–5, 323, 329

New School for Social Research, 251

news industry, MacGill on, 59

Newsome, Effie Lee, "The Bronze Legacy (To a Brown Boy)," 71

New Woman, 11, 71, 330; in Germany, 85–6

New York Radical Women, 226

Nietzsche, Friedrich, 6, 78, 268, 269; existentialism and, 154; on knowledge, 258; Nazism and, 81; *Thus Spake Zarathustra*, 130; Weber and, 18–19

Nigeria, 179, 180

nihilism, 156, 157, 158, 330

Nineteen Eighty-Four (Orwell), 100, 101, 102–3, 203

Nixon, Richard, 162

No Exit (Sartre), 159

nonlinear logics, 173, 330